BEACHAM'S ENCYCLOPEDIA
OF SOCIAL CHANGE

AMERICA
in the
TWENTIETH CENTURY

BEACHAM'S ENCYCLOPEDIA OF SOCIAL CHANGE

AMERICA *in the* TWENTIETH CENTURY

Edited by Veryan B. Khan

VOLUME 4: PAGES 1507–1999

Published by
The Beacham Group LLC

Beacham's Encyclopedia of Social Change: America in the Twentieth Century

Veryan B. Khan, Editor
Walton Beacham, Project Director
Deborah Beacham, Production Manager

While every effort has been made to ensure the reliability of the information presented in this publication, The Beacham Group LLC neither guarantees the accuracy of the data contained herein nor assumes any responsibility for errors, omissions or discrepancies. Errors brought to the attention of the publisher and verified to the satisfaction of the publisher will be corrected in future editions.

This publication is a creative work fully protected by all applicable copyright laws, as well as by misappropriation, trade secret, unfair competition, and other applicable laws. The authors and editors of this work have added value to the underlying factual material herein through one or more of the following: unique and original selection, coordination, expression, arrangement, and classification of the information. All rights to this publication will be vigorously defended.

Copyright © 2001
The Beacham Group LLC
P. O. Box 1810
Nokomis, FL 34274-1810

All rights reserved including the right of reproduction in whole or in part in any form.

Distributed worldwide exclusively by The Gale Group

Book Design by Jill Dible

Library of Congress Cataloging-in-Publication Data

Beacham's encyclopedia of social change: America in the twentieth century / edited by Veryan B. Khan.
   p. cm.
   Includes bibliographical references and index.
   Summary: Traces the evolution of social ideas and values in the United States during the twentieth century, using such indicators as advertising, crime and justice, family life, fashion, music, race and class, sex and gender, and work.
     ISBN 0-933833-62-8 (set: alk. paper)
     ISBN 0-933833-64-4 (v. 1: ak. Paper)
     ISBN 0-933833-65-2 (v. 2: alk. paper)
     ISBN 0-933833-66-0 (v. 3: alk. paper)
     ISBN 0-933833-67-9 (v. 4: alk. paper)

     1. United States—Social conditions—20th century—Encyclopedias, Juvenile. [1. United States—Social conditions—20th century—Encyclopedias.] I. Title: Encyclopedia of social change. II. Khan, Veryan B., 1970-

HN59.2 .B43 2001
306'.0973Bdc21   2001043141

Printed in the United States of America
10 9 8 7 6 5 4 3 2 1

COMMENTS AND SUGGESTIONS ARE WELCOME

The editors invite comments and suggestions from users of *Beacham's Encyclopedia of Social Change: America in the Twentieth Century*. You may contact us by mail at: The Beacham Group LLC, P. O. Box 1810, Nokomis, FL 34274-1810; by telephone at (941) 480-9644 or (800) 466-9644; or by facsimile at (941) 485-5322. Our email address is beachamgroup@aol.com

PHOTO ACKNOWLEDGMENTS

These photos are on the covers of all four volumes of *Beacham's Encyclopedia of Social Change: America in the Twentieth Century*: *U.S.S. Shaw*, Pearl Harbor, Hawaii, December 7, 1941, photograph. National Archives and Records Administration; Dr. Martin Luther King, photograph. The Library of Congress; Children in a parade of suffragettes, May 1913, Long Island, New York, photograph. The Library of Congress, George Grantham Bain Collection; Jim Thorpe, photograph. National Archives and Records Administration; Anti-Vietnam War protest at the Pentagon, Washington, D.C., photograph. National Archives and Records Administration; Dust bowl farm, parts of wagon wheels visible above sand, photograph. National Archives and Records Administration; President Franklin Delano Roosevelt shaking hands with Chief Noal Bad Wound, circa 1936, photograph. Hulton/Archive. Reproduced by permission; Laptop computer, Copyright © 2000 PhotoDisc, Inc. All rights reserved; Hindenberg flying over city, photograph. Archive Photos/Lambert. Reproduced by permission; Dorothy Dandridge, photograph. AP/Wide World Photos. Reproduced by permission; The Beatles wave to a crowd at an airport as they arrive in the U.S. for concerts and television appearances, photograph. Hulton/Archive. Reproduced by permission; Ulysses spacecraft in orbit, illustration. National Aeronautics and Space Administration (NASA). Reproduced by permission. All photos throughout the text are reproduced by permission from Hulton Archive/Getty Images.

CONTENTS

Introduction ix
Contributors xiii

Advertising and Consumerism 1:1
American Expansion 1:47
Automobiles and Highways 1:107
Business and Labor 1:127
Cities 1:163
Crime and Justice 1:195
Death 1:227
Economy 1:273
Education and Literacy 1:411
Emotional Change 1:443
Environment 1:471
Ethnic Minority Groups 2:499
Family Life 2:541
Farming 2:577
Fashion 2:619
Food 2:651
Health and Medicine 2:705
Housing and Architecture 2:745
Immigration 2:831
Individual Prosperity and the American Dream 2:869
Inventions 2:897
Law Enforcement 2:929
Laws and the U.S. Legal System 2:955
Leisure 2:985
Morality 3:1037
Music 3:1089
Occupations 3:1135
The Press and Democracy 3:1155
Race and Class 3:1189
Race and Minorities 3:1261
Radio and Television 3:1311
Religion and American Life 3:1351
Retirement 4:1507
Science 4:1533
Sex and Gender 4:1579
Soldiering: Life in Combat 4:1615
Towns 4:1667
Transportation 4:1699
Travel 4:1749
War and the U.S. Military: Drivers of Social Change 4:1779
Work and the Workplace 4:1857

TIMELINE 4:1907
INDEX 4:1947

INTRODUCTION

It is a time for reflection as America steps into the twenty-first century, a century which in some ways resembles the transition from the Dark Ages to the Renaissance, a century of excitement and turmoil, of hope and resignation, in which perceptions about humankind's significance was constantly changing through booms, depressions, and wars.

Perhaps as never before, the delineation between two centuries can be seen through the terrorists' attacks on the World Trade Center and the Pentagon on September 11, 2001. Rarely has a single event established such a clear differentiation between centuries; ironically, the Spanish-American War (1898-1902), which marked the end of U.S. territorial imperialism, ushered in a new century that would demand a completely new role for American leadership, just as the terrorists' attacks on September 11 a century later forces new directions for the United States for the twenty-first century in which world interests take precedence over the ambitions of individual countries. As the United States achieved a position of world dominance at the end of the twentieth century, it renewed some of the same social arguments that prevailed during the period of American imperialism a hundred years before.

The evolution of the century provides fascinating insight into the spirit, values, and ingenuity of the American people. From our roots as outcasts and nonconformists, we developed instincts for survival, respect for social order, and a passion for independence and personal freedom. From the bounty of our land we learned the potential of natural resources and the possibility of abusing them. And from our naiveté we blundered into wars that secured our independence, turned our nation against itself, liberated Europe from tyranny, forced generations to reject each other's values, and established the United States as the most powerful nation.

America is the story of slaves, immigrants, Native Americans, and a European ancestry that created paradox and energy. America in the twentieth century has not been so much a "melting pot" as a nuclear reactor. To understand and appreciate the road from Kitty Hawk to Cape Canaveral, from Jamestown to Montgomery, from barley soup to Lean Cuisine®, *Beacham's Encyclopedia of Social Change: America in the Twentieth Century* traces American history through forty-one key indicators of social change. Each of the chapters—"Advertising and Consumerism" to "Work and the Workplace"—explains the progress of American culture each step of the way. Through our journey we see how Americans made their own history.

In a traditional sense, this encyclopedia is a history book with the usual timelines and statistical charts, but we prefer to think of it as a story book in which ordinary people struggle, suffer, strive toward great accomplishment, and change. What does food or fashion, family life or morality tell us about American values? Plenty. In 1909, as the suffragette movement gained strength, designers abandoned the corset and created the freedom of the Gibson Girl look; in the 1920s, when the proliferation of automobiles provided young people with privacy to pursue their own lives, women wore scandalous clothing, only to retreat to practical clothing during the Depression and World War II years. In the prim and proper 50s women wore tailored clothes and pillbox hats, and in their rebellion against their prim and proper mothers, the 70s women burned their bras and adorned baggy, tie-dyed pants. The fitness generation of the 80s wore her Calvins and in the 90s her spandex running shorts. The times they were a-changing, and what people wore tells us something about their times.

Rather than approaching history from a universal perspective, we look at it piece-by-piece, decade-by-decade, from a human perspective. We attempt to place readers *in* the historical moment, not above it looking down. How did American soldiers during World War I spend their countless miserable hours in the trenches? How did World War II women on the home front contribute to the war? What was life like without men? How did African Americans contribute to the war effort? Prisoners? Native Americans? You'll experience immigration through Mary Hagen's first Christmas after leaving Ellis Island twelve hours earlier; you'll discover that Thomas Edison had a dispute with an employee that forever changed the use of electricity; you'll learn that the bikini is named from an atoll in the Pacific Ocean that the Allies used for testing the atomic bomb during World War II. The fascinating facts, the photos, the timelines, and the sidebars help the reader experience life during a different time.

HOW TO USE THIS ENCYCLOPEDIA • We think of this encyclopedia as comparative history. Each chapter presents a separate key indicator of social change, but they are all interlocked and together complete a picture puzzle of American culture. Fashion alone reflects something about society; when compared to the same timeframes for other key indicators, we begin to see the whole of American society.

To facilitate studying American social history through comparison, we present each key indicator in small units with associated dates. Using the margin date to generally locate a timeframe and the subhead dates to narrow the time period, researchers can compare what was happening across key indicators, and thus see the influence of one on the other. The timeline at the beginning of each key indicator is divided into two parts: the top section list events related to the key indicator while "Milestones" lists other interesting events during the same time period.

Other study features include a composite timeline, which is useful in seeing connections across key indicators, and for generating ideas for research projects. Most of the references in the composite timeline are discussed in the encyclopedia, so that research on any one of them can begin here, then continue through the bibliographies and Internet resources. The comprehensive index provides the gateway for researchers.

The story behind many key indicators begins before the twentieth century opens, and our authors provide the background as far back as necessary to understand the twentieth century. Business and labor practices, for example, established their roots in the 1800s, while modern warfare begins with the Civil War, and modern economy begins with the development of the corporation and industrialization after the Civil War. Other key indicators—modern farming, health care, leisure, and retirement, for example—did not begin until the turn of the century, and thus our story begins there.

Social history is different from the history of great moments. Famous people or intensive events tell only one side of a story—an extreme side. Most people did not fly solo across the Atlantic Ocean or create great wealth by mining gold in California. Most of us who have flown the Atlantic were taking vacations to Europe; most of the miners who rushed to California panned a lifetime without finding an ounce of gold. To identify with these people is to be aware of who Americans are. To appreciate the plights of peoples past is a signpost as to where we might be going. Customs, traditions and behaviors have evolved dramatically in the hundred years of this past century. Following these changes is exciting, fascinating, and fun.

We think that the key indicators provide a personal approach to learning about history and culture. Whether or not readers are concerned about the larger historical picture, they are certainly interested in specific topics: how did Barbie contribute to the women's liberation movement (Sex and Gender); who did the Ku Klux Klan persecute before it turned its wrath on African Americans (Crime and Justice); and most important—a subject that touches on every aspect of American culture—what part have immigrants played in our evolving country (every article).

Usually, social changes occur over a slow, evolutionary process in which history, years later, reveals the gradual development and discernible changes between past and present. However, with a single event, much like the Japanese attack on Pearl Harbor, the twenty-first century has already become unique; we know, without the benefit of history, that America is a different society. Modern-day terrorism, domestic and foreign, began its infancy in the late twentieth century through horrific attacks on American soil and against civilians; the utter destruction of the twin towers in New York City will lead to many changes during the opening years of the twentieth-first century, and the clues to where America will refocus society for a strangely different century are embedded in the key indicators in this encyclopedia.

Veryan B. Khan

Contributors

Kenneth Adderley
Upper Iowa University

James F. Adomanis
Maryland Center for the Study of History

Cara Anzilotti
Loyola Marymount University

Brian Black
Pennsylvania State University, Altoona

Benita Blessing
Fellow, Institute of European History, Mainz

Stephen Burwood
SUNY, Geneseo

Peter Cole
Western Illinois University

Joel S. Franks
San Jose State University

Richard A. Garcia
California State University, Hayward

Jennifer Hamil-Luker
University of North Carolina, Chapel Hill

R. Steven Jones
Southwestern Adventist University
Keene, Texas

Veryan B. Khan

Judy Kutulas
St. Olaf College

R. A. Lawson
Vanderbilt University

Joan D. Laxson

Christina Lindholm
Virginia Commonwealth University

Mark Malvasi
Randolph-Macon College

Greg Moore
Notre Dame College, South Euclid, Ohio

Marie Marmo Mullaney
Caldwell College, New Jersey

Don Muhm

Michael V. Namorato
University of Mississippi

Karen S. Oakes

Paul Ortiz
University of California, Santa Cruz

Diane N. Palmer

Judith Reynolds

Elizabeth D. Schafer

Peter N. Stearns
George Mason University

Kathleen A. Tobin

Peter Uhlenberg
University of North Carolina, Chapel Hill

Christopher Waldrep
San Francisco State University

James D. Watkinson
Randolph-Macon College

The publisher wishes to thank the contributors for their outstanding contribution to this project.

Walton Beacham

Retirement

~

(circa 1937) A government poster advertising the benefits of the social security system.

TIMELINE

1790-1879 ~ Recognizing the Need for Retirement

State legislatures introduced policies of mandatory retirement for some public officials between 1790 and 1820 / Business begins to regard unemployment as a distinctly different problem from poverty (mid 1880s) / 70 percent of American males over the age of sixty-five still work (1840) / Some, but not all, states require judges to retire due to advancing age (1860) / Congress establishes a system to provide pensions for disabled soldiers (1862) / American Express establishes the first railroad pension plan (1875) / Massachusetts is the first state to collect unemployment statistics (1878)

MILESTONES: Decline of the apprenticeship system (1820-1860) • Factories employ entire families of immigrants (1820s-1830s) • Old Immigration from England, Ireland, Scandinavia and Germany (1830-1870) • Census shows great increase in the types of occupations (1850) • One-fifth of the American population is killed in the Civil War (1861-1865) • First labor union formed in the U.S. (1866)

1880-1899 ~ Early Pension Plans

B&O Railroad pension plan is the first to allow employees to retire voluntarily at the age of 65 (1880) / Nearly half of all retired men live with their children or a relative (1880) / Business begins looking for ways to dismiss older, inefficient employees (1880s) / Civil Service Act makes removal of government employees who are no longer productive extremely difficult (1883) / Term "unemployment" appears to have been used for the first time (1887) / Most businesses do not have formal policies requiring retirement at a specific age (late 1800s) / Vast majority of railroads do not offer pensions to their elderly workers (1889) / Federal government begins to provide a pension for veterans of the Union Army (1890) / Treasury Department plan reduces salaries for employees aged 70 or above while requiring less output from them (1897)

MILESTONES: Interracial alliances of workers and farmers forge national organization, the Knights of Labor (1880s-1890s) • State courts rule that labor reform laws violate the rights of employers to enjoy the freedom to operate their businesses (1881-1900) • First professional football game takes place in Latrobe, Pennsylvania (August 31, 1885) • Knights of Labor call a strike against the railroads (1886) • Eight-hour work day inaugurated in Chicago (1886) • Capture of Geronimo ends formal warfare between whites and Native Americans (1886) • St. Andrews Golf Club at Yonkers, New York formed, marking the beginning of golf in the U.S. (1888)

1900-1919 ~ Industrial Efficiency and Older Workers

United States Civil Service Retirement Association is formed (1900) / Pension plan for soldiers and federal employees consumes 30 percent of the federal budget (1900) / Andrew Carnegie endows a foundation for the retirement of college teachers (1905) / Physician William Osler argues that men should retire from work at the age of 60 (1905) / Commission on Economy and Efficiency calls for compulsory retirement at age 70 and supports the creation of a pension fund financed at employee expense (1909) / Age discrimination worsens as older employees are required to take physical exams (1915)

MILESTONES: NYC Tenement House Act requires that no new tenement could occupy more than 70 percent of its lot (1901) • Andrew Carnegie gives $350 million for social causes (1900-1919) • Director D.W. Griffith produces the first feature length film, *The Great Train Robbery*, which lasted eleven minutes (1903) • Vaudeville is at the peak of popularity (1910) • AFL demands and receives better wages for workers (1917-1918)

1920-1949 ~ Social Security Act

Congress passes a law that allows civil service officials to receive retirement benefits at the age of 70; mechanics, letter carriers and clerks at 65; and railway clerks at 62 (1920) / Congress expands benefits to people already retired (1926) / Social Security Act provides social insurance for both the unemployed and the elderly (1935) / Social Security Act shifts pension responsibilities from local to federal government (1935) / Rate of unemployment for workers over 65 has increased to more than 50 per cent (1935)

MILESTONES: First miniature camera, the Leica, is produced in Germany (1925) • Babe Ruth hits sixty home runs (1927) • George Eastman invents the Kodak color film process (1928) • National Institute of Health established (1930) • Blue Cross hospital insurance program created (1933) • *Reader's Digest* has a circulation of over 1,000,000 readers (1935)

1950-1969 ~ Retirement becomes Acceptable

Social Security provision permits women to retire at age 62 (1956) / American Association of Retired Persons (AARP) founded (1958) / Beginning of the retirement industry (1960) / AFL-CIO founds the National Council of Senior Citizens to lobby for Medicare (1961) / Older Americans Act specifies a series of goals to improve the lives of the elderly (1965)

MILESTONES: Weekly earnings for production workers increases by 70 percent (1950-1970) • Interstate Highway Act passed to fund a vast network of high speed roads (1956) • Sam Walton establishes the first Wal-Mart (1962) • Marine theme park, Sea World, opens (1964) • MasterCard introduced (1966)

1970-2000 ~ Increase in Benefits and Number of Retirees

Social Security benefits are indexed to the Consumer Price Index (1972) / Social Security benefit levels increase five times between 1965 and 1975 / Age Discrimination and Employment Act raises the age for mandatory retirement from 65 to 70 (1978) / People may spend as much as a third of their lives in retirement (1990s) / Alliance for Retired Americans is founded to lobby for retired trade unionists (2001) / Number of eligible Social Security recipients is expected to double while the number paying taxes into the system will increase by less than 20 per cent (2030)

MILESTONES: Women make up 40 percent of the overall labor force and represent a substantial increase in married women who work (1970) • Cable use of satellites begins (1973) • Mysterious disease kills dozens of Legionnaires during a convention (1976) • Some Native American economies prosper from casino gambling (1982-2000) • Family and Medical Leave Act provides worker security during family emergencies (1993) • With the retirement of Wayne Gretzky, the NHL loses the most popular player in its history (1999)

INTRODUCTION

Before the beginning of the twentieth century in the United States, there seems to have been little concern about the issue of aging and its relevance for society. Retirement contracts existed in colonial America, but retirement in this time was more of a gradual transition that permitted the head of a household to transfer title to his property to an heir in exchange for money or services as required by the elderly individual or couple. These transitions were common in agrarian societies where land was the main element in production, and the contract represented the final step in a long process of transferring property. These contracts were part of a process designed to make sure that family control of the land was maintained.

American legislatures introduced policies of mandatory retirement for some public officials between 1790 and 1820. In 1860 some, but not all, states required state judges to retire due to advancing age. By the late 1800s, most businesses did not have formal policies requiring retirement at a specific age, and there were no laws that required the elderly to stop working simply because they reached a certain age. If businesses chose to eliminate older workers, they did so through informal processes. It appears older persons simply kept on working until they either could do so no longer or because they chose to stop. Also, the elderly apparently were regarded for their knowledge and wisdom, particularly as the United States entered into the process of industrialization and prepared to enter the world stage as a major power. In addition, older persons might serve as a source of moral guidance to the young, and because they were knowledgeable about farming, they were able to perform chores around the house or farm.

1800s

1800s • WORKING ALL YOUR LIFE ~ The lack of mandatory retirement can be explained a number of ways. Forced retirement was undoubtedly not suitable to the society of the nineteenth century. The majority of businesses were still too small to assume the financial burden of providing pensions for employees who might number no more than a few dozen or so. The small employee base made sharing the cost of retirement between them and their employer nearly impossible. Close personal relationships between employers and their employees may have made laying off or firing older workers distasteful and uncommon. Also, as late as 1890, most American workers were still engaged in farming, which was not an occupation where mandatory retirement was likely to occur. Skills and experience served as substitutions for declining strength and stamina in later years. Basically, society expected the elderly to remain productive and they apparently were for as long as they could be.

Mandatory retirement had not come into existence by the turn of the century because older workers were choosing to retire on their own. Certain industries such as textiles and the railroads employed enough people to allow for the development of a mandatory retirement system. The railroad industry did develop a pension system in the last quarter of the nineteenth century and the federal government provided a pension for veterans of the Union Army in beginning in 1890. These programs may have contributed to the decisions of some men to retire, although they were a long way from a mandatory retirement system. A system of voluntary retirement may have been better suited to the small-scale businesses that were common in the United States immediately following the Civil War.

American society, however, may not have developed a full system of mandatory retirement because some older workers were choosing to leave the work force before they were no longer able to continue to work safely or efficiently. In 1840 about 70 percent of American males over the age of sixty-five were working; yet in 1890, when industrialization had reshaped the American economy, the percentage was about the same. In that fifty year period the percentage of non-working men over the age of sixty-five had not significantly changed.

1880s • MOVING TOWARD MANDATORY RETIREMENT ~ By 1885, the face of American business was changing. Corporations had become the predominant form of economic organization. More and more workers were moving to the rapidly growing cities and were now working in factories and offices rather than at home. Railroads were playing a vital role in unifying the American marketplace, leading to increasing competition and an equally increasing desire to eliminate business rivals. This made a system of mandatory retirement possible because workers were being organized into more efficiently managed groups, and because it was becoming necessary. A mandatory retirement system could solve numerous problems for a variety of economic and social groups. Businessmen could reduce unemployment and turnover rates while maintaining a younger and more efficient labor force. Labor could use this system to shift the work from one generation to another, especially in overcrowded labor markets. Even churches could recruit a younger and more vigorous clergy.

While corporations were finding ways to restrict competition though trusts, monopolies and holding companies, they were also finding it desirable to reduce the numbers of elderly workers in their employ. Restrictions were placed on the number of older workers that could be hired and efforts were begun to create mandatory retirement programs. Increasing competition and shorter workdays helped to further promote these policies.

Older workers, though, were not retiring in sufficient numbers. The rates of employment for the elderly were the about the same in the industrial 1890s as they were in the agrarian 1840s. There was a significant difference between retiring to the family farm and retiring to a tenement flat in Philadelphia or Cleveland or, perhaps to the poorhouse. In the increasingly urban and industrialized society and economy at the turn of the century, American workers who had little or no savings and without community resources to fall back on in order to ease the financial burdens of retirement, desperately clung to their jobs.

1900-1935 • FEDERAL GOVERNMENT INFLUENCE ~ By 1900, the federal government had begun to assert itself in the capitalist economy of the United States. Federal involvement was increasingly viewed as necessary in order to solve political, social and economic problems that seemed too difficult for local institutions or the cooperative nature of corporations to resolve. Federal regulatory agencies and legislators in the twentieth century turned their attention to a variety of issues, including the question of mandatory retirement.

1887-1900

The expansion of the government's bureaucracy helped bring the question of retirement due to age or infirmity into sharper focus. By 1929, service workers in half a dozen states in the northeast and in the federal government were now subject to retirement provisions contained in new pension laws. Old-age assistance, once the domain of local governments and private charities, were now increasingly coming under the jurisdiction of state governments. The Social Security Act of 1935 would bring the federal government into the picture.

1887-1893 • THE ECONOMICS OF RETIREMENT ~ The changeover from an economy based on productivity to consumerism also had an effect on the emergence of mandatory retirement in the United States. Following the Panic of 1893, many businessmen concluded that the nation was producing more goods than the nation could absorb. While these beliefs contributed to the imperialism of the 1890s and the early twentieth century, they were also expressed in an increased emphasis on advertising, marketing and consumerism in order to develop untapped domestic markets. The Great Depression intensified the changeover from production to consumption, and the nation's elderly found themselves expected to retire and spend their accumulated benefits as part of the new emphasis on consumption. By the 1960s retirement had become an identifiable consumer item itself, sold to potential buyers in the same manner as any other product.

In the mid-1880s, unemployment was being thought of as a distinctly different problem from poverty and, as such, required greater attention from the state. The earliest attempts to collect unemployment statistics took place in Massachusetts in 1878, and the term *unemployment* appears to have been used for the first time in 1887. By the mid-1890s, with the nation in the middle of a severe depression, the word came into increasing use. The concept of unemployment encouraged employers to discriminate in their hiring and retention practices by emphasizing the benefits of outstanding workers and the liabilities of keeping inefficient ones. Thus, a shorter work life, marked by mandatory retirement, could help reduce unemployment. This idea was beginning to take hold in the 1890s and would become national policy with the enactment of social security and railroad retirement laws forty years later.

1875-1900 • PRIVATE PENSIONS ~ The growing desire of employees for status, security and fair practices, along with higher salaries, and the need business had for loyal, dedicated and productive employees led both sides to try and develop relationships that would suit both of their interests. One result of this was the development of private pension plans, which emerged from the struggle to establish a stable and efficient management-labor relationship. These plans were partly an expression of welfare capitalism, based on the belief that benevolent and generous programs such as standardized housing, recreational benefits, insurance, and profit-sharing would help create the stable, productive and loyal workforce businessmen were seeking. Out of this grew private pension programs.

Some companies continued to employ older employees in non-essential tasks, such as tending a gate at the company's entrance. If the employee suffered an incapacitating illness or became disabled, the company would provide a pension. Companies had to care for their elderly employees and often had to create pension plans, but they often did all they could to keep the worker busy in some manner. Many still regarded retirement as disgraceful and resisted going on the pension rolls. If an employee became a danger to the factory or to his fellow worker, then he might be compelled to retire.

The American Express Company established the first railroad pension plan in 1875. The Baltimore & Ohio railroad followed with a pension plan of its own in 1880, and the Pennsylvania Railroad established a plan in 1900. These plans were established as examples of corporate benevolence for employees, although they were also the result of efforts to retain employees and to deal with increasing union pressure to force the railroads to display greater concern for the welfare of their workers.

One of the central features of the B&O plan was the provision of old-age income protection, and the comprehensive plan became a model for future railroad pension plans. The plan allowed employees to retire voluntarily at the age of 65, or, if disabled, at age 60. Old age was treated as a disabling illness, which was a common view at that time, and the plan gave retirees the same benefits that workers who suffered long-term disabilities received. The B&O pension plan became a model for later railroad pensions.

The Pennsylvania Railroad's pension plan was innovative in that it established corporate innovation and control over the benefit plan. Earlier plans had left the administration of the benefits to company relief associations. The Pennsylvania Railroad altered this process by creating a relief *department* within the corporate structure that allowed the company to maintain control of the plan, while allowing management complete control over policy, administration and financial decisions. In this manner, the precedent was set for the development of modern personnel administration, which would be significant for the future of pension and retirement benefit packages. Other railroads followed suit and earlier railroad plans were revised to incorporate the features of the Pennsylvania Railroad's plan.

The railroads generally offered more non-cash benefits than other American businesses did, yet in 1889 the vast majority of railroads did not offer pensions or some sort of employment to their elderly workers. Many of those who took care of their older employees did so with light work assignments.

Out of the many family owned business that were industrializing by 1900, only a handful had developed and were operating some sort of pension plan. Undoubtedly some firms provided other forms of welfare capitalist approaches to the question of dealing with their older workers, but it is clear that few companies at the end of the nineteenth century were deeply concerned about the fate of their elderly employees.

The fact that pension plans required a long-term commitment may well have discouraged many firms from implementing them. Profit-sharing plans were far more popular with employers, and some of those who adopted pension plans did so by making them extensions of profit-sharing plans. Profit-sharing had the attraction of directing benefits to the active workforce as whole, while pensions provided benefits only to the elderly, and existed only as a distant promise to younger workers. The critical nature of such a long-term commitment meant

(circa 1955) Berry Pickers. Even as late as the 1950s many industries did not have retirement programs: migrant farm workers are seldom able to afford to retire. Seen here are berry pickers from Philadelphia sitting in the back of their labor contractor's truck in Burlington County, New Jersey.

1862-1890 that many corporations had no use for pension plans.

1862-1890 • THE UNION ARMY PENSION PROGRAM ~ Congress established the General Law pension system in 1862 to provide pensions for regular and volunteer recruits who were disabled as a direct result of military service. Payments were based on the degree of disability, and a board made up of three local doctors, who ruled on the degree to which the individual was disabled, screened applicants. The level of disability was determined by the applicant's ability to perform manual labor.

In June 1890, the federal government established a more general pension program for veterans of the Union Army. While the program originally was designed to provide assistance for disabled veterans, it contained the beginnings of a collective disability and old-age plan for soldiers who fought for the North during the Civil War. This new law provided a pension to any disabled Union veteran, whether the disability was due to the war or not. While old age was not recognized by law as a cause for receiving a pension, the Pension Bureau instructed doctors who examined pension applicants to grant a pension to all men 65 years of age or older, unless they appeared to be exceptionally energetic. This pension seems to have encouraged men to retire, and, in the early years of the twentieth century, Union Army veterans retired at a greater numbers than did non-veterans. This probably reflects the fact that for veterans, their pension payments represented a significant portion of their incomes. Also, the Union Army pension was the only available government sponsored retirement fund and veterans appear to have taken advantage of it. However poor health caused by disabilities received as a result of the Civil War may also help explain the higher rate of retirement.

By 1900 the extent of this pension plan had become huge. Consuming close to 30 percent of the federal budget and housed in its own office building (The Pension Building) in Washington, D.C., the program provided benefits to both veterans and their dependent children and widows. Despite the fact Confederate

1514 ~ RETIREMENT

veterans were ineligible and continuous immigration was swelling the population, a large percentage of Americans were receiving benefits. More than a third of white males between ages 55 and 59 received benefits, as did about one in five of those between 60 and 65, 15 percent of men 65 to 69 and just under 10 percent of those over the age of seventy.

The political power of Union Army veterans, like that of the elderly today, was significant, making pension issues an important element in the elections of the late nineteenth and early twentieth centuries. Also, like today's senior citizens, these veterans, despite their relatively small numbers, were very well organized. They maintained lobbyists in Congress and kept the ranks informed through local chapters and newspapers. They supported efforts of manufacturers to keep tariffs high and then lobbied to have the revenue from tariffs directed to the pension fund. Many Americans supported pensions for these veterans in recognition of their defense of the Union and because the economy was generally prosperous.

1870s • POOR HOUSES ∼ In the nineteenth century many retired men were dependent upon their families for support. Nearly half of all retired men in 1880 lived with their children or some other relative. A poem published in *Harpers' Weekly* in 1871, told the story of a widow who was passed from child to child until she ended up in an institution. This spawned a popular song three years later that retold the story, this time using an elderly man as its central character. Abandoned by his children, he finds himself on the verge on institutionalization. In the song's refrain, the old man bemoaned his fate:

For I'm old and I'm helpless and I'm feeble
The days of my youth have gone by,
Then over the hill to the poor house,
I wander alone there to die.
(Braham & Caitlin, 1874)

(1954) Visiting Old People. Some people in the welfare homes go months with no visitors. Seen here is an old man receiving a visit from a local townsperson.

1870s-1905

Films, poetry and songs all raised the issue of the future for the unemployed elderly worker and often suggested that his fate would ultimately be the poorhouse run by charitable organizations. At the turn of the century welfare reformers continuously summoned up the image of senior citizens being relegated to institutions as they became destitute. Advocates of pension plans argued that the existence of the poorhouse was a vivid demonstration of the helplessness of the elderly in the industrial age. More and more people seemed to be entering these institutions, and reformers argued that eventually most old people would end up as residents in asylums. Only measures such as the establishment of old age pensions could prevent such an occurrence, reformers insisted. In fact, only about two percent of elderly persons were institutionalized in the late nineteenth and early twentieth centuries, but the fear of being placed in an asylum had a dramatic impact on public perceptions of the fate of the elderly and on demands that the government provide some form of assistance.

1905 • Debate Over Retirement Age ~ Among the many popular notions held in the Progressive Era of the late nineteenth and early twentieth centuries, was that of "The Gospel of Efficiency." Relying on scientific methods for the collection of data, many reformers felt that "Scientific Management" could eliminate waste and inefficiency in business, government and society, while ending the impoverishment of many rural areas and overcoming problems such as poor health in the nation's cities.

Business leaders were particularly supportive of ideas that could result in efficiency, order and organization. Among the issues that required consideration was the role of the aging worker in the new industrial workplace, and in society in general. In 1905, William Osler, who was leaving Johns Hopkins University after serving some sixteen years as chief physician of the university's new hospital, offered some thoughts on the problem of older workers. In an address given in February, Osler stated his belief that men should retire from work at the age of 60. Osler believed that men were at their most productive between the ages of 25 and 40, and after that productivity gradually declined. From the age of 60 onwards, Osler argued, men should retire from work, for they were becoming, or had become, inefficient within the workplace.

Osler's remarks stimulated a debate over the issue of the productivity of the elderly. Critics argued that men could remain productive past the age of 60, while others raised the issue of how to support the elderly in the event of their retirement. Others felt that elderly workers could remain productive into their later years, but found a certain logic in the concept of retirement in one's later years. While Osler's ideas were criticized, Osler himself was arguing in favor of efficiency and productivity, and, while his remarks were directed to his own profession of medicine, they could be construed to apply to society as a whole.

In 1905, possibly influenced by Osler's address, Andrew Carnegie endowed a foundation for the retirement of college teachers. Admiral George Dewey warned that a future naval war could prove disastrous for the United States if the Navy was not placed under the command of younger men. The growing implementation of machinery in industry made it apparent that the work lives of many would be shortened by the growing use of technology. Thousands of local, state and national public workers no doubt saw the relevance of Osler's point of view, and either resisted or welcomed the concept of retirement as they tried to work out some form of agreement with the forces in support of productivity.

1905-1910 • PRODUCTIVITY AND SOCIAL PROGRESS

As an advocate of efficiency and progress, Osler supported ideas that threatened the continued employment of workers who were, or could seem to be, sources of inefficiency. Younger persons might interpret this view as the heralding of an age of opportunity. Those reaching an age where their productivity might be called into question could envision retirement as a form of leisure, earned from their working years yet separate from employment. Resistance would remain strong to the concept of retirement for another three decades, until the scarcity of work and the greater availability of pensions would allow the concept of retirement as a time of leisure to join with social security and become a part of mainstream thinking. But, Osler helped raise the image of an aging population in the United States, and defined the problem along the lines of productivity. By doing so, he helped to confirm certain values and fears of American culture as a whole. Osler pointed out that a society dedicated to progress and which permitted economic conventions to dictate the terms of advancement, would have to learn to set the older generation aside to make way for younger workers. Managers motivated by the desire to increase productivity or efficiency came to prefer younger employees and viewed older workers as burdens who hampered the efficiency of the business.

1915-1920s • AGE DISCRIMINATION

Although around 1915 some studies argued that older workers could be valuable to a business in terms of employee retention, among other things, age discrimination began to worsen in the United States. Job applicants began to find themselves required to take physical examinations, and some companies tended to apply the requirement more stringently to older job applicants than younger ones.

The growing cult of youth in the twentieth century also helped to intensify discrimination based upon age. Americans in the 1920s were beneficiaries of the industrial progress that had taken place to that point. The incredibly rapid development and spread of technology, particularly the automobile and the assembly line, left an indelible mark on American culture. The nation's young people now expected to have advantages their parents had not had, and the overall quality of their lives would be better than that of the preceding generation. America looked to its young to guide them into the future, rather than its older population.

These ideas infused the business community as well. The emphasis was on workers who were energetic and full of "pep" and vigor. While a small number of companies recognized that older employees had a certain value, the majority of managers preferred to hire younger workers. Retirement offered a way for business to restructure the age of its work force. Impersonal and equal in its application, retirement allowed business to balance the need for efficiency with labor-management relations that were still permeated with personal relationships. After 1925, retirement was recognized as a useful cure for the problems of unemployment in depressed industries and in the economy as a whole.

1883-1897 • Retirement in the Federal Government ~ After making pensions available to Union Army veterans on the basis of age in 1890, the federal government would take another thirty years to establish a retirement and pension program for its employees. Not until 1920 would a Republican dominated Congress pass a bill implementing a retirement package for civil service workers. President Woodrow Wilson signed the bill into law.

As was the case in business, the question of retirement for government employees also had to deal with the issues of efficiency and security. The Civil Service Act of 1883 made removal of government employees who were no longer productive or efficient extremely difficult at best. Civil service employees could be assured of a secure tenure and, while they were free to leave government work for other employment, the security offered by a civil service position encouraged the majority to remain in the employ of the government. As with the rest of the population of the country, aging was inherent within the federal bureaucracy. Many of these older workers were veterans of the Civil War, and as former members of the Union Army, were highly unlikely to be removed from their jobs for political reasons. These men remained on the federal payroll and were often shielded from salary reductions even when they became incapacitated and were no longer productive. And when a bureaucrat was removed from his job for inefficiency, pressure often mounted for his reinstatement. In fact, the civil service legislation undoubtedly contributed to the creation of an aging and increasingly inefficient bureaucracy by failing to provide effective machinery for the removal of increasingly unproductive older workers.

(circa 1912) The central courtyard inside the Pension Office Building, Washington D.C.

In 1897, Treasury Secretary L.C. Gage put into operation a program that would act as an informal pension for elderly workers in the Treasury Department. Gage's action included reducing salaries for employees aged 70 or above, while requiring less output from them. Gage's decision brought about opposition from his own employees as well as from supporters of Union Army veterans, who viewed this policy as the beginning of a genuine federal pension system and as an insult to employees who provided years of loyal service. The opposition to this course of action led to the attachment of a rider to an appropriations bill for the Treasury that prohibited the spending of any of the money in the appropriation on older employees. Led by Congressmen eager to restore efficiency to the government bureaucracy, passage of the bill forced Gage to let go those elderly workers he had identified in his program. However, Gage's actions sparked the debate on the question of a retirement and pension policy for civil service workers.

1900-1910 • FORMALIZING THE FEDERAL RETIREMENT POLICY ~ Over the next two decades a series of commissions would investigate this issue. The Gage action had created a level of interest among federal employees who now had to wonder if their jobs would remain secure, as they grew older, or if they faced a future of a forced retirement without a salary. Ironically, within the Treasury Department, the United States Civil Service Retirement Association (USCRSA) was formed in 1900.

The USCSRA spent several years collecting data and investigating ways in which a federal retirement policy and a method of funding it could be created. Support from the administration of Theodore Roosevelt came in the form of the Keep Commission. While the task of the commission was to find ways of improving government business methods, it allowed advocates of a formal retirement policy a forum to express their views, while it also gathered the first reliable information on older workers and their treatment within the government bureaucracy. Part of the Keep Commission's final report included statistical data that suggested older workers became increasingly inefficient.

Despite evidence to the contrary, many departmental supervisors continued to portray their departments as efficient. It seems that these supervisors were continuing to protect those older employees for whom they were responsible. Actions such as that of Gage or the firing of a number of elderly Post Office workers in 1907 were still unusual occurrences.

Mounting evidence indicated that the federal government was retaining older workers, and, as the data accumulated, the question of their efficiency was becoming more of a concern. By the time William Howard Taft assumed the presidency in 1909, more government departments were commenting on this issue. It was becoming apparent that the bureaucracy was operating a pension system but was not encouraging retirement. Taft had a dislike for bureaucracy and favored the idea of retirement. Under Taft, the USCSRA would be permitted to continue its lobbying efforts in favor of retirement.

Taft's commitment to retirement was further demonstrated with the formation of a Commission on Economy and Efficiency, and his acceptance of their recommendations on civil service retirement. The commission called for compulsory retirement at age 70, and supported the creation of a pension fund financed at employee expense. Taft justified his acceptance of these recommendations on the basis that compulsory retirement would increase the efficiency of civil service employees.

1910-1919 • DESIGNING A PENSION SYSTEM ~ The interest shown by Roosevelt and Taft helped the retirement movement within the government to grow. A division grew within the movement over the method of financing a retirement system. The USCSRA emerged from the desire to protect older workers, and was willing to accept a retirement system based on employee contributions in order to get Congress to act quickly on the issue. However, a newer organization, the National Association of Civil Service Employees (NACSE) argued for a direct pension system. The differences between the two were significant. By arguing for a pension system funded by the government, the NACSE was calling for a system that would foreshadow the creation of a true welfare state with benefits provided out of general revenues.

The question of efficiency and the carrying of older, non-productive workers on the government payroll continued during the Wilson Administration. Wilson, unlike Taft, opposed retirement and he did so primarily for political reasons. As a Democrat, he could not embrace a policy that had become identified with the Republicans. Democrats remained hostile to Republican support of Union Army veterans though the military pension, and many small-town and rural Democrats, who were the foundation of the party, were hostile to the idea of seeing the federal government financing the retirement of its employees with their tax dollars. Wilson had also angered southern Democrats by blocking their efforts to restore, to some extent, the old spoils system in order to gain more federal appointments for their backers. He could not afford to alienate them further by supporting a pension program for government workers, and so he took no action on the issue.

Wilson changed his mind in 1918 for reasons that are not entirely clear. He may have been influenced by a study on public employee retirement that pointed out how a pension system could serve as a promise to younger workers that their security would be taken care of as retirement drew near. Wilson was approached by a pair of senators in the last half of 1918, who showed him a proposed retirement bill. Wilson responded to the bill with enthusiasm. His support along with the return of a Republican majority to Congress in the election of 1918, made retirement legislation more likely.

1920-1926 • THE NEW LAWS ~ Due, in part to opposition from Southern Democrats, retirement legislation was not enacted until May 1920. The law provided for retirement of civil service officials at the age of 70 with at least fifteen years of service. Other employees, including mechanics, letter carriers and clerks were eligible for benefits at 65 and railway clerks could retire at 62. Benefits were determined by years of service. The bulk of the funding for the pension program came from a small salary deduction, although the government did contribute funds for the retirement of older workers who would be unable to make any significant contribution to the pension account. The law did not make retirement mandatory, for a worker could remain employed for a maximum of four years past his scheduled retirement date. A number of supervisors treated the law as requiring mandatory retirement, however, and compelled all those who reached the requisite age to retire.

The law was not entirely satisfactory. The original pension fund was insufficient to meet the needs of those who retired. Retirees had to adjust to a reduced standard of living, and in many cases the pension they received would not pay for a decent place to live and sufficient food and clothing. Many were forced to live with their children or needed charity in order to survive. Through efforts of organizations like the National Association of Retired Federal Employees, Congress was persuaded to amend the retirement law and offer a larger benefit in 1926, with those benefits going out to those who were already retired. The new law also provided for benefits for those between 45 and 55 with fifteen years of service who had been let go to reduce the work force. These persons became eligible for benefits at age 55. However, Congress rejected the concept of retirement based on years of service rather than age, believing that the concept was too costly and not likely to increase efficiency within the bureaucracy.

What is of interest is that the advocates of retirement within the civil service justified their views on the basis of improving efficiency. Yet they found themselves opposed by supervisors and managers who refused to admit the inefficiency of their older workers, despite evidence to the contrary. They continued to maintain nineteenth century values regarding the security of their employees even after the retirement legislation was passed in 1920. While the federal government, like American society as whole, was becoming committed to modernization, older values continued to remain rooted within the system.

1930s • SOCIAL SECURITY ~ In the 1930s, the Great Depression worsened the growing problem of unemployment and poverty among the elderly. By 1935 the rate of unemployment for workers over 65 had increased to more than 50 per cent. Pension benefits were of little help as private pension plans were failing, while state and local governments were scaling back or eliminating pension programs altogether.

There were legislative proposals for ending these problems, among them the Townsend Plan and the Lundeen Bill. The Townsend Plan called for a $200 payment monthly for older Americans with the provision that the money be spent within thirty days. The Lundeen Bill was designed to provide a payment at the level of existing local wages for all unemployed workers 18 years old and older. Elderly workers were to be included in the program. However, neither program was really focused on retirement. The Townsend Plan offered equal benefits to all persons over the age of 60, while the Lundeen Bill was directed more at the creation of jobs rather than limiting the supply of labor by separating certain age groups from the work force.

From the very beginning of the New Deal, members of President Franklin D. Roosevelt's administration argued for a program sponsored by the federal government that would provide social insurance for both the unemployed and the elderly. Leading the fight for a program of this sort was FDR's Labor Secretary, Frances Perkins. Two years into the New Deal, in 1935, Roosevelt publicly expressed his support for what would become the Social Security Act, which was passed by Congress that year. The Social Security Act of 1935 remains one of the most far-reaching and complicated laws ever to pass Congress.

(1939) A sign reading 'Restore America By The Townsend Plan' on a roadside near Walesco, Texas. The Townsend Plan was put forward by Dr. Francis Townsend to provide a pension for every American citizen.

1930s

1935 • STRUCTURING THE SOCIAL SECURITY PLAN ~ The existence of similar programs in the most industrialized nations of Europe provided some of the basis for the Social Security Act. Retirement and pensions had been less of a concern in agricultural America, where chores for older family members could always be found, and large families assumed the responsibility of caring for dependents. Urbanization, and the up and down nature of an industrial economy, however, was now forcing the federal government to assume some responsibility for providing social programs to assist the elderly.

A committee headed by Secretary Perkins drafted the measure. Taking the ideas of reformers from the Progressive Era and borrowing from social welfare programs in England and Germany, the act would establish a combined system that included the states and the federal government. The act established old-age pensions for workers, survivor's benefits for victims of industrial accidents along with aid for dependent mothers and children, the blind and the disabled. The funds from which pensions and benefits were paid came from taxes that were paid by both employers and workers. While the implementation of these taxes had the short-term effect of contributing to a recession in 1937 by taking money out of circulation, the program was politically sensible since workers would not permit the repeal of a program that they were contributing to.

The Social Security Act provided two types of assistance to the elderly. Those who were destitute at the time the act became law could receive as much as

$15 monthly in federal aid. Working Americans, meanwhile, were placed into a pension system funded by social security taxes. Eligible workers could begin receiving pension payments in 1942, with benefits ranging from $10 to $85 a month. The act also excluded many types of workers, including domestic servants, farm workers and self-employed individuals. Nor did it offer health insurance. However, it was an important beginning for what has become the nation's most important social program for its older citizens, and created the precedent for federal involvement in social welfare. Additionally, by encouraging older workers to retire when they became eligible, jobs could be opened up for younger workers.

1939 • ENTITLEMENT, NOT WELFARE ~ The goal of those who wrote the Social Security legislation was not a system of welfare, but one of insurance. Both the old-age pensions and unemployment insurance were similar in a number of ways to the programs offered by private insurance corporations, particularly in collecting funds from the participants while providing benefits for all. Yet the law also provided direct assistance to those in need as well. Originally the groups targeted to receive aid were thought of as small ones and truly unable to support themselves. Over time, though, the programs of direct assistance would expand until they took on aspects those who supported the original concept probably never considered. By 1939, some 45 million Americans were eligible for Social Security benefits. In later years benefits would increase and new groups of workers would be added to the eligibility lists.

When he signed the Social Security Act into law, FDR boasted that no politician would "ever scrap my social security program." Roosevelt's confidence that the law would remain in place was due to the fact that benefits were linked to payroll deductions. Since workers made contributions to the program, they had a vested interest in it and would feel they had a right to collect the pensions and other benefits the law promised them. Today, the program assists the elderly, the disabled and survivors of those whose payroll deductions contributed to the federal funds that are now paid out. Probably close to half the nation's elderly would be facing poverty if it were not for the checks they receive from Social Security.

2001-2030 • THE FUTURE OF THE SOCIAL SECURITY PROGRAM ~ Now, however, the expansion of the Social Security program has raised questions about its future. By the year 2030, the number of eligible recipients is expected to double, yet the number of those paying taxes into the system will increase by less than 20 per cent. The continuation and the viability of Social Security are threatened by the specter of huge deficits in the not too distant future. Results of a Gallup poll taken in March 2001 show that 52 percent of non-retired Americans expect to receive a Social Security benefit when they retire, while 41 percent do not. (www.gallup.com)

Even so, FDR's boast that politicians would not dare disband Social Security continues to hold true. The debate over the future of Social Security reflects divergent viewpoints about continued expansion of the federal government and its entitlement programs that date back to the New Deal itself.

Today there are fewer supporters of the notion that the federal government must assume responsibility for resolving social problems or providing social wel-

2030

fare than there were in the 1930s. In fact, since the 1960s there has been increasing resistance to the continued expansion of the federal government. There is also more support for private programs to replace those of the government, and even some talk of "privatizing" Social Security. Critics have suggested changes as extreme as providing benefits only to those who contribute to the system, and encouraging contributors to invest their Social Security accounts themselves, in the stock market for example, in the expectation of earning larger payouts.

Others argue for reform instead of drastically changing or eliminating Social Security. Opponents of privatization believe that doing so would eliminate the basic premise of Social Security – the guarantee retirees have of a dependable income. Critics further point out the risks of investing retirement savings due to the volatility of the market. There is always the hazard that one could suffer serious losses just as they were preparing to retire. And a private system might eliminate various special programs offered by Social Security to large families, couples where one partner has a small income or none at all, and low-income earners.

Suggested reforms include taxing all wage earners; many workers, especially state and municipal employees, do not pay Social Security taxes. The increasing life expectancy of Americans has led to proposals to extend the age at which pension benefits can be received in order to shore up the Social Security nest egg. Others have in mind a plan whereby the government would set aside its current investment policies in order to let a semi-private government agency manage the system's investments. The expectation is that these reforms would result in sufficient funding to allow Social Security to provide for the needs of the American people.

These arguments and criticisms regarding Social Security reflect earlier disagreements about the role and purpose of the federal government. Supporters and opponents of the involvement of the government in social issues today are continuing a debate that dates back to the turn of the century in the United States. At the heart of the issue of how to fund Social Security in the twenty-first century will be a debate over the nation's basic and most fundamental values.

1950s-1965 • THE GROWTH OF RETIREMENT

Despite the creation of Social Security, the availability of federal benefits did not hasten the process of retirement. Studies conducted by the Social Security Administration in the 1950s indicated that older workers made the decision to retire for health reasons rather than because benefits from the government were available. For most workers as late as the 1950s, economic reasons made retirement an option that was not attractive for many older workers. Because these benefits were fixed, or unchanging, the elderly recognized that their financial security in retirement was threatened. Fixed benefits would mean that the value of a pension would decline as a result of inflation, thereby reducing the spending power of a retiree.

Despite the concern about financial security, retirement as a social occurrence was on the rise in the 1950s. Private insurance companies helped to encourage retirement by marketing programs designed to prepare workers for eventual retirement. Social arguments suggested that the gradual surrender of authority and responsibility within society was a natural process that resulted from aging and should not be resisted. Indeed, social disengagement could be seen as a positive function for both the individual and society.

Postwar prosperity led to the view that retirement was a time of potential pleasure and creativity that was society's reward to the individual after a lifetime of work. The growth of leisure industries reinforced this perception and enhanced the marketing of retirement. Mass tourism and entertainment such as movies, television, golf and various spectator sports provided activities for the elderly at affordable prices. Mandatory retirement was not an issue; in fact, the trend was toward retirement before age 65. In 1956 women were able to retire at age 62, while men got the same privilege in 1962. In each case, early retirement was accompanied by reduced benefits from Social Security.

In the mid-1960s the issue of poverty among the elderly once more gained political prominence, largely as a result of the Johnson Administration's War on Poverty. Congress passed the Older Americans Act of 1965 that specified a series of goals that, if met, would lead to a significant improvement in the lives of the elderly. These objectives included the right of older people to enjoy an adequate income in their retirement years that would allow them to maintain a suitable standard of living along with the right to enjoy a healthy, honorable and dignified retirement.

1965-1978 • INCREASING RETIREMENT BENEFITS

It was during the presidency of Richard Nixon that the age of modern retirement came into existence. Although earlier amendments to the Social Security Act had brought more and more workers into the system, there had been no significant improve-

(1955) Rear view of elderly men sitting on a bench across the street from Charles Department Store and Woolworth's, Paris, Tennessee.

ment in the payment of retirement benefits. To this point there had been no challenge to the assumption that Social Security should serve as a supplement to retirement income rather than the primary source of income. However, the persistence of high rates of poverty among the elderly made complaints that benefits were no longer adequate seem credible. Benefit levels were increased five times between 1965 and 1975, and, in 1972, benefits were indexed in relation to the Consumer Price Index. These improvements in retirement benefits made it possible for retired Americans to maintain their standard of living. They also gave legitimacy to retirement as a social status that persons who made average incomes could afford to enter voluntarily. In 1978, amendments to the Age Discrimination and Employment Act raised the age for mandatory retirement from 65 to 70 in most occupations and removed mandatory retirement from the federal civil service.

Private pension plans were also reorganized during the 1970s. Passage of the Employee Retirement Income Security Act (ERISA) legalized vesting plans while providing workers with some protection against any loss of benefits. Private corporations now began to encourage early retirement as well, and, private plans began to offer greater benefits to those who opted for early retirement, instead of the reduced benefits that were common before. As a result, more elderly Americans were choosing to retire, and the poverty rate among retirees dropped.

1990s • RETIREES AS THE LEISURED CLASS ~ The lowering of the cost of recreational and leisure activities has particularly benefited the elderly, so that retired Americans have become a true leisured class. When one considers that a 20 year-old man in 1880 might look forward to spending two years of his life in retirement, while a 20 year old today can anticipate spending as much as a third of his life in retirement, the availability and lower cost of leisure activities take on greater importance. As one grows older the amount of time spent on leisure activities increases. Moreover, activities that interested younger persons tend to remain of interest or become even more attractive after retirement.

The elderly can now enjoy a greater variety of recreational activities than ever before. Continued technological change has allowed producers to satisfy increasingly narrower segments of the retirement market. Cable and satellite television, for example, offer a wider range of programming suited to a diversity of tastes. Watching television is the most common form of leisure activity in the United States, and cable has increased the selection of programs available to watch. Both radio and television have brought the city and rural areas closer together through media programming. National clubs and associations have also connected the recreational habits of persons nationwide and brought recreational habits of those in the country more in line with those in the rest of the nation. Retirement communities throughout the Sunbelt cater to the needs and interests of those retirees who inhabit them. The cost of recreation and leisure has fallen with the introduction of new and better products along with a greater variety of leisure time options.

But even with lower costs and a greater selection of recreational choices, it is still the elderly who partake of leisure activities the most. One reason for this may be that technological advances in home entertainment – improved televisions, VCR's and DVD players, and sound systems are less demanding physically and it is the older segment of the population that has benefited most as a result.

The elderly today are more capable physically of enjoying activities that their counterparts of the past could not. Walking, bicycling, swimming, square dancing, golf and even more strenuous pastimes routinely attract senior citizens today. It is not unusual to find persons well past the age of 65 running in marathons or lifting weights, for example. Undoubtedly, the improved health of the elderly allows them to participate in other endeavors, such as volunteer work, far more often than in times past.

1990s • Greater Prosperity for Retirees ~ Another explanation for why so much recreation is utilized by senior citizens may have to do with the tax structure of the American economy. The tax-exempt status of pension benefits makes saving for retirement less costly than savings would normally be. Many pensions provide an incentive for retirement by making retirement income almost equivalent to earning a salary.

Additionally, a reason for the greater consumption of leisure products and systems by the elderly may result from the benefits a company is willing to offer and the employee is willing to accept. Ideally, recreation could be spread more evenly over a person's life, but in order to do this, the individual would have to accept a lower level of compensation. Therefore, maximum use of leisure time activities is postponed until retirement. Retired individuals generally have more assets today than senior citizens did in the past. And while the hours in the workweek for a full

(circa 1965) A group of elderly women exercising in a 'keep fit' class, New York.

time worker may have declined, there are still only so many hours in a day a working person has for recreation.

Retirement also increases the opportunities for travel. People travel more frequently and for longer periods after they have retired than they did before retirement. The advent of recreational vehicles has created an alternative lifestyle based on travel for some retirees. These people often sell their homes and live out of their RV, perhaps wintering in the warmer climates of Arizona or Florida and then traveling around the country during the other months of the year. It appears that those retirees who adopt the nomadic lifestyle of the "RV'er" enjoy a greater sense of community and have fewer of the emotional problems that are common among the elderly than do those individuals who adopt other forms of retirement living. For a younger person, job requirements rules out the kind of extended travel that "RV'ers" and other retirees can take pleasure in.

Increased opportunities for leisure has helped make retirement a more attractive option for older workers than it has been in the past. Certainly the role of public and private pensions, retirement savings programs and improved health care have contributed to making retirement an acceptable alternative to working far into one's later years. The role of leisure is critical since it offers the retired individual the opportunity to replace the stimulation that work satisfaction may have offered with alternative forms of stimulus. Certainly there are those who have trouble adjusting to retirement, and most of those who express unhappiness with being retired trace their dissatisfaction to financial problems or poor health. The opportunities for leisure or recreation serve as a means for satisfaction among retirees, and serves as an additional inducement to retire as old age approaches.

1990 • WOMEN IN RETIREMENT ~ A number of factors make the work experience different for women than men. Commitments at home, later entry into the work force, and uneven work histories have a direct bearing on a woman's decision to retire, including affordability and the determination as to when to leave the work force.

In general women seem to have positive attitudes toward retirement. A positive outlook can come from the fact that a husband's pension serves as the primary source of financial support, that plans have been made for the transition to retirement, overall satisfaction with one's life or leaving working conditions that are not satisfying. However, women who have worked for a long time, are highly educated and committed to their work, and who spend a great deal of time in job-related activities tend to view retirement negatively. Professional women are as reluctant to retire as their male colleagues.

Although women plan and prepare for retirement, they plan less than men. Studies suggest that some women have a continued sense that they will be cared for in their old age, or because of their fear of growing old, that they are more reluctant to make plans for retirement. It is also likely that late entry into the work place, uneven work histories and a lifetime of lower wages cause women to approach retirement with fewer financial resources needed to plan effectively. Professional women appear to have the same regard for retirement planning as men.

As with men, the decision to retire for women involves a number of factors. A married woman's decision to retire is often influenced by her husband's decision to do so; however the opposite seems to occur less often. The husband's decision to retire, or family pressures, can play an important role in a woman's retirement decision. However, this is not always the case. A woman may not retire when her husband does, especially if she is employed in one of the professions. Joint retirement is more likely if she and her husband are close in age, less likely if they are farther apart in age.

The tendency is for unmarried women to remain in the labor force longer than married women. This is especially likely if the woman's entry into the labor force was delayed and her financial resources are fewer. On the other hand, widows are more likely to retire early. Widows often work until they are eligible for widow's benefits, and then retire. Women who are divorced or separated also are more likely to retire early. Resources available from the previous marriage may make early retirement possible in these cases. Women also find themselves forced to retire in order to assume family responsibilities such as taking care of a sick husband or aged parent.

Marital status may also be a factor. Women seem to plan, for the most part, to retire either early or late. Those who plan for early retirement generally were married, in good health and upper class. Those opting for later retirement more likely were unmarried, lower class and held a less positive view of retirement. Economic factors, in either case, were critical in the retirement decision.

Women seem to adjust well to retirement. Satisfaction in retirement may involve some of the factors that contributed to happiness while working, but can also include sufficient income, meaningful use of time, a positive attitude toward retirement, good health, social activities and friendship networks, particularly with other women, and opportunities for involvement in cultural events. How long one has been retired and whether or not a retired woman is married may also affect the adjustment to retirement. The health of a spouse can also have an effect on a woman's adjustment to life in retirement.

1958-PRESENT • THE ELDERLY AND POLITICS ~ The political power of the elderly has been expressed primarily through senior citizens' groups, which grew rapidly in the 1970s. These organizations have served to promote issues relevant to older persons, and they also are active in lobbying efforts and reporting on the views of politicians to their constituents.

The largest voluntary organization in the United States is the American Association of Retired Persons (AARP), which was founded in 1958. Originally organized to provide insurance to retirees, the organization has more than 30 million members in 4,000 chapters across the United States. While maintaining a nonpartisan stance, AARP lobbies on behalf of issues of importance to older persons. The organization's magazine, MM (formerly *Modern Maturity*), publishes voter's guides on the positions of political candidates regarding matters of concern to the elderly, and the AARP maintains a web site (www.aarp.com) that offers information and services to members.

The AFL-CIO founded the National Council of Senior Citizens in 1961 in order to lobby for Medicare. This organ-

(1996) U.S. senator Strom Thurmond sitting at the Republican National Convention, San Diego, California. In 1996, at the age of 93, Thurmond became the oldest person to serve in Congress.

1990s

ization focused primarily on retired trade unionists and, like the AARP, served as a lobbying group and offered services and benefits to its membership. The NCSC disbanded operations on December 31, 2000, and has endorsed the AFL-CIO's new organization, the Alliance for Retired Americans, which was founded on January 1, 2001. Like the NCSC, the ARA will direct its activities at retired trade unionists. It will lobby for issues of importance to this group of retirees, and will also offer members various benefits and services. Other organizations include the National Committee to Preserve Social Security and Medicare, and the National Association of Retired Federal Employees.

These organizations have effectively used their lobbying efforts to protect Social Security. Their real impact, however, is on the political agenda as a whole. While older voters do not appear to use their voting strength politically, politicians are concerned about their potential to affect elections. However, to this point in time, older voters have been able to do little more than maintain the existing system, and have made little headway in terms of persuading politicians to initiate new programs.

1990s • Retirees at Work ~ Many senior citizens continue to work in some capacity after retirement; as many as a third of all retirees work, either formally or informally. Historically individuals who work past retirement age or who re-enter the labor force come from two sources: well educated retirees with adequate income sources, and retirees with fewer resources who must work to maintain an adequate income. Retirees go back to work for three reasons: the need to survive, the need to preserve status, or from the desire to improve the quality of life for their families or communities.

Returning to work in order to survive means that the retiree lacks the financial resources to do so. They participate in jobs in the formal marketplace, work in cottage industries, or engage in domestic services for wages. Employment may be full or part-time, depending on circumstances. Other retirees who work may have adequate incomes, yet feel a loss of status because they are unable to consume at the levels they did while working. In order to maintain their sense of identity they continue to work, not because they need it to survive but in order to maintain a standard of living closer to what they were used to before retiring. These persons often work in temporary or part-time jobs for low pay, but are willing to do so in order to have spending money. Some of this work may be the continuation of part-time jobs they worked at while they were working full time. Others turn hobbies or crafts into moneymaking enterprises.

Finally, some retirees work in order to enhance the survival or status of their families or community. They may do so by providing services at less than the normal rate. This allows others to save money while continuing to consume and maintain social status. Parents may rely on retired grandparents to help with childcare. This kind of labor is usually unpaid and performed out of necessity in order to help the family make ends meet.

Retirees are often involved in unpaid community work as well. Many volunteer at local associations, hospitals, churches, schools and other organizations. They perform services or help raise money for various causes and by doing so, help raise the quality of life within the community. They derive a sense of satisfaction from the work they do and enjoy the fellowship of fellow retirees at the same time. These volunteer activities are often vital to the life of a neighborhood or community. As an example, by manning information desks or performing other services for patients, volunteers help hold down health costs since hospitals do not have to hire individuals to perform these tasks. Volunteers, although unpaid, often fill real needs within a community.

CONCLUSION

While retirement has roots in the nineteenth century, and even a bit earlier, it is truly one of the many byproducts of the process of social change that have come about as a result of the Industrial Revolution. Before industrialization, few people "retired" in the modern sense. Farmers might sign over the deed to the family farm to their children in return for a guarantee of support, but many elderly persons continued to work until they could no longer do so.

The increase in the number of older persons in the nineteenth and twentieth centuries and the desire to promote efficiency and productivity in the workplace helped to stimulate the process of modern retirement. However, the lack of financial resources made retirement an unpleasant prospect for many and there was considerable resistance to the concept. Only with the passage of Social Security and the growing availability of affordable leisure activities did retirement become a true social phenomenon in the United States. Yet many "retired" individuals continue to work today in order to supplement insufficient pension funds, to maintain a certain standard of living they were used to before retirement, to assist other family members or to maintain a certain level of satisfaction that be gained by performing a needed service.

The future of retirement as we knew it at the end of the twentieth century is difficult to predict. Growing concerns over the availability of Social Security funds in the future has led many to worry that it may not be possible to retire when the time comes. Among proposed reforms that have been proposed to assure continued availability of Social Security payments to the next generation of retirees is raising the retirement age to 67 or 70. Improvements in the quality of health care and medical technology have significantly extended the life spans of Americans and enabled them to work effectively and productively for more years. It is possible that the twenty-first century will see more and more Americans postponing retirement, possibly for economic reasons, but also because they are able to contribute to society and enjoy the satisfaction of productive careers well into what is now considered to be "old age."

BIBLIOGRAPHY

Carter, Susan B. and Richard Sutch. *Myth of the Industrial Scrap Heap: A Revisionist View of Turn-of-the-Century American Retirement.* Cambridge, MA: National Bureau of Economic Research, 1995.

Costa, Dora L. *The Evolution of Retirement: An American Economic History 1880-1990.* Chicago: University of Chicago Press, 1998.

Graebner, William. *A History of Retirement: The Meaning and Function of an American Institution, 1885-1978.* New Haven: Yale University Press, 1980.

Krajcinovic, Irina. *From Company Doctors to Managed Care: The United Mine Workers' Noble Experiment.* Ithaca, NY: ILR Press, 1997.

"Ohioans Retiring to full-time jobs." *The Akron Beacon Journal* (August 12, 2001).

Ransom, Roger and Richard Sutch. *The Trend in the Rate of Labor Force Participation of Older Men, 1870-1930, A Review of the Evidence.* Cambridge, MA: National Bureau of Economic Research, 1989.

Sass, Steven A. *The Promise of Private Pensions: The First Hundred Years.* Cambridge, MA: Harvard University Press, 1997.

Schaie, K. Warner and W. Andrew Achenbaum. *Societal Impact on Aging: Historical Perspectives.* New York: Springer Publishing Co., 1993.

INTERNET RESOURCES

AARP Foundation
601 E. Street NW
Washington D.C. 20049
www.aarp.org

AMERICAN ASSOCIATION OF HOMES & SERVICES FOR THE AGING
Represents non-profit organizations that provide health care services and assisted living arrangements for the nation's elderly
www.aahsa.org

NATIONAL EDUCATION ASSOCIATION
Website includes a section for members of the NEA who are retired
www.nea.org

NATIONAL COUNCIL ON AGING
Identifies federal and state assistance programs for older Americans
www.benefitscheckup.org

AMERICAN SENIORS HOUSING ASSOCIATION
Deals with issues regarding housing the growing number of elderly Americans
www.seniorhousing.org.

ALLIANCE FOR RETIRED AMERICANS
The Alliance is a voice for retirees and older Americans in national, state and local policy-making.
www.retiredamericans.org

NATIONAL COMMITTEE TO PRESERVE SOCIAL SECURITY AND MEDICARE
Grassroots citizens group serving as an advocate for continuation of Social Security and Medicare
www.ncpssm.org

Greg Moore
Notre Dame College
South Euclid, Ohio

SCIENCE

(1929) Portrait of the Edison Scholarship Committee standing outside the Edison Laboratories, West Orange, New Jersey. L-R: Dr. Lewis Perry, American inventor and industrialist George Eastman, American pilot Colonel Charles A. Lindbergh, American inventor Thomas A. Edison American inventor and auto manufacturer Henry Ford and American engineer and educator Dr. S.W. Stratton.

TIMELINE

1900-1909 ~ Quantum Theory, Aviation Science, Genetics, Statistics

German physicist Max Planck presents the quantum theory that speculates energy is emitted in pulses from heated objects in units he called quanta instead of being discharged continuously (1900) / Einstein theorizes that light is composed of particles he calls photons (1905) / Leo Hendrik Baekeland patents the first completely synthetic plastic, Bakelite (1907) / Albert A. Michelson becomes the first American scientist to win a Nobel Prize for his invention of the interferometer to measure stellar spaces (1907) / Hybrid corn is the most valuable U.S. crop, adding $1.6 billion to the economy (1908)

MILESTONES: About 20 percent of all children die before reaching age 5; less than half survive to age 60 (1900) • Color photo reproduction provides cheap, eye-catching images (1900) • Lee De Forest invents the vacuum tube, essential to the development of electronics (1906) • Indiana becomes the first state to pass sterilization laws of surgical implements; twenty-nine additional states pass sterilization legislation by 1935 (1907)

1910-1919 ~ Theory of Relativity

Einstein develops his initial theory of relativity (1910) / Water chlorination for purification initiated in the United States (1913) / Theodore W. Richards becomes the first American to win a Nobel prize for chemistry for his work with atomic weights (1914) / George Hale constructs a 254 centimeter telescope and learns that galaxies other than the Earth's Milky Way exist (1917)

MILESTONES: Flexner Report questions the adequacy of American medical schools and poor training of physicians (1910) • Measles discovered to be a viral infection (1911) • Mammography developed to detect breast cancer (1913) • Pasteurization of milk begins in large cities (1914) • / 675,000 Americans die during an influenza epidemic (1918)

1920-1939 ~ Evolution, Soil Dynamics, Eugenics

Robert A. Millikan wins a Nobel Prize for his work with electrons (1923) / John T. Scopes, a school teacher in Tennessee, is arrested and tried for teaching evolution to his students (1925) / Supreme Court decision, *Buck v. Bell*, rules that involuntary sterilization for eugenic purposes is constitutional (1927) / Ernest O. Lawrence's cyclotron accelerates nuclear particles to smash atoms and release energy from matter (1930) / Nobel Prize winning geneticist, Hermann J. Muller, attacks the eugenics movement for "lending a false appearance of scientific basis to advocates of race and class prejudice." (1930s) / Thomas Hunt Morgan becomes the first American to win a Nobel Prize in medicine and physiology (1933)

MILESTONES: Infant death rates fall by 20 percent (1920) • Insulin used to treat diabetes (1922) • Invention of the electrocardiograph (1923) • Charles Birdseye develops a quick-freeze technique, making frozen foods possible (1924) • George Papanicolaou develops the Pap test for diagnosing cervical cancer (1928) • Discovery of vitamin C (1928) • Discovery of the common cold virus (1930) • Sulfa drugs introduced to United States (1936)

1940-1959 ～ Atomic Age, Nuclear Transistors, Satellites, Microchips

Westinghouse Science Talent Search (later sponsored by Intel) is organized to identify high school students who have extraordinary scientific potential (1941) / Test pilot Chuck Yeager breaks the sound barrier in an experimental aircraft, the Bell X1 (1947) / Carbon14 dating methods accurately date objects thousands of years old (1947) / Émigrés George Gamow and Hans Bethe, with American physicist Ralph Alpher, propose the Big Bang theory to explain the origins of the universe (1948) / Julius and Ethel Rosenberg, avowed Communists, are executed for transmitting atomic secrets to the Soviets (1953) / Soviet Union's satellite *Sputnik I* successfully orbits the Earth (1957)

MILESTONES: New vaccines developed against typhus and tetanus (1940s) • Chemical sprays developed to control diseases spread by insects (1940s) • Penicillin and blood plasma become available for battlefield use (1941) • Isolation of DNA (1944) • Sickle-cell anemia, prevalent among African Americans, is described as a molecular disease (1949)

1960-1979 ～ Aerospace, Information Age, Computers, Energy Crisis, Environmentalism

John H. Glenn, Jr., becomes the first American to orbit the Earth (February 20, 1962) / American astronauts Neil Armstrong and Buzz Aldrin become the first people to walk on the moon (July 20, 1969) / Norman E. Borlaug, receives the Nobel Prize for genetically creating a strain of high-yield dwarf spring wheat(1970) / Arno Penzias and Robert W. Wilson win the Nobel Prize for refining the "Big Bang" theory of the beginning of the universe (1978)

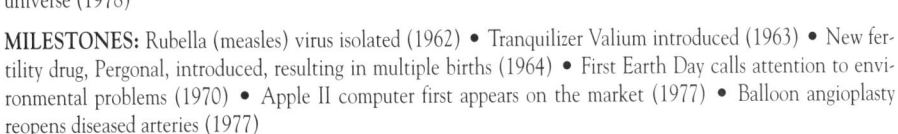

MILESTONES: Rubella (measles) virus isolated (1962) • Tranquilizer Valium introduced (1963) • New fertility drug, Pergonal, introduced, resulting in multiple births (1964) • First Earth Day calls attention to environmental problems (1970) • Apple II computer first appears on the market (1977) • Balloon angioplasty reopens diseased arteries (1977)

1980-1989 ～ Space Shuttle, Digital/Genetic Age, Global Warming

A reusable aerospace vehicle, the space shuttle *Columbia*, launched (1981) / Barbara McClintock becomes the first woman to win a Nobel Prize not shared by other scientists for her work in gene behavior (1983) / Russell Higuchi becomes the first scientist to clone an extinct animal's DNA segment (1983) / First liposuction surgery performed (1983) / First dual heart and liver transplant performed (1984) / First baby born from a donated embryo to an infertile mother (1984) / The Human Genome Organization founded (1988)

MILESTONES: World Health Organization announces worldwide eradication of smallpox (1980) • First successful surgery performed on a fetus (1981) • Sally Ride is the first American woman in space (1983) • First U.S. liver transplant using a living donor (1989)

1990-2000 ～ Human Genome Mapping, Biotechnology, Digital Technology, Space Station

Stem cells from human embryos used to alleviate the symptoms of nervous system disorders, raising ethical questions (1990s) / A four-year-old American girl is the first person to undergo gene therapy (1990) / Federal government withdraws funding for the Super Collider that scientists had used for high energy physics research (1993) / Huntington F. Wilard makes the first artificial human chromosome (1997) / Mapping of the first complete plant genome sequence, that of the mustard weed (2000) / Two scientific teams map the human genome, one of the twentieth century's most outstanding scientific accomplishments (2000)

MILESTONES: Scientists develop irradiation as a safety measure to kill bacteria and toxins such as *E. coli* in foods (1990s) • Norplant implantable contraceptive approved for women (1990) • First significant decline in AIDS deaths is attributed to new protease inhibitors (1997) • FDA approval of a chicken pox vaccine (1995) • U.S. scientists clone a male calf (1997)

INTRODUCTION

Scientists seek to comprehend the world in which they live. Derived from the Latin word *scientia*, meaning knowledge, science represents information gained from observation of subjects, evaluation of facts, and establishment of theories. Scientific experiments test and verify hypotheses. Depicting a variety of interests, such as studying the life cycles of animals determining if water exists on the planet Mars, scientists developed specialties within the branches of physical (examining nonliving matter) and life (studying organisms) science during the twentieth century. These specialties reflected common human interests throughout history: health, employment, communication, transportation, and entertainment. Humans recognized that science enabled them to understand and attain some control of the world. Science also provoked philosophical and religious examination of the purpose and role of humanity in the universe.

In the twentieth century, scientific fields became solidly professionalized by scientific societies focusing on specific subjects. These professional organizations established and enforced standards expected of scientific practitioners and published findings in refereed journals. Interdisciplinary fields, such as biochemistry, evolved to investigate parallel concerns such as the chemical processes in organisms. Mathematics was crucial for scientists to have precise means to measure and describe their data as well as to develop logical thinking skills.

Deductive logic is based on known scientific principles to develop a conclusion for one question. Inductive logic involves observing several experiments to devise a general conclusion. Methodology appropriated from the social sciences, especially economics and statistics, also described twentieth century scientific activity.

Throughout the twentieth century, scientific investigations intrigued scientists who discovered novel ways to perceive a singular topic such as the atom, brain, genetics, cell structure, the universe's origins, and botany. Some scientists pursued interdisciplinary research such as how genetics influences brain behavior. While some scientific queries were resolved and considered part of common knowledge, other aspects required additional investigation and still are not fully comprehended. Although most twentieth century scientists relied on scientific methodology and extended experimentation to form hypotheses, others benefitted from chance discoveries.

Progress was achieved when new scientific ideas expanded or replaced prior knowl-

---

"Modern civilization depends on science. . . . [S]cience is the pursuit above all which impresses us with the capacity of man for intellectual and moral progress and awakens the human intellect to aspiration for a higher condition of humanity."

Inscription by Joseph Henry, the first secretary of the Smithsonian Institution, on the National Museum of American History in Washington, D.C.

edge. Scientists demanded that replicability (a scientist using another scientist's data reproduces the same results) and verifiability (a scientist showing that another scientist's findings are valid by performing an experiment or through observation) were essential for credibility and acceptance of scientific knowledge as a fundamental principle or scientific law. Such peer review regarding scientific methodology retained the integrity of science in the twentieth century

Opinions vary as to whether science is beneficial, detrimental, or somewhere in between. Antiintellectualism during socially conservative periods attempted to stymie scientific philosophies. Scientists agree that science can enhance the quality of life, expand life spans, improve efficiency, and guide people to achieve a better understanding of the natural and physical aspects of the world. In the twentieth century the debate between detrimental science and beneficial science still continues. Either way the twentieth century witnessed more science-related improvements than occurred in any previous eras.

Periods of Modern Science

Historians have identified four main periods of science in the twentieth century: post-Industrial-Revolution, electrical-physical-atomic, information, and digital/genetic ages. Physics and biotechnology have produced the most groundbreaking discoveries. Prior to World War II, scientists mostly worked independently or for academic and industrial institutions and sought information to understand more clearly the basic aspects of science. The Second World War was the catalyst for the federal government to fund, oversee, bureaucratize, and direct teams of scientists investigating more specialized and sophisticated scientific topics useful for both military and peacetime purposes.

The twentieth century was a period in which partnerships were formed between American scientists employed by academia, industry, and governmental agencies. They were responsible for achieving increased understanding and developing new products, processes, and approaches to scientific problems. Research institutes and laboratories provided centralized places for scientists to collaborate and share expensive equipment. Cooperation with international scientists and multidisciplinary research enhanced scientific progress, and new disciplines and industries such as information technology and biotechnology emerged.

Historical Development

Scientific inquiry has been a component of American culture since settlers first began colonizing the eastern coast of the North American continent in the early seventeenth century. Curiosity about the new environment inspired some colonists to question why certain phenomena occurred and to initiate individual and rather amateurish experimentation. Native Americans had previously recognized natural phenomena such as celestial events, including eclipses, comets, and weather patterns that accompanied seasons, and they were well aware of indigenous flora and fauna and how they could be utilized for agriculture, medicines, clothing, and shelter.

1800s

Explorers in the fifteenth and sixteenth centuries had been preoccupied with looking for gold, subduing the natives, and assessing resources of possible value to European monarchs. Some of these adventurers, though, noted wondrous geological formations, wildlife, and plants in their travel accounts and sketched maps of areas that provided information for later scholars to investigate further. Such rudimentary scientific efforts provided a foundation for more learned and structured scientific endeavors.

American science gradually underwent a transition from amateurs indulging in scientific pursuits, such as botanical collections, expeditions, and stargazing to professionals earning credentials from established scientific institutions, including European universities and societies, and gaining authority as experts. Benjamin Franklin's electrical experimentation with lightning is one of the best-known examples of amateur American scientific activity. Pioneering professional scientists' names are mostly obscure and not part of popular culture.

Initially, American education consisted of classical curricula based on Latin, Greek, and the humanities and was only available to upper-class white males. The transition to scientifically oriented schools occurred in the mid-nineteenth century with federal legislation in the form of the 1862 Morrill Act, which established land grant colleges that began to gradually democratize the American educational process. Eighty years later, the G.I. Bill of Rights provided more Americans access to scientific educational opportunities.

The Civil War and nineteenth-century Industrial Revolution were conducive for creativity and invention necessary for

(circa 1920) American educator and scientist George Washington Carver (c. 1865-1943), born to slave, parents in Missouri. He joined the staff of the Tuskegee Normal and Industrial Institute in Alabama and became one of the nation's most prominent agricultural scientists.

technological advancement and escalated scientific research. Frustrated by farm life, many middle and lower class males took advantage of the new state universities to seek scientific and engineering training and secure urban careers. Course work included both theoretical and practical science instruction. Many of these newly graduated science professionals served in executive and administrative positions, influencing and determining business decisions in a dual role as scientist and entrepreneur. Late nineteenth and early twentieth century federal legislation such as the Hatch and Adams Acts encouraged further scientific investigation at land-grant schools. Similar laws were passed to promote science at African American landgrant colleges in the South.

1890s • Public Perceptions
Magazines such as *Scientific American* printed patent information and science news. Newspapers promoted science by printing articles about notable experiments such as American efforts to replicate Wilhelm Roentgen's X-ray demonstration in the 1890s. Science was often relegated to lectures and displays in parlors at local study clubs, which were popular around the turn of the century. Many Americans were aware of, but unfamiliar with, science. They were either suspicious of it or enthralled by it, considering it almost magical, possibly dangerous, and religiously questionable. Although scientists claimed their work ensured future prosperity and security, most people remained dubious about the practicality and profitability of science.

Clearly Americans encountered mixed messages about science. The populist movement of the late nineteenth century interrupted the advancement of scientific measures, especially scientific agricultural practices, because organizations attempted to entice farmers and rural residents to align with them for political motives and goals, such as controlling market prices instead of encouraging them to seek diversification and other scientific methods to increase yields. At the same time, demand increased for trained mechanics and engineers because of internal improvements in railroads, canals, and river navigation. The industrial revolution produced mills and factories utilizing newly invented machinery to process raw materials such as cotton and producing mechanical objects, including automobiles. Many Americans viewed engineering as a means to transform scientific knowledge into monetary profits.

1900s • Scientific Freedom
"We step upon the threshold of 1900," the *New York Times* commented on January 1, 1900, "facing a brighter dawn of civilization." Optimistically, the newspaper projected that new scientific discoveries and technological inventions would dramatically transform American culture in the twentieth century. For several decades, Americans had become aware of a variety of devices such as automobiles, washing machines, and film projectors that had been invented to reduce human labor, expedite transportation, improve housing, and entertain people. These inventions were mostly available only in urban areas, where factories and showrooms were located, and many rural Americans' access to these items were delayed. Technological developments in aviation were perhaps the most amazing and well publicized scientific events of this decade.

Science flourished in turn-of-the-century America because scientists were free

1900s to pursue their research. Unlike scientists in many other countries, American scientists were not controlled by their government. Economic support often came from foundations and industries eager to sponsor scientists who might produce marketable products for them. The technological and theoretical achievements of American and European scientists during the previous quarter century set the stage for a flurry of scientific activity in the early 1900s. American scientists were motivated by the culture of free enterprise and individual liberty to take risks and explore topics, initiate experimentation, and innovate new methods and tools. The membership of the American Association for the Advancement of Science (AAAS) increased by 400 percent during the first decade of the twentieth century.

Science was considered primarily as a marvel. Many Americans did not understand the basic concepts of science nor did they regularly encounter individuals who were scientists. More flamboyant aspects of science provided a popular form of entertainment for many urban Americans who had their hands and purses X-rayed at club meetings and watched magic shows based on scientific principles such as magnetism and optical illusions. Many people viewed science as a social activity. People became aware of science through question/answer columns, articles, and illustrations in newspapers.

1904 • WORLD'S FAIR ~ The 1904 World's Fair in St. Louis, Missouri, popularized science. Exhibits familiarized fair attendees with scientific instruments and processes. Treats such as CocaCola represented scientific endeavors. Chemists originally developed that concoction as a pharmaceutical. Americans could purchase goods made from Bakelite, the first completely synthetic plastic patented by Leo Hendrik Baekeland in 1907 or buy

---

Chronological List of Selected American Science Societies by Date Founded

American Philosophical Society http://www.amphilsoc.org	1743
Franklin Institute http://www.fi.edu	1824
American Association for the Advancement of Science http://www.aaas.org	1848
National Academy of Science http://www.nas.edu	1863
American Chemical Society http://www.acs.org	1876
Sigma Xi http://www.sigmaxi.org/	1886
National Geographic Society http://www.nationalgeographic.com	1888
American Astronomical Society http://www.aas.org	1899
American Society for Microbiology http://www.asmusa.org	1899
National Research Council http://www.nas.edu	1916
Optical Society of America http://www.osa.org	1917
Science Service http://www.sciserv.com	1922
American Institute of Physics http://www.aip.org	1931
National Association of Science Writers http://www.nasw.org	1934
National Science Teachers Association http://www.nsta.org	1944
American Institute of Biological Sciences http://www.aibs.org	1947
National Science Foundation http://www.nsf.gov	1950
American Astronautical Society http://www.astronautical.org	1954

products originally designed in the General Electric laboratories. Other commercial research laboratories, including AT&T's Bell Labs, Dow Corning, and Du Pont, further promoted commercialization of science. More people recognized the merits of science for humanitarian uses. The Progressive Era encouraged reformers to seek scientific remedies for social concerns such as public health and combating infectious diseases and infant mortality. Science was equated with progress. Health sciences evolved as more and more immigrants inhabited cities and the cities discovered health hazards.

1900-1910 • SUPPORTERS AND DISSENTERS ~ At the turn of the century, politicians were more reform-minded and friendly to the work of scientists than in previous decades. They supported scientific pursuits that addressed social concerns by approving funding and legislation. For the most part, the scientific community explored theoretical science. Academic communities were nuclei of proponents of scientific and technological advancement, and supportive colleagues listened to research ideas and encouraged original experimentation. Scientists in related fields discussed and analyzed concepts and theories and provided books on advanced work in their specialized fields of study. Outside of college towns, such intellectual stimulation was mostly absent, and many people were reluctant to accept science, choosing to reject it in favor of traditions often based on religion, superstitions, and folklore.

In the early twentieth century, critics of science thought that industrialization and commercialization related to science threatened their current lifestyles and conflicted with their traditional religious

(1904) Participants in the New York to St. Louis automobile parade, part of the Louisiana Purchase Exposition in 1904 (St. Louis World's Fair), St. Louis, Missouri. A ferris wheel stands in the background.

and cultural beliefs. Antiscience individuals wanted to retain the traditions of their ancestors and expressed distrust of external and unfamiliar ideas, preferring the familiar, even if it was outdated, incorrect, or prevented advancement. Many people also considered practical experience more valuable than academic instruction. Public forums modeled after religious camp meetings often were the most effective method to expose rural peoples to scientific concepts that might be useful in their lives.

Extension and home demonstration programs affiliated with colleges attempted to share information about scientific agriculture and domestic concerns such as nutrition and sanitation. The insufficient number of scientifically trained agents prevented many people from gaining access to progressive ideas endorsed by scientific colleges. Business interests, however, began to provide financial support, and this work expanded. Philanthropists such as Julius Rosenwald, John D. Rockefeller, and Andrew Carnegie provided funds to improve educational institutions and create facilities conducive to scientific advancements. By showing people how science could benefit them, instead of relying on discussing abstract ideas, some transfer of improved methods occurred.

1900-1915 • EINSTEIN ~ American scientists were aware of international researchers' ideas that transformed how physical phenomena was perceived. Albert Einstein, a German physicist who later immigrated to the United States, posed two theories concerning relativity in the first fifteen years of the twentieth century. He stated that mass moves through space and time relative to other objects in the universe and that rest and motion are always relative to each other. His revelation was an epiphany for scientists worldwide who realized that their previous understanding of how to observe reality accurately was limited and that their grasp of scientific knowledge was not absolute. Considering new ways to approach problem resolution, people began to question existing scientific principles based on physical laws credited to seventeenth-century scientist Sir Isaac Newton. Einstein's theory caused scientists to consider the motion of an observer when considering basic space and time problems. He also formulated the equation $E=mc^2$, showing that mass and energy were equivalent. This equation led to the realization that if an atom could be split, it would release previously unimaginable amounts of energy. His theories revolutionized physics.

1890-1916 • ATOMIC PHYSICS ~ In the 1890s, European scientists had begun to realize that atoms were not solid objects as previously believed. Electrons and radioactivity were described, and scientists began to look for an internal structure in atoms. American scientists learned about these ideas and initiated atomic examinations that contributed to the future development of quantum mechanics and transformation of physics. In 1900, the German physicist Max Planck presented the quantum theory, which speculated that energy was emitted from heated objects in units he called quanta instead of being discharged continuously. Five years later, Einstein stated that light is composed of units of energy which he later described as particles that became known as photons. Matter was examined for its components which existed in what was referred to as the microcosm. Scientists determined that matter existed as particles and energy as waves, but that both forms could be converted within the microcosm to behave as the other. Energy sometimes acted like particles, and matter could behave similarly to waves.

Research into the structure of the atom expanded rapidly. In 1911, the British physicist Ernest Rutherford theorized that the mass of an atom is concentrated in a tiny nucleus, which is surrounded by electrons traveling at tremendous speeds. But his theory did not deal with the arrangement of electrons. In 1913, Niels Bohr, a Danish physicist, proposed a description of electron structure. Bohr suggested that electrons could travel only in a set of definite orbits around the nucleus.

Harvard chemist Theodore W. Richards, researching atomic weights, discovered the existence of isotopes. Gilbert N. Lewis combined studies of physics and chemistry to postulate his theory of atomic structure in 1916, saying that electrons surrounded an atomic nuclei. General Electric physicist Irving Langmuir applied this information to develop the concentric shell theory in 1919, which stated that an element was chemically active because of electrons completing the outer shell. Inspired by Einstein's theory, American scientist Robert A. Millikan experimented with methods to measure the charge of electrons. Millikan sandwiched an oil drop between two charged plates. When he altered the charge on a plate, the drop of oil moved up or down according to the plate's charge. Millikan estimated the drop's mass and strength of its electrical charge based on its behavior.

This new understanding of physics and chemistry resulted in useful applications of radioactive elements such as chemist Bertram B. Boltwood assessing rocks' ages by measuring the ratio of uranium and lead. During World War I, scientists and engineers were recruited for defense research and commissioned for temporary military service. Industrial chemists created chemical weapons, poisonous gases, and explosives during World War I. Their efforts foreshadowed the massive scientific mobilization for the Second World War.

Although the Nobel Prize, financed by Swedish industrialist Alfred Nobel, was first awarded in the categories of physics, chemistry, and medicine/physiology in 1901, an American did not receive that honor until six years later. Albert A. Michelson was the first American scientist to win a Nobel Prize, receiving the 1907 prize in physics. The principles of the interferometer that he invented to measure stellar spaces proved significant at the close of the twentieth century for astronomers seeking planets in distant solar systems. Theodore W.

Distribution of American Nobel Prize Winners

	Physics	Chemistry	Physiology/Medicine	Economic Science
1901-1909	1	0	0	—
1910-1919	0	1	0	—
1920-1929	2	0	0	—
1930-1939	3	2	4	—
1943-1949	3	3	6	—
1950-1959	9	4	14	—
1960-1969	10	5	13	—
1970-1979	13	6	15	8*
1980-1989	11	14	14	7
1990-1999	17	14	15	15
TOTALS	69	49	81	30

* First year the prize for Economic Science was offered.

SOURCES: *The Nobel Prize Winners. Physiology or Medicine and Chemistry*, edited by Frank N. Magill, 1990-91; *Nobel Prize Winners*, edited by Tyler Wasson, 1987; *The New York Times 2001 Almanac*, edited by John W. Wright, 2000.

Richards was the first American to win a Nobel for chemistry in 1914 for his work with atomic weights. Robert A. Millikan won a Nobel Prize in 1923 for his previously mentioned work with electrons. During the twentieth century, American scientific societies developed other awards to recognize scientific excellence.

1890-1920 • GENETIC RESEARCH

Genetics was another European idea imported by American scientists. Since the colonial era, some Americans had been aware of a scientific basis for certain characteristics in sexually-reproducing organisms. For example, Paul Dudley hypothesized that the wind transported reproductive material between rows of Indian corn with red, blue, white, and yellow kernels, which caused some ears of corn to be multicolored, but geneticists ignored his theory until the twentieth century.

1890-1920

Aware of Gregor Mendel's nineteenth century pea breeding experiments, Thomas Hunt Morgan, an American biologist, introduced the concept of genes and chromosomes to early twentieth-century American culture. He and his co-researchers identified genes as the transmitters of characteristics that offspring inherit from their parents. They also revealed that genes are placed in a predictable order along cellular structures called chromosomes. Morgan elaborated by showing where fruit fly genes were located on chromosomes and defined which genes determined traits such as eye color and the shape of wings. He also noted that some traits were linked to gender. Morgan's students studied genetic mutations. Such specialized research caused genetics to be established as a distinct branch of biology. In 1933, Morgan was the first American to win a Nobel Prize in medicine or physiology.

Agricultural scientists applied genetic research findings to hybrid seed technology, which first gained ground in the early twentieth century and foreshadowed the controversial dominance of biotechnology near the end of the century. Previously, agriculturists might have intuitively bred the best plants and animals to produce higher quality stock without understanding why the quality improved. The United States Department of Agriculture, created during the Civil War, encouraged scientific research by financing investigations, collecting data, and publishing yearbooks. Federally-supported agricultural extension services and experiment stations assisted farmers and implemented vocational education programs which incorporated scientific agriculture. Such governmental intervention in agriculture preceded legislation in the 1950s that extended to other scientific fields. Federal officials suggested that scientists pursue hereditary experiments, and they devised high-yielding hybrid seeds that transformed American agriculture. For example, in 1908, hybrid corn was the most valuable U.S. crop, adding $1.6 billion to the economy.

1910-1920 • HEALTH ISSUES ~ A medical crisis revealed the need for scientific investigations to preserve public health. Approximately 675,000 Americans died during the 1918 influenza epidemic. Scientists gradually recognized the relationships between microorganisms and diseases during the late-nineteenth century, but treatment procedures were more successful than determining preventative measures. Medical scientists focused on finding new ways to destroy disease-causing bacteria, developing antibiotics and producing more effective pharmaceuticals. Manufacturing pharmaceuticals became a vital industry in the American economy, and scientists were employed to create drugs to combat resistant new strains of bacteria and to mitigate new infectious diseases that plagued Americans during the century. Flu and pneumonia inoculations became a routine injection for many Americans to ward off potential health complications.

Water chlorination for purification was initiated in the United States in 1913 for additional public health efforts. Mental health procedures were influenced by Austrian physician Sigmund Freud's theories of psychoanalysis, which interpreted the unconscious mind. In addition to human health research, veterinarians focused on animal health issues to ensure healthy meat and milk supplies and prevent transmission of parasites and deadly diseases such as rabies, brucellosis, and tuberculosis.

1920s • ATOMIC STRUCTURE AND HEALTH SCIENCE ~ During the conservative and prosperous post-World War I decade, science experienced both progress and setbacks. Science was appropriated by some Americans to support radical causes and was often misunderstood and vilified. On the other hand, public infatuation with aviation blossomed, and scientists strived to produce instruments, materials, and fuels to make aircraft fly higher and longer distances. The National Advisory Committee on Aeronautics (NACA), established in 1915, coordinated research by universities, industry, and the federal government for both civil and military aviation.

Many scientists looked beyond the Earth's atmosphere. George Hale had constructed a 254-centimeter telescope in 1917 and learned that galaxies other than our home Milky Way existed. During the 1920s, astronomers observed and described new discoveries in the universe. Edwin Hubble said that the rapid stellar movement in many directions indicated that the universe was expanding. The farther away the celestial objects were from Earth, he explained, the faster their movement. This finding contradicted previous scientists' hypotheses that the universe was static and unchanging.

Scientists expanded their knowledge of quantum physics, realizing that wave theory caused previous physics principles to become invalid and inadequate. Physicists became aware of new subatomic particles in the microcosm named quarks and leptons and observed behavior such as particles spinning, decaying, and transforming into other particles. As physicists learned more about atomic structure and behavior—such as electron arrangement and discovery of the neutron—chemists applied this knowledge to experiments with chemical bonds. Not only did such research result in the production of new compounds, synthetic fibers, and plastics, but the information enabled scientists to comprehend more about the origins of the universe.

(circa 1925) A pair of enormous amplifiers used by the U.S. Naval Air Service for locating and contacting aeroplanes by day and night.

Chemistry was also essential for the life sciences. Scientists determined that vitamins were nutritionally essential. Vitamins supplement diets to prevent diseases caused by malnutrition, such as scurvy and rickets. European medical advances such as chemotherapy and penicillin were adapted for use in American hospitals. Researchers also discovered that deoxyribonucleic acid (DNA) and ribonucleic acid (RNA) were both fundamental to genetic inheritance. In the 1920s, Hermann J. Muller began using X-rays to cause mutations in organisms for which he later won a Nobel Prize. Laboratory advances influenced social scientists of this period who began to adopt scientific research methodology and statistical analysis to describe human patterns. Madame Curie's 1921 visit to the United States, including a White House reception, excited many Americans about the possibilities of women in science.

Fields Represented by Scientists Starred from *American Men of Science*, 1906, 1921, 1927

(Note: The totals are the same for each year, showing how these fields remained constant for 20 years.)

Field	Total Number of Scientist Each Year
Anatomy	25
Anthropology	20
Astronomy	50
Botany	100
Chemistry	175
Geology	100
Mathematics	80
Pathology	60
Physiology	40
Psychology	50
Physics	150
Zoology	150

SOURCE: *American Men of Science*, 1906, 1921 and 1927.

1920s • AGRICULTURAL SCIENCE
One of the most notable human social patterns of the 1920s was the demographic shift to urban areas. Historians cite the 1920s as the watershed decade in which more Americans lived in urban areas than in rural locations. As a result, fewer farmers had the responsibility to produce sufficient agricultural goods to feed and clothe a growing group of consumers. Agricultural science provided solutions to increase agricultural yields for the swelling urban populations in the United States and abroad. Historians explain that agriculture was static in the nineteenth century and that such sudden, fundamental changes as twentieth-century agricultural science were revolutionary.

Science enhanced the quality and quantity of crops and livestock and enabled economic growth. Such scientific developments as chemical fertilizers, insecticides, weed killers, and genetics increased yields and agricultural profits to purchase more scientific tools, thus perpetuating a cycle of efficiency. Science also saved time, which farmers used to learn more progressive farming methods. Science created employment opportunities in agriculturally related industries, increased agriculturists' earning potential, modernized rural lifestyles, secured professional respect for agriculturists, and encouraged farmers' children to stay on family farms and continue rural traditions because they had more earning potential.

Scientific research in dual fields such as agronomy and engineering resulted in original methodologies such as soil dynamics established by Mark L. Nichols at the Alabama Polytechnic Institute in the 1920s. An agricultural engineer, Nichols developed scientific methods to design reliable, predictable machinery to work with different soil types found in the United States. He also studied how soils provided support and traction for machines and how machines compacted and manipulated soil because compaction hindered production. The science of soil dynamics enabled efficient agricultural mechanization and permitted farming to become engineered and more stable than previous trial and error implement design attempts.

Nichols's research helped agricultural engineering become a recognized engineering profession, advanced industrial standards for rural implements, and enhanced farmers' attitudes toward technology by making tractors enjoyable to use. Soil dynamics emerged as a significant science by the 1950s, aiding implement manufacturers to create improved machinery with better traction thus conserving fuel and increasing yields. Soil dynamics knowledge aided the application of artificial intelligence and robotics to sophisticated agricultural machinery and was applied to other scientific fields such as tire design for automobiles and the lunar rover.

1920s • Backlash to Science ~ Despite its apparent benefits, science was skewered and misrepresented in a highly publicized court case. Most American scientists had been intrigued by English scientist Charles Darwin's evolution theories. The American public, however, were less eager to embrace evolutionism. The 1920s was a decade in which conservatism and fundamentalism prevailed and anti-intellectualism thrived. A resurgence of religiosity somewhat like the antebellum Great Awakening had emerged. Many religious groups viewed science as suspicious and warned followers to reject scientific ideas.

In Dayton, Tennessee, science was placed on trial when John T. Scopes, a schoolteacher, was arrested for teaching evolution to his students. The sensationalized Scopes Monkey Trial, as it came to be called, in 1925 revealed the antagonism between scientists and religious figures who denounced evolution for being contrary to the Biblical account of creation. Although defense attorney Clarence Darrow lost his case, the theory of evolution received national attention and scrutiny. Seventy years later, a similar protest was staged in Kansas where detractors unsuccessfully attempted to remove lessons about evolution from classrooms.

1920s • Eugenics ~ In addition to enduring attacks, science was also misappropriated during the 1920s. Eugenics was a sociopolitical effort by self-appointed elitists to control minorities, immigrants, and impoverished Americans by seizing their reproduction rights in a form of social Darwinism. Charles Darwin's cousin, Francis Galton, initiated the eugenics movement in late nineteenth century Great Britain, hoping to encourage people whom he considered to be superior humans to reproduce. He did not advocate the extreme measures used by American eugenicists who hoped to improve the genetic qualities of individuals and protect and purify the Caucasian race somewhat like livestock and plant breeders sought perfection with their stock. Politicizing genetics, eugenicists discouraged reproduction through sterilization. Eugenics became more popular in the twentieth century United States as some middle class Americans felt threatened economically by the lower classes. Such attitudes were reinforced by studies that made false claims justified with pseudo-scientific findings. Americans' emerging awareness of new biological theories that had been formed at the turn of the century aided the eugenicists' manipulation of this information as the foundation of their prejudices and hatred toward certain social groups.

Eugenicists complained that charitable support of poor people interfered with natural selection and blamed medical reforms for the survival and reproduction of so-called inferior groups. They emphasized that the people they considered genetically unworthy of reproduction should willingly submit to sterilization as their civic duty. In 1907, Indiana was the first state to pass a sterilization law, and twenty-nine additional states passed similar legislation by 1935. State eugenics agents examined individuals' heredity and ordered the arrest and sterilization of people they considered questionable, denying individuals the right to make personal reproductive decisions.

Geneticist Charles B. Davenport established the Eugenics Record Office at Cold Spring Harbor, New York, and estimated that the federal government paid $100 million annually to support people that he considered inferior. More than 70,000 people, predominantly poor and institutionalized, were involuntarily sterilized in the United States between 1907 and 1945. Several victims unsuccessfully challenged sterilization laws. A 1927 Supreme Court decision, *Buck v. Bell*, ruled that involuntary sterilization for eugenic purposes was constitutional.

During the 1930s, scientists began to discredit eugenicists' propaganda and separate themselves by exposing the movement's science as whitewashed racist rhetoric. Many scientists publicly denounced eugenicists for stereotyping groups, manipulating evidence, and not securing scientific proof for their beliefs. The Nobel Prize winning geneticist, Hermann J. Muller, attacked the eugenics movement for "lending a false appearance of scientific basis to advocates of race and class prejudice, defenders of vested interests of church and state, Fascists, Hitlerites, and reactionaries generally." The Nazis' horrifying use of eugenics during World War II further eroded the American eugenics movement.

1930s • HARD TIMES FOR ALL ~ In contrast to the prosperity of the previous decade, the 1930s witnessed a climate of despair during the Great Depression. Scientists suffered economic misfortunes. Many researchers and professors lost positions because schools and industries were unable to pay salaries and overhead costs. Scientists continued experimentation when possible. Some scientists were employed by federal relief programs to collect data. Others were fortunate to retain access to their laboratories and some funding despite the national economic emergency.

Although scientific instruments and supplies were sometimes too expensive and scarce, scientists persevered. One significant accomplishment was Ernest O. Lawrence's use of a cyclotron, that accelerated nuclear particles to smash atoms and release energy from matter in 1930. Producing radioactivity, physicists experimented with fission by splitting uranium nuclei to generate nuclear energy.

Electricity was also generated by dams along the Tennessee and Colorado Rivers that scientists helped to design and build during the Depression. Scientists found electricity useful to conduct scientific investigations. Chemist Wallace Hume Carothers created nylon in 1934. Scientific products were displayed at the 1933 Chicago World's Fair which appropriately had the theme "The Century of Progress." The 1939 World's Fair at San Francisco also showcased to the public scientific achievements of the decade.

1920-1950 • WOMEN, MINORITY AND ÉMIGRÉ SCIENTISTS ~ In the first half of the twentieth century, most scientists holding significant research positions or academic appointments were white males. Despite laws that promised social justice and equity, female and black scientists constantly faced barriers. Women scientists were often denied the prestige of academic or laboratory positions or competitive fellowships for which they were qualified. They worked as assistants to male scientists or served as temporary lecturers or researchers. Because of rules against nepotism, wives were prohibited from becoming faculty members at colleges where their husbands worked. Women's colleges employed many female scientists. African American scientists mostly worked at segregated institutions or moved to Europe where they enjoyed less racial discrimination. Women such as Ida Hyde also found more scientific opportunities abroad. Tuskegee Institute's George Washington Carver prospered in a predominantly African American environment where administrators, faculty, students, and residents appreciated his practical botanical contributions. Cytologist Ernest E. Just, however, was frustrated at all black Howard University and preferred European laboratories for research.

As America's disenfranchised groups retreated to Europe for opportunities, a mass migration of European scientists sought political refuge in the United States. Concerned when Adolf Hitler and the National Socialist German Workers' Party gained power in Germany and posed a threat to Europe's intellectual community, especially Jews, some scientists emigrated to America to escape the restrictive and punitive social climate. The scientific refugees included nuclear physicists who revealed in the late 1930s that enormous amounts of energy could be released by splitting uranium atoms. Despite many Americans'

(1950) In the first half of the twentieth century, most scientists were white males despite laws that promised social justice. In 1950, when these students were performing laboratory experiments, women were discouraged by society from pursuing careers or challenging men to compete for scientific positions.

tendency toward xenophobia and isolationism in the 1920s and 1930s, these physicists and chemists were mostly welcomed at educational institutions and think tanks where they contributed their intellectual prowess to pressing scientific concerns. The émigrés most notably provided scientific knowledge essential for the success of the Manhattan Project during World War II, resulting in the development of the world's first nuclear weapons. They also were among the first targeted for charges of treason.

1940s • Renaissance of American Science

The Second World War was a watershed for American science, introducing millions of people, both men and women, to scientific processes and enabling federal direction of a national science policy. U.S. science and engineering resources mobilized for military needs at home and abroad. Prior to the United States entering the war, American educators and industrial leaders, aware of possible wartime scientific needs, strived to encourage students to concentrate on science research that might be militarily valuable. In 1941, the Westinghouse Science Talent Search—later sponsored by Intel—was organized to identify high school students who had extraordinary scientific potential.

One week after Germany invaded France, Vannevar Bush, the president of the Carnegie Institution of Washington who had been the Dean of Engineering at Massachusetts Institute of Technology (MIT), contacted President Franklin D. Roosevelt on June 12, 1940. Bush recommended that Roosevelt establish a National Defense Research Council (NDRC) to determine how best to prepare and organize American science resources for potential wartime service. Roosevelt named Bush chairman of the NDRC. Within one year, Roosevelt issued an executive order to establish the Office of Scientific Research and Development (OSRD) which had more authority to deal with the increased military concerns of the war.

Functioning within the Executive Office of the President, the OSRD's purpose was to "serve as a center for mobilization of the scientific personnel and resources of the Nation in order to assure maximum utilization of such personnel and resources in developing and applying the results of scientific research to defense purposes." The order also stated that the OSRD was "to coordinate, aid, where desirable, supplement the experimental and other scientific and medical research activities relating to national defense carried on by the Departments of War and Navy and other departments and agencies of the Federal Government." Bush was named director of the OSRD.

Anticipating U.S. entry into World War II, Bush coordinated efforts with officials in the Departments of War and Navy to determine which defense-related research projects should receive priority. Also, he directed the identification and equipping of scientists to work on these projects. Scientific personnel and resources were spread among the nation's academic, government, and industrial institutions. Of the $345 million spent on research and development (R&D) in 1940, industry expended $234 million, the federal government $67 million, and academic institutions $31 million. The remaining $13 million came from foundations, research institutes, and state governments.

Prior to World War II, the United States federal government had not funded university research except for several aviation projects. Sometimes professors privately served as consultants for governmental agencies. The federal government preferred not to fund academic research to avoid interfering in institutional matters. Before the Second World War, most academic scientists received monies from grants, industries, foundations, endowments, and states. During the war, however, these scientists retained their civilian status and were encouraged to remain at their academic institutions to perform defense research. Industrial scientists also remained at their peacetime locations.

Rejecting the centralized World War I scientific defense system, Bush preferred decentralization, encouraging a partnership between academia, industry, and government rather than the government controlling academic and industrial scientists. In some cases, scientists worked at one location, such as the people who developed radar at MIT's Radiation Laboratory. Others were grouped together for top secret projects. Wartime research required academic scientists to conceive and undertake risky, unique ideas, which resulted in the development of nuclear weapons and radar systems. Military science applications also underscored the need for scientists to retain intellectual integrity by being as detached as possible from political processes despite receiving federal funds and adapting science for political agendas.

1942-1945 • THE ATOMIC AGE BEGINS

∽ Warned that Adolf Hitler's scientists were working on a bomb that could unleash the energy pent up in the atomic nucleus, American government leaders decided to assemble a team of American and European scientists who cooperated in a secret program known as the Manhattan Project. Beginning in 1942, leading scientists and engineers joined Bush to produce an atomic weapon. Charles Dunham led a scientific team at New York's Columbia University to separate uranium's rare, fissionable isotope U235 from the more common U238 by using a gaseous diffusion process. Italian émigré Enrico Fermi directed scientists at the University of Chicago to produce a controlled plutonium chain reaction in 1942. Reactors at Hanford, Washington, produced plutonium, and workers at an Oak Ridge, Tennessee facility called "Dogpatch," separated U235 with Dunham's process. At Los Alamos, New Mexico, scientists gathered at the secret Site Y where Robert Oppenheimer guided efforts to integrate the scientific components achieved at each of the other sites to produce atomic bombs.

(1948) Rockets powered by carbon dioxide are fired at a ball representing an atom of uranium 235 at the Westinghouse Research Laboratories' 'Theatre of Atoms'. The rockets represent neutrons and upon striking the balloon they release 'atomic fragments' in the form of smaller balloons.

The first successful trial occurred at the Alamogordo Desert in July 1945. Shortly thereafter two bombs were dropped on major industrial cities in Japan. Each explosion was equal to detonating 20,000 tons of dynamite. The resultant death and destruction led to the surrender of Japan in the Pacific and the end of World War II. Industry, academia, and government cooperated to make the Manhattan Project successful. For example, researchers from around the country worked at Los Alamos, a military base; University of California academics worked under a research and development contract with the Army; and the General Electric Company managed the Oak Ridge facility at the University of Chicago.

1944 • THE NATIONAL SCIENCE FOUNDATION ~ Although the public was unaware of this secret scientific activity, high-level politicians and officials in Roosevelt's administration knew about science's crucial role for national security and believed that governmental monitoring of science should be extended to peacetime. In 1944, Senator Harley M. Kilgore introduced a bill in the U.S. Senate to establish a National Science Foundation (NSF). Kilgore was a member of a Select Committee that investigated the war production effort; Senator Harry S Truman was the committee's chairman. Kilgore stated that the proposed NSF would fund federal laboratories and issue research contracts and scholarships to academic institutions. Reluctant for the federal government to assume control over science policy, senators refused to begin hearings regarding the bill until after the war concluded.

Ten days after he was reelected to a fourth term, President Franklin D. Roosevelt wrote Bush a letter, requesting advice on how wartime experiences mobilizing scientists and engineers could be applied to peacetime "for the improvement of the national health, the creation of new enterprises bringing new jobs, and the betterment of the national standard of living." Roosevelt had four questions of foremost concern. First, he was concerned about declassifying results from secret war research, particularly the Manhattan Project. Second, Roosevelt wanted Bush to specify the national need for a government program to support health-related scientific investigations. Third, he wondered how the government could issue aid for research through both public and private organizations. And fourth, he was interested in identifying potential scientists and developing their talents.

Bush, a proponent of academic scientific research, organized scientists not affiliated with the government into four committees, and each group was assigned a question and ordered to report their findings and offer suggestions. After Roosevelt's sudden death, Germany's surrender, and anticipating Japan's defeat, President Harry S. Truman urged continued examination of what the government's postwar role in science should be. By July 1945, Bush prepared his report, "Science—The Endless Frontier," with four appendices addressing Roosevelt's questions. The report emphasized that "without scientific progress no amount of achievement in other directions can insure our health, prosperity, and security as a nation in the modern world." Because existing governmental agencies were unprepared to regulate scientific activity and too political, the report stressed the "imperative" need for the NSF to be established and isolated as possible from politics and guided by members who the president appointed and who were "persons of broad interest in and understanding of the peculiarities of scientific research and education."

The proposed NSF would fund nongovernment, nonprofit research institutions that conducted scientific investigations, including medical and civilian defense research. The NSF would also grant fellowships and scholarships. Funds were to be allocated according to merit as determined by qualified professionals assessing applicants. At the time, suggestions that the federal government had the authority to support basic research, mostly in universities and the responsibility to assist the professional development of aspiring scientists was a daring departure from the status quo. Bush wanted university scientists to move from the periphery of American research to become the nucleus of scientific inquiries.

Consistent with previous procedures, Bush discouraged the government from interfering with industrial research except in cases of national defense. American industries had predominantly relied on basic research by European scientists, but laboratories and research facilities had been destroyed and scientists were killed during the war, causing American industries to seek American scientists to pursue research. Bush stressed, "The most important ways in which the Government can promote industrial research are to increase the flow of new scientific knowledge through support of basic research, and to aid in the development of scientific talent."

1945-1947 • LEGISLATING SCIENCE

∼ In late July 1945, Senator Warren Magnuson introduced legislation promoting the NSF, and Senator Kilgore consulted with Bush before reintroducing his revised bill several days later. The two bills presented divergent forms of a National Science Foundation with varying administrative structures and funding priorities. At joint hearings beginning in October 1945, senators disagreed about how the NSF should be organized and function. From 1945 to 1950, the issue of national science policy was publicly debated. Even the youthful Westinghouse Science Talent Search winners traveled to Washington, D.C., to testify before a congressional committee debating the merit of the NSF legislation. They stressed that federal support for science in the form of the NSF would benefit future scientists.

While politicians argued about the formation of the NSF, two research agencies, the Office of Naval Research (ONR) and the National Institutes of Health (NIH) as part of the Public Health Service, were formed in 1946 and 1948 respectively, lessening the extent of the disputed NSF and allocating funds to university researchers. In 1946, after hearing the testimony of scientists involved in World War II nuclear research, Congress created the Atomic Energy Commission (AEC), governed by a presidential-appointed civilian commission, to deal with the issue of whether the military or civilians should have control of nuclear energy. These agencies' experiences with non-government scientists established a framework for future federal science policies.

Because the federal government's role overseeing national scientific activity rapidly expanded, President Truman created the President's Scientific Research Board (PSRB) on October 17, 1946. John R. Steelman served as chairman and directed the compilation of a five volume report titled "Science and Public Policy" which was distributed in August 1947. Analyzing the national science system, the report commented on cooperation between academia, industry, and government and assessed the quality of science education from elementary levels to advanced graduate curricula. The report criticized the lack of coordination between science programs overseen by numerous agencies and urged that a central committee be formed to synchronize scientific research and monitor federal expenditures to each agency. Steelman also believed that science policy must be considered with other national policy issues and that a representative for science policy have close access to the president.

Immediately after the war ended, the facilities used for World War II scientific research were still staffed by academic and industrial personnel, many of whom had been employed at those facilities during the war. They were funded through contracts with federal agencies such as the Department of Energy. These postwar facilities were called "federally funded research and development centers" (FFRDCs). New FFRDCs for basic research conducted by university-affiliated scientists were established after World War II, including the Fermi National Accelerator Laboratory and the Stanford Linear Accelerator Center.

1946-1950 • Peacetime Science ～ Statistically, 1,900 people earned science doctorates in 1941, and this number declined to fewer than 800 science Ph.D.s in 1945. Researchers continued their work and accomplished notable scientific achievements related to military concerns during the war and immediately following it. During the war, scientists worked on developing more efficient fuels for military vehicles and aircraft. The jet stream was discovered as a result of jet aircraft flying at high altitudes and traveling long distances to reach the war front. Climate and altitude conditions encountered in the war inspired Vincent J. Schaefer to study how to remove ice from airplane wings. He also discovered a process to seed clouds with dry ice to cause precipitation.

Because the United States emerged from the war as a global leader, postwar research continued to examine the uses of nuclear energy as a weapon while also exploring its capacity to produce civilian energy resources. Wartime experimentation resulted in better power sources and radioactive tracers for use in medicine. Supersonic flight became possible when test pilot Chuck Yeager broke the sound barrier—traveling faster than the speed of sound—in an experimental aircraft, the Bell X1, in 1947. That year, Willard Libby introduced carbon14 dating methods.

Émigrés George Gamow and Hans Bethe, with American physicist Ralph Alpher, proposed the Big Bang theory in 1948 to explain the origins of the universe. American physicists William B. Shockley, Walter Brattain, and John Bardeen designed a point-contact transistor in 1947 that provided scientists an alternative to using vacuum tubes and were the catalyst for the semiconductor revolution. The trio won the Nobel Prize in 1956, and Bardeen was the first scientist to win the physics Nobel Prize twice when he won in 1972 with colleagues Leon Cooper and John Schrieffer for presenting the first plausible theory of superconductivity. Claude Elwood Shannon developed mathematical information theory that would be essential for communication and computer science applications.

In 1947, approximately 137,000 scientists, engineers, and technicians were active in research and development (R&D) in the United States, and 25,000 of these scientists possessed a doctorate in a field of physical or biological science while also teaching at academic institutions. In that year, 1,600 students completed their Ph.D. in science, but a shortage of qualified science personnel required at least 3,800 doctorates be produced annually in the next decade in order to provide sufficient science resources needed to meet national science policy goals. Although the total number of scientists in the United States had increased from 131,440 in 1941 to 324,145 in 1945 then to 462,890 in 1947, more scientists were sought.

1942-1949 • FOREIGN SCIENTISTS IN THE UNITED STATES ~ Foreign scientists provided one means to increase the population of scientists in the United States quickly. Throughout the twentieth century, international science ties had introduced American scientists to numerous scientific theories and instruments that were essential for scientific advancement. Furthermore, American scientists recognized the contributions of émigrés who had arrived before the war and welcomed renewing ties with colleagues in foreign countries, inviting them to do their research in the United States. Many foreign scientists were eager for this opportunity because research and academic institutions in Europe and Asia had been destroyed during the war.

American science helped to rebuild Europe and Asia after the war and to reinforce democracies during the Cold War. Federal funds paid for American scientists to travel abroad for conferences and for foreign investigators to visit the United States and enroll in American universities. Perhaps the most controversial group of World War II foreign scientists were the Germans, known as the rocket team, who had built the V1 for Hitler. Settling in Huntsville, Alabama, near Redstone Arsenal, these scientists under the leadership of Wernher von Braun provided much of the scientific knowledge that resulted in America's successful space program in the 1960s. Their wartime allegiances with the Nazis and accusations of their inhumane treatment of slave laborers tainted their accomplishments, however. Because of cultural limitations in the 1940s and 1950s, specifically segrega-

(circa 1945) With the growing number of scientists in the United States, science became a popular field of study for teenagers at mid-century. Seen here is an interior of a science classroom and laboratory where students study at their desks and conduct experiments, Litchfield High School, Litchfield, Connecticut.

tion and sexism, the recruitment of foreign male scientists took precedence over the encouragement of African Americans and women scientists.

1950s • COLD WAR OPPORTUNITIES FOR SCIENCE ~ Congress passed the National Science Foundation Act of 1950, establishing the NSF as an independent agency in May 1950 "to promote the progress of science; to advance the national health, prosperity, and welfare." The NSF's primary purpose was to collect, analyze, and distribute data regarding the status of American science and technology. According to this act, the NSF's leadership consisted of a director and a National Science Board of 24 members "eminent in the fields of basic sciences, medical science, engineering, agriculture, education, and public affairs."

This legislation was pivotal in twentieth century American science history because governmental involvement sanctioned by this act continued through the rest of the century and set policies for funding and protocol that determined the fate of all future scientific research. No longer were scientists primarily individuals privately pursuing research objectives in personal, industrial, or academic laboratories. The NSF was the catalyst for science to become a very public process, pondered and dismissed in committees by politicians who were usually not qualified to assess investigational proposals but who often judged the merit of projects based on political agendas.

The beginning of the Korean War in June 1950 exacerbated the need for President Truman and Congress to make defense-related scientific R&D a priority. The National Science Board first met on December 12, 1950, at the White House. President Truman spoke to the group, establishing the precedent for the board's chairman to report the board's actions to the president. Initially, the board elected chemist and Harvard president James B. Conant, who had directed the National Research Committee during World War II, as chairman and established an executive committee. The board also created a committee to suggest people whom President Truman might consider for appointment as the NSF director. A week later, the board urged President Truman to appoint a science advisor who could focus on mobilizing scientists for defense needs and also monitor the comprehensive federal science system.

The urgency of the Cold War era resulted in more opportunities for American scientists for both military and civilian applications. At a February 1951 meeting, the National Science Board released a public statement denying that the NSF was involved in defense-related research and stressed that "the fundamental objective of the National Science Foundation is the promotion of basic research and education in the sciences throughout the country." Despite this disclaimer and to encourage partnerships to pursue the expanded national scientific goals, the Scientific Advisory Committee to the White House Office of Defense Mobilization (SAC/ODM) was organized in April 1951. With its science structure firmly established, and only being altered to adapt to socioeconomic and political demands, the role of the federal government at this time in science was to promote cooperation among academic, industrial, and government scientists and to advance and increase basic research for the interests of national security.

Because most of the innovative research for World War II military applications had been conducted at universities or similar institutions, universities became the primary location of basic research after the war, directly contrasting to academia's limited research role before the 1940s. This transition from industrial to educational research environments was uniquely American. One example of this change was the fact that from 1951 to 1980 industry contributed less to national R&D investments than the government. The federal government recognized the need to enrich and build human resources through education to achieve scientific objectives. American graduate science education and research soon gained global prominence, and students traveled from around the world to study at American institutions.

1950-1955 • ATOMIC RESEARCH ~ Atomic research intensified during the Cold War. Scientists detonated a hydrogen bomb in 1952, replicating the fusion of hydrogen and helium nuclei that occurs naturally in stars. Scientists' research resulted in nuclear fusion occurring for the first time outside of a star. Nuclear weapons research was continued to maintain America's role as the free world's guardian; politicians were concerned that Communist countries, specifically China, the Soviet Union, and North Korea, might achieve nuclear capabilities. Scientists applied knowledge of how to control nuclear reactions to power submarines and American homes. Submarines benefited from nuclear power because nuclear submarines needed minimal refueling. This allowed the nuclear submarines to have longer periods of time in sustained dives without refueling. American homes benefited from nuclear power because above-ground reactors to generate inexpensive energy.

The atomic era witnessed trials against people accused of spying and stealing nuclear secrets and selling them to America's enemies. Klaus Fuchs was imprisoned in 1950 for divulging to the Russians information he acquired while working on the Manhattan Project. After he was released, East Germany employed Fuchs to conduct nuclear research. Julius and Ethel Rosenberg, avowed Communists, were executed in 1953 for transmitting atomic secrets to the Soviets that Ethel Rosenberg's brother, David Greenglass, provided them while he worked at Los Alamos. The Rosenbergs' executions were controversial because many Americans blamed the hysteria of McCarthyism, a political assault on suspected American Communists, for escalating charges against the Rosenbergs.

1950S • DNA, POLIO VACCINES, AND TRANSPLANTS ~ By mid-century, physicists had found new elementary particles and proved that antiparticles, which had electric charges or properties that were the reverse of other atomic particles, existed. Chemists produced radioactive elements derived from uranium that were added to the periodic table. Genetics research advanced quickly during the 1950s. In 1953, biologists James D. Watson, an American, and Francis H.C. Crick, from Great Britain, described their discovery of DNA's doublehelix structure. Their model enabled scientists to comprehend how the genetic code was distributed in molecular units that were paired and bonded to form runglike pieces of a three-dimensional structure that resembled a twisting ladder. These DNA strands could be separated to achieve replication.

Scientists specializing in anthropology gained information about the origins and

(1968) A model of a DNA molecule.

1957-1961 lives of early humans. Geologists developed plate tectonics theory to describe why and how the Earth's crust changes. Medical scientists studied amino acids, enzymes, and micro-organisms. For example, pioneering research by 1954 Nobelist Prize winners Frederick C. Robbins, John F. Enders, and Thomas Weller who cultivated polio viruses in human tissue, provided the foundation for Jonas E. Salk and Albert B. Sabin to develop injectable and oral polio vaccines. Medical scientists also helped develop methodologies for organ and tissue transplants and improved surgical techniques. The public was fascinated by such intriguing research, and schools expanded their science curricula and hosted science fairs to encourage innovation. Post-World War II education emphasized competency in science not only to create skilled scientists but also to enable Americans to have an adequate scientific knowledge to benefit their lives.

1957-1961 • THE SPACE RACE
One month after the Soviet Union's satellite *Sputnik I* successfully orbited the Earth on October 4, 1957, President Dwight D. Eisenhower reorganized the SAC/ODM into the Presidential Science Advisory Committee (PSAC). He selected MIT's president, James R. Killian, Jr., to serve as his science advisor. Satellite science became an important aspect of late 1950s research. University of Iowa physicist, James Van Allen, and the former "German rocket team" leader, Wernher von Braun, headed America's race for space against the Soviet Union. As early as July 29, 1955, the United States had announced plans to launch a satellite for the International Geophysical Year (IGY). The Soviets informally responded the following day that they would launch a satellite too. The IGY was scheduled from July 1, 1957 to December 31, 1958, and was sponsored by the International Council of Scientific Unions, which wanted scientists to conduct polar and equatorial observations during that year. Scientists envisioned using satellites capable of orbiting Earth to measure and evaluate the planet from space thus meeting IGY goals.

The Cold War atmosphere thrust the United States and the Soviet Union into a heated contest to produce the first successful artificial satellite. When *Sputnik* orbited the globe, American space scientists were dismayed that it weighed more than they thought was aeronautically possible. Two months later, the Soviet Union launched *Sputnik 2* with a dog aboard. Upset American politicians pressured rocket scientists to produce a working satellite. An intense scientific race occurred between two American military branches, the Army and Navy, each claiming the right to launch the first satellite. The Army optimistically outlined a fifteen-year plan for manned satellites and a moon base, while the Navy conducted satellite research at the Naval Research Laboratory (NRL) in Washington, D.C., and oversaw Vanguard, America's official satellite program. The United States Air Force also tested rocket-powered aircraft. Each service branch realized that success would result in future aerospace assignments for the scientists who achieved an orbiting satellite.

In November 1957, the Jet Propulsion Laboratory (JPL), an Army research laboratory in Pasadena, California, was selected to build the satellite *Explorer I* and its scientific instruments, communication devices, and launch vehicle. JPL Director William Pickering and Army General John B. Medaris assembled experts, including Van Allen and von Braun with personnel from the Army Ballistic Missile Agency from Huntsville, Alabama. They built a fourteen kilogram stainless steel cylinder and a Jupiter-C rocket to propel *Explorer I* into space on January 31, 1958, from the missile test center at Cape Canaveral, Florida. People crowded the streets of Huntsville and other cities with space science connections to celebrate the event.

The orbit of *Explorer I* is considered the beginning of the U.S. space program. The National Advisory Committee for Aeronautics was renamed the National Aeronautics and Space Administration (NASA), a civilian space agency, in October 1958 to reflect the changing nature of research. Scientists used *Explorer I* to study energetic particles in the ionosphere with miniature electronic geodetic devices including Geiger counters and micrometeoroid detectors. *Explorer I* sent scientific data via transmitters to Earth during orbits. Van Allen built a cosmic ray detector for the satellite, and this scientific instrument relayed data that ultimately resulted in the discovery of radiation bands encircling the Earth, which were named the Van Allen Radiation Belts. *Explorer III* and *IV* and the space probe *Pioneer III* confirmed the existence of these radioactive areas in the upper atmosphere which have provided scientists information about physical interactions between the Sun and Earth. Although they were launched after the Sputniks, the Explorer satellites collected more valuable scientific information than the Soviet spacecraft did.

The Navy was hindered by weather problems and technical malfunctions and failed to launch the *Vanguard I* until March 17, 1958. The Navy's satellite collected data about radioactivity and verified that the Earth was thicker along the equator as geologists had hypothesized. *Vanguard I* still circles the Earth, and a website provides statistics about the number of orbits, hours, and miles that it has completed in space. These 1950s satellites seem simplistic in comparison with modern space technology such as the 1997 Mars *Pathfinder*, and their scientific achievements were overshadowed by the political demands of the space race to demonstrate national power during the Cold War.

1962-1969 • GOING TO THE MOON
The Cold War space race intensified in the 1960s. Aerospace scientists investigated the many aspects related to space trav-

1962-1969

el, including physiology and nutrition. Space exploration captured the public's imagination and inspired Americans to become more aware of the universe and to comprehend the Earth's relationship to its celestial surroundings. NASA's goal was to land humans on the moon before the Soviet Union achieved that objective. Both countries launched unmanned robotic lunar probes, intensifying efforts to achieve a moon landing. Although the first group of astronauts, selected in 1959, were primarily military test pilots, NASA emphasized its civilian status, and space centers such as the JPL were transferred from military control to NASA's direction. In 1958, the National Academy of Sciences created the Space Science Board to advise the federal officials regarding scientific research conducted in space. Congressional committees were formed to address space-related concerns.

NASA's Mercury program focused on developing spacecraft that could successfully orbit the Earth. On February 20, 1962, John H. Glenn, Jr., was the first American to orbit the Earth. Scientists such as Vance Marchbanks, an African American physician, monitored Glenn's vital signs and collected medical data from the ground. Although Soviet astronauts had orbited the Earth, Glenn's three orbits were heavily publicized internationally and inspired people worldwide to promote the American space program. Gemini missions studied American astronauts' physiological reactions to extended space travel and prepared for docking and landing maneuvers necessary for the Apollo lunar missions. On July 20, 1969, American astronauts Neil Armstrong and Buzz Aldrin were the first people to walk on the moon. On other lunar landings in the late 1960s and early 1970s, astronauts charted the moon's surface and collected samples to conduct scientific investigations, especially geological examinations collected by astronaut Harrison H. Schmitt, Jr.

While astronauts traveled into space, astronomers on Earth achieved new knowledge about the universe through the use of radio telescopes. These scientific instruments became possible because of English researcher Susan J. Bell Burnell's discovery of pulsars. Radio telescopes recorded and assessed radio waves emitted by objects in space, and astronomers used this information to measure the size and structure of the universe and to seek proof of its origins. These tools enabled astronomers to identify quasars, pulsars, and previously unknown celestial objects. In 1964, World War II German émigré Arno Penzias and Robert W. Wilson became aware of unfamiliar radio noise, and they determined that this cosmic interference picked up by their satellite-tracking radio dish was cosmic microwave background radiation that came from all directions of the universe. They hypothesized that this radiation was a remnant of an explosion when the universe was formed and presented it as convincing evidence for the Big Bang theory. Penzias and Wilson won the 1978 Nobel Prize for this work. Around this same time period, mathematicians Edward Lorenz and Mitchell Fingelbaum developed chaos theory, which hypothesizes that physical actions such as a human's heartbeat, no matter how small, are interdependent, unstable, and not predictable.

1950s • Practical Applications for Scientific Research ~ Technology benefited from science in the 1950s. Scientists used quantum physics principles to miniaturize transistors, enabling Texas Instruments researcher Jack Kilby to invent the integrated circuit known as the computer chip in 1958. Kilby won a Nobel Prize in physics in 2000 in recognition for microchips being the catalyst for the information age and dissemination of computers for commercial and personal use. Microchips had practical applications, opening new possibilities and sources of knowledge for scientists. Since Kilby first designed these semiconductors, researchers estimated that they have doubled their speed and capacity every eighteen months while being successfully reduced in physical size. Microchips replaced the bulky vacuum tubes used in early computers, radios, and televisions.

Science was crucial for the dramatic transformation that American agriculture underwent after 1950. Farming became commercialized and industrialized as governments and corporations dictated what crops would be grown and where they could be sold. The stereotypical independent farmer, providing food for his family and selling surpluses at local markets, began to vanish almost as quickly as fertile rural acreage was developed into interstates and malls near expanding urban areas. The agricultural revolution occurred because farmers were forced to embrace scientific techniques to meet production demands for adequate, nutritional food supplies during World War II. While the amount of American farm land and labor declined, populations worldwide increased rapidly.

Scientific applications to agriculture since 1950 have been primarily beneficial. Agricultural processes sped up, produced more food and fiber per acre, increased farmers' earning potential, and saved time. In 1945, a farmer spent an average of nineteen hours per acre of corn harvested; fifty years later, an agriculturist relying on science invested less than one hour per acre of corn.

1959-PRESENT • HONORING SCIENTISTS ~ The President's National Medal of Science is the United States' highest scientific honor and is administered by the National Science Foundation, an independent governmental agency created by a 1950 Congressional act. Responsible for establishing national science policy, the National Science Foundation funds research, education, and teacher training. The National Medal of Science was established in 1959 and is given to a maximum of twenty people per year who have contributed significantly to science and engineering and who are chosen by the President's Committee on the National Medal of Science.

1960s • BIG SCIENCE ~ The 1960s were a period in which science activity expanded in several directions. In the 1961 *Science* article, "Impact of Large-Scale Science on the United States," Oak Ridge National Laboratory director Alvin Weinberg defined the concept of Big Science which had emerged during World War II and expanded in the following decades. Funded by the federal government of international agencies, scientists and support personnel worked as teams in largescale facilities on comprehensive projects such as the Apollo program. Entire communities, such as Oak Ridge, were built as research centers. Scientists with managerial and fundraising skills were valued for administrative duties. Publications presenting data and achievements of Big Science groups were credited to many, sometimes hundreds, of authors. Some people protested Big Science, especially students at campuses that hosted military-related research.

To meet research demands, more scientific fields, positions, laboratories, doc-

1960s

toral programs, and professional societies and awards were established. Government regulation assured the availability of more research grants and increased the role of bureaucracy in science. Civil Rights legislation strived to make science careers more equitable for minority scientists and women. At the same time, U.S. involvement in the Vietnam War and confrontations with the Soviet Union in Cuba during the 1960s increased scientific activity related to defense, leading to more accurate missiles and effective toxic substances such as napalm and Agent Orange.

1960s • ORGANIC FARMING ~ The government's involvement in science research and development to meet military objectives caused some scientists to question the motives of politicians and military leaders and their ethical accountability for the possible harmful effects of defense-related scientific applications. The public also was outspoken about some scientific investigations in the 1960s. Inspired by Rachel Carson's writings, such as *Silent Spring*, protesters questioned the potentially detrimental effects of agricultural science techniques on human consumers and the environment. The organic farming movement and sustainable agriculture gradually gained strength through the end of the century. Organic farmers raise crops without chemical substances, and sustainable agriculture consists of methods that assure plentiful food supplies for present and future generations while protecting the environment. Farmers were encouraged to act as amateur scientists and experiment with varying crops and ground cover to replenish soil, prevent erosion, and maintain a symbiotic balance between humans, Earth, and organisms.

In the 1960s, the Green Revolution introduced bioengineering methods to less industrially-developed countries in an attempt to ease hunger. Norman E. Borlaug, a plant pathologist, genetically created a strain of high-yield dwarf spring wheat with sufficient protein and calories

(1926) Throughout the twentieth century farmers were encouraged to act as amateur scientists and experiment with varying crops and ground cover to replenish soil, prevent erosion, and maintain a symbiotic balance between humans, Earth, and organisms.

to alleviate malnourishment. Borlaug was credited with saving millions from dying of starvation and received a Nobel Prize in 1970.

1970s • THE INFORMATION AGE
Scientific investigations in the 1970s built on work from the previous decades. The population of scientists grew from 201,292 in 1960 to 312,644 in 1970. The latter decade was a period in which Vietnamese and Cambodian refugees fled to the United States, and many of those immigrants contributed their scientific expertise to universities and industry. Anticipating further globalization, Congress passed legislation in December 1975 urging Americans to convert voluntarily to the metric system within a decade. Although scientists now primarily use the metric system, average Americans still do not understand or use the metric system.

The Internet was born in the 1960s. Computing advances in microchips resulted in faster processors and smaller machinery. The Internet was initially established for defense uses. Government, industrial, and academic researchers used the early Internet to share scientific information quickly and privately. This form of transmission enabled scientists in different parts of the country to communicate without having to send documents by slow delivery methods. Developed for military use, the Internet was not at first envisioned as a massive public international communications network open to users with access to computers and for storage of non-military information.

Geneticists developed recombinant DNA techniques for gene splicing in the hopes of curing inherited diseases. Stanley Cohen and Herbert Boyer placed a designated gene in a bacterium in 1973, which marked the beginning of genetic engineering. Boyer founded Genentech, the first genetic engineering company in the world. Scientists hoped to refine this genetic engineering technique by identifying and removing genes that controlled certain characteristics and functions in one multicellular organism and splicing them into another organism. Scientists produced artificial insulin through such methods. They also successfully derived Taxol, an anti-cancer drug, from Pacific Yew tree bark.

Space science advanced in the 1970s when astronauts conducted experiments on the *Skylabs*. Aerospace and physics research contributed to the miniaturization of electronic equipment, including calculators. Computer processing speeds increased as mainframes became smaller. Lasers revolutionized daily life and enabled scientists to conduct research with more precise tools and develop practical applications such as using lasers to perform delicate surgical procedures in small spaces. Lasers were also used for computer printers and barcode readers.

Despite these scientific advances, an anti-science backlash continued to gain momentum as environmentalists criticized scientific use of pollutants and hazardous materials, emphasizing the mishandling of toxic wastes at Love Canal in 1978 and the nuclear power plant breakdown at Three Mile Island in 1979 as proof of science being out of control. Protesters also peaceably denounced the use of animals as research subjects, while some animal liberation groups freed laboratory animals and damaged laboratory facilities. Scientists were asked to act responsibly and to be accountable for their actions. As scientists secured more control over natural processes, some people worried if scientists might use that power improperly, such as using lasers for destruction or to alter people's genetic composition negatively.

During the 1970s, the NSB released the first report of *The Science and Engineering Indicators* series. NSB is legally required to prepare these documents biennially. Each report provides information and analysis about the status and trends of American science. Some of the main points made in each report are how NSB compares to programs internationally and the need to assist scientists, policymakers, and the public to comprehend possible developments and uses of science. The indicator reports are designed to evaluate and revise the federal government's science policy.

In 1971 the acknowledgment of the importance of female scientists was represented by renaming the leading directory of America's significant researchers from *American Men of Science* to *American Men and Women of Science*.

1980s • BOOM ERA FOR SCIENTIFIC RESEARCH ~ By the 1980s, there were more than 700,000 research scientists in American industries and academic institutions. The national R&D expenditures totaled $62 billion. The pace of scientific activities and discoveries accelerated as more people participated and as additional money was invested in scientific investigations. Instrumentation such as electron microscopes to analyze and measure samples became more powerful and precise. The quantity of scientific achievements expanded rapidly, while the quality of scientific applications improved.

Computers became essential to process and communicate information in a standard, recognizable form to other scientists. The large amount of data and the complexity of calculations made it impossible for humans to solve intricate equations without the assistance of computers. Computer modeling soon became an essential step in modern scientific experimentation. Scientists used computers to simulate and model experiments to test hypotheses without using physical specimens. Computers enabled scientists to manipulate digital objects in a way impossible to do with physical specimens. Students could dissect virtual frogs on computer screens.

1980s • DIGITAL IMAGING ~ Other equipment that aided scientific achievements in the final quarter of the twentieth century included enhanced particle accelerators designed to help physicists study the composition of atoms, quarks, and other subatomic units of matter. Telescopes with lenses capable of greater magnification and improved storage techniques recorded digital images of objects farther and farther away from Earth. Space probes relayed information about distant planets and celestial objects, while satellites and other orbiting devices served as collectors of information about Earth and its atmosphere. Scientists used magnetic resonance imaging (MRI) to create images of internal organs and tissues for medical evaluations. Such imaging devices were also used to examine mummies and other scientific and archaeological specimens.

1980s • GENE RESEARCH ~ American genetics achievements in the 1980s included Martin Cline and his colleagues moving a functioning gene from one mouse into another. J.W. Gordon and F.H. Ruddle manually placed genes into fertilized eggs; these offspring passed the genes on to their children, thus resulting in the first transgenic animals.

Kary B. Mullis devised the polymerase chain reaction to copy DNA sequences without living cells. In 1983, Barbara McClintock became the first woman to win a Nobel Prize not shared by other scientists. In previous decades, she had demonstrated how genes moved on chromosomes, and this fundamental understanding of gene behavior altered all future genetic work.

1980s • SPACE SHUTTLE EXPERIMENTS

A reusable aerospace vehicle, the first space shuttle, *Columbia,* was launched in 1981. Later shuttle missions flew secret Department of Defense payloads, which were scientifically oriented and included sensor technology experiments. The European Space Agency's *Spacelab* featured international scientific investigations. College and younger students were encouraged to compete for their science experiments to be flown on shuttles, and commercial companies paid for shuttle space. Astronauts and specialists on board performed the experiments.

The study of zero gravity's effect on humans, plants, and small organisms was the theme of most shuttle experiments. The zero gravity environment of the space shuttle enabled researchers to produce pharmaceuticals with the Continuous Flow Electrophoresis Experiment that they would have been unable to manufacture on Earth. In addition to life sciences, shuttle scientists investigated plasma physics, solar physics, astronomy, materials processing, and communications. In addition to all of these investigations, The Great Observatories Program also initiated the deployment of the Gamma Ray Observatory.

The Hubble Space Telescope collected valuable images for Earthbound scientists. The Atmospheric Laboratory for Applications and Science (ATLAS) was used for atmospheric studies. The space shuttle also allowed for digital imaging of the Earth's entire surface. The International Space Station created an orbiting laboratory where astronauts could stay long enough to monitor experiments of long duration. The results of space science investigations were applied to practical technology such as velcro.

Scientists also designed unmanned robotic spacecraft to explore and examine solar, atmospheric, and astronomical phenomena using remote sensing devices on missions. A variety of weather, military, navigation, and communications satellites performed crucial tasks such as storm warnings, credit card transactions, television broadcasts, and agricultural evaluations.

(1995) Cosmonaut Valery Polyakov appears at a window of the Russian space station Mir during the STS-63 rendezvous with the American shuttle Discovery. Polyakov boarded Mir on January 8th 1994 and left it on 22nd March 1995, setting a record of 438 days in space.

1980s-1990s

CONSUMER PRODUCTS

On Earth, scientists contributed to the development of improved plant varieties and livestock breeds, as well as agricultural chemicals for fertilizer and pest control. They also contributed to rapidly rising production costs. Many farmers who have been unable to meet these rising costs have been forced to quit farming and sell their land. A farm crisis in the 1980s resulted because of increased agricultural costs and declining profits. Since 1925, the number of farms in the United States decreased from about 6,500,000 to about 2,050,000 (See Farming).

The commercialization of scientific research often resulted in public awareness and recognition, to some degree, of scientific developments. Through genetic studies and careful selection of breeding stock, researchers at Auburn University had scientifically developed a strain of cattle that produced the lowfat meat that McDonald's used for its McLean hamburgers. Veterinary scientists developed heartworm preventatives and flea and tick repelling treatments that protected American pets. Zoologists described wild animal behavior on talk shows, at zoo programs, and through other forms of popular culture, which resulted in unusual exotic animals becoming familiar. Chemists created new synthetic polymers for use in products such as clothing and vehicles. Scientific artifacts, both past and present, were displayed in museums, often in interactive learning stations.

1980s • POPULARIZING SCIENCE

As computers became more accessible, computer games and toys resulted in more people becoming aware of how to operate computers. Other science activities, sold through such popular venues as the Sears catalog, introduced children and adults to scientific ideas, methods, and tools. Science became a popular topic in comic strips and on television shows, making scientific subjects more familiar. States established high schools especially for students to study science and mathematics, and more scientific competitions, such as the Olympiad and Mathcounts, were held.

Some Major American Science Museums

National Air and Space Museum
http://www.nasm.si.edu

Museum of Science and Industry
http://www.msichicago.org

The U.S. Space & Rocket Center
http://www.spacefun.com

American Museum of Science and Energy, Oak Ridge, Tennessee
http://www.amse.org

DNA Learning Center, Cold Spring Harbor
http://vector.cshl.org

California Science Center
http://www.casciencectr.org

Carnegie Museum of Natural History
http://www.CarnegieMuseums.org/cmnh

Franklin Institute Science Museum
http://sln.fi.edu/tfi/welcome.html

National Medals of Science
http://www.nsf.gov/nsb/awards/nms/start.htm

SOURCE: *Magill's Science Annual 2001*, edited by Joseph L. Spradley, 2001.

1990s • A Breakthrough Decade

~ The final decade of the twentieth century emphasized the intense acceleration of scientific activity that gradually had been developing since 1900. The 1990s was a vibrant period of scientific breakthroughs and the continued globalization of science. Approximately 34,700 scientists were included in the 2000-2001 volume of *Who's Who in Science and Engineering*, representing at least 110 specialties.

Scientists were aided by accompanying technological developments that enabled more precise measurements and assessments of data. The digitization of computing clarified information and permitted accurate computer models to explore scientific hypotheses. Computing advances allowed scientists to process massive amounts of data at fast rates; distribute theories, data, and results via the Internet; and to store data in physical and cyber-databases accessible to other researchers. Information technology resulted in electronic commerce and digital libraries, which impacted Americans' daily lives at home, work, and school. Science and engineering education and training were emphasized as necessary to maintain and advance the American economy in a global market.

1990s • Genome and DNA Research

~ Perhaps the most outstanding scientific breakthrough of the 1990s concerned genetic research. The mapping of the first complete plant genome sequence—that of the mustard weed—occurred in 2000. This plant's genomic information provided scientists valuable information about chromosomal structures called centromeres, which benefitted molecular biology and ecological and evolutionary research.

American Men and Women of Science
Biographical Subjects By Region

	1992	1995	1998
Northeast	58,325	58,716	56,006
Southeast	39,769	41,472	41,313
North Central	19,846	20,171	19,699
South Central	12,156	12,539	12,169
Mountain	11,029	11,505	11,675
Pacific	22,550	26,055	25,703
TOTAL	166,675	170,458	166,565

SOURCE: *American Men and Women of Science* by R.R. Bowker Database Publishing Group, 1992, 1995, 1998.

American Men and Women of Science
Biographical Subjects by Fields

	1992	1995	1998
Agricultural and Forest Science	7,360	7,600	7,488
Biological Sciences	36,604	37,385	35,777
Chemistry	25,760	25,883	24,700
Computer Sciences	5,406	5,543	5,652
Engineering	23,997	24,368	24,153
Environmental, Earth and Marine Sciences	10,427	10,676	10,526
Mathematics	11,722	12,337	12,303
Medical and Health Sciences	19,476	19,936	19,292
Physics and Astronomy	16,973	17,174	16,809
Other Professional Fields	8,950	9,606	9,865

SOURCE: *American Men and Women of Science*, by R.R Bowker Database Publishing Group, 1992, 1995,1998.

In 1984, Robert Sinsheimer suggested that all human genes be mapped, and the Human Genome Organization was organized in 1988. By 2000, two scientific teams led by J. Craig Venter and Francis S. Collins mapped the human genome, which is considered one of the twentieth century's most outstanding scientific accomplishments. With this information, researchers hoped to understand how genes influence human development and to determine how such information could be utilized to improve health care and the quality of life. Companies, meanwhile, planned to use the human genome sequence to manufacture pharmaceuticals and other biomedical goods. Scientists plan to further understand the three billion nucleotides that compose human DNA to develop diagnostic tests and treatments for diseases. The scientific management of all of this new genetic information is called Bioinformatics. In 1990, a four-year-old American girl was the first person to undergo gene therapy when a gene for adenosine deaminase was placed in her DNA. Seven years later, Huntington F. Wilard made the first artificial human chromosome. Despite genetic advances, in January 2000, a patient who had undergone human gene therapy testing died, causing the safety of that procedure to be questioned.

During the 1990s, DNA's value as criminal evidence resulted in more scientists testifying as experts in courts. DNA provided reliable identification of some criminals or exonerated victims of false allegations. Some unnamed and otherwise unidentified criminals were labeled and indicted based only on the unique genetic code found in saliva or semen left on their victims' bodies. Law enforcement agencies retained this information in case a known suspect ever matched that DNA data. In 1998, DNA tests were used in an attempt to determine whether President Thomas Jefferson was the father of a child born to his slave, Sally Hemings. Although results suggested that Jefferson probably was the child's father, many Americans refused to believe the results of the tests.

Genetics tests can be used to help individuals become aware of hereditary defects and the diseases they might develop. Genetic engineering also poses potentially problematic ethical situations, however, such as parents genetically designing their children. Genetic analyses might be used to deny people employment and health insurance, as well as controlling marginalized ethnic or socioeconomic groups similar to the eugenics laws upheld earlier in the century.

1990s • Transgenic Organisms

Biotechnology emerged as a controversial genetic application in the 1990s. Using bioengineering techniques, scientists manipulated organisms' genes to control growth and biochemical activity. They strived to create perfect specimens by identifying the genes for certain qualities and removing those that express negative traits. During the process of recombination, scientists isolated specific genes on one DNA strand and spliced them into another strand. Scientists genetically altered plants to repel and kill harmful insects and to manufacture their own fertilizer, thus saving money spent on chemical pesticides and lost due to ruined crops.

Many bioengineered plants can withstand extreme environmental stresses. In 1998, an estimated 69.5 million acres globally were cultivated with bioengineered crops. In addition to these plants, scientists developed specially devised polymers to lubricate plows so they could cut through sticky soils with minimal friction, decreasing energy requirements by thirty percent and saving 1,500 million gallons of gasoline annually. Global Positioning Satellites (GPS) monitor the moisture content and soil quality of fields where various bioengineered crops are planted to predict agricultural yields. Computer models permit engineers to test and refine machinery designs to meet different requirements, and crops are sometimes genetically altered to be more compatible with harvesting and processing technology.

Scientists' bioengineered livestock to be immune to contagious diseases. They developed such additives as a bovine growth hormone that increases the size of beef cattle with less feed. In 1983, Russell Higuchi became the first scientist to clone an extinct animal's DNA segment. By the 1990s, scientists successfully cloned livestock in an effort to replicate superior specimens and produce ample sources of high-quality milk, meat, wool, and hides. Pigs were genetically engineered to create organs for human transplants. Corporations invested in bioengineering methods and items that quickened the transformation of agriculture from subsistence to commercial production. During genetic experimentation, researchers discovered they could move genes between species and create animals such as the geep, a goat-sheep cross. Biotechnology is also used to manufacture agriculturally based pharmaceuticals. Protesters label bioengineered product as "Frankenfood" and try to implement bans on genetically modified foods. In January 2000, 130 countries signed the first international treaty concerning the trade of bioengineered goods.

Several thousand Americans die annually after eating contaminated foodstuffs, and millions become sick. In the 1990s, scientists developed irradiation as a safety measure to kill bacteria and toxins such as *E. coli* in foods, including meat, vegetables, and fruits. The process of irradiation involves exposing foods to an electron beam which not only kills microscopic organisms and pests but also prevents meat from spoiling. Some Americans are reluctant to eat irradiated foods, however. Irradiation proponents say that this attitude resembled people's initial reaction when milk pasteurization was introduced in the nineteenth century. Insisting that agricultural facilities should be sanitized to eliminate toxins, activists boycott irradiated foods.

1990s Scientific Quests

MEDICINE ~ Scientists used computer modeling and microarrays to conduct cellular immunology investigations, specifically how the immune system and inhibitory receptors respond to pathogenic invasions. The mysterious Gulf War Syndrome in which veterans exhibited symptoms of numerous diseases and conditions but not a uniquely identifiable pathological ailment puzzled medical investigators. The threat of biological warfare resulted in scientists at the Centers for Disease Control to cultivate and isolate deadly viruses such as smallpox in order to seek ways to counter bioterrorism.

After isolating Human Immunodeficiency Virus (HIV) as the cause of Acquired Immunodeficiency Syndrome (AIDS) in 1983, researchers continued to seek cures and made progress in treating AIDS patients in the 1990s. Stem cell research was one of the most controversial biomedical issues of the 1990s. One of the reasons why stem cell research is considered controversial is that stem cells mostly come from the human umbilical cord. Obviously the only ways to obtain the stem cells is either after the birth process or to abort the pregnancy and take the umbilical cord from the remains. Despite the controversy, scientists showed how stem cells could be used to alleviate the symptoms of Parkinson's disease and other nervous disorders. Many people questioned the ethics of such procedures because many stem cells were taken from human embryos.

SPACE ~ Awed by the reappearance of the HaleBopp comet in 1997, aerospace scientists experienced many successes in the 1990s such as the *Sojourner* rover landing on Mars in July 1997. High resolution images relayed by the Mars Global Surveyor spacecraft showed geological formations that suggested the presence of a dry ocean bed on Mars. The spacecraft *Magellan* mapped the surface of Venus. Ice crystals were also detected in moon soil. Scientists utilized optical and near-infrared imaging and spectroscopy to locate possible planets beyond the Earth's solar system. The Cosmic Background Explorer examined radiation to verify that the universe had been formed 15 billion years ago by a cataclysmic event supportive of the Big Bang theory. The international space station was constructed to aid global cooperation for aerospace investigations.

Aerospace equipment was used to monitor the Earth's topography. Cold War-era military satellites, aircraft, ships, and sonar collected intelligence and mapped the Earth's topography. In the 1990s, scientists studied global warming and weather phenomena such as El Niño and La Niña. Researchers studied plate tectonics and climatology and investigated methods to predict and prepare for natural disasters such as hurricanes, tornadoes, and earthquakes. They warned that the ozone's hole had increased in size, exposing life on Earth to harmful ultraviolet rays.

Scientific achievements near the conclusion of the twentieth century included scientists slowing the speed of light, discovering new elements, linking an enzyme to Alzheimer's Disease, and developing Interferon to combat Multiple Sclerosis. Paleontologists found a dinosaur heart and the largest, best-preserved Tyrannosaurs rex skeleton to date. Each finding helped scientists learn more about dinosaurs, such as that they moved slower than previously hypothesized. Princeton University scientists determined that adult monkeys grow new brain cells unlike humans.

Although United States presidents in the 1990s continued to address scientific meetings and promote science issues, the federal government decreased its support for science. In 1993, the government withdrew funding for the Superconducting Super Collider that scientists had used for high-energy physics research. NASA had to readjust its goals and methods in the face of a reduced budget. The arrest of Wen Ho Lee, a Chinese-American nuclear scientist at Los Alamos Labs, for allegedly stealing nuclear secrets became controversial when there was a lack of evidence that Lee did anything with the intention of leaking secrets.

CONCLUSION

During the twentieth century, American science became bureaucratized. It expanded to include new fields of study and witnessed new means to organize scientists and scientific information using new ways to transmit knowledge gained. Twentieth century science slowly became more inclusive. While minorities—particularly members of ethnic and racial groups and women, and socioeconomically impoverished Americans—were excluded from science in favor of privileged white males in the nineteenth century, scientific opportunities became more equitable because of political and social issues that were pivotal in the twentieth century.

World War II created an overwhelming demand for capable individuals, regardless of social class, who could contribute scientifically to military victory. Many veterans benefited from having access to scientific training during the war and meeting scientifically-minded individuals in service. Veterans also took advantage of benefits provided by the 1944 G.I. Bill of Rights to obtain higher education and to pursue scientific careers. The postwar Civil Rights and feminist movements aided recognition of minority scientists.

After the war ended, the federal government became an active participant in scientific investigations, evaluating and funding projects and carefully monitoring scientific policy. Government agencies oversaw specialized scientific activity such as defense work, and budgets often determined the extent to which scientists could explore specific research concerns. Private foundations and laboratories also sponsored researchers, enabling scientists to have more funds to pursue their interests. Academic institutions supplied varying levels of support to scientists depending on institutional resources and agendas. Both public and private scientific supports were accompanied by restrictions such as directives concerning ownership of intellectual property.

Despite scientific advances, some limitations included a predominating focus on science that did not address concerns of lower socioeconomic classes or women. For example, most twentieth-century medical research concentrated on experimentation with male subjects, which was not always applicable to female health concerns. On the other hand, much research in the last part of the century focused on women's issues, including breast and ovarian cancers, and diseases such as sickle cell anemia linked genetically to American blacks. Some scientific research was developed with specific impoverished groups in mind, such as feeding and vaccinating residents of undeveloped countries with high-yield wheat and yellow rice which contains beta carotene—an antioxidant that converts to vitamin A in the body.

Although science underwent an amazing period of growth during the twentieth century, scientists continued to encounter skepticism and disrespect toward their work from the general public and even among their colleagues. Antagonism among scientific peers either stimulated or retarded research progress through competition or discouragement. For the most part, the twentieth century provided an invigorating environment for a varied group of American scientists to explore questions, contribute novel insights, and create a foundation for further scientific experimentation.

The knowledge, methodology, and scientific tools developed in the twentieth century provided keys to unlocking new awareness of genetics and other scientific mysteries that can advance the quality of life for humans in future centuries while raising potential ethical dilemmas. Science can also be the means for discovering such needed resources as new, nonpolluting energy sources.

Notable Twentieth Century Scientists
* indicates Nobel Prize winner

Alabama
George Washington Carver
*Frederick C. Robbins
Robert J. Van de Graaf
Wernher Von Braun
Charlotte Ward
Edward O. Wilson
Alaska
John C. Eichelberger
Wilford F. Weeks
Arizona
William K. Hartmann
Ian L. Pepper
Arkansas
Norman F. Williams
Duane C. Wolf
California
*Luis W. Alvarez
Hebert Boyer
*Felix Bloch
*Owen Chamberlain
*Max Delbruck
*Renato Dulbecco
*Joseph Erlanger
Colorado
*Willard F. Libby
*Edward L. Tatum
Connecticut
*John F. Enders
*Barbara McClintock
*John A. Van Vleck

Delaware
Thomas Buchter
*Daniel Nathans
District of Columbia
Katherine Ralls
Laurence E. Skog
Florida
Roy C. Herndon
Indra K. Vasil
Georgia
John K. Spitznagel
Charlie E. Rogers
Hawaii
Russell C. Schnell
Fred I. Kamemoto
Idaho
*James Rainwater
Jeanne M. Shreeve
Illinois
*Robert A. Millikan
*James D. Watson
Indiana
*Wendell M. Stanley
*Harold C. Urey
Iowa
*Norman Borlaug
Wallace Hume Carothers
James Van Allen
Kansas
Donald W. Kaufman
*Earl W. Sutherland, Jr.

Kentucky
*Thomas Hunt Morgan
Donald W. Slocum
Louisiana
David E. Pope
Richard E. Defenbaugh
Maine
Muriel T. Davisson
Michael J. Herz
Maryland
Louis H. Miller
*Peyton Rous
Massachusetts
Bertram B. Boltwood
Vannevar Bush
James B. Conant
Gilbert N. Lewis
Richard John Roberts
Michigan
Hilary Clayton
*Alfred Hershey
*Glenn T. Seaborg
Minnesota
*Melvin Calvin
John T. Shepherd
Herbert E. Wright, Jr.
Mississippi
H. Wyman Dorough
Larry G. Pardue

SOURCES: *American Men and Women of Science* by R. R. Bowker Database Publishing Group, volumes issued throughout the 20th century; and *Who's Who in America* by Marquis Who's Who, published annually.

Missouri
*Carl F. Cori
*Gerty T. Cori
Edwin P. Hubble
Harlow Shapley
Montana
Jerome A. Onsager
Edward T. Ruppel
Nebraska
*George W. Beadle
*Val L. Fitch
Nevada
DeLyle Eastwood
Billy M. McCormac
New Hampshire
Henry N. Andrews
*George H. Whipple
New Jersey
*Albert Einstein
*Joshua Lederberg
New Mexico
Edward U. Condon
Harrison H. Schmitt
Jr., George Zweig
New York
*Irving Langmuir
*Hermann J. Muller
Robert Oppenheimer
*Burton Richter
Jonas E. Salk
Vincent J. Schaefer
*Rosalyn S. Yalow

North Carolina
William R. Davis
Alan E. Stiven
North Dakota
Leonard R. Joppa
Ronald E. Kirby
Ohio
*Arthur Holly Compton
J.W. Gordon
Mark L. Nichols
F.H. Ruddle Wright
Oklahoma
John A. Bantle
Robert A. Maddox
Oregon
*Linus C. Pauling
Lynda P. Shapiro
Pennsylvania
Stephen J. Benkovic
Rachel Carson
Kenneth C. Parkes
Rhode Island
Johanna M. Schmitt
Mildred Widgoff
South Carolina
Thomas C. Cheng
Ernest E. Just
*Charles H. Townes
South Dakota
*Ernest O. Lawrence
Joann Tall

Tennessee
*James M. Buchanan
Mary Engle Pennington
Texas
*Robert B. Merrifield
*Robert W. Wilson
Utah
Sharon B. Emerson
Peter J. Stang
J. Craig Venter
Vermont
Laurence K. Forcier
Hal McSweeney
Virginia
Francis S. Collins
Eric O. Hartwig
Cleveland P. Hickman
Washington
Leland H. Hartwell
Gerard D. Schellenberg
West Virginia
Diana S. Beattie
Alan R. Biggs
Wisconsin
*John Bardeen
*William P. Murphy
Wyoming
Frank C. Craighead, Jr.
Walter T. Grandy, Jr.
Vance H. Marchbanks

BIBLIOGRAPHY

Allen, Garland E. *Life Science in the Twentieth Century.* Cambridge: Cambridge University Press, 1979.

Asimov, Isaac. *Asimov's New Guide to Science.* New York: Basic Books, 1984.

Ben-David, Joseph. *The Scientist's Role in Society: A Comparative Study.* Chicago: University of Chicago Press, 1984.

Blanpied, W.A. *Impacts of the Early Cold War on the Formulation of U.S. Science Policy: Selected Memoranda of William T. Golden.* Washington, DC: American Association for the Advancement of Science, 1995.

Bowler, Peter J. *Evolution: The History of An Idea.* Rev. ed. Berkeley: University of California Press, 1989.

Bridson, Gavin. *The History of Natural History: An Annotated Bibliography.* New York: Garland, 1994.

Buchwald, Jed Z., ed. *Scientific Practice: Theories and Stories of Doing Physics.* Chicago: The University of Chicago Press, 1995.

Bush, Vannevar. *Modern Arms and Free Men: A Discussion of the Role of Science in Preserving Democracy.* Westport, CT: Greenwood Press, 1985.

Channell, David F. *The History of Engineering Sciences: An Annotated Bibliography.* New York and London: Garland Publishing, 1989.

Clarke, Adele E., and Joan H. Fujimura, eds. *The Right Tools for the Job: At Work in Twentieth-Century Life Sciences.* Princeton, NJ: Princeton University Press, 1992.

DeVorkin, David H. *The History of Modern Astronomy and Astrophysics: A Selected, Annotated Bibliography.* New York: Garland, 1982.

Doyle, Jake. *Altered Harvest: Agriculture, Genetics, and the Fate of the World's Food Supply.* New York: Viking, 1985.

Elliott, Clark A. *History of Science in the United States: A Chronology and Research Guide.* New York: Garland, 1996.

Finn, Bernard S. *The History of Electrical Technology: An Annotated Bibliography.* New York: Garland, 1991.

Galison, Peter. *How Experiments End.* Chicago: University of Chicago Press, 1987.

———. *Image and Logic: A Material Culture of Microphysics.* Chicago: University of Chicago Press, 1997.

Galison, Peter, and Bruce Hevly, eds. *Big Science: The Growth of Large-Scale Research.* Stanford, CA: Stanford University Press, 1992.

Gillespie, Charles Coulton, ed. *Dictionary of Scientific Biography.* 18 vols. New York: Scribner, 1980-1990.

Gingerich, Owen, ed. *Astrophysics and Twentieth-Century Astronomy to 1950.* Cambridge: Cambridge University Press, 1984.

Good, George A., ed. *Sciences of the Earth: An Encyclopedia of Events, People, and Phenomena.* New York: Garland, 1998.

Goodling, David, Trevor Pinch, and Simon Schaffer, eds. *The Uses of Experiment: Studies in the Natural Sciences.* Cambridge: Cambridge University Press, 1989.

Greenberg, Daniel S. *The Politics of Pure Science.* New York and Toronto: New American Library, 1971.

Haber, Louis. *Black Pioneers of Science and Invention.* Reprint. San Diego: Harcourt Brace Jovanovich, 1991.

Heitmann, John L. *Scaling Up: Science, Engineering, and the American Chemical Industry.* Philadelphia: Center for History of Chemistry, University of Pennsylvania, 1984.

Hellemans, Alexander. *Timetables of Science: A Chronology of the Most Important People and Events in the History of Science*. New York: Simon and Schuster, 1988.

Holton, Gerald, and Stephen G. Brush. *Physics, the Human Adventure: From Copernicus to Einstein and Beyond*. Piscataway, NJ: Rutgers University Press, 2001.

Hurt, R. Douglas, and Mary Ellen Hurt. *The History of Agricultural Science and Technology: An International Annotated Bibliography*. New York: Garland Publishing, 1994.

Jacob, Margaret C., ed. *The Politics of Western Science, 1640- 1990*. Atlantic Highlands, NJ: Humanities Press, 1994.

James, Portia P. *The Real McCoy: African American Invention and Innovation, 1619-1930*. Washington, DC: Smithsonian Institute Press, 1989.

Kass-Simon, G., and Patricia Farnes, eds. *Women of Science: Righting the Record*. Bloomington: Indiana University Press, 1990.

Kessler, James H., et al. *Distinguished African American Scientists of the 20th Century*. Phoenix: Oryx Press, 1996.

Kevles, Daniel J. *In the Name of Eugenics: Genetics and the Uses of Human Heredity*. Cambridge, MA: Harvard University Press, 1995.

———. *The Physicists: The History of a Scientific Community in Modern America*. Cambridge, MA: Harvard University Press, 1995.

Kevles, Daniel J., and Leroy Hood, eds. *The Code of Codes: Scientific and Social Issues in the Human Genome Project*. Cambridge, MA: Harvard University Press, 1992.

Kuhn, Thomas S. *The Structure of Scientific Revolutions*. 3rd ed. Chicago, IL: University of Chicago Press, 1996.

Larson, Edward J. *Sex, Race, and Science: Eugenics in the Deep South*. Baltimore and London: The Johns Hopkins University Press, 1995.

Magill, Frank N., ed. *Great Events From History II: Science and Technology*. Pasadena, CA: Salem Press, 1991.

Marcus, Alan I. *Agricultural Science and the Quest for Legitimacy: Farmers, Agricultural Colleges, and Experiment Stations, 1870-1890*. Ames: Iowa State University Press, 1985.

McMurray, Emily J., Jane Kelly Kosek, and Roger M. Valade III, eds. *Notable Twentieth-Century Scientists*. 4 vols. Detroit: Gale Research, 1995.

Midgette, Nancy Smith. *To Foster the Spirit of Professionalism: Southern Scientists and State Academies of Science*. University: University of Alabama Press, 1991.

Mount, Ellis. *Milestones in Science and Technology: The Ready Reference Guide to Discoveries, Inventions, and Facts*. 2nd ed. Phoenix: Oryx Press, 1994.

Neufeld, Michael J. *The Rocket and the Reich*. New York: Free Press, 1995.

Noble, David F. *America by Design: Science, Technology, and the Rise of Corporate Capitalism*. New York: Alfred A. Knopf, 1977.

Numbers, Ronald L. and Charles E. Rosenberg, eds. *The Scientific Enterprise in America: Readings from Isis*. Chicago: University of Chicago Press, 1996.

Olson, Richard, ed. *Biographical Encyclopedia of Scientists*. 5 vols. New York: Marshall Cavendish, 1998.

Porter, Roy, ed. *The Biographical Dictionary of Scientists*. 3rd ed. 2 vols. New York: Oxford University Press, 2000.

Pursell, Carroll W., Jr. *Astronomy in America*. Chicago: Rand McNally, 1967.

Rainger, Ronald, Keith R. Benson, and Jane Maienschein, eds. *The American Development of Biology.* New Brunswick: Rutgers University Press, 2001.

Rosenberg, Charles E. *No Other Gods: On Science and American Social Thought.* Baltimore: The Johns Hopkins University Press, 1978.

Rossiter, Margaret W. *Women Scientists in America: Before Affirmative Action, 1940-1972.* Baltimore, MD: The Johns Hopkins University Press, 1995.

———. *Women Scientists in America: Struggles and Strategies to 1940.* Baltimore, MD: The Johns Hopkins University Press, 1982.

Rothenberg, Marc, ed. *The History of Science in the United States: An Encyclopedia.* New York: Garland, 2000.

Sarton, George. *Introduction to the History of Science.* 5 vols. Huntington, NY: R.E. Krieger Pub. Co., 1975.

Schlager, Neil, ed. *Science and Its Times: Understanding the Social Significance of Scientific Discovery.* 7 vols. Detroit: Gale, 2000-2001.

Scientific American. *Scientific American Science Desk Reference.* New York: John Wiley & Sons, 1999.

Smith, Robert W. *The Space Telescope: A Study of NASA, Science, Technology, and Politics.* New York: Cambridge University Press, 1989.

Suplee, C. *Physics in the Twentieth Century.* New York: Harry N. Abrams, Inc., with the American Physical Society and the American Institute of Physics, 1999.

Turner, Janet, Constance Carter, and Ruth Freitag, comps. *Biographical Sources in the Sciences.* Washington, DC: Science Reference Section, Science and Technology Division, Library of Congress, 1988.

United States, Office of Scientific Research and Development. *Science, the Endless Frontier: A Report to the President* by Vannevar Bush, Director of the Office of Scientific Research and Development. Washington, DC: U.S. Government Printing Office, 1945.

Ward, Charlotte R. *This Blue Planet: Introduction to Physical Science.* Boston: Little, Brown, 1972.

Webster, Raymond B. *African American Firsts in Science and Technology.* Foreword by Wesley L. Harris. Detroit, MI: Gale Group, 1999.

Williams, Trevor, ed. *Biographical Dictionary of Scientists.* New York: HarperCollins, 1994.

INTERNET RESOURCES

Intel Science Talent Search
http://www.sciserv.org/sts/

Internet History of Science Sourcebook
http://www.fordham.edu/halsall/science/sciencesbook.html

National Institute for Science Education (NISE)
http://www.wcer.wisc.edu/nise/

New Scientist (online magazine)
http://www.newscientist.com

The Nobel e-Museum
http://www.nobel.se

On Being A Scientist: Responsible Conduct In Research (online publication)
http://www.nap.edu/readingroom/books/obas/

Science Daily
http://www.sciencedaily.com

Science Learning Network (SLN)
http://www.sln.org/

Science Reading Room (Library of Congress)
http://lcweb.loc.gov/rr/scitech/

SciQuest Corporate Page – E-solutions for Scientists
http://www.SciQuest.com/

The Ultimate Science Fair Resource
http://www.scifair.org

The Why Files: The Science Behind the News
http://whyfiles.news.wisc.edu/

An online science site useful for students, teachers, and parents:
http://www.thescientificworld.com

JOURNALS

American Scientist
http://www.amsci.org/amsci/amsci

Daily University Science News
http://unisci.com

Isis
http://www.journals.uchicago.edu/Isis/home.html

National Science Teachers Association
http://www.nsta.org

Odyssey Magazine
An excellant children's science magazine for young readers, ages 10-16.
http://www.odysseymagazine.com

Online Science-athon
http://scithon.terc.edu

Osiris
http://www.journals.uchicago.edu/Osiris/home.html

Popular Science
http://www.popularscience.com

Safe Science Online Course
http://www.practicingsafescience.org

Science
http://www.sciencemag.org/

Scientific American
http://www.sciam.com

Science News
http://www.sciencenews.org

Elizabeth D. Schafer

SEX AND GENDER

(circa 1965) Thirteen international stewardesses, who were entrants in the Miss New York Aviation contest, sit with travel bags from their respective airlines in front of the U.N. building, New York City. L-R: Georgia Johnson, Jo Ann Zorek, Barbara Hart, Sue Todd, Kay McLaughlin, Nicole Savoye, Adrian Magally, Patricia McCormick, Rhonda Spotton, Rosemary Maisonet, Margaretha Zecevic, Souriya Anwar, Marilyn Mennenga.

TIMELINE

1830-1899 ~ Domesticity and Morality

Cult of Domesticity relegates women to homemaking (1830-1880) / Seneca Falls, First Women's Rights Convention, held (1848) / Female moral reformers attack prostitution as the product of male lust (1850s) / Wyoming is the first state to grant women the vote (1869) / Seven out of ten working women hold jobs as domestic servants (1870) / Passionlessness marriages controls birth rate (1870s-1880s) / Women begin to express favorable opinions about sex but in moderation (1890s)

MILESTONES: Interracial alliances of workers and farmers forge national organization, the Knights of Labor (1866) • Transatlantic telegraph cable laid to Europe (1857-1866) • Darwin's *Origins of the Species* theorizes that man is descended from apes (1859) • Thomas Edison invents the light bulb (1879) and one horsepower generator (1881) • St. Andrews Golf Club at Yonkers, New York is formed, marking the beginning of golf in the U.S. (1888)

1900-1919 ~ Breaking the Chains

Women engage in activism on behalf of social change (1900-1920) / Supreme Court rules in favor of restricting working hours for women (1908) / Emergence of the New Woman and the ideal of companionate marriage (1890-1910) / Women enrolled in college rises from 20 percent in 1870 to 40 percent in 1910 / Mann Act makes it illegal to transport women across state lines for the purpose of prostitution (1910) / World War I provides new roles and opportunities for women (1917-1919)

MILESTONES: About 20 percent of all children die before reaching age 5; less than half survive to age 60 (1900) • Queen Victoria dies, ending the repressive Victorian era; Edwardian era begins (1901) • Alice Ramsey becomes the first woman to drive a car across the U.S., capturing Americans' imagination and interest in automobiles (summer 1909) • Percentage of women in clerical positions rises from 34 percent in 1910 to 49 percent in 1930 • Nineteenth Amendment (Women's Suffrage) enacted (1919)

1920-1929 ~ The New Woman

Roaring Twenties produces the emergence of the Flapper and the sexual revolution (1920-1930) / Cable Act declares that an American woman married to an alien loses her citizenship (1922) / George Papanicolaou develops the Pap test for diagnosing cervical cancer (1928)

MILESTONES: Presbyterians and Baptists split into smaller denominations (1920s) • Mail order catalogues and magazines bring fashion awareness to every household (1925-1929) • Supreme Court decision, *Buck v. Bell*, rules that involuntary sterilization for eugenic purposes is constitutional (1927)

1930-1939 ~ Work for Men Only

Working wives are publicly criticized as selfish and "a menace to society" (1930) / Women dominate the professions of teaching, nursing and social work (1930) / Economy Act stipulates that married employees be discharged (1932) / President Roosevelt appoints women to prominent posts within his administration (1932) / Frances Perkins becomes the first woman cabinet member (1933)

MILESTONES: Under pressure, the movie industry enacts the Production Code, addressing crime, sex, vulgarity, obscenity, profanity, costumes, dancing and religion (1930) • Women's golf becomes popular with the emergence of Mildred "Babe" Didrikson who ranks among the greatest athletes of the twentieth century (1930s) • Amelia Earhart is the first woman to complete a solo transatlantic flight (1932) • Synthetic hormone diethylstilbestrol treats menopause symptoms (1939)

1940-1959 ~ Changing Roles of Men and Women

Five million women enter the labor force (1940-1944) / Establishment of the All-American Girls Professional Baseball League (1943) / The Baby Boom generation (1946-1964) is born / 86 percent of Americans believe married women should not work (1946) / Kinsey report on sexual behavior of the human male published (1948) / Kinsey reports that more than half of the nation's women are not virgins when they married (1953) / *Playboy Magazine* inaugurated (1953) / Barbie doll creates public debate about her unattainable body standard (1959)

MILESTONES: Women, blacks and immigrants increase the work force from 46 million in 1940 to 60 million in 1945 • Wartime restrictions on goods cause fashion to become more austere (1942-1944) • Madame Chiang Kai-Shek visits the United States (1943) • *Seventeen Magazine* is founded (1944) • Christian Dior introduces his "New Look" for American women (1947) • Decade of 'correct' fashions and complicated rules of behavior (1950s) • Ultrasound examines fetuses in the womb (1958)

1960-1969 ~ Sexual Revolution

Oral contraceptive pills approved (1960) / First Lady Jackie Kennedy sets standards for elegance (1960) / Intrauterine contraceptive devices developed (1961) / Women's liberation movement encourages smaller families and free access to the birth control pill (1960s) / Mary Quant creates the miniskirt (early 1960s) / Ms. magazine reflects a revolution in women's thinking (1960s) / Bra burning protests symbolize women's liberation (1963) / Betty Friedan's *The Feminine Mystique* attributes women's problems to a sex-based society and not to the personal failure of women (1963) / New fertility drug, Pergonal, introduced, resulting in multiple births (1964) / Female hormone estrogen discovered to prevent osteoporosis (1965)

MILESTONES: Billy Jean King holds the mark for career wins for Wimbledon titles: six singles, ten doubles, and four mixed doubles championships (1961-1979) • Kennedy administration introduces Civil Rights legislation, which will not pass until 1964 (1962) • Boston Strangler murders thirteen women (1962-1964) • First national women's basketball championship tournament (1966) • Army Math Research Center at the University of Wisconsin bombed by student protesters (1968) • Film industry drops the Hays Code, lifting its ban on political and moral content in movies (1968) • California is the first state to permit "irreconcilable differences" divorce, leading the way to no-fault divorce (1969)

1970-1979 ~ Setting Records

Women make up 40 percent of the overall labor force and represent a substantial increase in married women who work (1970) / Women fight against wage discrimination (1970-present) / Title IX requires schools to provide funds for girls' sports (1972) / Courts uphold the right to abortion in *Roe v. Wade* (1973) / Billie Jean King defeats Bobby Riggs, and women symbolically assert their strength, in the so-called Battle of the Sexes in straight sets 6-4, 6-3 and 6-3, before a record crowd at the Houston Astrodome and a television audience of 50 million (1973) / Chris Evert sets the modern tennis record of fifty-six consecutive victories (1974)

MILESTONES: KPFK radio in Los Angeles refuses to turn over to the FBI Symbionese Liberation Army kidnapping tapes of Patty Hearst, continuing a series of battles between the press and law enforcement officials about sources of information (1974) • First "test-tube baby" born in England (1978) • Supreme Court limits strip searches (1979) • Jerry Falwell founds Moral Majority, Inc. and pledges to use its political influence to re-establish traditional values in American society (1979)

1980-2000 ~ Fear of AIDS

AIDS recognized as responsible for a worldwide death toll and first diagnosed in the U.S. (1981) / Barbara McClintock becomes the first woman to win a Nobel Prize, not shared by other scientists, for her work in gene behavior (1983) / Sally Ride is the first woman in space (1983) / First baby born from a donated embryo to an infertile mother (1984) / Norplant implantable contraceptive approved for women (1990) / Viagra introduced, a drug to treat sexual dysfunction in men (1997) / Fewer men and more women smoke cigarettes (1999)

MILESTONES: Fashion industry creates Supermodels to conceal the fact that fashion is in a slump (1985-1987) • *Challenger* space shuttle explodes killing six astronauts and the first private citizen, teacher Christa McAuliffe (1986) • AIDS becomes the second leading cause of death (following accidents) among American men aged 25-34 (1989) • Primetime television broadcasts sexually explicit programming (1990s) • Family and Medical Leave Act provides worker security during family emergencies (1993) • Trendy teen glossies, *Teen Vogue*, *Cosmogirl*, *Teen People*, *Teen* and *Elle Girl*, publish frank articles about self-empowerment, racism, eating disorders, rape, sexual diseases, pregnancy and depression (1995-2000)

Introduction

The relationship between the sexes has generated a great deal of attention since the beginning of the Women's Liberation movement in the 1960s. The struggle for equality and the demand for a reappraisal of gender roles has led to a call to reassess what it means to be male or female and what the roles of men and women should be in modern American society. The women's movement and the sexual revolution of the 1960s and 1970s has prompted this appraisal, but many Americans therefore assume that before that turbulent period, gender roles and sexuality were static elements in America's past. In fact, sex and gender are both dynamic issues that have always prompted discussion, dismay and reconsideration.

1830-1880 • Purity and Sentimentalism ~ The colonial understanding of woman as the weaker vessel, physically, mentally and morally weaker than man, gave way in the early nineteenth century to a new appraisal of woman as society's moral guardian, a being who through her piety, purity and passionlessness would influence her family and her community and help those around her curb their baser instincts. This new assessment of woman and her place in American society led to challenges of traditional legal restrictions placed upon her. Until the middle of the nineteenth century, married women could not own property, they could not engage in business transactions, they could not vote, hold public office or sit on juries. But the republican ideals of equality and independence that defined the new nation also helped to redefine the relationship between men and women in American society. There were men and women who began to challenge male domination in social relations and to argue that patriarchy ran counter to these ideals. They called for greater equality between the sexes.

Another contributing factor to this cultural shift was the popularity of sentimentalism, a cultural movement that emphasized emotions and feelings, an appeal to the heart rather than the mind. Influenced by this new movement, a reaction against the rationalism of the Enlightenment, American couples began to marry for love rather than for more pragmatic considerations, like wealth or status. Prospective brides and grooms sought partners who were "calculated to promote my happiness," as one young woman explained. The emphasis was now on "companionate marriage," an ideal that emphasized equality and mutual respect as well as affection. But the ideal did not necessarily reflect the reality, as husbands still retained control of property and even of their wives' bodies according to the law.

1830-1880 • Providing Moral Guidance ~ Throughout the nineteenth century American women continued to make the home and the family the focus of their lives. In fact, middle class women who were no longer productive members of the family economy were encouraged to focus ever more attention on their domesticity, caring for their husbands and children. With the advent of industrialization, a sharp distinction between male and female spheres emerged in American society, one the public world of business and politics and the other the private world of home and family. While men were expected to be assertive, aggressive and individualistic (all traits that would help them succeed in the competitive world of business), women needed a different set of characteristics to fulfill their roles as wives and mothers. They were expected to be pious, gentle, affectionate, nurturing and self-sacrificing. In connection with the rise of these separate spheres, a Cult of Domesticity emerged, glorifying women's domestic role and responsibilities.

As family life came to be increasingly privatized and separated from the world of commerce, and as fathers engaged in business were spending increasingly large amounts of time away from home, the household became a woman's realm. Within her home a woman played a central role, raising and caring for her children, seeing to her husband's needs. She was to create a haven from the demanding, corrupting world of business. As one advice manual author noted, a man's home should be "an Elysium to which he can flee and find rest from the stormy strife of a selfish world." More importantly, women were increasingly viewed as possessing a much higher degree of morality and piety than men, so that they were also held responsible for the moral guidance of their family members. Women were now charged with instilling morality in their sons and daughters, with curbing the moral lapses of their spouses, and therefore with safeguarding the virtue of the nation itself.

1830-1880 • FRIENDSHIP AND RELIGION

This new emphasis on separate spheres led to a new emphasis on the bond between women. Female friendships came to play an increasingly central role in women's lives. Because they shared a place in American society, women could turn to one another for support and security. Such relationships provided an emotional outlet that women could not necessarily establish with men. As one woman explained, "I do not believe that men can ever feel so pure an enthusiasm for women as we can feel for one another. Ours is nearest the love of angels." These bonds of affection often spanned years, unbroken by marriages or physical distance. Women maintained these female friendships through extensive correspondence and lengthy visits.

Within their sphere, women were responsible for the moral welfare of their husbands and children. In carrying out that responsibility, they turned to religion, and formed the core of the religious revivals of the Second Great Awakening. Female converts outnumbered males by a margin of three to two. Participation in religion gave women a legitimate way to expand their influence beyond the confines of their own homes. Their very visible presence within their congregations gave women an opportunity for community activism. During the early nineteenth century, American women devoted themselves to a variety of church sanctioned causes, including Bible societies, missionary societies and charity associations. But they were warned about assuming too public a role or aspiring to leadership positions within these organizations. They were to concentrate their efforts on personal persuasion of family and friends. Still their acknowledged moral superiority gave women an increased sense of self-esteem.

1830-1880 • FROM LUST TO RESTRAINT

The emphasis on women's morality was a sharp break with the past.

(circa 1911) Women in the West were often called upon to take on traditionally male rolls, like carrying weapons for protection. Seen here, a woman leans against a claim shack surrounded by snow in Newell, South Dakota.

During the colonial period, women were generally described as lustful creatures that required male oversight in order to protect them from moral lapses. By the early nineteenth century, female purity had come to replace female lustfulness in public discourse, and it was generally assumed that women were devoid of sexual impulses. Purity came to be regarded as a distinctly female trait, and women were expected to use it and the resulting self-restraint to curb the baser instincts of men. Because women were "passionless," as the scientific literature attested, they were uniquely suited to safeguard the morals of American society. As one physician observed, "the majority of women (happily for them) are not much troubled with sexual feeling of any kind." This assumption about women's asexuality provided them with a justification for curtailing the frequency of sexual intimacy within their marriages, and as a result, gave them some measure of control over their fertility.

1900 • LIMITING BIRTHS ~ In fact, family size declined steadily among American couples over the course of the nineteenth century, from nearly eight children per couple in 1800 to less than four children per couple in 1900. Passionlessness therefore became an asset for families desiring to limit births and therefore increase the assistance they could offer to each child. This was especially true for the middle class, for whom a large family had ceased to be an economic asset. Of course, abstinence was not the only method of family limitation practiced by American women during the nineteenth century. *Coitus interruptus* (withdrawal) was also used, as were douches, sponges and condoms. But the fact that couples were refraining from sexual intimacy is suggested by the dramatic drop in the rate of premarital pregnancy. While as many as 30 percent of all brides were pregnant at their weddings in the late eighteenth century, that number had declined to 10 percent by the middle of the nineteenth century.

Despite their enhanced status, though, women were still regarded as subordinate to men. Once married, they lost their separate identity and with it many of their rights. Early in the nineteenth century, married women could not own property or sign contracts in their own names. Everything they brought with them to the marriage immediately became their husbands' property. They could not take legal action in their own behalf, and they could not retain custody of their children if their marriages failed. A woman's wages, personal possessions, labor and even her body were legally the property of her husband.

1848 • First Women's Rights Convention ~ It was increasing concern over women's rights that led a small group of activists to organize the first convention to address this issue. The meeting was held at Seneca Falls, New York in 1848. Women's involvement in charitable organizations and reform crusades, particularly abolition, had created a social climate in which women demanded change in their own lives, and particularly in their legal status. As women were drawn into charitable and reform organizations in the middle of the nineteenth century, they expanded their activism beyond Sunday schools and missionary societies and took up a variety of other causes. Women who lived in urban areas were acutely aware of the effects of poverty and vice on society, and reached out to poor women and children in an effort to improve the social landscape. Their work in a host of benevolent associations allowed these women to expand their moral reach beyond their own homes, and involved them in a world of reform work where their skills as managers and fund raisers were well utilized.

As they visited working class neighborhoods, prisons and poor houses, these female reformers acted on their desire to assist poor women while putting a halt to a number of social ills. In that effort they targeted men and set about promoting a fundamental change in male behavior. In particular they were concerned with eliminating the double standard that governed sexual behavior in American society. These female moral reformers intended to implement a single standard of morality on all Americans. They sought to hold men responsible for their behavior as seducers and adulterers. They also wanted to eradicate prostitution by exposing the customers while saving the fallen women who they viewed as victims of male lust. Anti-prostitution advocates gathered outside brothels where they sang hymns and recorded the names of customers. They turned to state lawmakers in an effort to establish legal penalties for seduction. And they offered employment alternatives to the prostitutes, generally as domestic servants.

As activists, women believed that they were especially obligated to help other women. They sought to address "moral pollution" in every aspect of American society, and many came to the conclusion that they could not adequately address the plight of women if they ignored the particular horrors faced by female slaves. Northern women drawn into the anti-slavery crusade were conscious of the suffering of all those held in bondage, but understood that for women, slavery was particularly devastating. Black women were deprived of legal marriages (as property, they were not allowed to enter into binding contracts), they lived without the benefit of male protection (considered a woman's right), they were denied parental rights to their children (who were legally the property of their masters), and were frequently the targets of sexual abuse. "We should be less than women," wrote one female anti-slavery group, "if the nameless and unnumbered wrongs of which the slaves of our sex are made the defenseless victims, did not fill us with horror." As women, they felt themselves responsible to save other women from the horror and degradation of slavery.

1848 • WOMEN AND SLAVES ~ It was through their anti-slavery activism that some women came to see a powerful connection between women and slaves. Both groups were deprived of basic rights in American society. The first women's rights convention, held at Seneca Falls in 1848, grew out of the frustration of female abolitionists that they were being denied a leadership role, and even criticized for their activism, in a movement of which they made up the rank and file of supporters. That first meeting led to the adoption of a document known as the Declaration of Sentiments, a list of grievances against the "absolute tyranny" of men. At this meeting, those attending drew up a reform agenda, calling for a host of legal rights for women, including property ownership, child custody, access to higher education and the vote. They saw these reforms as necessary steps to bring about the moral reformation of all of American society.

Certainly not all women embraced the call for equal rights. One activist received a letter from her sister stating "I don't believe woman is groaning under half so heavy a yoke of bondage as you imagine; I am sure I do not feel burdened by anything man has laid upon me, to be sure I can't vote, but what care I for that, I would not if I could." But whatever their views on women's rights, middle class women continued to agitate for change in American society.

1870s • WORKING-CLASS WOMEN ~ In fact, the years after the Civil War ushered in sweeping changes, some for better, some not. As the United States industrialized, Americans became uncomfortably aware of the negative consequences of the country's economic transformation. While the middle class grew in size and experienced a marked improvement in their standard of living, the working class enjoyed no such benefits. While Americans were all largely in agreement that a woman's place was in the home, working class and immigrant women entered the workforce in increasing numbers. The workplace was a gender segregated place, with a powerful sexual division of labor that relegated female workers to low skill, low wage jobs.

In 1870, seven out of ten working women held jobs as domestic servants. But with the advent of industrialization, new jobs were created and employers recruited large numbers of young women. Most working women were young and single, and they considered paid labor to be a temporary phase of the life cycle, to be replaced by marriage and motherhood.

1880-1910 • PROSTITUTION ~ There was some anxiety about the growing numbers of women in the workforce. One source of concern was the fact that many of these young women were living away from home for the first time, with no family members to oversee their activities. Some of these women turned to the burgeoning "sexual service sector" for employment in dance halls or brothels. In fact, prostitution became a major source of middle class anxiety, prompting calls for reform. Anti-prostitution activists were particularly concerned about "white slavery," insisting that young women, the victims of seduction, entrapment or kidnapping, were delivered by unscrupulous men into a life of prostitution. Reformers finally prevailed upon the federal government to pass legislation to deal with the situation. The Mann Act, passed in 1910, made it illegal to transport women across state lines for the purpose of prostitution. Much of the concern about white slavery stemmed from the fact that middle class reformers could not imagine that young women would choose to become prostitutes. In reality, prostitution was often the best of a limited range of economic options available for women. While a female factory worker might earn six or seven dollars a week for her efforts, a prostitute could earn ten dollars in an afternoon. For some women, the choice was an obvious one.

1850-1900 • THE WORKPLACE FOR WOMEN ~ Another great source of anxiety stemmed from concerns that women's presence in the labor force might limit job opportunities for men because women could be hired at lower wages. This fear was unfounded, though, because women were generally hired only in certain industries (clothing manufacturing, canneries, laundries) or were given only "women's jobs," those that required the least skill (bottle washers in breweries). Still, labor unions excluded women workers. Groups like the American Federation of Labor argued that women did not need jobs, and even lobbied for equal pay for women as a ploy to drive them out of the workplace. The belief was that if an employer had to pay the same wage to a woman as to a man, he would certainly hire the man. Protective legislation, intended to safeguard women on the job by limiting the hours they could work or mandating improvements in working conditions, actually hurt their employability by making them less easily exploitable. Such measures were also supported by labor unions. One union leader remarked that "we cannot drive the female out of the trade but we can restrict her through factory laws."

Wage Gap: Women's earnings relative to men's

1900	50 percent
1945	63 percent
1973	57 percent
1980	61 percent
1985	65 percent
1990	71 percent
1997	74 percent
2000	72 percent

The reformers who had called for the introduction of protective legislation had been motivated by the desire to make the workplace safer for women. During the second half of the nineteenth century, middle class men and women, concerned by the plight of the nation's working class poor, embarked upon an ambitious and wide ranging reform campaign known as Progressivism. The regulations they called for did take steps to improve wages and working conditions for women, but also limited women's job opportunities by mandating that they could not work at night, lift heavy objects or take jobs in dangerous settings, whether physically (mines) or morally (bars). Such protective legislation created tensions between the middle class women who lobbied for them and the working class women such laws were intended to help.

1870-1910 • WOMEN BECOMING EDUCATED ~ Many of those who called themselves Progressives at the turn of the twentieth century were young women, the college-educated daughters of the middle class. As their families prospered due to industrialization, these young women were given an unprecedented opportunity for higher education. Women comprised only 21 percent of college students in 1870. By 1910 40 percent of college students were female. In addition, more girls than boys graduated from high school in 1900. There was some opposition to higher education for women, particularly from those who believed that the intellectual strain would ruin a woman's physical and mental health. One doctor maintained that education would make women feeble and sterile. To answer these critics, women's colleges sought to prepare students for a life of service to both their families and society. College educated women would make "efficient housekeepers" according to one administrator. To that end, many colleges established separate curriculums for male and female students, relegating young women to courses of study that included home economics (often called "domestic science"), child care and "sanitary chemistry."

The access to higher education proved to be a mixed blessing to the daughters of the middle class, though. For many the dilemma was what to do after graduation. There were few outlets for women with college degrees, few careers open to them. As one Radcliffe graduate observed in 1900, "I hang in a void midway between two spheres; a professional career puts me beyond reach of the average woman's duties and pleasures; but the conventional limitations of the female lot put me beyond the reach of the average man's duties and pleasures." These young women found themselves channeled into traditional women's work, becoming teachers, librarians and nurses. In this way they did not challenge traditional gender roles, as these female professions were generally viewed as an extension of traditional women's responsibilities.

1900 • SINGLE WOMEN ~ Female college graduates raised concerns not just because they might endanger their health or challenge men in the workplace, but also because they were challenging society's expectations of them. These young women married later than their peers and a growing number chose not to marry at all. The spinster, once thought of as a marginal member of society, looked on with pity, now came to represent new opportunities for women. Single women came to represent the vanguard of female reform efforts. Armed with an education, American women had options at the end of the nineteenth century that had not been available to their mothers. And many chose to forego marriage and motherhood in favor of careers and female associations. It became so common for young women to establish same sex households that observers devised a name for the phenomenon – Boston marriage. These romantic friendships (sometimes sexual, often not) linked female couples in long-term relationships, creating alternative family units that provided emotional support for single women.

1890S • MODERATION IN SEXUAL ACTIVITIES ~ Still, marriage and motherhood was the ultimate career for 90 percent of American women. But

(1913) A car taking part in a suffragette parade in Long Island, New York.

even here there were important changes ushered in by the era of the New Woman. Family size continued to decline as women gained more control over their reproductive lives. New expectations of "social purity" allowed middle class women to insist upon restraint in their sexual relations. Dr. Clelia Mosher surveyed a group of middle class women in the 1890s and found that while they expressed generally favorable opinions about sex, respondents also desired moderation in sexual relations with their spouses. While these couples had intercourse on average once a week, wives reported that once a month would be preferable. Attitudes towards sexuality corresponded with more general attitudes towards men and marriage. By the late nineteenth century women insisted on a greater degree of emotional satisfaction in their marital relations. When expectations were not met, the divorce rate began to rise. While both men and women increasingly expressed dissatisfaction with marriage, at the turn of the century, nearly two-thirds of all divorces were granted to women.

1900-1920 • ACTIVISM ∼ As she sought greater satisfaction within marriage, the New Woman of the early twentieth century also set out to extend her influence beyond the confines of her home and family, and to help usher in meaningful reforms in American society. Progressive era reform campaigns and formal women's clubs provided middle class women with an outlet for their talents and gave them an entrée into the public realm. Organizations like the Women's Christian Temperance Union (WCTU) allowed women to take on a leadership role in moral reform without leaving entirely the traditional female sphere of charitable work. Female activism on behalf of social change gave rise to "the woman movement," uniting women across the country with the belief that "women, as women, had something distinctive and significant to contribute collectively to public life." By the early twentieth century, women had come to think of themselves as "social housekeepers," determined to participate fully in the transformation of American society.

Through their reform efforts, women became increasingly convinced that only through full political participation could they effect lasting changes. Without the vote, they could not effectively influence state and national legislators to enact meaningful reform measures. But the challenge was to convince American men and women alike that women's suffrage would be a benefit to society, rather than a detriment. In fact, one of the greatest obstacles to the enfranchisement of women was women themselves. For the most part, they were apathetic to the suffrage campaign. There were also vocal critics, including the Senator who argued that giving the vote to women would lead to "a state of war, and make every home a hell on earth." Anti-suffrage rhetoric cautioned that giving the vote to women would "wreck our present domestic institutions," and would have "a dangerous, undermining effect on the character of wives and mothers." Women were thought to be too sentimental, too emotional to engage in the logical, rational debate about political issues and legislative measures. But women countered that female suffrage would elevate politics to a purer, more altruistic level. Suffragists emphasized women's moral superiority and their ability to "lift men into the higher realm of thought and action."

Ultimately, it was political expediency that gained for women the right to vote on the national level. This had been the case in separate state suffrage measures.

Wyoming was the first state to grant women the vote, in 1869. There was little opposition for the measure, because as one observer pointed out, "Wyoming gave women the right to vote in much the same spirit that New York or Pennsylvania might vote to enfranchise angels or Martians." Likewise, the Mormon political leadership in Utah enfranchised women in an effort to protect Mormon control of state government.

With the world at war in 1918, Congress passed a constitutional amendment calling for women's suffrage. Women's work on behalf of the war effort finally won them widespread support in their call for a political voice. In 1920, Tennessee ratified the Nineteenth Amendment, gaining for American women the political right many had so long desired. With the franchise women took an important step closer to real equality with men. As one historian has written, the woman suffrage victory thus crushed two fundamental assumptions: that women depended on men and that men held authority over women. As an attack on gender hierarchy, in short, the suffrage movement has no match.

1917-1920 • NEW WORK FOR WOMEN

Women's suffrage did not usher in the profound changes (for better or for worse) that many Americans had predicted. Despite widely held assumptions, women did not organize and vote as a bloc. In fact, many women failed to vote at all. And those that did cast ballots voted in harmony with their husbands, fathers and brothers. It was not the vote that changed day-to-day gender relations in the United States in the early twentieth century. Powerful changes were ushered in, but they were the result of an increasing shift in the employment picture that saw large

1917-1920

numbers of women in the workforce. Women had been an ever growing proportion of American workers since the late nineteenth century, but their entrance into the realm of paid labor accelerated dramatically with the United States' involvement in the first world war. The war left a void of workers that women stepped forward to fill. Before 1917, female laborers had been relegated to a small collection of low paid, low skill jobs generally regarded as "women's work." But the war's drain on manpower presented women with new opportunities.

Young women who were anxious to find a new place for themselves in the workforce set out to abandon any notion of "sex-consciousness." Rather than identifying themselves with other women and women's causes and concerns as female Progressives had done, this new generation of American women sought ways to emphasize their individuality. According to one historian, "these women wanted to emancipate themselves from each other, from their families, and from the assumption that women were more virtuous than men and more responsible for social welfare." The early twentieth century saw a dramatic change in American society and gender relations. The Progressive Era gave way to a much more conservative age in which the New Woman, with her desire to foster social reform was replaced as a social barometer with a very different persona, the Flapper. As one contemporary observed, "Cigarette in hand, shimmying to the music of the masses, the New Woman and the New Morality have made their theatric debut upon the modern scene."

Young women who had gained a degree of independence by entering the workforce now set out to achieve an unprecedented degree of self-fulfillment as well. They dressed to suit themselves, in short, revealing skirts with their stockings rolled down around their knees or sometimes their ankles. They bobbed their hair in a further rebellion against the Victorian feminine ideal, and they wore makeup, once the sure sign of immorality. They smoked, drank alcohol and dated unsupervised, all adding to an aura of overt sexuality. The Flapper, who took her name from the flapping sound she made as she walked with her galoshes unbuckled, looked upon her place in the labor force as a temporary sojourn, time spent between high school and marriage. And though many young women talked about their desire to continue working after they wed, to combine marriage with a career, this was more the ideal than the reality.

In fact, married women who held jobs were openly criticized for threatening the stability of the family. They were accused of being selfish for putting their own needs before those of their husbands and children, as well as for taking jobs away

(1924) An American businesswoman at her desk with her Ford sedan outside. From Good Housekeeping magazine, 1924.

from men with families to support. While the emphasis for unmarried women was individuality, the same was not true for their married counterparts. Instead, American society placed renewed importance on the role of mother. So the 1920s promoted two feminine ideals, the fun-seeking, fast-living Flapper and the nurturing, self-sacrificing housewife.

American women overwhelmingly aspired to marriage and motherhood. The percentage of spinsters declined dramatically by the 1920s, to only five percent. In fact, psychologists began to describe unmarried women as social deviants, neurotics who left their true destiny unmet. Female friendships also became suspect, as women were told that their attention should be focused on men. Other women became competition, not a source of emotional support. The experts reminded American women that their greatest source of fulfillment was marriage and motherhood. But wives were also led to expect a greater degree of emotional and sexual satisfaction within marriage. That expectation led to a sexual revolution.

1920S • THE NEW MORALITY ~ The "new morality" of the 1920s had its roots in the Victorian era with the development of more positive attitudes about sexuality, particularly women's desire for sexual gratification. Changes in sexual standards and behavior were under way before World War I, but significant emphasis on sexuality and changing ideas about morality became widespread by the 1920s. This is due in part to the fact that record numbers of young women were economically independent.

Newly liberated from parental support and control, they embarked on a new path of personal freedom in thought as well as behavior, and in the process provoking a generational rift. The writings of Sigmund Freud and Havelock Ellis found a new, mainstream audience, leading to widespread acceptance of sexual urges as natural and healthy. Ellis emphasized the existence of "sexual impulse in women" as distinct from "reproductive instinct." As one historian has noted, the new morality proclaimed equality of desire. Discarding purity for sexuality, women could now claim a facet of male privilege. The double standard of morality was gradually being replaced.

As young women entered the workforce, they took their places in what had been largely a man's world. Mingling, flirting, dating all became easier and more commonplace as women's presence in office buildings and factories increased. Leisure hours were also spent in public places catering to a youthful clientele, like dance halls, amusement parks and movie

(1926) A cinema poster advertising 'The Temptress', the second American film starring the Swedish born American actress Greta Garbo and the Spanish born star Antonio Moreno.

1910-1930

houses. Without chaperones, young couples were free to indulge in sexual experimentation. Young women gained access to amusements and to a higher standard of living than they could afford on their salaries alone through the system of "treating," in which young men impressed the opposite sex with meals and entertainment, while their dates reciprocated with sexual favors.

Such youthful indulgence was a dramatic departure from the previous generation. Of American women born in the decade 1890 to 1900, nearly three quarters were virgins at marriage. Yet that was true of less than one third of the women born after 1910. This increase in sexual activity could reflect the fact that women coming of age after 1900 felt free to engage in sexual experimentation to a much greater degree than their mothers had, or that they experienced more pressure to consent to sexual activity.

Premarital Sex: Proportion of women who were virgins at marriage

Before 1890	90 percent
1890-1900	74 percent
1900-1910	51 percent
1910-1930	32 percent
1950-1960	50 percent
1980-present	20 percent

1910-1930 • COURTSHIP ~ American courtship practices were fundamentally altered during the early twentieth century. The Flapper helped to redefine femininity in American society, as she was both a temptress and companion at the same time. In her short skirt, silk stockings and make up, the Flapper exuded sex appeal and exerted sexual power over men. And yet as she claimed male privileges like driving, playing sports, smoking and engaging in sexual relations, she became the competitor and equal to her male companions. Even her physical appearance evoked this dual identity – the sexual siren and the sport. While she wore revealing dresses made of sheer, clingy fabric, she also wore her hair short and bound her breasts. And as she shunned older norms of feminine identity, she also turned her back on more traditional modes of courtship. The nineteenth century practice of young women receiving suitors in the parlor of the family home had given way to dating away from home and parental supervision, a practice that was made much easier thanks to the automobile, the house of prostitution on wheels, according to one critic.

1920s • BIRTH CONTROL ~ This sexual revolution was further advanced by the availability of contraceptive information and devices. Activist Margaret Sanger first used the phrase "birth control" to describe her efforts to provide reliable methods of contraception to working class women.

While working as a visiting nurse in some of New York City's poorest neighborhoods in 1912, Sanger was frustrated by her inability to provide contraceptive information and devices to the working class women she served. Her own knowledge was limited, and she found the medical establishment unwilling to provide her clients with the information they needed to control their fertility. She knew, too, that women among the urban poor were producing more children than they could support, and were resorting to the services of untrained abortionists or were attempting "knitting needle abortions" at home in order to terminate pregnancies. They were often dying as a result.

Sanger determined to defy the laws that prohibited the dissemination of contraceptive literature. The Comstock Law, passed in 1873, classified any literature dealing with fertility as pornographic, and made it illegal to send both information about contraception and contraceptive devices through the mail. State laws barred the manufacture, sale or distribution of such devices. The fear was that access to such information would lead to promiscuity. In addition, by the 1870s there was widespread fear that native-born, middle-class Americans were committing "race suicide" by producing too few children, so that any interest in family limitation was viewed as highly suspect.

As Sanger insisted in her journal, the *Woman Rebel*, "women cannot be on an equal footing with men until they have full and complete control over their reproductive function." She published a pamphlet providing specific information entitled "Family Limitation," then fled the country to avoid arrest.

In Europe, Sanger visited state sanctioned birth control clinics, and determined that they were the answer to the problem of how to get the information to the women who needed it most—the working class. In 1916 she opened the first birth control clinic in the United States, in a working class neighborhood in Brooklyn, New York. In advertising the services of the clinic, Sanger offered to help women avoid having more children than they desired. Explicitly anti-abortion, Sanger's handbill read "do not kill, do not take life, but prevent. Safe, harmless information can be obtained of trained nurses at 46 Amboy Street." Though she was arrested and sentenced to 30 days in jail for her actions, Sanger's clinic brought a tremendous amount of publicity to her cause, and generated a great deal of popular support. With the backing of middle class women, Sanger established the American Birth Control League in 1921 (forerunner to Planned Parenthood). The aim of this organization was to educate women regarding family limitation in order to end the misery and poverty of the working class poor. But she reached a wider audience by arguing that birth control would protect the nation from the "over fertility of the mentally and physically defective," (thereby gaining the support of eugenicists) while contributing to "sexual satisfaction" for women and their partners. It was the support of the well-to-do that ultimately led to widespread acceptance of birth control and freed women from the danger and burden of "involuntary motherhood."

1890-1920s • FIGHTING FOR CONTRACEPTION ~ Sanger's interest in this cause was not unique. During the late nineteenth century, some reformers had advocated "voluntary motherhood," but they focused on a woman's right to abstain from sexual relations with her spouse. Sanger took a much more radical approach by insisting that all women had the right to limit their fertility through access to safe, effective contraceptive measures. Contraception allowed couples to limit family size, but also to disconnect sexual intimacy from procreation. Some middle class couples had made use of contraceptive devices including condoms, diaphragms (called "pessaries"), douches, sponges and cervical caps since the mid-nineteenth century. But by the 1920s, use of birth control measures was widespread, with as many as 60 percent of American women making use of various devices.

1890-1920s

Working class women were far less likely than their middle class contemporaries to practice birth control for a variety of reasons. Most had no access to private physicians who could prescribe contraceptives, and many had a very rudimentary understanding of fertility. Working class couples often relied upon the rhythm method, though medical texts often incorrectly reported that a woman's "safe" interval (the period in which she was least likely to conceive) was midway between menstrual cycles. Withdrawal was also advocated, though it demanded a great deal of self control. Many men refused to use condoms, and douches generally could not be used by women who had no indoor plumbing. In addition, many working class women were Catholics, either immigrants themselves or the daughters of immigrants, and their religious beliefs offered a powerful moral deterrent against the use of contraceptive devices. It was these women that Margaret Sanger hoped to reach with her publications and her Brooklyn, New York, birth control clinic.

The sexual revolution of the 1920s, with its emphasis on sex as a means of personal expression, increased public acceptance of birth control. But it also redefined marriage as a source of intimacy and emotional fulfillment. The message delivered to young women from their peers, at school, in advertising and the movies spelled out their future: man, marriage and domesticity. On college campuses, the new study of "Euthenics" prepared coeds for a career as homemakers with courses like "Husband and Wife," "Motherhood," and "The Family as an Economic Unit." Hollywood likewise promoted a domestic ideal for women. While the movie heroine of the 1920s

(1928) Lady Biker. The so called 'flapper' life style for young women of the 1920s saw not only women taking on larger roles in the area of sex but also in experimenting with daredevil activities. Seen here is a woman sitting on an Indian motorcycle on top of a wood planked bridge in Oregon.

> ## Screen Vixens of the 30s
>
> For four years, 1930-1934, between the coming of sound and before the Production Code lowered the boom on sex and violence, Hollywood produced more than 50 movies in which the female stars carried the banners from the previous decade's achievements over the battle for women's rights. In *Ladies They Talk About*, Barbara Stanwyck (1933) is the lookout and brains for a gang of bank robbers. In *A Free Soul* (1931) Norma Shearer doesn't want to marry; she just wants to enjoy her illicit lover affair with gangster Clark Gable. Femme fatales Stanwyck, Jean Harlow and Mae West saw suffering as a fool's game; they had no illusion about men's desires and weaknesses, and so they relied on their own resources. Sin is sexy and sex is a free ride as long as you've got a limousine, alimony, and a penthouse where you will remain forever young.
>
> *She Done Him Wrong*, Mae West (1933)
> *Red Headed Woman*, Jean Harlow (1932)
> *Baby Face*, Barbara Stanwyck (1933)
> *Three on a March*, Bette Davis (1932)
> *Red Dust*, Jean Harlow (1932)
> *A Free Soul*, Norma Shearer (1931)
> *Susan Lennox: Her Fall and Rise*, Greta Garbo (1931)
> *The Animal Kingdom*, Myrna Loy (1932)
> *The Divorcee*, Norma Shearer (1930)

was worldly, assertive and sensual, she was also determined to get her man and to live happily ever after in domestic bliss. But for many women, that bliss proved elusive. Marriage had been redefined by the 1920s. It was to be a "romantic-sexual union." But the sharp rise in the divorce rate suggests that many couples found the new ideal difficult to attain.

1930s • RETURN TO TRADITIONAL ROLES ~ By 1930, American couples faced new strains. The onset of the Great Depression led to a retrenchment in society's attitudes about women and gender roles. The Flapper gave way to a more traditional feminine ideal, the homemaker who sacrificed her individualism to see to her family's physical and emotional needs. Americans abandoned the assumption that it was their right to seek self-fulfillment and personal satisfaction. Instead, the family once again became a central element in people's lives and returned to its place as an economic unit as well as a source of emotional security. Society now expected women to leave the workplace to make way for unemployed men with families to support. In fact, the working wife was publicly criticized as selfish, "a menace to society," as future Secretary of Labor Frances Perkins argued in 1930.

During the Depression, 82 percent of those responding to a Gallup poll said that wives should not work if their husbands had jobs. The reality of course was that many married women were forced to work, because their husbands were unemployed or had deserted them. The argument that working women were taking jobs away from men also did not reflect real life, as most women were employed in traditionally female occupations. Still, local, state and federal government officials bowed to public pressure. A New York state assemblyman said that women who continued to work even though their husbands had jobs were "undeserving parasites." Some cities insisted that women should be fired if their husbands were working. In some communities, female teachers lost their jobs if they got married. Several states called for legislation that limited married women's access to government jobs. In 1932, Congress passed the Economy Act, stipulating that married employees be discharged first when the government cut back on jobs. (The measure was repealed in 1937.)

Within their homes, women's contributions took on new importance. To conserve family resources, they canned fruits and vegetables, sewed clothes, baked their own bread and found many ways to stretch limited budgets. Some women also found creative ways to make a little extra money, for instance by taking in boarders, doing laundry or sewing for others. But the economic devastation contributed to personal catastrophes as increasing numbers of men abandoned families they could no longer support. Desertion rates soared during the 1930s.

Conversely, the divorce rate dropped, but that simply reflected the fact that many couples could not afford the fees a legal separation entailed. At the same time, the marriage rate also declined sharply, simply because young couples lacked the resources to establish independent households. Those already married were not having children. The birthrate in the United States dropped to its lowest level ever during the Depression. The desire to limit family size led to the widespread acceptance of birth control in American society. In 1930, there were 55 clinics nationwide dispensing contraceptive devices and literature. By 1938, there were three hundred.

1932-1945 • WOMEN IN GOVERNMENT
~ It was in the realm of politics that women were able to bridge the gap between the career woman of the 1920s and the nurturing housewife society expected in the 1930s. Franklin D. Roosevelt determined to appoint women to prominent posts within his administration. He named the first female cabinet secretary in American history, and called women to serve in virtually every agency in the federal government. These women put a human face on Roosevelt's New Deal, by trying to ensure that women benefited from the programs being established.

But it was another national emergency, war, that led the American public to drop its protests against women in the workforce. Following the Japanese attack on Pearl Harbor in 1941, the United States prepared for war by expanding and transforming the economy from production of consumer goods to military supplies. The transition to a wartime economy, and the departure of tens of thousands of men from the labor force, opened up unprecedented opportunities for women. By 1944, the number of women in the workforce had jumped from 12 million to 18 million, a 50 percent increase. Americans now extolled the benefits of "womanpower." Women also became a visible component of the armed services, as Army WACs, Navy WAVES, Coast Guard SPARS and even as WASPs, Women's Airforce Service Pilots, whose job was to test new military aircraft and deliver planes to military bases throughout the United States.

1941-1945 • WARTIME JOBS FOR WOMEN ~ For the first time, women had an unprecedented opportunity to reach beyond traditional female occupations and to take jobs that had been held exclusively by men. Women worked as bus drivers, railway employees, security guards and in manufacturing. The largest employers were those companies devoted to war industry, and in these factories women took jobs as welders, riveters, electricians operated lathes, band saws and drills, and made everything from parachutes to battleships. Previous bans against women working in heavy industry were set aside, and many states suspended laws that had prohibited women from working at night or overtime. Women also took "white collar" jobs, many within the federal government, so that by 1945 clerical work had become identified as a female occupation.

While there was some concern about women, particularly married women, entering the workforce in huge numbers, manufacturers were quick to assure the public that factory work would not diminish a woman's femininity. Housewives were encouraged to take jobs as their patriotic duty, and were told that they would find factory work no more challenging than housework. Recruiters insisted that women would adjust to using power tools "as easily as to electric cake mixers and vacuum cleaners." But the entry of so many women into the labor force did not usher in an era of true equality. Rather, society was simply adapting to a state of national emergency. Women played no role in policy making, and were paid less for their efforts than men who were performing the same tasks. On the job, female employees were sometimes subject to hostility or sexual harassment. Most Americans believed that women's work, while necessary, should also be temporary, "for the duration."

1942-1945 • WARTIME SEX ~ As young men became scarce on the domestic front, young women found new challenges to traditional gender relations, but new opportunities for sexual experimentation. By 1944, so many men were in the service that among Americans aged 20 to 24, there were two women for every man. But as one young woman observed, "Chicago was just humming, no matter where I went. The bars were jammed, and unless you were an absolute dog, you could pick up anyone you wanted to." The social dislocation of the war years led to a change in young people's attitudes towards sex. "Victory girls" made the patriotic gesture of engaging in sexual relations with soldiers and sailors about to ship out. Many married couples, separated for extended periods of time, succumbed to extramarital affairs. Experts warned of the threat of "'sexual laxity,' moral decay and the destruction of the family." And they urged women to prepare to vacate jobs in favor of returning servicemen once the war was over.

1946-1950 • AFTER THE WAR ~ In fact, the majority of women who entered the workforce during the war years wanted to keep their jobs. But as early as 1943 the Office of War Information began a campaign to return women to their traditional place in American society. Most women left the factories voluntarily, while others were laid off to make room for men reentering the civilian workforce. Though she had been a symbol of patriot-

1946-1950s

ism during the war, the working woman became a threat to traditional society by war's end. In 1946, a Gallup poll reported that 86 percent of Americans believed married women should not work.

Following nearly two decades of national emergency, Americans were eager for a return to traditional gender roles and domestic bliss. The family became the symbol of stability and security in a nation recovering from depression and war. During the 1950s, American couples raced to the altar, marrying in record numbers. They also married younger. Nearly a third of all brides were teenagers. And they had record numbers of children. The Baby Boom became a powerful symbol of domesticity and Americans' search for security in an insecure world.

1946-1950s • Femininity and Domesticity ~ In 1947, one scholarly journal reported that the American family had returned to a "semi-patriarchal form in which a dominant husband 'brings home the bacon' and a submissive woman plays a traditional wife and mother role." Women were encouraged to embrace their femininity and to seek fulfillment through domesticity. Homemaking became the career goal for the vast majority of young women. In fact, those women who rejected the domestic ideal were labeled maladjusted and neurotic. "Independent woman," according to a prominent sociologist, was a contradiction in terms. Young women, in particular, embraced the message that their identity and happiness revolved around domesticity. In the mid 1950s, the *New York Times* reported that "girls feel hopeless if they haven't a marriage at least in sight by commencement time."

1950s • The Sexual Double Standard ~ For American women, the road to matrimony had to be carefully negotiated in order to land the man

---

The Good Wife's Guide

~

- Have a delicious meal ready when he returns from work.
- Touch up your make-up, put a ribbon in your hair, and be fresh looking.
- In the cooler months, light a fire. Caring for his comfort will provide you with immense personal satisfaction.
- Prepare the children. Wash their hands and faces, comb their hair, and change their clothes if necessary. They are little treasures and he would like to see them playing the part.
- Be happy to see him. Greet him with a warm smile and show sincerely your desire to please him.
- Let him talk first. Remember, his topics of conversation are more important than yours.
- Never complain if he's late for dinner or stays out all night. Don't question him about his actions, his judgment, or his integrity. He is the master of the house and as such will always exercise his will with fairness and truthfulness.
- Remember, a good wife always knows her place.

From *Housekeeping Monthly*, May 13, 1955

Playboy

In December, 1953, a glossy monthly magazine made its debut, unabashedly catering to an emerging new audience. *Playboy* capitalized on the demand for sexually explicit material, and sent a message to young men that personal sexual fulfillment, not commitment, was the goal and that they should "enjoy the pleasures the female has to offer without becoming emotionally involved." Marriage, the magazine warned, was a financial and emotional trap, leading to drudgery and domination. *Playboy* gave voice to male frustrations, labeling women as "money hungry" or as "parasites" intent upon forcing men into commitment. The first issue featured an article entitled "Miss Gold-Digger of 1953," that set the tone for future warnings to its readers. The key was learning how to play the game.

Women wanted commitment, men wanted sex. The magazine provided tips on how to get the latter without succumbing to the former. Hugh Hefner, *Playboy's* creator, was an outspoken critic of what he perceived as American society's "ferocious anti-sexuality," and saw his magazine as "a symbol of disobedience, a triumph of sexuality, an end of Puritanism." Hefner's publication contributed to the creation of a singles culture in the United States, a culture supported by singles bars, singles apartment complexes, dating services, all geared toward the quest for casual encounters. *Playboy's* message was liberating on one point, that virginity in women was not important, and was not necessarily desirable. Instead, men were told that women were always ready and willing to engage in sexual encounters. The sexual revolution, then, was initially driven by a male desire to be liberated from family responsibilities and family values.

but avoid any drastic sexual missteps. Attitudes about sexuality had loosened by the middle of the twentieth century, but the double standard was still a powerful social force. Girls had to safeguard their reputations, particularly protecting against pregnancy, at the same time that they were told that it was their sex appeal that attracted boys. It was up to them to set the limits in their sexual encounters with the opposite sex. In this social climate, dating took on particular importance and specific risks. How far was too far? How did a young woman manage sexual experimentation without risking her desirability? The double standard allowed boys a great deal of latitude in this regard–even expected them to pursue sexual relationships, while it demanded virtue from girls. As one young woman lamented, "How are you supposed to know what they want? You hold out for a long time and then when you do give in to them and give your body they laugh at you afterwards and say they'd never marry a slut, and that they didn't love you but were just testing because they only plan to marry a virgin and wanted to see if you'd go all the way."

Still, nearly half of all young women engaged in premarital sexual relations. Sexual attraction was understood to be a very important criteria for choosing a spouse, but experts warned against overemphasizing sexuality. One actually outlined a formula for selecting a partner, claiming that "60 percent profound affection and respect [and] 40 percent intense sex attraction" would lead to a happy mar-

1950s

riage. The reverse would likely ensure divorce. Women struggled to meet society's expectations of morality while securing their future by catching a husband. Girls were instructed in the art of attracting boys through magazines and movies. A key skill was to act the part of the subordinate. As one college coed explained, "I may be wrong, but I am just old fashioned enough to believe that men (at least the type I want to marry) still want their wives to be feminine, domestic, dependent and just a little inferior mentally."

Once married, social expectations seemed to keep women at home. Despite the rhetoric, large numbers of married women, in fact, remained in the workforce. The post-war economic boom demanded their labor, though they were once again relegated to low wage women's work. Women's pay declined by more than 25 percent from the mid 1940s to the 1950s. And working wives felt compelled to justify their employment by explaining that they were saving money to make special purchases—a new car, appliances—or to pay for a family vacation or college tuition for their children. They justified their jobs on the basis of family need, not personal desire. Women were warned that their absence from the home might have powerful negative consequences for themselves and their families. Those who desired something more than domesticity were accused of "penis envy" and "masculine strivings." Marynia Farnham and Ferdinand Lundberg argued in their best-seller, *The Modern Woman: The Lost Sex*, that education and careers would produce masculine women and "enormously dangerous consequences to the home, the children dependent on it, and the ability of the woman, as well as her husband, to obtain sexual gratification."

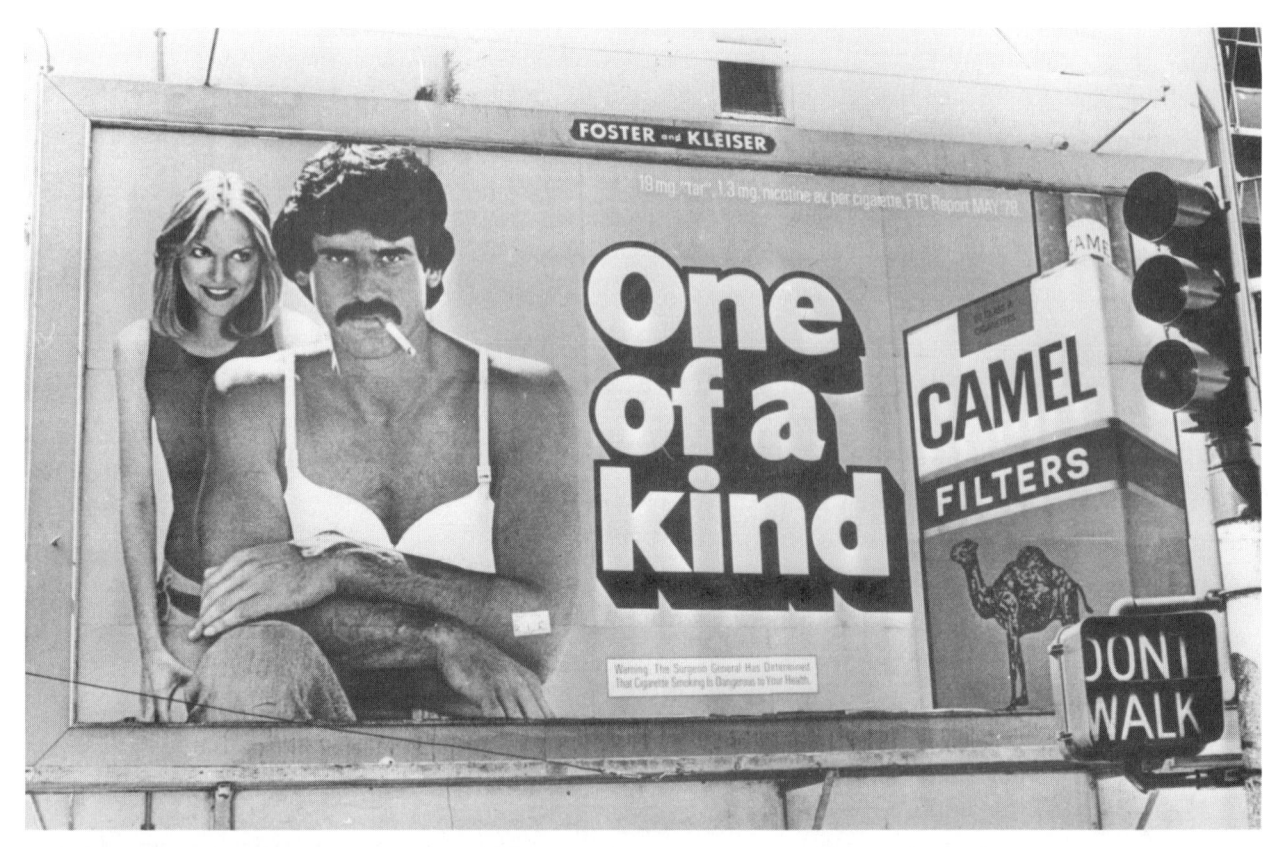

(1978) A billboard advertising cigarettes in San Francisco which has been enhanced by the addition of a giant brassiere by members of the Billboard Liberation Front, objecting to the use of male bodies in advertisements.

1960 • CHALLENGING TRADITIONAL ROLES ~ By 1960, the social climate in the United States was changing, and the conservative nature of gender relations that had marked the post-war years was beginning to soften. The birthrate was dropping, the marriage age was rising, and the divorce rate, which had stalled during the 1950s, was once again on the upswing. At the same time, women were beginning to challenge the notion that they should find their greatest fulfillment as homemakers. In fact, many women felt personally unhappy with their lives, and responded with enthusiasm to the publication of *The Feminine Mystique* (1963), a path breaking book that called upon women to question the myth that a woman's true destiny lay in her domesticity. The book's author, Betty Friedan, set out to dispel the myth and to identify "the problem that has no name," the powerful dissatisfaction that so many American women felt with their confinement to a passive, subordinate role in society. In particular, educated, middle class women experienced powerful discontent and began to lobby for greater sexual equality both in the home and in the workforce.

1965-1975 • THE SEXUAL REVOLUTION ~ Young women born in the post-war baby boom came of age just as older women were reasserting demands for equality. By the 1960s, record numbers of married women were in the workforce, while record numbers of their daughters were in college. These coeds found themselves in an egalitarian world where they were faced with the same demands and enjoyed the same benefits as men. But if they enjoyed intellectual equality, these young women did not necessarily find social equality. In one study, published in 1972, women admitted their fears that "any kind of achievement, in college or career, would undercut their attractiveness and limit their options." American women were also confronted with a dramatic change in the sexual landscape as the 1960s ushered in a new sexual revolution.

(1962) Glamorous hostesses called 'Bunnies' at work in 'The Playboy Club', one of America's most successful key clubs. The club was allied with publisher Hugh Hefner's 'Playboy' magazine.

Fueled in part by young men's resistance to commitment and domesticity, and enhanced by increasingly liberal social views, Americans looked for personal satisfaction and self fulfillment through sexual relationships. During the 1950s, sociologist Alfred Kinsey's research identified female sexuality. William Masters and Virginia Johnson followed up on Kinsey's work with a study of female sexual responsiveness and found that women were not the sexually passive beings that they had been labeled. Rather, Masters and Johnson

1964-1975

argued that women's sexuality equaled or even surpassed that of men. Their landmark study, *Human Sexual Response*, was published in 1966. Other authors built on Masters and Johnson's success. One of the most popular advice books of the 1960s, *Open Marriage: A New Life Style for Couples*, argued that "equal opportunity infidelity" was the surest way to promote intimacy and trust in a relationship. Americans began to celebrate this newfound female sexuality. On Long Island, 13 housewives were arrested for participating in a suburban prostitution ring. In Marin County, north of San Francisco, middle class couples participated in wife swapping parties. The rules were changing, and domesticity seemed to be falling by the wayside.

The availability of the birth control pill facilitated this shift in attitudes about sexual behavior by providing an easy, effective and private form of contraception. A single standard of morality now applied to both women and men, but as a result, women came to be viewed increasingly as sexual objects. Young women were now expected to make themselves available to a variety of sex partners. *Playboy* magazine encouraged men to "enjoy the pleasures the female has to offer without becoming emotionally involved." As a contributor to Ms magazine observed, "Women have been liberated only from the right to say 'no.'" Sexual violence against women increased in part due to this objectification. Rape was regarded as a crime of sexual passion, and the behavior and sexual history of the victim were closely scrutinized. Only in recent years has rape been redefined as a violent assault, and the perpetrators have been identified as husbands, dates, classmates and coworkers as well as strangers.

1964-1975 • SEXUAL EQUALITY

During the 1960s, young women found that despite liberated social attitudes regarding sex, sexism was still a pervasive force in American society. Through their efforts in the Civil Rights campaign, the anti-war effort and the Free Speech movement, college educated women became increasingly radicalized, and increasingly aware of the need for a movement to demand true sexual equality in American society. They were powerfully disillusioned when they realized that even within these campaigns advocating radical social change, gender roles remained traditional. Women were still expected to cook, clean, perform the menial secretarial tasks and serve as sexual partners for the men in the movements. Within the Civil Rights movement, young women began to openly challenge those expectations. They wrote that "the assumption of male superiority is as widespread and deep-rooted and as crippling to the woman as the assumption of white supremacy is to the Negro." Radicalized by their experiences, female activists sought a movement of their own.

In this effort they were joined by middle-aged, middle-class women who had organized themselves to demand reform. The National Organization for Women and the Women's Liberation Movement grew out of the realization that women would have to fight to overcome sexism and the assumption that women by virtue of their sex should be relegated to a subordinate place in society. In August of 1970, women across America participated in a national protest, "Women Strike for Peace and Equality," bringing the issue of sexual equality powerfully to the public's attention. Women participated in a range of activities from very personal "consciousness raising" meetings to very public campaigns to raise society's awareness of women's second class status. President John F. Kennedy had taken some steps to address this inequality with the establishment of the President's Commission on the Status of Women and Congress had responded to the issue with the passage of the Equal Pay Act in 1963. But much more needed to be done. In 1970, following protests against the portrayal of women on television, CBS executives called for "a new image of a woman as a doer, as an educated, serious-minded individual person." Across the country, cars sported bumper stickers that read "A Woman Without a Man Is Like a Fish Without a Bicycle." Feminists were beginning to challenge the powerful social convention that insisted that a woman should be defined by, and should find her own personal fulfillment in, her role as wife and mother.

1970s • Backlash to Feminism

Conservative forces in the country responded to the resurgence of feminism with a powerful backlash. Many women, in fact, rejected feminism and it's political campaign for an Equal Rights Amendment to the constitution. They felt that feminists criticized them for the fact that they chose motherhood over careers, and demeaned the full time homemaker's contributions to society. They particularly objected to the feminist characterization of the housewife as an oppressed victim of male domination. The Stop ERA campaign, spearheaded by Phyllis Schlafly, organized American women in an effort to block ratification of a constitutional amendment that would guarantee that "equality of rights under law shall not be denied or abridged by the United States or by any State on account of sex." Those opposed to the measure argued that the ERA posed a grave threat to the family. They feared the breakdown in traditional gender roles that the amendment represented. As one anti-feminist said "Women are ordained by nature to spend themselves in meeting the needs of others." The campaign for equality would corrupt this selfless image and promote competition for domination between the sexes. In addition, according to its opponents, passage of the ERA would mean an end to a husband's responsibility to support his wife, to alimony payments in the case of divorce, and to protective legislation for women in the workforce. Anti-feminists warned of the dangers of "desexegration," and raised the spectre of communal restrooms, same sex marriages and women in combat. The amendment failed in 1982 as the deadline passed for ratification without the necessary state votes.

Despite the backlash, though, women's issues became national issues. At the forefront of the debate over women's rights was the abortion question. Until the U.S. Supreme Court upheld a woman's right to seek a medical abortion in the landmark case of *Roe v. Wade* in 1973, women seeking to terminate an unwanted pregnancy had to resort to the services of abortionists. Nearly 10,000 American women died annually as a result of complications from the procedure. Despite the risks, abortion was common. Nearly one quarter of the married women surveyed by Alfred Kinsey in the 1950s reported that they had terminated a pregnancy, and 90 percent of out-of wedlock pregnancies were aborted. The Supreme Court's ruling that the constitutionally guaranteed right to privacy "is broad enough to encompass a woman's decision to terminate a pregnancy" gave women full control over their fertility.

1970s-1990s

1973 • LEGALIZING ABORTION ~ In 1973, the United States Supreme Court handed down a ruling on the very controversial topic of abortion that would have far reaching social implications. Rather than settle the issue of a woman's right to terminate a pregnancy, the Supreme Court's decision spurred the creation of the right to life movement. Pro-life advocates argued that abortion was murder, and that it threatened the family as a central element in American society. Very few Americans supported the idea of abortion on demand. Though most accepted the need to terminate a pregnancy if the mother's life or health was in danger, many rejected such action for economic or personal reasons.

While many have assumed that the Court was ruling specifically on a woman's right to an abortion, that is not entirely correct. The decision itself was not about a woman's right to control her own body. The case centered on a young, unmarried Texas woman's desire to terminate a pregnancy. "Jane Roe's" lawyers argued that laws barring abortion violated a woman's right to privacy and threatened doctor-patient confidentiality. The court upheld this argument in a seven to two decision, ruling that the decision to terminate a pregnancy was a private, medical matter between a woman and her doctor. Nonetheless, the ruling struck down state statutes that had banned abortion.

As a result, nearly 30 percent of all pregnancies are terminated by abortion, as women have come to rely on this as a means of birth control. But in the process, pro-life activists have succeeded in limiting access to abortion by cutting off Medicaid funding for the procedure for poor women, and in some states requiring a twenty-four hour waiting period prior to abortion or insisting that teenagers gain parental consent. Pro-choice advocates have gained a recent victory with the FDA's support of the abortion pill, RU-486. (The pill prevents the implantation of a fertilized egg in the uterus, leading to miscarriage.) While the Supreme Court has upheld its position as first outlined in *Roe v. Wade*, a New York Times poll found that half of the women surveyed supported greater restrictions on abortion. The pro-life/pro-choice debate is far from being resolved.

1970s-1990s • CHANGING ATTITUDES ABOUT HOMOSEXUALITY: ~ Until the 1970s Gay Liberation Movement, homosexuality was a taboo topic in American society. There had been a flourishing underground gay culture during the 1920s, but by the 1930s homosexuals were regarded as perverts and treated with hostility. Anti-homosexual attitudes intensified during the Cold War years, and gay men and lesbians were openly discriminated against. They were barred from military service or government jobs because they were labeled a security risk—the fear was they could be easily blackmailed by agents from hostile governments seeking classified information. Homosexuality was considered to be a lifestyle choice, and a

~

A federal court ruled in 2001 that private employers who offer prescription coverage for drugs must also cover birth control for women. The case arose in part because women who didn't have coverage for birth control pills were angered when Viagra, which is for impotent men, was added to prescription coverage lists soon after it debuted in 1997.

~

deviant one. By the early 1970s, a gay rights movement was underway, modeled on the Women's Liberation Movement and sparked by a riot that erupted after New York City police officers raided a gay bar in July, 1969. The Stonewall Riots raged for two days, and led to calls for gay men and lesbians to acknowledge their identity and to demand an end to discrimination. They challenged the public with the slogan "We're queer, we're here, get used to it."

By the 1990s, there was evidence of growing acceptance of homosexuals in American society, with 85 percent of those polled responding that gays should be treated equally in the workplace. But gay men and women still face powerful public disapproval, particularly regarding their right to marry and raise children. Less than a third of those polled supported same sex marriages. And some states denied same sex couples the ability to adopt. In some states, gay parents can lose custody of their children. Researchers have found that the sexual preference of parents does make a difference in children's attitudes and behaviors.

The offspring of gay men and lesbians are more open to same sex relationships than are the children of heterosexuals. Boys raised by same sex couples are less aggressive in their play, and tend to be more nurturing and affectionate than boys raised in a more traditional family setting. As teenagers, the sons of same sex couples are more restrained in their sexual behavior than their peers who are raised in traditional households, and teenage daughters of homosexuals tend to be less restrained than their contemporaries. In contrast to young women raised in heterosexual households, daughters of lesbians tend to show greater interest in activities with both masculine and feminine qualities, and they are more inclined towards occupations that are not traditionally female.

The distinctions can be attributed in part to maternal behavior. Heterosexual women "were significantly more likely to prefer that their boys engage in masculine activities and their girls in feminine ones," while homosexual mothers' "preferences for their children's play were gender-neutral." In terms of self-esteem and social adjustment, there was no difference noted between children of gay parents and children of heterosexual parents. Despite the findings, the subject continues to raise concerns.

But science is also dismantling the notion that homosexuality is either a lifestyle choice or a mental illness. New research indicates that sexual orientation may be fixed at birth, a product of a child's intrauterine environment. Scientists are examining such possible factors as a maternal immune reaction to the presence of foreign (male) cells in her blood during pregnancy, or the fetus's exposure to higher than normal levels of male or female hormones. Whatever the scientific outcome, noted one gay activist, "it shouldn't matter, because everyone deserves to be treated with dignity and respect."

1980s-Present • Gender Roles

The renewed emphasis on "family values" that has come to dominate discussions about American society has led to a reappraisal of gender roles. As women have sought career success and have struggled to balance career and family, many men have taken up the same burden. While careerist wives with stay-at-home husbands are still very rare, within two career marriages, men and women are much more likely to share household and childcare duties now than they were

1980s

in the past. One study suggests that men are not particularly pleased with the changes. Fifty-five percent of the men responding to a 1989 poll agreed that the women's movement had "made things harder for men at home," complaining that it had led to increased expectations that men take on more household responsibilities. This attitude reflects society's ambivalence about changing gender roles. Women as well as men feel the challenges of changes in modern life.

While married couples feel the strain of adapting to new roles and expectations, marriage itself has come to be regarded as only one of several options. Society's acceptance of extramarital sexual relations has led to a decline in the marriage rate in the United States. In the 1950s, fewer than half of American women were sexually active before marriage. By the 1990s, more than three-quarters were. Today, approximately 75 percent of Americans, both male and female, are sexually active by the age of seventeen. Cohabitation has become an increasingly common arrangement, with some couples choosing to raise children together outside of marriage. Gay men and lesbians experience a much greater degree of acceptance in American society, though there is still powerful public anxiety about the suitability of gays as parents, teachers or even Boy Scout troop leaders. Still, a more open attitude about sexuality has had some positive effects. A woman's reputation is no longer as fragile as it once was.

But while a woman's reputation is no longer as fragile as it once was, social concerns have not been completely eliminated. The sexual double standard has largely been obliterated. But that does not mean that Americans are comfortable with more liberated ideas about sexuality. The majority of a group of middle school students responding to a questionnaire agreed that a woman who went out at night in "seductive" clothing was "asking" to be raped. This demonstrates the persistence of the notion that it is a woman's responsibility to establish sexual limits. As a society, Americans receive mixed messages about sex, and those messages come largely from the media. Advertisers make frequent use of sexual images and sexual stereotypes in order to promote consumer response. Clothing manufacturers and retailers often feature models in provocative poses, but they are hardly unique. Advertisers have realized that sex sells. Music videos frequently contain overtly sexual images, playing to male sexual fantasies. In addition, movies

(1976) Harry Britton walking New York's Fifth Avenue campaigning for husbands' rights using sandwich boards.

and television programs contain increasingly sexual content, so that the lines between mainstream entertainment and pornography have blurred.

Recent studies, though, have dismissed earlier claims that pornography is a legitimate form of artistic expression that simply entertains but does no harm. Since the 1970s, some feminists have maintained that pornography led to increased violence against women. Researchers have now studied the effects of pornography on men and women, and have made some disturbing findings. One study found that men exposed to erotic depictions of rape reported that they fantasized about assaulting women or were more likely to commit rape themselves. This has led some anti-pornography groups to call for severe restrictions on such material, categorizing it as hate speech.

Despite the current open attitude toward sexuality, the casual sexual relationships that were so prevalent in the 1970s and 1980s have decreased, due in part to the AIDS epidemic. In addition to AIDS, other sexually transmitted diseases continue to cause concern, especially as they affect teenagers and even pre-teens. Middle school teachers have become increasingly alarmed by the numbers of adolescents engaging in sexual relations. Children as young as twelve or thirteen are reporting sexual activity. In fact, the United States has a rate of teen pregnancy and abortion that is twice as high as that in any other developed nation. Most of these young people lack basic information about sexuality. Young girls are often also under the impression that only promiscuous females use some form of contraception. Those who become pregnant are also typically emotionally needy rather than liberated and independent. Recent studies indicate that sexual education in the United States is woefully inadequate. One survey, conducted in 1992, found that less than 10 percent of American children "receive comprehensive sexuality education from kindergarten through adulthood." Most students are exposed to some information about physiology (changes at puberty), reproduction, and sexually transmitted diseases (particularly AIDS), and are also urged to practice abstinence. Safe sex is seldom discussed, and acceptable topics vary widely by state. In Utah, for example, teachers cannot mention condoms to their students unless they have received parental consent to do so. One study has found that teenagers most want information about birth control, abortion and coping skills for dealing with sexual feelings while 75 percent of instructors surveyed prefer that students be taught to abstain from sexual relations.

But the message of abstinence is largely contradicted by the more pervasive sexual imagery young people encounter daily. Clothing, accessories and cosmetics have always played a powerful role in defining an individual, in terms of gen-

Women as a percentage of those employed in certain fields (1988)

Airline pilot	3 percent
Child Care Worker	97 percent
Dentist	9 percent
Elementary school teacher	85 percent
Lawyer	20 percent
Physician	20 percent
Police Officer	13 percent
Nurse	95 percent
Secretary	99 percent

SOURCE: *The American Promise* by Roark, Johnson, Cohen, Stage, Lawson and Hartmann, 1998.

(1994) John Wayne Bobbitt testifying in court in Manassass, Virginia, against his estranged wife, Lorena, during her trial for cutting off his penis.

1970-PRESENT der, ethnicity or class. But personal display also sends a powerful sexual message, often intended, sometimes unconscious. The introduction of the miniskirt in the 1960s came with a thinly veiled sexual message. Its designer said "am I the only woman who has ever wanted to go to bed with a man in the afternoon? Any law-abiding female, it used to be thought, waits until dark. Well, there are lots of girls who don't want to wait. Mini-clothes are symbolic of them." In the late 1990s, the trend was to expose underwear. Young men wore their trousers slung low on their hips so that the waistband of their boxer shorts was visible. Young women displayed their bra straps. The message was subtlely sexual. Cosmetics, once exclusively used by women, are now also available for men. Likewise, cosmetic surgery has found a new market in men desiring to appear younger, thinner, more desirable. Men and women in the United States spend billions of dollars annually in the quest for youth and beauty. While the impetus may be vanity, the reality is that American society has come to idolize youth and beauty, and personal success, whether in romance or in the workplace, is determined to a degree by appearances.

Women in particular have felt the need to conform to society's expectations. During the 1980s, as women were making inroads into previously male occupations, they adopted the business suit and tie as their wardrobe. Dressing for success meant downplaying one's gender. By the late 1990s, women had largely abandoned the drab, gender neutral attire that had marked their exit from the "pink collar ghetto" and their entrance into the professional ranks. But clothes still made the man or woman, and dressing for success remained imperative. If women wanted to succeed in the workplace, they had to be professional and feminine simultaneously.

1970-PRESENT • WAGE DISCRIMINATION ISSUES ~ Wage differentials between male and female workers remain in place in many companies, despite laws to the contrary. Women who work full time still only earn about seventy-two cents for each dollar earned by men. There are various explanations for the difference, including outright discrimination, sex stereotyping that keeps women in lower wage occupations or the fact that working mothers would rather have flexible schedules than higher pay. Despite gains in many fields, women are still segregated in the job market. The majority still hold "pink collar" jobs. Sexual harassment, repeated and unwanted sexual advances, still plague women in the workplace, but the courts now recognize such behavior as a violation of a woman's civil rights, and corporations have had to take steps to change corporate culture to address the problem and save themselves from lawsuits. Women continue to struggle for equality in the workforce while they face difficult personal choices about marriage, family and personal fulfillment.

Conclusion

During the 1992 presidential campaign, Marilyn Quayle, wife of former Vice President Dan Quayle, told Republican delegates that "most women do not want to be liberated from their essential natures as women." She was arguing for a return to a conservative domestic ideal, but there is no consensus concerning a woman's "essential nature." It is certain, though, that women can no longer be defined solely by their domestic role.

Though nine out of ten women in the United States marry, a greatly expanded job market and higher levels of education give women many more options today than they had in the past. Eighty-five percent of teenage girls graduate from high school today, and 22 percent of young women in America complete a college degree. In the professions, 20 percent of all doctors and lawyers today are women. American women marry later than they did at the turn of the century, and have fewer children. Still, the task remains to renegotiate the domestic landscape so that women can be as free as men to pursue their interests and meet their personal goals. Gender equality is a right that women can expect and that all Americans can benefit from once bestowed.

Bibliography

Anderson, Karen. *Wartime Women: Sex Roles, Family Relations, and the Status of Women During World War II*. Westport, CT: Greenwood Press, 1981.

Bailey, Beth. *From Front Porch to Back Seat: Courtship in Twentieth-Century America*. Baltimore: Johns Hopkins University Press, 1988.

Bailey, Beth. *Sex in the Heartland*. Cambridge: Harvard University Press, 1999.

Chafe, William H. *The Paradox of Change: American Women in the 20th Century* New York: Oxford University Press, 1991.

Coontz, Stephanie. *The Way We Never Were: American Families and the Nostalgia Trap*. New York, NY: BasicBooks, 1992.

Cott, Nancy F., ed. *No Small Courage: A History of Women in the United States*. New York: Oxford University Press, 2000.

Degler, Carl N. *At Odds: Women and the Family in America from the Revolution to the Present*. New York: Oxford University Press, 1980.

D'Emilio, John and Estelle B. Freedman. *Intimate Matters: A History of Sexuality in America*. Chicago: University of Chicago Press, 1997.

Douglas, Susan Jeanne. *Where the Girls Are: Growing Up Female with the Mass Media*. New York: Times Books, 1994.

Ehrenreich, Barbara. *The Hearts of Men: American Dreams and the Flight from Commitment*. Garden City, NY: Anchor Press/Doubleday, 1983.

Evans, Sara. *Personal Politics: The Roots of Women's Liberation in the Civil Rights Movement and the New Left*. New York: Vintage Books, 1979.

Fass, Paula S. *The Damned and the Beautiful: American Youth in the 1920s*. New York: Oxford University Press, 1977.

Filene, Peter G. *Him/Her/Self: Sex Roles in Modern America*. 3rd ed. Baltimore, Md: Johns Hopkins University Press, 1998.

Friedan, Betty. *The Feminine Mystique*. New York: Norton, 1963.

Garrow, David. J. *Liberty and Sexuality: The Right to Privacy and the Making of Roe v. Wade*. New York: Macmillan, 1994.

Ginsburg, Faye D. *Contested Lives: The Abortion Debate in an American Community*. Berkeley: University of California Press, 1989.

Gluck, Sherna B. *Rosie the Riveter Revisited: Women, the War and Social Change*. New York: Penguin Books USA, 1988.

Goldin, Claudia D. *Understanding the Gender Gap: An Economic History of American Women* New York: Oxford University Press, 1990.

Gordon, Linda. *Woman's Body, Woman's Right: A Social History of Birth Control in America*. New York: Grossman, 1976.

Hartmann, Susan M. *From Margin to Mainstream: American Women and Politics Since 1960*. New York: McGraw-Hill, 1996.

Hartog, Hendrik. *Man and Wife in America: A History*. Cambridge: Harvard University Press, 2000.

Horowitz, Helen L. *Alma Mater: Design and Experience in Women's Colleges from their 19th Century Beginnings to the 1930s*. New York: Knopf, 1984.

Inness, Sherrie A, ed. *Delinquents and Debutantes: Twentieth-Century American Girls' Cultures*. New York: New York University Press, 1998.

Kaledin, Eugenia. *Mothers and More: American Women in the 1950s*. Boston: Twayne Publishers, 1984.

Kennedy, Susan Estabrook. *If All We Did Was to Weep at Home: A History of White Working Class Women in America*. Bloomington: Indiana University Press, 1979.

Kessler-Harris, Alice. *Out to Work: History of Wage-earning Women in the United States*. New York: Oxford University Press, 1982.

Kunzel, Regina G. *Fallen Women, Problem Girls: Unmarried Mothers and the Professionalization of Social Work, 1890-1945*. New Haven: Yale University Press, 1993.

Melder, Keith E. *Beginnings of Sisterhood: The American Woman's Rights Movement 1800-1860*. New York: Schocken Books, 1977.

Meyerowitz, Joanne J. *Women Adrift: Independent Wage Earners in Chicago 1880-1930*. Chicago: University of Chicago Press, 1988.

Meyerowitz, Joanne J., ed. *Not June Cleaver: Women and Gender in Postwar America, 1945-1960*. Philadelphia: Temple University Press, 1994.

Mintz, Steven and Susan Kellogg. *Domestic Revolutions: A social History of American Family Life*. New York: Free Press, 1988.

Pivar, David J. *Purity Crusade: Sexual Morality and Social Control 1868-1900*. Westport, CT: Greenwood Press, 1973.

Reed, James. *From Private Vice to Public Virtue: The Birth Control Movement and American Society Since 1830*. New York: Basic Books, 1978.

Rosenberg, Rosalind. *Divided Lives: American Women in the Twentieth Century*. New York: Hill and Wang, 1992.

Rothman, Ellen K. *Hands and Hearts: A History of Courtship in America*. Cambridge: Harvard University Press, 1984.

Russett, Cynthia Eagle. *Sexual Science: The Victorian Construction of Womanhood.* Cambridge: Harvard University Press, 1989.

Scharf, Lois. *To Work and to Wed: Female Employment, Feminism, and the Great Depression.* Westport, CT: Greenwood Press, 1980.

Stansell, Christine. *City of Women: Sex and Class in New York, 1789-1860.* Urbana: University of Illinois Press, 1987.

Wandersee, Winifred D. *Women's Work and Family Values, 1920-1940.* Cambridge: Harvard University Press, 1981.

Ware, Susan. *Beyond Suffrage: Women in the New Deal.* Cambridge: Harvard University Press, 1981.

Woloch, Nancy. *Women and the American Experience.* 3rd ed. Boston: McGraw-Hill, 2000.

INTERNET RESOURCES

Expansive site that discusses the history and contemporary issues surrounding abortion.
http://www.religioustolerance.org/abortion.htm

A site provided by the Sexuality Information and Education Council of the United States. It provides valuable information targeted at different ages and demographic groups.
http://www.siecus.org

A comprehensive site to about the AIDS virus.
http://hiv.com

Information about the Planned Parenthood organization.
http://www.plannedparenthood.com

The home of the Gay and Lesbian Alliance Against Defamation.
http://www.glaad.org

A forum from teens to learn about and discuss sexuality.
http://www.iwannaknow.org

This site seeks to help people deal with issues regarding trans-sexuality.
http://www.genderweb.org

Cara Anzilotti
Loyola Marymount University

Soldiering: Life in Combat

~

(1916) Members of the Women's Signalling Corps drilling.

TIMELINE

1898 — Spanish American War

200,000 men volunteer for the Spanish American War (1898) / U.S. fleet conquers the Spanish navy in a one-day fight at Manila Bay in the Philippines (1898) / Only 17,000 U.S. troops make it to Cuba in time to liberate the island (1898) / Spoiled food and yellow fever kill U.S. troops in Cuba (1898-1899)

MILESTONES: General Allotment Act wipes out the communal lands of Native American nations (1887) • Louis Pasteur first demonstrates use of antibiotics in France (1887) • Modern electric motor opens way for consumer appliances (1888) • Open door policy with China initiated (1899)

1917-1918 — World War I

200,000 U.S. troops arrive in France under the Command of John J. Pershing (1917) / General Pershing breaks the German front in France and ends the war (1918) / Diseases and unsanitary conditions in the trenches claim many lives (1917-1918) / Chemical warfare and airplanes introduced as a new weapons of war (1914-1918)

MILESTONES: Garrett Morgan invents the gas mask to keep firefighters from being overcome by smoke (1912) • Ford perfects assembly line production (1913) • First transcontinental phone line is established between New York City and San Francisco (1915) • Workers demand an eight-hour day and equal pay for women (1918)

1941-1945 — World War II

Two Oceans Navy Bill appropriates funds for construction of more than 1.3 million tons of new warships (1940) / Penicillin and blood plasma become available for battlefield use (1941) / Japanese attack Pearl Harbor, forcing the U.S. into WWII (1941) / Japan conquers the Philippines (1942) / U.S. ships defeat the Japanese navy at Midway and at Guadalcanal (1942) / General Eisenhower invades North Africa (1942) / Allied troops invade Normandy on D-Day (June 6, 1944) / Allied tank divisions race across France and into Germany (1944) / German forces surrender unconditionally on May 7, 1945 / Capture of Iwo Jima and Okinawa put Japan within range of heavy American B-29 bombers (1945) / *Enola Gay* drops an atomic bomb on Hiroshima, destroying forty-seven square miles of the city (August 6, 1945)

MILESTONES: Lanham Act authorizes housing at defense plants and military bases (1940) • Selective Service Act permits conscientious objectors to serve in non-combat positions (1940) • President Roosevelt forced to end racial discrimination in war production facilities (1941) • Brewery workers are granted draft deferments and 15 per cent of the beer produced is reserved for the military (1942-1945) • First atomic explosion occurs in Los Alamos, New Mexico (1943)

1950-1953 ~ Korean War

North Korean troops invade South Korea, starting the Korean War (1950) / President Truman dismisses General MacArthur for expanding the campaign (1951) / With no victory, the U.S. and U.N. negotiate an armistice with North Korea (1953)

MILESTONES: 10 billion cans of foods are produced each year in the U.S. (1950) • First coast-to-coast television broadcast (1951) • McCarran-Walter Act permits Japanese to apply for citizenship (1952)

1964-1975 ~ Vietnam War

Gulf of Tonkin Resolution officially starts U.S. involvement in Vietnam (1964) / Tet Offensive turns the war in favor of the Viet Cong (1968) / My Lai massacre of women and children horrify the American public (1968) / U.S. troops pull out of Saigon, which falls into Viet Cong control (1975)

MILESTONES: The Beatles appear on *The Ed Sullivan Show* (1964) • Martin Luther King, Jr. and Robert Kennedy are assassinated (1968) • The Gap clothing store opens, catering to "generation gap" buyers (1969) • Four students are killed by the Ohio National Guard at Kent State University (1970)

1991 ~ Gulf War

Iraqi troops invade Kuwait (1990) / Gulf War ends in decisive defeat for Iraq (1991)

MILESTONES: "Magic" Johnson announces he has AIDS (HIV) and retires from professional basketball (1991) • Successful heart surgery performed on a fetus in the womb (1991)

INTRODUCTION

Throughout history, soldiers at war have experienced a dual life, one alternately of boredom and sheer terror. In the twentieth century, however, the moments of boredom became fewer as mechanized armies, no longer reliant on horses and dependent on summer weather for movement, could campaign virtually year round. The moments of terror, conversely, became more frequent – and varied. Throughout the twentieth century industry and technology made killing more horrible and efficient. The global reach of twentieth-century wars, too, put soldiers in many adverse climates. And while the United States lost fewer men in the wars of the twentieth century than many other belligerent nations, its soldiers suffered some of the worst privations imaginable.

1898

1898 PRELUDE: THE SPANISH-AMERICAN WAR

When the United States levered Spain into a war over the freedom of Cuba in 1898, it was ill prepared to fight. American soldiers, full of patriotism and ready to help Cuban nationals free themselves from "tyrannical" Spain, were caught in an outdated war. Their equipment was often poor, some of it Civil War surplus. The government's war mentality, too, was surplus, not from the Civil War, when Union war-making abilities were hitting their stride, but from the Indian Wars of the 1870s when small-army attitudes were back in vogue.

The rush to war in 1898 swelled the regular Army from nearly 29,000 men to almost 59,000. Two appeals from President McKinley also brought another 200,000 volunteers into service. The American military bureaus responsible for purchasing war material, then supplying it to field armies, were traditionally slow to mobilize for war. They had ultimately done a good job in the Civil War, beginning to hit their stride and proficiency in 1863 with two years of war to go. But by the time they achieved some level of efficiency in the Spanish-American War, by late July and early August 1898, the war was over. Even as European nations were functioning with general staffs – agencies assigned to plan and make mobilization contingencies for future wars – the United States had nothing like that. Congress, too, was loath to make any peacetime military appropriations save those for defense. Simply, the United States considered itself peaceful and isolationist; it did not want to consider war until war was upon it. Thus, the soldiers who fought the Spanish-American War had to contend with problems that were not necessarily symptoms of incompetent war planners – for a generation earlier, in the Civil War, the United States had proved it could fight a quasi-modern war – but symptoms of the American preference for remaining "non-militarized" until crisis struck. Nevertheless, the problems could be devilish for soldiers in the field.

1898 • FIGHTING THE SPANISH-AMERICAN WAR ~ The war dragged the United States into operations in two theaters, Cuba and the Philippines, quite considerable given the United States had never been involved in a foreign war. In May 1898, Commodore George Dewey, commander of the United States' Asiatic fleet, conquered the Spanish navy in a one-day fight at Manila Bay in the Philippines. It would be August, though, before enough troops arrived to fully occupy the islands.

Then American attention moved to Cuba, the primary objective of the war. The army at first considered attacking Havana, the Cuban capital, but later decided to attack Santiago, on the southeast end of the island. Attention focused there when the Spanish Caribbean fleet under Pasqual Cervera headed that way, only to have the United States Navy blockade it in Santiago Harbor. Major General William R. Shafter, veteran of frontier assignments and by this time so fat that he could barely withstand the rigors of campaigning, got command of the army's Fifth Corps, assigned to the invasion of Cuba. When the expedition finally sailed in mid-June, it took only about 17,000 men, all regulars save for Roosevelt's volunteer cavalry and two other volunteer regiments.

The war was short. The Fifth Corps landed unopposed at Siboney and Daiquiri on June 22-23. Shafter's men moved inland. On June 24, dismounted cavalry under General Joe Wheeler (a former Confederate cavalry commander whom McKinley had convinced to volunteer to help unite former northern and southern enemies) chased a Spanish contingent from Las Guasimas, a chokepoint on the road to Santiago. Shafter then planned to attack El Caney, San Juan Hill, and Kettle Hill – high points outside of Santiago that would give Americans command of Santiago and southeast Cuba, and make Cervera's position in the harbor untenable.

But Shafter had to move fast. Spanish reinforcements were approaching the Santiago heights, and, possibly worse, his supply line was threatening to collapse. Shafter had only one boat to ferry supplies from ocean transports to the beach, and only one trail to get supplies from the beach to his men. As the army progressed inland, the difficulty of supply increased exponentially. Time was of the essence.

1898 • ROUGH RIDERS AND BUFFALO SOLDIERS ~ The Cuban campaign had one dramatic day—July 1, when Americans attacked and victoriously carried the heights. The battles for Kettle and San Juan hills were of great social import, as volunteers and black regular troops carried them out. Teddy Roosevelt's Rough Riders took Kettle Hill in dramatic fashion, advancing under heavy Spanish fire. Once at the top, they turned and advanced across a saddle of land to San Juan Hill, where elements of the black Ninth and Tenth Cavalries, also fighting dismounted, were charging.

The black soldiers were military ancestors of men mustered into service in the second half of the Civil War. Northern prejudice at the time, however, mandated that white officers were in command of black troops; the situation had not changed, and now John J. Pershing (destined to command American troops in World War I) was commanding them. He earned the nickname "Blackjack" for his willing service with black troops. Black soldiers had earned a stirring reputation in the Indian Wars, earning from Native Americans the sobriquet "Buffalo Soldiers," a term of respect, for Native Americans depended on buffalos for much of their subsistence.

The Rough Riders and the Buffalo Soldiers took the hills, but the fighting was tough. So tough that, with more Spanish defenses ahead and Santiago not yet taken, Shafter considered retreating to a position more easily supplied. But

(circa 1898) Future American President Theodore Roosevelt (1858 - 1919) (R) stands outdoors in a field with the 1st U.S. Volunteer Cavalry Regiment, known as the 'Rough Riders', and their horses during the Spanish-American War.

the situation became fluid. Within days American ships destroyed Cervera's fleet. That victory convinced Shafter to stay put, and soon the Spanish commander at Santiago surrendered. A planned expedition to Havana became unnecessary when Spain signed a peace treaty with the United States later in the year.

1898 • Equipment Problems in Cuba ~ It is not accurate to say that the American soldiers of the Spanish-American War had poor equipment. Better to say that the American War Department was slow to equip them properly. Problems showed up most noticeably in weapons, uniforms and food rations.

The regular Army's primary issue rifle was the Model 1896 Krag-Jorgensen, a bolt-action piece that used a five-round magazine. The army had adopted Krags in 1892, and the rifle had undergone some modifications for the 1896 model. It was superior to the Army's other main combat arm, the .45-70 "trapdoor" Springfield, in several ways. First, obviously, Springfield was a single-shot weapon, requiring soldiers to reload after each shot. (Ironically, the U.S. War Department was wary of the Krag's five-shot magazine a literal lifesaver in combat – believing it would encourage troops to waste ammunition.) Second, the .45-70 still used regular black powder; the Krag fired smokeless powder, which would not reveal a soldier's position when fired. Spanish troops in Cuba also used smokeless powder. The Krag was also easier to aim and fire accurately. The Krag, however, fired a .30-40 cartridge, giving it less killing power than the .45-70. But its biggest drawback was that it was in short supply.

Enlistments out-distanced the supply of Krag-Jorgensens in spring 1898 so that volunteers (with some exceptions, most notably the Rough Riders who got carbine versions of the Krag-Jorgensen) were issued the black-powder Springfields. In the end, of course, the Spanish-American War became a war of regular troops, with only a few volunteers seeing action in Cuba. Thus, most of the Springfields stayed home and the Krag-Jorgensens went to fight, but presumably a few of the black-powder rifles made it to Cuba. That would have been enough, however, for Progressive-era, muckraking journalists to capitalize on. Seeking out any malady of governmental performance, the journalists would expose it in hopes of remedying it. Thus, one often gets the sense that Americans in Cuba used primitive firearms against modern European firepower. Had that been truly the case, the resolution of the war may not have been entirely different, but perhaps longer in coming. Ultimately, American industry was able to turn out enough Krag-Jorgensens for all, but the fighting was over by that time.

Doubtless, volunteer troops who never left Florida ultimately had little gripe with obsolete weapons; but they could find plenty to gripe about in outdated clothing. The United States Army had campaigned throughout the steamy South in the Civil War; it had also campaigned in the arid desert Southwest during the Apache wars. Repeatedly, officers had petitioned the War Department to adopt a summer-weight, tropical uniform for use in hot climes. European colonial nations, with troops stationed in Africa and Asia, many near the equator, were adopting light khakis for service in lieu of colorful but heavy woolens. The United States government, however, issued Civil War surplus blue wool shirts and trousers for the men while they trained in some fifteen southern camps for the war.

New York Herald war correspondent Richard Harding Davis commented on the dire state of American uniforms. "Nothing our men wear is right," he said. "The shoes, the hats, the coats, all are dangerous to health and comfort; one-third of the men cannot wear the regulation shoe because it cuts the instep, and buy their own." Theodore Roosevelt, in fact, designed and purchased his own khaki uniform, which soon became a model for amended regulation issue. American clothing manufacturers were able to produce enough tropical uniforms for the army by the end of the war, but, like the Krag-Jorgensens, they arrived too late to benefit the mass of soldiers.

1898 • TRANSPORTATION AND FOOD PROBLEMS ~ Food was another problem area. Not that there was not enough food, there was. It just was not in the right place at the right time. Transportation proved as big a problem as anything else.

In the Civil War, the Union government had undertaken to run military railroads. It did not do the same in the Spanish-American War; plus, in the main theater of debarkation, the American South, railroad mileage still lagged behind that of the North. So, what railroads were available for government usage became clogged and confused under the burden of a military mobilization. The result played havoc on all supplies, but especially foodstuffs.

The army apparently purchased enough food. There was plenty of canned corned beef and vegetables, and for the first time the army could use refrigerated train cars to deliver food. But delivery systems were a mess. The Quartermaster's Department, a symbol of efficiency and economy in the Civil War, failed to adequately provide for

1898

unloading boxcars of provisions. Rail sidings backed up for miles with fully loaded cars. Quartermasters did not mark the cars or even properly label manifests, so they did not even know what supplies were in what cars. Once unloaded at rail terminals, army mule wagons had to transport the goods over rough roads to the training camps. Unfortunately, at the close of the Indian wars the army had downsized its rolling stock of wagons so that even the final leg of delivery was botched.

The volunteers at Florida camps could content themselves, at least, with the fact that they were not on the combat line. Regulars in Cuba did not even have that. There, transportation problems caused true deprivation and even tactical problems.

General Shafter well knew that his men would have to debark for Cuba from Port Tampa, a deficient harbor with only one pier for loading men and supplies aboard ship. His own staff officers had worked out a plan for debarkation in late May and early June, but McKinley's administration could not offer Shafter a firm debarkation date. When McKinley finally set a date, it came in a rush so that the end effect was a free-for-all of packing and loading in Tampa, with Shafter's plan going out the window. Shafter finally announced that the expedition would leave on June 7 with whoever was aboard ship.

The scramble to get aboard ship played havoc with the Rough Riders. Fortunately, Roosevelt had made sure the cavalry regiment was camped close to the debarkation point, lest they not make the trip at all. But the army did not even have room on its boats to make the transport, and when it came time for loading the Rough Riders, chosen for their horsemanship, they had to leave their mounts behind. The army promised to bring them along, but the transport problem forced the Rough Riders to make their famous charge up Kettle and San Juan hills on foot.

Landing on the southeast part of the island below Santiago, Americans encountered horrid roads and the problems mirrored those in Florida. Shafter's landing zone prohibited the quick unloading of provisions. When they did make it ashore, supplies then had to follow inland behind the advancing American army, often on trails that would only accommodate pack-mules. Only after army engineers widened the roads could the army's limited number of wagons move to the front. Surprises abounded. In Florida, food rations, very important to the troops, were loaded first. However, first on meant last off, and much of the food was ruined by the time it came ashore.

Food that made it ashore was, in general, bad – not rotten or rancid, it simply didn't taste good. Soldiers in the expeditionary force did not get regular rations of corned beef, but rather rations of what the army called canned fresh beef. It was boiled, unseasoned, gray and stringy. It had no taste and was as unappealing to the eye as to the palate. While Shafter's quartermaster maintained it was quite good when boiled in a stew with vegetables, supply problems prevented vegetables from catching up to the troops for some time. In close contact with the enemy there was little time to concoct fine stews, so men opened their cans, dug out the boiled beef with their knives and stomached it as best they could.

1898 • DISEASE AND MEDICAL CARE

While transportation affected medical supplies to the front, and army doctors used amputation frequently (as they had in the Civil War) to treat war wounds, the typical American soldier in Cuba would not have expected to die in combat. His real enemy was disease. Estimates say between 2,400 and 5,400 American soldiers died in the war, but only some 400 from combat. The rest fell prey to tropical diseases (many of them in Florida), most to an outbreak of Yellow Fever.

While the causes of Yellow Fever were unknown, its symptoms and lethality were. Yellow Fever produced high fever, muscle and joint pains. While some afflicted appeared to recover, they could relapse, turning yellow as their livers ceased to function, then vomiting black blood. They would soon die.

Yellow Fever tended to strike in July and August, the same time that the American army was investigating the garrisoning of troops at Santiago, Cuba. While they may not have known why, army commanders had long known it was best to keep armies sanitary and evenly spaced, and situated on well-ventilated ground. In Cuba, units were packed together in horrific settings. After winning at Santiago, top commanders including Roosevelt and Leonard Wood, petitioned the War Department to let them move to new ground. The army was eventually moved completely out of Cuba, back to the United States, but not before Yellow Fever had taken its toll.

The United States Army continued to garrison Cuba until 1902. During that time, a team of Army doctors, including Walter Reed, began investigating the causes of Yellow Fever. Soon, most agreed that mosquitoes spread the disease. As governor-general of Cuba, General Leonard Wood ordered islanders to take measures against mosquitoes, such as keeping water supplies in covered containers, or covering open water supplies with a layer of oil. The measures worked, and the numbers of Yellow Fever deaths declined. Prevention spread to the Gulf Coast of the United States as well, where Yellow Fever struck with summer regularity. The results were the same; by 1905, the United States had seen its last major Yellow Fever epidemic. Walter Reed would earn more notoriety later when he helped clear the Panama Canal Zone of disease, enabling American workers to build the canal.

Many of the problems American soldiers faced in the Spanish-American War stemmed from the fact that the army had changed little in its outlook and methods of operation since 1775. The Civil War, a true, industrial war, had not permanently changed the army. But the Spanish-American War catapulted the nation to a world, colonial status. While not yet a superpower, the United States was a world power. The next war would force it to radically change its order of business.

1917-1918 • AMERICANS FIGHT THE GREAT WAR ~ A European arms race, colonial aspirations and a delicate alliance system plunged Europe into World War I in the summer of 1914. The United States, seeking the rights of a neutral nation, stayed out as long as possible, but German submarine warfare forced the United States into the war in early 1917. A rapid social and industrial mobilization had to occur before Americans could send troops to Europe, and soldiers did not arrive until late 1917. They came just as the Bolsheviks took control of the Russian government and signed an armistice with Germany. With Russia out of the war, Germany was free to concentrate all its military power on the Western Front, where England and France struggled to hold on and waited impatiently for United States troops to arrive.

John J. "Blackjack" Pershing, former

1918

commander of the black Tenth Cavalry in the Spanish-American War, and more recently commander of a punitive military expedition into Mexico to hunt down bandit and revolutionary Pancho Villa, commanded American troops in France, now collectively known as the American Expeditionary Force (AEF). Pershing arrived in France in June 1917, and by December four American divisions (200,000 troops) had arrived as well. But the numbers were well below the million-plus American soldiers the Allies both expected and wanted. They were also little comfort when the Germans launched a staggering new offensive in March 1918.

1918 • GERMAN OFFENSIVE ~ On March 21, the reinforced German Army began a series of attacks designed to end the war before the United States could come aground in any serious numbers. Suddenly the war, locked in trenches for almost four years, became fluid and mobile. The increased mass in troops enabled Germans to come out of their trenches and send the Allies reeling. In fighting near the Somme River, Germans drove some forty miles. Fighting ensued to the north in Flanders in April, and to the south, closer to Paris along the Marne River in May and June.

1918 • AMERICANS TIP THE BALANCE ~ Americans joined the fray. Pershing had long resisted Allied efforts to integrate – or "amalgamate" – American divisions into and alongside British and French units. Rather, Pershing wanted Americans to fight independently. But during the spring crisis of 1918, with only about four

(circa 1918) American 23rd Infantry of the Second Division of the U.S. Army firing a 37mm gun at German troops in the Argonne Forest during World War I.

divisions ready to fight, Pershing allowed them to fight alongside the Brits and French. Americans began collecting battlefield honors. In May the American First Division attacked Germans at the village of Cantigny and recaptured it. In July American divisions helped stall the German drive along the Marne River toward Paris. They successfully held in the Battle of Chateau-Thierry, a critical forty miles from the French capital. Then the American Second Division launched a counterattack and recaptured Belleau Wood. American Marines in the battle fought so tenaciously that they won the grudging respect of the German Army. Grateful French later renamed Belleau Wood the "Wood of the American Marines." American troops had helped stop the German push; it would be Germany's last offensive effort.

Now Pershing could launch a long-planned American offensive on the southeastern end of the front. Between September 12-16, Pershing's First Army broke through a German salient at St. Mihiel. Then Pershing positioned his troops to participate as the right wing of a concentrated Allied campaign, the Meuse-Argonne offensive set to begin September 26. Americans battered through successive lines on the German left flank in non-stop fighting that lasted six weeks. At the same time, British troops to the northwest swung around the German right flank while French troops pressed the middle. On November 10, American broke through German lines between Sedan and Metz. The Germans were crippled as their front collapsed along with supply lines to the rear. Germans, so hopeful of victory in March, now had no choice but to lay down their arms. Armistice came at the eleventh hour of the eleventh day of the eleventh month: 11 a.m., November 11, 1918.

1914-1918 PECULIARITIES OF WORLD WAR I

1854-1918 • TRENCH WARFARE
When American troops arrived in Europe in 1917, they entered a battleground greatly changed from any their forefathers had experienced. The Western Front in France, where Americans would fight, was a hellish, surreal place. Three years of shellfire had cratered the land between the Allied and German lines; fire had scorched it. Trees, even in springtime, were shattered and bare. Occasionally, birds would light on their limbs, but not for long. The unrelenting smell of death hung in the air, unventilated by breezes. The war Americans entered was far different from the one their fathers might have known in 1898; different still from what their grandfathers and great-grandfathers might have known in the Civil War, and yet that war foreshadowed what was perhaps the most unique element of World War I combat – the trenches.

Trenches were not new to war, besieging armies had been digging them as a matter of course for some centuries. But they began to reach a complex fruition in the mid-nineteenth century when rifled projectiles cast the advantage in war to the defender and forced all soldiers to take cover. The Crimean War in 1854 saw trench usage, but the American Civil War made trench digging a soldier's art. When General Ulysses S. Grant, in command of combined Union armies, besieged Petersburg outside of Richmond, Virginia, from mid-1864 to April 1865, troops on either side dug extensive trenches and earthworks. The trench systems, if stretched out, would have run for miles. Forward trenches had firesteps and loopholes for firing through logs that protected a soldier's head even when standing.

Angled approach trenches connected forward lines to rear lines where soldiers built kitchens and sleeping areas. Some men built "bombproofs"—areas covered with logs and dirt that could sustain direct hits from cannon and mortar fire.

If a modern observer was to take a photograph of Petersburg, Virginia, in late 1864, with no soldiers or buildings to denote its place or time, and compare it with a like photograph of France in 1916, he would be hard pressed to tell Civil War from World War I. The scars in the landscape indicating the trenches were the same, but the trenches in France were more extensive. When French and German troops reached a stalemate in the First Battle of the Marne in August 1914, they began to entrench. British soldiers did the same when they pulled into line on the left of the French. As armies tried to execute flanking maneuvers, their enemies responded by extending their trench line. It is not exaggeration to say that soon an ugly trench line stretched from the English Channel to the Swiss frontier.

Combat on the Eastern Front, where Germans and Austro-Hungarians clashed with Russians, remained somewhat fluid. But the Western Front was a perpetual stalemate. The trenches dominated the life of any soldier who fought there. Two books, Erich Maria Remarque's *All Quiet on the Western Front* (1929), and Siegfried Sassoon's *Memoirs of an Infantry Officer* (1931) give chilling descriptions of trench life.

DISEASE IN THE TRENCHES ~ The trenches were filthy, stinking holes. Rainwater collected and stagnated, spreading disease. Men on front line duty would relieve themselves in a corner of the trench, adding to the stench and potential for disease. Wounded men fell back and bled in the trenches; many died there. Armies, of course, attempted to remove their dead and wounded to the rear as quickly as possible, but in times of heavy bombardment or fighting, corpses might linger in the trenches for hours or days.

Wet, cold conditions in the trenches led to other types of sickness. Bronchitis was common, as was pneumonia. Human waste and blood in the standing trench water spread dysentery, long the bane of campaigning soldiers. It would seem, too, that regularity evaded soldiers in the trenches, for if they were not diarrhetic they were often constipated; supply difficulties frequently kept sufficient potable water and vegetables from the front lines for long periods.

The trenches of World War I introduced many phrases into the world's vernacular. "Trench mouth" sprang from wretched hygiene at the front; "trench foot" accurately described soldier's feet rotting in standing water. The problem came when, once wet, soldiers did not or could not dry their feet and don dry socks and boots. Wet leggings or wrapped puttees (leggings) became heavy and constricted circulation. Constantly wet, the feet and ankles would become numb and develop sores, blacken and begin to rot. If not treated quickly, gangrene could set in, mandating amputation of the foot or leg. In extreme cases, trench foot could kill its victim. Armies began combating the disease with extra pairs of boots and socks, and line officers ordered changes of socks and boots two to three times a day.

Trenches were frequently home to more than soldiers. Rats invaded the trenches, nibbling on the dead and living alike. Lice were a bigger problem. Lice had the run of the trenches on both sides, crawling over walls and into gear, and laying eggs in the seams and creases of uniforms. A soldier's body heat would help incubate the eggs and quickly nits, then full grown lice, were all over the soldiers, biting them and leaving red marks on their bodies. Soldiers would pick lice out of their clothes, off themselves and each other, then crush the bugs between their fingers. Armies set up baths for the men and disinfectant laundering methods for clothes, but fighting lice seemed to be an unending battle. Nearly every man in the trench system became lousy at one time or another. In extreme personal infestations, lice could infect soldiers with "trench fever," which caused high temperatures and painful legs. Treatment called for hospitalization of up to three months.

1914-1918 • ATTACKING ACROSS NO-MAN'S LAND ~ Trenches were not just defensive positions – they were the springboards for attacks. Despite the fact that the trenches were excellent defensive works, made even better by machine gun nests anchoring key points, generals on both sides continued to believe that the best way to dislodge his enemy was to order troops to hop out of their own trenches and charge the enemy in a frontal assault. To make such an assault, attackers had to climb out of their works and cross "No-Man's Land," a wide expanse between trenches that neither side possessed but which both sides had strung with razor-wire to prevent such passage. Preceding an attack, rear echelon artillery would pound the enemy works, attempting to soften it up, and pound No-Man's Land, attempting to blow holes in the wire. Such shelling, obviously, eliminated the element of surprise and created fresh craters in the expanse through, over and around which attackers had to run. Such assaults were frequent, murderous and absurd given defensive capabilities of the time. Ground gained by armies in such attacks could be measured in yards, not miles. Army units lucky enough to gain their enemy's works usually found their own positions untenable, as enemy reinforcements had only to come up from the rear of their own trench lines to surround the invaders and repel them.

(1918) American soldiers carry wounded fellow soldiers along a muddy path as they advance upon Aeuse, France, during World War I.

1914-1918 • CHEMICAL WEAPONS ~ Though trenches were not new in World War I, other combat elements were, including poison gas. Poison gas came in several varieties; most common were chlorine and mustard gasses. Chlorine gas was especially effective against troops in trench lines. Heavy, it hugged the ground as it spread, dropping into depressions and trenches rather than dispersing in the wind. When soldiers breathed the gas, it seared their lungs, causing them to suffocate on a bloody froth. Its wartime method of delivery was in artillery shells. While the gas was devastating, soldiers quickly learned to recognize spreading gas clouds and guard against them. All belligerent nations outfitted their troops with gas masks that would filter gas from the air before soldiers breathed it.

Mustard gas (so named because it smelled to soldiers like mustard or garlic), could kill in two ways. Like chlorine gas, it could attack the lungs, but it could also attack any moist area of the body. Classic film footage from the Western Front shows files of men, their eyes injured in mustard gas attacks, walking blindfolded by bandages and clinging to each other's shoulders for support and direction. Eyes weren't the only danger spots. Mouths, lips and sweaty armpits and groins were just as susceptible. Gas mask construction countered mustard gas attacks. Manufacturers incorporated eye lenses and full head covering to the breathing apparatus so that, coupled with a helmet, soldiers could have virtually full head protection. Greatcoats, later known as trench coats, offered another degree of protection. With collar turned up, front buttoned, and cuffs buckled, the coat, combined with gloves, pants, puttees, and boots, offered full body coverage for soldiers.

1914-1918 • AIRPOWER ~ Death could come floating across the ground in a gaseous cloud, but it could also come from the sky, carried on a new military platform – the airplane. Two Americans, Wilbur and Orville Wright, had invented the first workable, powered aircraft in 1903. But in the ensuing years, the initiative of aircraft production had passed from the United States to Europe. Whereas the United States Army initially saw little military value in airplanes, Europeans were more progressive. By the early days of World War I, all the belligerents had significant air forces.

Aircraft of the day were small and light. Wooden spars and struts formed the skeletons of the planes. Fabric, stretched tight over the wooden frame, then covered with a doping solution that dried and made it even tighter, formed the aircraft's skin. For the most part, the aircraft were biplanes, with two wings instead of just one. Aircraft designers recognized that more wing surfaces gave more maneuverability to the relatively slow-moving aircraft. A litany of aircraft names soon became well-known among ground soldiers, who learned their silhouettes and could spot them from the trenches: the English SE-5s, SE-5As, and Sopwith Camels; the French Neuports; the German Fokker D-7s. Perhaps the most famous airplane of World War I, the German-built Fokker Dr 1, had three wings. While many of them saw service, the best known was a brilliant red machine, piloted by the Prussian officer Baron Manfred von Richtofen – the Red Baron. Richtofen, leader of the famed German squadron called the "Flying Circus" (so named because all their planes were colorfully painted) downed eighty Allied planes before he himself died in combat in 1918. While an American flyer, Roy Brown, is often credited with downing von Richtofen, it seems likely that Australian ground troops, firing skyward with rifles, killed the ace as he flew over their lines.

1914-1918 • EVOLUTION OF DOGFIGHTING ~ Air combat developed gradually. At first, airplanes simply served as aerial forward observers, with pilots flying over enemy positions and scouting them with binoculars. Early in the war, planes were not armed. Encounters between enemy craft usually resulted in nothing more than a chivalric exchange of salutes between pilots. But quickly, army commanders realized that aerial spies were a real threat, and they dispatched armed planes to knock them down. Early on, arming an aircraft meant simply giving the pilot a pistol, or giving an observer in the rear seat of a two-seater aircraft a rifle. It was also not unheard of for pilots or observers to toss hand-grenades, rocks or bricks at enemy aircraft. Soon, two-seaters were fitted with machine guns that traversed a metal ring fixed around the rear seat. But most aircraft were single-seaters, and if pilots were expected to fly and evade enemy fire, his method of discharging a weapon had to become somehow more efficient and automated. Many aircraft went aloft with machine guns affixed to the top wing, but for ease of sighting, the best place to mount machine guns was immediately forward of the cockpit, in line-of-sight between the pilot and his prey. However, firing a machine gun from this position would quickly shred a pilot's own propeller. Engineers tried to solve the problem by putting angled pieces of metal on the backside of prop blades, which would simply deflect bullets. But ricochets were often detrimental to both plane and pilot. Not until engineers perfected a synchronization system did real aerial combat arrive. The system linked machine guns to the engine. Whenever a propeller blade came up in line with a machine gun barrel, the gun momentarily shut off, starting again when the blade passed. All the pilots had to do now was fly, evade and target enemies. The days of the dogfight were born.

1918 • AIR "ACE" EDDIE RICKENBACKER ~ To become an aerial "ace" required a pilot to score twenty "kills." He could not simply return from a sortie and report that he had downed a plane, but he had to provide witnesses to the downing as well. Certainly, von Richtofen was the top ace of the war, but the United States had aces as well, the most famous of whom was Captain Eddie Rickenbacker. Born in 1890, Rickenbacker loved automobiles and by the time of the war was a well-known racecar driver and speed demon. Rickenbacker became part of the United States 94th Aero Pursuit Squadron, known as the "Hat-in-the-Ring" squadron. The air group got its name from insignia painted on the sides of their aircraft depicting an Uncle Sam star-spangled top hat floating in the middle of a ring – the United States, as it were, had finally thrown its hat in the ring of World War I. The 94th actively engaged von Richtofen's Flying Circus, and by the end of the war Rickenbacker had downed twenty-six planes.

Not only did aircraft target each other, they attacked enemy observation balloons and ground troops as well. Observation balloons rose above trench lines, linked to ground winches with cables. Susceptible to attack, observers dangling from the balloons in baskets went aloft with parachutes so they could quickly abandon punctured balloons.

Troops in the trench lines became the targets of strafing aircraft, or worse, bombing aircraft. By the end of the war, belligerents had developed "bombers," but fighter aircraft did most of the bombing. Bombing was rudimentary. Initially, pilots – with little or no means of targeting – would fly over a target, lean over the side of the cockpit, and drop one or two bombs by hand. Later, bombs were

(1918) American pilot and fighter ace Eddie Rickenbacker (1890 - 1973). In later life he went into business with General Motors and Eastern Airlines.

1917-1918 fixed to the undersides of planes and released by a mechanism in the cockpit. It was never very efficient or highly accurate, but the new aerial threats created a new kind of despair for ground troops.

1917-1918 • Doughboys ~ A variety of death and destruction awaited Americans by the time they came ashore in France in 1917. To combat it, they arrived with an mixture of gear, much of it patterned after European styles. Their spirit, however, was completely American.

The Americans came with the unlikely epithet of "Doughboys." There is no satisfactory origin for the word as applied to American soldiers, but it seems to date from the Mexican-American War of 1846-48. The term may derive from a doughy biscuit that infantrymen cooked in camp, or perhaps from dust in the American Southwest that caked to uniforms and gave soldiers a "doughy" look.

Regardless, Americans in France in 1917 and 1918 were all "Doughboys," and they came to wear the name proudly.

1917-1918 • World War I Uniforms and Weapons ~ Doughboys were outfitted in fatigue shirts and pants, greatcoats, puttees and boots. On the drill field they wore a distinctive American campaign hat, but in combat they wore the famed "Tin Hat" – a saucer-shaped helmet that the United States Army adopted from the British and used until the early days of World War II. The helmet, officially the Mk. 1 to the British, M-1917 to the Americans, was flat olive drab and rode on the wearer's head by means of a web lining. Reportedly, it could withstand the impact of a .45-caliber bullet at ten feet.

American soldiers were equipped with the Model 1917 Enfield Rifle, and what was to become one of the classic sidearms of all time, the Model 1911 Browning Colt .45 automatic pistol. With a seven-round clip and superior stopping power, the Colt quickly became a favorite of American troops. The war spurred production of the weapon, and by mid-1918 manufacturers were turning out 2,200 pistols a day, still not enough, though, to supply every American in France. The popularity of the weapon surpassed the war. American troops used it in World War II, Korea and Vietnam. Other nations, as well, adopted it as a standard sidearm. It was standard until the late 1980s when NATO standardization replaced the Colt .45 with 9mm weapons.

1917 • MUSIC TO RELIEVE THE MONOTONY ~ Soldiers had little to relieve the drudgery of war, but music helped, and World War I produced some classic songs that were popular on both sides of the Atlantic. As the United States mobilized for war, Broadway songwriter and producer George M. Cohan created the signature song for Americans headed for France. "Over There" became a smash hit. It was a marching anthem full of American attitude, and was not subtle in the message that it was going to take Americans to straighten out the European mess.

Over there, Over there
Send the word, send the word
Over there
That the Yanks are coming,
The Yanks are coming,
The drums rum tumming everywhere
So prepare, Say a prayer
Send the word, send the word to beware.
We'll be over, we're coming over.
And we won't be back till it's over
Over there!

In 1940, acknowledging the patriotic contributions of Cohan's "Over There" and "You're a Grand Old Flag" (1906), the American Congress issued him a special Medal of Honor.

Perhaps the doughboys' favorite song involved the "Mademoiselle from Armentieres," an enigmatic woman of questionable morals. Soldiers could easily insert one set of lyrics for another, depending on their mood. Usually the lyrics were ribald or bawdy, providing a good laugh for soldiers in the trenches. Some versions included:

Oh, Mademoiselle from Armentieres,
Parley-vous
Oh, Mademoiselle from Armentieres,
Parley-vous
Mademoiselle from Armentieres,
She hasn't been kissed for forty-years!
Hinky-dinky, parley-vous?

Oh, Mademoiselle from Armentieres,
Parley-vous
Oh, Mademoiselle from Armentieres,
Parley-vous
She's the hardest working girl in town,
But she makes her living upside down!
Hinky-dinky, parley-vous?

Oh, Mademoiselle from Armentieres,
Parley-vous
Oh, Mademoiselle from Armentieres,
Parley-vous
She'll do it for wine, she'll do it for rum,
And sometimes for chocolate or chewing gum!
Hinky-dinky, parley-vous?

The mademoiselle may in fact have represented the first sexual encounter for many a young American boy, fresh from the small town or farm. In truth, Americans were experiencing a different world. Debarkation from New York City, then travel through London and Paris gave many men their first look at a big city. Mixing with men from different regions and of different temperaments and mores moderated and changed their own. Another popular song lamented — with a great deal of accuracy —"How Ya Gonna Keep 'Em Down on the Farm, After They've Seen Paree?"

While music and leave-taking in the big city may have tempered the war for some soldiers, the fact remained that their combat lives were made up of mud, blood, noise and suffering. It is little wonder that many men developed "Shell Shock." Now known as Post-Traumatic Stress Disorder (PTSD), Shell Shock was the negative emotional response to combat or prolonged duty on the front lines. Medicine had no real response for it.

By the end of the war in November 1918, more than two million American soldiers had arrived in Europe. Americans suffered 116,708 total killed; 53,513 of those were outright battle deaths, the remainder died of other causes, such as disease or accident. Americans killed and wounded totaled 320,710. American losses were far less than the million-plus casualties suffered by Germany and France, and the near million suffered by England. The comparison is not entirely accurate, since U.S. troops were only in Europe about a year, compared to more than four years of fighting for the other combatants.

1941-1945
WORLD WAR II

When American soldiers sailed off to World War I, they proudly sang that they wouldn't be back until "it's over over there!" The naïve implication was that, with just a little American muscle, the war would be over in no time. Comparatively, for the United States at least, it was. When the United States entered World War II in late 1941, Americans were not so cocky. Certainly, the fighting spirit and patriotism that had forged the country were still there, but the world had become a more frightening place. Dictators and militarists ruled much of the globe, men who were equally at ease taking the lives of enemies or fellow countrymen. World War I—the War to End All Wars —had not done so, nor had it made the world "safe for democracy," as Woodrow Wilson had intoned in 1917. Scared, Americans had taken an isolationist position again for two decades and only tentatively wanted a part of another world war. Forcing an American entrance into the war, the Japanese attacked the United States naval base at Pearl Harbor, Hawaii on December 7, 1941, and steeled Americans for what was to come. Most everyone could sense that, with fighting raging around the globe, this would not be a short war.

The diligence of President Franklin D. Roosevelt and some internationalists in Congress had created an American peacetime draft in 1940, so the army and navy were already expanding, albeit hesitantly, when war came. The mobilization experiences of World War I proved an effective classroom for World War II, and the Japanese attack – which most Americans deemed treachery – spurred volunteerism. It was not long before the United States was fighting back.

The strategies of World War II would be nothing like those of World War I. The dreaded trenches would be gone. The rise of tank warfare had made combat more mobile. Broad, sweeping, penetrating strikes that threatened supply lines were the order of the day. Achieving and maintaining air superiority was a must. Commanders had to be comfortable with quick, bold decisions.

FIGHTING WORLD WAR II

Franklin Roosevelt and British Prime Minister Winston Churchill had always agreed that, whenever the United States entered the war, Germany would be the first Allied target. Soviet leader Josef Stalin agreed too, for Hitler had disregarded a 1939 Non-Aggression Pact with the Soviet Union and attacked her in June 1941. However, events conspired to make the Pacific the United States' first concern.

Three days after the attack on Pearl Harbor, on December 10, 1941, Japanese troops attacked the Philippines, with the goal of clearing out Americans and Filipino allies on the way to the Dutch East Indies. By May 1942, despite dogged American resistance on the Bataan Peninsula and Corregidor Island, Japan had conquered the Philippines and moved south. Japan took control of the East Indies, New Guinea, the neighboring Solomon Islands, and threatened to take northern Australia.

Ragged but resolute, Americans fought back. In April, flying B-25 medium bombers from the aircraft carrier *Hornet*, American flyers staged a bomb raid on Tokyo itself. The raid was token; it did little damage. But it hurt the morale of Japanese who believed the U.S. could not stage any kind of strike in the wake of Pearl Harbor.

1942 • TURNING THE TIDE: MIDWAY AND GUADALCANAL ~ After a disastrous five months, the tide of war in the Pacific began to turn in favor of the Allies. Since 1939, the United States had been attempting to break Japanese radio codes with a secret operation named "Magic." By the end of 1940, Americans had cracked the important Japanese "Purple" code and began deciphering Japanese diplomatic and military intelligence. Before Pearl Harbor, Magic intelligence suggested a coming attack, but American inexperience at interpreting large amounts of intelligence limited its usefulness. After Pearl Harbor, though, American intelligence masters streamlined their operations. The results were dramatic. Capitalizing on United States intelligence, the U.S. Navy moved to counter a Japanese invasion force in the Coral Sea attempting to move within striking range of Australia. In the Battle of the Coral Sea, May 7-8, 1942, the U.S. Navy halted Japan's southern momentum.

More naval intelligence enabled the American navy, under Admiral Chester Nimitz, to intercept a Japanese force headed for Midway Island 1,000 miles west of Hawaii. Midway held little strategic value for Japan, but Admiral Yamamoto reasoned that a strike there would pull American carriers into the open where Japanese naval aircraft could destroy them. Due to military intelligence from Magic, Nimitz surprised the Japanese and instead defeated them, destroying four enemy aircraft carriers in the Battle of Midway, June 3-6, 1942.

Midway proved to be the turning point of the Pacific War. It permanently halted Japan's spread across the Pacific and put the nation, which had been on the offensive since invading Manchuria in 1931, on the defensive. It also proved something else. When Yamamoto designed the Pearl Harbor attack, he told his superiors it would keep the United States out of the

(1942) Battle of Midway. Midway proved to be the turning point of the Pacific War. It permanently halted Japan's spread across the Pacific. Seen here a Japanese aircraft carrier under attack during the Battle of Midway.

1940s

1940 • BUILDING THE FLEET ~ The United States Navy has been an integral part of the American military since the Revolution. The *U.S.S. Constitution* had been a commissioned ship in the navy since the 1790s. Ulysses S. Grant used joint army-navy operations to reduce Forts Henry and Donelson and Vicksburg during the Civil War. That war also saw the first combat between ironclad ships. As the nineteenth century closed, the navy was becoming more important in foreign policy with American interest in imperialism. Certainly Commodore George Dewey became a true naval hero when he quickly subdued the Spanish Pacific fleet at the Battle of Manila Bay in 1898.

World War I had not been a navy war for the United States. German U-boats had done much to damage British shipping and drag the United States into the war. But the Battle of Jutland between England and Germany in 1916 had ended big fleet battles before the United States ever entered the war. It was not until World War II that the twentieth-century American navy really came into its own.

Obviously, the surprise Japanese attack on Pearl Harbor made its entry into World War II touch-and-go for the Navy. However, the Japanese had failed to kill any American aircraft carriers in the attack, and the United States Navy was already operating under the Two Oceans Navy Bill of 1940, an expansion/appropriations plan that okayed the construction of more than 1.3 million tons of new warships. That the nation was already on something of a war footing enabled the navy to come out fighting within six months of Pearl Harbor.

1942-1944 • NAVAL AIRPOWER ~ Aircraft carriers proved to be the workhorses of the Pacific war, and both Japan

war only six months, not eighteen like they wanted. The Battle of Midway ended one day shy of the six-month anniversary of Pearl Harbor.

Now the United States went on the offensive. In an attack designed to crack the southern Japanese defensive line, American Marines landed at Guadalcanal in the Solomon Island chain in August 1942. The battle lasted six months and involved naval as well as land operations. By its end, the Japanese had lost 25,000 troops and Americans had firmly seized the initiative in the Pacific.

and the United States built fleets around them. Carriers themselves were lightly defended, relying on their aircraft to do that job. The Navy began the war with the feisty Grumman F4F Wildcat as its main fighter, with the Grumman TBF (torpedo, bomber, fighter) Avenger doing steady work in a variety of assignments. (It was as pilot of a TBF Avenger that future president George H.W. Bush was shot down late in the war.) By late 1942, the Navy was replacing the Wildcat with the Grumman F6F Hellcat, which performed stupendously and went far toward establishing American air superiority over the Pacific. The United States Marines – the ground-fighting component of the Navy – had used the gull-winged F4U Corsair (considered a remarkable fighter) for some time before the Navy picked it up as a carrier based plane in 1944. In all, American manufacturers built more than 50,000 aircraft for the Navy during the war years.

1942-1945 • Service Aboard Ship

∼ Service on any naval vessel could be alternately boring and tedious, then exciting and horrible. Depending on a sailor's destination, he could find himself either in freezing arctic temperatures, struggling to stay warm and dry on a night watch, or in 100-degree tropical heat and humidity, trying to catch a breeze in an above-deck hammock for a few hours sleep. (In the Pacific, near the equator, the inside of steel-plated crew quarters could become like ovens with heat, nearly impossible to stay in for long.)

Crews became like floating families: close, often too close; friendly at times, edgy and bickering at others. Captains set the tone for the ships. Without fail, the best of them could maintain a loose discipline without becoming an autocrat. The stickler for rules and regulations got little respect from the crew, especially one that had been seasoned by combat.

Daily duties included cleaning, painting, and routine maintenance. Everyone stood watch on a rotational basis, watching for enemy ships and aircraft. In an attack, a ship horn would sound "General Quarters" and each man would run to his battle station. Some manned heavy, long range guns; others operated lighter machine guns or anti-aircraft guns. Others fed ammunition to the guns; still others coordinated fire or handled communications. The men below decks manning the engines or internal systems couldn't see what was going on topside and were also subject to the clanging and banging of explosions; they would also likely be the first to die (or be trapped in a flooding compartment), if their ship got hit by a bomb or torpedo.

While aircraft carriers became the centerpiece of the Pacific force, the Navy operated a variety of other vessels during the war, including battleships, cruisers, destroyers, submarines and PT boats. All told, the Navy received more than 5,750 new warships of all classes during the war years, and more than 66,000 landing craft for Marine Corps invasions. Naval personnel went from 203,000 in 1940 to 486,000 by December 1941. It jumped to a whopping 4,064,455 by the end of the war. The Pacific was not the only naval theater of World War II. The United States Navy also saw action in the North Atlantic from 1941 to 1944, and navy battleships supplied covering fire for the Allied landings in North Africa, Sicily and Normandy.

> Of special concern to sailors in the last half of the war were Japanese kamikazes. These suicide pilots were assigned to pilot "flying bombs" – aircraft stuffed with explosives – into enemy ships, destroying themselves but wreaking devastation in the process. Ship gunners would throw up curtains of anti-aircraft fire, knowing that they had to stop the kamikazes well away from their ship, lest forward momentum carry even a damaged Japanese plane into its target. Kamikaze planes would explode in mid-air, raining aircraft parts and the bloody remains of pilots down on American crews.

1942-1944 Navy battleships, cruisers and destroyers served as cover for the many amphibious landings Marines made in the Pacific. Before any given landing, the ships – as well as carrier-based aircraft – would shell and bomb the target island, hoping to reduce enemy resistance before the Marines hit the beach. Often, though, Japanese defenders retreated into holes and caves, surviving the bombardment to unleash death on the invaders.

1942-1944 • SUBMARINE AND PT SQUADRONS ~ Sailors could, perhaps, find more romantic service in the American submarine squadrons. By World War II, all the major powers had significant submarine fleets. American subs primarily saw duty in the Pacific, where they soon outpaced Japanese subs. American subs – 195 of them by the end of the war – targeted Japanese merchant ships, sinking nearly 1,000 of them during the war and crippling oil supply lines running from the Dutch East Indies. American subs also sank about one-third of all Japanese ships lost during the war.

A sailor could also find romantic service on the PT Boats. PT stood for "patrol-torpedo." The boats, made of plywood, were extremely light and quick. They were unsuitable for attacking large ships, but could be a nuisance in close quarters against individual, smaller enemy craft. They carried two to four torpedoes and some guns, and perhaps depth or smoke charges depending on version. Americans found them quite useful in the 1942-43 campaigns in the Solomon Islands.

Young John F. Kennedy was captain of a PT Boat that was split into two pieces by a Japanese cruiser. Kennedy led his crew to a nearby island, where they were ultimately rescued. During Kennedy's 1960 presidential campaign, family publicists exploited his adventure, turning Kennedy into a full-blown war hero. The experience was dramatized in the movie *PT-109*.

1942-1943 • INVASION OF NORTH AFRICA ~ While the U.S. Navy was coming into its own in the Pacific, the Army was joining the fight in the European theater. Many American war planners wanted to immediately mass troops in England and launch an invasion of German-occupied France across the English Channel. Stalin, in Russia, wanted just such a second front to relieve pressure on his worn troops. But Churchill demurred on the plan, suggesting it would be too much for green American troops to accomplish. Besides, he pointed out that training for and supplying a cross-channel invasion would take more than a year, not just a few months. He suggested, instead, an invasion of Vichy-held North Africa. Such a stroke would relieve British troops defending colonial Egypt and the Suez

Canal against German desert troops, give American soldiers needed experience, and, hopefully turn North Africa into a base from which to strike across the Mediterranean at what Churchill called the "soft underbelly" of Hitler's Europe.

Roosevelt agreed with Churchill, and planners created "Operation Torch," code name for the invasion of North Africa. American General Dwight D. "Ike" Eisenhower, a staff officer with a penchant for coalition building and management, got command of Torch. The invasion began in November 1942. While the fighting was sometimes severe and American skill often amateurish, the invasion was a turning point. When Vichy French troops, supposedly loyal to Hitler, failed to halt the invasion, Hitler disbanded the Vichy government altogether; that forced him to divert more troops to garrison southern France. It also enabled Soviet troops, bottled up for months in the German siege of Stalingrad in the southern Soviet Union, to stage a breakout and ultimately trap the besiegers.

1943-1944 • INVADING SICILY AND FRANCE ~ In 1943 American and British troops did indeed cross the Mediterranean and invade Sicily, then Italy. War planners expected victory to come easily against weak Italian troops, but Hitler committed crack German soldiers to Italy's defense. Dogged fighting in the rugged Apennine foothills slowed Allied advances. Rome did not fall until June 4, 1944.

Meanwhile, Allied armies were indeed planning for a cross-channel invasion of France. Throughout 1943 and the first half of 1944, U.S. industrial output turned England into a natural aircraft carrier. American and British bomber groups pounded German bases in France, and industrial sites in Germany proper as the armies amassed supplies in England. Eisenhower commanded the coalition force for the coming assault, code-named "Operation Overlord." Shortly after midnight June 6, 1944, after weather delays, paratroops began dropping into the French countryside behind the beaches of Normandy, about 100 miles south of England. Then, at sunrise, four divisions of Allied troops that had crossed the channel in the dark began storming the Normandy beaches. While German resistance on some beaches was slight, at others, including Omaha Beach in the American sector, it was heavy. A day's fighting, however, gained Allies a foothold in France.

Within weeks, American and British troops broke off the beaches of Normandy

1942-1944

(circa 1941) Explosive Action. Artillery units of the Allied Army during the North African campaign.

SOLDIERING: LIFE IN COMBAT ~ 1637

1943-1944

and drove into the French interior. German lines crumpled as Allied armor advanced. On August 25, 1944, Allies captured Paris, then they rolled on. Supply became a problem, as divisions, especially those under Third Army commander General George S. Patton, outdistanced supply trains. Supply difficulties, an abortive assault planned by British Field Marshall Bernard Montgomery on river bridges in Belgium and Holland and finally, a massive German counterattack, known as the Battle of the Bulge, in Belgium stalled Allied progress by the end of 1944.

1945 • Crushing Germany ~ The next year, however, saw renewed vigor as British and Americans doggedly crossed the Rhine River into Germany, then punched through the Siegfried Line, defensive works protecting the German frontier. The Soviet Army was pressing Germany also, but from the east, so that Germany was caught in a pincers. Planning conferences between the Allied "Big Three" leaders—Roosevelt, Churchill and Stalin—had already decreed that Allied countries divide up Germany into zones of occupation after the war. They also divided the capital city of Berlin. As such, Eisenhower devoted no effort to taking Berlin. The costs could be high, he reasoned, and the United States would get its share of the city just the same. Still, the city had to be won. With Soviets in place to do it, Ike let them pursue Berlin

The battle for Berlin was vicious, house-by-house, building-by-building urban fighting. Hiding in a bunker under the city, Hitler committed suicide as Soviet troops rolled overhead. City defenders surrendered on May 2. On May 7, 1945, all German forces surrendered unconditionally; Eisenhower announced the victory in Europe on May 8 – VE (Victory in Europe) Day.

President Roosevelt did not live to see the victory. In April 1945, after winning a fourth term in office, Roosevelt died at his vacation home in Warm Springs, Georgia. Vice-President Harry S. Truman became president.

1944-1944 • Island Hopping in the Pacific ~ Meanwhile, the war in the Pacific slogged on. It came in two combat theaters. To the south, General Douglas MacArthur, supreme commander of Allies in the Pacific, plotted a campaign to take back New Guinea from the Japanese. MacArthur had left the Philippines before their disastrous fall to become Allied commander based in Australia. He had vowed to return to the Philippines, and New Guinea was the way to get there. From late 1942 to early 1944, American and Australian troops fought their way up New Guinea, with MacArthur executing sometimes-brilliant "leapfrogging" moves up the coastline that isolated Japanese contingents and forced them to die on the vine behind American advances.

The second major campaign was in the central Pacific, where Admiral Nimitz used the navy to move Marines from one island to the next, chipping way at the Japanese defensive perimeter. Beginning at Tarawa in the Gilbert Islands on November 20, 1943, Nimitz launched a ten-month campaign that saw the capture of islands, including the Marshalls, Saipan, Guam, and Tinian. Nimitz advanced 4,500 miles, destroyed hundreds of Japanese aircraft and ships, and helped converge the two Allied battle lines on the Philippines.

In October 1944, Allies began their

reconquest of the Philippines. While the last Japanese defender did not surrender until war's end, Allies liberated most of the island chain and were now coming threateningly close to Japan itself.

1945 • Battles for Iwo Jima and Okinawa ～ In February 1945, Marines landed on the volcanic island of Iwo Jima to the southeast of Japan. Japan considered Iwo Jima essential to home defense and committed 23,000 troops to hold it. Americans hit the island, sustaining 2,500 casualties the first day. It took nearly a month for Marines to pacify the island. In the process they lost 5,300 killed and another 17,400 wounded. They killed all but 200 of the Japanese defenders.

In April, Allies launched an invasion of Okinawa, in the Ryukyu chain of islands off the southern tip of Japan. Fighting there was as bad as at Iwo Jima. The Japanese lost a staggering 130,000 men trying to hold the island. Americans lost just over 12,500 men taking it.

Capture of Iwo Jima and Okinawa put Japan within range of heavy American B-29 bombers. They raided at will over Japan, dropping not only high explosives but firebombs as well. One fire raid leveled fifteen square-miles of Tokyo. Collectively they knocked out many of Japan's industrial areas, killed some 260,000 Japanese, and left more than nine million homeless. These bomb runs, as well as similar firebombings on Germany in 1945, were the logical extension of strategic bombing thought (namely, bomb nations' internal, industrial infrastructures, regardless of civilian loss) that had begun only twenty years before. As a result, the private citizens of Germany and Japan had become full combatants in world war.

1945 • The Atomic Bombs ～ Allies now poised themselves for an invasion of Japan. President Truman reeled under casualty estimates for such an invasion (some sources placed them as high as one million men), and American soldiers just freed from the war in Europe fearfully opened orders sending them to the Pacific for the invasion. But, while attending a post-war conference at Potsdam outside Berlin, Truman received ominous news that the United States had just successfully tested a super bomb.

Truman had only known about it for weeks, but years earlier Roosevelt authorized scientists to work on creating an atomic bomb. Their operation, the Manhattan Project, was perhaps the most closely guarded secret ever in American history. They raced against time, fearing that Hitler, too, was about to achieve an atomic bomb. Now Truman had a device that could possibly end the war with no more American casualties.

For fifty-six years now, some critics have decried Truman's use of the bomb, citing evidence that Japan may have been ready to surrender anyway. In truth, given the context of the time, Truman probably had no moral or political option. The Soviet Union had just taken most of Eastern Europe in its campaign against Germany and was refusing to give it back. Now it was about to enter the Pacific War, and Truman wanted the conflict over before Soviets could take more territory. Also, the fighting on Iwo Jima and Okinawa revealed how desperately the Japanese would fight the closer war came to their homes. Even if casualty estimates for the invasion were grossly inflated, Truman saw a way to save American lives, and he took it.

On August 6, 1945, the B-29 *Enola Gay* dropped an atomic bomb on Hiroshima,

(1945) The mushroom cloud spreading over Nagasaki after the second atomic bomb of World War II was dropped there.

1941-1945 destroying forty-seven square miles of the city. Japan did not surrender; militarists in charge of the country could not bring themselves to do so. On August 9, the B-29, *Bock's car* dropped a second atomic bomb, this one on Nagasaki. Death estimates were 240,000 in the two blasts. Finally Japanese Emperor Hirohito, silent throughout the war, told government leaders to end it. Japan called for a cease-fire, and formally surrendered on September 2, 1945 – VJ Day.

1941 • OUTFITTING THE G.I.s

American soldiers started World War II as extensions of the Doughboys of World War I. Their uniforms were similar, and they still wore the saucer-shaped Tin Hat—a barely updated version of the M-1917 helmet. But American battle gear was evolving. When they were totally outfitted, American soldiers were all "Government Issue"—G.I.s. Soldiers had always used and worn government issue gear, but the term G.I. came to distinguish World War II soldiers just as "Doughboy" had those of World War I.

In late 1940, during the peacetime armed forces buildup, the United States Army Infantry Board embarked on a plan to replace the Doughboy's Tin Hat with a new helmet. By January 1941, the board was sifting through a variety of plans, and discovered that the crown of the World War I helmet offered superior protection for the top of the head, but that the sides needed modification. After consulting various designers, and even getting help from the New York Museum of Modern Art, the infantry board hit on the helmet design that would become the classic symbol of American soldiers for the next forty-two years—the M-1 helmet, more popularly known to soldiers as the "Steel Pot."

The Pot came in two parts: the steel outer helmet, and a plastic inner liner that contained the adjustable webbing that fitted to the wearer's head. Weighing about six pounds, the helmet rode comfortably on the head, did not slip, permitted excellent vision, and did not impede marksmanship. The helmet came with chin traps, but American infantry frequently adopted the more cavalier style of letting the straps dangle or hooking them up around the helmet. Paratroops, who faced heavy gravitational forces that tended to separate helmet from liner and pull the assembly from their heads, received modified M-1s with bulkier, more complex chin straps, which they wore.

The helmets were painted in a flat olive drab, but depending on need, soldiers could camouflage them in a variety of ways. Soldiers invading the beaches of Normandy, France, on June 6, 1944, and the parachutists dropping into the interior of Normandy a few hours earlier, frequently stretched a cotton net, soaked in a creosote preservative, over their helmets as a camouflage webbing. Into the net they could stick leaves and twigs for disguise in wooded and overgrown areas. The Marine Corps adopted the M-1, and Marines storming islands in the Pacific often put a cloth leaf-pattern camouflage cover over their helmets. They could wear the cover with a green-side or brown-side facing out, whichever best suited the terrain. The Navy adopted the M-1 as well for use aboard ship, and painted its helmets navy gray. Navy Corpsman and Army Medics wore the helmet as well, frequently adorned with a Red Cross in a white circle on the sides. Corpsmen in the Pacific, however, soon began wearing helmets with no medical designation when they learned that Japanese soldiers considered American medics prime targets.

1941 • WEAPONS ~ American soldiers went to war well armed. In all theaters, the M-1 Garand rifle was the primary infantry weapon. It fired a .30-caliber bullet and used an eight-round magazine that loaded into the top of the weapon and popped up when empty. It's superb stopping power made it a powerful combat weapon. It's little sister was the M-1 Carbine, a semi-automatic weapon that packed short-range (only effective at up to 300 yards) stopping power in a light-weight package. It replaced some pistols as a favorite for personal defense. Still, pistols were used in combat, usually in the hands of officers and non-commissioned officers, such as sergeants. The Colt .45 was still a favorite, as were Smith & Wesson .38-caliber revolvers. Submachine guns were deployed as well. Marines preferred the M-3 submachine gun (sometimes called a "grease gun" for its distinctive shape), a .45-caliber weapon with a thirty-round clip. In Europe, American infantry officers tended to carry the .45-caliber Thompson submachine gun. That weapon had already won fame in the United States as a favorite of Prohibition- and Depression-era gangsters.

Back in the Civil War, in the days of linear tactics and muzzle-loading rifles, the prime military unit had been the 1,000-man regiment; in World War II, thanks to automatic weapons, increased firepower, and maneuverability it was the twelve-man squad. One can rightly say that, on many a battlefield, American infantrymen "made it up as they went." The exigencies of war necessitated it, and American G.I.s were good at it.

Historian Stephen E. Ambrose credits American flexibility and ingenuity at the small-unit level with winning the war. But there was a base infantry tactic from which everything else spread. Essentially, the twelve-man teams were divided into thirds: the squad leader and two men formed a scout section, four others were a fire section, and the remaining five were a maneuver and assault section. The leader and the scouts would pinpoint enemy targets, then call for covering fire from the fire section. That section included one man with a Browning Automatic Rifle—the famed BAR—a .30-caliber weapon with a high rate of fire and deadly capabil-

---

The M-1 helmet often saw double duty. In combat, it protected the wearer from some bullets (it would not stop them all), shrapnel, rocks and debris. But in many a camp and foxhole, the helmet, turned upside down, often became a wash basin and shaving bowl.

1940-1945

ities. Under that section's fire, the third section would move up and assault or flank the enemy. German soldiers considered the BAR man so critical that they often laid out ambushes for American units, holding their fire until the BAR man came within range, taking him out first then handling the rest.

Some fire teams also used the heavy Browning .50-caliber machine gun, of the same type used in American bombers but fitted for ground use with a tripod. The eighty-two-pound weapon required two men to carry and operate, and could fire 450 rounds per minute using 100-round ammo link belts. Enemy tactics and defensive works, terrain and plain old experience frequently mandated changes in American tactics, especially in France in 1944 where dense hedgerows around farmers' fields posed almost impassable barriers and excellent German defenses. Squads began using tanks as fire and assault support; tankers began installing radios in their vehicles to coordinate support with other tanks. Soon infantrymen began getting help from fighter airplanes which could strafe and bomb targets.

1940-1945 • ARMOR ~ American tanks were a shade above mediocre, at best. The main American battle tank, the M-4 Sherman, carried a 75 or 76-mm gun, but was always under-armored and outgunned by German tanks, especially the Tigers and Panthers, which carried superior 88-mm or better guns. Where the Sherman had the advantage was in speed (it's lighter weight made it less cumbersome than German tanks); reliability; and numbers—ultimately the United States built almost 50,000 of them. Late in the war, Americans began outfitting the Shermans with 105-mm guns, giving them more of a punch. Armor-piercing projectiles also added lethality to the Sherman's firepower. Shermans saw service in every theater, in a variety of roles. In the hedgerow country behind Normandy, soldiers welded pieces of angle-iron (which German Field Marshal Erwin Rommel had placed in the surf off the beaches to prevent invasion) to the fronts of the tanks. The iron formed a sort of wicked plow that tankers used to rip up the rugged hedges and create passages for infantrymen. Other tanks were fitted with extending arms on the end of which were rotating drums with flailing chains. The chains were designed to explode land mines before soldiers crossed a suspect piece of ground.

While tanks frequently served as infantry support, they were fierce assault weapons on their own. German generals had started the war in 1939 with new tank tactics—the Blitzkrieg—that made tank units into spearheads that overran enemy positions. In 1944, Allied commanders threw Blitzkrieg in reverse and used tank divisions to race across France and into Germany. The best of them was, without doubt, General George S. Patton, Jr., commander of the U.S. Third Army. Patton had studied tank tactics since the 1920s, and used them as the key to his advance. Foul-mouthed and opinionated, Patton was frequently a public relations problem for Allied Supreme Commander, Europe, Dwight D. Eisenhower, but he got results. Patton's units were the first to cross the Rhine River into Germany in 1945.

ARTILLERY ~ American soldiers could always expect to hear the roar of artillery. The main combat field-pieces were the 105-mm howitzer and the 155-mm gun. The 105 was light and maneuverable, packed a tough punch, firing up to seven miles. Its big cousin, the 155, also known as the Long Tom, could fire twice as far. On the Allied push through France and Germany, and on many island campaigns in the Pacific, guns fired night and day. One soldier in Germany remarked how odd it was to hear the guns go silent when Germany surrendered in May 1945.

RATIONS ~ Campaigning soldiers stashed in their knapsacks, along with changes of socks and underwear, the much-maligned K- or C-rations. These were prepared, canned meals, including pressed meat, some vegetables, biscuits, bouillon powder, salt, coffee, a spoon, some toilet paper and cigarettes. (The army put high value on keeping plenty of cigarettes at the front; without them morale would suddenly plummet.) Soldiers had high energy foods, too: M&Ms were developed for consumption in World War II, and the Hershey company produced a higher-calorie chocolate bar that provided instant energy.

MEDICINE ~ World War II soldiers could expect better medical treatment than their World War I counterparts. Sulfanilimide had been discovered in the mid-1930s to stop many bacterial infections, and G.I.s were issued medical kits that contained a quantity of sulfa powder. As a matter of course they would sprinkle sulfa powder on any open wound; army medics and navy corpsmen (who served as medics for Marines in their Pacific island assaults) also liberally used sulfa, which probably suppressed American battlefield deaths.

The other big gun of World War II medicine was penicillin. Scottish scientist Alexander Fleming had discovered in 1928 that secretions of mold had antibacterial properties, and by 1941, on the eve of war, American pharmaceutical companies were producing penicillin-based antibiotics. Penicillin injections both on the battlefield and in hospitals fought infection and saved lives. Penicillin also frequently and successfully combated venereal diseases in soldiers who had failed to use the condoms the army passed out as liberally as cigarettes.

Blood plasma also saved soldier's lives. The process of separating plasma, the liquid portion of blood, from whole blood had been perfected, and by the time American soldiers were on the battlefields of World War II, medics could supply plasma to boost blood pressure, maintain electrolyte balance and prevent shock. Plasma was a boon to hospitals as well.

Hitching A Ride

~

The lot of an infantryman has always been to walk, but World War II G.I.s rode as much as they could, hitching rides on tanks, half-tracks, four-wheel-drive Jeeps (which made their initial appearance in this war), or the workhorses of the army, two-and-a-half ton trucks, known as the Deuce-and-a-Half. Soldiers hitched rides with good reason; they were their own pack mules. Depending on his combat assignment, a man might carry sixty to eighty pounds of clothing and equipment. Helmets, knapsacks, weapons, ammunition, canteens, first-aid kits, radios, perhaps flame-throwers, BARs or bazookas —it all added up.

1940-1945

From a medical standpoint, soldiers had a better chance of surviving World War II than they had World War I. But one element of combat hit them just as frequently, and medicine still had little response to it—shell shock, now called combat fatigue. Men in combat frequently just wore out, became used up, unnerved. There was little they could do about it, and while doctors attempted to deal with battlefield depression, anxiety and panic, their best solution was to let men recuperate for a while in rearward hospitals, then shove them back to the front. Often the anticipation of going back to combat was worse than remembering fights they had already been in. In a classic incident in Sicily, 1943, General George Patton slapped a soldier confined to the hospital with a case of nerves. Patton denigrated the man a coward, and probably revealed how many commanders felt about combat fatigue. Eisenhower forced Patton to apologize, but medical treatment was as much at fault for having no better response to combat fatigue.

1943-1945 • AIRPOWER ∽ In World War II, a soldier's hell was not limited to the ground – it could be in the sky as well. Air superiority was the key to battle. Allies wanted to dominate the skies of Europe before they invaded France in 1944. Americans wanted to dominate the skies over island chains in the Pacific before they invaded them in 1943, 1944 and 1945. In Europe, Allied planes flew out of England; in the Pacific, American planes flew off aircraft carriers, then island bases that approached Japan itself. American planes became legendary, and many a schoolboy could identify them by silhouette as if he was a spotter in some forward position. The great fighters included the P-40 Warhawk, made famous by the Flying Tigers, Americans flying against Japanese in China even before the war began; the P-38 Lightning, a twin-boomed, twin-engine fighter; the P-47 Thunderbolt, known as the "Jug" for its milk-bottle shape (and unbeatable in a dive); and the spectacular P-51 Mustang, the best fighter of that, or perhaps any other age. (In 1964, when Ford Motor Company engineers designated their new breed of car the Mustang, they named it not for the unbroken horse of the American West, but for the fighter of World War II.) Great bombers included the light B-25 Mitchell, the B-26 Marauder, the slab-sided but reliable B-24 Liberator, and the graceful, trim B-17 Flying Fortress. Later came the blunt-nosed B-29 Superfortress, which would drop atomic bombs on Japan.

Fighters performed several functions. They dueled with enemy fighters, such as the Messerschmitt Bf-109 and Focke-Wulf FW-190 in Europe, and the Zero in the Pacific. They staged light bomb runs over tactical targets and strafed targets on the ground. They also escorted long-range bombers over areas swarming with enemy fighters.

By today's standards, the planes were small. Bomber cockpits were something less roomier than an office cubicle. B-24s and B-17s were only slightly longer than today's F-14D Tomcat navy fighter. But the bombers carried large crews: ten on the B-17s, eight on the B-24s. They performed various functions—pilot, co-pilot, navigator, bombardier, radioman, waist gunners, ball turret gunner, tail gunner. They were connected to each other with an intercom system, and they flew high enough they had to wear oxygen masks and heavy, quilted and lined uniforms in the unpressurized aircraft.

In Europe, throughout 1943 and early

1944, bombers flew daily missions over France and Germany with two objectives—wreck war-supporting industry in Germany and bases in France. In the process, fighter escorts and bomber machine gunners would target German fighters who flew up to stop the bombers, knocking down as many as they could. By destroying planes, air bases and manufactories, Allies could hope to have air superiority when they invaded France.

Until the "D" version of the P-51 arrived with external fuel tanks and longer ranges, bombers over occupied Europe were on their own for much of the trip. In theory, the bombers were self-protected, with machine guns laying out overlapping fields of fire that interconnected with those of other bombers in formation.

But plans and formations always went awry. Flak—anti-aircraft fire shot skyward from German guns, usually the deadly 88-mm cannon—was the nemesis of Allied bombers. It exploded red in the sky, then turned smoky black. Flak was like a shotgun blast, with fragmentation bits spraying through the sky. Flak hit planes from the bottom up, causing men excessive concern for their genitals. Flak jackets—heavy, armored vests—had extended crotch pieces to cover the vital areas; some men chose to sit on the vests rather than wear them. Flak could disintegrate a plane, blow its tail off, and rip a wing off. Enemy fighters would search for holes in a bomber's defenses, perhaps where a waste gunner was already dead, or a ball turret had ceased to function. Swooping in, they would target men, engines, tail surfaces and wings where the fuel tanks were located.

Many pilots nursed a broken B-17 or B-24 back across the English Channel to a landing in England. Others had no choice but to ditch their craft. If the command came to abandon ship, men, wearing parachutes, would scramble for an exit, perhaps the bomb bay, maybe a door or window, or the nose gear door. One gunner, his airplane on fire, paused to urinate on the blaze as a last act of defiance before he bailed out.

A tour of duty in a bomber could be harrowing, and bomber crews sought to break the anxiety with a new form of artistic expression—nose art. Nose art ran the gamut, from patriotic to lewd, fierce to funny, all of it an effort to personalize a government issue plane, and instill in its crew a unifying spirit. The government officially did not recognize the painting of anything on an aircraft except unit designations; but commanders also realized that nose art was an outlet for men living on the edge, and they tacitly accepted, if not openly embraced, the tradition. Nose art decorated the side nose panels of B-17s, B-24s, B-26s and A-20s, and it spread to fighter airplanes as well.

Sometimes air crews found professional artists to do their painting, sometimes a guy who had a flare with a brush and sometimes they just did it themselves, regardless of talent. The resulting art was sometimes brilliantly colored and shaded, with excellent perspective and anatomical dimensions; sometimes it was flat and awkward like a grade school mural. Some artists got paid for their work, maybe a few dollars and a bottle of whiskey.

Plane design often suggested artwork. The chins of B-24s and P-40 fighters leant themselves greatly to tiger- or shark-mouth designs. Patriotic themes graced other noses, and a good likeness of Dwight Eisenhower appeared on at least one bomber. Some planes used the Skull-and-Crossbones theme; others just painted on a name, perhaps reflecting a hometown or regional affiliation. The female form, how-

1943-1945

(1945) The PV-3, the largest U.S. helicopter prepares for a test flight in Pennsylvania, watched by a group of American servicemen. With a capacity for 12 people, the PV-3 was designed for U.S. Coast Guard and air-sea rescue missions, and can make emergency landings on water.

ever, was the most popular airplane decoration. Photos of pinup girls (movie stars Betty Grable and Rita Hayworth were favorites) graced the footlockers and wallets of many infantrymen, and the pinup style found its way onto the airplanes. Women usually represented wives or girlfriends back home, or simply universal male fantasy, and they were usually in some state of undress. They carried names, often double entendres like "Virgin on the Verge" and "Mountain Time."

Nose art wasn't the only decoration, however. For every successful bomb run, crews were allowed to paint on a bomb emblem; for every confirmed enemy plane the crew shot down, they got to paint on a kill mark—a swastika if they were in Europe, a Rising Sun flag if they were in the Pacific. Kill marks did as much for the crew's morale as the pinup girl on the nose.

1943 • HELICOPTERS ~ Airplanes were not the only aircraft flown in World War II. In 1943, the world's first production helicopter, known as the Sikorsky R-4, appeared in service. It was a two-man vehicle, capable of less than 90 miles per hour. While only 127 were built, the U.S. Army Air Force and the U.S. Navy both used it for reconnaissance and rescue. Helicopters, of course, would see a marked increase in service in Korea, where they effectively evacuated wounded troops to hospitals, and in Vietnam where they served both as transport and gunships.

ENTERTAINMENT ~ Just as the nose art helped alleviate the tensions of war, so, too, was entertainment vital to men in combat. United Service Organization (USO) shows toured the rear-echelons of all the major theaters, bringing live entertainment to soldiers. By far the most popular of the touring USO stars was Bob Hope (who would continue the practice in every American conflict through the Persian Gulf War in 1991). Touring with big bands, guest stars and always surrounded by beautiful women, Hope brought the men a frequently irreverent but always uplifting show.

G.I.s could also find a bit of humor in the army's own official publication, *Stars and Stripes*. A young cartoonist, Bill Mauldin, began the war in the 45th Infantry Division, and soon landed a job with the army newspaper. Creating a couple of dog-faced G.I.s named Willie and Joe, Mauldin used them as American everyman soldiers. His cartoons satirized everyday army life, and made particular fun of officers and top brass. While the hierarchy found him irreverent, the men loved him. Mauldin won a Pulitzer prize for his wartime work, and after the war he published several compilations of his cartoons. The exploits of Willie and Joe also became movies in the late 1940s.

1942-1945 • THE ENEMIES ∼ Fighting in both major theaters of the war was fierce and horrible; no man in France could claim he had it worse than a guy in the Pacific, or vice versa. As Allies pursued Germans through France, German soldiers fought back with everything they had. American G.I.s gained every inch with blood. When German troops counterattacked in Belgium in December 1944, touching off the Battle of the Bulge, they pinned Americans down in blizzards and deep snow. English-speaking Germans, passing themselves off as American G.I.s, infiltrated American lines, killed soldiers and wreaked havoc until Americans weeded them out. Fighting and freezing in foxholes, suspecting Germans all around them, Americans were miserable and scared. They broke out, though, with the help of sunshine and aerial provision drops, and the Battle of the Bulge marked Germany's last offensive operation. But the German army was not yet defeated. As Allies crossed the Rhine, they encountered the German "Siegfried Line," a line of defenses that proved tough to crack. Germans, retreating now for more than six months, dug in and held fast, fighting better than they had in years. Germans at home called the defense the "Miracle of the West," not surprising since they were now fighting to defend their homeland.

1942 • THE JAPANESE BUSHIDO CODE
∼ American soldiers fighting in the Pacific had to face one phenomenon of this war that their European counterparts did not – the Bushido Code. When militarists took control of the Japanese government in the 1920s, they resurrected the ancient Samurai code of Bushido. In its original form, Bushido represented military nobility and honor, but the militarists perverted it. They claimed Bushido as the nobility for military aspirations: to die for country and emperor was an honor. Indoctrination ensued in which even young boys were taught handle weapons. Japanese instilled with the Bushido philosophy believed it would be a disgrace to be taken prisoner in battle, and they looked with contempt on anyone who allowed himself to become captive. Bushido led to many suicides and fierce battles.

Bushido first became evident after the Battle of Bataan in spring 1942. Soon after attacking Pearl Harbor, Japanese bombers attacked American airbases in the Philippines preparatory to invasion. American war planners had previously

1942-1945

adopted War Plan Orange Three in case Japan attacked the islands. It called for Americans to build strong concrete defensive works across the neck of the Bataan Peninsula on south Luzon Island, then withdraw behind them in the face of attack. There they could hold off Japanese onslaughts until American ships resupplied them. But American Commander on the Philippines, General Douglas MacArthur, believed no Japanese attack could come before spring 1942, and thus he let War Plan Orange Three slide. In an emergency, he would defend the beaches of Luzon instead. When Japanese troops invaded on December 22, 1941, the stunned MacArthur ordered his troops onto the unprotected Bataan Peninsula. Fighting raged until May 1942, as Americans and Filipinos pulled back, survivors ultimately hopping across to Corregidor, an island in Manila Bay. The U.S. War Department pulled MacArthur out, moving him to Australia to command all Allied troops in the Pacific, and leaving General Jonathan Wainwright to surrender Allied troops in the Philippines.

The ensuing episode was one of the bitterest of the war. Japanese began assembling all of their prisoners on Bataan, then force-marched them back up the peninsula for dissemination to prisoner of war camps. They had not counted on taking so many American military personnel, Filipinos and civilians, and they did not have provisions enough for everyone. Starvation and sickness was rampant; prisoners began falling out of line. They could expect no mercy from the Japanese, for Bushido would not allow it. Japanese soldiers regarded the prisoners as subhuman, for they had allowed themselves to be taken captive. The Japanese left men who fell out of line to starve to death, or worse, they kicked or beat them with rifle butts. At times, Japanese soldiers attacked prisoners for no apparent reason. This became known as the Bataan Death March.

Bushido was evident at other places as well. Marines and soldiers fighting in the Solomons and on New Guinea saw it; Marines saw it again on the islands of the central Pacific. It manifested itself in Japanese determination to fight to the death for every inch of ground leading to Japan, to never surrender, to kill as many Americans as possible before they fell. On Iwo Jima in February 1945, Marines had to kill nearly 23,000 Japanese soldiers to take the little volcanic island. Often they had to flush the enemy out of caves with flame throwers to finish the job. On Okinawa, the gateway to Japan itself, Marines killed more than 100,000 Japanese soldiers and civilians, sealed another 30,000 or so in caves, and took 10,000 prisoner.

Bushido could spur Japanese soldiers on to bold Samurai charges, blades flashing in the sunlight. At Okinawa, it inspired pilots to buckle into planes packed with explosives and fly them into Allied ships. They were called Kamikazes (the name meaning Divine Wind), and in the spring of 1945, thousands of Kamikaze raids sank twenty-six Allied ships and damaged 160 others. The implications of Bushido for Japanese defense of their home island in the event of an Allied invasion were a reason for President Harry Truman's decision to drop atomic bombs on Japan in August 1945.

1940-1945 • FOREIGN CIVILIANS IN WARTIME ~ World War II was total war; as such, operations extended beyond the battlefield and frequently included belligerent civilians. Depending on their loyalties, those civilians could either help or hinder American G.I.s.

Those in the former category included resistance movements to the German and Japanese totalitarian regimes. Resistance movements were many and varied. While they existed in both major theaters of the war, those fighting against German occupation in Europe tended to be more organized and efficient than those fighting against Japan in the Pacific.

A common enemy was sometimes the *only* thing resistance movements had in common. In Europe—especially Eastern Europe—movements frequently grew from political cells that had formed in the post-World War I governmental upheavals. Nationalists segregated themselves from Communists. Some Communist groups got direct aid from the Soviet Union, much to the chagrin of the Western Allies, the United States and England. Others, such as Josip Broz Tito's Yugoslavian Communist resisters, regained territory from Germany with more aid from Anglo-American allies than from Stalinist Russia.

To most Americans, the most familiar resistance movement is the French Resistance, or French Underground. A rudimentary resistance began soon after Germany defeated France in the fall of 1940. Resisters helped downed English and French pilots escape capture, and helped POWs escape prison. They helped French Jews flee the Nazis' grasp, and they published underground leaflets urging resistance. Their resistance was against both Vichy France and Germany.

At the outset, French Resistance came in several forms. One group, loyal to Charles DeGaulle who had established Free France in London after the Germans took France, was known as his "Secret Army." Another, loyal to General Henri Giraud, the U.S.-backed French leader in North Africa, was the National Council of Resistance. French Communists, dedicated to fighting German occupation, remained aloof from both these groups.

The Allied invasion of France in June 1944 helped coalesce French resistance. Resisters plagued German troops by sabotaging railroads, cutting telegraph lines and by feeding them false information, for example, that the Allied invasion site would be Calais rather than Normandy. Such efforts were popularized later by Cornelius Ryan's classic account of the Normandy invasion *The Longest Day: June 6, 1944* (1959), and the subsequent movie of the same name. Resistance work was risky, at best. An estimated 75,000 members of the French Resistance died fighting the German occupation.

In the Pacific, Japanese occupation troops also faced resistance. In the Philippines, many Filipinos retreated into the mountains rather than surrender in 1942, and from there waged a guerilla war for the duration. In China, Mao Tse-tung led a Communist movement against the Japanese, suspending for the war his ongoing clash against rival nationalist Chinese. And in French Indochina, otherwise known as Vietnam, a group of Communist partisans kept up a desultory war against Japanese occupiers from 1940 to 1945. They were the Viet Minh, and their leader was a man who would soon plague the United States, Ho Chi Minh.

1940-1945 • ESPIONAGE ORGANIZATIONS ~ To be sure, many resistance groups dealt in spying on the enemy and passing information on to Allied military commands. But World War II saw many organized espionage units as well.

Germany had several, including the Abwehr for military intelligence; the Gestapo, a thuggish police force with both uniformed and covert members; and the *Sicherheitsdienst* (SD), which began as

1940-1949

the Nazi party's intelligence squad, but became the national espionage unit when Hitler consolidated power in the 1930s. The Abwehr's loyalties were frequently questionable, and in 1944 several of its operatives were implicated in a plot to kill Hitler with a bomb. Ultimately the SD eclipsed the other two branches as Germany's prime intelligence unit.

England had an effective intelligence unit, the Special Operations Executive, or SOE. Its primary objective was to help local resistance movements, and carry information from them back to military commands. It was a chief conduit of aid to Tito in Yugoslavia.

The United States also had an intelligence unit, the Office of Strategic Services, or OSS. Forerunner of today's Central Intelligence Agency (CIA), the OSS patterned itself after Britain's SOE. With an operative force of more than 12,000 worldwide, the OSS engaged in foreign intelligence, disinformation, resistance movement liaisons, guerrilla operations and sabotage.

Resistance movements and espionage groups used coded radio transmissions to pass information, but others made use of public radio programs to demoralize enemy troops. Famous incidents came from both Germany and Japan.

1944-1949 • Radio Propaganda: "Axis Sally" ~ Shortly before D-Day, June 6, 1944, many American G.I.s in England preparing for the invasion heard a radio play broadcast on shortwave bands by Radio Berlin. Not knowing exactly when or where, but that an invasion of continental Europe was inevitable, Germany was attempting to frighten the troops who would make the crossing. The play, entitled "Vision of Invasion," featured an American mother who received a gruesome visit from the spirit of a son killed in the attack. Soldiers who had been in the European theater for any amount of time could recognize the main voice behind the play as that of "Axis Sally," one of Radio Berlin's chief on-air propaganda personalities.

Axis Sally (American troops hung the name on her; on the air, she only referred to herself as "Sally") was in fact Mildred Gillars, an American woman born November 29, 1900, in Portland, Maine. Educated in American colleges, she failed as an actress and went to Europe in the early 1930s, ostensibly to study music. In Germany, she became involved with Radio Berlin program director Max Otto Koischewitz, and during the war she did propaganda programs for him.

Typically Gillars would play sentimental American songs, then intersperse them with digging commentary. She implied to American boys that their sweethearts and wives back home had given up on them and become unfaithful. She passed herself off as a Red Cross helper and interviewed American prisoners of war, extracting from them statements which she later twisted out of context and presented on-air to show that German POW camps were friendly places and that Americans much preferred them to fighting Germans.

In 1946, intelligence tipped Americans to Gillars' presence in Berlin. They arrested her and took her back to the United States, where a court indicted her on ten counts of treason the next year. In 1949, she was convicted on one of the counts, that one stemming from the "Vision of Invasion" broadcast. Tapes of the radio play helped convict her. She was fined $10,000 and sentenced to ten to thirty years in prison. She served twelve of them, getting paroled in 1961.

Gillars entered a Catholic convent in Columbus, Ohio. She died in 1988.

1943-1948 • "Tokyo Rose" ~ In 1948, the United States tried another woman for treasonous radio broadcasts. She was Iva Toguri, purported to be "Tokyo Rose," although American G.I.s hung that collective name on many female radio broadcasters for Radio Tokyo during the war.

Toguri was a Japanese-American born in Los Angeles. She was visiting relatives in Tokyo when the war began, and could not return. Japan ordered her to make radio propaganda broadcasts. She later maintained that she always inserted subtle subterfuges in her broadcasts more damaging to Japan than to Americans.

Regardless, in 1948 the United States tried her for treasonous broadcasts in which she mentioned the loss of American ships in a Pacific battle. The actual indictment is vague; indeed, folklore claiming that Toguri taunted American Marines by telling them their support fleet was gone and they were stranded in the Pacific is more dramatic, though false.

Toguri was convicted, fined $10,000, and given a ten-year prison sentence. She served six years before receiving parole. In January 1977, President Gerald Ford gave Toguri a full pardon.

1945 • G.I.s and the Holocaust ~ As Allied troops spread across Europe, squeezing Germany from west and east, American troops found themselves facing horrors they never expected to see. Since 1941, Hitler had been ordering the mass execution of Jews in occupied territory. By spring 1945, the number of dead from Nazi death camps had reached six million.

Allied troops began uncovering the death camps as they pressed the offensive. In the west, Americans liberated twelve camps in April and May 1945. They included the now infamous Buchenwald and Dachau camps. By the time American troops entered the camps, German troops were usually running or had been long gone. Nevertheless, the crematoria ovens, where Germans incinerated the bodies of dead Jews, were often still burning. Slowly, realizing the armed men outside their barracks were Americans and not returning Germans, camp inmates ventured outside to greet their liberators. The Americans were appalled. They found living skeletons; humans nearly starved to death, with gray skin stretched over bone.

Near the gas chambers and oven were bodies—thousands of them—neatly stacked and awaiting incineration. The unmistakable smell of death hung over everything. General George Patton, elements of whose Third Army liberated Buchenwald, reportedly vomited at the site. So did Ike Eisenhower, who toured the camps. "I visited every nook and cranny of the camp [Buchenwald] because I felt it my duty to be in a position from then on to testify at first hand about these things in case there ever grew up at home the belief or assumption that the stories of Nazi brutality were just propaganda," Ike reported to Army Chief of Staff George C. Marshall. Most of the men were overcome with emotion. Images of the death camps would haunt many for the rest of their lives.

1945 • World War II Ends ~ Wherever they had served, American soldiers at the end of 1945 were confident they had completed a job well done by smashing tyranny and defeating two of the best armies the world had ever seen. In Europe, as Americans had liberated

1945-1953

(1944) American soldiers on a truck drive past a cheering crowd during the liberation of Paris, France.

city after city, confetti, flags, champagne and women greeted them. They returned home to virtually the same. As a group, they were also the last American soldiers to feel any real sense of accomplishment for some time to come.

1950-1953 KOREA

For American soldiers, the Korean War (never an officially declared war, Korea was a United Nations-sanctioned attempt at containment of Communism) was in many ways an extension of World War II, save for one very important factor. Allies had waged World War II to force unconditional surrender on their Axis enemies, but Korea was a limited war, a byproduct of the United States' commitment to containment of Communism. As such, American soldiers would fight a war that was never declared, a war that most of their friends and family back home knew little about, a war that had unclear goals and a war in which victors would be hard to identify.

After defeating Japan in 1945 and ending its colonial hold on Korea, the United States held influence over the southern part of the country, below the 38th Parallel. The Communist Soviet Union and, after 1949, Communist China considered North Korea their satellite country. The Korean War began in the summer of 1950 when Chinese- and Russian-backed North Korean troops invaded South Korea, hoping to unite the country into one Communist nation. Elements of Lt. General Walton Walker's Eighth U.S. Army, stationed in Japan, crossed to Korea and, fighting with South Korean troops, stalled the Communist advance on a semi-circular defensive line at the tip of the Korean peninsula known as the Pusan Perimeter. The United Nations sanctioned widening the war,

1652 ~ SOLDIERING: LIFE IN COMBAT

authorizing the United States and allied nations to send more troops to Korea. The United States was senior member of the U.N. coalition, and its chief Pacific commander, World War II veteran General Douglas MacArthur masterminded an invasion of South Korea at Inchon Harbor that would force Communist troops to withdraw to the north.

Only five years after World War II, the United States was not ready for the war. Domestic manufacturers had retooled from the heady days of World War II, and were once again making washers, radios and toasters instead of war supplies. The landing at Inchon Harbor in September 1950, required the U.S. Army, Navy, and Marines to use leftover equipment from World War II, and even buy old landing craft from local Japanese fisherman. While the landing had a make-do flavor to it, Marines successfully scaled the seawalls at Inchon, and within days approached the South Korean capital of Seoul.

Soon after the invasion succeeded, North Korean troops were withdrawing to the north with U.N. troops in pursuit. As North Koreans retreated, U.S. troops gave chase. Upon reaching the 38th Parallel, Americans had essentially fulfilled the obligations of containment. But MacArthur pressed Truman to let him go further. The United States certainly wanted to see all of Korea unified under South Korean rule, and Truman pressured the U.N. to let U.N. troops go further. Finally, the U.N. agreed.

U.N. troops stepped beyond containment and into liberation when they crossed the 38th Parallel and pushed toward the Yalu River, the border between North Korea and China. As U.S. troops discovered that North Koreans were using Soviet weapons, and that some prisoners of war were Chinese, fear spread that this would escalate into a larger conflict. In late November, it did escalate as 300,000 Chinese troops poured across the border. The Chinese loosed horrid charges, blowing bugles and tossing grenades. Winter weather and night movements impeded U.S. air power, which MacArthur had been counting on. American and allied troops were now in retreat.

The retreat, through blizzards and sub-zero temperatures was harrowing, but it produced its share of heroes. Marines caught at the Chosin Reservoir in North Korea had to cut their way south, through snow and mountain passes, fighting Chinese all the way. A Marine commander dryly noted that his men were not retreating, just "attacking in another direction."

Back south of the 38th Parallel, the allied gains of the fall were erased, and in April 1951 MacArthur ran afoul of President Truman after the general questioned the wisdom of fighting a limited war. Truman was committed to such a war—the Chinese intervention conjured precedents of World War III and nuclear disaster for many Americans—and Truman fired the general and replaced him with another World War II veteran, General Matthew B. Ridgway. A solid, no-nonsense, popular commander, Ridgway orchestrated two months of pounding attacks on the Communists that drove them back above the 38th Parallel. Communists agreed to go to the negotiating table with Americans, but talks proved fruitless until they reached an armistice agreement two years later in the summer of 1953. In the meantime, troops jostled for position, attacking and defending, fighting and dying.

(1954) American broadcast journalist Edward R. Murrow (C) sits in a trench with a microphone in his hand, interviewing an African-American U.S. Marine during the Korean War for his CBS television show 'See It Now,' Korea. The company was holding a ridge on the Korean Front.

1950-1953

1950-1953 • THE AMERICAN TROOPS OF KOREA ~ American troops in Korea were very much like their World War II counterparts of a few years earlier. They wore virtually the same uniforms, with white camouflaging covering up O.D. and leaf-pattern cloth for much of the 1950 campaign. They wore the same helmet, the M-1. Sherman tanks prowled around the front lines and 105-mm howitzers still pounded away with rhythmic regularity. Overhead, sky battles were different. Even though men could still see the sleek P-51 Mustang (now designated the F-51; "F" standing for fighter, where the old "P" had stood for pursuit) in flight, most of the American aircraft were jets. Germany had introduced jet fighters late in World War II, and they became standard in aerial warfare. The United States Air Force flew F-86 Sabre jets and F-80 Shooting Stars; the Navy the F9F Panther. In Korea they first encountered Soviet-made aircraft in the deadly MiG-15. In dogfights, Americans could hold their own.

Korea could be mild in the summer, brutally hostile in the winter. Unfortunately, the United States' bitterest defeat in the war came during the winter of 1950. Americans faced not only Chinese soldiers but freezing cold as they repelled from the Communist attack in late November. Marines retreating from the Chosin Reservoir endured such frostbite and misery that their battleground is forever known as "Frozen Chosin" and themselves the "Chosin Few."

At other times, especially during the stalemate along the 38th Parallel, Korea could take on a lunar appearance, pocked with shell holes and littered with strewn earth. Men might battle for a hill here, or a few yards there, but, like another stalemate back in World War I, the line changed very little. At other times, such as the rapid and fluid combat of late 1950, the battleground, with rumbling tanks and trucks bringing up supplies, was much like that of World War II.

The men of World War II knew their objective—total defeat of the Axis powers. In Korea, it was not so simple. Did victory mean holding at the 38th Parallel? The Yalu? Crossing into Red China, as MacArthur had intimated? Or something else? Even when the armistice came in 1953, no one could be sure who had won, or if anyone had truly won.

For Korea, the United States government did not mobilize the public as it had for World Wars I and II. The draft had never fully ended, so restarting it was not an issue. Government bonds were still sold. But there were no great bond drives or rationing, no great patriotic drives, speeches or posters. National Guardsmen and Reservists, many of whom had served in World War II, worried about being called to active duty. Many of them were called, and they served, but the manpower dent of Korea was nothing like it had been in the 1940s. Industry went on manufacturing the goods of a growing nation, new homes went up in suburbia, and the Baby Boom continued. In short, American life went on with little regard for what was happening in Korea.

The Americans who fought in Korea were of a new breed. They fought, and fought well, for limited objectives. A defensive line here, a hill there. They won most of their engagements, but could never be sure if they won a war. They met no parades when they came home. They did it all in obscurity. They paved the way for a coming generation of young men who would fight another limited war in another Pacific nation. But while Korea faded away into the memory of the 1950s, that next war—in Vietnam —would rip the United States apart and change forever the attitudes of American fighting men.

1964-1975 VIETNAM

The United States became involved in Vietnam in the 1950s, first sending financial aid to France, trying to restore colonial order after World War II. When Communist Vietnamese forces under Ho Chi Minh forced France out of the country, the United States filled the vacuum, backing anti-Communist southern forces and political leaders. In the early 1960s, when Communist aggression became overt, and both North Vietnamese troops and South Vietnamese Communist sympathizers—the Viet Cong—attacked southern military installations, cities and hamlets, the United States became a military presence. President John F. Kennedy authorized sending American troops, advisors he called them, to help South Vietnam fend off the Communists. Such was in line with the American policy of containment.

Lyndon B. Johnson became president upon Kennedy's assassination in November 1963, and he maintained the American advisorship role in South Vietnam. American troops were engaged in sporadic fighting, some dying, but wholesale bloodletting had not yet begun.

The next year saw a turning point in American involvement. In August 1964, American warships in the Gulf of Tonkin off North Vietnam reported that Communists had fired on them. Using that as a lever, Johnson, a former senator and consummate politician, got Congress to okay the Gulf of Tonkin Resolution, giving him full reign to combat North Vietnamese aggression. Johnson, a Democrat, was running for president in his own right that year, and he did not immediately seek an escalation of hostilities. As he campaigned, he said he sought no "wider" war. Johnson beat Republican candidate Barry Goldwater by a wide margin.

1965 • AMERICAN ESCALATION
In February 1965, Communist troops attacked an American base at Pleiku in South Vietnam's central highlands. The attack brought American reprisals, and Johnson ordered the opening of a bombing campaign against military targets in southern North Vietnam. The campaign, called Operation Rolling Thunder, did little good but sought to appease hawkish conservatives at home.

1965-1973

(Military planners knew the bombing would not bring an end to hostilities. Contrary to what bombing theorists in the 1920s had believed, heavy bombing in World War II had not stopped ground troops in either Europe or the Pacific, nor had it done so in Korea. Ground troops were still key to winning victories.) And while Rolling Thunder dropped hundreds of thousands of tons of explosives on enemy positions, it was still a limited operation. Johnson feared a total bombing campaign of the North would bring China into the war, or worse, the Soviet Union. Even though Johnson over the next two years approved an expanded list of targets, some nearing the northern capital of Hanoi, the bombing remained limited in character and result.

In July 1965, Johnson authorized sending 50,000 additional combat troops to South Vietnam, and he gave General William Westmoreland, overall commander in South Vietnam, a free hand to use them as he saw fit. Westmoreland would periodically call for more troops, and Johnson would okay them, driving the number of American troops to 540,000 by 1969.

American military branches seemed to sidestep their responsibilities in Vietnam. They never gave Johnson truly creative strategies for victory in Vietnam. Claiming that the jungles of Vietnam negated the possibility of classic, conventional warfare, the army used American troops as a counter-insurgency force, which demoralized the American troops, as it provided for no clear victories. It was also unnecessary. In 1975, when Communists overran South Vietnam, they did it with conventional tactics reminiscent of World War II.

1966-1973 • COMBAT IN VIETNAM

Combat in Vietnam had its own peculiarities. North Vietnamese troops were elusive. They entered South Vietnam not over the national boundary at the 17th Parallel, but down a 600-mile-long route that ran from North Vietnam, through Laos and Cambodia, then reentered South Vietnam at a variety of places. It was called the Ho Chi Minh Trail. The trail enabled NVA troops to effectively supply and link up with Viet Cong insurgents in the South, attack American and South Vietnamese bases, then quickly disappear into the "neutral" countries of Laos and Cambodia. Such fighting popped up all over the South, and was not limited to a clearly defined "front" as it had been in other American wars.

To combat such guerrilla tactics, Westmoreland adopted a system called "search and destroy." It was essentially a war of post, with American troops establishing bases in response to individual Communist raids. It involved major campaigns, such as a 30,000-man campaign in 1967 to shut down the Iron Triangle, a Communist area near Saigon, the capital of the South. But more characteristic were the squads and platoons of men who trekked through jungles and rice paddies, river deltas and highlands looking for enemies who were there one minute, gone the next; who blended with the terrain and struck without warning; who left booby traps that killed with no enemy present. Troops used dogs to help sniff out the enemy, and odor-sensing devices that could do the same. Using helicopters for quick transport and frequently calling on Air Force fighter-bombers to rain death on enemy positions, American troops had the advantage of superior firepower.

Aircraft dropped defoliants on jungle areas, hoping to strip the land and deny cover to Communist troops. (One such defoliant, Agent Orange, was later discovered to cause cancer in men exposed to it.) When attacking a known enemy position, American troops might ring the position, then call down air strikes to bomb it into submission. Some bombs were loaded with napalm, a sticky, jelly-like substance that stuck to targets – even human targets – and burned.

Search and destroy was as limited as bombing. It was like punching at air, and it failed to effectively curtail Communist incursions. The tactic had no overall strategy, such as cutting off the Ho Chi Minh Trail to the Communists, and it presented the American public with no verifiable victories. By the end of 1967, people at home were wondering just how the United States could know if it was winning. The Pentagon assured Americans that the U.S. was winning, but could only offer as evidence "body counts" of killed Communist soldiers. Eventually the media discovered that the U.S. commanders had inflated the numbers to make the campaigns seem more successful.

1968 • TET OFFENSIVE ~ Although the American campaign achieved some success from 1965 through 1967, 1968 proved to be a turning point in favor of the Viet Cong. Both sides had traditionally called a cease fire to observe Tet, the Vietnamese Lunar New Year observed in January and February. But in 1968 the North Vietnamese designed an extensive series of surprise attacks throughout South Vietnam during the Tet holiday.

They struck first at Khe Sanh, a Marine base in northern South Vietnam. Their siege convinced American military leaders that Khe Sanh was the focus of the new campaign. Americans were diverted north when, on January 30, 1968, North Vietnamese and Viet Cong soldiers struck all over the South, using Ho Chi Minh Trail outlets to strike many

---

Military Life

~

Millions of Americans served in the military either as volunteers, draftees, or professional soldiers, and their experiences have been the subject of movies about military life other than during wartime. The absurdity of some facets of military life have provided material for comedies, as well as the tragedy of risking lives and losing families in the service of country. Here is a sampling of movies about the peacetime military.

Strategic Air Command (1955)	*An Officer and a Gentlemen* (1982)
The D.I. (1957)	*Top Gun* (1986)
No Time For Sergeants (1958)	*The Presidio* (1988)
On the Beach (1959)	*The General's Daughter* (1999)
Fail-Safe (1964)	*The Hunt for Red October* (1990)
The Great Santini (1979)	*Crimson Tide* (1995)
The Right Stuff (1979)	*The Three Kings* (1999)
Private Benjamin (1980)	*The Astronaut's Wife* (1999)
Stripes (1981)	*Rules of Engagement* (2000)

1968-1973

places at once. They hit thirty-six of forty-four provincial capitals; sixty-four district capitals; the ancient capital of Hue; and in Saigon, the American base of operations, they hit the American Embassy, the Vietnamese Presidential Palace and Tan Son Nhut Airport.

American manpower and firepower, plus the fact that many Communist attacks were mistimed, restored the advantage to U.S. troops. Ultimately, American and South Vietnamese troops pushed the Communists back, retaking lost targets. On the books, Tet became a decisive defeat for the Communists; but in reality, it was a defeat for the United States.

Much of the Tet Offensive played out on American evening news broadcasts, forcing Americans to wonder how the United States could be winning the war, when it seemed that the North Vietnamese had so much fight left. Teacher and student protests against the war had been going on since 1965, but prior to 1968 protesting seemed to be the province of a radical, liberal extreme. After Tet, however, what little public support there was for the war seemed to dry up. Conservatives began to question United States methods and objectives. Tet drove Lyndon Johnson out of the 1968 presidential race. In November 1968, Richard Nixon beat Vice-President Hubert Humphrey for the presidency, promising to pull the United States out of Vietnam.

This is when the tide turned for American soldiers. Men who had fought well early in the war now sensed that the public at home no longer supported the war, or the soldiers fighting it. Americans had lost interest, and the soldiers lost interest as well. Nixon quickly made good on his promise to start disengaging American troops. Adopting a policy of Vietnamization, by which South Vietnamese troops would gradually take over more and more of the fighting, Nixon began bringing American soldiers home. To men in the field it appeared that the United States was calling it quits; they questioned why should they continue to fight and risk their lives if the U.S. was pulling out. The withdrawal took until 1973, with periodic escalations of fighting, ensuring that the North knew the United States was not weakening. The long, drawn-out disengagement was very difficult for American combat troops who continued to question why should they fight a war that their own country now deemed worthless. No American wanted to be the last soldier to die in Vietnam.

1968-1973 • TROOP MORALE IN VIETNAM ~ In such an atmosphere, American troop morale plummeted. The average age of the combat soldier in Vietnam was nineteen. Young Americans at home had begun experimenting with drugs—marijuana, heroin, opium and a variety of psychedelic drugs, and some men who were drafted continued to use drugs on duty. More than fifty percent of soldiers in Vietnam had smoked marijuana; more than a third had tried harder drugs. Alcoholism among troops, a perennial problem in armies at war, took a sharp upturn. Some of the phenomena was an extension of domestic dissatisfaction with the war, but no doubt much of it was a soldier's attempt to escape the horror of jungle warfare and the feeling their country had abandoned them. Frustration among troops was rampant.

In the field, soldiers could not easily differentiate between friends and enemies, as Viet Cong were, in fact, South

Women Soldiers - 3rd March 1966. Adding to morale problems, the soldiers found it increasingly hard to identify their targets. As seen here, three young women from South Vietnam with rifles on their shoulders. American soldiers found it difficult to kill women.

Vietnamese and wore no special markings to indicate their political affiliation. Troops believing they were passing through a friendly hamlet might quickly be gunned down by women, even children. Americans began to suspect everyone, and in some instances patrols began shooting anyone in sight on the grounds that they were "just gooks," (the derogatory term Americans applied to all Vietnamese.) In March 1968, an American contingent under Lieutenant William Calley killed more than 200 civilians—old men, women and children—in the hamlet of My Lai. Calley's unit had been told that the hamlet was a Viet Cong stronghold, and to expect heavy resistance. Finding no soldiers there, Calley's men opened fire anyway. Ultimately, Calley was court martialed and convicted of murder in 1971. After a series of political maneuvers and interventions, Calley was paroled in 1974, but the incident indicated the severity of combat troop frustration.

1969-1971 • FRAGGING ~ The troop frustration manifested itself in other ways as well. Sometimes, when assigned an objective, a platoon might decide to "search and not destroy," just walk around in a safe area for a few days, then return to base and report no contact with the enemy. Officers who did not go along with avoidance policies might quickly find themselves the target of a "fragging" – tossing a fragmentation grenade at a troublesome officer to get him out of the way. Troops might also frag officers who were simply incompe-

(circa 1970) American POW L. Hughes (center), a lieutenant colonel in the U.S. Air Force, is paraded barefoot and with a bandaged face through the street by two Vietnamese soldiers during the Vietnam War.

tent and in danger of leading them into ambushes. (As the war progressed, the quality of low-level officers did indeed fall. College ROTC programs dried up as support for the war vanished, and the army drew officers from draftee pools, and put them through hurried officer training programs.) In 1969, fraggings and suspected fraggings numbered 126; that number rose to 333 in 1971. Officers sometimes fragged troublesome enlisted men, and both might frag Vietnamese soldiers simply because they were Vietnamese. At the same time, cases of American soldiers going AWOL (Absent Without Leave) increased, as did desertions. Cases of mutiny went up. Never had the morale of American troops been so low.

Post-Traumatic Stress Disorder

Men who completed their tour of duty frequently left Vietnam with Post-Traumatic Stress Disorder (PTSD), the new name for shell shock and battle fatigue. Conditions at home frequently exacerbated their problems, as war protesters labeled them criminals and baby killers. Today the image of the mentally scarred Vietnam vet, bearded, stoned, alone and suicidal is clichéd. But in the mid-1970s, the image had its basis in truth. The incidence of Vietnam-era PTSDs caused the army to look anew on the phenomena and its causes. Now the army spends a great deal of time educating soldiers about the mental and emotional effects of combat and teaching them to watch for signs of fatigue. It also quickly debriefs men, offering them counseling after they come out of combat.

The final American pullout came in 1973. Americans who had fought in Vietnam could not help but wonder what it had been for. No matter what face the Nixon administration put on it—withdrawal with honor, it was called—soldiers believed that the United States had lost a war. Evidence seemed to bear that out, for in 1975 North Vietnamese troops overran South Vietnam, uniting the country under a Communist banner. Containment in Indochina had failed, and more than 50,000 American soldiers died in the process.

1975-1990 • POSTSCRIPT: SAIGON TO KUWAIT CITY – REBUILDING ~ After Vietnam, the United States military services lived with stained reputations. It took sixteen years for American troops to point proudly at a clear victory. In spring 1975, North Vietnam finally overran South Vietnam, spreading communism throughout the country and renaming Saigon, the former U.S. base, Ho Chi Minh City. Communists also took over neighboring Laos and Cambodia. When soldiers of Cambodia's Communist Khmer Rouge faction boarded the U.S. merchant vessel *Mayaguez* off the coast of Cambodia in May 1975, United States Marines nearly botched their recovery. While the Khmer Rouge returned the hostages, the Marines found themselves pinned down on a nearby island and very nearly cut off from rescue.

The next few years did little to help the image of the United States military. When forces loyal to the Ayatollah Khomeini deposed the Shah of Iran early in 1979, then captured fifty-two American hostages later that year, the United States seemed powerless to intervene. In 1980, President Jimmy Carter (who had won the office from Gerald Ford in 1976) authorized a helicopter-borne rescue of the hostages. But something went awry at a desert checkpoint. Three of eight Marine helicopters were damaged in a sandstorm, one of them when it collided with an Air Force C-130 cargo plane. Three Marines and five Air Force servicemen died. Carter cancelled the operation, and he was never able to affect the hostages' release. Iranians, released them on January 20, 1981, the very day Ronald Reagan, victor in the November 1980 presidential race, took the oath of office as president.

1975-1990

Reagan vowed to restore luster to the American military. In 1983, ground forces invaded the tiny Caribbean island of Grenada to rescue American college students there from the grip of a dictatorial power. The mission, however, proved that the military was still in disarray after Vietnam. Soldiers had difficulty taking objectives, orders were frequently fouled and enemy resistance on the island sometimes hard to overcome. By 1989, things went more smoothly when the Army invaded Panama to remove president and drug-runner Manuel Noriega from power.

1990-1991
PERSIAN GULF WAR

The real test of the army's revitalization came with the Persian Gulf War in 1991. On August 1, 1990, Iraqi President Saddam Hussein sent his armies into neighboring Kuwait, capturing that country's vital oil fields and annexing the country to Iraq. Immediately, United States President George Bush vowed that Hussein's action "would not stand," and he

1990-1991

authorized the Pentagon to work on plans to oust Iraq from Kuwait. Throughout the rest of 1990, Bush forged an international coalition, headed by the United States and Great Britain, to fight Iraq if Hussein persisted in holding Kuwait. He also corralled Congressional support for military action, as the War Powers Act of 1973 mandated.

Hurriedly, the United States Army's Central Command, assigned responsibility for the Middle East and commanded by General H. Norman Schwarzkopf, moved men and equipment to Saudi Arabia, which the United States would use as a staging area much as it had used England in World War II. Troops were deployed from bases in the U.S. and Germany. Those troops had seen their primary mission—guarding western Europe against Soviet invasion—change as Communism crumbled between 1989 and 1991. Now, much of the army that would cross the desert to fight Iraq was composed of units that had been trained to fight nothing less than World War III.

In January 1991, the United States Air Force, backed by British, French and Saudi air forces, launched a six-week bombing campaign designed to hammer Iraqi desert defenses and the nation's capital, Baghdad, the site of command and control installations. But American war planners knew from history that bombing alone had not brought Germany to her knees in 1944 and 1945, nor had it North Vietnam in the 1960s and 1970s. Complete victory required a land campaign to achieve objectives.

While fostering enemy beliefs that he would attack Kuwait from the front, Schwarzkopf planned a flanking armored sweep through the desert, its spearhead pointed at Baghdad well behind Iraqi front lines, that would force Iraqis to withdraw from Kuwait. The move was very similar to MacArthur's invasion of Inchon in 1950, and it had the same results. Hammered on all fronts, Iraqis broke from their lines; Allied air forces slaughtered many of them who maintained belligerent postures as they fled Kuwait City. Other Iraqi soldiers seemed to welcome American troops as they surrendered, often on televised reports. The Allied ground war secured the sovereignty of Kuwait; it lasted 100 hours.

DESERT EQUIPMENT ~ American troops in the desert were outfitted superbly. They used versions of the M-16 rifle, standard infantry arm since Vietnam, and wore uniforms of desert camouflage. The old M-1 helmet, the steel pot, was gone. Now troops wore a helmet and vest made of bullet-turning Kevlar. The outfit was known as the Personnel Armor System Ground Troops (PASGT). Troops first wore the PASGT helmet in combat in Grenada. But extended sides offering seventeen percent more protection than the M-1 made the PASGT helmet look something like German helmets of World War II, and it took some time for purists in the army and the public to accept the new helmet.

Water was essential to troops in the desert heat. Each man was encouraged to drink up to eight gallons of it a day. The army flew in planeloads of bottled water. Troops no longer ate old K- or C-Rations as they had in World War II. Now they ate MREs—Meals Ready to Eat. Each came in a black plastic pouch and contained full, albeit compressed meals, with such items as meat entrees, fruits and juices, Tabasco seasoning, coffee and toilet paper. As it had in World War II, the Hershey company again produced a high-energy chocolate bar for the troops. This one, called the Desert Bar, could with-

(1991) American airforce F-15 C fighters flying over a Kuwaiti oil field which had been torched by retreating Iraqi troops during the Gulf War.

stand intense desert heat without melting. It quickly became a favorite.

DESERT VEHICLES ~ Tank crews drove the speedy M-1A1 Abrams tank. The tank, on good terrain, could reach a top speed of near forty-five miles per hour. It proved perfect for the desert war with its systems holding up well under heat and sand. The Abrams mounted a 120-mm main gun, two 7.62 mm machine guns, and a .50-caliber machine gun. Its four-man crew had access to night-vision gear. A cooling system allowed the men to button up inside the tank so that they were protected from chemical agents.

The Abrams' little sister on the battlefield was the Bradley Fighting Vehicle, a step-up from the old armored half-track personnel carriers of World War II. The Bradley carried a crew of three and could transport six infantrymen. It had a 25mm main gun in a turret and a 7.62 mm machine gun. Two TOW missiles (Tube-launched, Optically-tracked, Wire-guided) gave the Bradley a long-range punch. Fully tracked, the Bradley could make thirty-eight miles per hour.

Mechanized infantrymen went to battle in Bradley fighting vehicles or HUMVEES, which had replaced the indefatigable Jeep in the mid-1980s. Officially designated High Mobility Multipurpose Wheeled Vehicles (HMMWV), soldiers quickly began calling the odd-looking vehicles HUMVEES or Hummers. With an enclosed cab, the HUMVEE could mount machine guns or rocket launchers on its flat roof.

Some troops made it to Kuwait City in militarized dune buggies. Sporting little armor but a good bit of armament, the buggies offered great speed and maneuverability on the desert sands.

CONCLUSION

When the Persian Gulf War ended, President Bush declared that the U.S. Army had whipped the stigma of Vietnam. Indeed, the army appeared to have learned several lessons from its Vietnam days. First, it quickly mobilized its Reserve and National Guard forces. It had not done that in Vietnam, and missed a valuable tool to lever public support. With servicemen from all areas of the United States service, the public could little help but support the men at arms. Thus, in 1991, many men and women who had joined the Reserve and Guard simply to cash in on the college benefits of the New G.I. Bill found themselves on active duty in a real, live shooting war.

American troops did well in every war they fought during the twentieth century. From Cuba to Saudi Arabia, they laid down a winning heritage. Sometimes, as in Vietnam, true victory proved elusive, but the American G.I. gave it his all just the same. As the century progressed, technology gave American troops better equipment, but the measure of victory always came down to personal training, stamina and bravery.

The life of the American soldier in combat improved as a result of better equipment over the twentieth century. Mental stress from the possibility of instantaneous death as a result of the improved technology and weaponry created a new environment requiring commanders to recognize the emotional as well as physical conditions of their troops. In the twenty-first century, American armed forces indoctrinate troops to the possible sights and smells of the battlefield before they ever reach it. They also quickly debrief soldiers after combat, removing them to the rear as soon as possible. Such measures, the Army hopes, will reduce the incidence of PTSDs.

But no matter how technical or sophisticated it becomes, combat is still combat. Regardless of climate, from the snows of Korea or the burning sands of Iraq, regardless of their computers, lasers, and radars, soldiers still have to define military objectives and take them by force. The collective experience of a century and the backing of an industrial nation, much less naïve than it had been in 1898, go far to making an American soldier's life "easier." But, just as it had in the Belleau Wood in 1914, or on Normandy Beach in 1944, the measure of victory is often still given by the age-old qualities of guts, perseverance . . . and luck.

BIBLIOGRAPHY

Adkin, Mark. *Urgent Fury: The Battle for Grenada*. Lexington, MA: Lexington Books, 1989.

Ambrose, Stephen E. *Americans at War*. Jackson: University Press of Mississippi, 1997.

———. *Citizen Soldiers*. New York: Simon and Schuster, 1997.

———. *D-Day*. New York: Simon and Schuster, 1994.

Blair, Clay. *The Forgotten War: America in Korea 1950-1953*. New York: Doubleday, 1987.

Bradley, James. *Flags of Our Fathers*. New York: Bantam, Doubleday, 2000.

Fahey, James J. *Pacific War Diary, 1942-1945*. New York: Berkeley Medallion Books, 1973.

Freeman, Roger A. *The Mighty Eighth: A History of the U.S. Eighth Air Force*. Garden City, New York: Doubleday and Company, 1970.

Freidel, Frank. *The Splendid Little War*. New York: Bramhall House, 1958.

Herring, George C. *America's Longest War: The United States and Vietnam, 1950-1975*. New York: Alfred A. Knopf, 1986.

Jeffers, H. Paul. *Colonel Roosevelt: Theodore Roosevelt Goes to War, 1897-1898*. New York: John Wiley and Sons, 1996.

King, Otis H. "Karl." *The Alamo of the Pacific: The Story of the Famed "China Marines on Bataan and Corregidor and What They Did to the Enemy as POWs*. Fort Worth, TX: 1999.

Lewy, Guenter. *America in Vietnam*. New York: Oxford University Press, 1978.

Lord, Walter. *Midway: Incredible Victory*. New York: Harper and Row, 1967.

Manchester, William. *American Caesar: Douglas MacArthur, 1880-1964*. New York: Dell Publishing, 1978.

McCullough, David. *Truman*. New York: Touchstone Books, 1992.

Millett, Allan R., and Peter Maslowski. *For the Common Defense: A Military History of the United States of America*. New York: The Free Press, 1984.

Norton, Mary Beth, et al. *A People and a Nation: A History of the United States*. 5th ed. Boston: Houghton Mifflin, 1999.

Perret, Geoffrey. *A Country Made by War: From the Revolution to Vietnam – the Story of America's Rise to Power*. 1989. Reprint. New York: Vintage Books, 1990.

Prange, Gordon W. *At Dawn We Slept: The Untold Story of Pearl Harbor*. New York: Penguin Books, 1982.

Reynosa, Mark A. *U.S. Combat Helmets of the 20th Century*. Atglen, Pennsylvania: Schiffer Military/Aviation History, 1997.

Ryan, Cornelius. *A Bridge Too Far*. New York: Popular Library, 1974.

———. *The Longest Day*. 1959. Reprint. New York; Popular Library, 1974.

Schwarzkopf, H. Norman. *It Doesn't Take A Hero*. New York: Bantam Books, 1992.

Stokesbury, James L. *A Short History of World War II*. New York: William Morrow and Co., 1980.

———. *A Short History of the Korean War*. New York: William Morrow and Co., 1988.

Summers, Harry G. *On Strategy: A Critical Analysis of the Vietnam War*. New York: Dell Books, 1984.

Tanks and Weapons of World War II. New York: Beekman House, 1973.

Weigley, Russell F. *History of the United States Army*. Bloomington: Indiana University Press, 1967.

———. *The American Way of War: A History of United States Military Strategy and Policy*. New York: Macmillan Publishing, 1973.

Wheal, Elizabeth-Anne, Stephen Pope, and James Taylor. *A Dictionary of the Second World War*. Peter Bedrick Books for Military Book Club, 1990.

INTERNET RESOURCES

U.S. MILITARY COMBAT HANDGUNS OF THE TWENTIETH CENTURY
Get the history of various handguns and find out what conflicts they were used in. Also includes photos and basic technical statistics.
http://www.wwa.com/~dvelleux/milhguns.htm

Aircraft Noseart and Decorations
www.Library.Arizona.edu/noseart

Humvee military vehicle data
www.Hummer.com

ARMY QUARTERMASTER FOUNDATION
Includes info on military rations
www.Qmfound.com

AIRCRAFT CARRIERS, BATTLESHIPS, NAVAL FORCES
Includes aircraft specifications
www.Skytamer.com

Spanish American War Centennial Site
www.Spanam.simplenet.com/mailbag/mmtokyorose.html

Information on Tokyo Rose
www.Straightdope.com

WORLD WAR I TRENCHES ON THE WEB
Contains info on the people, places, and events that comprised World War I
www.Worldwar1.com

U.S. Army official homepage which includes army alumni, association database, personnel locator and a center for military history.
http://www.army.mil/

U.S. NAVY HISTORY
Naval Historical Center provides introduction, FAQs, history of the Navy, with bibliographies and a list of publications.
http://www.history.navy.mil/

U.S. NAVAL INSTITUTE
Includes press, membership, seminar and exposition, and contact information. Also link to a naval history or proceedings magazine.
http://www.usni.org/

A vast collection of Korean War photographs from official and personal sources.
http://history1900s.about.com/cs/koreanwarphotos/index.htm?rnk=r2&terms=soldiers+in+combat

R. Steven Jones
Southwestern Adventist University
Keene, Texas

Towns

(1953) A drive-in movie theater marquee announces Sunday drive-in chapel services. By the 1950s, the drive-in theater had become a social hub of nearly every town in America.

TIMELINE

1565-1799 ~ Establishing Towns in Colonial America

Establishment of St. Augustine (1565), Jamestown (1607), Santa Fe (1610), Boston (1630) / New England port towns connect English trade routes to many parts of the world (1650-1750) / Annapolis, a seaport with considerable commerce, becomes the capital of Maryland (1694) / Puritan towns develop, through cooperative efforts, a public school system, town meeting government, and the comprehensive organization of the Congregational Church. (1700-1775) / By 1700, 120 towns are established in Massachusetts, Connecticut, Rhode Island and New Hampshire with more than 100 new towns founded in the next fifty years / By 1765, almost one-fifth of Pennsylvanians live in towns / Industrial Revolution reaches New England, generating a new type of town, the textile mill town; by 1812 there are twenty-two textile mills in New England (1780-1812)

MILESTONES: First African slaves arrive in America at Jamestown, Virginia (1619) • Savannah, Georgia is established as America's first planned city (1733)

1800-1899 ~ Opening the Frontier to Settlement

Number of incorporated towns grows from 56 in 1820 to 368 in 1860 / The transportation revolution of canals and railroads causes towns to quickly grow (1815-1860) / Half of all American commercial shipping is carried on the Mississippi River system (1840) / Discovery of Gold in California and Colorado cause mass migration westward and many new mining towns to be established (1848-1859) / Between 1867 and 1887, some 5.5 million cattle are driven north from Texas through central and western Kansas / Homestead Act of 1862 offers 160 acres of free public land to anyone who is 21 years old or the head of a family / Population west of the Mississippi River rises from 6.8 million in 1870 to 16.8 million in 1890

MILESTONES: The first public railroad, the Baltimore and Ohio (B & O) begins operations (1830) • Steamboat era causes towns to flourish along major rivers (1830-1930s) • Steampowered railroad opens the American West to settlement (1840-1950s) • Debates rage over restricting slavery in the western territories (1850) • Irish and Chinese laborers build a transcontinental railroad across the U.S. completing it at Promontory Point, Utah (1862-1869) • Alaskan gold rush begins after the discovery of gold in the Klondike (1896)

1900-1949 ~ Golden Days for Towns

Automotive revolution dramatically changes the character of towns (1920s) / U.S. Supreme Court in *Village of Euclid, Ohio v. Ambler Realty Co.* upholds the legality of zoning laws separating land uses, a step towards the widespread development of suburbs (1926) / Drive-in theaters become an important source of amusement in small towns (1933-1950) / Levittown, New York, a huge low-cost, homogeneous new town, is developed (1947)

MILESTONES: Ford Motor Company begins mass production of the automobile (1913) • Federal Aid Road Act begins government assistance to construct roads (1916) • For the first time more Americans live in urban than in rural areas (1920) • Rural Electrification Act brings electricity to rural areas (1935)

1950-1999 ~ Decline and Rebirth of Towns

The ratio of people to cars is four to one (1950) / Proliferation of regional shopping centers in suburbia (1950s) / Federal urban renewal programs attempt to revive inner cities (late 1950s) / First enclosed shopping mall in the U.S. opens near Minneapolis.(1956) / Interstate Highway Act funds a vast network of high-speed roads and opens vast new territory for suburban development (1956) / More Americans live in suburbs than in cities and there are twice as many people living and working in suburbs as those who commute to jobs in cities (1970s) / Interstate highways create commerce on the edges of towns and cause town centers to collapse (1970s) / White flight to the suburbs increases urban deterioration (1970s) / Ratio of people to cars is two to one (1990)

MILESTONES: Baby Boom, low unemployment, and increase in life expectancy create more housing demand; housing starts reach 1.7 million (1950) • Proliferation of ranch-style houses (1950s) • Establishment of nationwide motel chains (1950s) • Federal home loan programs discriminate against minorities (1950s-1960s) • First McDonald's opens (1952) • Expansion of mobile home and condominium apartments market (1960s) • Housing Act includes mortgage interest subsidies for low- and moderate-income rental housing and condominiums, and a subsidy for apartments for the elderly in public housing projects (1961) • Increase in single person households creates demand for condominiums (1980s) • High inflation, high interest rates, high unemployment reduce housing starts (1980s) • Proliferation of attached two-story single-family housing in suburbia (1980s) • Housing and Urban-Rural Recovery Act provides funds for housing for the elderly, handicapped, and homeless (1983) • Savings-and-loan institutions begin collapsing, causing the worst banking crisis since the Depression (1988) • First major Housing Act since 1974, National Affordable Housing Act provides matching funds for new construction and rehabilitation of renter-occupied and owner-occupied housing (1990)

INTRODUCTION

A town is a human settlement, generally a group of neighborhoods, larger than a single-neighborhood village. Social historians debate at what size towns can be classified as small cities, but a town may be defined as much as a product of function as of size. Towns incorporate a mixture of commercial and residential uses, churches, and schools, all within a close proximity. Towns are formed when a physical settlement with an interdependent community joins together under some type of incorporation. Towns, in American history, ideology, and actuality have been the source of a sense of place, an identity, and a social and spiritual rootedness. In his *Cities on the Move* (1970), Arnold Toynbee said in this regard that "man cannot live in a state of spiritual rootlessness....man is by nature a social being....he must continue to have neighborly personal relations with a small enough group of fellow human beings to allow the relations between him and them to be close and intimate." Autonomous small towns have long been an American ideal, a concept that was highly favored by Thomas Jefferson, who believed that cities were not a desirable form of settlement.

Although towns arbitrarily might be said to have populations generally ranging between 1,500 and 20,000, population cannot be the sole measure. Towns have more limited economic functions than cities and have more homogeneous populations. They also serve a much smaller tributary area or hinterland that depends on the distance people are willing to travel to procure the goods and services available in the town. In the seventeenth and eighteenth centuries, the Atlantic seacoast towns had populations of fewer than 15,000, but they participated in international trade and their citizenry included a wide range of merchants, shippers, artisans, whalers, professionals, and laborers. These towns also served a large tributary area and functioned more like small cities than towns even though their population was less than city size.

The economic base of towns is generally a primary activity such as agriculture, forestry, fishing, manufacturing, or mining. Towns can also be engaged in tourism or seasonal recreation and therefore have a population that varies during the course of a year. Towns also engage in secondary activities such as retailing, construction and the provision of professional services and entertainment. Cities engage in the tertiary, or third level of economic activity, distributing manufactured goods and providing a broad and complex variety of services to a large population. There are wide overlaps in these categories and often towns, although small, provide a variety of services to their consumers.

1820-1860 • THE FOUNDING OF TOWNS

Most towns in the United States were established in the eighteenth and nineteenth centuries and were separated by horse-and-buggy distances. The forty years preceding the Civil War were a period of very rapid town development. In 1820 there were only fifty-six incorporated towns numbering between 2,500 and 25,000 residents. By 1860 there were 368 towns in that category, 300 with populations of 2,500-10,000 and 68 with 10,000 to 25,000. Of the sixty-eight larger municipalities, 43 were in the Northeast and Middle Atlantic states, 13 were in the eastern part of the Midwest, one was in California, and 11 were in the Southwest and the southern portions of the Ohio and Mississippi valleys. With the exception of the older seaports and the newly-settled towns of the frontier, most of these towns were developed to serve established rural areas. Using 2,500 as the minimum population of an urban area as the Census Bureau does, the United States was only six percent urban in 1800, 40 percent in 1900, 51 percent in 1920, and more than 75 percent in 2000. Most of the urban growth in the last half of the twentieth century has been suburban to cities; cities per se have diminished while relatively few towns have been created in the twentieth century.

THE STRUCTURE OF TOWNS ~ The layout of towns can best be seen from an airplane, a viewing position that reveals more clearly the spatial arrangements of buildings, the roads that connect one town with another, the physical relationships of towns to natural features such as waterways and harbors, mountains and valleys, or the open plains. Towns generally were developed with formalized patterns rather than haphazard spatial arrangements.

MAIN STREET USA ~ Town patterns vary regionally. New England towns are distinctive with their clusters of white frame buildings, among them the characteristic tall-spired church, the town hall, the town commons, the variety of small shops, and the dignified white frame houses sheltered by large trees. The spatial arrangements of towns in the Pennsylvanian culture area, which are most evident in southeastern and central Pennsylvania and Piedmont Maryland, are quite different. Those towns have closely-situated, even attached, mostly brick buildings in linear arrangements centered on a town square. Residences are often intermixed with commercial and institutional structures.

(circa 1950) A signpost at the center of Pennsylvania Dutch territory. The province of the Mennonites or 'plain' people, the towns and hamlets bear unusual names.

1820-1860

The most characteristic pattern is that of the Main Street town in the Midwest where towns are simple grids of streets, regular and at right angles, with only the railroad cutting through them on the diagonal. There is one principal street, along which are two- and three-story brick commercial buildings that house banks, stores, barber shops, perhaps a movie theatre, and a cafe or two. The functions are rigidly separated, with the residences located away from the business section. Many towns in other parts of the country that were not developed until the nineteenth century adopted the basic Midwest town plan.

Towns in the Southwest that reflect a Spanish influence are centered on a large plaza, once a marketplace, now a park, lined on four sides by businesses and often a large church. Other business streets radiate out from the plaza.

1815-1860

Centrality is the principal organizing feature of towns in general. The business, social, and sometimes religious life of the town is centered on Main Street, the plaza, the courthouse square, or the town commons. In these centers are situated the tallest and most prominent and significant buildings, the courthouses and town halls, the banks and other important businesses. Exceptions, placed away from the center, typically include factories, hospitals, and high schools.

In New England, which began as a theocracy (God-centered community), Congregationalist meetinghouses were always central. In the Midwest, the center of town includes the banking corner, where a prominent brick or stone bank building or two dominate Main Street. Churches in the Midwest are usually located around the periphery of the commercial core, between it and the residential districts. Density, height, and the durability of building materials are also characteristic of town centers. The lower density uses or those that require the greatest space are located on the outer periphery. These can be larger residential lots, baseball fields, fairgrounds, golf courses, or small industries.

In addition to the cultural significance and symbolism of centrality, locating the commerce, churches, and entertainments in town centers permits the most convenient access for the greatest number of people. This principle also explains the spacing of towns, which ideally are located in the center of the market region they service. In cases where towns are located on waterways and the downtown area is directly on the waterfront, the typical concentric circle formation of town centers is interrupted by the water. If there is a bridge, a second half of the circle will often develop on the opposite shore.

Because of their small size, towns are more egalitarian than hierarchical; that is, the town functions more as a unit than as separate parts. To be sure, there are distinct differences between classes, but the prosperity of everyone, including the wealthy, generally depends upon the general prosperity of the town. Social differences, particularly in the sizes, locations, and conditions of houses are described in Henry Bellamann's novel *King's Row* (1960), which is set at the end of the nineteenth century: "Union Street was the town's principal business street. It ran north and south and passed the imposing west front of the courthouse, which occupied the center square of the town. Federal Street, next in importance, ran east and west and lay on the north side of the square. West of Union was Walnut Street; east of it was Cedar. On these four streets, within a few blocks of the courthouse square, was the best residence section of the town. . . . These were social boundaries. Every step away from these clearly marked precincts took one a step downward in the well-defined and perfectly understood social order of Kings Row."

Where towns arose to serve an already-established rural settlement area, their initial purpose was generally to store and market surplus agricultural products. Towns next provided inns or hotels and eating places for travelers and began to supply the consumer goods and personal services needed by those in their tributary area. Social and entertainment functions followed and towns also became communications centers as the publication of newspapers flourished.

1815-1860 • CANALS AND RAILROADS LINK TOWNS ~ The development of transportation systems was key to the history of town development in the United

States. Henry Adams wrote in 1889 of the bad roads and untamed rivers that had remained unchanged for a century. Ocean trips to Europe, he said, were more comfortable and more regular than the voyage from New York to Albany or through Long Island Sound to Providence. Transportation problems retarded the growth of trade until the turnpikes and canals that were built after the war of 1812 began to link western farmers and merchants with manufacturers in the Northeast and to serve developing industries. For example, the catalyst for most of the growth of Kingston, New York was the Delaware and Hudson Canal, built during the 1820s to connect the coal fields of Pennsylvania to the Hudson River Valley where the town was located. By 1840 after a decade of canal operations, the town's population had doubled to 6,000 and by 1860 it exceeded 15,000. It was transformed by what has been termed the transportation revolution of the period between 1815 and 1860.

The most impressive transportation advance in U.S. history was the building of the railroads. Railroad construction began in the United States around 1830 and by 1930 there were more than 400,000 miles of track. The shipment of products from coast to coast by railroad made the country a functional economic whole and towns that were on the railroad had a much greater chance of economic success.

THE CONCEPT OF COMMUNITY

The concept of community in towns is based on the principle that the individual is a member of a society of interdependent parts, which might be said to be a distillation of the various philosophies and ethical systems of civilization. Relationships in towns between individuals are based on detailed knowledge of character, family history, and current status. Most of the people encountered on a daily basis are familiar, whereas in cities the majority of people encountered are strangers. If the community of interdependence principle is honored, inhabitants of towns have an assurance of their value to the community that is much more difficult to achieve in a city. The other side of this social construct is that towns are small enough to allow any person's reputation, whether of honor or shame, to be known to others and this operates as a controlling social force that is not always welcome.

Towns are part of the visual, humanized landscape of America. They are geographical places overlain with social and cultural meaning and context. The interrelationship of structures, streets, natural features, and inhabitants, makes the town an emotionally significant place, a source of human identity. The combination of the physical reality and the social exchanges, successes and failures experienced in the community creates a mental map by which members of the community find and keep their bearings. Towns provide a sense of chronological connection in the continuum of history.

The historian Frederick Jackson Turner contended in his 1893 essay "The Significance of the Frontier in American History," that the most important effects of the ever-moving-westward American frontier were the promotion of democracy and the development of a distinctly national character. It was on the frontier that immigrants were Americanized and that the rare individual initiative of Americans was developed. Turner's theory was subsequently challenged by other historians, who pointed out that the new Western state constitutions were based on those of the East and that the ideas and institutions that the pioneers carried into the West were more important than their experiences after they settled there. In other words, the new states were democratic because they were settled by people who believed in democratic ideals. Nevertheless, the image of the frontier town as a bastion of social equality and individualism is a popular one that has persisted and towns in general, by extension, became the essential America.

1650-1775 AMERICAN TOWNS BEFORE THE REVOLUTION

NEW ENGLAND ~ The colonial economy was a coastal one in its initial period. Travel and transport were predominantly by water so the earliest towns were mostly on river harbors close to the ocean. They served as collection points for raw materials and agricultural products that were exported and for the return flow of imported manufactured goods as well as supplying the auxiliary services to this trade.

In New England, poor soils, a harsh climate, and few natural resources resulted in an economy based on the ocean. Fishing, whaling, timber exports, shipbuilding, and shipping services became mainstays. New Bedford and Nantucket were the centers of the whaling fleet. New Englanders established shipbuilding towns on nearly every navigable river that was near an accessible supply of timber. English trade routes connected many distant points of the world between 1650 and 1750 and the New England port towns became a vital part of that system.

These New England towns founded for reasons of religious utopianism were physically, and in some ways administratively, patterned on the English towns that the colonists had known. Thirty to forty families, the Puritan leaders believed, were the ideally-sized groups for constituting a town, small enough for adequate social exchange and large enough to provide some social balance. Towns and church congregations were initially one and the same and the town government was undertaken as a covenant.

The physical layouts of these Puritan towns harked back to feudal manor patterns in England. The towns were either nucleated, i.e., clustered around a center that contained the meetinghouse, the town market, and the town commons, or strung out along a wide central street. Town leaders tried to keep the towns compact and complete and to prevent dispersion. At first people who lived in these small clustered local communities went out the surrounding area each morning to tend their fields and came back to the town at night. Eventually though, more people moved to live on their farms as they acquired additional land. Still there was an extraordinary cohesion in the New England towns. The religious unity, although attenuated over time, was the social cement that held the New England towns together and allowed their governance by consensus. Before the American Revolution the Puritan towns had developed, through cooperative efforts, the public school system, town meeting government, and the comprehensive organization of the Congregational Church.

New Englanders were extremely loyal to their towns and were characteristically suspicious of outsiders. They used words such as "townsman" and "town-born." Even in Boston, on the night of the Boston massacre, the cry went out, "Town-born, turn out!" Animals were branded with each town's mark rather than with an individual's mark. Loyalty to community was exemplified by a Massachusetts Puritan statute requiring that "no man shall give his swine any corn but such, as being viewed by two or three neighbors, shall be thought unfit for any man's meat."

The Puritans brought governance from England in the form of town meetings, town selectmen, town covenants, and town records. When problems arose, the leaders of the town called general meetings to decide the issues. Throughout the smaller municipalities of New England, town meetings have remained an institution over the history of the nation.

By 1700 there were 120 towns in Massachusetts, Connecticut, Rhode Island and New Hampshire with more than 100 new towns founded in the next fifty years. The number of towns established in New England grew from an average of six per year before 1760 to eighteen per year between 1760 and 1776, a total of 283 new towns in sixteen years. In 1790 there were 101 towns in Connecticut alone.

CHESAPEAKE BAY COLONIES ~ The Chesapeake Bay colonies also had a predominantly coastal economy although it was very different from that of New England. Along the magnificent estuary that is the Chesapeake Bay, 200 miles long with 50 navigable rivers and 8,000 miles of shoreline, were extensive acreages of alluvial soil, well-suited for growing tobacco, a crop for which there was a huge European demand. The rivers, creeks, and inlets of the Bay provided the needed water egress for the transport of tobacco to waterfront warehouses where it was inspected, weighed, graded and shipped out. By the end of the century, tobacco was the leading source of income for the Chesapeake Bay colonies of Virginia, Maryland, and North Carolina.

Except for the coastal shipping ports, towns did not develop at first in this setting. The early settlements were at first crude outposts near the water; later there were neighborhoods of small planters struggling with owner-operated farms, aided by indentured servants who were hoping to become tobacco planters on their own. The settlers encountered a climate that was extremely unhealthy; diseases such as malaria, dysentery, and typhoid fever produced a frightening degree of mortality. There was a high incidence of mobility and out-migration. Without towns the settlers felt threatened and isolated. Robert Beverley, in his seventeenth century *History and Present State of Virginia*, wrote that the colonists on the Bay had "fallen into the same unhappy form of settlements, altogether upon country seats without towns." Instead, houses, churches, schools, stores, and mills were scattered here and there over the countryside. The era of the small planters dwindled at the end of the seventeenth century giving way to the great planters who presided over the cultivation of huge tracts of land worked by contingents of black slaves. These plantations assumed the functions that would normally be those of towns with the lords of the manor controlling the civil and religious institutions of the society.

There was some town development at the beginning of the eighteenth century. Annapolis, a seaport with considerable commerce, became the capital of Maryland in 1694. It prevailed as a colonial center of wealth and culture although its population remained fewer than 5,000 people. Williamsburg was designated the capital of Virginia in 1699 and was the economic, educational, reli-

(1786) The Maryland State House where the Annapolis Convention took place in 1786.

gious, social, and governmental center of Virginia until 1779 when the capital was moved to Richmond.

Port Tobacco, in Charles County, Maryland, was the largest of the county's market towns and the busiest river port on the Maryland side of the Potomac before the Revolution. At least a thousand hogsheads, containing more than a million pounds of tobacco, passed through its nearby inspection warehouse. This tobacco was shipped from the town of Port Tobacco to Britain, France, Holland, and Russia. In the 1750s Port Tobacco had a population of only seventy but it included several inns, a goldsmith's shop, and a brewery with a kiln and a two-story, sixty-foot-long malthouse. There was a public square where farm produce was sold, a church, a courthouse, merchants' and artisans' shops, and an assortment of houses. There were also a jail, a whipping post, and a gallows in the public square. The dirt streets were strewn with crushed oyster shells.

Within a ten-mile distance of Port Tobacco were two smaller towns, Newport and Nanjemoy, which between them, added another million pounds of tobacco to Charles County's annual outbound shipments. Benedict, on the Patuxent River, was the second largest town in Charles County. It was nineteen miles east of Port Tobacco and served as the trade center for the northeastern part of the county. Benedict exported seven hundred hogsheads of tobacco each year. Channeled back through these towns were the imports that the colonists needed: fabrics, clothing, china, housewares and furnishings, bridles, saddles, whips, paper, books, garden tools, rope, twine, and nails.

The pace of urban development accelerated after 1720. In addition to tobacco ports, new towns developed to service the wheat and corn economies that were emerging around the edges of the tobacco region; these were towns such as Chestertown and Norfolk in the 1720s and 1730s, Frederick and Winchester in the 1740s and 1750s, and Baltimore, Alexandria, Fredericksburg, Richmond, and Petersburg in the 1760s and 1770s. Whereas the tobacco towns had limited populations and a limited array of merchants and craftsmen, these newer towns had much larger populations and provided many more services and stores. The Chesapeake colonies were at last becoming more urbanized, although just prior to the American Revolution approximately 85 percent of the population remained engaged in agriculture.

1710-1770 • TOWN DEVELOPMENT: NEW YORK TO FLORIDA ~ The Middle Colonies of Delaware, Pennsylvania, New Jersey, and New York began with a pluralistic society made up of a variety of ethnic and religious groups, unlike New England and the Chesapeake, both of which were settled mainly by the English. Quakers, Mennonites, Amish, and Scotch-Irish, from Germany, England, and the north of Ireland combined to increase the population of the Middle Colonies from 63,000 in 1710 to 520,000 in 1770. The economy was diverse and balanced by the eighteenth century, but wheat and grain exports predominated, being as important to these colonies as tobacco was to the Chesapeake.

In Pennsylvania tightly-organized Quakers, Mennonites, and Amish settled in an open-country pattern. William Penn's attempts to establish agricultural villages failed almost totally. Family farms in neighborhoods without centers were the primary source of early economic production.

Philadelphia and New York, towns that grew into cities in the eighteenth century, soon exceeded Boston in both population and commerce. Smaller urban centers after 1730 included towns such as Burlington, Perth Amboy, New Brunswick, Trenton, Elizabethtown, and Newark, New Jersey; Newcastle, Delaware, and Albany, New York; Albany had nearly four thousand inhabitants by 1775. During this period, 55 new towns emerged in Pennsylvania and Delaware as county seats and transport and processing centers. By 1765, almost one-fifth of Pennsylvanians lived in towns.

Further south, Charleston, an ocean port that was the first permanent settlement in South Carolina, functioned for years as an adjunct to the West Indian economy, sending large quantities of agricultural products, naval stores, and Indian slaves to Barbados, the Leeward Islands, and Jamaica, in return for sugar products and black slaves. Rice became a very profitable export after 1690, forming the basis of South Carolina's enormous wealth in the mid-eighteenth century. North Carolina Atlantic ports, on the other hand, remained quite small during the colonial period.

Savannah was established by James Oglethorpe in 1733 on the Savannah River eighteen miles from the Atlantic Ocean. As a town it was unique in colonial America because of its beautiful and distinctive plan of monumental public squares on which faced generously-sized residential lots and dedicated public building lots over a 900-acre area.

Further south on the Atlantic Coast, heat, humidity, insects, and disease hindered town development in East Florida. Many early attempts to establish settlements there were tragic failures. The Spanish, however, had established St. Augustine in East Florida in 1565 and Pensacola, in West Florida in 1696. The British took over the Spanish garrisons at the ports of Pensacola and Mobile in West Florida in 1763 where they set about establishing towns. Another port came into being in the 1770s at the dilapidated Mississippi River fort called "The Natches." At this beautiful and fertile spot with its high cliffs above the river, the elegant town of Natchez would soon develop.

1680-1750 • NEW ENGLAND INDUSTRIAL TOWNS ~ As the Puritans began to disperse from their original covenanted towns, or as the phrase goes, as the Puritans became Yankees, some began to speculate in land, acquiring thousands of acres to sell at a profit. In the Connecticut River valley, the Pynchon family developed Springfield in the western part of Massachusetts as a company town by securing much of the land and creating a monopoly of trade. The Pynchons owned all of the gristmills and sawmills and employed a large proportion of the adult males in their many agricultural, processing, and trading enterprises. By 1680 approximately fifty percent of the adult males in Springfield were dependent on this company town, locked into an exploitative socioeconomic system that was in stark contrast to the original New England egalitarian towns.

In the late eighteenth century, the industrial revolution reached New England, generating the development of a new type of town, the textile mill town. In 1812 there were twenty-two textile mills in New England. The Merrimac River mill towns north of Boston included Lowell, one of the best known. There, in a revolutionary development, the young women from the farm areas around the town attained jobs in the mill and advanced socially and economically. By 1841 they had accrued $100,000 in the Lowell Savings Bank. For years Lowell was the showplace of the textile industry.

After 1850, however, when the mill owners began paying much lower wages to an immigrant labor force and requiring that they work "from dark until dark" and then with the invention of gas lighting, from twelve to fourteen hours a day, the mill towns of New England became places of social unrest. Women made up more than three-fifths of the mill labor forces and a significant proportion were children under the age of twelve. Organized labor began to agitate for shorter working hours and higher conditions and the mills were unionized. Because they were dependent on southern cotton, they could no longer compete after the Civil War when the South opened its own textile mills with a local supply of cotton and non-union labor. By the twentieth century the manufacture of textiles was primarily a southern industry in the United States.

1800-1900 • RIVER TOWNS ~ Prior to the building of the railroads, settlers in Kentucky and southern Ohio had to follow a very circuitous route to transport their produce and livestock to Eastern markets. At first flatboats were poled down the Ohio and Mississippi Rivers to New Orleans, then their cargoes were loaded on sailing ships and delivered by sea to the northern ports. Soon packet boats, which were keelboats with passenger cabins, made regular trips up and down the two rivers. After 1812, steamboats, laden with cotton and passengers, traveled constantly up and down the Mississippi and the Ohio for sixty years. By 1840, half of all American commercial shipping was carried on the Mississippi River system by some 3,000 steamboats and smaller boats. In the

(1870) Two river boats belch black smoke in a Great Race on the Mississippi. One is the U.S. Mail carrier, 'Natchez' and the other the pleasure boat 'Robert E Lee'.

1870s, passenger travel on the rivers was replaced by the railroads, which reduced the travel time to one third of what it had been on the river.

River towns along the Mississippi River system were unique in American history. The centers of these towns were the river wharves. Mark Twain, who grew up in Hannibal, Missouri, yearning to be a riverboat pilot—a dream he later fulfilled—revisited the river towns of the Mississippi in the 1880s and wrote about what he saw in *Life on the Mississippi*. The towns ranged from sleepy small places that only came to life when river boats arrived to constantly bustling cities such as New Orleans. There were the old French towns such as St. Genevieve, sixty miles below St. Louis, which had been settled by the French "when one could travel from the mouth of the Mississippi to Quebec and be on French territory the whole distance." Some of the towns were rough places where the brawling river crews went to drink, fight, and sometimes murder each other. Many were pretty towns set on the hills above the river. Hannibal was no longer a mere village when Twain visited it in the 1880s; it now had "a mayor, a council, and water-works... and fifteen thousand people." The towns that Mark Twain saw and described on his trip were all scenic places that had once been successful because of their location on the river, but the ones that were prospering in the 1880s were the ones that had been reached by railroads.

Show boats were another special feature of the river towns. Theatrical troupes traveling by boats to the river towns brought melodramas, minstrel shows, and vaudeville along with brass bands and steam calliopes on small boats at first and then later on larger and larger boats, culminating in the largest productions on the paddle-wheel steamboats. Show boats became less popular after the Civil War and by 1900 only about 25 were left.

1800-1900

1840-1900 • MINING TOWNS

By the 1840s, frontier settlement had reached the eastern edge of the Great Plains. Settlement then leapfrogged over the "vast American wasteland," as the Great Plains were called, to the Pacific Coast. Settlers had already been streaming to California when gold was discovered at Sutter's Fort in 1848. Some 80,000 people came to California and mining camps and towns emerged overnight. In 1859 a gold strike near Pike's Peak in Colorado started a rush to the eastern edge of the Rocky Mountains and by 1860 the population of the Territory of Colorado was 35,000. The Colorado towns of Black Hawk, Golden, Central City, Mount Vernon, and Nevada City were all founded in 1859; Breckrenridge, Empire, Gold Hill, Georgetown, and Mill City were founded in 1860 and 1861.

Also in 1859 Nevada was carved out of Utah after the Comstock Lode, the world's richest vein of silver, was discovered in the mountains near Lake Tahoe. Virginia City, Nevada became the most famous mining town of the Far West. Gold was also discovered in 1860 in eastern Washington and in Idaho and Montana, leading to new settlements. Gold was discovered at French Creek in the Black Hills of South Dakota in 1874. The town boomed to a population of 6,000 by the winter of 1875-1876. The gold at French Creek was soon exhausted and the rush to Deadwood, South Dakota began. People surged into South Dakota and in the next decade the population had more than tripled to 330,000. Another mining town was Tombstone, Arizona, established in 1879. In 1896 there was a gold strike in the Klondike region of Alaska that brought 30,000 miners in two years.

Mining towns were often lawless, wildly exuberant, and out-of-control places. Dr. Henry F. Hoyt, who set up his medical practice in Deadwood, South Dakota for a while in the 1870s, wrote in *A Frontier Doctor* about the town: "Miners came into town in droves on Saturday nights, and surely made the dust fly. One night I heard a commotion and down the street came a woman on a horse at full gallop. She had a Colt forty-five in each hand, and both were in action, the bullets flying in every direction, while the rider emitted a good imitation of an Indian war-whoop at every jump of her mount. This was my first closeup of that well-known figure of the pioneer West, Calamity Jane. She was dressed in soldier's uniform and was the first female I had ever seen riding astride."

Sometimes lynch law, popular courts, and self-appointed vigilantes had to enforce order. There were several committees of vigilance in San Francisco during the gold rush. The first was formed in 1851 when the city administration failed to control gangs of outlaws. The vigilantes seized and executed one outlaw leader, then sentenced his gang members to death, deportation or whipping, which frightened other outlaws out of town. Other vigilance committees took direct action against corrupt law officers in the mining towns of Montana and Idaho. In January of 1864, vigilantes tried and executed Henry Plummer, who doubled as sheriff in the daytime and a leader of highwaymen at night. In the spring of 1866 Idaho vigilantes executed David Updyke, who acted both as sheriff and a leader of horse thieves and highwaymen.

The influx of miners into new areas also frequently caused difficulties with Indian tribes. The Smoky Hill Trail across Kansas Territory, which was used by the Butterfield Overland Express across the 600 miles between Atchison and Denver, ran through the heart of Cheyenne and Arapahoe hunting grounds. The Army set up forts to protect travelers on the trail as they did in other areas of the United States where the federal government was forced to take a hand in protecting those rushing to the mining sites.

The miners led the way for other settlers to follow into these new and untried areas of the United States. They also created, along with the wild cattle towns of the West, a store of colorful American folklore that has provided much subject matter for books and films.

1860-1890 • CATTLE TOWNS
Cattle towns were another genre of quickly-growing, and difficult-to-control towns, this one arising from the realization by Texas ranchers in the 1860s that the wild grasses that had supported the buffalo in such huge numbers on the prairies could also provide excellent nutrition for cattle. The ranchers began driving Longhorns north through the plains to railheads so they could be shipped to the cattle markets in the northern and eastern parts of the country.

Abilene, in central Kansas, became the major railroad nexus between Texas cattle ranchers and cattle buyers. Between 1867 and 1887, some 5.5 million cattle were driven north from Texas through central and western Kansas. Joseph G. McCoy conceived the idea of establishing a place where the herds from Texas could be safely assembled without having to go through what was at that time a very dangerous area along the Kansas-Missouri border where gangs of outlaws waited to steal the cattle and rough up and sometimes kill the drovers.

McCoy established Abilene as the first cow town of the West in 1867. Initially, he couldn't decide whether the new shipping point would be on the prairies or on some southern river, but after meeting with cattle buyers and railroad officials, he settled on a rail connection on the newly-built Kansas Pacific to the Missouri River and on the Hannibal and St. Joseph Railroad from the Missouri River to Chicago.

When neither Salina nor Solomon City welcomed the idea of becoming a cow town, McCoy selected Abilene, a town that had been laid out in lots in 1860, but still had very little development. As he wrote: "Abilene in 1867 was a very small, dead place, consisting of about one dozen log huts, low, small, rude affairs, four-fifths of which were covered with dirt for roofing; indeed, but one shingle roof could be seen in the whole city. The business of the burg was conducted in two small rooms, mere log huts, and of course, the inevitable saloon, also in a log hut. . . . " McCoy believed that Abilene was the farthest point east at which a good cattle depot could be established. He bought a trainload of pine from Hannibal, Missouri and built stockyards, pens, and loading chutes, and within sixty days he had the facilities for 3,000 head of cattle. He then set out to inform Texas cattlemen of the availability of the new shipping center.

Abilene became the endpoint of the Chisholm Trail, the most traveled of the great Western cattle trails. Thirty five thousand cattle were shipped out of the town that first fall, most of them to Chicago and points farther east. In the next four years an additional 1,425,000 cattle were brought to Abilene for shipping. By 1870 the town had four hotels, ten boardinghouses, five dry-goods stores,

1860-1890

a dozen saloons, and a large red light district. The largest of the hotels was the Drover's Cottage, built by Joseph McCoy. The Drover's Cottage had a hundred rooms and barns and corrals accommodating fifty carriages and a hundred horses. The red light district was confined by the town council to the southeast section of town, where the prospering prostitutes built houses, beer gardens, dance halls, dancing platforms, and more saloons. After riding 600 miles from Texas and surviving dust, rustlers, Indians, prairie fires, stampedes, rattlesnakes, and some very long hours and hard work, the drovers, after they had delivered their cattle to the rail yards and had their wages in their pockets, were ready to have some fun. They had a few drinks, a hot bath, bought some new clothes, and took on the town. Along Texas Street, or "Hell Street," as it was called by the law-abiding citizens of the town, the saloons were open twenty-four hours a day. These ranged from those that catered to the cow hands to the more elegant ones, patronized by the trail bosses, cattle dealers, and those with real money to lose at the gambling tables.

The cow hands regularly shot up the town, especially when one of their number was put in jail, and strong lawmen were needed. After marshal Tom Smith was killed in 1870, the town hired Wild Bill Hickok as the new marshal. A few days after his arrival in the spring of 1871, Hickok was very unpopular with the cowhands. With his long hair and long moustaches and dressed in a Prince Albert coat, checked trousers, embroi-

(circa 1900) A young Dwight David Eisenhower (1890-1969) with his brothers outside the family house in Abilene, Kansas. General Eisenhower was Supreme Commander of the Allied troops in Europe during World War II and served as President of the United States from 1952-1958.

dered vest, and sometimes a cape lined in red silk, he rigidly enforced the no-guns ordinance, and unlike Tom Smith, he did it without talking politely first. "Talk about a rule of iron," Joseph McCoy later wrote, "We had it in Abilene. We had to rule that way. There was no fooling with the courts of law. When we decided that such a thing was to be done we did it. Wild Bill cleaned up the town and kept it clean, but we had to kill a few roughs to do it" (from O'Connor's *Wild Bill Hickok*). By 1885, the railroads had been extended into Texas and Abilene's days as a wild cattle town ended.

There were many cattle towns: Dodge City, Kansas was notorious for its frequent murders and wicked ways. In fact, the press called it "the wickedest little city in America." In 1870, the population of the townsite area consisted of only the 427 people at the Fort Dodge military installation, which had been organized nearby to protect travelers on the Santa Fe Trail. A trading post was established nearby for buffalo hunters in 1872, the same year the Atchison, Topeka, and Santa Fe Railroad came through and soon the cattle trade was booming. By 1880 a half million steers a year were being shipped out of Dodge City and the drovers were there in the thousands.

Railroadmen, soldiers, cowboys, hunters, and freighters mixed on Dodge City's Front Street and made the town world famous for being unable to curtail its violence and wild living. In one year alone, 25 victims of gunslingers were buried in Dodge's Boot Hill Cemetery. Kansas passed a prohibition on alcohol in 1880 in an attempt to curtail the lawlessness of the cattle towns.

The Texas longhorn trade in Dodge City was at the level of 300,000 per year until late in 1884, when a state-ordered quarantine on the driving of southern cattle into the area, which was by then being settled by farmers, ended it for all time.

1870-1900 • TOWNS OF THE GREAT PLAINS

The population of the area west of the Mississippi River rose from 6.8 million in 1870 to 16.8 million in 1890. The center of the corn and wheat belts shifted from the old Granger states of Illinois, Wisconsin, Minnesota, and Iowa, to the Populist states of Kansas, Nebraska, the Dakotas, and western Minnesota, mainly in response to the Homestead Act of 1862 that offered 160 acres of free public land to anyone who was 21 years old or the head of a family. The homesteader would receive patent to the land after five years' continued residence. By 1870, 14 million acres had been granted and by 1900, more than 80 million acres.

Towns led agriculture in the development of the Great Plains. They were often settled first, or at least concurrently with the influx of farmers and ranchers. The locations of towns generally followed the rail lines, which preceded settlement west of the 98th meridian, whereas east of that line development of the railroads had followed the population, connecting one town to another. A location on a rail line with a station stop was the best guarantee of success for a Great Plains town. Town commissions raised money through revenue bonds to pay for the construction of stations. Towns that could not attract rail lines soon lost population unless they could compensate by establishing a county seat or some other major economic function that would draw people and funds to their town.

There was a great deal of capitalist promotion in the settlement of the towns of the Great Plains. Speculators bought up town sites, divided them into lots, and sold them, hoping to make large profits. Towns were promoted shamelessly in all kinds of boomer literature that claimed that the Great Plains was a virgin paradise only waiting to have the sod broken and planted to make it the new Garden of Eden and that the particular town in question was a potential center of civilization and refinement with abundant commercial opportunities. The railroads participated in this boomer literature, recruiting immigrants from the Eastern states and from Europe. The writings even claimed that increased rainfall would follow cultivation of the semi-arid lands west of the 98th meridian.

Some Great Plains towns were rudimentary with their crude hotel, railroad station, and a line of flimsy one-story wooden structures that extended upward with false fronts clinging together along a truncated Main Street, but others were prodigiously developed by their promoters. WaKeeney, Kansas, named after its developers, Albert Warren and James Franklin Keeney, was one of the latter kind. Keeney was a Chicago real estate developer, a graduate of the University of Rochester, who had participated in the development of the Chicago suburbs of Ravenswood and South Evanston. He and Warren, after seeing the Kansas exhibit at the Centennial Exposition in Philadelphia in 1876, bought and optioned 340,000 acres of Kansas Pacific Railroad land in Trego County, Kansas. The railroad, in return, agreed to build a major depot with Keeney and Warren providing a Chicago architect. The two developers laid out eighty-foot-wide streets just like the ones in their Chicago suburbs. Through extensive lobbying, they had the location of the U.S. Land Office, which would handle the homestead claims and sales for fifteen counties, moved to their new town. By 1878, 40,000 acres had been sold to settlers and all the land within a ten-mile radius had been taken. A steam-powered flour mill and a stone hotel were built. Main Street was soon lined with an impressive array of stores.

However, even such energetically-developed towns as WaKeeney soon suffered setbacks as the economic downturns of the 1880s dried up financial credit and the exigencies of Great Plains weather cut crop yields to unprofitable levels. The railroads, in a fury of unregulated and highly competitive activity, had overbuilt all over the Great Plains in this period, even though the construction crews had to fight their way through herds of buffalo and stave off Indian attacks. There was little if any industry to be developed on the treeless prairies, only farming, and the aridity, plagues of

(1891) Emigrants searching for a place to settle in the wild American west.

grasshoppers, and extremes of hot and cold soon revealed how tenuous an economic basis farming was. As a result town development in the Great Plains in the late nineteenth century was tragically over-expanded on the basis of an anticipated rapidly growing population that did not materialize. The excessive numbers of businesses that were established in towns relative to their population bases led inevitably to many business failures.

The Great Plains towns that did survive and prosper were the ones on main railroad routes that were not too close to other towns with more drawing power, the ones that were county seats and therefore had a governmental function that created employment, or the ones that in the twentieth century served the emerging oil and gas industry.

1900-1920s • CHANGES IN TOWNS ~ Towns in the United States at the beginning of the twentieth century varied widely in their physical development, but they were all similar in that there were very few automobiles and none of the automobile-related features that later so revolutionized American life. Town streets at the beginning of the century were designed for horse-drawn vehicles, from wagons in country towns to fine carriages, hansom cabs, and fire wagons in the larger ones. Horse-drawn delivery wagons brought ice and dairy products daily and the sound of hooves formed a constant background to town life. Hitching posts and water troughs lined commercial streets and livery stables, harness makers, and blacksmiths were necessary town businesses. Many towns did not install paved streets, electric street lighting, public water systems, and concrete sidewalks until the prosperous years of the 1920s.

Prior to World War I American towns typically had a wide variety of small shops and stores, all within easy walking distance of one another. Often there were several stores of any one kind. There were dry goods retailers, milliners, bootmakers, jewelers, creameries, meat markets, confectionaries, stationary stores, pharmacies, grocery stores, with the customers in all served by the proprietor or the clerks. General stores combined the sale of all kinds of merchandise in country towns. The undertakers sold furniture as well as caskets. Hardware sales were combined with lumber yards. Piano stores sold sheet music. The presence of a railroad station with passenger service insured that there would be at least one hotel in the downtown area and often more than one. Most towns had a variety of restaurants, saloons, and cafes as well as opera houses where live stage shows were presented on a regular basis. Banks, real estate offices, and doctors' and lawyers' offices were interspersed with the stores. Often proprietors lived with their families over their stores. Doctors might have their offices over drug stores and lodges would meet on the second floors of banks. This lively mix presented a dynamic and active focus to town life.

Houses in American towns in the early years of the century were a mix of Georgian and Victorian architectural styles and enough of these have survived to let us know how they looked. What hasn't survived is the character of the yards that surrounded them, a sharp contrast to the flower gardens and neat green lawns of the latter part of the twentieth century. These earlier yards were until World War II embellished with large vegetable gardens, windmills, flapping clothes on clotheslines, outhouses, chickens roaming about, cats and dogs on the loose, stables, and even the occasional mother pig and piglets.

SMALL TOWN SOCIETY ~ The social atmosphere of towns in the pre-automobile and pre-television era was an active one. Towns had numbers of lodges and clubs, literary societies, and town bands. Plays were presented by dramatic societies throughout the year. The literary societies met regularly and children as well as adults were given chances to recite poems or take part in debates. Band concerts were held outdoors in the summer in the town park. Churches and clubs sponsored pie socials and box suppers. Towns of all sizes had baseball fields and sometimes horse racing tracks.

The big days of the year were those of a patriotic nature, Memorial Day (called Decoration Day) and Independence Day. A typical Independence Day celebration consisted of a grand street parade, with individuals representing each state of the union and many floats presenting patriotic themes. Several bands would participate and there would be an orator. There were footraces and horse races, a baseball game with a neighboring town, and often a steam merry-go-round. On Decoration Day with the memory of the Civil War still fresh in everyone's mind and many Civil War veterans still alive, there were elaborate celebrations sponsored by patriotic organizations such as the Grand Army of the Republic and the Women's Relief Corps. The celebrations always included an address by some notable speaker and a flag drill by the children. A parade down Main Street featured children dressed in white, carrying baskets of flowers followed by the veterans. The parades continued to the cemeteries where bouquets of flowers were placed on the graves.

(1918) American soldiers driving through streets during July 4th celebrations.

After World War I, a period of disillusionment and introspection somewhat dampened the enthusiasm of Americans for their wholesome and unaffected town-centered way of life. The United States had entered World War I with a crusading spirit and in the beginning it was a popular war, but in the end it seemed to many of its participants and observers an unheroic nightmare of blood, filth, and unspeakable suffering brought about by members of an older generation who did not have to die in its despicable trenches.

Young writers and painters survived the war to write bitterly about their experiences. The 1920s were characterized in general by an intellectual revolution against religion, Victorian propriety, and the ideals of community, all of which were typical of small town life. Sinclair Lewis, who grew up in Sauk Centre, Minnesota, satirized the narrowness of life in midwestern towns in his 1920's novel *Main Street*. His fictional town of Gopher Prairie is a somewhat ugly little town with pretentious aspirations to high culture that are laughable in any wider context. To the Swedish immigrants who farm around it and send their daughters to town to become domestics, Gopher Prairie is wonderful. To its heroine, who grew up in St. Paul and has a university education, but has been persuaded to marry one of Gopher Prairie's young doctors, it is shockingly unenlightened. The self-important denizens of the town look down on the Swedish farmers and servant girls and spend a lot of time gossiping. After a year of marriage, the heroine suddenly realizes that she has trapped herself in a very limiting way of life. Lewis was also subtly satirizing those who criticize small town life without offering a better alternative.

(circa 1930) American novelist Sinclair Lewis (1885 - 1951), the first American to win the Nobel prize for Literature. His novels, including 'Main Street' and 'Babbitt' expose the hypocrisy as well as the community feeling of small town life in America's midwest.

1920s • THE AUTOMOTIVE REVOLUTION

The 1920s were an era of trolley lines and railroads, the automobile revolution was responsible for the radical change in the function of towns and cities. Hitching posts and horse troughs began disappearing from America's Main Streets, replaced by traffic lights and signs; paved roads between towns became more common.

Cars revolutionized the American way of life. The freedom afforded by ready transportation allowed people to move away from the family home and the little town. Young people old enough to drive suddenly found a greatly expanded world available to them, not just in terms of distance, but also in social relation-

1920s-1940s

ships. In the mid-1920s Robert and Helen Lynd undertook a sociological examination of Muncie, Indiana, which they re-named "Middletown." They subjected the town to a "total situation study," which revealed that it had gone through many changes in social norms. In 1923 there were 6,221 passenger cars in Middletown, one for every 6.1 persons and two for every three families. Socially, cars were required. People were mortgaging their houses to buy cars. One woman told the Lynds it was more important to own a car than a bathtub. There was a new type of parent-teenager conflict over use of the family car, curfews, and the sexual freedom the car offered dating couples. Cars also became the despair of ministers as they lured people away from Sunday services. The Sunday afternoon drive became part of the Sunday ritual.

Many new popular forms of real estate development emerged that were the result of the mobility cars offered. There were the travel courts and camps, the precursors of motels that were sometimes established defensively by towns on their peripheries, the diners, and the curb-service restaurants with their canopies and car-hops. In later years many of these automobile-related innovations were standardized because of the influence of trade associations, chains, and franchises. However, before the 1960s, they were still interesting, attractive, and different, and they brought a new dimension to town life.

1920s-1930s • Entertainment ～ Radio and movies expanded the horizons of the Americans in small towns, beginning in the 1920s and 1930s. These became much needed diversions during the gloom of the thirties. Radio shows such as "Fibber McGee and Molly," "Henry Aldrich, the Great Gildersleeve," "Our Gal Sunday," "Pepper Young's Family," and many others, were set in towns; some of the most popular movies, however, led people's imaginations away from town life, depicting the glamorous lives of wealthy people in beautiful clothes living refined lives in cities. Fred Astaire and Ginger Rogers danced, Clark Gable and Carole Lombard cavorted in sophisticated comedies, and Nick and Nora Charles drank martinis and solved murders.

Every town in America had at least one movie theater before World War II and the new medium quickly became the most popular small town entertainment, replacing the opera house traveling shows and the amateur concerts and dramatic productions. Movie theater architecture aided the escapist theme of movies by enticing audiences with Art Deco, Southwest, Egyptian, Mayan, or Aztec buildings even in the smallest American towns. In 1933, Richard Hollingshead of New Jersey introduced a new idea in motion picture entertainment to the public, the drive-in theatre. Within twenty years, there were over 3,000 drive-in theatres in the United States, many of them on the edges of small towns.

1930s-1940s • The Depression: A Turning Point for Towns ～ The Great Depression and the Second World War slowed the movement of city people to the suburbs. The dust storms and loss of mortgaged farms increased the populations of many towns in rural areas as people retreated from the despair of agriculture. Then when World War II came, people left towns in large numbers to serve in the military and work in the war production industries in the cities. After the war, many in the two groups decided not to return to their home towns.

Population in the Great Plains peaked in the 1930s and then began a steady downslide that by the end of the twentieth century had culminated in a widespread emptying out of the center of the country. At first, during the Depression, the population of towns increased although overall population was decreasing. The towns were better able to survive the Depression than the rural areas. However, this was the beginning of a centralization trend with people gathering first in the small towns, then after World War II, in larger towns and cities. By the end of the twentieth century, only a few Great Plains towns were growing, benefiting from ongoing oil and gas production or the meat packing industries. From eastern Montana and North Dakota through South Dakota, Nebraska, Kansas, Oklahoma, and West Texas, the population dwindled until in 2000 there were in some areas many new "frontier counties," defined by the Census Bureau as having only two to six people per square mile. Towns that fell victim to this syndrome went through several predictable phases. The brightest of the high school graduates left for opportunities in other places, people traveled to larger towns to shop and then eventually to work, the stores on Main Street closed, the school districts consolidated to serve larger and larger areas with fewer and fewer students, churches merged with other churches and then closed, buildings were torn down and not replaced, and finally there were no businesses, only houses occupied by those who wanted to save money by living there.

As the Great Plains continues to lose population, the long-waged battle to establish agriculture against the forces of nature and to develop towns where there was little economic basis except for agriculture, seems to be exhibiting a losing turn. Towns in the Great Plains have not benefited from the return to small-town life that characterizes more attractive places such as Colorado, where the towns that were drying up in the 1970s and 1980s have experienced a turn-around in growth. The towns that remain in the Great Plains states have something of the character of an oasis in the desert with the unremitting wilderness reclaiming dominance in between, evoking memories of prairie grasslands, herds of buffalo, and the nomadic life of the earlier inhabitants, the Plains Indians.

1950s • THE CHANGING FUNCTION OF TOWNS ~ Towns in general in the United States appeared to be prospering in the 1950s. Downtown businesses were generally doing well; in some towns there were so many cars that public parking lots or parking meters had to be installed. There had been many changes in the types of stores in towns. Chain stores such as J.C. Penneys, Woolworths, A & P, and Western Auto, as well as department stores, had replaced many of the older types of retailing. Stores had become self-service and were larger. Nevertheless, the drug stores and dress shops, the restaurants and that new phenomenon, the motels, were still independently owned. Movie theaters, drive-in restaurants, and soda fountains all were thriving. Golf courses were being built in almost every town in the country so that by the 1970s twelve million Americans played golf on 10,500 courses and spent more than a half billion dollars each year on golf equipment. What had been a rich man's or an old man's game had become a sport for everyone.

1950s

Travel from one town to another allowed people in the 1950s to experience different qualities, not only varying physical settings and buildings, but also local customs, crafts, and cuisines. These differences could reflect ethnicity, climate, or the economic bases, whether they were water-related activities, mining, manufacturing, or agriculture. Some towns were flourishing because they were college towns. In a time when baseball was the national pastime and there were sixteen major league baseball teams in ten cities, many towns had unifying minor league farm teams. Some towns had race tracks; some were beach or mountain resorts. There were many fishing towns along the coast where the seafood was incomparably fresh. Some were company towns, where a single industry prevailed and almost everyone in town was an employee of that industry.

By the late 1950s, however, there were obvious ominous portents for American towns. Railroads cut their passenger service as more and more people were driving rather than taking the trains. Shopping centers were being built where they could be more easily accessed by cars, outside of existing town development. Suburban development on the edges of cities had burgeoned after World War II and by the 1960s was the obvious continuing trend. The suburban life style began to eclipse the small town life style. Older houses in small towns were consistently replaced with the ubiquitous suburban ranch houses with double garages and wide expanses of grass lawn. Living near the golf course in a one-story ranch house was considered preferable to living in a traditional house in the older residential section of town. At the same time people were regularly driving out of towns to shop at bigger stores and malls.

Before 1970 towns near cities and on major highways generally continued to do well. Other towns, not so advantageously located, began to lose their downtown businesses, although they maintained their residential component to some extent. Between the late 1960s and 1980 the small-town and rural population of the country actually grew faster than the metropolitan population, reversing a century of faster urban growth. After 1981, however, the rate of growth of metropolitan areas began to accelerate.

At some point towns lost their autonomy. Whereas once they were centers of local life governed by well-respected citizens who served without pay because it was an honor as well as a responsibility, in time towns became more or less extensions of federal and state governments. Every town has outposts of the Department of Agriculture, the Social Security Administration, state welfare agencies, and recruitment offices for the military. Although they still conduct transactions with municipal and county offices, town citizens also deal directly with government personnel in the offices of the distant power centers.

This trend began in the 1930s, as a result of the Great Depression, when it became necessary for those in political power to save the country from a socialist revolution by the creation of federal agencies that brought assistance directly to the people. The federal government intervened in the areas of agriculture, housing, social welfare, and the conservation of the natural environment and established local offices to carry out these functions. Entitlements (automatic government payments) such as Social Security, Medicare, Medicaid, veterans' benefits, welfare subsidies, food stamps, unemployment insurance, vocational training, disaster relief, and farm subsidies, among others, are paid to a majority of the American people. As a result local control of towns has been attenuated over the course of the twentieth century. Also towns are subject to the control of state and/or federal governments in the areas of property taxation, historic preservation, use of water and other natural resources, environmental pollution, and in many cases land development. This overall trend has produced towns that are more homogeneous, less subject to local idiosyncracies, and in which citizens may feel that they have less of a role to play. Nevertheless, town governments still have considerable influence and control over many areas of town development and life.

Towns have continued to exist but their development patterns have shifted. New commercial buildings—malls, furniture stores, discount stores, convenience stores, gasoline stations, drive-ins then fast-food restaurants, and motels—have been increasingly placed at the edges, not at the centers of towns because of more convenient automobile access. As highway interchanges were built outside of towns, new development grew around these interchanges. As this happened, the centers of towns began to fade and then collapse, as the energy moved to the edge.

Beginning in the 1960s, and increasingly thereafter, almost all commercial development not in central cities was engineered for the automobile. The endless suburban sprawl along the country's roadways is distinguished mainly by its lack of architectural appeal and its ready accessibility by car. The mostly one-story, mostly concrete, fast-food restaurants, motels, shopping centers, big-box stores, warehouses, and auto service facilities that line the streets, highways, and throughway interchanges of the country, together with their signs and their endless acres of parking, have created economical convenience for car travel and at the same time a loss of landscape, regional character, and beauty. Too many urban places now fit Gertrude Stein's description of Oakland, California: "What was the use of my having come from Oakland. . . there is no there, there." Simon Schama wrote in Landscape and Memory (1995) that we identify as human beings with what we see spread out before us and that it reflects back to us our idea of what we are. The desolation of the highway strip development that so dominates the American landscape conveys little in the way of permanence, culture, or beauty.

1970s • COMPOUNDING THE PROBLEMS DOWNTOWN ∼ The 1970s were a period of malaise in the United States. Due to the economic prosperity of the post-World War II period, much of the architectural and town planning fabric of the country had been thoroughly revamped. The sterility of modern architecture prevailed. New zoning concepts removed residences from commercial areas, and home offices and apartments from residential areas; and they proportioned and scaled construction for the accommodation of the automobile. Downtowns without parking garages and parking lots had been deemed non-functional, and consequently towns constructed hideous parking structures that interrupted the flow of commerce and imperiled pedestrians in what had been beautiful downtown areas. Town planners, dismayed at the decrease in the number of downtown shoppers, began devising ineffectual remedies, such as closing off selected streets to automobiles. This ploy, together with the creation of one-way streets to move rush-hour traffic, made downtown shopping even more inaccessible, motivating more people to drive to a shopping center.

1970s • Returning to Visually Stimulating Communities ~ During the 1970s many architects continued to express the Modernist wonders of technology in their work, but trends of discontent were developing. In 1966 Robert Venturi had published an influential work *Complexity and Contradiction in Architecture* that chastised the Modernist movement for its rejection of tradition. He favored a "messy vitality" in the fabric of towns and the symbolism of traditional shapes and forms such as gabled roofs on houses and roof cornices on Main Street stores. In the 1970s architects and town planners began to recognize that the dynamism of mixed-uses and the variety of styles, heights, and colors that had been eliminated by the Modernist movement were what made downtowns exciting and interesting places to be and that there needed to be neighborly relationships in the design and siting of houses. Streets needed to connect, not separate, buildings and people. However, recognizing the problem, although a beginning, still left the enormous task of undoing the damage done to towns by Modernism and the automobile economy.

1980s • Urban Sprawl ~ By 1980 traditional town life had been largely eclipsed by the development of suburbs around cities. Suburban development has existed in the United States since the mid-nineteenth century, but it played a minor role until the post-World War II period. In 1950 some 70 million Americans lived in cities and their suburbs in areas totaling approximately 13,000 square miles. By 1990, more than 140 million Americans lived in cities and their suburbs covering over 60,000 square miles. By the end of the century suburban sprawl was taking over farmland at an annual rate of 1.2 million acres and causing the average suburban family to make ten car trips per day and commuters to spend 500 hours per year in the car getting to a job an hour's drive away.

This huge expansion of suburban sprawl resulted from the desire of most home buyers to have a spacious new house on a spacious lot in a safe, clean, location with access to jobs and good schools, all at an affordable price. Existing towns, although they provided some of these attributes, often lacked the jobs and modernity that millions of Americans wanted. The suburbs provided what appeared to be the best possible alternative in that they were separated from the problems of the old center cities while still allowing access to employment, they were semi-rural in atmosphere, and the housing was spacious and affordable. The ease of owning and using a car made the suburban lifestyle accessible to the majority of Americans.

Suburban sprawl as the answer to the American quest for the ideal place to live has come at a high price that includes a loss of community and sense of place, the loss of human scale and beauty in architecture and the ongoing diminution of open space and farmland. The costs include greater and greater automobile traffic, unhealthy lifestyles that result in too little exercise for both children and adults, and the potential loss of a viable environment for human habitation on the Earth.

1980s • Not in My Backyard ~ By the 1980s suburban sprawl had also become a political issue. Those objecting to further development in their immediate area included the so-called NIMBYs (not in my back yard) and the BANANAs (build absolutely nothing anywhere near anything). These activists used zoning and subdivision regulations to create bureaucratic barriers to new development so that home builders were forced to jump over developed areas to build on vacant rural land further out, thereby worsening the sprawl. By the 1990s eco-terrorists were burning and defacing new subdivision houses in their protests against sprawl.

1980-2000 • RETURNING TO TRADITIONAL TOWN LIFE ~ The last two decades of the century brought about a return to regional architecture and to an espousal of traditional town life as it existed before Modernism came to dominate architecture and town planning in the middle years of the twentieth century. Leon Krier led a revival of Neoclassical architecture and the traditional town plans of the pre-Modern period in Europe. He favored a return to town squares, arcades, and distinctive public and private structures. In both Europe and the United States architects and town planners, following the ideas of Robert Venturi and Leon Krier, began to turn away from quirky postmodern designs to more accurate classical interpretations.

There had also arisen in the United States an academic interest in the relationships between architecture and the social relationships it engenders between people. The historic preservation movement that had emerged to fight redevelopment and to preserve America's pre-Modernist architectural heritage fostered an interest in restoring some old buildings and adaptively reusing and updating others. The historic preservation movement also brought a concern for not wasting the existing infrastructures of towns; why build everything on the edge where new streets and utilities had to be constructed at an enormous cost when there already was an existing infrastructure in place in the middle of town?

1980s • THE NEW URBANISM ~ At the same time there developed an intensified concern with the environmental problems caused by population growth, widespread use of automobiles, too much technology, too much industrialization, and too little regard for the elimination of forests, all of which were polluting the air, heating up the Earth's climate and thinning the atmosphere's protective ozone layer. The return to regional architecture, to pre-Modernist town planning and Neoclassical architecture, the historic preservation movement, and concern for the environment all combined to produce the movement known as the New Urbanism.

The New Urbanism movement is based on the idea that land uses in traditional towns, which were clustered together, rather than zoned apart, provided a better way of life, one that fostered civic pride and a connection with our history and our future as a people and a nation. Furthermore the New Urbanists believe that the automobile ought not to dictate the quality of American architecture. New Urbanism advocates a full circle return to the small American town, to a human scale of built environment, to community, to walking on sidewalks to the store, to the dynamism of mixed uses, and the appropriate scaling of buildings, streets, and trees, to create civic pride, a reintroduction of dignity, permanence, centrality, and a special sense of place.

The New Urbanism has led to newly-built planned communities and a revival of well-located older towns. Planned communities are not a new concept but they have been revised by the precepts of the New Urbanism and have taken on a new importance at the beginning of the twenty-first century. An important element in the development of towns based on New Urbanist principles is the provision of mass transportation, such as a light-rail system, that can partially supplant the use of cars. New urbanist towns provide a mix of housing types that include rental apartments, home-office town houses, and detached single-

Utopia, or the Ideal Small Town?
Seaside, Florida: A Planned Community

When Robert Davis decided to create a holiday town on the 80 acres he had inherited in the Florida Panhandle almost 20 years ago, he wanted to recall the idyllic vacations he had spent there with his family within the context of a traditional small town. He probably had no idea that he was about to build the model and catalyst for an international movement: The New Urbanism.

Davis had done some real estate development in the Coconut Grove area of Miami and had spent a year visiting the towns and cities of Italy while he was a resident scholar at the American Academy in Rome. Both of these experiences whetted his appetite for the quest: to reclaim the charm and civility of the traditional small town or neighborhood.

Teaming with his wife, Daryl, and the young architectural/planning team of Andres Duany and Elizabeth Plater-Zyberk, Davis set out to define what makes a small town so desirable and then to put that definition to work on his property near Destin, Florida.

Definitions, it was agreed, had to be simple, devoid of mystery and development double-talk, pragmatic and practical. So, the two couples set out to visit small cities and towns in the South, hoping to discover what makes a good town work, what makes a bad development bad. "Good" and "bad" were defined in terms of daily civic life: what is there about the ambiance that creates civic pride, neighborliness, charm and solid property value? What discourages these things?

The visits, which they made aboard an enormous 1950s-era convertible dubbed "The Land Yacht," soon uncovered some interesting concepts. People who know what is happening on their street tend to take pride in it and in their part of maintaining the streetscape. People who know each other, while they may not be close friends, usually watch out for each other and — more important — for each other's children. Streets that are narrow and sheltering discourage high-speed traffic. When the daily necessities — the bottle of milk, the box of cereal, the newspaper, dry cleaner or post office — are part of the neighborhood, people will walk to them, reducing the number of cars on the streets and increasing street life. Streets that are full of people, day and night, are seldom the sites of crime.

The Davises and Duany/Plater-Zyberk (now best known by the name of their firm, DPZ) found that the inhabitants of the most charming neighborhoods — those whose streets had become outdoor living spaces, overhung with trees, lined with houses close to the street behind picket fences — shared their public life easily, chatting from front porch to sidewalk, from side yard to side yard, over the fence, meeting on the walk to, or at, the mom-and-pop grocery store or pharmacy or newsstand. So, the team began to arrange these accidental attributes into a system which eventually became the "Seaside Code."

family houses. Houses are designed and sited to provide attractive people-scaled streetscapes and to be pedestrian friendly. Stores are located at walking distances from residences. Cars are recognized as necessary but are not allowed to dominate or take precedence over aesthetics or human needs. Public buildings are located in squares at the crossing of important avenues. Trees are used to soften the hard edges of streets. Streets are accorded the importance they held in traditional towns where they provided efficient access for pedestrians and vehicles between all parts

1980s

Today, Seaside is an enormously successful development. Its narrow streets are lined with cottages, mostly in the Cracker Vernacular style, close to the street, each with its owner-designed picket fence. The houses are built to the Seaside Code, which specifies that they be constructed of wood, with metal peaked roofs, front porches and small native-vegetation-only yards. Sandy alleys thread through the neighborhoods, providing shortcuts to the store and perfect places for the sunset game of hide-and-seek. Downtown fills in around the mom-and-pop (in this case Charlie and Sara Modica) grocery store, where neighbors meet and children can get an ice cream bar on the family tab under the watchful eyes of the Modica family (who don't allow more than one treat a day without checking with Mom). And, if Junior falls off his bike, the Modicas know whom to call. Restaurants, art galleries and the inevitable t-shirt shops are also part of the downtown scene.

Each street ends in a gateway that serves as a monumental portal to the beach. Designed and built by various architects, they also provide a gathering place and shelter. A village green is the site of informal ball games and public events, while the Lyceum area is the educational center of the town, already the site of a charter school, the Seaside Neighborhood School. Ruskin Place provides an urban setting: townhouses around a common green.

Seaside is, in the words of Robert Davis, a holiday town. Very few of the homeowners live there year-round, but there are more long-term residents than ever. Neighborhood associations are active in protecting the character of the town, which is probably more upscale than originally intended. If Seaside is visually too perfect (a factor which may have led to its being the location for the film *The Truman Show*), it is also a testament to planned communities that are not cookie-cutter monotonous.

As a laboratory for the study of civic life, a role encouraged by the Seaside Institute's schedule of conferences and artist residencies, Seaside offers lessons to all the municipalities around the world that seek a way out of the sterile strip malls and empty downtowns that afflict the American landscape. A stroll down its leafy streets at sunset brings the nostalgic sound of kids playing in the alleys, families at their dinner tables, laughter in the kitchens as the family washes dishes, the sun dropping into the Gulf of Mexico off white beach dunes, the regulars at the bar of one of the restaurants. Seaside represents the best of America's small towns, too often lost to an automotive culture and high tech society. Some social historians might argue that Seaside is an unrealistic dreamworld available only to a privileged few, but the Davises and Duany/Plater-Zyberk have convincingly demonstrated that the lessons learned from this utopian experiment are valid and compelling for all.

Sidebar by Richard Storm

of the town as well as serving as promenading routes for social exchange, but they are limited to widths that are in proportion to the buildings that are adjacent to them. The New Urbanism celebrates the street as an essential part of the social fabric of a town; it allows parallel parking of cars as a protective barrier for those who walk on sidewalks.

The revival of existing towns has taken place where there is an economic basis and employment opportunities from local industry, proximity to a city, tourism, a retirement destination, a university, or some other special purpose or attraction. Some of the towns that have survived more or less intact with a viable commercial Main Street, mixed commercial and residential uses, and pleasant neighborhoods of architecturally diverse houses and tree-lined streets with sidewalks, are towns that have resisted the incursion of shopping malls and the big-box discount retailers. There are organized programs that help towns maintain the integrity of their commercial downtowns. One of these is the Main Street program of the National Trust for Historic Preservation.

Conclusion

At the beginning of the twentieth century, the ideal American lifestyle was to be found in the world of the towns, or so we came to believe. Towns, cities, and countryside were three distinct and delightfully different entities. At the end of the century the distinction has been blurred by the sprawl of the seemingly endless and centerless suburbs of the huge metropolises. The boredom and banality of the American suburban life was brilliantly depicted in the Oscar-winning film *American Beauty* (1999).

It is no wonder that travelers seek respite in the colorful towns that remain in the United States or else travel to other countries to find them there. Towns such as Nantucket and other colorful New England towns, the seacoast towns of Maine, the fishing towns of the Eastern Shore of Maryland and Virginia, the hunt country towns of Piedmont Virginia, the Wine Country towns of California, St. Augustine, Florida, and many others, remain beautiful and viable, although many of them are of necessity sustained by tourism. What these towns lack, and what makes them attractive to the traveling and dreaming American public is mainly the fact that they are not as overwhelmed by the automobile culture as the rest of the country. It is more comfortable once one reaches these towns, to park the car and walk or bicycle. They still have charm, regional character, distinctive architecture, individually-owned shops and restaurants, and their hostelries are bed and breakfast, inns, and hotels, not motels.

These colorful and interesting towns are travel destinations, not places where most Americans can live, but they offer evidence that we once had towns to live in that provided a psychological, social, and physical setting that was both comprehensible and stimulating and that we to a large extent surrendered town life for suburban life.

Bibliography

Abler, Ronald, John S. Adams, and Peter Gould. *Spatial Organization: The Geographer's View of the World.* Englewood Cliffs: Prentice-Hall, 1971.

Adams, Henry. *History of the United States During the First Administration of Thomas Jefferson*. New York: Charles Scribner's Sons, 1889.

Bailyn, Bernard. *Voyagers to the West: a Passage in the Peopling of America on the Eve of the Revolution*. New York: Vintage Books, 1986.

Blumin, Stuart M. *The Urban Threshold: Growth and Change in a Nineteenth-Century American Community*. Chicago: The University of Chicago Press, 1976.

Curti, Merle. *The Making of an American Community: A Case Study of Democracy in a Frontier County*. Stanford: Stanford University Press, 1959.

Fischer, David Hackett. *Albion's Seed: Four British Folkways in America*. New York: Oxford University Press, 1989.

Greene, Jack P. *Pursuits of Happiness: The Social Development of Early Modern British Colonies and the Formation of American Culture*. Chapel Hill: The University of North Carolina Press, 1988.

Greene, Jack P. and J. R. Pole, eds. *Colonial British America: Essays in the New History of the Early Modern Era*. Baltimore: The Johns Hopkins University Press, 1984.

Hoyt, Henry F. *A Frontier Doctor*. New York: R.R. Donnelley & Son, 1979.

Jordan, Terry G., Mona Domosh, and Lester Rowntree. *The Human Mosaic: A Thematic Introduction to Cultural Geography*. New York: HarperCollins, 1994.

Kunstler, James Howard. "Home from Nowhere." *The Atlantic Monthly*. September 1996.

Ladd, Everett Carll. *Ideology in America: Change and Response in a City, a Suburb, and a Small Town*. Ithaca: Cornell University Press, 1969.

Lee, Jean B. *The Price of Nationhood: The American Revolution in Charles County*. New York: W.W. Norton, 1994.

Lynd, Robert S. and Helen Merrell Lynd. *Middletown: A Study in American Culture*. New York: Harcourt, Brace & World, 1929.

Martindale, Don Albert and R. Galen Hanson. *Small Towns and the Nation*. New York: Greenwood Publishing Corporation, 1969.

Miner, Craig. *West of Wichita: Settling the High Plains of Kansas, 1865-1890*. Lawrence: University Press of Kansas, 1986.

O'Connor, Richard. *Wild Bill Hickok*. New York: Doubleday & Company, 1959.

Spencer, J.E. and William L. Thomas. *Cultural Georgraphy: An Evolutionary Introduction to Our Humanized Earth*. New York: John Wiley and Sons, 1969.

Toynbee, Arnold. *Cities on the Move*. New York: Oxford University Press, 1970.

Twain, Mark. *Life on the Mississippi*. New York: Harper & Brothers, 1900.

Webb, Walter Prescott. *The Great Plains*. Omaha: University of Nebraska Press, 1981.

INTERNET RESOURCES

GHOST TOWNS OF AMERICA
Take a tour of the towns that time forgot. Provides background info on hundreds of ghost towns, plus tips for tourists and recommended reading.
http://ghosttowns.com/

U.S. TOWNS AND CITIES WITH DUTCH NAMES
The Dutch West India Company settled a large parcel of land in the eastern

United States, which in the 1600's became known as New Netherland.
http://www.netherlands-embassy.org/c_townname.html

CITY AND TOWNS MAPS HOME PAGE
Map Collections, Cities/Towns, Conservation/ Environment, Discovery/ Exploration, General Maps, Cultural Landscapes, Military Battles/Campaigns, from the Library of Congress.
http://rs6.loc.gov/ammem/gmdhtml/cityhome.html

Townhall USA provides free web sites for towns, cities, and municipalities.
http://www.townhallusa.com/

Liveable small towns and villages
http://www.townsandvillages.com/

Judith Reynolds

Transportation

(1939) How much room is in a Studebaker trunk?

TIMELINE

1830-1899 ~ Moving across America

Steamboat era (1830-1930s) / Steam-powered railroad era (1840-1950s) / Orphan trains transport homeless or impoverished children from urban to rural areas (1853-1929) / Transcontinental railroad lines completed (1869) / Electric rail transport and gasoline-powered automobiles introduced (1880s) / Subway systems introduced (1890) / Modern submarines developed (1890s)

MILESTONES: Thousands of Native Americans die during forced relocation on the "trail of tears" (1831-1838) • Fugitive Slave Law requires people to return runaway slaves (1850) • First petroleum well discovered in Pennsylvania by Edwin Drake (1859) • The great cattle drives (1865-1870) • Thomas Edison invents the motion picture (1889)

1900-1919 ~ Airplanes and Automobiles

New York introduces first law governing speed (1901) / Wright brothers' gasoline-engine aircraft successfully flies at Kitty Hawk (1903) / President Theodore Roosevelt is first president to dive in a submarine (1905) / Alice Ramsey becomes the first woman to drive a car across the U.S., capturing Americans' imagination and interest in automobiles (summer 1909) / Theodore Roosevelt is the first president to ride in an airplane (1910) / Airmail service inaugurated (1910) / First American transcontinental flight (1911) / Harriet Quimby becomes the first American woman to earn a pilot's license (1911) / Ford Motor Company initiates mass production of the automobile (1913) / Federal Aid Road Act begins government assistance to construct roads (1916)

MILESTONES: Mexicans strike against the Pacific Electric Railway company for equal wages and parity (1903) • Ford introduces the first inexpensive car, the Model T (1908) • Henry Ford institutes the five-dollar day for his factory workers (1914) • World War I provides new roles and opportunities for women (1917-1919) • Race riots erupt in St. Louis, Chicago, and Washington, D.C. (1917-1919) • John J. Pershing breaks German front in France to end WWI (1918)

1920-1929 ~ Milestones in Flight

United States Army pilots begin transporting mail by air (1918) / First transcontinental airmail route transports mail between New York City and San Francisco (1920) / First diesel engine railroad put into service (1920) / First commercial aircraft flights for passengers and cargo begin (1920) / Traffic signal technology developed by an African American (1920s) / Bessie Coleman becomes first African American female pilot, earning her license in France because of segregation in the United States (1921) / Route 66, the first completely paved road across U.S., is begun (1926) / Charles Lindbergh completes nonstop transatlantic flight on "The Spirit of St. Louis" (May 20 and 21, 1927) / Amelia Earhart becomes the first woman to fly across the Atlantic, as a passenger (1928)

MILESTONES: First commercial radio broadcast (1920) • Pig Stand in Dallas is the first drive-in restaurant (1921) • One out of every eight American workers is employed in automobile-related industries, including rubber, steel and petroleum (1920s) • First motel is built in San Luis Obispo, California (1925) • First national radio networks begin, NBC (1926), CBS (1927)

1930-1939 ~ Freeways and Commercial Flights

Streamliners popularize railroad travel (1930s) / Wiley Post and Harold Gatty are the first people to circle the globe in an airplane (1931) / Amelia Earhart completes a solo transatlantic flight (1932) / Twin engine Boeing 247, the first modern commercial aircraft, put into service (1933) / First Freeway, Pennsylvania Turnpike, opens (1940) / First jet aircraft put into service (1939) / Ukrainian immigrant Igor Sikorsky builds the first successful helicopter (1939)

MILESTONES: President Hoover's programs fail and the American banking system is on the verge of total collapse (1932) • Hitler rises to power (1933) • *Reader's Digest* has a circulation of over 1,000,000 readers (1935) • Nazis banish Jews to ghettos (1936) • Sulfa drugs introduced to U.S. (1936) • African American Marian Anderson sings before 75,000 at the Lincoln Memorial (1939) • First commercial televisions displayed at New York World's Fair (1939)

1940-1959 ~ Atomic Submarines and Super Highways

Chuck Yeager breaks the sound barrier (1947) / First nuclear submarine, the *Nautilus*, put into service (1950) / Rosa Parks arrested, starting the Bus Boycott in Montgomery, Alabama (1955) / Louise Arner Boyd is the first woman to fly over the North Pole (1955) / Interstate Highway Act funds a vast network of high speed roads (1956) / President Dwight D. Eisenhower is the first president to dive in an atomic submarine (1957) / First nuclear submarine, the *Nautilus*, passes underneath the North Pole (1958)

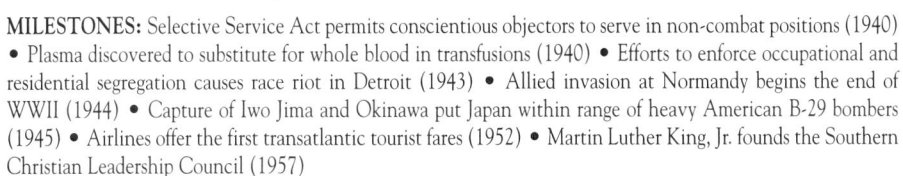

MILESTONES: Selective Service Act permits conscientious objectors to serve in non-combat positions (1940) • Plasma discovered to substitute for whole blood in transfusions (1940) • Efforts to enforce occupational and residential segregation causes race riot in Detroit (1943) • Allied invasion at Normandy begins the end of WWII (1944) • Capture of Iwo Jima and Okinawa put Japan within range of heavy American B-29 bombers (1945) • Airlines offer the first transatlantic tourist fares (1952) • Martin Luther King, Jr. founds the Southern Christian Leadership Council (1957)

1960-1969 ~ Traveling to Space

Number of deaths due to automobile accidents increases 46 percent (1960s) / Boeing's jumbo 747 jet developed (1960s) / Soviet cosmonaut Yuri Gargarin is the first man in space (1961) / Alan B. Shepherd, Jr. becomes the first American in space (1962) / John H. Glenn, Jr. is the first American to travel in orbit (1962) / Boeing 707 explodes over Elkton, MD, becoming the first lightning-caused American air disaster (1963) / *Apollo 1* launch pad fire kills 3 astronauts (1967) / Neil Armstrong becomes the first person to walk on the moon's surface (July 20, 1969)

MILESTONES: President Kennedy commits to landing an American on the moon by 1969 (1961) / President Kennedy vows support to West Germany (1962) / Rachel Carson's *Silent Spring* calls wide attention to pollution (1962) / 200,000 civil rights supporters march on Washington with Dr. Martin Luther King, Jr (1963) / NBC TV introduces color programming (1964) / Gulf of Tonkin Resolution begins official U.S. involvement in Vietnam (1964) / Army Math Research Center at the University of Wisconsin bombed by student protesters (1968)

1970-1979 ~ Fast Trains and Planes

Rail Passenger Service Act establishes Amtrak to transport passengers on intercity routes (1970) / Electrically powered light rail systems put into service (1970) / Airlines deregulated (1970) / NASA engineers build Skylabs, orbiting scientific laboratories, predecessors of the International Space Station (1970s) / Supersonic *Concorde* developed for passenger flight (1970s) / Federal laws require use of safety belts (1971) / American Byron Allen crosses the English Channel in a mylar and polystyrene aircraft (1979)

MILESTONES: Clean Air Act attempts to minimize vehicle produced pollution (1970) • Four students killed by the Ohio National Guard at Kent State University (1970) • Soviet Union purchases $1 billion of U.S. wheat (1972) • American Indian Movement occupies Wounded Knee for two months (1973) • Home Box Office (HBO) becomes the first national cable network (1975) • Alaskan Pipeline constructed (1977) • Three Mile Island meltdown causes backlash to nuclear reactors (1979)

1980-1989 ~ Space Exploration

Air traffic controllers strike (1981) / First space shuttle, *Columbia,* is launched (April 12, 1981) / *Voyager* airplane flies nonstop around the world in nine days without refueling (1986) / *Challenger* space shuttle explodes killing six astronauts and the first private citizen in space, Christa McAuliffe (1986)

MILESTONES: MTV begins (1981) • U.S. restores sovereignty to Native American nations (1982) • Housing and Urban-Rural Recovery Act provides funds for housing for the elderly, handicapped and homeless (1983) • Exxon *Valdez* oil spill in Alaska (1986)

1990-2000 ~ Improving Transportation

Intelligent Transportation Systems developed (1990) / Smoking banned on all U.S. domestic flights of less than 6 hours (1990) / GM introduces the first mass-marketed electric car, the Saturn EV1 (1990) / Dissolution of the Soviet Union ends the Cold War (1991) / Clean Air Act requires automobile manufacturers to begin developing alternative fuel vehicles (1991) / Failure of a Mars lander causes many Americans to question the value of space travel (1999) / High-speed passenger trains between Washington, Boston, and New York City inaugurated (2000)

MILESTONES: World Wide Web is created (1990) • Travel and tourism is the second largest industry in the U.S. after health (1992) • Number of farm workers declines from 13.6 million in 1915 to 2.85 million in 1995 • *e. Coli* bacteria in contaminated hamburgers kills several people (1998) • Heart disease, cancer and stroke account for 60 percent of all deaths (1999)

INTRODUCTION

Twentieth-century transportation dramatically transformed how Americans live and perceive their community, state, country and world. Humans throughout history have relied on various modes of transportation to migrate to geographical sites and convey supplies for both economic needs and recreational enjoyment. Transportation has been crucial for trade and the establishment of civilizations. Initially, people relied on their own power and strength for transportation on land by walking or running to reach destinations, deliver messages, sell agricultural produce, hunt game and other activities. Humans appropriated animals for transportation to carry loads, pull wheeled vehicles or drag sleds.

People designed transportation methods useful for varying topographical conditions. Water provided humans means to travel between land masses or within the interior of continents. Constructing rafts, boats and ships, people traveled on naturally occurring bodies of water such as rivers and oceans. Scientific knowledge and technological tools later guided humans to transform creeks and adjacent land to create canals between geographic locations.

Basic modes of land and water transportation aided settlers who migrated to North America between the sixteenth and eighteenth centuries from Europe, Africa, Asia and South and Central America, including the Caribbean islands. By the nineteenth century, Americans welcomed new, more elaborate means of transportation. The concept of engine-powered vehicles, which emerged as early as the late eighteenth century, ultimately transformed American transportation in what many historians consider a revolutionary development. Networks of railways were built, connecting the east and west coasts by 1869 with steam railroad service to transport both passengers and cargo. The first automobiles were introduced in the late nineteenth century. Internal combustion engines gradually emerged as the preferred power source, and highways were built across the country in the twentieth century to accommodate growing transit requirements.

Because transportation was essential for trade and made daily routines more convenient, Americans innovated new transportation methods and designs to adapt existing transportation technology into more efficient, sophisticated machinery and devices to meet socioeconomic and cultural needs. Such advances are ongoing as engineers,

> "We recognize that the transportation system is about more than concrete, asphalt, and steel; it is about people and their daily lives. It is about their dreams and aspirations, their connection to the economy and to each other. Transportation is the tie that binds."
>
> William T. Coleman, Jr., Secretary of Transportation, in a 1977 report, "National Transportation Trends and Choices."

scientists and inventors strive to produce more fuel-efficient, higher-capacity and faster transportation to fulfill global trade and travel demands. Transportation has become an industry that produces and serves vehicles with commercial and military applications in addition to personal uses for consumers. People dedicate their professional careers to a variety of transportation fields.

Transportation is comprised of land, water and air crafts which are powered by diesel, gasoline or jet engines or naturally-generated power such as solar, wind, water or muscular energy. Engine-powered transportation tends to be quicker, more reliable and capable of carrying larger and heavier loads than non-engine transportation. Incorporating sophisticated navigation instruments and systems, engine-powered transportation often costs thousands to millions of dollars per vehicle and requires highmaintenance accessories such as rails and ports in addition to expensive fuels. Many Americans tend to associate types of transportation and specific brands with their socioeconomic status.

Transportation not only distributes people and goods, but also spreads ideas and indigenous products from one country to another even if the countries are very far away from each other. Transportation intertwines expertise in numerous specialties such as civil, mechanical, aerospace and agricultural engineering. Authorities focus their skills on building and improving five main forms of transportation in the United States: road, rail, water, air and pipeline. These types of transportation are further divided into transporting freight or passengers (with the exception of pipelines), and they can be public, private or commercial.

Creating American heroes and martyrs, transportation has encouraged humans to seek distance, speed and endurance records with various transit modes, and provided the surreal drama of catastrophic events and mysterious disappearances. Transportation themes and figurative language are prevalent in popular culture as plots and symbols in poetry, ballads and literature. Transportation represents the American dream for adventure, freedom, opportunity, mobility and imagination.

1880-1900

1880-1900 • Transportation By Land ~ Motorized vehicles in the form of automobiles, trucks, buses, taxis and motorcycles are the primary form of transportation with which most modern Americans have daily contact. In contrast, in 1900, most Americans traveled on foot within their communities or by train to distant places. Some people used bicycles, and even unicycles, to move within their neighborhood or surrounding areas. Both roller and ice skates were used for recreation and to reach destinations as were scooters and sleds. Humans pulled small wagons to transport groceries and other goods and hauled larger conveyances on intracity railways.

Few people had access to automobiles in 1900 because cars were considered recreational toys for sporting activities indulged in by wealthy people. The first cars were expensive and seemed intimidating and complicated to operate to people who were unfamiliar with machinery and motors. Chauffeurs often accompanied early automobile owners to maintain vehicles. On August 22, 1902, President Theodore Roosevelt became the first United States president to ride in a car, making a public appearance in a

(circa 1903) A man drives a model of one of the first gasoline motorized carriages in the United States.

Columbia Electric Victoria at Hartford, Connecticut. Since then, presidential Cadillacs, Lincolns and limousines equipped with safety devices have transported presidents and those cars are often equated with prestige, power and elitism. The convertible in which President John F. Kennedy was assassinated in 1962 is one of the most infamous of these presidential cars.

Automotive builders, many of whom were bicycle mechanics who applied that mechanical knowledge to automobiles, experimented to refine and improve original designs and to appropriate aspects of other inventors' machinery. Most early automobiles resembled a buggy and had an open cab with a removable cover and a cushioned seat. Air conditioning and heat were comforts unavailable in vehicles for decades. Instead of a steering wheel, drivers moved a stick connected to gears. Vehicles had three and four wheels. A few vehicles pulled trailers for passengers and supplies. Some vehicles were enclosed to form early vans. Most vehicles were powerful enough to climb small hills. Many were displayed in circuses to attract public attention. Because they cost several hundred dollars each, few of the first cars that were manufactured were sold to individual consumers.

Automobile production attracted so many eager engineers that determining who was the first person to achieve certain transportation design milestones is often difficult. Late-nineteenth century European manufacturers such as Daimler-Benz, who had pioneered automotive design and displayed their machines at American expositions, influenced many American automobile designers. At a Chicago, Illinois, exposition, Gottlieb Daimler demonstrated a motorized quadricycle, which was the first gasoline-engine vehicle exhibited in the United States. Carl Benz received an American patent for his vehicle in 1888. Both men were recognized for successfully developing their ideas into practical machinery. Many aspiring automobile creators examined the Germans' vehicles and pondered the possibilities of gasoline-powered transportation.

1879-1927 • THE FIRST AUTOMOBILES
~ Some Americans, however, claimed that their inventive ideas to motorize wagons and buggies had preceded those of their European rivals. On May 8, 1879, New York attorney George B. Selden had applied for an automobile patent even though he had not built a vehicle. Sixteen years later, he received U.S. patent 549,160 which acknowledged that he was the inventor of the automobile in the United States even though other people had already received national publicity regarding their mechanized vehicles. Most contemporary automobile inventors dismissed Selden's patent as unoriginal, and automotive historians generally give credit to other designers as the automobile's pioneering inventors.

Brothers Charles E. and J. Frank Duryea are considered by some historians to be the creators of the first gasoline-powered automobile in the United States. The Duryea, a carriage with an electrical ignition and one-cylinder gasoline engine, was first operated on September 21, 1893, in Springfield, Massachusetts. On November 2, 1895, J. Frank Duryea and one competitor, Oscar Mueller, raced in a match sponsored by the *Chicago Times-Herald* over a 92 mile course in the Chicago area. Suffering damage when he drove into a ditch to avoid a horse and wagon, Duryea lost. Six cars raced through ice and snow in a November 28 rematch, which was designated the first American automobile race. Duryea's car was awarded for achieving the best performance. Both regional and national press coverage of the race told Americans about the possibilities of motorized transportation.

Some scholars credit John William Lambert as the inventor of the first internal-combustion automobile in the United States. He built a single-cylinder, gasoline-powered automobile in 1890. During the 1890s, Ransom Eli Olds and James Ward Packard focused on gasoline-engines after working with steam-powered vehicles. Approximately fifty American automobile companies had been established by 1898. The Oldsmobile became the first commercially successful car manufactured in the United States. Increasing sales from 425 automobiles in 1901 to 5,000 in 1904, Oldsmobile's success inspired other manufacturers. By 1908, 241 additional automobile companies began producing gasoline-powered vehicles. In 1911, Charles F. Kettering sold to car companies electric automobile starters that he had invented. Replacing hand cranks, these starters made the gasoline-powered car easier to operate.

The Ford Motor Company, incorporated in 1903, is perhaps the best known automobile manufacturer. Creating 1,700 cars in 1904, the Ford Motor Company standardized designs and initiated mass production by 1913 which made cars cheaper to make and more popular with consumers. In contrast, most early twentieth-century automobiles were handmade from parts that were in low supply, thus making production and repairs both time-consuming and expensive. Henry Ford built his first car, the Quadricycle, in 1896 and sold it for $200 to build more automobiles. Introduced in 1908, the Model T was Ford's first best-selling automobile design. Assembled at Ford's Highland Park, Michigan, factory, the Model T, known as the Tin Lizzie, represented the first car with which most Americans were familiar. Detroit became the nucleus for car manufacturing.

Wanting to create a family automobile, Ford devised a standard Model T design made from simple parts that were affordable to install and replace. The cars were painted black. From 1908 to 1927 when they were discontinued, 15.5 million Model T's had been manufactured on assembly lines. Workers made a car in ninety-three minutes. Within five years of being first sold, Model T's comprised almost half of the cars manufactured in the United States. In 1920, Tin Lizzies represented half of the cars being driven globally, and some states had more registered automobiles than were driven in all the European nations and Great Britain. By 1930, American automotive manufacturers produced eighty-five percent of cars in the world. Few technological innovations were applied to automobiles, which retained nineteenth century design features, during the first half of the twentieth century. Quantity, not quality, was the most significant aspect of early automobile history.

LAW AND ORDER

When cars first became available, Americans already had experienced traffic congestion. Almost every day, horse-drawn trolleys and vehicles blocked the streets of New York City and other major urban areas. Some sources estimated that at least one person died each day because of chaotic traffic. William Phelps Eno was eight years old in 1867 when his family's carriage was delayed in traffic on Broadway in New York; everyone was clueless about how to resolve the problem and prevent future congestion. As an adult, Eno developed traffic rules for safety, which were adopted in New York City in 1903, and then worldwide, and have remained in effect mostly unchanged.

Eno, an avid horseman, devised his regulations based on horsemanship practices. Drivers were told to stay in line in right lanes and to signal other drivers about their intentions to pass and stop. Eno also stated that drivers who broke the rules should be ticketed. He also recommended speed limits to prevent accidents due to speeding, traffic signs, crosswalks for pedestrians, markings on pavement, vehicle registration and driver's licenses. He established the Eno Transportation Foundation in 1921 to promote traffic management and reform. Garrett A. Morgan, an African American inventor, developed traffic signal technology in the 1920s that supplemented Eno's efforts to bring order to chaos at intersections.

Eno's ideas became more crucial as the number of automobiles in the United States increased during the prosperous

United States Factory Sales of Cars, Trucks, and Buses

Year	Total Number Sold
1900	4,192
1910	187,000
1920	2,227,349
1930	3,362,820
1940	4,472,286
1950	8,003,056
1960	7,869,271
1970	8,239,257
1980	8,067,309
1990	9,774,954
1997	12,222,703

SOURCE: *Ward's Motor Vehicle Facts and Figures*

1879-1927

(circa 1923) Traffic Control. William Phelps Eno developed traffic rules for safety, which were adopted in New York City in 1903, and then worldwide, and have remained in effect mostly unchanged. Here, a police officer directs traffic in Kearny Street, San Francisco, California.

1920s. The Tin Lizzie appealed to people because of its low price and practical upkeep and use. In addition to manufacturers' statistics regarding the number of American automobiles, local and state governments implemented registration systems as Eno suggested to keep track of cars. Over twenty million cars had been registered by 1930. Almost one third of America's six-and one-half million farmers owned an automobile to transport goods to urban markets.

At first, private drivers were not required to be examined for driving proficiency, but most states demanded that chauffeurs be licensed. Gradually, because of Eno's insistence, states began implementing licensing procedures, and by 1954 every state required drivers to be licensed. As of 1959, every state stipulated that drivers must have attained a specific age, usually sixteen years old, and pass tests about their knowledge of traffic laws, driving ability and vision to receive a license. Earning a driver's license has become a rite of passage for most American teenagers.

1909-1915 • PATHFINDING ~ As the number of drivers and automobiles grew, especially in the economically prosperous 1920s, demand for good, surfaced roads became urgent. In the colonial period, roads had been created as settlers migrated to settlements and drove livestock to markets. Many people followed Native American and animal paths or paths along natural topographical landscapes such as mountain valleys and rivers. These paths formed the basis of modern transportation routes. The nineteenth century National Road between Cumberland, Maryland, and Vandalia, Illinois, was one of the most

Licensed Drivers in the United States

Year	Drivers
1950	59,300,000
1955	74,685,949
1960	88,852,000
1965	99,033,694
1970	111,542,787
1975	129,815,000
1980	145,972,000
1985	156,224,000
1990	167,015,250
1995	176,628,482
1998	184,980,177

SOURCE: *Federal Highway Administration*

Motorized Vehicles Registered in the United States

Year	Number of Cars	Total Number of Motor Vehicles (cars, trucks, buses)
1900	8,000	8,000
1905	77,400	78,800
1910	458,377	468,500
1915	2,332,426	2,490,932
1920	8,131,522	9,239,161
1925	17,481,001	20,068,543
1930	23,034,753	35,653,515
1935	22,567,827	26,546,126
1940	27,465,826	32,453,233
1945	25,796,985	31,035,420
1950	40,339,077	49,161,691
1955	52,144,739	62,688,792
1960	61,671,390	73,868,682
1965	75,257,588	90,370,182
1970	89,243,557	112,010,000
1975	106,705,934	109,675,000
1980	121,600,843	159,029,000
1985	131,664,029	170,237,000
1990	143,549,627	188,655,462
1995	136,066,045	201,530,021
1998	131,838,538	211,616,553

SOURCE: *American Automobile Manufacturers Association*

prominent American routes. Trails that had guided western pioneers remained travel routes. Most early roads were dirt, although some were covered with gravel for drainage and traction.

When Alice Ramsey became the first woman to drive a car across the United States in the summer of 1909, she captured Americans' imagination and interest in automobiles. With three female companions, Ramsey navigated from New York City to San Francisco in a Maxwell touring car. The Maxwell Company sponsored Ramsey, hoping to sell more cars as a result of publicity. Guided only by landmarks, Ramsey repaired the car when it broke down, extricated it from mud and managed to steer up steep hills. She often traveled where no roads existed. The next year, Blanche Scott drove an automobile across the United States alone.

Americans began to prefer automobiles to trains for transportation, and motorized vehicles became the primary method to transport passengers. By 1915, more miles of surfaced roads than railways existed in the United States. A decade later, half a million miles of surfaced roads transported cars, reaching one million miles within ten years. Americans traveled by automobile to reach locations for both commercial and personal reasons. Cars moved more quickly than traditional transportation methods like wagons and trains. Headlights enabled drivers to travel at night, and windshield wipers enhanced visibility during storms.

1909-1915

Individuals benefited from having more control over when, where and how they sent their goods to distant markets by trucks or cars. Americans embraced the freedom automobiles presented to travel beyond their communities to experience other geographical regions. Highways promised easier, more spontaneous and often more affordable and enjoyable travel than boats and trains. Because of increased motorized vehicle usage, an automobile tourism industry emerged which offered travelers food, shelter, fuel, repairs and entertainment. These services financially strengthened local economies.

1916-1938 • THE FIRST NATIONAL HIGHWAY SYSTEM ~ State and municipal governments were expected to maintain and upgrade roads until the Federal Aid Road Act was passed in 1916, promising federal supervision and financial support of highway construction between states. At that time, the Bureau of Public Roads began overseeing construction of highways across the country including the Lincoln and Dixie Highways, but there were only several hundred miles of paved roads to support several million automobiles.

In 1919, the United States Army's First Transcontinental Motor Convoy traveled from Washington, D.C., to San Francisco to evaluate the condition of American roads for possible military use. Participants noted such traffic obstacles as muddy roads and unstable bridges. After World War I, General John J. Pershing directed a committee that established a national defense highway system. The Pershing Map was issued in 1922 to identify American roads that could be used for military maneuvers if necessary. These routes became eligible for federal financial funding and identification that was the foundation of a national highway system. During wars, tanks and jeeps were designed for military transportation, and the latter vehicle became a popular peacetime vehicle.

One of the most significant transcontinental highways was the 2,448-mile Route 66, which linked Chicago and Santa Monica, California, in 1926. Route 66 became the first completely paved road crossing America in 1938 and was considered the most significant twentieth century east-west migration route in the United States. During the Dust Bowl era between 1935 to 1940, one-half million people known as Exodusters migrated to California on Route 66, which John Steinbeck called the "Mother Road" in his novel *The Grapes of Wrath* (1939). Post-World War II migrants traveled on Route 66 to seek economic prosperity in California. Bobby Troup wrote the song, "Get Your Kicks on Route 66!" to celebrate tourism along the highway, and an early television program, "Route 66," expanded the mythology of the highway.

1938-1956 • ROAD EXPANSION ~ After the Depression had temporarily halted automobile manufacturing, more Americans purchased cars in the late 1930s and demanded highways capable of supporting increased traffic. Traffic planners envisioned roads with multiple lanes to accommodate many cars simultaneously traveling at high speeds. They also realized that east-west and north-south highways across the continent would permit travelers to use direct routes without detours to reach major destinations. The Federal Aid Highway Act of 1938 issued funds to evaluate President Franklin D. Roosevelt's plan to construct toll highways, but World War II interrupted this endeavor. Wartime industry and rationing resulted in fewer Americans buying and using automobiles. Before the war, the first United States freeway opened in 1940 when the Pennsylvania Turnpike from Middlesex to Irwin and the Arroyo Seco Parkway between Pasadena and Los Angeles were completed.

The Federal-Aid Highway Act of 1944 approved building more than 40,000 miles of interstate highways but did not legislate construction resources. The Bureau of Public Roads, renamed the Public Roads Administration, began listing routes that should be developed and outlined design standards with the American Association of State Highway Officials. The Federal-Aid Highway Act of 1952 approved funding for road building. Because production of luxury items such as cars accelerated in the 1950s, President Eisenhower stated that adequate highways were essential for American economic success and national security. Although the Federal-Aid Highway Act of 1954 allocated $175 million in funding, Eisenhower demanded financial cooperation between the federal government and states to build an interstate system.

Eisenhower signed the Interstate Highway Act in 1956, implementing transportation that transformed the United States and changed how Americans lived, worked and played. The Interstate Highway Act resulted in the decline of Route 66 and other primarily rural roads as main travel routes. Interstates linked urban areas and were a catalyst for economic development.

The National Defense and Interstate Highway Act of 1956 initiated the largest American public works project. Supporters of the act believed that the standardized interstates would improve traffic safety and offer defensive measures in case of military attacks and terrorism within the United States, as well as evacuation routes during natural disasters such as hurricanes or nuclear attacks. Interstates were required to have a straightaway every five miles for emergency military aircraft landing sites. The military emphasis reflected the Cold War atmosphere. Because war veterans and unemployed laborers were hired for interstate engineering and construction, the system was sometimes considered the final New Deal project in which Americans benefited from applying their ingenuity and skills to shape the countryside landscape for efficient transportation. The interstate system is the only human-made structure besides the Great Wall of China that is visible from outer space.

1960s • INTERSTATE IMPACT ~ The interstate highway system's political, cultural, and technological accomplishments modified the way Americans perceived and utilized their society. Suburbs built in rural areas surrounding metropolitan centers were perhaps the most significant cultural change resulting from interstate construction. Many Americans became commuters, adding to traffic and parking demands. Employees and students traveled longer distances in carpools and buses to work at businesses and attend schools outside their immediate community. Some rural residents took advantage of interstates to seek new educational, employment, commercial or cultural opportunities. Suburbs and interstates symbolized the emerging American middle class. Interstates, such as the Washington, D.C., Beltway, were built to accommodate heavy traffic traveling to and from an urban nucleus.

Interstate highways boosted the economic growth of adjacent areas. Billboards along interstates advertised new busi-

(circa 1965) Aerial view of onramps to the National Interstate Highway System, which was developed to accommodate the nation's growing prosperity and need for civil defense.

1960s nesses, including fast food restaurants, drive-in movies and motels (a term coined from the words "motorist" and "hotel" in the 1950s). Burma Shave signs amused travelers with snippets of humorous messages displayed on billboards placed at intervals along the road. Franchises gradually displaced independently owned businesses that could not compete with brand-name gasoline stations and fast-food chains that offered quick, predictable and convenient products and services. Although many historic houses and scenic landscapes were destroyed for interstate construction, some portions of the highways were designed to be compatible with regional environments such as providing passages beneath the interstate for panthers in the Everglades and overpasses for the Appalachian Trail. Claudia "Lady Bird" Johnson, the wife of President Lyndon B. Johnson, promoted the beautification of American highways with wildflowers, and most states sponsor roadside programs in which people and groups can adopt a mile of highway or local roads to keep clean of debris. Mrs. Johnson was also responsible for limiting signs, including billboards, on interstate highways.

In addition to linking the forty-eight contiguous states, interstate highways connected American trade to Mexico and Canada. Interstate 35 runs through the center of the United States from Texas to Minnesota with major trading centers near the Mexican and Canadian borders. This route became vital after the passage of the North American Free Trade Agreement (NAFTA) in 1994. As a result of the interstate highway, the North American trading region is the world's largest free trade market.

Freight trucking expanded due to interstates, and large cargo vehicles, generally referred to as eighteen-wheelers or semis, were designed to transport specific goods in trailers which also could be moved by railroad. Some trucks carried smaller vehicles to automobile markets, and refrigerated trucks moved perishable foods grown in specific regions, especially fruits and vegetables from the southern states, to consumers across the country. Private shipping businesses such as Federal Express and United Parcel Service were established to transport packages and documents via interstate highways, in addition to airplanes, to compete with the United States Postal Service in an effort to achieve prompt and affordable delivery.

Because of the use of interstate highways for transporting both raw materials and finished products, industrial parks were developed to service and supply trucks. Factories were built in remote areas near interstates for the convenience of employees, suppliers, and buyers. Nearby truck stops and rest areas offered drivers places to refuel, eat, and sleep. Passenger bus lines such as Greyhound and Trailways improved their service with the interstate highways.

1970s-Present • The National Highway System ~ Some sources state that the interstate system of 45,000 miles was completed in December 1977 when the final section of Interstate 75 was opened, while others insist that interstate construction has continued. Instead of building new highways, such work represents 3R improvements: "Resurfacing, Restoration and Rehabilitation." Legislators have passed regulations to supplement the 1956 interstate act to implement new requirements such as vehicles' weight limits, emission standards and the transportation of hazardous materials.

The National Highway System of 160,000 miles of frequently-traveled roads—including the interstates and state highways and routes—and other significant transportation facilities such as ports, was established in 1995. Road signs to guide motorists along these highways indicate east-west routes with even numbers and north-south routes with odd numbers, with the lowest numbers representing roads in the northeast and the highest numbers representing roads in the southwest. Engineering standards determine roads' foundations, thickness and surfaces in addition to how many lanes are built in high-traffic areas and how steep roads over hills and angle of curves can be for average motorists to traverse safely.

By 2000, the United States had almost four million miles of roads of varying quality to accommodate 35 percent of the world's automobiles. Other types of roads include expressways designed for speed, toll roads which charge fees for drivers' use, and parkways which tend to be well landscaped and limited to passenger automobiles. Most highways are funded with taxes collected from fuel sales and vehicle registrations.

United States Road Mileage of All Roads Used for Transportation

Year	Total Miles	Percentage Paved
1905	2,351,000	
1920	3,150,000	
1930	3,259,000	
1940	3,287,000	
1950	3,313,000	23.5%
1960	3,546,000	34.7%
1970	3,731,000	44.5%
1980	3,860,000	53.7%
1990	3,867,000	58.4%
1998	3,906,000	61.2%

SOURCE: U.S. Department of Transportation

Accidents

Vehicular accidents and fatalities statistics have increased throughout the twentieth century, representing the growing population and reliance on automobiles for transportation. By 2000, an average of 1.1 million car crashes occurred annually. More people die in car accidents than in any other form of transportation. An estimated ninety percent of fatalities result from drivers disobeying traffic rules, driving recklessly or being incapacitated by alcohol, drugs or drowsiness. Others die

1970S-PRESENT

in weather-related accidents such as pile-ups in fog or sliding off icy roads. Earthquakes also cause driver injuries and destroy roads and bridges. Pedestrians hit by cars are considered vehicular casualties. Some transportation experts emphasize that interstates have actually reduced the number of accidents that might have happened on more congested, less improved roadways and that motorists can maneuver their vehicles more defensively from hazards on wide, straight interstates than on narrow, twisting roads.

SAFETY

Aware that vehicles can have potentially lethal mechanical flaws, such as the treads peeling off tires, the United States Secretaries of Transportation have implemented new standards for manufacturers, including making vehicles with air bags and a third brake light in the rear window. They also enforce required product crash testing. States have passed seat belt laws and insist that all drivers purchase automobile insurance. Traffic planners use computer modeling to design better ways to cope with traffic flow at peak hours. Intelligent transportation systems to improve vehicle transportation include electronic tolls and automatic vehicle tracking to identify vehicles involved in accidents or breaking road laws. Salt and sand are used to melt snow and ice on roads and provide traction. Snowplows push snow off roads into ditches. Fiber optics lighting systems on snowplows alternate colors which is easier for automobile drivers to see than flashing halogen lights when driving near a plow.

Organizations such as Mothers Against Drunk Driving have striven to promote safe, sober driving to reduce the number of automobile deaths. Incidents of road rage, often provoked by motorists' frustrations with traffic congestion, have resulted in the deaths of drivers and passengers. Automobiles have been used to commit crimes such as drive-by shootings and robberies. Notorious fugitives such as the bank robbers Bonnie and Clyde lived and died in their automobile. Some drivers use their cars as weapons to intimidate others and force them off roads. Car theft and carjacking frequently occur, with car parts being harvested to sell.

THE AUTOMOTIVE CULTURE

Many Americans identify themselves through their car by their choice of brand, model and color. Personalized license plates and bumper stickers reflect person-

---

Motor Vehicle Casualties

Year	Casualties
1915	3,978
1920	9,103
1925	17,571
1930	29,080
1935	34,183
1940	32,245
1945	28,706
1950	34,763
1955	38,300
1960	38,137
1965	40,000
1970	54,800
1975	54,633
1980	53,172
1985	46,600
1990	46,814
1997	43,200

SOURCE: *National Safety Council*

List of Most Dangerous U.S. Intersections

1. Pembroke Pines, FL: Flamingo Road and Pines Boulevard
2. Philadelphia, PA: Red Lion Road and Roosevelt Boulevard
3. Philadelphia, PA: Grant Avenue and Roosevelt Boulevard
4. Phoenix, AZ: 7th Street and Bell Road
5. Tulsa, OK: 51st Street and Memorial Drive
6. Tulsa, OK: 71st Street and Memorial Drive
7. Phoenix, AZ: 19th Avenue and Northern Avenue
8. Frisco, TX: State Highway 121 and Preston Road
9. Metairie, LA: Clearwater Parkway and Veterans Memorial Boulevard
10. Sacramento, CA: Fair Oaks Boulevard and Howe Avenue

SOURCE: State Farm Insurance Company. www.statefarm.com/media/danger.htm

---

al attributes and opinions. Automotive terms such as "lemon," indicating a faulty car, have become part of American jargon. Some internet sites warn motorists of speed traps and construction zones. Many Americans tow recreational vehicles or drive motor homes. Others add hydraulics so their cars will bounce.

Golf carts, mopeds, three-wheelers, dune buggies and motorized scooters are other forms of recreational land transportation. Race-car driving has become a popular pastime, with leading drivers such as the late Dale Earnhardt becoming sports heroes. In addition to sport, automobile racing helps engineers develop and test more streamlined cars, more durable materials and more efficient fuels.

IMPROVEMENTS IN CARS

Automobiles use half of America's energy resources. Because of diminishing petroleum supplies available to Americans and increased automotive pollution, alternative fuel sources that have been tested include ethanol, made from corn, and electrical cars. Some automotive designers experiment with solar cars which store power gathered by solar panels in batteries. Every two years, college engineering teams compete in the transcontinental Sunrayce to demonstrate the

(circa 1970) A U.S. sheriff's dune buggy, in use by the Los Angeles Police Force, on Malibu Beach. The buggy is equipped with a two-way radio and flashing light bar and is used for patrolling coastal areas.

potential of solar cars. During energy crises, smaller cars are promoted as the best way for motorists to conserve fuel.

Improvements in tires have included thicker treads, patterns for traction and rayon being used for strength. In 1952, B.F. Goodrich patented tubeless tires. Using computer modeling, radial tires with steel belts were designed for durability. Advanced automotive technology includes satellite guidance systems which drivers can use to determine directions as well as to seek help. Vehicle entertainment systems have switched from AM radios to CD players, and communications have been upgraded from CB radios to cell phones. Nostalgic car collectors have restored older cars which are displayed in parades, automotive shows, and museums such as the Smithsonian Institute in Washington, D.C. and the Henry Ford Museum and Greenfield Village, in Dearborn, Michigan.

1897-PRESENT • SUBWAYS ~ Land transportation requires technology to move people and products beneath, through or above natural obstacles such as rivers and mountains. Some transportation moves underground to avoid inclement weather or to increase use of crowded urban areas. Subways move workers and goods beneath city streets. Boston's subway opened in 1897, and New York City's subway began operation on October 27, 1904, with almost two hundred miles of tracks. Traffic on surface transportation decreased by seventy-five percent on that subway's first day. People sang the "The Subway Glide" and danced the "subway express two step." New York City's demographics shifted as people built and lived in housing away from the city's nucleus because they could commute by subway.

After World War II, subway ridership decreased because people preferred auto-

United States Railroad and Vehicular Tunnels

Name and Location	Year Opened
Holland, Hudson River, New York/New Jersey	1920
Liberty Tubes, Pittsburgh, Pennsylvania	1923
Moffat, Rocky Mountains, Colorado	1928
New Cascade, Cascade Mountains, Washington	1929
Yerba, Yerba Buena Island, California	1936
Lincoln, Hudson River, New York/New Jersey	1937
Queens Midtown, East River, New York	1940
Allegheny Tunnels, Pennsylvania Turnpike	1940, 1965, 1966
Brooklyn Battery, East River, New York	1950
Hampton Roads, Norfolk, Virginia	1957
Baltimore Harbor, Maryland	1957
Flathead, Rocky Mountains, Montana	1970
Fort McHenry, Baltimore, Maryland	1985

SOURCE: American Society of Civil Engineers; Federal Highway Administration

> ## Snow Sports
>
> Americans travel by dogsleds for exploration, such as Will Steger's expeditions to Antarctica and the North Pole, and sport, including Susan Butcher's victories in the Alaskan Iditarod. Humans ride on ski lifts, first built by Union Pacific engineers in 1937, and snowmobiles for winter transportation.

mobiles. In the 1980s, the Metropolitan Transportation Authority improved the deteriorating subway with new equipment, cheaper fares and better service. By 2000, New York's subway included seven hundred miles of track and carried one billion people annually. Escalators and conveyor belts move people to subway stations deep underground. In the 1970s, electrically powered light rail systems, which are cheaper to build than subways, were first constructed in California commuter communities. Tunnels transport cargo through mountains and under rivers and bays. In 1920, the Holland Tunnel opened between New York and New Jersey, and it was the first major underwater tunnel for automobiles.

1970s • PIPELINES ~ Pipelines both above and below ground transport petroleum and natural gas from deposits to distribution centers which send the energy resources throughout the United States. The TransAlaska Pipeline stretches 1,287 miles from Prudhoe Bay to Valdez and is capable of transporting approximately 2.145 million barrels of oil daily. Built in the 1970s, half of the pipeline is elevated to prevent the permafrost from melting because of the oil's frictional heat. The pipe rests on supports and is coated with Teflon so that it can move during earthquakes. Where caribou migrate, another section of the pipeline is underground and insulated with fiberglass and brine to keep the surrounding soil frozen. Some parts of the pipeline are buried underneath rivers, while others are placed on bridges such as the one spanning the Yukon River. In case the pipeline ruptures, engineers are transported in special vehicles within the pipeline to close valves and repair leaks.

1869-PRESENT • RAILROADS ~ By the twentieth century, railroads crossed the United States, connecting ports and metropolises. Steam engines first pulled railcars in the early nineteenth century on lines such as the Baltimore & Ohio. On May 10, 1869, the first transcontinental railroad was completed when workers from the Central Pacific and Union Pacific Railroads united their tracks at Promontory, Utah. Attaining speeds as high as sixty miles per hour, trains could carry heavy loads that would require hundreds of horses to transport. In one week, a person could travel from New York City to San Francisco, a trip that would take months by horse-pulled vehicles. Fares and freight rates became affordable, and people accepted the idea of moving quickly by train.

Cities were built along railroads, and the daily railroad schedule affected community activities. Fannie Flagg's novel,

1869-PRESENT

Fried Green Tomatoes at the Whistle Stop Cafe (1987), depicts the unifying nature of railroads in rural towns. Functional depots and elaborate stations were built to accommodate passengers and cargo. Demand increased for more and faster trains. Most passenger and freight trains continued to be powered by steam until gasoline and diesel engines became the preferred energy source in the early twentieth century. Railroad companies were established and merged, and the Burlington Northern, Santa Fe, Union Pacific and the Nickel Plate became household names.

Train engines and cars were made from wood then steel and alloys throughout the twentieth century. The twentieth Century Limited was a luxury train between New York City and Chicago that the New York Central introduced in 1902. Conductors rolled out a crimson colored carpet for passengers that started a well-known saying, the "red carpet treatment." The railroad's golden age began in the 1920s. In the 1930s, the streamliners became popular passenger trains. Made from stainless steel, the streamliners were more streamlined than other trains, resembling a long bullet. Powered by a diesel engine, the streamliners transformed train travel before World War II when war transportation became the priority.

> The Santa Fe Railroad's "Super Chief" first transported people between Los Angeles and Chicago in 1936 and was a favorite form of travel for Hollywood celebrities. On January 14, 1952, 226 people were stranded on the streamliner "City of San Francisco" during a blizzard in the Sierra Nevada mountains.

Because the government regulated the railroads, even taking control of them during war, and subsidized other forms of transportation, railroads lost customers. In 1945, railroad executives decided to modernize railroads and invest primarily in diesel engines and new equipment. Most steam locomotives were replaced by the late 1950s. Declining railway use continued through the 1960s, and one-fourth of American railroads filed for bankruptcy because they could not compete with subsidized transportation, government regulations and taxes. Mergers of railroad companies also occurred. Congress passed the Rail Passenger Service Act in 1970 that established Amtrak, the National Railroad Passenger Corporation, to transport passengers on intercity routes. The 1980 Staggers Rail Act limited railroad regulation by the Interstate Commerce Commission that had overseen railroad commerce since 1887. As a result, some railroads such as Conrail were privatized to offer consumers choices.

By the year 2000, 75 percent of 80 million annual railroad passengers were commuters. More than 1.38 trillion ton-miles of freight were transported by rail. High-speed passenger trains run between Washington, D.C., Boston and New York City, moving as fast as 150 miles per hour. Magnetic levitation, or maglev, trains are pushed forward by magnetic forces emitted from a single track. Engineers worked on designing a maglev train that might one day speed safely at three hundred miles per hour.

RAILROAD ACCIDENTS

Despite their efficiency, trains posed perils for their crews and passengers. The speed of travel resulted in catastrophic results when trains collided or were derailed. Trains often fell through rotting bridges, slid off broken or worn rails or skidded when landslides covered tracks. From 1876 to 1905, 207 postal clerks died in 9,355 wrecks of trains specified for transporting mail across America. Newspapers printed accounts of train crashes, commenting on the gory accident scenes and casualties. Some survivors and witnesses composed ballads that narrated the circumstances of each wreck. Although accidental collisions were considered tragedies, some Americans attended staged train wrecks for entertainment. Railroad crossings are often the site of collisions of trains with automobiles whose drivers do not yield the right of way. Railroad companies sponsor educational programs about cautious crossing and have track replacement programs to repair and maintain tracks for safety.

1853-1929 • THEY ALSO RODE THE RAILS ~ Orphan trains transported approximately 150,000 homeless or impoverished children from urban to rural areas between 1853 and 1929. Agents working for the Children's Aid Society, founded by Charles Loring Brace in New York City, identified children who they thought would benefit from a country home. Booking passage for groups at discount rates, the agents accompanied the children on passenger trains heading west and south from eastern cities. Traveling for several days, the children slept on the trains. When the orphan trains reached communities where the children's arrival had been advertised, the children disembarked for possible selection by residents. Most children found nurturing homes where they were educated and well-provided for, while some reported being abused and treated as servants. Other charity groups

---

One Pullman railroad car was designed for the United States president in the twentieth century. The Ferdinand Magellan, or Presidential Rail Car, U.S. Number 1, was approved for presidential transport in 1942. Previously, presidents had traveled in several different Pullman cars designated for general service, but this one was prepared especially to protect the president while he traveled within the United States. Some presidential candidates used trains during their campaigns, speaking to people at whistle stops.

(1900) A poster advertising the comforts of Pullman dining cars on the Cincinnati, Hamilton and Dayton Railroad.

1853-1929

conducted similar programs to transport needy children to new homes. The final orphan train was sent to Sulfur Springs, Texas, in May 1929.

1900-1930s • ESCAPE ~ Like automobiles, the railroad represented freedom and adventure for many Americans. Especially during the Depression, many

Major Twentieth Century American Railroad Disasters
(Casualty figures vary by source and because many injured people died later from their wounds)

Date	Place	Dead
September 27, 1903	Danville, VA	9
December 23, 1903	Laurel Run, PA	53
August 7, 1904	Eden, CO	96
September 24, 1904	New Market, TN	64
March 16, 1906	Florence, CO	35
October 28, 1906	Atlantic City, NJ	40
December 30, 1906	Washington, DC	53
January 2, 1907	Volland, KS	33
January 19, 1907	Fowler, IN	29
February 16, 1907	New York, NY	22
February 23, 1907	Colton, CA	26
May 11, 1907	Lompoc, CA	36
July 20, 1907	Salem, MI	33
September 25, 1908	Young's Point, MT	21
January 15, 1909	Dotsero, CO	21
March 1, 1910	Wellington, WA	96
March 21, 1910	Green Mountain, IA	55
July 27, 1911	Hamlet, NC	10
August 25, 1911	Manchester, NY	29
July 4, 1912	East Corning, NY	39
July 5, 1912	Ligonier, PA	23
August 5, 1914	Tipton Ford, MO	43
September 15, 1914	Lebanon, MO	28
March 29, 1916	Amherst, OH	27
September 28, 1917	Kellyville, OK	23
December 20, 1917	Shepherdsville, KY	46
June 22, 1918	Ivanhoe, IN	68
July 9, 1918	Nashville, TN	101
November 1, 1918	Brooklyn, NY	97
January 12, 1919	South Byron, NY	22
December 20, 1919	Onawa, ME	23
February 27, 1921	Porter, IN	37
December 5, 1921	Woodmont, PA	27

people became hoboes, sneaking onto freight trains to escape impoverishment and unhappiness at home. Millions of Americans rode the rails or hitchhiked along highways during the 1930s to seek economic opportunities and to see the country. Traveling by boxcar was often dangerous and always a hardship. Illegal

Date	Place	Dead
August 5, 1922	Sulphur Spring, MO	34
December 13, 1922	Humble, TX	22
September 27, 1923	Lockett, WY	31
June 16, 1925	Hackettstown, NJ	50
October 27, 1925	Victoria, MS	21
September 5, 1926	Waco, CO	30
December 23, 1926	Rockmart, GA	20
June 19, 1938	Saugus, MT	47
August 12, 1939	Harney, NV	24
April 19, 1940	Little Falls, NY	31
July 31, 1940	Cuyahoga Falls, OH	43
August 29, 1943	Wayland, NY	27
September 6, 1943	Philadelphia, PA	79
December 16, 1943	Rennert/Buie, NC	72
July 6, 1944	High Bluff, TN	35
August 4, 1944	Stockton, GA	47
September 14, 1944	Dewey, IN	29
December 31, 1944	Bagley, UT	50
August 9, 1945	Michigan, ND	34
April 25, 1946	Naperville, IL	45
February 18, 1947	Gallitzin, PA	24
February 17, 1950	Rockville Centre, NY	31
September 11, 1950	Coshocton, OH	33
November 22, 1950	Richmond Hill, NY	79
February 6, 1951	Woodbridge, NJ	84
March 27, 1953	Conneaut, OH	21
January 22, 1956	Los Angeles, CA	30
September 15, 1958	Elizabethport, NJ	48
October 30, 1972	Chicago, IL	45
September 22, 1993	Big Bayou Conot, AL	47
March 15, 1999	Bourbonnais, IL	11

SOURCES: *The World Almanac and Book of Facts*; *Scalded to Death by the Steam* by Katie Letcher Lyle, 1991.

Electric trains and streetcars were first used in the 1880s, and almost 15.7 billion Americans annually rode streetcars by the mid 1920s. Some cities have elevated trains, operating on above-street tracks, or light rail vehicles such as streetcars powered by an electrified rail or overhead wire. Some of these systems are computer operated and driverless. Traffic complications between automobiles and streetcars resulted in buses replacing most streetcars circa 1950.

(circa 1900) The elevated 'El' train tracks running along Third Avenue past tenement buildings, New York City. A Jewish store with signs in Hebrew is in the foreground.

1900-1930s

passengers risked being arrested. Trains were often crime scenes where people were murdered or accused of crimes committed while traveling aboard, such as the notorious Scottsboro Trial in 1931 when two white women claimed they had been raped by a gang of black men on a train en route from Tennessee to Alabama. The 1933 movie, *Wild Boys of the Road*, attempted to depict freight hopping's hazards but actually made riding the rails seem appealing to many Americans.

During the first half of the twentieth century, African Americans used the railroad to flee from restrictive lives in an exodus from the South called the "Great Migration." Moving from impoverished rural areas to the industrialized North and Midwest where labor shortages existed, blacks hoped to find economic opportunities and more tolerant social policies and possibly full citizenship rights they were denied in the South.

Transportation symbolized freedom and mobility to these migrants, many of whom had been enslaved or were aware how previous generations of African Americans had been restricted to specific geographical places. Railroad routes were accessible throughout the South to northern destinations, and between 1916 and 1919, half a million blacks migrated from the South. Another one million African Americans moved north in the 1920s prior to the Depression, and another five million relocated north from 1940 to 1970. Some migrants learned to build ships and automobiles at northern factories to earn money, and others purchased expensive cars to flaunt their newfound prosperity. Although the antebellum Underground Railroad was not a physical technological system, its name foreshadowed the role of trains for future African Americans.

1880s–1960s • DISCRIMINATION In contrast to helping minorities attain autonomy, many forms of transportation were used to discriminate against minorities in the United States. Railroads especially were utilized to segregate blacks from whites. Before the 1950s and 1960s Civil Rights Movement, African Americans were required to sit in separate train cars, but many blacks refused to abide by discriminatory regulations. African American journalist Ida Wells Barnett sued the Chesapeake & Ohio Railroad in 1884 when she was physically expelled from a whites-only train seat. She based her legal action on the railroad's failure to provide separate but equal facilities for African Americans as stipulated by law. She won her case, but the Tennessee Supreme Court overturned the ruling.

African Americans were also expected to sit in designated seats on buses and in segregated areas of ships. Alice Coachman, the first African American woman to win an Olympic gold medal in 1948, had to travel in segregated sections of transportation separate from her white teammates. The arrest of Rosa Parks for refusing to relinquish her bus seat in 1955 was the catalyst for the Montgomery Bus Boycott in Montgomery, Alabama, and brought national attention to the plight of Civil Rights advocates in the Deep South. When public schools were integrated in the 1960s and 1970s, many Americans protested busing of black students into traditionally white neighborhoods. Freedom Riders were firebombed on buses in the 1960s.

1800s • BY WATER Bodies of water have influenced American demographics and settlement patterns and have provided a means to transport people and goods to and from the United States as well as within the country. Sailing vessels were used for shipping and military ventures, and steamships, introduced in the early 1800s, became the preferred form of water transport by the next century. Early settlers developed ports, shipyards, and canal systems from natural harbors and transportation routes that provided a foundation for twentieth century naval activity. Pioneering inventors devised modes of water transportation which have been improved to meet modern needs. Watercraft are used for tasks such as fishing, patrolling, ferrying and rescuing.

Americans have utilized waterways efficiently as trade routes. The Mississippi River, flowing from Minnesota to the Gulf of Mexico, is a major transportation system. In the nineteenth century, the United States Army Corps of Engineers built jetties in the river's mouth to eliminate buildup of sediment and sandbars. The army engineers constructed a series

(1859) The landing stage for the ferry which provides transport across the Hudson River between Garrison and West Point, New York State.

TRANSPORTATION 1723

1800s-1960s

of twenty-nine hydraulic dams and locks in the river from St. Louis to St. Paul and levees on land in the 1920s and 1930s to prevent flooding. These engineering improvements made the Mississippi River navigable by most vessels, including those with deep drafts, because deep water is pooled in each lock.

Barge traffic, usually accompanied by tugboats unless the barges are motorized, moves agricultural goods from the Midwest to southern ports where goods are shipped internationally. The locks usually prevent the Mississippi River from undergoing seasonal changes such as extremes of flooding and drought. With an annual operating budget of $110 million, the dam system insures consistent transportation on the Mississippi River from spring through autumn. The Corps of Engineers dredges the river to clear passage channels. Recreational boats in addition to houseboats and riverboat casino and tourist boats also move through the locks. Occasionally, more barges than can pass through each lock at a time line up, causing delays and congestion that affects the profitability of agriculture. Critics of the dams also cite how the system harms the habitats of wildlife, which costs an estimated $20 million annually to repair damages to the ecosystem.

Prior to the twentieth century, canals offered travelers and traders direct routes to destinations. Modern canals incorporate advanced technology, including hydraulic locks and computerized controls that link major metropolises. The St. Lawrence Seaway, a cooperative engineering project between Canada and the United States, is a significant transportation route. The United States Army Corps of Engineers and Environment Canada monitor the seaway for coastal erosion, implementing shoreline protection and management plans. They also supervise water level fluctuations and use Geographic Information Systems for comprehension of the entire seaway's status.

The Gulf Intracoastal Waterway along the Gulf Coast connects the St. Marks River, Florida with Brownsville, Texas (1,180 miles), connecting coastal and inland ports, and the Atlantic Intracoastal Waterway runs 1,329 miles from Key West, Florida to Norfolk, Virginia.

1960-PRESENT • PORTS ~ Ports and shipyards were built along America's coasts and in large inland bodies of water such as the Great Lakes, encouraging both domestic and international trade using cargo ships. These sites provided accessibility to inland forms of transportation, such as trucks and railroads, and benefited local communities' economies when manufacturers, industries, and businesses established factories and stores selling supplies and offering services near harbors. The Shipping Act of 1916 established that ship lines would discuss and set competitive rates acceptable to all companies. The Federal Maritime Commission was

Major United States Canals

Name	Year Canal or Sections Opened
Erie	1825
Chesapeake and Delaware	1829
Gulf Intracoastal Waterway	1892, 1897, 1905, 1941, 1949
St. Lawrence Seaway	1895, 1915, 1931, 1959
Houston	1914
BeaumontPort Arthur	1916
Atlantic Intracoastal Waterway	1938

SOURCE: American Society of Civil Engineers

Top U.S. Ports by Tonnage, 1996 (millions of tons)

South Louisiana, LA	189.8
Houston, TX	148.2
New York, NY & NJ	131.6
New Orleans, LA	83.7
Baton Rouge, LA	81.0
Corpus Christi, TX	80.5
Valdez, AK	77.1
Plaquemins, LA	66.9
Long Beach, CA	58.4
Texas City, TX	56.4
Pittsburgh, PA	50.9
Mobile, AL	50.9
Tampa, FL	49.3
Norfolk Harbor, VA	49.3
Lake Charles, LA	49.1
Los Angeles, CA	45.7
Baltimore, MD	43.6
Philadelphia, PA	41.9
Duluth-Superior, MN & WI	41.4
Port Arthur, TX	37.2
Beaumont, TX	35.7
St. Louis, MO & IL	30.2
Portland, OR	29.7
Pascagoula, MS	29.3
Chicago, IL	27.9

SOURCE: U.S. Corps of Engineers

established as an independent government agency in 1961 to regulate commercial shipping in American waters.

1940-1960 • IMPROVEMENTS TO SHIPS ~ Advances in cargo ship design such as refrigeration has enabled the global distribution of perishable produce grown in only certain regions of the world. Tankers were built after World War II. Ship composition changed from wood to steel during the twentieth century. Diesel ships dominated waters when the century began, and after World War I, turboelectric drives were improved and gradually adopted in vessels. Welding replaced rivets in ship manufacturing during World War II. Lighter-aboard ships (LASH) carried numerous barges loaded with over one thousand containers that could be delivered to shallow ports where the larger LASH could not dock. The first nuclear-powered ship, the *Savannah*, was launched at Camden, New Jersey, in 1960.

1900-PRESENT • RECREATIONAL BOATS ~ In addition to shipping commercial goods, steampower vessels transported passengers on transoceanic voyages for lines such as Cunard and White Star. Perhaps the best known ocean liner, the *Titanic*, hit an iceberg and sank in April 1912 with many influential Americans aboard. Four years before that tragedy, the *Republic*, a vessel carrying 742 people, and the *Florida*, transporting approximately 750 Italians evacuated from their homes after an earthquake, collided near Nantucket, Massachusetts. Both ships sank, but, unlike the Titanic, casualties were minimized because a wireless operator, Jack Binns, called for help successfully. At the time, such communications technology was considered a luxury, but modern transportation and communications are inseparable to assure safety and efficiency.

On vacations, Americans travel on cruise ships, primarily to Caribbean and Alaskan destinations. At home, they use almost 16 million pleasure boats. Post-World War II technological advances improved boating. Electric starters simplified operation of outboard motors that

EARLY 1900s

(1939) Passengers from the luxury liner 'Queen Mary' arrive at the New York customs center after their four-day trans-Atlantic crossing.

were mechanically improved to function more reliably. Many mechanical advances for boats were developed since World War II.

Outboard motors became more dependable and powerful, increasing from 3 horsepower in 1940 to 200+ horsepower by 2000, and less expensive. Lightweight aluminum alloys replaced heavy cast iron for motor composition. Aluminum, as well as fiberglass, also was used for hulls, and these materials required less maintenance than wood. Dacron and nylon were used for sails instead of cotton. The development of automobile-pulled boat trailers meant that people could store small vessels at home and transport them to launching ramps. More marinas were built to store and fuel recreational boats.

The federal government established boating laws and regulations which the United States Coast Guard enforces and vary whether boats are on inland, river, the Great Lakes or international waters. Boats with ten horsepower or greater motors are registered with states and the Coast Guard. Although federal law mandates that people who are employed to operate boats must be licensed, many states do not stipulate that recreational operators should be licensed. For safety reasons, each boat is required to be equipped with life preservers for everyone aboard.

1844-1919 • RACING BOATS ~ In 1844, the first American yacht club was organized in New York City, establishing a precedent for similar boating associations that held annual competitions. Motorboat races not only test drivers' skills in speed and distance trials but also results in improvement in boats' and engines' designs based on performance. The American Power Boat Association (APBA) was established in 1903 to implement racing rules for lake, river and ocean competitions and to provide honors for sporting achievements. During the twentieth century, racing motorboats

1904-1999 Twentieth Century American Shipwrecks

Date	Craft	Cause	Place	Dead
June 15, 1904	General Slocum	burned	New York, NY	1,030
July 24, 1915	Eastland	capsized	Chicago River	812
October 25, 1918	Princess Sophia	sank	Alaska waters	398
September 9, 1919	Valbanera	lost	Florida waters	500
June 12, 1924	USS Mississippi	exploded	San Pedro, CA	48
November 12, 1928	Vestris	sank	Virginia waters	113
September 8, 1934	Morro Castle	burned	Asbury Park, NJ	134
May 23, 1939	Squalus	sank	Portsmouth, NH	26
April 16, 1947	Grandcamp	exploded	Texas City, TX	510
May 26, 1954	Pennington	sank	Rhode Island coast	103
July 26, 1956	Andrea Doria and Stockholm	collided	Nantucket, MA waters	51
December 19, 1960	Constellation	fire	Brooklyn, NY	49
November 10, 1975	Edmund Fitzgerald	sank	Lake Superior	29
October 20, 1976	George Prince and Frosta	collided	Luling, LA	77
February 12, 1983	Marine Electric	sank	Chincoteague, VA	33
May 1, 1999	excursion boat	sank	Lake Hamilton, AR	13

SOURCE: *The World Almanac and Book of Facts*

were equipped with gasoline, diesel, jet and turbine engines that became more sophisticated. Racing boats differ by boat size, hull shape and engine power.

In 1904 on the Hudson River, the APBA initiated its most prestigious race, the Gold Cup, an annual competition for hydroplanes, which are boats that skim above the water surface, on a two-mile or longer circular course. Alexander Graham Bell designed the Hydrodome IV that set a world record of seventy miles per hour in 1919. In the late twentieth century, champion drivers such as Dave Villwock travel at speeds near two hundred miles per hour, risking personal injury in crashes. Villwock had two fingers amputated after a racing accident. Because boat racing is expensive, corporate sponsors often own the racing vessels, which are covered with merchandising logos, and hire teams of drivers and support personnel.

1873-1957 • PRESIDENTS AT SEA

Starting with the *USS Despatch* in 1873, American presidents have had several yachts to play and work on as a refuge from the White House. President Franklin D. Roosevelt dubbed the presidential yacht the "Floating White House" during the fishing trips he enjoyed. The first working submarine was tested in 1898, and, on August 25, 1905, President Theodore Roosevelt was the first president to be submerged in a submarine, spending fifty-five minutes in the *Plunger* at a depth of twenty feet in Long Island Sound near Oyster Bay, New York. Roosevelt was permitted to handle the submarine's controls. President Harry S. Truman traveled briefly in a captured U-boat near Key West, Florida, on November 21, 1946.

On September 26, 1957, President Dwight D. Eisenhower was the first president to dive in an atomic submarine, spending fifteen minutes at a sixty feet depth on the *Seawolf* near Newport, Rhode Island. Nuclear submarines could remain submerged for long durations and travel thousands of miles before refueling. In 1958, the first nuclear submarine, the *Nautilus*, passed underneath the North Pole with a navy crew commanded by William R. Anderson.

1903-1908 • THE WRIGHT BROTHERS

~ Flying has intrigued inventors throughout history. Since the late eighteenth century, Americans had experimented with balloon and kite flight, and developed gliders by the turn of the twentieth century. Inventors competed to be the first to fly a heavier-than-air engine-powered airplane. Like some early automobile designers, the brothers Orville and Wilbur Wright transferred their expertise in bicycle mechanics to the problem of how to design a machine that could carry a pilot.

Requesting aviation information from the Smithsonian Institute, the Wright brothers researched other people's attempts to create a machine capable of sustained flight. The experimental failures of Samuel Langley, the secretary of the Smithsonian, and Otto Lillienthal, a German pilot who died falling from a glider, aided the Wright brothers in how to approach the engineering problems. The brothers also consulted noted American aviation engineer Octave Chanute, who had designed and flown gliders successfully on hundreds of flights prior to the Wright Brothers. They determined that there were three concerns. First, a successful aircraft would need wings that could lift the combined weight of the airplane and pilot off of the ground. Second, the aircraft needed a power source to move through the air. And, third, control devices were needed to navigate the aircraft in flight. The brothers considered the last problem to be the most difficult to resolve.

Their mechanical experiences resulted in them considering the technical problem of manned flight in a way unique from other inventors. The brothers could visualize how mechanical devices operated and how components could be redesigned or applied to other forms of technology such as transferring bicycle methods to aircraft. Aware that successful bicycle riding depended on the rider's balance and movement with, instead of against, the bicycle's propulsion, the Wright brothers also observed flying birds. They constructed a box kite with wires in the wings that could twist them in opposite directions, like birds twisted their wing tips to turn and balance in the air. Naming this process wing warping, the brothers tested their design and were pleased at the control they achieved with the kite. The brothers' wing design relied on calculations Lillienthal had made.

Based on information from the United States Weather Bureau, the brothers traveled to the sand dunes of Kitty Hawk, North Carolina, where the nearby ocean contributed to the presence of consistent winds needed for flying experiments. They built a glider that incorporated a wing warping device that raised or lowered the wing's rear edge, and they also included a forward elevator which moved the nose up and down. Because the glider was unable to rise with a passenger, the brothers flew it like a kite to test their control tools and techniques.

The next year, the Wright brothers built a glider with larger wings, which they thought would be sufficient to lift a passenger. Hindered by pouring rains, they were eventually able to test the glider, but Wilbur lost control of it during a turn and injured his forehead when it crashed. Returning to Dayton, the frustrated brothers contacted Chanute and told him that they believed that Lillienthal's wing information contained errors. The brothers built a wind tunnel in their bicycle shop and experimented with various wing shapes to determine which one would provide the most lift. They also realized that the tail rudder should be hinged and connected to the wingwarping device to achieve successful control of the glider in flight.

1903-1908 • FAILURE AND SUCCESS

In order to transform their glider into an airplane, the Wright brothers contemplated power and propulsion sources, including an engine and propeller. They determined that the propeller actually functioned as a rotating wing that created thrust that moved the airplane forward. While the Wright brothers fine-tuned their design, Samuel Langley used $50,000 of United States Army funds to build a machine he called the Aerodrome. Flown by Charles Manley, Langley's aerodynamically-weak and uncontrollable aircraft crashed into the Potomac River in December 8, 1903.

The next week at Kitty Hawk, on December 17, 1903, the Wright brothers' gasoline-engine aircraft Flyer successfully lifted from a launching rail, carrying Wilbur for twelve seconds and flying 120 feet. The first heavier-than-air machine to complete a sustained, controlled flight later transported Orville 852 feet during

(1903) One of the Wright Brothers first flights at Kitty Hawk, North Carolina.

1903-1927

59 seconds. An eyewitness recorded the feat with a camera. Worried about possible patent infringements by competitors, the Wright brothers guarded public announcements of their achievement. Because of their secrecy and general skepticism, few people believed that manned flight had occurred.

European aviators received more publicity than the Wrights. Frustrated when the United States War Department rejected their proposal to develop military aircraft, the Wright brothers decided to market their aircraft abroad. The brothers continued to work on airplane designs and secured a patent in 1906 that helped convince President Theodore Roosevelt of the airplane's military potential. In 1908, the United States Army Signal Corps gave the Wrights $25,000. While Wilbur demonstrated the Wright's flyer in France, Orville flew a craft at Fort Myer near Washington, D.C., completing a seventy-minute flight. According to the Army contract, Orville flew with a passenger, Signal Corps Lieutenant Thomas Selfridge, who died from injuries sustained when they crash landed. He was the first person to die in a powered airplane accident. On October 11, 1910, former president Theodore Roosevelt became the first president to ride in an airplane, flying over St. Louis, Missouri, with Archie Hoxsey.

1909-1927 • BARNSTORMING ~ In 1909, the Wright brothers formed the Wright Company for airplane manufacturing. People worldwide flew aircraft or machines resembling the Wrights' design. The Wrights constantly sought damages for patent infringement because many people incorporated their designs and ideas. Others developed planes with unique attributes. During the early 1900s, Glenn Curtiss, also a bicycle mechanic, built airplanes with powerful engines. In 1914, his seaplane flew over Tampa Bay between Tampa and St. Petersburg, Florida, initiating the world's first commercial airplane service. Curtiss aircraft were adopted for a variety of aviation purposes.

Most people had never seen airplanes, thus aviation became a popular form of entertainment. This entertainment came in the form of watching pilots who performed daring spirals, rolls, figure eights and tailspins at air shows. Aerial circuses toured the United States. Barnstormers performed aerobatics with planes and thrilled audiences with daring maneuvers such as wing walking, and transferring between planes in the air and from automobiles and boats to low-flying airplanes.

Calbraith P. Rodgers flew from Brooklyn, New York, to Long Beach, California, in eighty-four days in 1911. This was the first American transcontinental flight. Rodgers was actually in the air for three days, ten hours and fourteen minutes during that time. In 1912 at Jefferson Barracks, Missouri, Albert Berry was the first person to parachute from an airplane. Aviators also participated in races such as the Belmont Park International Aviation Tournament. Some of the barnstormers owned aviation schools such as the Moisant School of Aviation on Long Island which offered training for student pilots to learn fundamental skills and maneuvers to earn licenses from the Aero Club of America.

Charles Lindbergh became the most famous barnstormer when he flew "The Spirit of St. Louis" solo, thirty-three hours nonstop from Roosevelt Field on Long Island, New York to Paris, France, on May 20 and 21, 1927. He was the first pilot to complete successfully a transatlantic flight. Lindbergh had learned to fly in the Army Air Service Reserve and was an airmail pilot who first flew the mail route between St. Louis and Chicago, using a railroad map for guidance. An international celebrity after he landed in Paris, Lindbergh returned to the United States on a warship assigned by President Calvin Coolidge, and more than four-and-a-half million New Yorkers waited to see him at the New York Harbor and along Broadway. Lindbergh later established new air routes and participated in goodwill tours to other countries.

1918-1937 • WOMEN PILOTS ~ Most early pilots were men because the public did not think women were capable of the strength and courage believed necessary to fly. Some American men learned to fly airplanes during World War I when aviation benefited from the military crisis because of increased demand for aircraft and pilots. After the war, non-military uses of airplanes resulted in improved designs and flying methods. Aviation veterans returned to the United States and earned money flying airplanes as test pilots for the military and airplane manufacturers. Others became corporate pilots for businesses or joined flying troupes that presented performances. Many pilots charged fees to take customers for rides. Pilots were employed for aerial advertising and transportation services. Ruth Law earned $9,000 a week by commercial and demonstration flying. She flew a record 590 miles nonstop solo from Chicago en route to New York City on November 19, 1916 before she was forced to land, delaying reaching her intended destination.

Blanche Scott was the first woman to fly an airplane solo. In 1911, Harriet Quimby was the first American woman who earned a license, breaking aviation gender barriers and proving that women should be given the opportunity to fly. An extraordinarily attractive journalist, Quimby was appealing to the public, and her talent for attracting publicity resulted in more Americans becoming aware of aviation and its potential to improve transportation. She was the first woman to fly solo across the English Channel. Quimby's flying accomplishments stressed that technology was becoming accessible to more people and established a foundation for future aviatrixes. For magazines, she wrote about the commercial possibilities aviation offered for passenger services, mail routes, and aerial photography and cartography.

Bessie Coleman was the first African American female pilot, and she had to earn her license in France in 1921 from the Federation Aeronautique Internationale because of segregation in the United States. She proved that both women and blacks were capable of mastering flight and demonstrated the potential of diverse uses of aviation technology. Coleman was a pioneering black barnstormer and stunt pilot. Both she and Quimby died when they fell from the open cockpits of their planes because they did not wear seatbelts. By 1929, federal regulations concerning low altitude flying resulted in many barnstormers retiring.

Amelia Earhart learned to fly from pioneering aviatrix, Anita Snook, at her school in Los Angeles. In 1928, Earhart became the first woman to fly across the Atlantic as a passenger, and she completed a solo transatlantic flight in 1932. She had participated in the first Women's Air Derby in 1929, racing from Santa Monica, California, to Cleveland, Ohio, and was the first president of the Ninety-Nines, a women's pilot organization. From 1928 to 1931, she served as vice-president of

(1931) American aviator Amelia Earhart (1898 - c.1937) climbs into the cockpit of her airplane at Willow Grove, Pennsylvania, just before embarking on a trip to California.

1915-1929 Luddington Airlines, Incorporated, an early passenger service in the East. Earhart set numerous altitude and speed records, popularizing aviation in America. She made the first solo flight from Honolulu to the U.S. mainland in January 1935, then completed the first nonstop Mexico City to New York flight in May. Her disappearance in 1937 with copilot Frederick Noonan in the Pacific is one of aviation's most puzzling mysteries.

1915-1929 • AIRMAIL AND PASSENGERS ~ Congress created the National Advisory Committee on Aeronautics (NACA) in 1915 to report on the status and future of flight science. Committee members included aviation experts and government and military representatives. World War I stimulated the mechanical advancement of airplanes to carry heavier loads more quickly for longer time periods over greater distances. After the armistice, public interest in aviation waned. Magazines published articles that encouraged airmindedness and the development of commercial aviation. American children joined model airplane clubs.

The first transcontinental airmail route began in 1920, transporting mail between New York City and San Francisco. In the early twenties, the federal government became active in developing civil and commercial aviation. Government agencies created numerous transcontinental airmail routes and placed beacons for night flights. Because airplanes at that time could not attain high altitudes, mountains hindered service. Transcontinental Air Transport and the Pennsylvania Railroad cooperated to alternate rail and aviation services to overcome these landscape obstacles. In 1925, the Kelly Air Mail Act opened airmail contracts to private companies based on competitive bids. As a result, not only was service guaranteed, but it was also flown by the lowest bidders.

In order to earn extra money, airmail carriers began to transport passengers in the 1920s. For example, Western Air Express first offered passenger service

---

Earle Ovington strapped the first airmail letter approved by the United States Postal Department to his knees on September 23, 1911, and took off at the Nassau Boulevard air meet on Long Island. He flew five miles to Mineola where he dropped the mail for delivery to the post office. In 1918, United States Army pilots began transporting mail by air until civilian pilots performed that service for the postal department. These flights were hazardous, with pilots landing in fields and navigating with flashlights. Approximately thirty-one of the initial group of forty airmail pilots died in service.

(circa 1925) A U.S. Aerial Mail Service biplane, a pilot, postal workers and a postal automobile on an airfield in Cleveland, Ohio. This was the inaugural flight for the service between Cleveland and Chicago.

between Salt Lake City, Utah, and Los Angeles on April 17, 1926. Several aviation companies, including Boeing, were formed to fly the airmail routes. In October 1928, Lillian Gatlin, President of the National Association of Gold Star Mothers, was the first woman to cross the continent by air. Flying as a special delivery package in a mail plane because no commercial passengers-only services existed, she traveled from San Francisco to Long Island to promote aviation.

As civilian and commercial air traffic expanded, regulation became necessary. President Calvin Coolidge signed the Air Commerce Act on May 20, 1926. This act authorized the Secretary of Commerce to encourage aviation by creating airways, supporting navigation instrumentation research and development, overseeing pilot licensing and aircraft examinations and investigating accidents. Such rules and policies helped Americans consider aviation as a serious pursuit instead of a novel entertainment. In 1924, sixty airplanes were manufactured in the United States, increasing to 5,500 by 1929.

1920s-1970s • IMPROVEMENTS IN AIRCRAFT ~ In addition to designing automobiles, Henry Ford created, then improved, the Ford Trimotor with stronger radial engines to travel at swifter speeds. Possible airplane speed increased from 100 to 150 miles per hour. John Northrup and the Lockheed Aircraft Company built the lighter-weight radial-engine, wooden-skinned Vega of 1927, which could carry a pilot and six passengers and served as a model for future commercial airplanes.

In 1931, Wiley Post and Harold Gatty were the first people to circle the globe in an airplane. Post repeated the trip solo in 1933. He developed a high-altitude flying suit that allowed him to attain a height of 49,000 feet.

1920s-1967

Boeing produced an airplane made completely of metal with retractable landing gear. The twin-engine Boeing 247 made in 1933 is considered the first modern commercial aircraft because it was more maneuverable and safer than trimotors and could be flown in an emergency with one engine. Boeing was unable to fill Transcontinental and Western Airlines' order for this type of airplane, and the Douglas Company built a smaller version, the DC2/3, which some authorities state is the most significant of the early commercial planes because of its versatility. Later aircraft included pressurized cabins so that the airplanes could rise to higher altitudes. The 1940 Boeing Stratoliner could reach 14,000 feet and fly 200 miles per hour because of four supercharged engines that could lift the weight of extra fuel to travel long distances.

Aerospace researchers designed more sophisticated jet airplanes based on World War II aviation developments and experiences. Chuck Yeager broke the sound barrier on October 14, 1947, when he flew a Bell X1 rocket at speeds exceeding 670 miles per hour. Six years later, he piloted a BellX1A at more than two-and--a-half times the speed of sound.

In the late 1940s, the first nonstop transoceanic propeller-driven airliners reduced traveling time from the U.S to Europe from four days on a ship to one day in the air. Commercial jet airliners with multiengines began to transport passengers regularly within the United States and abroad in the 1950s.

In the next decade, Boeing's jumbo jet, the 747, carried several hundred passengers plus freight long distances. Supersonic modes of transportation such as the Concorde were developed in the 1970s to make long journeys quicker as people moved faster than the speed of sound to reach global destinations. The expensive airfares for the Concorde based on the large amounts of fuel burned in transit limited the number of passengers who chose that service.

1938-1967 • GOVERNMENT REGULATION ~ The Civil Aeronautics Board had been created in 1938 to oversee American airline transportation and was terminated after Congress deregulated the airline industry in 1978. In 1958, the Federal Aviation Act outlined domestic aviation regulations and formed the Federal Aviation Agency that became the Federal Aviation Administration (FAA) in 1967. The FAA oversees commercial airlines, regional and commuter airlines, helicopters and cargo carriers and has set

Busiest U.S. Airports in 1999

Airport	Number of Passengers
Atlanta/Hartsfield	77,939,536
Chicago/O'Hare	72,568,076
Los Angeles/LAX	63,876,561
Dallas/Fort Worth	60,000,125
San Francisco	40,387,422
Denver	38,034,231
Minneapolis/St. Paul	34,216,331
Detroit	34,038,381
Miami	33,899,246
Newark	33,814,000
Las Vegas	33,669,185
Phoenix/Sky Harbor	33,533,353
Houston	33,089,333
New York/JFK	32,003,000
St. Louis	30,188,973
Orlando	29,173,491

SOURCE: *Airports Association Council International*

noise limits for air traffic. The Air Transport Association of America is the airlines' trade organization.

1939-1942 • CIVIL PILOTS DURING WORLD WAR II ~ During World War II, many Americans learned to fly in the Civilian Pilot Training Program (CPTP), which the Civil Aeronautics Authority sponsored from 1939 to 1942 at American colleges and universities. Rose Rolls Cousins was the first black female solo CPTP pilot. She traveled to Tuskegee, Alabama, in hopes of joining the Tuskegee Airmen, the African American military pilots, but was denied permission because of her gender despite being told that her piloting skills qualified her.

Members of the Women's Airforce Service Pilots (WASP) were civilians who ferried supplies and airplanes to troops. Some American women, such as the Curtiss Wright Cadettes at Grinnell College in Iowa, also attended ground schools to learn aviation mechanical skills such as assembling engines so they could fix airplanes during World War II. After the war, women had few employment opportunities in the aircraft industry despite their training and experience. Women with financial resources, such as Louise Arner Boyd continued Earhart's legacy of setting aviation records. In 1955, Boyd was the first woman to fly over the North Pole.

Hot air balloons regained popularity for recreation and sport in the late twentieth century. In 1979, American Byron Allen crossed the English Channel in the Gossamer Albatross, a mylar and polystyrene aircraft powered by Allen pedaling a mechanism similar to a bicycle. Dick Rutan and Jeana Yeager flew the Voyager nonstop around the world in nine days without refueling in 1986.

1939-1970S • SPECIAL DUTY AIRCRAFT ~ Ukrainian immigrant Igor Sikorsky built the first successful helicopter in 1939. Airplanes and helicopters are used for search and rescue missions and to drop relief parcels and food to stranded people and livestock such as during a December 1967 blizzard in the Southwest. Although helicopters cannot carry many passengers or much freight, they are more maneuverable than airplanes and are used to medevac accident victims to hospitals. Helicopters also serve as vehicles to monitor highway traffic for television and radios stations and to seek fugitives for law enforcement agencies. Both specially-equipped helicopters and airplanes are used to fight forest fires.

Airplanes and helicopters are also modified to transport military troops, politicians, and the United States president and staff. Air Force One is the best known form of presidential transportation. That term is a radio call sign that refers to either of the Boeing 747-200B's or any Air Force aircraft on which the president is aboard. The first presidential aircraft was the "Sacred Cow," a commercial Boeing 314 Clipper Ship, which transported President Franklin D. Roosevelt to the Casablanca Conference in January 1943. He was the first United States president to fly while in office.

Various aircraft carried successive presidents, and the call sign Air Force One was initiated during President Dwight D. Eisenhower's term to prevent confusion when other aircraft had the same number as the Air Force craft that transported him. Initially a classified call sign, it was publicized during President John F. Kennedy's administration. The C-137C which transported Kennedy's body from Dallas, Texas, to Washington, D.C., after his assassination and where

1937-1997

President Lyndon B. Johnson was pictured taking the oath of office is one of the most familiar presidential airplanes.

The flying Oval Office transports presidents to domestic and foreign meetings. The presidential airplanes have twice the wiring of normal 747s to protect the aircraft from electromagnetic pulses that would disrupt electronic equipment in case of a thermonuclear blast. Eisenhower was also the first American president to fly in a helicopter, and presidential helicopter landings on the White House lawn became a common occurrence. Cargo planes transport security and administrative personnel and communications equipment and supplies required for presidential trips.

1937-1997 • AIR HAZARDS ~ On August 3, 1981, the Professional Air Traffic Controllers Organization (PATCO) began a strike. The 15,000 PATCO members were federal employees who had been seeking higher wages, fewer hours and different retirement requirements. Air traffic controllers stated that their jobs were more stressful than other federal employment, causing many air traffic controllers to retire at younger ages. Because the PATCO strike was illegal, President Ronald Reagan fired 12,000 air traffic controllers who did not resume their duties. While training replacement controllers to assist the nonstriking controllers to direct domestic flights, the government reduced the number of flights by twenty-five percent. Passengers experienced delays and worried about aviation safety. The airlines lost approximately $30 million daily. President Reagan said that the striking controllers

(1936) The Hindenburg airship (LZ-129) flies over the Hudson River and downtown Manhattan, New York City.

had quit their jobs and were told that they would never be rehired or eligible for any federal employment. The government decertified PATCO, and pro-union groups criticized the government's anti-labor attitudes.

The 1981 air traffic controller strike foreshadowed safety concerns of late twentieth-century air transportation. By 2000, 733 million people flew annually on commercial airlines, and aviation travel became more hazardous and timeconsuming. Because of increased demand and pilot, mechanics and crew labor strikes, many flights were canceled or delayed, and incidents of air rage increased from passengers angered by sitting on runways for hours. Although most experts claim that air travel is safer than automobiles, when airplane disasters or hijackings occur, they are usually catastrophic and dramatic. One of America's best-known air calamities was when the German dirigible, the gas-powered *Hindenberg*, exploded and burned over Lakehurst, New Jersey, on May 6, 1937. Within thirty-seven seconds, flames consumed the *Hindenberg*, killing thirty-six people. Sixty-two passengers survived. Because the airship fire was the first to be filmed, many people were shocked by the tragedy.

Aircraft disasters have killed passengers and crew-members in addition to people on the ground. Airplanes crash because of mechanical malfunctions, poor weather conditions, wind shear, crowded runways and inadequate air traffic management. Besides jet airplane wrecks, which cause the deaths of hundreds of people, private aircraft also are involved in hundreds of collisions annually. Some hobbyists have been killed in ultralight aircraft that larger airplanes cannot see and run into. Private pilots have died in both propeller-driven aircraft and small, private jets. Notable aircraft casualties in the twentieth century included singer Richie Valens, John F. Kennedy, Jr. and golfer Payne Stewart, whose jet flew hundreds of miles on autopilot after the pilot and all the passengers had lost consciousness due to a failure in the cabin pressure, crashing only after it ran out of fuel. Another pilot gained temporary notoriety when he crashed his plane into the White House and died.

> On December 8, 1963, a Boeing 707 exploded northeast of Elkton, Maryland, when lightning struck it. All eighty-one people aboard were killed. Eyewitnesses included skaters at the Merryland Roller Rink in nearby Glasgow, Delaware, who thought an atomic bomb had been detonated. Other people saw an orange glow they thought was a meteor before realizing that it was a burning airplane. As the jet plummeted, burning fragments fell into a field and set corn stubble on fire. The fuselage punched a huge crater in the ground. As a result of this first lightning-caused American air disaster, the Federal Aviation Administration formed a lightning protection committee that required lightning repelling devices on aircraft.

1937-1997

1926-1986 • SPACE FLIGHT

Although most Americans will never be transported aboard spacecraft, they are familiar with the vehicles that astronauts have used to explore space. Robert H. Goddard launched the first liquid-fueled rocket in 1926 at Auburn, Massachusetts. That rocket rose forty-one feet in the air. After the Soviet Union was the first country to launch a successful orbiting

Twentieth Century American Air Disasters

(casualty totals include victims killed on the ground)

Date	Aircraft	Place	Dead
May 6, 1937	Hindenburg, German zeppelin	Lakehurst, NJ	36
July 28, 1945	U.S. Army B25	New York, NY	14
December 20, 1952	U.S. Air Force C124	Moses Lake, WA	87
October 6, 1955	United Airlines DC4	Medicine Bow Peak, WY	66
November 1, 1955	United Airlines DC6B	Longmont, CO	44
June 20, 1956	Venezuelan Super Constellation	near Asbury Park, NJ	74
June 30, 1956	TWA Super Constellation/United DC7	Grand Canyon, AZ	128
December 16, 1960	United DC8/TWA Super Constellation	New York City	134
December 8, 1963	Boeing 707	over Elkton, MD	81
July 19, 1967	Piedmont Boeing 727/Cessna 310	Hendersonville, NC	82
May 3, 1968	Braniff International Electra	Dawson, TX	85
November 14, 1970	Southern Airways DC9	Huntington, WV	75
September 4, 1971	Alaska Airlines Boeing 727	Juneau, AK	111
December 29, 1972	Eastern Airlines Lockheed Tristar	Miami, FL	101
July 31, 1973	Delta Airlines jet	Boston, MA	89
December 1, 1974	TWA727	Upperville, VA	92
June 24, 1975	Eastern Airlines 727	New York, NY	113
December 13, 1977	U.S. DC3	Evansville, IN	29
September 25, 1978	Boeing 727/Cessna 172	San Diego, CA	150
May 25, 1979	American Airlines DC10	Chicago, IL	275
January 13, 1982	Air Florida Boeing 737	Washington, D.C.	78
July 9, 1982	Pan Am Boeing 727	Kenner, LA	153
August 2, 1985	Delta Air Lines L1011	DallasFt. Worth, TX	137
August 31, 1986	Aeromexico DC9/Piper PA28	Cerritos, CA	82
August 16, 1987	Northwest Airlines MD82	Romulus, MI	156
July 19, 1989	United Airlines DC10	Sioux City, IA	111
September 8, 1994	USAir Boeing 737300	Aliquippa, PA	132
October 31, 1994	American Eagle ATR72210	Roselawn, IN	68
May 11, 1996	ValuJet DC9	Everglades, FL	110
July 17, 1996	Trans World Airlines Boeing 747	near Long Island, NY	230
January 9, 1997	Comair Embraer 120	Detroit, MI	29

SOURCE: *The World Almanac and Book of Facts*; *Natural Disasters*, Marlene Bradford and Robert S. Carmichael, eds, 2001.

1926-1986 satellite in 1957, a space race began. The United States soon launched satellites, then sent space probes and landers to the moon. The American engineers included a team of rocket experts who had emigrated from Germany after World War II. In 1958, NACA became the National Aeronautics and Space Administration (NASA) which recruited military jet test pilots to become the first astronauts.

Jerrie Cobb and twelve female pilots also passed the rigorous tests to qualify as Mercury astronauts and called themselves Fellow Lady Astronaut Trainees or Flats. Although Cobb trained for three years, she was assigned publicity duties and never traveled into space.

The Mercury flights were launched with Redstone and Atlas rockets that carried capsules that could orbit the earth with one astronaut. Alan B. Shepherd, Jr., was the first American in space, and John H. Glenn, Jr. was the first American to travel in orbits. The Gemini missions, lifted by Titan rockets, paired astronauts to practice rendezvous and docking with other spacecraft, space walking, and changing orbital paths. These astronauts also remained in orbit for longer durations.

The Apollo capsules, boosted into space by Saturn rockets, prepared for the lunar landing. On July 20, 1969, Neil Armstrong became the first person to walk on the moon's surface. On additional Apollo missions, astronauts collected lunar samples. President Nixon was the first United States president to watch a manned space flight launch when he observed the liftoff of Apollo 12 on November 14, 1969, at Cape Kennedy, Florida.

Additional groups of astronauts were selected, and space centers expanded near scientific industries and military air bases. In the early 1970s, NASA engineers built Skylabs, orbiting scientific laboratories that were the predecessors of the International Space Station. A final Apollo mission in 1975 united American and Soviet space travelers. The space shuttle was developed as a form of reusable space transportation to deploy and repair satellites and the Hubble telescope and to study microgravity. The first shuttle, *Columbia*, was launched on April 12, 1981. Future shuttle missions included the Spacelab for international scientific investigations. Students were encouraged to compete for their science experiments' inclusion on the shuttle.

The United States space program has also endured tragedies that caused many Americans to criticize NASA. The worst accidents were the *Apollo 1* launch pad fire on January 27, 1967, in which three astronauts died, and the *Challenger* explosion on January 28, 1986, in which six astronauts and the first private citizen, Christa McAuliffe, a teacher who was selected from thousands of applicants, were killed. The astronauts on the *Apollo 13* mission resolved a malfunction that threatened to cause that spacecraft to fail. Despite numerous successful space probes, the failure of a Mars lander in 1999 resulted in many Americans questioning the value of space travel, especially to Mars, where many aerospace researchers aspired to transport humans. These diverse disappointments caused NASA's purpose to be scrutinized and its budgets cut by the end of the twentieth century. Social critics have long questioned the morality of spending so much money on what they regard as fantasy science when so many Americans are sick and hungry.

1914-PRESENT • TRANSPORTATION AND GOVERNMENT ~ Although most American transportation forms are privately owned, the federal government helps finance facilities such as air traffic control centers and regulate transportation. Such intervention has occurred since the late nineteenth century when the federal government wanted to prevent railroads from imposing unfair rates. By the 1980s, such regulation was eased because critics demanded more competition to encourage transportation providers to improve their services. Although American transportation was considered the world's best in 1900, the lack of government funding resulted in American services declining while state supported transportation in Europe gained eminence. Increased government subsidies have resulted in American transportation becoming comparable to superior European systems, especially rail.

Established in 1966, the U.S. Department of Transportation (DOT) is America's primary federal agency regulating motorized vehicles and aircraft. The first Secretary of Transportation in the presidential cabinet was appointed in 1967. Those officials have monitored national transportation concerns and recommended actions to resolve problems that threaten to interrupt transportation. The DOT enforces fuel-mileage standards, drafts transportation legislation in cooperation with other agencies, and sets manufacturing and operation standards such as exhaust limits. Transportation secretaries suggest required safety devices such as air bags and rear window brake lights, and encourage the implementation of seat belt laws. State DOTs monitor local transportation needs, which the federal DOT assists and coordinates.

In 1991, Congress approved the Intelligent Transportation Systems (ITS) which researches how state-of-the-art information and communication technologies can improve traffic safety by applying them to transportation devices and vehicles. The government also encourages the improvement and expansion of public transit and intercity transportation facilities to make them an attractive transportation source for motorists to choose instead of relying on automobiles. Mass transit systems are essential for the thirty percent of adult urban Americans who do not own cars.

Some urban areas designate special traffic lanes for buses and cars with a certain number of passengers. Future plans call for automated roadside inspection services. Intelligent vehicles will have onboard instrumentation to notify authorities immediately when vehicles are involved in accidents, and lanekeeping and collision-avoidance technology will prevent crashes in heavily congested areas where vehicles travel at high speeds. Just as interstate construction required innovative civil engineering skills, future ITS technology necessitates new applications of electronics, communication, and systems engineering which are still being devised.

An independent federal agency, the National Transportation Safety Board (NTSB) investigates major transportation accidents such as train derailings. The NTSB also examines the accident scene of every American civil aviation accident. Analyzing the data collected from these accidents, the NTSB prepares safety guidelines in an effort to prevent future transportation disasters. In 1965, consumer watchdog Ralph Nader published *Unsafe at Any Speed*, charging that vehicle design flaws were the cause of fatal accidents. Congress passed legislation the next year, establishing the National Safety Bureau, which became the National Highway Traffic Safety Administration (NHTSA). This agency monitors crash testing of new automobiles and provides information about how vehicles can be made safer for passengers through the use of restraints for adults and children. Programs also emphasize correct driver behavior, such as sobriety, and educate how to prevent accidents. Issuing recalls, the NHTSA investigates vehicular defects that threat-

United States Secretaries of Transportation

Alan S. Boyd	1967-1969
John A. Volpe	1969-1973
Claude S. Brinegar	1973-1974
William T. Coleman	1975-1977
Brock Adams	1977-1979
Neil E. Goldschmidt	1979-1981
Drew Lewis	1981-1983
Elizabeth Dole	1983-1989
Samuel K. Skinner	1989-1991
Andrew Card	1991-1993
Federico F. Peña	1993-1997
Rodney E. Slater	1997-2001
Norman Y. Mineta	2001

SOURCE: U.S. Department of Transportation

en safety, odometer fraud and consumer complaints about vehicles. That agency decides and regulates fuel economy standards and antitheft measures.

In an effort to minimize vehicle-produced pollution, the Environmental Protection Agency (EPA) and state agencies oversee vehicle emission standards established by the Clean Air Act of 1970, its 1990 amendments and the Energy Policy and Conservation Act of 1975. The Federal Highway Administration monitors interstate trucking. The Surface Transportation Board regulates railroads. The Federal Maritime Commission watches the shipping industry, and the Federal Energy Regulatory Commission regulates natural gas and oil pipeline companies.

The United States Postal Service has played a significant role in shaping transportation. Colonial Postmaster General Benjamin Franklin outlined mail roads to expedite service. Throughout its history, the postal service adopted new delivery modes and improved transportation methods within the United States. In addition to generating funds for highways, mail contracts provided revenues for railways and aviation facilities. Rural free delivery (RFD) was initiated in the late nineteenth century, resulting in rural Americans becoming less isolated socially and culturally and having more access to news and information. Roads were improved and extended into remote areas where industries were built and contributed to rural economies. The postal service utilized new technology as mail delivery underwent a transition from stagecoaches to trains to jet airplanes. The final railway route was canceled in 1977. Large trucks transport mail within postal zones, and fleets of small, motorized vehicles are used for distribution within communities. In 1914, Congress approved the first federally owned motor vehicle service for the Washington, D.C. Postal Department.

Politicians have found transportation issues crucial to winning elections and public opinions of their performance in office. Huey Pierce Long, Jr., pledged transportation reforms that helped his election as Louisiana's governor in 1928. President Ronald Reagan was both praised and criticized for the firing the protesting air controllers during the 1981 strike which disrupted commercial aviation. Politicians debate possible outcomes of mergers of major transportation carriers that might limit competition and negatively affect consumers and constituents. Partisan conflict in Congress is often about transportation issues such as construction contracts, environmental concerns and transportation workers forming unions such as the United Auto Workers and Teamsters to demand equitable salaries and safe working conditions.

CONCLUSION

In 1900, the function of American transportation was primarily to move freight from one location to another. By 2000, passenger conveyance was transportation's primary purpose. Business and engineering schools offer majors in transportation studies, traffic planning and aviation management. Approximately ten percent of the American workforce is employed in the transportation industries, whose companies produce and sell transportation vehicles, devices, and fuel; carry passengers or freight; and offer transportation-related services. Transportation manufacturers are the leading American manufacturers. Producers of steel, glass, rubber and petroleum for transportation also are major national profit-earners. Road construction contractors, new and used car dealerships and transportation-related service businesses form the core of American business.

Cars and trucks remain the primary transportation tool. Railroads are convenient for delivering passengers into cities, while airports usually are on urban peripheries, necessitating use of rental cars, taxis, buses or other modes to reach desired destinations near the airport. In 1940, 8.3 billion people rode streetcars but by 2000, few lines still operated because bus use had replaced streetcars in the last half of the twentieth century. However, buses were unable to compete economically with more affordable transit modes.

Intermodal transportation is the shipping of freight by several methods. For example, containerization has been used since the mid-twentieth century to pack products into large metal containers, which can ride on flatcars on the railroad, be towed by trucks or placed by crane on ships. In the 1990s the Intermodal Surface Transportation Efficiency Act and the Transportation Equity Act for the 21st Century approved flexible use of highway funds for transportation alternatives.

BIBLIOGRAPHY

Berlow, Lawrence H. *The Reference Guide to Famous Engineering Landmarks of the World: Bridges, Tunnels, Dams, Roads, and Other Structures*. Phoenix, AZ: Oryx, 1998.

Bilstein, Roger E. *The American Aerospace Industry: From Workshop to Global Enterprise*. New York: Twayne, 1996.

———. *Flight in America: From the Wrights to the Astronauts*. 3rd ed. Baltimore: The John Hopkins University Press, 2001.

———. *Flight Patterns: Trends of Aeronautical Development in the United States, 1918-1929*. Athens: University of Georgia Press, 1983.

Brown, John K. *The Baldwin Locomotive Works, 1831-1915: A Study in American Industrial Practice*. Baltimore: The Johns Hopkins University Press, 1995.

Cohen, Norm. *Long Steel Rail: The Railroad in American Folksong*. Urbana: University of Illinois Press, 1981.

Corn, Joseph J. *The Winged Gospel: America's Romance with Aviation, 1900-1950*. New York: Oxford University Press, 1983.

Crouch, Tom D. *Aiming for the Stars: The Dreamers and Doers of the Space Age*. Washington: Smithsonian Institution Press, 1999.

———. *The Bishop's Boys: A Life of Wilbur and Orville Wright*. New York: W.W. Norton, 1989.

———, ed. *Charles A. Lindbergh: An American Life*. Washington, D.C.: National Air and Space Museum, Smithsonian Institution Press, 1977.

———. *A Dream of Wings: Americans and the Airplane, 1875-1905*. Washington, D.C.: Smithsonian Institution Press, 1989.

———. *The Eagle Aloft: Two Centuries of the Balloon in America*. Washington, D.C.: Smithsonian Institution Press, 1983.

Cudahy, Brian J. *Cash, Tokens, and Transfers: A History of Urban Mass Transit in North America*. New York: Fordham University Press, 1990.

———. *Under the Sidewalks of New York: The Story of the Greatest Subway System in the World*. Lexington, MA: The Stephen Greene Press, 1988.

Davies, Richard O. *The Age of Asphalt: The Automobile, the Freeway, and the Condition of Metropolitan America*. Philadelphia: Lippincott, 1975.

DeVorkin, David. *Science With a Vengeance: How the Military Created the U.S. Space Sciences After World War II*. New York: Springer-Verlag, 1992.

Douglas, George H. *All Aboard: The Railroad in American Life*. New York: Paragon House, 1992.

Federal Highway Administration. *America's Highways 1776-1976*. Washington, D.C.: Government Printing Office, 1976.

Flink, James J. *The Automobile Age*. Cambridge: Massachusetts Institute of Technology Press, 1988.

Gibbs-Smith, C.H. *Flight Through the Ages: A Complete Illustrated Chronology from the Dreams of Early History to the Age of Space Exploration*. New York: Crowell, 1974.

Glischinski, Steve. *Burlington Northern and Its Heritage*. Osceola, WI: Motorbooks International, 1996.

Hadfield, Charles. *The Canal Age*. 2nd ed. North Pomfrey, VT: David & Charles, 1981.

Hallion, Richard P. *Supersonic Flight: Breaking the Sound Barrier and Beyond*. Washington, D.C.: Brassey's, 1997.

———. *Test Pilots*. Washington, D.C.: Smithsonian Institution Press, 1981.

Hemming, Robert J., and Maury Graham. "Steam Train." *Tales of the Iron Road: My Life as King of the Hobos*. New York: Paragon House, 1990.

Hood, Clifton. *722 Miles: The Building of the Subways and How They Transformed New York*. Baltimore: The Johns Hopkins University Press, 1995.

Jackson, Donald C. *Great American Bridges and Dams*. Washington, D.C.: Preservation Press, 1988.

Jackson, Kenneth T. *Crabgrass Frontier: The Suburbanization of the United States*. New York: Oxford University Press, 1985.

Jakle, John A. *The Tourist: Travel in Twentieth-Century North America*. Lincoln: University of Nebraska Press, 1985.

Jakle, John A., and Keith A. Sculle. *The Gas Station in America*. Baltimore: The Johns Hopkins University Press, 1994.

Jakle, John A., Keith A. Sculle, and Jefferson S. Rogers. *The Motel in America*. Baltimore: The Johns Hopkins University Press, 1996.

Jenkins, Dennis R. *Space Shuttle: The History of Developing the National Space Transportation System*. 2nd ed. Marceline, MO: Walsworth Publishing Co., 1996.

Jennings, Jan, ed. *Roadside America: The Automobile in Design and Culture*. Ames: Iowa State University Press, 1990.

Lee, Allan E. *American Transportation: Its History and Museums*. Charlottesville, VA: Hildesigns Press, 1993.

Lemann, Nicholas. *The Promised Land: The Great Black Migration and How It Changed America.* New York: Vintage Books, 1991.

Lewis, David L., and Laurence Goldstein, eds. *The Automobile and American Culture.* Ann Arbor: University of Michigan Press, 1980.

Lewis, Tom. *Divided Highways: Building the Interstate Highways, Transforming American Life.* New York: Viking, 1997.

Lewis, W. David, ed. *Airline Executives and Federal Regulation: Case Studies in American Enterprise from the Airmail Era to the Dawn of the Jet Age.* Columbus: Ohio State University Press, 2000.

Lewis, W. David, and Wesley P. Newton. *Delta: The History of an Airline.* Athens: University of Georgia Press, 1979.

Lewis, W. David, and William F. Trimble. *The Airway to Everywhere: A History of All American Aviation, 1937-1953.* Pittsburgh, PA: University of Pittsburgh Press, 1988.

Liebs, Chester H. *Main Street to Miracle Mile: American Roadside Architecture.* Boston: Little, Brown and Company, 1985.

Logsdon, John M. *The Decision to Go to the Moon: Project Apollo and the National Interest.* Cambridge: Massachusetts Institute of Technology Press, 1970.

Lyle, Katie Letcher. *Scalded to Death by the Steam: Authentic Stories of Railroad Disasters and the Ballads That Were Written About Them.* Chapel Hill, NC: Algonquin Books of Chapel Hill, 1991.

Maiken, Peter T. *Night Trains: The Pullman Systems in the Golden Years of American Rail Travel.* Baltimore: The Johns Hopkins University Press, 1992.

Margolies, John. *Home Away From Home: Motels in America.* Boston: Little, Brown, and Company, 1995.

Martin, Albro. *Railroads Triumphant: The Growth, Rejection, and Rebirth of a Vital American Force.* New York: Oxford University Press, 1992.

May, George W. *Charles E. Duryea, Automaker.* Chillicothe, IL: River Beach Publishing, 1996.

Mazlish, Bruce. *The Railroad and the Space Program: An Exploration in Historical Analysis.* Cambridge: Massachusetts Institute of Technology Press, 1965.

McDougall, Walter A. *The Heavens and the Earth: A Political History of the Space Age.* New York: Basic Books, 1985.

McShane, Clay. *The Automobile: A Chronology of its Antecedents, Development and Impact.* Westport, CT: Greenwood Press, 1997.

Mead, Robert Douglas. *Journeys Down the Line: Building the Trans-Alaska Pipeline.* New York: Doubleday, 1978.

Middleton, William D. *Landmarks on the Iron Road: Two Centuries of North American Railroad Engineering.* Bloomington: Indiana University Press, 1999.

Moon, Henry. *The Interstate Highway System.* Washington, D.C.: Association of American Geographers, 1994.

Newhouse, Elizabeth L., ed. *The Builders: Marvels of Engineering.* Washington, D.C.: National Geographic Society, 1992.

Nock, O.S. *Railways of the USA.* New York: Hastings House Publishers, 1979.

Ordway, Frederick I., and Mitchell R. Sharpe. *The Rocket Team.* New York: Crowell, 1979.

Papageorgiou, Markos, ed. *Concise Encyclopedia of Traffic & Transportation Systems.* New York: Pergamon Press, 1991.

Patton, Phil. *Open Road: A Celebration of the American Highway.* New York: Simon & Schuster, 1986.

Petroski, Henry. *Invention by Design: How Engineers Get From Thought to Thing*. Cambridge: Harvard University Press, 1996.

Rae, John B. *The Road and the Car in American Life*. Cambridge: Massachusetts Institute of Technology Press, 1971.

Reynolds, Terry S. ed. *The Engineer in America: A Historical Anthology From Technology and Culture*. Chicago: University of Chicago Press, 1991.

Rich, Doris L. *Amelia Earhart: A Biography*. Washington, D.C.: Smithsonian Institution, 1989.

———. *The Magnificent Moisants: Champions of Early Flight*. Washington, D.C.: Smithsonian Institution Press, 1998.

———. *Queen Bess: Daredevil Aviator*. Washington, D.C.: Smithsonian Institution Press, 1993.

Richter, William L. *The ABC-CLIO Companion to Transportation in America*. Santa Barbara, CA: ABC-CLIO, 1995.

Roland, Alex. *A Spacefaring People: Perspectives on Early Spaceflight*. Washington, D.C.: National Aeronautics and Space Administration, 1985.

Rose, Mark H. *Interstate Express Highway Politics 1941-1989*. Rev. ed. Knoxville: University of Tennessee Press, 1990.

Scharff, Virginia. *Taking the Wheel: Women and the Coming of the Motor Age*. New York: Free Press, 1991.

Seely, Bruce E. *Building the American Highway System: Engineers as Policy Makers*. Philadelphia: Temple University Press, 1987.

Shallat, Todd. *Structures in the Stream: Water, Science, and the Rise of the U.S. Army Corps of Engineers*. Austin: University of Texas Press, 1994.

Siuru, William D., Jr., and Andrea Stewart. *Presidential Cars & Transportation: From Horse and Carriage to Air Force One, the Story of How the Presidents of the United States Travel*. Iola, WI: Krause Publications, 1995.

Solberg, Carl. *Conquest of the Skies: A History of Commercial Aviation in America*. Boston: Little, Brown, 1979.

Stover, John F. *Transportation in American History*. Washington, D.C.: American Historical Association, 1970.

Sussman, Joseph. *Introduction to Transportation Systems*. Boston: Artech House, 2000.

Warren J. *Americans on the Road: From Autocamp to Motel, 1910-1945*. Cambridge: Massachusetts Institute of Technology Press, 1979.

Vance, James E., Jr. *Capturing the Horizon: The Historical Geography of Transportation Since the Transportation Revolution of the Sixteenth Century*. New York: Harper & Row, 1986.

———. *The North American Railroad: Its Origin, Evolution, and Geography*. Baltimore: The Johns Hopkins University Press, 1995.

White, John H., Jr. *The American Railroad Freight Car: From the Wood-Car Era to the Coming of Steel*. Baltimore: The Johns Hopkins University Press, 1993.

———. *The American Railroad Passenger Car*. Baltimore: The Johns Hopkins University Press, 1985.

Wilson, Rosalyn A. *Transportation in America 2000, with Historical Compendium 1939-1999*. 18th ed. Washington, D.C.: Eno Transportation Foundation, 2001.

Wohl, Robert. *A Passion for Wings: Aviation and the Western Imagination, 1908-1918*. New Haven: Yale University Press, 1994.

Wood, Donald F., and James C. Johnson. *Contemporary Transportation*. Upper Saddle River, NJ: Prentice Hall, 1996.

INTERNET RESOURCES

United States Department of Transportation
http://www.dot.gov

National Transportation Library
http://www.ntl.bts.gov/

National Transportation Safety Board (NTSB)
http://www.ntsb.gov/

Bureau of Transportation Statistics
http://www.bts.gov/

National Highway Traffic Safety Administration (NHTSA)
http://www.nhtsa.dot.gov/

Intelligent Transportation Systems (ITS) Home Page
http://www.its.dot.gov/

Institution of Transportation Engineers
http://www.ite.org/

Automobile Association of America
http://www.aaa.com/

Federal Aviation Administration
http://www.faa.gov/

Federal Aviation Regulations
http://www.faa.gov/avr/AFS/FARS/far_idx.htm

Air Traffic Control System Command Center (ATCSCC)
http://www.fly.faa.gov/

AAA Foundation for Traffic Safety (AAAFTS)
http://www.aaafts.org/

Urban Mobility Study
http://mobility.tamu.edu

News, Car Reviews, Auto Shows
http://www.auto.com/

Automotive Learning On-line
http://www.innerbody.com/

Innovative Transportation Technologies
http://faculty.washington.edu/~jbs/itrans/

EV World (electric vehicle)
http://www.evworld.com/

Foster's Online-Science and Technology
http://www.fosters.com/special_sections/autos/

Fuel Economy Site
http://www.fueleconomy.gov/

Insurance Institute for Highway Safety
http://www.highwaysafety.org/

Truckers/Transportation Homepage
http://www.uky.edu/Subject/transport.html

N.A.D.A. Guides
http://www.nadaguides.com/

Airlines of the Web
http://www.flyaow.com/frames.htm

National Air and Space Museum Milestones of Flight
http://www.nasm.edu/galleries/gal100/gal100.html

To Fly is Everything-A Virtual Museum covering the invention of the Airplane
http://hawaii.psychology.msstate.edu/invent/air_main.shtml

United States Coast Guard
http://www.uscg.mil/

Naval Historical Center (NHC)
http://www.history.navy.mil/

Association of American Railroads
http://aar.org/

National Association of Railroad
  Passengers
http://www.narprail.org/

WEB JOURNAL

Transportation Quarterly
http://www.aashto.org/quarterly/a_quart.html

Elizabeth D. Schafer

Travel

~

(circa 1946) Designer Sergeant Clyde O. Peterson sitting in the cockpit of his invention, a car built from salvaged aeroplane parts.

TIMELINE

1825-1899 ~ Developing Transportation

George Stephenson builds the first public railroad, the Baltimore and Ohio (B & O) (1825) / First railroad sleeping cars constructed (1829) / Congress makes the first federal land grants for development of U.S. railroads (1850) / First transcontinental railroad completed at Promontory Point, Utah (1869) / Yellowstone, the first national park, is established (1872) / Philadelphia Centennial draws big crowds (1876) / Children's Aid Society of New York City offers a summer home for children at Bath, Long Island (1885) / Congress passes the Interstate Commerce Act to control certain economic practices of U.S. railroads (1887) / Chicago World's Columbian Exposition is held (1893)

MILESTONES: Fugitive Slave Law requires the return of runaway slaves (1850) • Colorado gold rush begins (1858) • Homestead Act promises land to pioneer settlers (1862) • Capture of Geronimo (Chiricahua Apache leader) ends formal warfare between whites and Native Americans (1886) • Thomas Edison invents the motion picture (1889) • Henry Ford begins production of the gas-powered automobile (1896)

1900-1919 ~ Cars and Boats and Trains and Planes

Introduction of color photo reproduction provides cheap, eye-catching images for ads (1900) / New York introduces first law governing automobile speed (1901) / Louisiana Purchase Exposition held in St. Louis (1904) / Sinking of the British ship, the *Titanic*, kills 1500 passengers (1912) / Ford Model T costs $290, down from $950 in 1908 (1915) / Grand Canyon becomes a national park (1919)

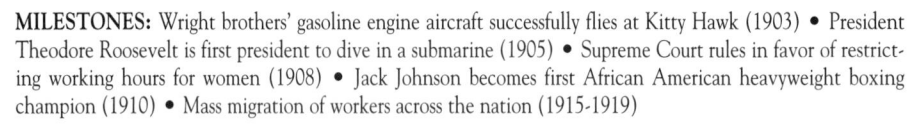

MILESTONES: Wright brothers' gasoline engine aircraft successfully flies at Kitty Hawk (1903) • President Theodore Roosevelt is first president to dive in a submarine (1905) • Supreme Court rules in favor of restricting working hours for women (1908) • Jack Johnson becomes first African American heavyweight boxing champion (1910) • Mass migration of workers across the nation (1915-1919)

1920-1929 ~ Proliferation of Travel

One out of every eight American workers is employed in automobile-related industries (1920s) / First set of traffic lights is built in New York City (1922) / First national road atlas is published by Rand McNally (1924) / The first motel (motor hotel) is built in San Luis Obispo, California (1925) / Construction begins on Route 66, beginning in Chicago and ending in Santa Monica (Los Angeles) will be fully paved by 1937, crossing 8 states and 3 time zones (1926) / Charles Lindbergh completes nonstop transatlantic flight on "The Spirit of St. Louis" (May 20 and 21, 1927) / First public parking garage is built in Detroit (1929)

MILESTONES: First commercial radio broadcast (1920) • First transcontinental airmail route established between New York City and San Francisco (1920) • Bessie Coleman becomes first African American female pilot, earning her license in France because of segregation in the U.S. (1921) • Alexander Fleming discovers penicillin in molds (1928) • Coca Cola sold in 66 countries (1929)

1930-1949 ~ Depression and War

First jet aircraft put into service (1939) / 30,000 Americans die in car accidents (1930) / Streamliners popularize railroad travel (1930s) / Wiley Post and Harold Gatty are the first people to circle the globe in an airplane (1931) / Amelia Earhart is the first woman to complete a solo transatlantic flight (1932) / First freeway, Pennsylvania Turnpike, opens (1940) / Chuck Yeager breaks the sound barrier (1947)

MILESTONES: Emergency Banking Act closes, then reopens failing banks (1933) • Blue Cross hospital insurance program created (1933) • The ocean liner *Queen Mary* commissioned for use as a troop carrier to and from Australia during World War II (1939) • Japanese bomb Pearl Harbor, forcing the U.S. into World War II (1941) • French ship, the *Normandie* burns in New York City harbor as it is being converted from a luxury liner to a U.S. troop carrier (1942) • Oral penicillin introduced (1945) • Mao Zedong's communist party seizes power in China (1949)

1950-1969 ~ International Travel Boom

Gerard Blitz creates the first Club Med with 23,000 members (1950) / U. S. liner *United States* commissioned, the fastest ocean liner ever built (1951) / Airlines offer the first transatlantic tourist fares (1952) / First McDonald's opens (1952) / Disneyland opens (1955) / Interstate Highway Act funds a vast network of high speed roads (1956) / Bank of America introduces credit cards (1959)

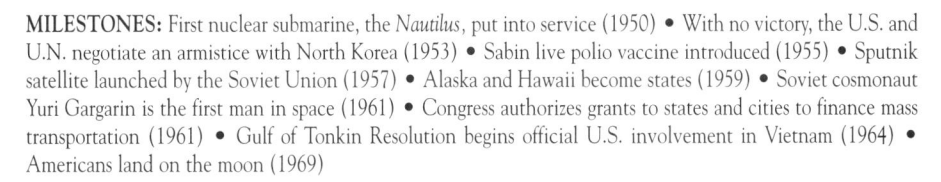

MILESTONES: First nuclear submarine, the *Nautilus*, put into service (1950) • With no victory, the U.S. and U.N. negotiate an armistice with North Korea (1953) • Sabin live polio vaccine introduced (1955) • Sputnik satellite launched by the Soviet Union (1957) • Alaska and Hawaii become states (1959) • Soviet cosmonaut Yuri Gargarin is the first man in space (1961) • Congress authorizes grants to states and cities to finance mass transportation (1961) • Gulf of Tonkin Resolution begins official U.S. involvement in Vietnam (1964) • Americans land on the moon (1969)

1970-2000 ~ International Travel Boom

Safari holidays, Kenya's major industry, attract many Americans (1970) / Rail Passenger Service Act establishes Amtrak to transport passengers on intercity routes (1970) / Ocean liner *Queen Elizabeth* burns in Hong Kong while undergoing renovations (1972) / Supersonic *Concorde* jet put into service for passenger flights (1972) / Travel/tourism is the second largest industry in the U.S. after health (1992)

MILESTONES: President Nixon resigns over Watergate scandal (1974) • First test-tube baby born in England (1978) • Hostages taken from the U.S. embassy in Teheran (1979) • President Reagan disbands the Air Traffic Controllers union (1981) • *Challenger* space shuttle explodes killing six astronauts and the first private citizen in space, Christa McAuliffe (1986) • Congress approves Everglades National Park restoration (2000)

INTRODUCTION

Wither shall I turn
By road or pathway, or through trackless field,
Up hill or down, or shall some floating thing,
Upon the river point me out my course?
                                            William Wordsworth

Two roads diverged in a wood, and I—
I took the one less traveled by,
                                            Robert Frost

Technically, a traveler is anyone going from one place to another by any means and for any purpose. Generally, a person would not be considered a traveler, however, if he or she went to the next door neighbor's or to a nearby friend's or relative's house, or to a store or shop. In the past, travel was undertaken principally for battle, trade, or pastureland. Travelers went by land or sea, across deserts or oceans, up or down rivers, or along caravan routes like the Silk Road of Asia. By the fifteenth century, or even earlier, men also set out to explore the unknown. Usually travel serves some purpose; however, travel can also be for no purpose at all.

Author Michael Crichton once said he traveled because "I felt a need for rejuvenation, for experiences that would lead me away from things I usually did, the life I usually led. From time to time I felt the urge to do something for no reason at all." Like most endeavors, travel has also had its share of heroes. Across the centuries, there have been thousands of travelers from all over the world who have had a tremendous influ-

(1977) NASA's Space Shuttle Urbiter mounted on top of a 747 carrier jet completes the first inert captive test flight at the Edwards Air Force Base in Lancaster, California.

ence on society at their destinations as well as at home. The earliest people who wandered the earth from Africa to Europe or from Asia across to North and South America were brave heroes to future civilizations. Odysseus, Marco Polo, Christopher Columbus, Francisco Magellan, and Zheng He are some of the most famous explorers and travelers who charted unknown seas and lands. By the twentieth century, some of the most courageous travelers would be pilots—Charles Lindbergh, Amelia Earhart, and astronauts.

Travel for the express purpose of leisure before the nineteenth century was done by very few people and usually limited to the wealthy. Very wealthy Alexandrians, Greeks, and Romans traveled to spas and summer resorts for rest and relaxation or to escape pestilence, such as malaria. It wasn't until the nineteenth and twentieth centuries, however, that a great many people traveled for leisure

IMPACT OF TRAVEL ON SOCIETY

It has been said that the history of civilization is a story of mobility, migration, settlement adaptation, and integration into a place. The primary means of investigating social reality in pre-industrial times was travel. The reports of travelers provided the raw materials from which statistical compilations were created; travel correspondence, so closely bound up with the art of travel, provided the reader with information and a great sense of place.

Whenever a person travels, he not only brings change, he experiences changes as well, however slightly or imperceptibly. Travel is a source of the new; it shapes history. Coming into contact with other people, places, and goods has an impact, positively or negatively, on a person. And a person impacts other persons, places, or goods, positively or negatively. It is interesting to contemplate this phenomenon as travel is discussed in terms of changing society. The strength of the impact is one of the factors to observe or to investigate.

Another factor is how changes in society affected travel—who traveled, where they traveled, and why they traveled. Technological inventions have affected how people travel as well as who travels and why. As more and more people traveled—for business or for leisure, they influenced multiple changes in society. For example, travelers need an infrastructure in order to travel; they must have places to stay and places to eat. As the demand for such services grows travelers also impact the natural environment. To understand the interaction of changes in travel and changes in society in the twentieth century United States, it is necessary to first look at developments in the nineteenth century.

WORK VS. PLAY

In trying to analyze whether society affects changes in travel or travel affects societal change more, it is also interesting to investigate the influence of the conflict between work and pleasure in the United States. American culture prides itself on the philosophy that working is good and idleness is not. Work brings financial safety, which idleness threatens. The American work ethic was shaped by the Puritan ideal and by the republican philosophy, which dominated early nineteenth century social and intellectual thought. The idleness of the "gentleman" was often derided. One of the most famous books on the subject was Thorsten Veblen's *The Theory of the Leisure Class*, published in 1899. In the work, Veblen attacked conspicuous consumption and the idle rich, and warned against the evils of both.

Tensions between work and play were exacerbated by the very success of the growing middle class in the nineteenth and early twentieth centuries. Industriousness and discipline helped make people middle class and earn them time and money to be able to take vacations. However, vacations embodied the very opposite of what the middle class most valued, hard work. The lessening of this tension is the story of the changes in travel for leisure and society in the twentieth century.

From the nineteenth century to World War II, changes in the United States fostered changes in travel and who traveled and why. Those who traveled in the first half of the nineteenth century were the elite, but by the turn of the century and up until World War II, the growing middle class joined the elite travelers. Since World War II travel has become a mass phenomenon in the United States. Social factors which brought this about included the change from an agricultural to an industrial nation; the growth of a vast transportation network; the growth of the middle class; and the increase in general prosperity and consequent leisure time.

IMMIGRANTS

It has often been said that the United States is a nation of immigrants. They have come from every country in the world, and at certain times there have been waves of immigrants. Immigrants are travelers who seek new locations because they are starving, persecuted, or just in search of a better future. Prior to the Civil War of 1860-1865, immigrants were mainly from northern Europe. Immigrants typically were and are intrepid travelers, with few resources, yet with a determination to seek better circumstances. When people migrate, especially in large numbers, their own cultural values, customs, and languages change the culture into which they immigrate.

1800-1865 • WHY THEY CAME AND WHERE THEY WENT ~ The Irish famine has been well documented and the numbers of immigrants who came to the United States as a result numbered in the millions. German peasants also came in droves in the nineteenth century because of a similar potato famine and because of political unrest. The Irish settled mainly in cities, especially Boston and New York, though in many others

Table 1: Percent of Foreign-Born in the United States in 1850

England and Wales	14
Ireland	43
Germany	26
Scandinavia	0.8
France	2
Austria-Hungary	—
Italy	0.2
Poland	—
Russia	—
China	—
Japan	—

SOURCE: *A Century of Population Growth: 1790-1900.* Genealogical Publishing Co. 1989.

as well. Germans settled more in the middle west, especially in Chicago and Wisconsin. Scandinavians settled in rural areas in the Midwest, Minnesota and the Dakotas. Table 1 demonstrates the origins of Americans by the mid-nineteenth century.

1865-1900 • What They Did ~ After the Civil War, immigrants, particularly the Chinese in the West and the Irish in the East, were employed to build the transcontinental railroads. Although immigrants built the railroads, they could rarely use them for travel; they built them for others. These immigrants had a tremendous impact on American society in every way. Initially they provided inexpensive manual labor that fueled the country's growing industrialization, but eventually they provided leaders in every occupation and level of society. Their impact was felt in urban and rural areas, in the growing factory movement and in farming. Just one example of the impact of immigrants is Andrew Carnegie who came from Scotland and built a steel empire in the nineteenth century. Today he is still well-known for his philanthropic works.

1870-1900 • The Wealthy ~ The wealthy traveler in the mid-nineteenth century traveled for reasons that had a tremendous impact on society. They were the first group of Americans to take vacations, defined as pleasure trips lasting at least a few days (previously known as excursions). In the nineteenth century the elite travelers went for rest and recuperation (R & R). They went to spas and resorts to cure illnesses and to enjoy

(1859) Monteagle House. Not only were spas a niche travel destination, but also a favorite honeymoon spot. Seen here is the Monteagle House, one of the many hotels built at Niagara Falls for tourists celebrating their honeymoons.

1830-1869

leisure time. Since ancient times the wealthy had gone to spas for the curative properties of drinking mineral waters or bathing in mineral springs. Europe had many famous spas. Nineteenth century Americans began to build such places in their own country to establish their own spa and resort culture.

One of the first American resorts was in Saratoga Springs, New York. Others such as White Sulphur Springs, West Virginia soon sprang up in the North and South. Cape May, New Jersey and Newport, Rhode Island were among the early seaside resort areas. Wealthy Southerners went to the mountains to escape the hot and humid climate of the plantations. Northerners went to the sea or mountains to escape the hot and gritty urban life. Such resorts catered to "genteel people and genteel pursuits." Though the motive for travel was R and R, resorts and spas became places to "be seen." Days were filled with constant activity for both men and women. A typical day in the first half of the nineteenth century included a promenade of an hour or so after each meal, with dancing and card playing in the evening.

1830-1860 • WESTERN TRAVEL

Throughout the nineteenth century thousands of American citizens and new immigrants traveled west, first across the Appalachians, then across the Plains and Rocky Mountains. They went to start new lives, or in search of adventure, riches, or land to farm. They built new societies as they went, supplanting the existing native society wherever they came into contact with it. These travelers, or pioneers, who ventured beyond the Mississippi River, contended with loneliness, hardship, and the inaccessibility of only a few scattered towns before they finally reached the western coast.

The Gold Rush of 1848 brought a huge wave of all kinds of travelers to the western United States. To reach the gold fields of California, people traveled by every conveyance imaginable—ship, cart, horse, or foot. They seldom settled in the Plains. As a result, California's development leapt ahead of the area between the Mississippi and the Pacific coast.

1825-1869 • RAILROADS

During the Civil War—1860-1865—resort-building declined, but the last half of the nineteenth century saw many changes in travel in the United States, not the least of which was a significant increase in it. One of the primary reasons for the increase in travel after 1865 was the development of the railroads, especially west of the Mississippi River. By the end of the century, trains were the primary means of long-distance travel.

Railroad building began in England where Richard Trevithick built the first steam engine in the early 1800s. In 1825 George Stephenson built the first public railroad. The first U.S. railroad was the Baltimore and Ohio (B & O), which at first went only from Baltimore to Ellicott City, Maryland, about twelve miles. In 1831 regular passenger service in the South began. By 1850 all states east of the Mississippi River had railroads, and the Northeast had a true rail network. Just prior to the Civil War there were about 30,000 miles of track.

The first railroads were uncomfortable and the food undesirable, but increased use brought rapid improvement. The first sleeping cars, called land bridges, were built in 1829. By 1836 there were regular sleeping trains between Baltimore and Philadelphia. After 1850 steel rails replaced wooden rails so train travel became smoother and more dependable. Trains could average 50-60 m.p.h.

On May 10, 1869, the first transcontinental railroad was completed when the Central Pacific and Union Pacific sections met at Promontory Point, Utah. Some 10,000 Chinese workers had constructed the Central Pacific sections across the mountains from Sacramento, California, beginning in 1863. Meanwhile, the Union Pacific railroad, using some 10,000 Irish immigrants had begun construction from Omaha, Nebraska in 1865. By the end of the nineteenth century, the United States had five transcontinental lines.

1860-1890 • IMPACT OF RAILROAD BUILDING ~ After the Civil War the first revolution in travel began. The combination of government land grants, business efforts, and the public's desire to move west came together to create a huge railroad construction boom. Railroads linked the nation coast to coast and opened up the vast, unsettled interior of the country. Railroads also became the first large-scale industry in the United States, and railroad construction was instrumental in creating other industries, including steel, timber, and coal. Between 1860 and 1890, over 130,000 miles of track were laid.

Railroads inspired the growth of towns wherever they made regular stops. Isolated rural families could come to town to purchase goods brought by the railroad or to ship their products to other cities and towns. In this way, a sense of community was created out of the vast emptiness of the plains. Communities became connected to the outside world. Clusters of "civilization" grew across the United States. Railroad building affected every facet of life and every group, creating ripples in a pond that seemed to spread endlessly, affecting people, capital, and natural resources.

> In the heyday of sleepers, the 1880s, there were three principal sleeping car makers, Webster Wagner, Theodore Woodruff, and George M. Pullman. Sleepers eventually became known as Pullman cars. William D'Alton Mann built compartment cars also, which were elegant but which held fewer passengers. Traveling by overnight train created a need for service workers. In 1867 George Pullman's Palace Car Company hired freed slaves as porters, one of the few places freed men could find jobs. From this came the Brotherhood of Sleeping Car Porters, a very strong, mostly African American union. In the twentieth century, A. Philip Randolph was one of its greatest leaders. The union finally went out of existence in 1978.

Certain railroad stops became cow towns, shipping points for the cattle industry. Abilene, Kansas was the first of these. Ranchers could ship their cattle to stockyards in Omaha or Chicago instead of driving herds hundreds of miles, often through hazardous conditions. Railroads also fueled the growth of the vacation and business travel industry, and they led to democratization of leisure and vacations as more people could afford the time and price of travel.

By the 1870s so many people were traveling that the railroad companies competed with travel agents for selling vacation trips. Thomas Cook opened one of the first travel agencies in England in the 1840s. After the Civil War, in 1865, he came to the United States to take advantage of the burgeoning market for travel. Many others soon followed.

Table 2: Important Dates in Nineteenth Century Railroading

1804   Richard Trevithick of England invents the steam engine locomotive

1825   The Stockton and Darlington Railway, built in England by George Stephenson, offers the first regularly scheduled steam-powered train service

1831   The South Carolina Canal and Railroad Company begins regularly scheduled steam-powered train service in the United States

1836   The Champlain and St. Lawrence Railroad begins operating Canada's first regularly scheduled steam-powered trains in Quebec

1850   Congress makes the first federal land grants for development of U.S. railroads

1869   The world's first transcontinental railroad is completed across the United States

1887   Congress passes the Interstate Commerce Act to control certain economic practices of U.S. railroads

1895   The Baltimore and Ohio Railroad starts the world's first electric main-line service in Baltimore

SOURCE: World Book Encyclopedia, 1995.

Railroads Then and Now
The present Amtrak system follows the paths of the first railroads

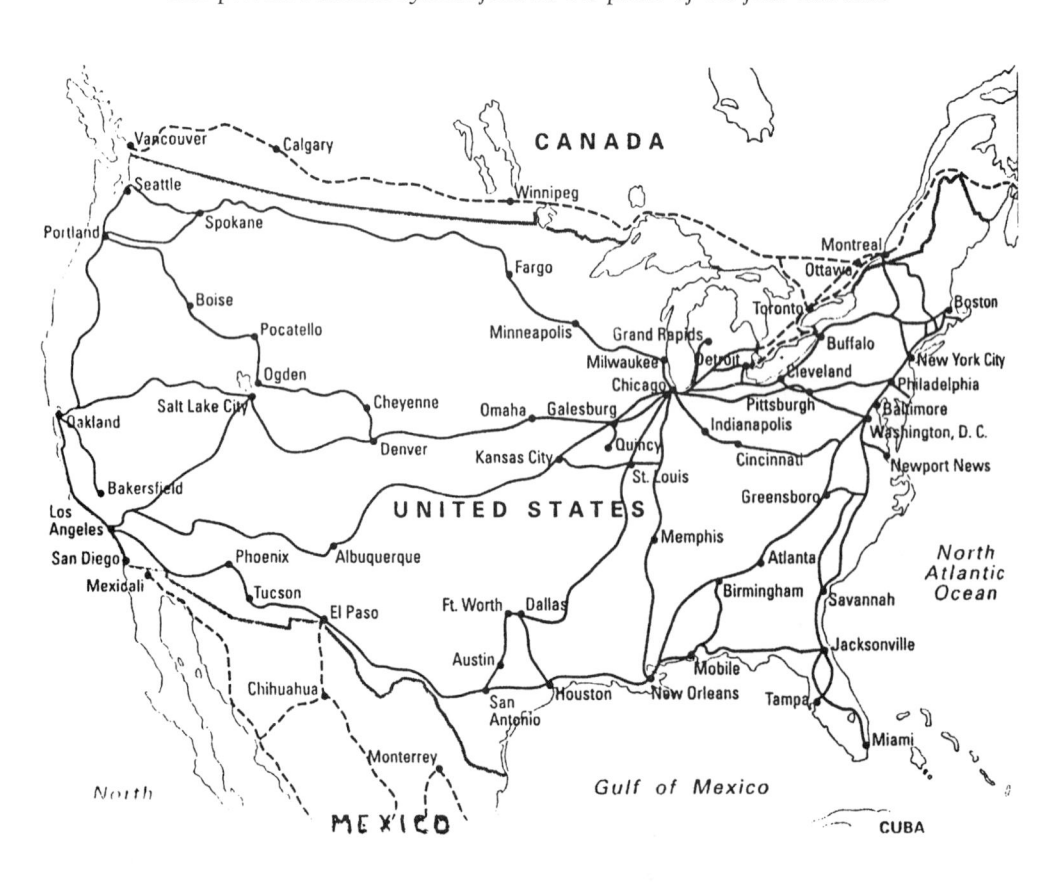

SOURCE: World Book Encyclopedia, 1995.

(circa 1900) An electric locomotive hauling a passenger train through the Baltimore Tunnel on the Baltimore and Ohio line—the first main line in America to use electric power (installed in 1896).

1880-1900 • NEW WAVES OF IMMIGRATION ~ In the late 1800s, there were new waves of immigrants coming to the United States. Before the Chinese Exclusion Acts of 1880 and 1882, great numbers of Chinese came to the West to work on building the railroads and in mining the gold fields in California and Alaska. Immigrants, mostly rural people, also flooded in to the East from Southern and Eastern Europe, settling mainly in cities where it was easier to find work in growing industries. Some of these immigrants also provided the labor needed to build the transportation systems of cities and towns—subways, trolleys, bridges, and roads—just as earlier immigrants had built the railroad lines.

Between 1820 and 1890 over 15 million immigrants had come from Ireland, Germany, and Scandinavia. Between 1891 and 1920 over 18 million came from Italy, Austria-Hungary, Romania, and Russia. The total from Northwest Europe in 1870 was 3.1 million; in 1900, 4.2 million. Compare this to 1.8 million from Central and Eastern Europe in 1870 growing to 4.1 million in 1900. In the ten years from 1890-1900, immigration from Central and Eastern Europe climbed from 1.7 million to over 3 million. While during that same time period immigration from northern and Western Europe declined from 3 to 1 million. The turn of the century also marked a time when immigration from Latin America began in earnest. For example, Mexican immigration in 1870 was 42,000; in 1900, 103,000. Over the last half of the nineteenth century, immigrants accounted for over 30 percent of the population growth of the United States. Table 3 compares the percent of foreign-born between 1850 and 1900.

1870-1900

Table 3: Percent of Foreign-Born in the United States

	1850	1900
England and Wales	14	9
Ireland	43	16
Germany	26	26
Scandinavia	.8	10
France	2	1
Austria-Hungary	—	6
Italy	.2	5
Poland	—	4
Russia	—	5
China	—	.8
Japan	—	.2

Note: The blanks represent a number less than one tenth of one percent. They are used for comparison.

SOURCE: *A Century of Population Growth: 1790-1900.* Genealogical Publishing Co. 1989.

1870-1900 • VACATIONS ~ In the last half of the nineteenth century, an infrastructure grew throughout the United States that supported the growth of a vacationing culture. Increasingly, work allowed for vacation time; there was a range of resorts in terms of location and type; and railroads and roads provided a safe and easy transportation network.

Vacation spots were often places where both men and women were active, often on an equal par. Some of the activities enjoyed by both sexes included bowling, hiking, billiards, fishing, swimming, croquet, dancing, and flirting. Women and children often spent the whole summer at a resort while their husbands and fathers continued to work in the city, occasionally visiting the family.

1870-1900 • IMPACT OF THE MIDDLE CLASS ~ After the Civil War the middle class grew rapidly. It included more than businessmen; clerks, salespeople, bookkeepers, managers, small entrepreneurs, even teachers earned enough money to be able to consider time for travel, at least to nearby locations. One of the most popular destinations for the middle class was camp meetings. These began as summer gatherings for religious rejuvenation. Gradually the social occasion of the camp meeting became as popular as the religious aspect of it. While there was no drinking or dancing allowed, staples of the resort crowd, camp meetings still provided socializing and became increasingly secular.

Often anxious about taking time off from work, the middle class traveler often looked for vacation spots that offered intellectual stimulation as well as relaxation. The Chautauqua Movement brought lecturers and concerts to the vacationers and offered short courses on a variety of topics, often in an outdoor setting. The movement began in Chautauqua, New York, but spread rapidly across the country, from Maryland to California, Minnesota to Texas. In the early twentieth century, there were also African American Chautauquas that emphasized individual self-improvement and racial pride. They also offered a forum for discussion of political problems and solutions.

Another popular nineteenth century destination for middle class vacationers was camping. It was an inexpensive and relaxing way to escape the hot drudgery of summer in the city. As camping grew in popularity, it became very important in making vacations part of the lives of working class Americans as well. One of the most popular camping books was William H.H. Murray's *Adventures in the Wilderness; or, Camp-Life in the Adirondacks*, published in 1869. He offered descriptions of campsites, nature, and the camping experience.

1870-1900 • TOURISM ~ As more and more Americans traveled for vacation, a new type of traveler developed, the tourist. The tourist does not travel in order to find employment. He goes to experience the travel, the place, and the sights. Tourism is a phenomenon concerned with leisure, but a tourist travels to see and do things, not just to relax. Tourism is a type of vacation, but it is not the same as a vacation. For example, business travelers can be tourists though they are not on vacation. From the earliest days of tourism, tourists were prone to try to cram as much "seeing" as possible into their allotted time.

Tourism aided in developing an "American" culture by increasing the knowledge of who and what America was; encouraging people to visit natural wonders, historic sites, and cultural attractions in cities. Many guidebooks at the end of the nineteenth century also recommended visiting workplaces such as factories, as well. One of the earliest tourist attractions in the United States was Niagara Falls in New York, still a major tourist location. The growing use of railroads made tourists out of travelers. They could see the country, but from an insulated perspective.

1876-1904 • FAIRS ~ Another tourist destination, which expanded the possibilities of travel destinations to more and more Americans, was world fairs. One of the biggest was the Chicago World's Columbian Exposition in 1893 (400 years after Columbus' voyage). It offered magnificent displays of inventions for industry and pleasure, as well as presentations from many other countries. Other major theme fairs to commemorate important events in history included the Philadelphia Centennial in 1876 and the Louisiana Purchase Exposition in St. Louis in 1904.

The fairs demonstrated also the growing diversity of travel in the United States. African Americans were usually allowed entrance to the fairs but were still segregated in other ways. For example, at the 1895 Atlantic Cotton States and International Exposition, African Americans could enter, but they could only buy food and drink in the Negro Building, and audiences were segregated at the shows.

1885-1904 • WORKING CLASS VACATIONS ~ As the concept of vacation travel broadened in the late 1800s, several organizations developed to aid poor urban children and women in experiencing the joys of fresh air in rural areas. In 1885 the Children's Aid Society of New York City (which still exists) offered a summer home for children at Bath, Long Island. In 1890 the New York Association for Improving Conditions of the Poor offered excursions for working class women and children. In 1904, in keeping with the middle class desire to continue learning at the same time as vacationing, Gad's Hill, north of Chicago, offered vacation school. By 1900, 17 cities offered fresh air relief programs for children. Others like the National Civic Federation and the Vacation Savings Fund offered advice and services for working women to get vacations.

1890s-1920s

TWENTIETH CENTURY

1890s-1920s • WHO TRAVELED ~ Trends in twentieth century travel began in the nineteenth century. For example, today the vast majority of Americans travel for work or pleasure and usually are tourists some time in their lives. This trend began in the late nineteenth century when more and more people moved into the middle class and had the time and money to travel. Increasingly in the early twentieth century, the working class was given the time and means to travel because of the adoption of labor laws and prosperity caused by industrialization; the middle class worked fewer hours and had larger disposable incomes so that by the 1930s a majority of the working class had some vacation time.

In the early twentieth century, businesses began to consider the value of giving workers vacations, especially during the slack summer season. National Cash Register Company began closing its plants for two weeks in the summer and paying for vacations. They believed vacations were good for workers, and, as a result, good for business. Only a few other companies, however, did the same until after World War I. Eventually, business owners began to reflect on the relationship between work, rest, and productivity.

1920-1960 • HOW THEY TRAVELED ~ After World War I and again after World War II, vast changes in modes of transportation brought vast changes in who traveled, why they traveled, and where they traveled. In the 1920s the

(1926) After World War II, in the 1950s, there was a third revolution in travel. Airplanes and cars became the primary vehicles of travel, surpassing ships and trains. To make travel more comfortable and seem more like train travel (only faster) sleeper airplanes were put into service in the 1920s.

automobile industry brought travel possibilities to more and more people because automobile prices declined as mass production made them cheaper to manufacture, impacting a whole new generation with the possibilities of individual freedom and independence. After World War II commercial airplanes had a tremendous impact on travel. Since the 1950s the travel experience has become common for Americans of all socio-economic groups. Increasingly since 1960, U.S. airplane travel has expanded to the whole world—not just the United States.

1900-1930s • WHY THEY TRAVELED ~ By 1906 travel for vacation purposes had already become so popular that both the *New York Times* and the *New York Herald* had Sunday travel sections. Travelers still went to resorts to relax, and the wealthy still traveled to Europe to see the "old" cities and to be seen at the expensive spas, but Americans increasingly traveled to places within the United States as well. The national park system championed by Theodore Roosevelt offered a way to appreciate American culture and the "great outdoors."

By the end of the 1930s vacationing had become a mass phenomenon; vacations were considered part of the culture. Interestingly, labor unions did not initially fight for vacation time for workers because they were principally interested in improving working conditions, managing working hours and securing decent wages.

1900-1930s • OCEAN LINERS ~ While more and more of the middle class traveled and took vacations by the end of the nineteenth and in the early twentieth centuries, there was one mode of transportation still enjoyed primarily by the rich. The early 1900s through the end of the 1930s was the great age of ocean liners. Sailing packets (passenger boats) attuned to passenger comfort had existed since the early 1800s, especially under the British Cunard and White Star lines. These Clipper ships had been fast, but they depended on wind. Steam-driven liners changed ocean travel.

Ocean liners were built for three classes of passengers. In the lowest level at the bottom of the ship, in the most primitive quarters, was third class. Around 1910 passage in third class from England to the United States cost seven British pounds. Thousands of immigrants arrived in the United States by travelling third class on ocean liners. (Thousands of others arrived on ships much less luxurious than the ocean liners.) Second class passage on ocean liners cost about ten British pounds from England to the United States. In stark contrast, first class passage in the upper decks, which were as luxuriously furnished as could be imagined, cost about 200 British pounds, and the ships were full.

One of the first of the glamorous ocean liners in the early twentieth century was the Cunard Line's ship *Mauretania*, which carried passengers from 1906-1935. The most famous, largest, and most luxurious ocean liners were the French *Normandie*, and the British *Queen Mary* and *Queen Elizabeth*. Ocean liners were up to 1,000 feet long and the fastest ships made the Atlantic crossing in four days.

The most famous of these ocean liners was the *Titanic*, a British ship 882.5 feet long and sumptuously furnished. It carried 2,200 passengers and crew. Its April 1912 maiden voyage ended tragically when the ship broke in two after hitting an iceberg. Some 1,500 people died, including one of the world's richest men, John Jacob Astor. In the inquest that followed, several reasons for the tragedy and enormous loss of life became evident. The steel used in its construction had become brittle in the cold waters of the northern Atlantic; it had been traveling at 21 knots, nearly its top speed, in an area teeming with icebergs; and there had not been nearly enough lifeboats.

The history of some of the other great liners ended tragically as well, though not with such great loss of life. One of them, the elegant *Normandie*, burned in New York City harbor in 1942 as it was being converted from a luxury liner to a U.S. troop carrier.

The *Queen Mary*, commissioned in 1934, was used as a troop carrier to and from Australia during World War II. It traveled some 600,000 miles and carried some 750,000 military personnel. The *Queen Elizabeth*, launched in 1940, was also used for military purposes until 1946. The two Queens were so valuable as military vessels that Hitler put a bounty on them, but never caught them. Beginning in 1947, the two Queens ruled the ocean as luxury passenger liners until the 1960s, when both were sold. The *Queen Elizabeth* burned in Hong Kong in 1972 while undergoing renovations.

Indicative of the end of the ocean liner era was the story of the U. S. liner *United States*. Built in 1951, it, too, was luxurious and the fastest ocean liner ever. The United States Government spent a great deal of money on the *United States* in anticipation for using it for carrying troops. As the Korean War dawned, the United States quickly readied the ship for this purpose during the Cuban Missile Crisis, however, it was never ready in time. As an ocean liner, its career ended in 1969 when ocean liners were unable to compete with increasingly popular air travel. Since the 1970s ocean travel has become mainly cruise travel—the trips are usually shorter and made for tourism in specific areas of the world, emphasizing vacation fun and relaxation, with package travel plans to fit the incomes of even middle class travelers. An example is the *QE2*, built in 1962. It is luxurious, carries 1700 passengers and crew, and can go at a speed of 33 knots. It sails across the Atlantic from April to December and then offers cruises around the world. People rarely rely on ocean liners as a means to travel from one place to another, but rather, to enjoy a vacation on the water.

1920s • THE AUTOMOBILE ~ After World War I there was a second travel revolution and the 1920s saw one of the greatest travel booms ever with the advent of the affordable automobile. In 1921, 1.5 million cars were produced. By 1929 the number grew to 4.8 million. In 1920 some 8 million cars were owned; by 1930 ownership had grown to 23 million. In the 1920s one out of every eight American workers was employed in automobile-related industries, including the rubber, steel, and petroleum industries.

It is true that until the 1950s trains still carried more travelers, but the growth in road construction, especially the interstate highway system begun in the 1950s, greatly expanded the range and variety of vacations, as well as the number of travelers. Particularly in the western United States, automobiles nearly brought a revolution in tourism. Railroads carried travelers only to specific places; cars allowed people to go in many different directions. Differences among the disparate regions of the country—North, South, East, West—were broken down and the nation made more homogeneous by the tourist and his car.

While the automobile gave people a sense of freedom and independence, it also brought people closer together. Roads now connected small towns that had existed miles away from any place else, allowing people who had lived in isolation to partake in medical care, business, education, or entertainment. Thousands of new suburban communities sprang up around cities. Automobiles allowed people to own a home in the suburbs, and to commute to the city for work.

1920s • Tourism Boom ~ The boom in advertising and popular culture of the Roaring Twenties also brought a boon to tourism and travel. In the 1920s tourist travel shifted from the tastes of the elites, from what has been called "heritage" or "cultural" tourism, the marketing of the historic, scenic, or mythic past. Tourists became more interested in experiencing America, especially the outdoors. This decade saw great expansion in nationally marketed recreational tourism, including skiing, hiking, and camping.

The ubiquitous automobile created many changes in the landscape. Cars had an especially great impact on camping. It was still the least expensive vacation, other than staying with friends or relatives. In the 1920s many towns and cities opened municipal automobile campgrounds complete with showers and bathrooms for the "auto campers." For instance, Kansas had over 200 such campgrounds along major highways.

As new highways were built, other "new" features sprang up. The first "motel," or motor hotel was built in San Luis Obispo, California in 1925; the first set of traffic lights was used in New York City in 1922; the first shopping center opened in Kansas City in 1924; the first

---

Jackson Hole, Wyoming typifies the development of the West for the sake of tourism. In the mid-nineteenth century, it was an area rich in beaver pelt trade. At the turn of the century, it was an area devoted to cattle ranching and alfalfa. But by then also, a few important people had "discovered" the area, including President Arthur in 1883 and the popular author Owen Wister in 1887. Early in the twentieth century, dude ranching became the rage with the wealthy, and Jackson Hole ranchers joined with developers in grabbing the tourist buck. Eventually lines were drawn between natives of the area and neonatives (those who moved there seeking a peaceful refuge). Natives wanted development of any kind; neonatives pressured for a limit on outsiders (though they had recently been outsiders themselves).

The creation of Grand Teton National Park in 1929 brought thousands of tourists, by car, not just railroad. Opening up huge ski resorts in the 1960s brought even greater numbers. By the end of the twentieth century, only the wealthy could afford to live there, and although the natives carry out the services of the resorts today, they often have to live long distances away in more affordable housing areas.

national road atlas was published by Rand McNally in 1924; and the first public parking garage was built in Detroit in 1929.

1920s-1930s • Transcontinental Highways ~ The 1920s began the boom also in long distance highway construction. Route 66 is the most famous of the early highways, or at least the most romanticized. One of its nicknames is "the Mother Road"; another, "Main Street of America." Route 66 began in Chicago, Illinois and ended in Santa Monica (Los Angeles), California. It was commissioned in 1926 and fully paved by 1937, crossing eight states and three time zones.

Another, longer highway, Route 50, cut nearly straight across the United States, from Ocean City, Maryland to San Francisco, California, including the midway point in the United States, Kinsley, Kansas. Highway 1 was equally important for the east coast, going all the way from northern Maine to Key West, Florida. All of these highways have now been broken up or superceded by the wider and faster Interstates, but they were critical both in opening up and in joining together vast sections of the nation.

1920s • Travel by Minorities ~ Cars even allowed for cultural diversity at certain vacation places such as Atlantic City, New Jersey, which became a popular destination for white and black citizens, and immigrants. Nevertheless, during the first half of the twentieth century segregation remained entrenched in most places, even though African Americans and Jews had money and time to travel. Consequently they often built their own resorts. African American vacation destinations included Highland Beach, near Annapolis, Maryland; Sag Harbor on Long Island, New York; Idlewild, Michigan; American Beach, Florida; and Shell Island, North Carolina.

(circa 1938) In the 1930s, service stations provided a full line of automotive care, even at night in some parts of the country.

> In the nineteenth century, Highland Beach, Maryland was a privately owned beach community for African Americans on the Chesapeake Bay, near the state capital, Annapolis. In 1922 Highland Beach became one of only two incorporated towns in Anne Arundel County, Maryland (the other is the state capital, Annapolis). In 1990 its population was 102. For over 100 years it has been a popular summer residence and travel destination for African Americans from Washington, DC and other locations.
>
> Two of its most illustrious summer residents were Frederick Douglass and Mary Church Terrell. Douglass was an ex-slave, a leading newspaperman and abolitionist and speaker on equal rights. He held several U.S. government posts. Mary Church Terrell and her husband lived next door to Douglass. She was a leading feminist, charter member of the National Association for the Advancement of Colored People (NAACP), and active civil rights advocate until her death in 1954 at the age of 90.

Jews on the East coast often went to resorts in the Catskill Mountains. Another major destination for Jewish travelers, and others, in the 1920s was southern Florida. In the 1920s Miami, Palm Beach, and Tampa became very popular. In 1926 tourists spent over a billion dollars in Florida resorts.

1930s • TOURISM AND THE DEPRESSION ~ Normally factors that affect travel, especially for pleasure, include political stability and affluence. Thus, it would be expected that the 1930s, the era of great world depression, would see a major decline in tourism and vacation travel. Table 4 demonstrates such a decline. However, by 1934, some six years before the end of the Depression in the United States, numbers at popular vacation sites had already begun to climb. Travel increased 20 percent from 1934 to 1935. Spending on vacations showed a similar pattern. In 1929 Americans spent $2.7 billion on vacations; in 1933, $1.7 billion; but in 1935, again over $2 billion. Even the Great Depression did not diminish for long the vacation spirit and the urge to travel.

The automobile and the government helped maintain the travel "bug" and travel destinations. The federally funded Civilian Conservation Corps built many paths for hiking and maintained urban and national parks. The Works Progress Administration (WPA) paid artists of all types to create their works and promoted

Table 4: Selected Vacation Sites and Number of Visitors

Vacation Site	1929	1932-33	1934
Niagara Falls	3,000,000	1,400,000	NA
Yellowstone National Park	261,000	162,000	NA
Grand Canyon	184,000	105,500	140,000

SOURCE: *Working at Play* by Cindy Aron, 1999.

1940s-1950s

exploring the arts (through museum visits and attendance at plays, for example) as vacation attractions.

In the 1930s the automobile also allowed thousands to leave the dustbowl of Oklahoma and other prairie states to migrate west in search of work. These people, so eloquently portrayed in John Steinbeck's *Grapes of Wrath*, depended on the transportation network of roads and on their cars to get them to California. They also often depended on their cars for temporary living quarters.

1946-1950 • POST WORLD WAR II ~ Travel during World War II was reserved almost exclusively for people connected with the military. During the war years new models of cars could not be developed and gasoline was severely rationed. Many civilians still took vacations, but they stayed closer to home. The railroad industry, however, thrived after the war by serving as the principal carrier of people and freight until Americans could be resupplied with automobiles. The diesel engines developed in the 1930s were more fuel-efficient than coal operated steam engines.

1950s • AIRPLANES ~ After World War II, in the 1950s, there was a third revolution in travel. This time it was fueled by airplanes. Airplanes and cars became the primary vehicles of travel, surpassing ships and trains. In 1952 airlines offered the first transatlantic tourist fares. By 1955, Boeing Company became a major builder of jumbo jets with its Boeing 707. By 1957 more people crossed the Atlantic Ocean by air than by sea.

One of the major benefactors of the increased airline travel was the travel agent. Between 1960 and 1974, tourism grew 10 percent per year. In 1974 tourists spent $29 billion, six percent of the total international trade. Travel agencies became a major industry in the growing service economy. Worldwide business travelers, as well as tourists, spurred this

(1949) Seen here are passengers exiting a TWA airplane via movable steps that are attached to the airplane upon landing.

growth. In the 1950s and 1960s, Americans provided most of the international tourists. The 1960s saw a boom in charter flights and package tours.

1950-1970 • IMPACT OF TOURISM
Between 1950 and 1970, worldwide tourism increased tenfold, especially for North Americans, Western Europeans, and Japanese. Among the conditions which encouraged this growth were increased leisure time, earlier retirement ages, better jet airplane travel, and low cost travel and accommodations. For example, before 1958, airplane travel from New York to Europe took 15 hours and the return up to 20 hours. The introduction of large fast jets decreased the time to six-and-a-half and seven-and-a-half hours.

One sign of how important tourist travel can be to world economies is that the United Nations designated 1967 as

---

The romantic travel packages of Club Med exemplify the blend of mass marketing appeal to the growing middle class traveler with the traveler's desire to leave cars behind and just relax. Affordable Club Med villages are scattered around the world on some of the most beautiful beaches, including many locations in the Caribbean, as well as Polynesia and Mexico. Gerard Blitz created the first Club Med in 1950 with 23,000 members. Soon the Polynesian hut style village became the Club Med resort look. Visitors to a Club Med do not even have to use currency. They can do nothing or participate in all sorts of activities day and night, as they wish. By the 1970s there were 100 villages. Now there are Club Meds in Europe and Colorado for ski vacations, as well as locations in Japan, Malaysia, Thailand, Morocco, and many other places. By 1994, some 20 million people had stayed at a Club Med at least once.

Table 5: Principal Tourist Generating Countries, 1985-1990

Country	_____Expenditure (in U.S. $bn)_____					
	1985	1986	1987	1988	1989	1990
West Germany	12.8	18.0	23.3	25.0	23.7	30.1
United States	25.1	26.7	30.0	33.1	33.5	38.7
United Kingdom	6.4	8.9	11.9	14.6	15.1	19.8
Japan	4.8	7.2	10.8	18.7	22.5	24.9
France	4.6	6.5	8.5	9.7	10.3	13.5
Top 5 countries	53.7	67.4	84.5	101.1	105.2	126.9
Rest of world	40.8	57.5	71.4	85.1	93.2	114.0
World total	94.5	124.9	156.0	186.2	198.4	241.0
Top 5 as % of world total	56.8	53.9	54.1	54.3	53.0	52.6

SOURCE: Derived from figures published by World Tourism Organization, (1988, 1992).

1950-1970

International Tourist Year. Those were the years of the syndrome: "If it's Tuesday, this must be Belgium." Tourists crammed as much into their travel and sightseeing as possible.

The growth of technology and wealth in the post-war period allowed a much greater segment of the population to travel, and because more people traveled, the cost of travel became relatively less. Thus, many travelers, not just the wealthy, could go to places unimaginable before World War II and have a great impact on a country's economy. For example, in the early 1970s safari holidays were Kenya's major export. In 1972 there were 65 safari companies in Nairobi, Kenya, catering mainly to wealthy tourists from Europe and North America.

Tables 5 and 6 demonstrate the value and power of tourist dollars and how much some countries depend on tourist travel.

Table 6: Travel Account Receipts as a Percentage of Gross Domestic Product (GDP)

All Europe	1.9 %
Austria	8.5
Denmark	2.5
Germany	0.7
Ireland	3.4
Italy	1.8
Portugal	6.0
Spain	3.8
Switzerland	3.8
United Kingdom	1.4
Australia	1.2
New Zealand	2.5
Japan	0.1
United States	0.8

SOURCE: OECD. 1992.

1960s • Impact of Airplane Travel

∼ Airline travel also made it possible for individuals and families to take vacations in the winter, as well as in the summer. This possibility brought a growth in year-round resort locations on coasts, as well as a tremendous expansion of the ski resorts, which, in turn, influenced the growth of industry connected to outdoor winter activities, from snorkeling equipment and beachwear, to ski equipment and ski slope outfits. New winter sports also became popular such as snowboarding and snowmobiling.

Airline traffic showed phenomenal growth in the last 40 years of the century.

Table 7: Passengers Enplaned (in the millions)

Year	Domestic	International
1960	52.4	5.5
1970	153.7	16.3
1980	272.8	24.1
1990	423.6	42.0
2000	655	
2010(est.)	1,000	

SOURCE: http://www.air-transport.org/public/industry

1960s-Present • Automobile Travel

∼ Just as air travel grew by leaps and bounds after World War II, so did automobile travel. Federal aid to highway construction had begun in 1916, but in the 1950s the federal government funded 90 percent of the cost of a superhighway system of turnpikes, now an interstate system which crisscrosses the entire country. The old, romantic Route 66, the "Mother Road," from Chicago to Los Angeles hardly exists anymore; it is now included in parts of Interstates 55, 44, 40, 15, and 10. There are now some 4 million miles of highways and roads in the United States. Some of the former toll roads or turnpikes still exist, especially east of the Mississippi River, but the Interstates are free.

Travel in the past was primarily done out of necessity—for business purposes or to find new opportunity. In the United States since the 1920s travel has become an expression of freedom and an escape from necessity and purpose. For Americans, the automobile symbolizes that expression of freedom.

1915-1970 • DECLINE OF RAILROADS

~ The growth of automobile travel meant a huge decline in passenger train travel. In 1915, 73 percent of travelers in the United States went by train; in 1955, only five percent did so. In 1919 there were 6,000 passenger trains in the United

(1946) Airborne Fashion. The airline industry was so popular with travelers that the industry made efforts to be even more fashionable. Model Jayne Kieth wears a plaid gingham sun dress with matching shorts and bolero jacket. The audience are Chicago journalists on a trip over the city in a Pennsylvania Central 59 passenger airliner.

United States Interstate Highway System

SOURCE: World Book Encyclopedia. 1995.

ATLANTIC CITY
The Playground of the World
TRAVEL BY TRAIN

(circa 1925) Crowds of holiday makers grace the promenade at Atlantic City, New Jersey, 'the playground of the world'.

Table 8: Important Dates in Railroading in the Twentieth Century

1925	First commercial diesel-electric locomotive in the U.S. begins service
1934	The Burlington *Zephyr*, first passenger train powered by diesel-electric engine, begins service in the U.S.
1964	Japanese trains begin operating between Tokyo and Osaka at speeds up to 130 mph
1970	Congress authorizes creation of Amtrak to operate intercity passenger trains
1976	Six bankrupt railroads in the northeastern U.S. are reconstructed by federal government as a private corporation (Conrail)
1980	Staggers Rail Act eases some regulations of Interstate Commerce Act
1987	U. S. government sells its Conrail stock to private investors

SOURCE: World Book Encyclopedia. 1995

1915-1970 States; by 1970 there were fewer than 300. In 1970 the Amtrak railroad system was created to provide passenger service between major cities, so it is still possible to travel by train across the United States. However, it is not a profitable industry, even in the crowded Northeast where Amtrak travel between Washington, DC and New York or Boston is often faster than by car or plane. In the Northeast corridor a high-speed train, the Acela, has recently been introduced to try to lure the traveler from cars or airplanes.

1950-PRESENT • TOURIST DESTINATIONS-THEME PARKS ~ As tourism has grown since World War II, the tourist industry has become a huge business. The tourism industry is one of the typical examples of the change from a manufacturing to a service economy. It produces nothing, but generates great amounts of economic activity. Post-World War II tourism is principally entertainment tourism. Often heritage or cultural tourism and recreational tourism are now combined in entertainment—in a theme park. Even the national parks also offer recreation and theme areas. Tourists can now allay their historic tensions about work and play and learn while on vacation, being entertained all the while.

World's fairs, theme parks, and international events attract millions of visitors a year. In the mid 1990s there were some 50-60,000 half- to one-day international events and some 6,000 events lasting two or more days. Forty-two states in the United States have theme parks. In the world there are some 700 theme or amusement parks in 28 countries. Disneyland alone has over 10 million visitors per year. The National Park Service maintains over 400 historic sites, monuments, cemeteries, and national parks.

1990s • Environmental Damage from Tourists ~ One of the problems with the excessive tourism of the late twentieth century is damage to the environment. As has been stated before, tourism drastically changes a location. One prime example in the United States is the Grand Canyon. It has been a popular travel destination since the late 1800s. It became a national park in 1919 so that the federal government could not only maintain it, but could also regulate visitors. In 1993 over 5 million people visited the canyon; the visitor rate has doubled every decade since 1919. The damage to the desert environment has been so tremendous that beginning in May 2001, the numbers of visitors and places they may visit was restricted. Vehicle traffic has and will also face specific restrictions, moving it farther away from the canyon.

1970s • Green Tourism ~ Because for many years Americans dominated the travel and tourist industry, the image of the "Ugly American" became synonymous with a selfish, ignorant, and insensitive traveler. Travelers demanded that conditions away from home be as familiar and as good, or better, than at home—from language (English) to food to air conditioning. As travel worldwide has grown, the Ugly American has become too often the "Ugly Tourist."

Because tourism and tourists have such a tremendous impact on the environment, recently a new idea in tourism has grown in response, the so-called "Green Tourism," which grew from the Green Movement in Europe in the 1970s. Green tourists develop or embody the caring traveler: respectful of other people, wildlife, and the environment. They are interested in historical and cultural points of view. Green tourism promotes personal, intellectual, and spiritual growth. Green tourists include conservancy visitors, volunteers such as Doctors Without Borders and the Peace Corps, and students studying aboard ships. Sir Edmund Hillary of New Zealand, the first mountain climber to reach the top of Mt. Everest, explains the need for green tourism.

"When I first went, I had no awareness of conservation. We left rubbish in heaps. As I spent more time in such areas [Himalayas], I saw more of the carelessness and became more aware of the environment. Initially I was as careless as anybody else, but I learned."

- Sir Edmund Hillary

A primary kind of green tourism may be the ecotourist who is interested in viewing, but also in preserving the environment. Ecotourism is any kind of tourism that focuses on and respects the natural environment, from flying around the world and stopping at certain natural preserves, to spending time at one location such as the Galapagos or a Costa Rican rainforest.

The Tirimbina Rainforest Center in Costa Rica exemplifies an ecotourism location. It promotes experiencing the rainforest through hands-on discovery—for children and adults. Its facilities are sustainable, that is, it uses natural wastewater treatment through certain plants, solar power, local building materials, and its own gardens for most food. It has a canopy skywalk observation bridge, carefully constructed without cutting any trees or vines. Also typical of good ecotourism facilities, it can only accommodate groups of 15 day-visitors and up to 70 overnight visitors. To further preserve the rainforest while allowing visitors, two-thirds of the Tirimbina Reserve is trail-less.

(1960) The Petrified Forest is a popular "nature" destination for tourists.

CONCLUSION

IMPACT OF TRAVEL AND TOURISM ~ The prospect of travel for business or pleasure has expanded to include middle classes in nearly every country of the world. The World Tourism Organization states that 9-10 percent of the world's population has entered another country as a tourist. Travel and tourism have many positive aspects, but also some negatives. Travel and tourism can be forces for better understanding; they can encourage opening up of regions such as China or Eastern Europe; or they can even lead to a reduction in international tension. Tourism can promote preservation of national treasures, improve income, job opportunities and industry, and improve communication and transportation. Travel and tourism, however, may also increase imports to meet tourist demands, speed the opening up of a society to non-compatible standards or behaviors, cause environmental destruction from the numbers of tourists as well as the construction of buildings to accommodate them, and cause pollution.

The cultural impact of travel and tourism is non-measurable, but is definite. Throughout the United States the impact of travel on types of food, music, and architecture can be observed. In other countries, or even in the United States, tourism can revive interest in traditional cultures—in dress, crafts, artifacts, and customs.

ECONOMIC IMPACT ~ The economic impact of travel and tourism is measurable. In 1992 in the United States, travel and tourism was the second largest industry after health. Six million people were directly employed by the travel/tourist industry. Domestic and international travelers spent $362 billion in the U.S. in 1992. Tourism is the second largest U.S. retail industry—over $200 billion in 1990.

World travel accounts for five percent of world trade, and money spent on tourism is the largest single item in world trade. (Tourism includes many elements such as transportation, food, services, accommodation, entertainment, and manufactured items from souvenirs to airplanes.)

Tourism accounts for major foreign exchange in many countries. For example, up to 75 percent of the U.S. Virgin Islands' economy is the tourist industry. Tourism is even a primary source of foreign revenue for such countries as Canada, Great Britain, France, Ireland, Italy, and Switzerland.

IMMIGRATION ~ Travel in the late twentieth century United States is as diverse as the country itself. Immigration continues at a fast pace—from all over the world. Today thousands more Asians and Latin Americans enter the country than a hundred years ago. They travel to the United States for the same reasons as their ancestors—work and refuge. Using the same categories as earlier in the chapter, it is possible to observe how the origins of immigrant populations have shifted over the century.

The trends in immigration from Asia and Latin America continue to emerge. Immigration patterns show up in population characteristics. From a nation of a vast white majority with some Native Americans and African American minorities in the eighteenth century, the United States is now over 29 percent minorities.

Table 9: Origins of Immigrants, 1870-1970
(In millions)

	1870	1910	1970
England	.8	1.2	.6
Ireland	1.8	1.3	.3
Germany	1.7	2.3	.8
Scandinavia	.2	1.1	.3
France	.1	.1	.1
Eastern Europe (Aust.-Hung.)	.07	1.3	.7
Italy	.02	1.3	1.8
Poland	.01	.9	.6
Russia	—	1.1	.6
China	.06	.06	.2
Japan	—	.07	.1
Latin America	.06	.3	2.0

SOURCE: *Historical Statistics of the United States.* 1975.

The population of the United States in 1999 was 72 percent white, 13 percent African American, 11.5 percent Hispanic, and four percent Asian. Travelers from abroad have had and will continue to have a tremendous impact on American society.

BUSINESS TRAVELERS AND TOURISTS ~ Business travelers move hundreds of miles on a daily basis. The airline shuttle service between Boston and New York City, for example, resembles the commuter traffic formerly at the railroad station in the morning and evening. Freeways and interstates are constantly jammed. One of the negative results of increased travel is congestion and pollution—of the road and the air. Newspapers often note the threats to safety of air traffic congestion.

Tourist travel depends on economic prosperity and the last decade of the

(circa 1950) Riders trekking along a path in the Grand Canyon, north Arizona.

twentieth century was a very prosperous one, so tourism continued to increase, the destinations as varied as the imagination. Tourism still includes the "traditional" camping, resort, recreational, and entertainment venues. However, adventure travel has grown rapidly recently. By the end of the century men and women, families, and seniors, enjoyed bungee jumping, shark diving, mountain biking, rock climbing, or whitewater rafting. There are some 100 adventure travel magazines and 8,000 outfitters.

Also recently there has been a small shift to what is called "special interest" tourism. This can be educational (languages or archaeology), arts and urban heritage, rural ethnic adventures, nature-based (rockhounds or trekkers). Many tourists today seek more of an integration into a place, not just transportation and accommodation.

Table 10 shows the numbers of tourists (those who are in a place for more than a

Table 10: Top Five Tourist Locations and Number of Tourists for the year 1998

France	70 million
Spain	47.7 million
United States	47.1 million
Italy	34.8 million
United Kingdom	25.4 million

SOURCE: World Tourism Organization

Table 11: Departures From and Arrivals to the United States, 1986-1994
(In millions)

	1986	1990	1994
Departures	232	340	485
Arrivals	329.4	458.6	507.1

SOURCE: P. Lengyel in Philip Pearce *The Social Psychology of Tourist Behavior*, 1982.

day) in the top five locations in the world. Table 11 demonstrates travel just to and from the United States over the last ten years.

Thanks to the expansion of transportation systems worldwide, travelers have nearly unlimited destinations and reasons for travel. Tourism can capitalize on any trend in American society or culture. During the twentieth century travel has aided in the democratization of world cultures. Or as some have stated, increased travel has also made life more homogeneous—holiday-makers, participants at a professional convention, archaeologists joining a dig, reporters covering an event, diplomats on missions and businessmen seeking markets are thrown together not only at airports, railway or bus terminals and in means of transport, but also often at the accommodation offered at their common points of destination.

Travel is no longer constrained by proximity and travel is ubiquitous. The expansion of travel in the twentieth century has vastly changed the culture of the United States, as well as the rest of the world. While some see U.S. culture as more homogenous, the individual parts that are blended are more diverse. For many, John Steinbeck's observation in *Travels with Charley in Search of America* (1962) rings true:

"When I was very young and the urge to be some place else was on me, I was assured by

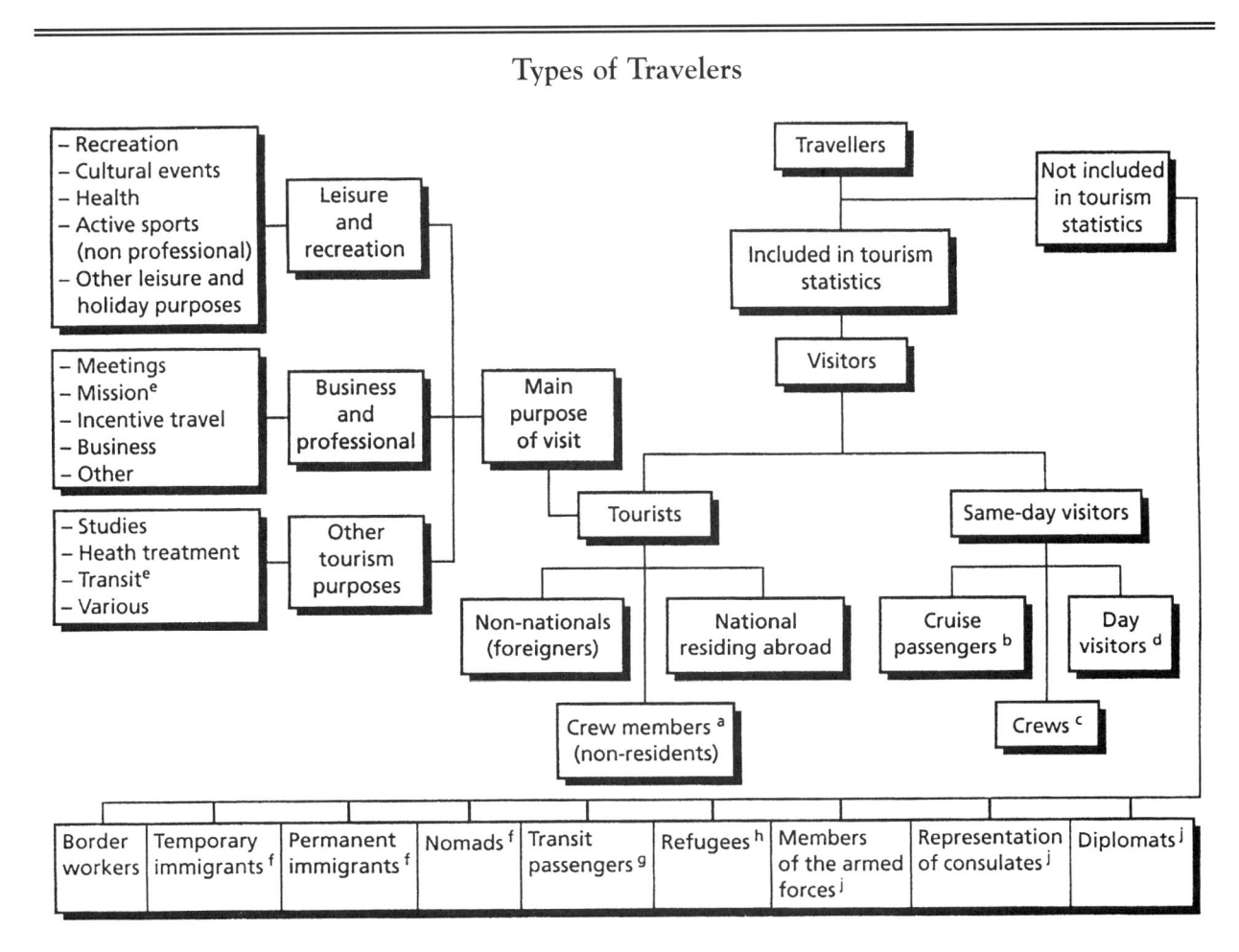

Types of Travelers

SOURCE: Cooper, et al. *Tourism: Principles and Practices*. 1993.

mature people that maturity would cure this itch. When years described me as mature, the remedy prescribed was middle age. In middle age I was assured that greater age would calm my fever. I fear that the disease is incurable."

Rothman, Hal. *Devil's Bargain: Tourism in the Twentieth Century American West*. Lawrence: University of Kansas Press, 1998.

World Book Encyclopedia. 1995.

BIBLIOGRAPHY

A Century of Population Growth 1790-1900. Baltimore: Genealogical Publishing Company, 1989.

Ambrose, Stephen. *Nothing Like It in the World: The Men Who Built the Transcontinental Railroad, 1863-1869*. New York: Simon & Schuster, 2000.

Aron, Cindy. *Working at Play: A History of Vacations in the United States*. New York: Oxford University Press, 1999.

Cooper, Chris, John Fletcher, David Gilbert, and Stephen Wanhill. *Tourism, Principles and Practice*. London: Longman Scientific and Technical, 1993.

Demographic Yearbook 1996. New York: United Nations, 1998.

Feifer, Maxine. *Tourism in History- from Imperial Rome to the Present*. New York: Stein and Day, 1985.

Goeldner, Charles R., et al. *Travel Trends*. Boulder: University of Colorado, 1970.

Jennings, Peter, and Todd Brewster. *The Century*. New York: Doubleday, 1998.

Pearce, Philip. *The Social Psychology of Tourist Behavior*. Elmsford, NY: Pergamon Press, 1982.

Ringholz, Raye. *Little Town Blues: Voices from the Changing West*. Salt Lake City: Peregrine Smith Books, 1992.

INTERNET RESOURCES

AIR TRANSPORT ASSOCIATION
Gives traffic summary statistics from 1960-2000
http://www.air-transport.org/public/industry

U.S. DEPARTMENT OF TRANSPORTATION
Tracks changes in international passenger and freight traffic in the U.S. *International Air Passenger and Freight Statistics* report.
http://ostpxweb.ost.dot.gov/aviation/international-series/

Theme parks around the world
http://themeparks.about.com

CENTRAL PACIFIC RAILROAD
PHOTOGRAPHIC HISTORY MUSEUM
On-line library of 19th century pictures (more than 2,300), maps and descriptions of railroad construction and travel
http://cprr.org/

UNION PACIFIC RAILROAD
History and photos of the development of the transcontinental railroad
http://www.uprr.com/aboutup/history/index.shtml

Diane N. Palmer

War and the U.S. Military: Drivers of Social Change

(1918) A pair of 'Handley Page Heavy Bombers' at an airfield near Dunkirk, Belgium.

TIMELINE

1860-1864 ～ Civil War

Telegraph / hot-air balloon / ironclad ships / submarines / repeating rifles / machine guns

MILESTONES: Silver rush (1860-1880) • Proliferation of sewing machines (1860s) • One-fifth of the American population is killed in the Civil War (1861-1865) • Homestead Act promises land to pioneer settlers (1862) • Indian uprisings (1862-1867) • Irish and Chinese laborers build transcontinental railroad across the U.S. (1862-1869)

1898-1902 ～ Spanish-American War and Philippine Insurrection

U.S. Imperialism / yellow journalism / women's nursing corps / Monroe Doctrine / Panama Canal begun

MILESTONES: Women enrolled in college rises from 20 percent in 1870 to 40 percent in 1910 • Henry Ford begins production of the gas-powered automobile (1896) • Alaskan gold rush begins after the discovery of gold in the Klondike (1897) • Spoiled food and yellow fever kill U.S. troops in Cuba (1898-1899)

1900-1914 ～ Pre-World War I

Military alliances forged in Europe / Schlieffen Plan

MILESTONES: August Otto, in Germany, invents the internal combustion engine (c. 1900) • Lee De Forest invents the vacuum tube, essential to the development of electronics (1906) • Harriet Quimby becomes the first American woman to earn a pilot's license (1911)

1914-1916 ～ World War I Begins in Europe

Lusitania sunk / German U-boat attacks / Zimmerman Telegram / conscription of soldiers

MILESTONES: Panama Canal completed (1914) • First voice communication by radio (1914) • Henry Ford institutes the five-dollar day for his factory workers (1914)

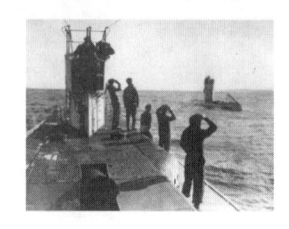

1917-1919 ~ United States Enters World War I

U.S. war propaganda / four-minute men / war bonds / War Industries Board / National War Labor Board / women and minorities in industrial jobs / war gardens / women and blacks in the military / Red Cross nurses

MILESTONES: Espionage Act prohibits openly criticizing the government (1917) • Vitamin D is discovered (1917) • Great flu epidemic begins in U.S. (1918) • Workers demand and receive an eight-hour day and equal pay for women (1918)

1918-1933 ~ Armistice Ends World War I

Versailles Peace Treaty / League of Nations / communist scare / first U.S. peacetime army established / Japan invades Manchuria (1931) / U.S. forms army air corps

MILESTONES: Invention of Freon makes widespread home refrigeration feasible (1920s) • KDKA in Pittsburgh, the first public radio station in the U.S., begins broadcasting on November 2, 1921 • Charles Lindbergh completes nonstop transatlantic flight on "The Spirit of St. Louis" (May 20 and 21, 1927) • Great Depression begins (1930)

1933-1939 ~ The Rise of Nazism

Adolf Hitler assumes power in Germany / Mussolini establishes Fascism in Italy / Hitler orders Jews to be impounded / Germany invades Rhineland (1936) / Germany signs non-aggression pact with Russia / Germany takes Sudetenland from Czechoslovakia; invades Austria; takes remainder of Czechoslovakia (1938) / Germany invades Poland, igniting World War II; Soviet Union invades Poland from the east, as well as Baltic countries (1939)

MILESTONES: First successful lung surgery removes cancerous lung (1933) • Twin engine Boeing 247, the first modern commercial aircraft, is put into service (1933) • Nazis banish Jews to ghettos (1936) • Sulfa drugs introduced to U.S. (1936) • Al Gross develops the two-way radio, or walkie-talkie, used extensively during WWII (1938) • Ukrainian immigrant Igor Sikorsky builds the first successful helicopter (1939)

1940-1945 ~ World War II

1940 – Germany overruns western Europe, attacks England / 1941 – United States wages undeclared war against Germany in North Atlantic; Japan bombs Pearl Harbor naval base on December 7, officially plunging the United States into World War II / 1942 – women join the military and industry / black men and women go to war/ Tuskegee airman and the Red Ball Express are crack African American units / Japanese Americans sent to internment camps / Holocaust expands / United States Navy turns tide of Pacific war at Battle of Midway in June; fight for Guadalcanal begins in August; U.S. and Allies invade North Africa in November / 1943 – Island Hopping campaigns begin in central Pacific; fight for New Guinea underway; Allies invade Sicily, then Italy; massive air bombing campaign waged over Europe / 1944 – MacArthur returns to the Philippines; Allies invade France on D-Day, June 6; Allies liberate Paris and sweep toward Germany; German counterpunch in December results in Battle of the Bulge, stops Allied drive for the year / 1945 – Allies in Europe invade Germany; Soviet troops pressing from the east take Berlin; FDR and Hitler die within weeks of each other; victory in Europe declared May 8; in the Pacific, American troops invade Iwo Jima in February, Okinawa in April; President Truman orders two atomic bombs dropped on Japan in August; Japan formally surrenders on September 2.

MILESTONES: Five million women enter the labor force (1940 -1944) • Once considered inappropriate, swing dancing becomes an acceptable method of releasing wartime tension (1942-1945) • National policy of rent control established (1942) • Coal, petroleum, steel, aluminum and rubber production expanded (1942-1944) • Repeal of Chinese exclusion law (1943) • "War brides" immigration permitted (1943-1946)

1946-1963 ~ Cold War Era

1946-49 – War crime trials of the Germans and Japanese / second Red Scare / The House Un-American Activities Committee formed / U.S. and European allies create NATO; Soviet Union explodes atomic bomb (1949) / French lose control of Indochina / McCarthyism breeds Red Scare hysteria in U.S. / 1950 – Korean War begins / 1953 – Armistice ends Korean War

MILESTONES: First electronic computer, ENIAC, is developed (1946) • Synthetic penicillin is produced (1946) • First television sets go on sale (1946) • Marshall Plan to restore Europe is implemented (1946) • Chuck Yeager breaks the sound barrier (1947) • Truman refuses to use atomic weapons against China (1952) • Soviet Union's satellite Sputnik I successfully orbits the Earth (October 4, 1957) • Boeing's jumbo 747 jet developed (1960s)

1964-1975 ~ Vietnam

1964 – U.S. commits "advisors" to Vietnam; Gulf of Tonkin incident commits United States to war in Vietnam / 1968 – Tet Offensive convinces many that the U.S. cannot win in Vietnam / Civil Rights movement peaks / massive antiwar protests in the U.S. / 1970 – U.S. invades Cambodia; Kent State students killed by National Guard / defoliation of jungle vegetation by "agent orange" / 1971 – Pentagon papers released / 1973 – Watergate scandal / Nixon administration diplomacy brings cease fire, ending U.S. involvement in Vietnam / 1974 – Nixon resigns / 1975 – South Vietnam falls to Communists

MILESTONES: Civil Rights Act declares that American citizens cannot be segregated in public accommodations (1964) • Fierce race riots occur in Los Angeles, Cleveland and New York (1965) • Miranda decision forces police to read a suspect his rights (1966) • Neil Armstrong becomes the first person to walk on the moon's surface (July 20, 1969) • Women make up 40 percent of the overall labor force and represent a substantial increase in married women who work (1970)

1976-2000 ~ Peace-keeping Missions

1983 – U.S. invades tiny Caribbean island of Grenada / 1989 – U.S. invades Panama / 1990 – Iraq invades Kuwait; U.S. leads coalition deploying in Saudi Arabia to force Iraq out of Kuwait / 1991 – Operation Desert Storm defeats Iraqi army, liberates Kuwait / Tailhook scandal / Veterans become ill with Gulf War Syndrome

MILESTONES: Hostages taken from the U.S. embassy in Teheran (1979) • Three Mile Island meltdown causes backlash to nuclear reactors (1979) • U.S. restores sovereignty to Native American nations (1982) • 400,000 Americans die of AIDS (1987-1999) • Rampage killing by students in their own schools (late-1990s)

INTRODUCTION

Writers have frequently called the twentieth century the "Violent Century"—with two world wars, the Cold War and its associated "hot wars," and hundreds of regional conflicts, the title seems well deserved. And while the United States certainly did not start the world wars (it was a latecomer to both), American action in each catapulted it to "superpower" status. Indeed, American influence, bought with warfare, earned the twentieth century another name—"The American Century."

Americans typically regard themselves as peaceful and peace loving. Yet in its 225 years as a nation—brief by many world standards—the United States has been involved in ten major conflicts, double that number of smaller ones, and countless battles with Native Americans. Indeed, historian Geoffrey Perret has called the United States "a country made by war."

Certainly, the American wars of the twentieth century have furthered American political—and sometimes imperial—interests. But they have also changed American society. The Spanish-American War of 1898, the point at which most scholars agree the American Century began, fostered levels of military volunteerism not seen since the first half of the Civil War. Simply, young men wanted to taste the glory they had heard their fathers and grandfathers attach to Civil War stories. One must assume that, with the wartime deaths of 630,000 Americans a mere three decades behind them, and even as many Civil War amputees still lived among them, those Spanish-American War volunteers chose to consider patriotic aspects of war over mortal ones. Regardless, once again American wives and mothers waited while their men marched to war, albeit a short one.

1898-1902 • SPANISH-AMERICAN WAR ~ The Spanish-American War made an imperial nation out of an isolationist one. In the 1890s, the United States was just waking up to the new idea of Social Darwinism, which maintained that a nation must grow and adapt to survive. With England, France, Germany and smaller European nations parceling up the world in imperialistic, mercantile systems during the nineteenth century, many American policy-makers believed the United States could do no less. It needed an empire to ensure the burgeoning American industrial sector had captive export markets. And, influenced by the writings of naval theorist Alfred Thayer Mahan, the United States Navy needed ports of call around the globe to anchor its growing strength.

Granted, the empire that the United States achieved after the Spanish-American War was small—Cuba, Puerto Rico, Guam, and the Philippines—but it augmented growing American possessions, which already included Alaska and the Aleutians and the strategically important Hawaiian Islands. But the first taste of empire, which included the surprising and bloody Filipino Insurrection (1898-1902), was bitter to many Americans. As quickly as they had become imperialist, many became anti-imperialist, a social sentiment that would echo in the politics of the early 1900s and once again make the United States isolationist.

1900-1917 • ISOLATIONISM ~ That isolationism continued until 1917, when the United States entered World War I, almost three years after it had erupted in Europe. U.S. entry into the war necessitated a social mobilization the likes of which Americans had not known before. The mobilization, in fact, could not have occurred had the country not already passed from the laissez faire, "hands-off" domestic political attitudes of the nineteenth century to the more "hands-on" interventionist attitudes of the Progressive Era and the twentieth century. The Progressive Era had made the federal government "big" (although it would get much bigger during the New Deal of the 1930s), and Americans were becoming more accustomed to governmental intervention. When President Woodrow Wilson announced far-ranging mobilization policies, few Americans balked. Wilson's policies included a national conscription (draft), the first since the Civil War; a War Industries Board, designed to match the needs of the U.S. armed forces with American industrial production; a food bureau, to do the same thing with agricultural production; and a Committee of Public Information—a propaganda bureau—assigned to get all Americans behind the war effort and keep them their for the duration. For the first time the federal government could manipulate many parts of Americans' lives, from the work they did and pay they received, to their very thoughts about the war.

Military action often causes severe reaction in the American public. Such was the case after World War I. The war, costing millions of lives worldwide, was a horrible shock to Americans. Retrenching, American politicians vowed to never again form military alliances that might drag the nation into another such war. Their reaction kept the United States out of the Wilson-designed League of Nations, and made it isolationist once again. Americans focused inward, concentrating on business-oriented conservatism in the 1920s and then, quite naturally, the devastating Depression of the 1930s. But even as war threatened in Europe again after Adolf Hitler assumed power in Germany in 1933, and in the Pacific after expansionist and militaristic Japan invaded Manchuria in 1931, the United States remained isolationist. As late as the presidential election of 1940, Democratic incumbent Franklin D. Roosevelt promised American mothers that he would not commit their sons to another foreign war; privately he never intended to keep that promise.

1940-1945 • A NATIONAL POWER IN THE MODERN WORLD ~ World War II saw American society mobilize as never before. While the United States' commitment to World War I lasted only 19 months, the nation was involved in World War II nearly four years. Men flocked to volunteer for service (some even lied about their age or medical condition so they would be accepted) after the Japanese attacked Pearl Harbor on December 7, 1941, and the draft affected American families most directly. Not just young men, but those as old as forty-five were subject to the draft, barring health, family or other deferments. The departure of millions of men to service, not to mention their triumphant return in 1945, caused a baby boom that still impacts American society.

But the war lasted long enough, and was so complex, that all of American society, not just the men slugging it out on the varied fronts of the war, became somehow "militarized." Everyone from school children to the elderly did their part for the war effort. Communities staged drives to collect old rubber tires, tin cans, aluminum foil, and countless other items to turn in to the government for recycling and military applications. Americans rationed every item imaginable, from sugar to gasoline and cigarettes, from meat to hosiery. Private citizens and big corporations bought war bonds, giving the government a steady cash flow and banking on a return with interest from a victorious United States. Americans planted "victory gardens" so they could grow their own food and not rely on commercial farmers, who were themselves supplying the American armed forces and many British troops as well.

Even when Americans went to the movies, they were still at war. First they watched the *Movietone News*, newsreels that were the 1940s equivalent of today's six o'clock news. The newsreels took viewers to the seat of war, offering a glimpse of war never before seen. Movie shorts were also patriotic. Cartoons featured Bugs Bunny or Daffy Duck battling Hitler, and Frank Capra (before he made *It's A Wonderful Life*) directed the now-classic *Why We Fight* series, calculated to keep Americans both abreast of and behind the war. The feature films were also war-related. Hollywood produced such entertaining but patriotic fare as *The Flying Tigers* (1942), *Bataan* (1943), and *Fighting Seabees* (1944).

The government had expanded into a bureaucracy during the Depression-era New Deal. Just as it was a short hop from Progressive reforms of the early 1900s to Wilson's World War I mobilization, it was equally short from FDR's New Deal to his World War II mobilization. Once again, the government would regulate war industries, industrial wages and jobs, food production and supply and public information. Government industrial contracts for aircraft carriers, bombers, fighters, helmets, M-1 rifles, and hundreds of other types of military equipment ended the Depression. Any American who wanted a job could have one, including blacks and women.

Women became true heroes in World War II. They flocked to the workplace in record numbers, many filling the formerly male jobs of heavy industry. They became welders and riveters, ran heavy equipment, and turned out the B-17s, B-24s, B-29s, aircraft carriers, Higgins Boats, anything you can name, that enabled the United States and her allies to defeat the Axis powers. Without the American woman in the workplace— Rosie the Riveter in her time—World War II would have been a good deal longer and a good deal tougher.

While the home front was so actively engaged, something subtler was happening—private citizens were becoming full-blown combatants of war. In truth, the change had been coming ever since William T. Sherman's armies burned their way through Georgia in 1864. In a variety of ways, either by growing food to feed armies, making their weapons, or simply encouraging soldiers, private citizens supported armies in the field. Commanders began to realize it, and they began waging war on a different front. If they could somehow incapacitate the public support structure, armies in the field would begin dying on the vine. The United States attacked belligerent public support in the Civil War; did it again against Native Americans in the Indian Wars of the 1860s-1880s. Other nations were doing it as well. The Allied bombing campaigns over Germany and Japan were in part to break the Axis civilian supports—bombing heavy industry was certainly that. But World War II bombers were not the precision instruments of 1991's Persian Gulf

1945-PRESENT

(1943) Women in the first U.S. Women's Army Auxiliary Corps (WAAC) unit in overseas service, 149th Post Headquarters Company, smile and wave from the back of a military vehicle as they leave for their assignment in North Africa. The Auxiliary Corps served in non-combat roles in the Allied campaign, filling crucial communications and clerical positions for less pay and protection than their counterpart ranks in the male military.

War missiles; the bombs were inaccurate, often unreliable, terrifying machines that killed private citizens, and the Germans proved their psychological terror with bombing raids on London. In the wars of the twentieth century, everyone became a combatant. In the 1940s, Americans could take comfort that bombers from Germany or Japan could not reach its shores; the intercontinental ballistic missiles of the post-war age would quickly change that.

1945-PRESENT • U.S. ROLE AS THE WORLD'S PEACEKEEPER ~ After World War II, Americans may have wanted to isolate themselves from the world once again, but it was impossible. The war had crippled other long-standing world powers, and made superpowers of two others—the United States and the Soviet Union. While they had been allied against Hitler, neither one trusted the other, and quickly a period of Cold War commenced. The era would last until the collapse of the Soviet Union in 1991, and include such skirmishes as the Berlin Airlift and the Bay of Pigs, and such full-blown wars as Korea and Vietnam.

The Korean War, 1950-1953, pulled many World War II veterans back into service, but drew in younger draftees as well. But unlike World War II just five years earlier, the American public did not mobilize. It went about its domestic business, barely taking notice of events in Korea. In fact, some historians have called Korea "The Forgotten War."

Similar societal attitudes held sway during the Vietnam War, but Vietnam is anything but forgotten. Unable to cope with new attitudes of limited war, the American public quickly grew tired of Vietnam. While one historian has said the United States had a chance to "win" in 1964, by 1966 it was too late. The war sparked protest, first among college professors, then among their students. The protest melded with those of Civil Rights activists, sparking riots in major American cities in the summers of 1965-68. Protests marred the 1968 Democratic National Convention in Chicago. Thousands of draft-age Americans burned their draft cards; some fled to Canada to avoid the draft. Far from supporting troops in the field, Americans turned against the soldiers in Vietnam, often labeling them as baby killers and spitting on them when they returned. Vietnam polarized Americans against themselves; middle-aged conservative Americans who could remember the clear-cut victories of World War II clashed with their children who could see no sense in sacrificing themselves in a futile war. The "Summer of Love" in 1967, and mottos such as "Make Love, Not War," became the younger generation's response to the older generation. "Flower children" became the symbol of a new generation rejecting many of the values of their parents, including patriotism for war. The Vietnam War left in its wake American generations distrustful of each other, and an American public distrustful of the federal government that ran the war. The latter rift, at least, has never fully closed.

The quarter-century since the Vietnam War has seen the American armed forces try to rebuild and attach new respect to themselves. The invasion of Grenada in 1983 was one such action; the invasion of Panama in 1990 another. But during Operations Desert Shield/Desert Storm, 1990-91, a renewed sense of military/societal cooperation developed. While the Persian Gulf War was short-lived, it did see the federal government learning from Vietnam and attempting to mobilize the public. American citizens, wary of the government and the army since Vietnam, responded tentatively, but did respond. Flag-waving and parades for returning veterans were once again fashionable, and while anti-war protests did occur, protesters made it clear that they opposed the war, not the men who fought it. The United States began the twentieth century with an isolationist attitude. It was a powerful nation, but so were many others. It finished the century a superpower. America's wars of the twentieth century, and the military branches that fought them, have had an indelible effect on American society.

1860-1865 • ON THE VERGE OF MODERN WAR ~ Many writers have called the American Civil War the first "modern war." While some, like historian Mark Neeley, find fault with that description, the Civil War was at least *nearing* modern warfare.

The war saw stunning advances in weaponry. It dawned with virtually all troops, both Union and Confederate, using rifles instead of smoothbore muskets. That made killing more efficient, enabling soldiers to hit targets at 500 yards instead of 100. It placed every advantage with defenders, immediately rendering obsolete the vaunted "frontal assault." It also outpaced battlefield tactics. Civil War commanders, both professionals and volunteers, were heavily influenced by Napoleonic battlefield maneuvers, which used linear tactics and block formations to mass short-range smoothbores for maximum impact. Unable to think of anything else, many

1860-1865

Civil War generals just kept marching their men forward like Napoleon would have done, even though the rifles were decimating their massed ranks before they could do any damage.

The Civil War was industrial. The North capitalized on an industrial infrastructure (of which the South had only a fraction) to place hundreds of thousands of shoulder arms and cannon in field; to feed, clothe, and supply a million soldiers; and to build a military railroad network that made provisioning the front lines efficient.

The Civil War saw a wealth of new military technology. Armies extensively used telegraph lines to transmit orders; they used hot-air balloons to collect intelligence about enemy lines. Navies inaugurated the use of ironclad—or armored—steamships, and they experimented with submarines. Before it was over, the Northern army had seven-shot repeating rifles—which Confederates complained could be loaded on Sunday and fired all week—and a rudimentary machine gun in the form of the Gatling Gun (although it saw only limited use in the war). Both North and South used some form of conscription—a draft—to ensure manpower for their armies.

The types of fighting in the Civil War were varied. There was trench fighting in this war, at Petersburg, Virginia—an eerie foreshadowing of World War I. Ulysses S. Grant's brilliant and mobile campaign to take Vicksburg in 1863 would have fit on any World War II planner's map.

For the North, the war became a crusade. President Abraham Lincoln effectively communicated his war aims to the American people. In the first stage of the

(circa 1865) Delaware Indians resting after a reconnaissance mission on behalf of the Union Army during the American Civil War.

war, 1861-62, it was about preserving the Union. From 1863 to the end, it was about ridding the nation of the evil of slavery. It was always about destroying the spark of rebellion. Americans would harken to the "crusade against evil" theme some eighty years later in World War II.

Most notably, the Civil War saw warfare change from some that only occurred on battlefield between armies. Before it was over, the American Civil War classified even civilians and combatants.

Embarking on the campaigns of 1864, top Union generals Grant and Sherman agreed with Lincoln that the Southern populace had to be punished. Women and clergymen in the South had encouraged their men to go north and kill Yankees. Southern farmers, plantation owners, and merchants supported the war. The top Union command had realized it was not fighting just soldiers, but a whole society. And so, after taking Atlanta in September 1864, Sherman staged a devastating march across Georgia, taking what his army needed to survive and burning the rest. Then he turned north and did the same thing in the Carolinas. In Virginia, cavalry commander General Phil Sheridan waged a similar campaign in the Shenandoah Valley.

When the Civil War ended, much of the South was in smoking ruins. Americans, indeed the world, had to take notice. Warfare had become as total as it could be in 1865.

1890-1910 • AMERICAN IMPERIALISM, SOCIAL DARWINISM AND NEW INTERNATIONALISM ~ By 1890, a new spirit had settled over much of the United States, one that would alter the course of the nation. If someone had pressed the average American farmer or shopkeeper to name that spirit, they would probably have simply called it "patriotism," borne aloft by a forty-four-star American flag and the martial air of John Philip Sousa's popular marches. The big businessmen of the industrialized American Gilded Age and politicians with a world view regarded that spirit as a necessity to fuel American enterprise. Sociologists and historians call it Social Darwinism.

Borrowed from naturalist Charles Darwin and coming to American politics via the business world, Social Darwinism would have great impact on the way the United States formed and fielded its military arms. Earlier in the century, Darwin had argued that living species had, over time, adapted to survive in a variety of climates and against a variety of enemies. Essentially, only those species that could adapt to change would survive. Business entrepreneurs co-opted that notion of "survival of the fittest." In an age when Populist reformers argued against big business and monopolies (especially in the railroad industry) and lobbied to have the federal government intervene in the operation of those entities, business owners applied Social Darwinism to their own situation. Government should not, they said, intervene in their operations. There should be no regulation of rates, wages or hours. The competitive nature of business would naturally cull out unfit organizations; monopolies would naturally occur as weaker corporations died. The meddling hand of government, they believed, would only muddle the process.

1890-1919 • POPULISM, PROGRESSIVISM, AND EMPIRE ~ The Populist Midwestern reform movement evolved into the Progressive Era in the mid-1890s and forced government to indeed become interventionist in private business; Social

1890s

Darwinism lived on elsewhere. American policy makers, now in league with some of the same businessmen they were curbing in other areas, began applying the notion of "survival of the fittest" to the nation itself. Looking across the Atlantic Ocean they could see England and France still thriving, in part, because they held overseas empires. The empires, scattered widely through Africa, the Pacific, and Asia, provided captive markets for home-country products. The colonies ensured exports for domestic producers, and at the same time ensured a global military posture for the imperial country. In short, empires equaled money and power. Germany, a united country for only twenty years, had taken notice and was vying with Great Britain to become the greatest world colonial power. Japan was recognizing the fact also, and by the turn of the century would be venturing onto the imperial stage.

1890s • IMPERIAL U.S. ~ The United States, too, was taking a new look at empire building, ironically, some thought, as the country had been founded by a revolution against an empire. But American industry had been booming since the end of the Civil War. Could not the United States also benefit from an empire? Industrialists claimed that the tenets of Social Darwinism called for no less. As American military historian Russell F. Weigley noted, "When other powers embarked upon a new round of economic and colony building competition overseas, the United States grew tempted to join the game."

Something else was afoot in the United States as well— a renewed patriotism. In just over a hundred years the nation had bridged a continent, both territorially and with a railroad. Seemingly, by 1890, the nation had resolved most of its long-running domestic issues. The Civil War, Reconstruction and the Indian Wars were over. And, as if to punctuate the close of an era, the United States census bureau proclaimed that, as of 1890, population density in the West made it no longer a frontier, but a settled region. While Progressivism was still to transform domestic politics, the United States began to look beyond its own borders. Political isolationism gave way to a "New Internationalism" and ultimately imperialism.

Empire inherently meant conquest of one type or another, and conquest entailed the use of arms. If the United States was to become an imperial power, even a modest one, its armies and navies had to be up to the task.

1890s • SIZE OF THE U.S. ARMED FORCES ~ Problem was, much of the American military had been rusticating since the end of the Civil War. The United States had never favored a large standing peacetime army, opting instead to rely on citizen soldiers to expand a regular army cadre in time of crisis. While American volunteers could become quite professional in wartime, when the fighting ended, the citizen soldier went back home to work.

Americans saw no need to keep much of an army at all in peacetime. Between 1865 and 1876, the army dwindled to a prescribed strength of 27,442, but it rarely reached that number. The army scattered regiments among 255 posts around the nation. Private soldiers tended to be of low caliber—men who had failed in private life, could not make a living otherwise, or were on the run from a local constabulary. Military training was almost non-existent. Officers were generally better trained, most having served in the Civil War. But they were frequently frustrated. Men who had attained a brevet—or temporary—rank of brigadier or major general during the war found themselves returned to their permanent rank, usually a colonelcy, after the war. Promotion during peacetime would come agonizingly slow. Also, those on the frontier found tactics and strategies that had worked against the Confederacy inadequate against Native American cavalries.

The size of the navy, too, was in reversal. By 1870 it had dwindled from 700 ships to fifty-two. And it had backed away from the armored steamboats that had dominated Union naval victories during the Civil War and returned, remarkably, to the age of sail and wood.

How could these military arms take the United States into an age of empire and, subsequently, to the status of world power? They both developed top theorists. And they both came along at just the right time.

1870s • EMORY UPTON ~ The United States Army found its theorist in a young Civil War veteran officer, Emory Upton. Upton, West Point class of 1861, became a brevet major general in the Civil War. He stayed in the army after the war and became interested in professionalizing the army. His work captured the attention of General William T. Sherman, who became his mentor. Sherman sent Upton to Europe to observe the Prussian Army, which had recently led the unification of Germany. Upon his return, Upton wrote a treatise, *The Military Policy of the United States*, which he never completed. Upton became despondent over the state of the army and the fact that few politicians, at least, seemed to care. Depressed, Upton killed himself in 1881.

Army officers began passing around Upton's unfinished text, pondering his thesis. Upton argued that, because the United States had always relied on volunteers as the backbone of its army, it had always been unready for war. Unless that reliance changed, it would be unready for future wars. Upton realized, of course, that citizen soldiers had won the Civil War, and he was not calling for their ouster. But he decried government policies that neglected the professionalization of the regular army and did not call up civilians long enough for them to become experienced soldiers.

Certainly, the reliance of the United States on civilian armies would not change, but thanks in part to Upton the army did begin to professionalize. It began to institute more specialized schools for artillerymen and cavalrymen. Officers received extended training, and Sherman eventually created the School of Application for Infantry and Cavalry, forerunner of the Army Command and General Staff School.

1890s • ALFRED THAYER MAHAN ~ The navy's chief theorist was Alfred Thayer Mahan. Mahan, son of venerated West Point commandant Denis Hart Mahan, had entered the navy, but he hated going to sea. He sought duty landside, and ultimately realized his long suit was writing and teaching naval history. By 1890 he had published the watershed book *Influence of Sea Power Upon History*.

Almost as if by design, Mahan's *Influence* lent itself directly to the mood of Social Darwinism. It suggested that, throughout history, the great nations of the world had become great because they had large, effective navies. From Rome to the British Empire, the story was the same. Social Darwinists and Nationalists, such as up-and-coming New York Republican

1890s

Theodore Roosevelt, could make the leap easily – if the United States was to become a player on the world stage, it had to have a bigger, better navy.

There was more. Mahan advocated building better defenses at American harbors so the U.S. Navy did not have to be trapped in coastal defense; enlarging the American merchant fleet; building a canal through Central America to link Atlantic and Pacific Oceans; and acquiring bases in the Pacific and Caribbean while preventing other nations from doing the same.

In Emory Upton and Alfred Thayer, Social Darwinism had met the American military. Mahan, in fact, sounded much like the business entrepreneurs who had first espoused Social Darwinism when he wrote, "War is not fighting, but business." The army and navy of the United States were about to pave the way for an American empire.

THE SPANISH-AMERICAN WAR

1890s • CAUSES ~ Social Darwinism, American industrial desire for markets and resources, and a resurgent military converged in 1898 to create the highpoint of American imperialism—the Spanish-American War. Though brief, the war destroyed what was left of the once-great Spanish Empire and handed the United States a short list of colonies in the Caribbean and Pacific.

While the war involved the Philippines and Guam, Spain's last Pacific holdings, its focal point was Cuba. In the early 1500s, Cuba had been the jumping-off spot for Spanish explorers in the New World. Through a series of colonial revolutions in the early nineteenth century, Spain had managed to hang on to Cuba, but now it was wracked by its own revolution as

---

Spanish-American War

~

Colonel Theodore Roosevelt – TR to some, Teddy to others – was arguably the most dashing and colorful character of the rather short war. When the war began, he resigned his position as Assistant Secretary of the Navy, then joined the army as a volunteer and helped raise the First U.S. Volunteer Cavalry – the Rough Riders. Roosevelt had been a cowboy in North Dakota some years earlier, and knew western men to be perfect riders. Such was the requirement for a cavalryman, Roosevelt figured. In the horrid supply tangle of the Army in Florida, however, the Rough Riders' horses were left behind, and they made their classic assault on San Juan Hill afoot.

Before joining his regiment, Roosevelt had stopped off at a New York haberdashery where he ordered a custom-designed uniform. All buff and khaki, it reflected improvements that the British were making in tropical uniforms. On the way up Kettle and San Juan Hills, however, Teddy doffed the jacket and went in khaki breeches, blue shirt, suspenders, boots, and a short-crowned hat which he adorned with a blue polka-dot bandanna.

TR carried something else, too. Horribly myopic, he was lost without his glasses. Before shipping out, he had ordered ten pair of his prescription spectacles. On this charge – the one that would so change American world stature – TR carried several pairs of glasses inside the crown of his hat. Just in case he lost a pair in the attack, he wouldn't have to miss history because he couldn't see.

Cuban nationalists, fighting guerrilla style, tried to win their independence. Fighting had first erupted in Cuba in 1868 and lasted ten years. While that conflict had sparked the interest of many American interventionists, including President Ulysses S. Grant, Congress was not interested in assisting the Cuban revolution and the United States stayed neutral.

Renewed violence in 1895, however, caught more American attention, first from businessmen. Warfare in Cuba disrupted an important commerce link; Americans had established business interests on the island, most notably in the sugar cane fields, which the war frequently laid waste

The American public began to identify with Cuban patriots; after all, the United States had itself rebelled against an imperialist power. While many Americans called for intervention, President Grover Cleveland officially proclaimed American neutrality in the conflict in June 1895.

1890S • YELLOW JOURNALISM ~ Neutral or not, Americans had a constant stream of news, or at least stories, from Cuba to keep their interest piqued. Newspaper moguls William Randolph Hearst and Joseph Pulitzer, both imperialists and fierce competitors, used their papers, the *New York Journal* and the *New York World* respectively, to inflame American readers against Spain. Both Hearst and Pulitzer put reporters in Cuba, who indeed supplied copy and photographs to the home papers. But the publishers demanded fantastic tales, and increasingly newspaper stories were more fiction than fact. Stories were often lurid, featuring women defamed at the hands of the Spanish. Artwork was graphic. The newspapers devoted "extras" to Cuban stories, often printing them on attention-grabbing yellow paper, giving rise to the phrase "yellow journalism."

1896 • "BUTCHER" WEYLER AND RECONCENTRATION ~ In 1896 Spain handed American reporters more fodder for print when it adopted a new strategy. Captain General Valeriano Weyler arrived in Cuba and soon began a policy of "reconcentration." Patriot guerrillas could not operate without a support system of families and friends who lent them supplies, provided them shelter, and covered their tracks. Reconcentration would cut that supply base by arresting known guerrilla supporters and concentrating them in cities and towns, which Weyler would fortify against attack. Then he would lay waste to the countryside to deprive the patriots of its cover and resources.

The policy was not new in war. The Union Army had pursued a type of concentration policy against the families of rebel guerrillas in Missouri during the Civil War and Sherman had burned crops as he marched through the South to deprive the soldiers of food and pressure civilians to surrender. But Weyler's action inflamed Americans. Reporters called Weyler a "butcher." They said Cuba had become an island prison. That Americans should become so enraged shows a certain innocence and naiveté about changes in warfare. Even before the dawn of the twentieth century, even before two world wars had come to pass, warfare was dragging all people—soldier and civilian alike—into a modern equation.

1898 • AMERICAN INTERVENTION IN CUBA ~ Ohio Republican William McKinley won the presidency in 1896 and replaced Cleveland in March 1897, inheriting from him the Cuban question. Even

1898

though the United States acquired Hawaii as a territory under McKinley, he was a reluctant imperialist and something of a pacifist. He had been in the Civil War (in fact, he was the last Civil War veteran to be elected president), and he noted once how he remembered the Civil War dead stacked up like chopped wood. He had seen one war, he said, and did not want to see another. The threat of American intervention in Cuban affairs scared him.

But events pulled McKinley along. Even though Spain pulled Weyler out of Cuba, the yellow press kept Americans agitated. McKinley's administration tried diplomacy with Spain, and Spain was honestly trying to stay on good terms with the United States while attempting to hold Cuba.

1898 • BATTLESHIP MAINE ~ An escalation of violence in early 1898 prompted McKinley to order the battleship *U.S.S. Maine* to Havana harbor to protect American interests. The ship's mission would be the catalyst for war. Riding at anchor on February 15, 1898, the *Maine* exploded; 260 of her crew died. Spain immediately offered help with rescue and salvage, but Americans charged treachery, believing the Spanish had torpedoed the ship. (An American investigation later determined the blast was internal—an accident.)

The sinking of the *Maine*, coupled with an intercepted Spanish diplomatic letter that slandered McKinley, fueled American hawkishness. Popular culture, from songwriters to ministers, reflected the mood, and the catch phrase of the day was "Remember the Maine."

Something else was in the air. Progressivism was becoming the prevailing political wind, and Progressivism demanded government intervention and reform in many areas—work place safety, meatpacking, food and drug purity. That spirit of reform translated to an American

(1898) The battleship U.S.S. Maine, entering Havana harbour, where it later blew up, triggering the Spanish-American War.

desire to help the Cuban nationals. As Spanish-American War historian Frank Friedel said,

Perhaps it [the war] can be attributed in part to American restlessness in the 1890s, and in part to a desire to see the United States function like a great nation, complete with a powerful navy and strong overseas bases. More than those factors, it was crusading morality. Above all, the reform element in the population— those who had been Populists and those who became Progressives—clamored for the United States to rescue the Cuban people from Spanish malefactors.

That same spirit affected the pacificistic McKinley. He could see that the reform sentiment of the American public could cost Republicans the mid-term elections in November 1898 if he did not act.

1898 • SPANISH-AMERICAN WAR BEGINS ~ McKinley at first hoped active diplomacy would forestall war. In March 1898 he told Spain to grant Cuba full independence. Spain refused. On April 11 McKinley sought Congress' permission to use U.S. force to intervene in Cuba; Congress agreed on April 19. Two days later United States warships were blockading Cuba, and on April 25, 1898, Congress declared war on Spain.

1898 • BATTLE OF MANILA BAY ~ The United States Navy, remade in the image of Mahan, acted quickly. Assistant Secretary of the Navy Theodore Roosevelt, who received the job for vigorously supporting McKinley in 1896, was acting head of the navy department in the absence of Secretary John D. Long. Sensing war, Roosevelt had already warned Commodore George Dewey, commander of the American Pacific fleet, in harbor at Hong Kong, to be on the alert. As soon as Dewey learned of the declaration of war, he sailed to the Philippines and attacked the Spanish fleet at Manila Bay. In a brief battle on May 1, 1898, Dewey's squadron destroyed the Spanish fleet, and, for all real purposes, took control of the Philippines. Occupation, however, would not be complete until army troops could arrive. For the time being, Dewey would rely on a few Marines and some Filipino insurgents, already staging their own insurrection against Spain, to hold the archipelago.

1898 • BUILDING AN ARMY TO FIGHT IN CUBA ~ Infantry ground action, targeting Cuba, would move slower, but it would more directly affect American society. The regular army numbered only about 25,000 troops, and the War Department quickly determined that would not be enough for an extensive campaign. McKinley issued a call for 125,000 volunteers, more than the army expected but a number roughly equal to that in National Guard units; politically, McKinley could not afford to alienate any of them by denying them a spot in the war. Later he would call for another 75,000 volunteers. Volunteerism was rampant. By late May the army had most of the initial 125,000 request.

No doubt many of the men came with a "crusading" spirit, believing that they were going to right wrongs in Cuba. But they were also the sons, nephews, and grandsons of Civil War veterans. They had grown up on stories that increasingly focused on the glory of war, not the grisly death it had produced. In the age of Social Darwinism—survival of the fittest—many may also have had the belief of Teddy Roosevelt, who thought war was a purifying agent, trying men by fire and culling out the weak. Roosevelt himself resigned his spot in the Navy Department and, with regular army friend Colonel Leonard Wood, raised the First United States Volunteer Cavalry—the Rough Riders. Roosevelt had recruited the men for their riding skills—cowboys from the West and polo players from New York. Ironically, their horses had not arrived from Florida by the time they went into action, and the Rough Riders made their famous charge up Kettle and San Juan hills on foot.

The rush to war resembled greatly the early days of the Civil War. Men paraded through streets amid cheering crowds. Flags and bunting decorated buildings. Politicians made speeches. The men marched to trains that took them to assembly points across the nation, but Georgia and Florida were their main destinations. Volunteers realized that army life was not glorious at all, but rather sweaty, dusty, dull and routine. National Guardsmen realized their home training had been insufficient. The Army realized it too, and regular soldiers were especially frustrated because state National Guards had repeatedly promised that their troops were ready for service. As it was, when the time came to fight, the Army left the ill-trained Guardsmen behind in Florida. This would be a regulars' war.

1898 • THE FIGHTING IN CUBA ~ Under the command of General William O. Shafter, an old, out-of-shape frontier veteran, the United States Fifth Corps, with the regiments of Indian "Buffalo Soldiers" and a few regiments of volunteers, including Roosevelt's Rough Riders, left Florida for Cuba in June 1898. Plagued by supply and transport problems, the army never landed more than 17,000 troops in Cuba. As it turns out, it didn't need more.

Shafter landed in southeast Cuba, targeting Santiago and its adjacent port instead of the capital of Havana to the northwest. At Santiago, he could coordinate with the navy that had trapped the Spanish Caribbean fleet in Santiago Harbor. Key to taking Santiago were the heights outside of the town, and American troops rushed them on July 1, 1898. Fighting that day included the Rough Riders' classic charge up Kettle Hill supporting other regiments charging San Juan Hill. (American folklore traditionally has Roosevelt's men going up San Juan Hill proper.) Americans carried the day, and while an official cessation of hostilities would be several weeks coming, the fighting was over.

1898 • AMERICAN WOMEN IN THE SPANISH-AMERICAN WAR ~ Camp life in Florida and occupation duty in Cuba proved more treacherous than combat for U.S. soldiers as epidemics of typhoid fever struck both camps. Army corpsmen (medics) proved insufficient to combat the disease and a call for 6,000 more volunteers failed to reach desired numbers. Quickly the army began appointing women as nurses. Dr. Anita Newcomb McGee headed the new nursing service. Although it was an auxiliary—nurses worked under a civilian contract without military rank—more than 1,500 women volunteered for service between 1898 and 1901. That service would see them stateside, in Cuba and in the Philippines where U.S. troops fought a Filipino guerrilla war until 1902.

The nurses' exemplary service convinced Army Surgeon-General George M. Sternberg that the female service was a necessary addition to the army. In 1901, he backed legislation creating the Army Nurse Corps. McGee again headed the

(1898) Troops from the 71st Regiment, wearing uniforms and carrying rifles, walk up the steps of the New York City armory upon their return from fighting in Cuba during the Spanish-American War.

corps. Even though it was now something more than an auxiliary, women in the Nurse Corps still had no military rank, status, pay, or benefits. In 1908, the U.S. Navy created a similar nursing system, again without rank and privileges.

1900-1914 • BETWEEN THE SPANISH-AMERICAN WAR AND WORLD WAR I
~ A great spirit of victory thus spread over the United States at the turn of the century, but reality quickly dampened it. Troops had to garrison in Cuba until the United States granted it independence in 1902, and they had to stay in the Philippines longer. Spain was gone, but Americans did not believe Filipino insurgents could effectively govern themselves. Congress decided to keep the Philippines, angering the island patriots and touching off a bloody war between Filipinos and American troops. Americans soldiers fought well, but the insurrection surprised the American public. Diplomacy ended the insurrection, and Americans began thinking better of imperialism.

Teddy Roosevelt, McKinley's vice-president after the election of 1900, became president in 1901 when an assassin killed McKinley. Roosevelt did not endeavor to increase the American empire, but he kept a firm hold on the one it already had. He issued the Roosevelt Corollary to the Monroe Doctrine, warning European nations to stay out of the Caribbean, and he began the American project to build the Panama Canal.

The United States Army realized things could have gone better in Cuba, and it set about professionalizing itself even more. It created a true General Staff to plan strategies for potential wars, and it tried to beef up the National Guard.

But it was laboring again in a spirit of isolationism, for the American public wanted no more of war or imperialism for the time being.

WORLD WAR I

1900-1914 • EUROPEAN CAUSES

World War I began of a long-running colonial contest and arms race between European nations. England, France, the newly united Germany, and, to a lesser extent, Belgium, the Netherlands and Italy had extended their colonial reach around the globe, taking territories in Africa, Asia, and Southeast Asia. The dual-monarchy of Austria-Hungary, too, was colonial, but it could only grasp control over Balkan countries. Czarist Russia also had eyes on the Slavic people of the Balkans as, with a sizeable Slavic population herself, she took on the role of protector of the Balkans.

The nations realized that they had to protect their holdings from each other, and an arms race ensued. They dispatched troops to their colonies, and they began to build bigger and better weapons. England, long the world's major sea power, drew competition from Germany, and soon the German Navy rivaled England's.

With Europe becoming an armed camp, national leaders recognized the need for military alliances. German Chancellor Otto von Bismarck created one in the early 1870s. Germany had just defeated France in the Franco-Prussian War, 1870-1871, and he knew that another war with France was likely sometime in the future. He convinced Kaiser Wilhelm I to forge an alliance with Austria-Hungary, Italy and Russia. Russia was key. Far to the east of Germany, if it entered a war on the side of France, the two could engage Germany in a fatal two-front war. While the size of Russia's armies and their preparedness were military unknowns, Bismarck reasoned it was better to be allied with her than against her.

The alliance system was the lynchpin of Bismarck's foreign policy until, in 1890, Wilhelm II fired him, taking over foreign policy himself. He quickly let the Russian alliance drop. Alone and scared in a hostile Europe, Russia sought a new alliance; France was eager to oblige. French authorities knew Russia lagged behind in the industrial development that had, in part, spawned the arms race. In return for a military alliance, they offered Russia money and industrial expertise to better industrialize. Russia quickly agreed. The French-led alliance, which soon included England, became known as the Triple Entente; the German alliance was the Triple Alliance. (During World War I, however, French and British forces will become known as the Allies; Germany and her allies as the Central Powers.)

THE SCHLIEFFEN PLAN

But Germany was not fazed, and the German General Staff developed a plan to combat a two-front war. Called the Schlieffen Plan, it relied on speed, mass, and Germany's rail network. If a war broke out, Germany would leave a bare-bones defensive force on her eastern frontier to combat Russia, then quickly shift the critical mass of her troops to the western front via railroads, quickly march through Belgium (ignoring that country's neutrality), move into northern France and occupy Paris, thus knocking the country out of the war. Then, with a garrison force staying in France, the German army would entrain for the eastern front and there destroy Russia.

1914 • Flashpoint in the Balkans ~ The year 1914 became the critical one for Europe. Nationalists in the Balkans had long wanted to break away from Austro-Hungarian rule. In July 1914 Austria sent its Archduke Franz Ferdinand (next in line to the Austrian crown) to convince them otherwise. While Ferdinand and his wife were riding in a motorcade in Sarajevo, Bosnia, a Serbian assassin killed both of them.

Austria-Hungary demanded that Serbia allow Austro-Hungarian troops within their borders to root out the assassin and his supporters. Serbia said no. Then Austria-Hungary asked Germany for permission to invade Serbia; as senior member in the Triple Alliance, Germany had to approve and back everything its allies did. Kaiser Wilhelm II said okay, and promised support if needed.

1914 • European Mobilization ~ Mobilization is the process by which nations get their troops prepared for war. When Austria-Hungary mobilized against Serbia in July 1914, the whole European alliance system went into effect. Russia mobilized against Austria-Hungary, Germany against Russia, France and England against Germany. By August, all the major European powers were at war. The conflict that Europe and the Western world had long feared was at hand. People would not call it World War I until, obviously, World War II erupted. Instead they called it the Great War, or, more ironically, The War to End All Wars.

1914 • Attack – and Stalemate ~ Germany put the Schlieffen Plan into effect, but by now the new chief of the General Staff, Helmuth von Moltke the Younger, had become scared that a bare force on the eastern front would not hold back imagined Russian hoards. So he diluted the force attacking Belgium and France, leaving troops behind in the east and depriving the western punch of the force it needed to carry through to Paris. The Germans indeed swung through Belgium and into northern France, but French troops, surprising Germans with their speed, spirit, and élan, met them full-on at the Marne River about forty miles north of the capital.

Deprived of their mass, the Germans could not press on; neither could the French route them and drive them back toward the Rhine, even with the addition of the British Expeditionary Force, which stepped across the English Channel to fight on the French left. All the combatants used machine guns now, a weapon that inherently gave advantage to defenders. Commanders on both sides could not figure how to defeat the machine gun. Time after time they ordered nineteenth-century style charges against enemy works; time after time their men collapsed under heavy fire. The private soldier on the Marne did what instinct told him to do—seek the protection of the ground. Men began digging trenches, nothing new in warfare, but the magnitude and intricacy of the trenches eclipsed anything in previous wars. Before 1914 ended, a trench line extended from the English Channel to the Swiss frontier. The war stalemated.

1914-1915 • The United States Attempts Neutrality ~ While Europe burned, the United States endeavored to stay out of the conflict. Isolationist for most of the twenty years since the Spanish-American War, and still harboring a bad taste from the Filipino Insurrection, the United States

1915-1915

wanted no part of world affairs. Events would prove, however, that the world had grown too small for a nation the size of the United States to completely ignore the European war.

In a contradictory stance, the United States demanded that the European belligerents grant her neutral rights on the high seas. Simply, the United States wanted to trade freely with England, France, and Germany. But those countries were locked in a death grip. Part of the struggle was to deny materiel of war (virtually any product, not just weapons, that might help a war effort) to the enemy. To that end, England had blockaded German ports; Germany had spread a ring of unrestricted submarine warfare around the British Isles in which subs—or U-boats—prowled and sank merchant ships. Neither the Allies nor the Central Powers could tolerate the United States trading with their enemies.

1915 • THE SINKING OF THE LUSITANIA ~ The situation worsened in May 1915 when a German U-boat sank the Cunard line luxury cruiser *Lusitania* off the coast of Ireland. The *Lusitania* was a passenger liner but not totally innocent—it carried in its hold a supply of ammunition for the Allies. Before the ship had left New York harbor five days earlier, Germany had placed ads in New York newspapers warning Americans not to travel on the ship. It would be crossing through a zone of submarine warfare, the ads warned, and passengers would be in grave danger. More than 1,200 people died on the *Lusitania*, including 128 Americans.

Wilson cried foul and sent strident diplomatic protests to Berlin; the United States was neutral, he said, and now German U-boats had dragged Americans into the war. Berlin ignored Wilson. Its U-boat war was indeed crippling British shipping and front-line supply operations. Over the next year, more Americans would be killed or wounded in U-boat attacks.

1916 • RESTRICTED SUBMARINE WARFARE ~ Wilson stepped up his protests and fractured his own presidential cabinet. Secretary of State William Jennings Bryan—a former Populist, presidential candidate, and avowed pacificist—believed Wilson's protests were hypocritical and wrong. He was already angry that the United States was making war loans to England and France, and manufacturing arms for them as well. Such "neutrality," he argued, would ultimately place the United States in the war. He also cautioned Wilson against stepping up his rhetoric against Berlin. Wilson did not budge, and Jennings resigned his post.

Wilson's rhetoric worked, though. In 1916 it elicited from Germany a promise to begin a "restricted" type of submarine warfare, one in which sub commanders would surface their vessels before striking, warn enemy ships of an impending attack, and give neutrals time to leave the ship. In hindsight the notion seems romantic and naïve; certainly it did not last long.

Wilson faced reelection in 1916, and his campaign managers successfully used the slogan "He kept us out of war" to secure him another term in the White House. But before he could make his second inauguration speech, Germany resumed unrestricted U-boat warfare around England.

1917 • ZIMMERMAN TELEGRAM AND U.S. DECLARATION OF WAR ~ When U-boats once again began killing at will in January 1917, Wilson broke

German U-Boats – 1915. Two German submarines, the U35 and U42, surface off the Mediterranean coast. When U-boats began attacking at will in January 1917, President Wilson broke diplomatic relations with Germany—the penultimate step to war.

diplomatic relations with Germany—the penultimate step to war. England, seeing the United States about to join the fray, shoved it over the line. Some time earlier, the British had intercepted a telegram from German foreign minister Alfred Zimmerman to a German ambassador in Mexico City. The message, now known as the Zimmerman Telegram, encouraged Mexico, in the event the United States entered the war, to side with Germany. After a German victory in Europe, Zimmerman said, Germany would help Mexico reclaim land it had lost to the United States at the end of the Mexican War in 1848. (That land would include California, Nevada, Arizona, Utah, New Mexico, part of Colorado and, presumably, Texas). England leaked the telegram to the American public, and the drift to war became a rush.

In April 1917, Wilson approached Congress seeking a declaration of war against Germany. He got it. The United States was in the War to End all Wars.

1917 • AMERICAN MOBILIZATION

The United States has traditionally been unprepared for its entry into large military conflicts. But such is the temperament of a democracy. It feared large standing armies; equated them with dictatorial rule or revolution. Even when the army began to professionalize itself in the post-Civil War years, it remained a society within itself, segregated from the American mainstream. To do otherwise, to give too much attention to war planning and things military, reasoned most Americans in the early twentieth century, was to risk "Prussianizing" the United States.

1917

So the United States may be blamed and then excused for not being ready to fight World War I when it entered it in 1917. But the fact remained, it had joined the contest, and now must do something about it. Mobilization meant for the United States, just has it had for England, France, Germany, and Russia, enlisting the troops, equipping them, paying for them, feeding them, getting them to the front, and keeping the public behind them—all at the same time. One can argue that the American mobilization of 1917 could not have occurred had not the Progressive Era come before it, had not presidents Roosevelt, Taft, and Wilson himself—along with enough reformers of either party in Congress to do the job—created the fundamental American bureaucracy. War mobilization in 1917 was both progressive and bureaucratic.

1917 • Mobilizing the Public

When Wilson asked for the declaration against Germany, he was by no means assured the American public would back him. Some still believed the true enemy was England; after all His Majesty's ships had denied American neutrality early on as well. The United States was also a land of immigrants, many of them German. Germans had settled American cities, fought in the Civil War, mined for gold, and helped build the Transcontinental Railroad; German-Americans were as American as anyone, they would say. Another group might just as soon fight the English also—Irish-Americans. Ireland had long wanted autonomy from England, had fought for it in the nineteenth century, and in 1917 they were smarting after the British had brutally suppressed the Irish "Easter Rebellion" the year before. And yet another group wanted to fight no one. Socialists, while never big players in American federal politics, had carved niches for themselves in local politics. Tracing their roots to German Marxism, moderated by American pragmatism, borne on by industrialism and finding some expression in Progressivism, Socialists were anti-war.

Wherever Wilson looked he could find someone who did not like his war aims; yet he needed the public solidly behind the war. The key to it was propaganda, or to put it in a more genteel way, public information.

Propaganda, public information, advertising, whichever name it went under, had been around for some decades. As American industry boomed in the 1880s and 1890s, producers discovered they had to convince millions of Americans they needed what manufacturers produced. Advertising became the key. Entrepreneurs used it to sell everything from oatmeal to Ivory soap, toothpaste to Coca-Cola. Later, in the Progressive Era, propaganda came in another form—magazine articles and books by "muckrakers," crusading journalists who wrote to expose corruption and bring reform in a variety of social arenas. Muckrakers brought about election reform, oversaw the demise of city "boss" systems, and agitated for temperance and suffrage reform. Perhaps the most famous of them, Upton Sinclair, brought reform in the meatpacking industry with his novel *The Jungle* (1906).

In the early days of World War I, both England and Germany had kept propaganda offices in the United States. Both anticipated American entry into the war; both wanted the United States on its side. English information officers deftly melded the image of Germans (Huns, they called them, or the Bosche) into machine-gun wielding barbarians. Their favorite fodder was the Schlieffen Plan's violation of Belgian neutrality in 1914. Stories described the German rape of Belgian women, and how victorious Germans marched down streets with Belgian babies on their bayonets.

1917 • George Creel and the Committee of Public Information

~ Wilson required image management to gain support for this war. In 1917, he and Congress created the Committee on Public Information (CPI), and appointed former Progressive journalist George Creel to head it. Creel kept the image of the German Hun before Americans; before he was finished, everything German was unpatriotic if not diabolical. People began Anglicizing Germanic names: frankfurters became hot dogs; Muellers became Millers; Schmidts became Smiths; and so on. He also played on American patriotism and gave it a logo—Uncle Sam. Bedecked in top hat, stars, and stripes, Uncle Sam had been around for some time before Creel adopted him. But Creel used him effectively in the famous "I Want You" campaign, with Uncle Sam pointing and gazing down young American men, almost shaming them to march straight to the enlistment office.

Four-minute Men

Knowing that word-of-mouth and street-corner debate were perhaps the most effective propaganda tools, Creel adopted another method of public information as well. Across the country, he enlisted men of all ages and occupations, men who could speak well and command local respect, to give impromptu speeches on the war effort. They were called Creel's "four-minute men" because, when a conversation turned their way or they heard people decrying American war aims, they could deliver a four-minute speech on any aspect of American mobilization, strategy, aims or patriotism.

1917 • Curtailing Civil Liberties

~ Just as George Creel was crafting public opinion, the Wilson administration moved to make sure unauthorized voices did not attempt to do the same. Opponents saw Wilson's measures as an unconstitutional curtailment of civil liberties; proponents saw them as necessary war measures. First, Wilson backed passage of the Espionage Act in 1917. It mandated severe penalties for anyone found guilty of interfering with the draft or encouraging disloyalty to the United States. Next, he backed the Sedition Act in 1918, a more widespread supplement to the Espionage Act. The act extended penalties to anyone suspected of abusing the government in print. Taken together, the two acts essentially made it illegal to question or rebuke the United States government. The Civil Liberties Bureau challenged the acts, claiming they trod on the basic right of free speech guaranteed in the Constitution; however, the Supreme Court upheld the acts.

Most Americans agreed with the Court and Wilson, believing that drastic times called for drastic measures. In fact, Americans were becoming accustomed to handing over large measures of discretionary power to the federal government. They had started doing so with the Progressive Era, believing the government was the only agency big enough to combat big business. Now, the government was the only agency big enough to combat the Central powers of Europe.

(circa 1920) Reserve officers of the XI Corps firing artillery during a training session at Fort Devens, Massachusetts. During WWI civilians were "quick trained" for combat.

The trend would continue through another world war and the Cold War, as Americans perceived foreign menaces so great that the federal government must be given wide latitude to fight them.

1917 • INDUSTRIAL AND FINANCIAL MOBILIZATION ~ World War I changed the warring countries. Each had to recraft its society around the war; each had to structure the aims of industries and farms, private citizens and public to the war effort. The United States was no different.

With Creel working on maintaining public sentiment for the war, Wilson knew that the government also had to ensure its armies were equipped. The government had to point all of American industries at producing war materiel and delivering to the army. Despite American industrial prowess, when the United States entered the war it had shortages of military supplies, and American railroads —undoubtedly the best in the world— still could not make deliveries with the efficiency the army demanded. The situation required streamlined economic and industrial mobilization.

Some progress was already underway. Watching the war's economic consumption of nations, the War Department, Navy Department, and Chamber of Commerce formed committees in 1915 and 1916 to study industrial mobilization. That resulted in the Naval Consulting Board, the Industrial Preparedness Committee of the Chamber of Commerce, and the Advisory Committee to the Council of National Defense. Successful civilian entrepreneurs and businessmen comprised those committees. They saw quickly that centralization was the key to efficiency, but the Progressive government had just spent twenty years combating industrial centralization—monopolies. They feared reactionary Progressives might opt to nationalize industry, cutting owners out of war-time profits. They proposed instead a system of voluntary self-regulation, offering to work closely with the military departments to ensure supplies.

1917 • WAR INDUSTRIES BOARD ~ A major result of the plan was the War Industries Board (WIB) created in 1917. Its job was to consult with the army and navy, ascertain their needs, then meet them. Consultants would set quotas, and then allocate resources for their fulfillment. Of course, carving out this niche for American military demands had to happen without disrupting the flow of goods and supplies to the already strapped British and French. The WIB proceeded haltingly. Wilson and other Progressives never fully trusted the WIB or got over the nagging feeling they were allowing the rise of another monopoly.

While the WIB never completely solved the problems of industrial mobilization, it did perform a vital function in the first total mobilization of the United States. It hit its stride in 1918 after Wall Street speculator Bernard Baruch, one of seven original members of the board, took over direction of the WIB and made it run more efficiently.

The nationalization of industries that civilian businessmen had feared did, to a limited degree, occur. Operating as individual companies, railroads could not solve delivery problems. To make railroads more efficient, Wilson nationalized them. They ran as a single system, not competing businesses, for the duration of the war. Populists had wanted such a measure in the 1880s to curtail railroad abuses. But it had smacked too much of socialism then; in 1917 it sounded like common sense, albeit temporary.

1917 • NATIONAL LABOR RELATIONS BOARD ~ Although the heyday of labor unions was yet to come, some unions sensed that, with industry desperate to meet quotas and deadlines, it might be a good time to demand better conditions and wages, reinforcing the demand with strikes if necessary. Such activities could not occur without chaos, the government knew, and it created the National War Labor Board (NWLB) in 1918. The board aimed to smooth relations between labor and owners to avoid strikes and slowdowns. As such, the board endorsed collective bargaining; guaranteed eight-hour workdays in return for no-strike agreements; and secured higher wages for many laborers.

1917-1920 • WOMEN AND AFRICAN-AMERICANS ON THE HOMEFRONT ~ The heavy industrial demands of World War I on United States manufacturing meant businesses suddenly needed more manpower. But that was the paradox—just as manpower demands went up, millions of men joined the armed services. As contractors faced WIB deadlines, they turned to other sources of labor—blacks and women.

Jobs for women opened up in all areas, from industrial manufacturing to office work and retail sales. Women worked in heavy industry, making munitions, artillery pieces, and ships. They joined labor unions. They were indeed the forerunners of the more famous "Rosie the Riveter" of World War II. After the war, when servicemen returned, those women ultimately had to relinquish their jobs. But they had begun to break down sexual barriers in the workplace.

1917-1918

African Americans, too, benefited; in fact, war-time opportunities caused a "Great Migration" of blacks from the South to the North. The post-Reconstruction South had been a difficult place for blacks. Despite the assurances of freedom, citizenship, and voting rights that the Thirteenth, Fourteenth, and Fifteenth Amendments had provided, by the 1890s most southern states had enacted "Jim Crow" laws—local mandates that sought to get around federal civil rights laws. Jim Crow segregated blacks from whites, and greatly impeded their right to vote. The Ku Klux Klan was resurgent, and lynchings were on the rise. When war-time northern industry beckoned, it is no wonder that African Americans responded. Between 1917 and 1920, some 500,000 people moved north.

The North, however, did not completely welcome them. Northerners had long since feared some type of black migration into their section, and feared blacks taking white jobs. In many regards, racial prejudice was as heavy in the North as in the South. The Great Migration sparked race riots in 1917, which continued sporadically in larger American cities until 1921.

1918 • FOOD ADMINISTRATION ~ Not only did the army need manufactured equipment, it needed food for both men and horses. It was clear that agriculture required the same type of close management the WIB was giving industry. Thus, Congress created the United States Food Administration. At its head was Herbert Hoover, an affable Republican who had sponsored a benevolent relief effort to help Belgium after the start of the war. (Hoover would also soon oversee Red Cross operations and would, in 1929, be the unfortunate U.S. president who presided over the Wall Street crash and first years of the Great Depression.) Hoover promoted increased production and urged farmers to bring more acreage under cultivation; the government would buy all they could grow.

Hoover and the administration encouraged Americans to conserve food; after all the boys going to war needed it. The Food Administration encouraged Americans to set aside certain days of the week to give up designated commodities, such as meat or wheat products. Americans responded, and even planted their own "War Gardens." These gardens, in lots near their homes or in communal lots outside of town, were designed to decrease individual dependence on commercial growers, who could, in turn, furnish more food to the army.

Temperance reformers got an unlikely boost from the food conservation movement. The Army needed barley, rye, grapes and other produce necessary to distill liquors and wines. Reformers reasoned that distillation was a waste of war materiel; that to drink it up as spirits was unpatriotic. They convinced Congress to pass legislation putting the Eighteenth Amendment, which prohibited the production and sale of beer and alcohol, before the people for ratification. The war was over by the time states ratified it in 1919.

1917-1918 • TROOP MOBILIZATION ~ All of this social mobilization would, of course, have been for nothing had the United States not had an effective fighting force ready to go to Europe. The truth is, in 1917, it did not.

The army was working on the problem of troop strength, though, and had been since the turn of the century. The United States Army General Staff had recognized after the Spanish-American War that the United States' military needs had changed. The war, the acquisition of an empire, and the Filipino Insurrection made it clear that the army must change from an Indian-fighting army of 25,000 men to one capable of defending overseas territories and meeting challenges from major world powers.

1916-1917 • NATIONAL DEFENSE ACT ~ The General Staff called for more men. Neither the public nor Congress would accept a peace-time draft, but there were ways around conscriptions. In 1901, Congress approved a gradual increase of troops in the regular army, calling for an army of more than 100,000 men; by 1915, with Europe already at war, the American army reached nearly 106,000 officers and enlisted men. But warily watching events in Europe and making war plans, the General Staff recognized the United States needed an army of at least one million men if it ever entered the war. Passing the National Defense Act of 1916, Congress cautiously approved the gradual elevation of regular troop strength to 175,000 men.

Another part of the National Defense Act of 1916, however, moved to guarantee the regular army a reserve force by attempting to improve the National Guard. But the Guard was all volunteer, and while the General Staff wanted its number at 450,000, by early 1917 it could count only 174,000 troops. Simply, when the United States entered World War I, it did not have the troops the General Staff said were necessary to fight it. It would fall to a patriotic flourish of volunteerism and a national conscription to fill the ranks.

1917 • SELECTIVE SERVICE ACT ~ A national conscription was the only answer. In May 1917, Congress passed the Selective Service Act. It called only for men between the ages of twenty-one and thirty years old to register for the draft (later the range would be expanded to eighteen to forty-five years old). The national government would not handle the draft, leaving the duty to local boards. That way, the leading men of any given community had the final say on who was conscripted. Local doctors would judge the fitness of young men for service; board members could judge exemptions on a case-by-case basis. The system gave a hometown, communal feel to selective service. By June 1917, ten million men had registered for the draft. Draft boards called up three million of those, but judged only 500,000 of them suitable for service.

Even though the selective service appeared to move sluggishly, the military services were approaching their initial manpower needs. Just as Congress passed the Selective Service Act, the army and National Guard embarked on massive recruiting drives. Those efforts ultimately netted some 700,000 volunteers. Thus regulars, volunteers, and conscripts together put the United States land force in 1917 at 1.2 million men, satisfying initial General Staff requests.

1918-1920 • WOMEN IN THE ARMED FORCES ~ Conscription and volunteerism involved mostly white men, but other groups joined military forces as well. For the first time, women joined the army. They were not drafted and they did not serve in combat roles, but rather as volunteers in nursing or secretarial and clerical roles. The Army Nurse Corps grew from 400 members to 20,000 during America's time at war; the Navy Nurse Corps grew from 400 to 1,400 in the same

1917-1920

time. Army nurses served all over Europe in mobile and stationary hospitals, as well as on troop transport trains and ships. Three nurses won the Distinguished Service Cross, twenty-three others the Distinguished Service Medal.

Modern, industrialized warfare created a larger rear-echelon service in World War I than in previous wars, with many noncombatant functions necessary to the operations of the army. AEF commander General John J. Pershing recognized he needed skilled workers at clerical jobs in his headquarters. American women, trained in the new industrial/clerical workplaces back home, were the key, but Pershing never received as many as he requested. Still, hundreds did serve in clerical positions as members of the army, and did another 5,000 women who served in adjunct civilian capacities.

The navy, too, used women in clerical roles—some 12,500 of them worldwide. Following the Navy's lead, both the Marines and Coast Guard had nursing and clerical corps of women during the war.

1917-1920 • AFRICAN-AMERICANS IN THE WAR

Black men, too, served in large numbers, continuing the impressive military heritage they had begun during the Civil War. Some 400,000 enlisted. Half of those served in Europe, and 30,000 of those had front-line combat duty, the remainder working in essential if unsung support services behind the lines. If African Americans were looking for equality in the armed forces, though, they were sorely disappointed. The navy accepted black recruits, but relegated them to kitchen duty. The Marine Corps accepted no African Americans. The United States Army remained segregated until the 1950s, and black units kept to themselves.

On many bases whites and blacks clashed, but the worst incident occurred

(1917) Dispatch Rider. While the American navy formally enlisted women, granting them rank and status, the U.S. Army did not. Nurses in both services also remained in auxiliary status. Nevertheless, women in World War I proved their necessity. Another war would prove their worthiness of rank. Seen here is a woman dispatch rider for the AID during World War I.

in Houston, Texas, where white civilians goaded a black regiment into fighting back. The black troops killed 16 whites, and the army court martialed 156 of them for mutiny. The army convicted many of them and 19 were hanged. American prejudice traveled to Europe as well. Infighting between white and black officers tainted the reputations of even the best black regiments.

1917-1918 • THE AMERICAN RED CROSS ~ Founded in 1881, the American Red Cross had served on a limited basis in the Spanish-American War, relaying correspondence between American troops and their families. But in World War I it became the battlefield aid organization so familiar to millions of Americans.

During the war, American Red Cross chapters blossomed from 562 chapters to 3,724 chapters and more than 31 million members. Red Cross volunteers went to Europe to help soldiers of all the combatant nations, but in 1917, after American entry into the war, Doughboys became their primary aid group. Some 18,000 Red Cross nurses served with the army and navy during World War I and cared for sick and wounded soldiers both at home and in Europe. After the war, many of those nurses stayed on duty fighting a flu epidemic that began in 1918. The flu killed an estimated 500,000 people (some estimates ranges as high as 700,000) in the United States, and between 20 million and 30 million people worldwide. It did not abate until 1919.

1917 • THE UNITED STATES OVER THERE! ~ Mobilization of the type that World War I required took time, but in April 1917 America's allies needed help quickly. In fact, 1917 proved to be a bad year for the Allies, and, as the United States swung into motion, events seemed to turn irreparably against the British and French.

First, the German resumption of unrestricted submarine warfare was crippling the British. The Royal Navy's hunt-and-kill missions against the subs were ineffective. The Admiralty finally began sending merchant ships across the ocean in convoys with naval escorts, but only after the United States recommended it. Convoys traveled in safe numbers, forcing U-boats to expose themselves to heavy firepower if they wanted to attack. The new tactic worked, reversing the trend in the North Atlantic by late 1917.

1917 • RUSSIA EXITS THE WAR ~ But the story on the ground in Europe was grim throughout 1917; by the end of the year the British and French found themselves fighting a *single-front* war against an invigorated German army. In 1917, domestic revolt rocked Russia, which the war had already bled white on the eastern front. By October, the Communist Bolsheviks had taken control of the government in the Russian Revolution. Under the leadership of V.I. Lenin, the Bolsheviks promised that, once in power, they would take Russia out of the war. They made good on the pledge. Ignoring Russia's earlier agreement with the Allies not to sign a separate peace with Germany, Communist Russia made terms with the Germans in the Treaty of Brest-Litovsk in early 1918. Now the strategic land situation turned dramatically against the Allies. With German troops disengaged in the east, they were free to move to the western front where the battle had been stalemated since 1914.

WAR AND THE U.S. MILITARY ~ 1809

British and French war planners fretted as they waited, both for German and American troops to arrive. But the Americans would be slow in coming, and the Allies feared they would lose before the Yanks arrived.

1918 • TIDE OF BATTLE TURNS

Germany did, in fact, plan an offensive for March 1918, but Americans, albeit few in number, got to France before it began. American commander General John J. "Blackjack" Pershing arrived in mid-summer 1917 and established an American headquarters. By December, he had about 200,000 soldiers at his disposal, and he committed those to defending against the German spring push. Americans were crucial to holding the Allied line, putting an end to Germany's last offensive operation. In Fall 1918, American troops spearheaded the Allied Meuse-Argonne campaign, which broke Germany's back and forced her to surrender in November 1918.

In 1918, the tide of war turned on the battleground, and mobilization at home began going smoother. Bernard Baruch became head of the WIB, and Wilson and other Progressives began to entrust the board with a degree of centralization. Enlistments, flagging after the first blush of patriotism in 1917, rose again, especially after Congress authorized widening the draft eligibility age to eighteen to forty-five years old. (While millions of men in this new age bracket registered for the draft, few were actually drafted. Instead, the threat of drafting from these then-extreme ages prompted new enlistments from those in the 20-31 age bracket.) Now conscriptions averaged 275,000 men per month. Transportation and supply problems began to clear; shipping started to hit its stride. Then the war ended.

1918 • VERSAILLES PEACE TREATY

As Germany prepared to stack arms in November 1918, its top military commanders, Generals Paul von Hindenburg and Eric Ludendorf convinced Kaiser Wilhelm that he should turn over power to a provisional, liberal government. That way the militaristic, Prussian-led government that had started and prosecuted the war would not have to be present at any treaty table with the Allies. The provisional government would thus have to negotiate and treat for terms. The move would have consequences for Europe within only a handful of years.

Woodrow Wilson had long been convinced that the United States would, and indeed should, have a large say in the restructuring of post-war Europe. Early in the war he thought the U.S. could wield the most power by staying neutral until the end; as the most powerful of the world's neutrals, surely Europe would listen to his opinions. But gradually, perhaps as early as the *Lusitania* sinking, Wilson came to understand that the war's victors would listen to no one who had not shared in the cost of the war, both in money and blood. So, as grueling as the war was, Wilson could see possibilities for American influence in post-war Europe. In November 1918, after U.S. troops, equipment and money had turned the tide for the Allies, he expected to have a large say at the treaty table. Wilson did not carry the backing of his own people. Happy and relieved that the United States had been victorious, they wanted nothing more than to return to a normal life; that didn't include worrying about the state of post-war Europe.

Treaty talks were set for early 1919 at Versailles, just outside of Paris. Wilson went to France, where ebullient Parisians hailed him as a great leader. But if the parade crowds were warm to Wilson, the Allied leaders at the treaty table were cold.

Wilson brought with him a plan for a new Europe. He called it his Fourteen Points. He had written them months earlier, in fact he had presented them in rough form to the American Congress. They contained a variety of proposals, including limiting empires and letting colonial nations decide their own governmental fates through "national self-determination." He wanted to limit arms races. The most important point of all, the fourteenth point, called for a worldwide "League of Nations," an idea Wilson had borrowed from philosopher Immanuel Kant and which would enable member nations to solve their grievances through negotiation before resorting to war.

1918 • Punitive Nature of Versailles ~ The Allies at Versailles were in no mood for Wilson's high-minded plan or oratory. They had Germany on the ground and intended to kick her. They demanded that Germany sign a war guilt clause, admitting that she had started the war. They demanded that the German army be stripped to a size suitable only for defense; after all, Germany had invaded France now twice in the last fifty years. To add insult to injury, they made Germany agree to pay war reparations, staggering monetary retributions payable to England, France and the United States as repayment for the devastation Germany had caused. The only point of Wilson's plan the Allies accepted was the League of Nations.

1917-1919 • Wilson Campaigns for the League of Nations ~ Wilson returned home disappointed and his mood would not change upon his arrival. The nation was in the midst of the awkward, often painful shift from war-time to peace-time. American troops were returning and wanted their old jobs back. They displaced many of the black workers who had performed so ably. Tensions between blacks and whites strained once again, erupting into violence in the summer of 1919. Men displaced women, too, from some of their war-time jobs, but women turned their accomplishments into political capital. Pointing out that the war would not have ended as quickly had they not gone to work, women suffragists levered passage of the Nineteenth Amendment through Congress, then ratification by the states. It gave American women the right to vote, after more than a century of suffrage reform action. Once again the war had brought social change.

Most of all, the American public was sick of war. World War I had cost millions of lives, most of them European. Although the United States had lost only about 100,000 men in the war (53,000 in combat, the rest from disease or accident), the shock of the war had worn the public thin. They wanted no more of it. As soon as the Armistice had begun in November, the United States started its course back to isolationism.

As such, Americans wanted none of Woodrow Wilson's League of Nations. The League charter committed member nations to defend each other in case of attack. That was a military alliance, and had not military alliances helped start World War I?

1917 • First Red Scare ~ Something else frightened Americans, too. American capitalists had long feared Communists, who predicted the violent downfall of capitalism as the workers of the world overthrew capitalist industrialists to create a utopian state. American businessmen feared being on a Marxist hit list, and they had kept a wary eye on suspected Marxist cells in the late nineteenth century. But now, after the Bolshevik Revolution of 1917, there was a full-blown Communist nation in Russia. It was growing, forming the Union of Soviet Socialist Republics (U.S.S.R), and becoming aggressive. Americans became paranoid (not for the last time) that the Soviet Union would infiltrate the United States. Under J. Edgar Hoover, the Federal Bureau of Investigation began hunting down suspected Communists and jailing or deporting them.

To most Americans, the world had become too dangerous a place to venture into. Better to just retrench, stay home, and become isolationist as it had after the foray into imperialism at the turn of the century. In such an environment, the League of Nations was dead. Even though Wilson went on the stump for the League (in fact, he broke his health doing so), the United States would never join it. While not exactly still-born, the League of Nations was always powerless without the United States; obviously, it would fail to halt the coming of another world war.

1920s • The Interwar Years: Conservatism, Hedonism, Isolationism

∼ The 1920s were a mix of "isms," all largely wrought by World War I. The brutality of the war—the suddenness and efficiency of mass death—caused the great rural middle of the United States to retrench in biblical, moral conservatism. But many veterans had returned from France demoralized by death and the sense that their efforts had been for naught. Young Americans in the cities, convinced now that life was too short and that they must quickly grab all the pleasure they could, partied, drank illegal liquor and set the fashion rage of the decade. Business thrived and, for the first time since the 1890s, government became *laissez faire* again. The United States Army and Navy groped forward with new doctrinal policies, but the isolationist mood of the country held them in check.

1920 • Conservatism and Prosperity

∼ In 1920, conservative Republican Warren G. Harding captured the presidency. He won, in part, by calling for a "return to normalcy." Although no one knew what "normal" meant, it nonetheless struck a chord. He wanted a world where the United States was not involved in foreign affairs, and where government took a breather from Progressivism. Certainly, Progressive reforms would not be undone, and the governmental bureaucracy born of Progressive thought would not crumble, but Harding believed government could take a more "hands-off" approach to commercial regulation and let businesses steam ahead on their own. Harding was conservative, as was his successor, Calvin Coolidge. Pro-business, Coolidge said the "business of America is business," and under him the nation experienced what people then called "Coolidge Prosperity."

But not everyone shared it. When the war ended and England and France no longer needed the support of American agriculture, middle-American farmers fell into a recession. The poor rural economy lingered, rolling right into the Great Depression when the rest of the country fell on hard times in 1929.

1920s • Hedonism

∼ In hard times, as before, Christian conservatism thrived in rural America, but in urban America, the scene was quite different – Americans in their early twenties were seeking a different life. Such was perhaps normal, for they were looking at life differently. Veterans of World War I had stared death in the face, lived through the trenches, the mud, and the stench of war. They had a sense that life was short, and many of them adopted a hedonistic attitude. They had also been to France, a country free of the moralistic constraints of the United States. While Blackjack Pershing had endeavored to keep French prostitutes away from American troops, the men had been with French women just the same, and they returned home with a different moral outlook. The outlook, of course, spread to men who had not been in the army, too young perhaps, or ineligible for service, but who could enjoy the changing social climate anyway.

Many urban women, too, discovered that the war had freed them from Victorian fetters. They had gone to work, been an integral part of the American war effort. They adopted a new practicality, doffing corsets and long skirts in favor of shorter, less confining garments. They cut their hair, which the traditional Victorian woman would not think of doing. When they assumed male jobs during the war, they also assumed some male vices, like smoking and drinking. Liquor was readily available, even during Prohibition, but you had to know where to get it. Speakeasies (back-alley joints, some lavish and run by organized crime, where you had to whisper a code word to enter) thrived. Women, called "flappers," attending these places wore short, beaded dresses, drank champagne, smoked cigarettes from long cigarette holders and disregarded the old sexual codes. They had sex whenever, with whomever they wanted. While they were a minority of American women, they and their male counterparts were a social expression of the post-war years.

(circa 1920) A poster, published by the League of Women Voters, urges women to use the vote which the 19th Amendment gave them. This poster reflects another previously male-dominated activity now the privilege of women after the war.

1920s • INTERWAR ARMED FORCES

The United States Army and Navy, aware that mobilization for war in 1917 and 1918 had not been adequately anticipated or planned, sought to avoid the same problems in any future war. The Army General Staff promoted a new

1920s-1930s

National Defense Act in 1920, aimed at beefing up the American peace-time army. While it provided more slots for regular and National Guard troops (and again sought to professionalize the Reserve arm even more), it politically could not call for peace-time conscription. In the end, enlistments remained shy of Army General Staff hopes.

Industrial mobilization, too, had been central to America's war effort. Bernard Baruch, head of the old War Industries Board, helped design a new Industrial Mobilization Plan (IMP). But many in Congress, indeed the nation, thought it was simply a disguised cabal of businessmen trying to corner government contracts and make money off armaments. Later, in the 1930s, the Congressional Nye Committee would verify such sentiments when it blamed World War I on "merchants of death"—industrialists who made and sold military equipment, thus propounding an arms race that led to the war. The reasons for the Great War, of course, were more complex, but the Nye Committee's findings merely reflected the mood of the nation.

1930s • Rise of an Air Power Doctrine ~ In the United States, Army General Billy Mitchell wrestled with making airpower a central arm of the United States Army. He proved, to the Navy's chagrin, that bombers could sink battleships; in fact, he said that bombers and fighter aircraft should be America's front-line defense, not seacoast batteries and naval fleets. Mitchell's claims caused interservice fighting between the army and navy, and intraservice fighting within the army alone, and ultimately drove him to court martial and resignation.

But Mitchell was tapping into the ideas of Italian General Guilo Douhet. Douhet said that bombers, massed together and armed for self-defense, could wreak havoc on warring nations' support systems—their industrial plants, their oil supplies, and their business centers. That, of course, meant taking war to civilians in a degree never before possible, or thought of. It was now obvious that civilian and industrial mobilization was critical to any nation's war effort. This was the age of total war and, as far as any military planner was concerned, civilians were combatants.

That idea would lead to the downfall of Germany and Japan in 1945. Civil targets in the contiguous United States have never been bombed (although Japan tried with clumsy, automated bombing balloons in World War II), but

---

Civilians become Targets

~

During World War I something subtle was happening to societies, both in the United States and around the world – they were becoming civilian targets in the next war. Airplanes had played a role in World War I, and while aerial dogfights became the new romantic notion of war for many young boys, airpower went largely untapped. One of its most ominous uses came, however, when Germany sent huge zeppelins across the English Channel to bomb England. Bomb loads were light and inaccurate, but the raids began carrying war in a new way to the civil populace.

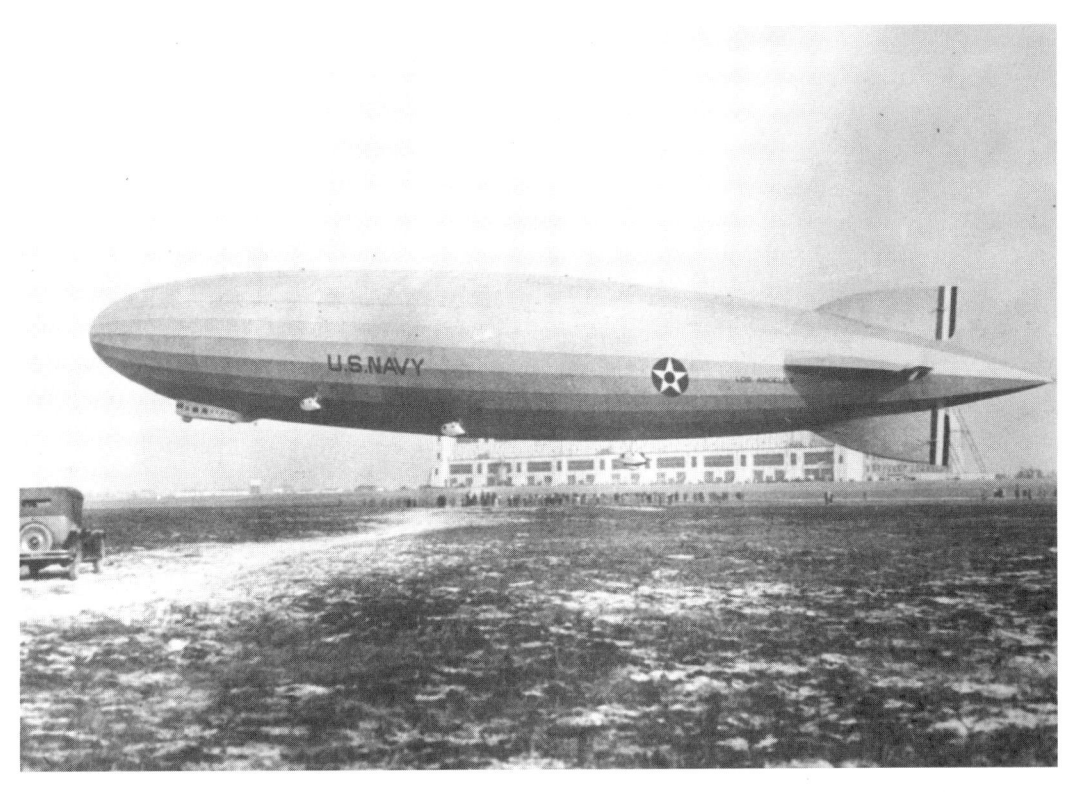

(1923) A helium filled U.S. Navy dirigible, 'Los Angeles', is at her mooring mast. Formerly the ZR3 built by the Germans, the U.S. took possession of this craft as part of war reparations.

Americans slowly became aware that they could be just as vulnerable as anyone in Dresden or Hiroshima. It would take another age, however, an age of intercontinental ballistic missiles, to drive the point fully home.

WORLD WAR II ~ World War II grew out of the rubble of World War I and the vitriol of Versailles. Three nations, Germany, Italy and Japan—one outright crippled by Versailles, the other two disgruntled—began marking new paths in the 1920s. The paths led to renewed warfare on a scale theretofore unimaginable.

1930S • ITALY ~ Italy was one of the disgruntled ones. On the winning side in 1918, Italy felt cut out of the spoils of war. In the early 1920s, a new political figure in Italy promised to renew Italy to the glory that had once been imperial Rome. Benito Mussolini, a World War I veteran and sometime journalist, began to amass power with his Fascist Party. Levering himself into power, Mussolini quickly made himself a dictator and set up the first fascist state. Fascism relied on fear to keep power—a strong military, an active secret police force, an effective propaganda unit. While Adolf Hitler would later master fascism, Mussolini was the father of it. Mussolini bullied the Pope into passing no judgment on Italian actions, then he set about creating an empire. In 1935 Italy attacked primitive little Ethiopia in eastern Africa, trying to conquer the territory that sat between its current colonial holdings. Italy easily won the war.

1930S • JAPAN ~ Japan, too, came away from Versailles disgruntled. She had been on the side of the Allies, taking control of some German islands but contributing little to victory. Showing the first stirrings of imperialism before

1930s

the war, Japan had bested Russia in the Russo-Japanese War of 1905. In an American-brokered peace ending that war, Japan took control of Korea. Feeling, like Italy, cut out of the spoils of Versailles, Japan demanded in the 1920s portions of the Caroline, Marshall and Mariana Islands in the central Pacific. The League of Nations acquiesced to the demand, and granted Japan this "Japanese Mandate."

The Japanese government fell into the hands of militarists, who espoused the ancient warrior code of "Bushido" and demanded an aggressive Japanese imperialism. In 1931 Japanese soldiers invaded Manchuria on mainland China, devastating the city of Nanking, raping its women and murdering innocents. The aggression brought response from Russia, and for a time Japanese soldiers indecisively fought Soviet soldiers on the frontier. Despite a half-hearted protest from the isolationist United States, Japan spent the rest of the decade crawling down the China coast.

1930s • GERMANY ~ The biggest aggressor was Germany. While the country spent the 1920s under the Weimar Republic, a liberal government, internal discord constantly boiled. Various activist cells—leftist and rightist, Marxist, socialist and nationalist— agitated for power. A little-known World War I veteran, Adolf Hitler took control of one of those cells. Austrian by birth, Hitler was a failed artist of little ambition before the war. He discovered a home in war, however, winning decorations for bravery. Hitler had a talent for politics and oratory, and soon he had established himself as leader of the National Socialist Party (the Nazis).

Hitler had a platform, but it was based mostly on mythology and hate. He proclaimed that Versailles had blotted out the greatness of Germany; that Germany had been and should be again a dominant world power. He couched his rhetoric in Teutonic mythology, and if his oratory had a musical score it would have been Wagner's *Ride of the Valkyries*. But the biggest myth of all was the "stab-in-the-back" myth. Quite simply, Hitler charged that the liberal Weimar government, taking over from the Kaiser in the closing days of the war, had sold out to the Allies. Surrender, he said, had been unnecessary. Left to the militarists, Germany would have won. Of course, the militarists had crafted the liberal government as a fall guy, and they had escaped blame. Regardless, the myth fit the mood of the time. Germany was broke, surrounded by more powerful nations, embarrassed. Inflation was rampant. Hitler blamed everyone for Germany's fall—English, French, Americans, Soviets, Jews, blacks, democrats, gypsies, and secretly he was vowing to wipe them all out.

In a Munich beer hall in 1923, Hitler and his Nazis declared themselves the new government of Germany. The coup—known as the Beer Hall Putsch—failed, and the state convicted Hitler of treason. Politically, though, Hitler had become powerful, and he spent only a few months in jail, and that in easy confinement. During that time he wrote *Mien Kampf*, a blueprint for his takeover of Germany and subsequent restoration of German greatness. Had anyone read it or taken it seriously, it was also a blueprint for genocide.

Released from prison, Hitler continued to agitate and consolidate power. He became a master Fascist, building a police force known as the Brown Shirts (which he destroyed when they became too powerful) and a propaganda office. In 1932

Hitler ran for president against incumbent (and largely figurehead) president Paul von Hindenburg. Hitler lost, but he and his Nazis made a good enough showing in national and local elections that Hindenburg's advisors convinced him to make Hitler chancellor to appease much of the country.

1933-1939 • Hitler Assumes Power
Hitler became chancellor in 1933, almost at the same time as Franklin D. Roosevelt was becoming president of the United States. When Hindenburg died, Hitler declared emergency powers and refused to call another election. The Weimar Republic ceased to exist, and Hitler had command of Germany.

Immediately he started to reindustrialize Germany. He re-militarized it as well, despite the limitations of Versailles. And he plotted German control of central Europe. In 1936 Germany reoccupied the Rhineland, traditional German territory which had been demilitarized since Versailles. Nazis also sponsored a coup attempt in Austria; when that failed, Hitler simply took the country by force. In 1938 Hitler sought control of a ring of land around the western edge of Czechoslovakia known as the Sudetenland. He claimed the territory was traditionally German, and the Germanic people there wanted it returned to Germany. Top European officials, led by English Prime Minister Neville Chamberlain, tried to stop Hitler, then relented when he promised not to bother the rest of Czechoslovakia. He got the Sudetenland, and the next year he took all of Czechoslovakia anyway. In 1939, Hitler told Poland to relinquish the Polish Corridor that had divided parts of Germany since Versailles and given Poland access to the Baltic Sea. Poland refused and Hitler vowed war. England and France stepped in, said they had had enough, and vowed war themselves if Hitler persisted.

Hitler suspected England and France were bluffing, but just in case, he wanted one European nation on his side – the Soviet Union. He approached Soviet leader Josef Stalin with a deal. (Stalin had assumed power in the early 1920s upon the death of Lenin. In philosophical theory, the socialist Stalin was the extreme opposite of the nationalist Hitler, but he was just as much of a dictator, basing his power on fear. In the 1920s and 1930s, Stalin had murdered tens of millions of his own people who had disagreed with his policies.) Hitler coaxed Stalin into the Non-Aggression Pact; when war started, not only would they leave each other alone but Stalin could take half of Poland and some coveted Baltic territory as well.

Hitler also kept up an alliance with Italy. Mussolini was always junior in the relationship and, ultimately, Italy would be more a detriment to Germany than an asset. This alliance gave the German-allied powers their name—the Axis powers—for a geographical axis line ran through Berlin and Rome, seemingly through the middle of Europe.

1939-1940 • German Invasion of Poland, Start of World War II
Hitler invaded Poland on September 1, 1939, touching off World War II. Polish troops resisted, dramatically so, but German generals had practiced armor tactics in the interwar years, and they had devised a tactic known as *Blitzkrieg*—lightning war. Matched up with airpower, German columns rapidly slammed into enemy positions, taking them by shock and storm. The static defenses and

trenches of World War I were now obsolete. Germany took its half of Poland in a matter of weeks; the Soviet Union soon did the same.

In the spring of 1940 Germany rapidly took Norway, prized for its North Sea outlets. Then, unleashing Blitzkrieg on France, Germany took that country by June. German troops occupied the northern half of the country, but some French authorities agreed to administer the southern half as well as France's colonial holdings in North Africa and Asia for Hitler. Their agreement freed up Hitler's troops and established the Vichy government of France, named for its political base in the town of Vichy.

In late summer 1940, Hitler plotted to invade England, too. But that would be across the English Channel and tricky. His air force needed to establish air superiority over the island first, and they could not do it. The steadfast resistance of the Royal Air Force during the Battle of Britain forced Hitler—for the first time—to abandon his plan.

1930s • Japan's Continued Aggression

Far to the east, in the Pacific, Japan saw the chaos of the European imperial nations as well as American isolationist inaction and became more aggressive. She took larger chunks of China, some British territories farther south, and Vichy-controlled French Indochina (Vietnam). Hitler did not care, for he had little interest in the region at the time. In fact, Hitler and his junior partner in European mayhem, Mussolini, soon signed the Tri-Partite Pact with Japan, vowing non-aggression against each other, and mutual defense should a then non-combatant nation (the United States) attack one of the member nations.

Emboldened, Japan planned more conquests. But the island nation had limited resources, and it was running out of oil—the one thing conquering armies and navies needed to sustain themselves in modern war. For most of the 1930s, Japan had run on American oil. But by 1939, the United States was slowly stirring from isolation and had begun constricting the flow of oil to Japan. In 1940, the U.S. threatened to cut it off altogether unless Japan pulled out of China and stopped all aggression.

1941 • Japan Bombs Pearl Harbor

Militaristic Japan would not agree, but instead plotted an invasion of the Dutch East Indies to gain control of rich oil supplies there. But one obstacle geographically stood in the way—the United States territory of the

(1941) Heavy black smoke rising from ships and waterfront buildings in Pearl Harbor, Oahu Island after a surprise bombing raid by the Japanese which brought America into WW II.

Philippines. Japan knew that, no matter how cautious the U.S. had been with the Eurasian conflict until now, it would not let Japan cross the geographical line of its own Pacific influence. Japan attempted negotiation with the United States, but American rhetoric grew tougher. Secretly, Japan planned another option—a knockout punch on American army bases on the Philippines and the Pacific fleet base at Pearl Harbor, Hawaii. Japanese planners believed such a decisive blow would keep the United States out of the war for eighteen months, enough time to allow Japan to consolidate its hold on the Dutch East Indies, take northern Australia for protection, and establish a defensive line through the central Pacific. (Admiral Yamamoto, designer of the Pearl Harbor attack, knew better. He had studied in the United States, and suspected his attack would only delay the United States six months.) Diplomacy crumbled in November. On December 7, 1941, flying from aircraft carriers to the north, Japanese fighters and dive bombers attacked Pearl Harbor, destroying much of the American fleet riding naïvely at anchor there. (American aircraft carriers, the true backbone of the World War II navy, were not in port. Missing them later proved deadly to Japan.) On December 8, the United States declared war on Japan. On December 11, although not bound to do so by the exact wording of the Tri-Partite agreement, Adolf Hitler declared war on the United States. Isolationist since 1919, the United States was now in World War II.

1935-1940 • THE UNITED STATES MOBILIZES, AGAIN

World War I had, of course, been a training ground in many ways. The United States had learned about modern war mobilization, both military and social. And, the country was not as flat-footed as its official isolationism made it appear. This time, it would not take so long for the United States to join the fight.

Even though his country was not, President Franklin Roosevelt was an internationalist; even in early 1940 he believed the United States should be in the war. Back in 1935, when Italy invaded Ethiopia, Roosevelt sought a "moral embargo" on U.S. oil to Italy to damage its war making ability. American businessmen ignored him. In 1935, 1936 and 1937, the United States Congress passed neutrality acts, and mandated that foreign buyers pay for U.S. goods in cash and carry them home in their own cargo holds. This Cash-and-Carry plan sought to ensure the United States did not get caught in the same shipping mess that had dragged her into World War I.

But later, as Europe burned, Americans more readily listened to Roosevelt. In early 1939, he convinced Congress to allocate $552 million for defense. American government contracts for ships, airplanes, and tanks, plus British and French orders for airplanes, began lifting the country out of the Great Depression.

1940 • DESTROYERS-BASES DEAL

Hitler's aggression shocked the United States into some sort of action. On June 22, 1940, Congress passed the National Defense Tax Bill, authorizing $1 billion annually in new taxes for defense spending. Later that year Roosevelt received little opposition when, by executive order, he made the Destroyers-Bases deal with England's Prime Minister Winston Churchill. With the Battle of Britain raging in the skies, English and German navies also grappled for control of the

North Sea. Great Britain was on the ropes, and Churchill asked Roosevelt for the use of some outdated American World War I destroyers. Roosevelt traded fifty of them to England in return for leases to some British naval bases in the Western Hemisphere.

1940 • PEACE-TIME DRAFT ~ In September 1940, Congress passed the Selective Training and Service Act, the first peace-time draft in American history. The act called for registering all men aged twenty-one to thirty-six, and drafting for a year 1.2 million regular soldiers and 800,000 reserves. Given the alarm that the world situation had produced, the American public accepted the need for the draft. Production of American war materiel stepped up to match the needs of the trainees.

In November 1940, Roosevelt won election to his third term in office. Elected first in 1932, he had presided over the Depression, attempting to mitigate it with his New Deal. As the domestic emergency melted into a foreign one, FDR urged voters to keep him at the helm. He also appealed to American mothers, promising that their sons would never fight in a foreign war. Of course, it was not a promise he could keep.

1941 • LEND-LEASE ~ Throughout 1941, the United States came as close as it could to waging war without declaring it. In March, Congress passed the Lend-Lease Act, which allowed the United States to build needed equipment, vehicles, airplanes and ships, then lend them to Allied nations or lease them for nominal fees. This went far to making the United States what FDR called an "arsenal of democracy." The U.S. began sending lend-lease materiel across the western Atlantic under naval escort until the British navy could pick them up. By September the escorts were taking casualties at the hands of German U-boats. The United States also placed troops in Greenland and Iceland to guard North Sea shipping lanes.

At home, the United States seized Axis assets. In August 1941 Roosevelt met Churchill off Newfoundland and struck the Atlantic Charter. The two tacitly agreed that, whenever the United States officially entered the war, Germany would be their first target. For the meantime, Churchill understood that FDR was doing all he could to help until the United States formally shook off isolationism. At the same time, the U.S. Congress reaffirmed the Selective Service Act, but only by one vote, an indication that isolationism had not completely died. Four months later, however, Pearl Harbor dealt isolationism a death blow.

Since 1941, many FDR opponents have suggested that the president knew the attack was coming, kept the information from army and navy commanders, and allowed the attack to drag the country into the war. Nothing is farther from the truth. True, Americans had cracked much of the Japanese military codes, and intelligence officers had an idea the Japanese Navy was planning a strike *somewhere* in the Pacific. But Americans were inexperienced at the intelligence game, and analysts suspected the strike would come at the Philippines, if it came at all. The army and navy put American bases throughout the Pacific on alert; commanders at those bases responded lackadaisically, thinking they were safe. Pearl Harbor was more a result of an American naiveté born of isolationism than treachery from the White House.

(1941) Inmates of the Federal Penitentiary in Atlanta, Georgia, do their part for the war effort by manufacturing portable canvas water tanks for the U.S. troops. The caricature of Adolf Hitler, emblazoned with the words 'Let us help defeat him' was painted by one of the prisoners.

1941-1944 • MANPOWER MOBILIZATION

While the Selective Service operated throughout the war, Pearl Harbor spurred volunteer enlistments. World War II would see the greatest manpower mobilization in the nation's history, before or since. At war's end in 1945, the American combined services had about 12.1 million personnel, both men and women. The government compelled men ages eighteen to sixty-four to register for the draft, but rarely did draft boards, again locally-operated as in World War I, draft men over the age of thirty-eight. Draft boards also granted many deferments to men on the basis of health, family and work considerations. In the end, the draft selected about 10 million men for active service, or roughly one-sixth of the United States' total male population, a smaller proportion than other warring nations.

1941-1945 • WOMEN IN WORLD WAR II SERVICE

Women, while not drafted, also served in great numbers. More than 400,000 served during the war, and in 1945, 266,000 of them were in uniform. They worked in a variety of services including the Women's Army Auxiliary Corps (WAACs), the naval Women Accepted for Volunteer Emergency Service (WAVES), Women's Reserve of the U.S. Marine Corps, Army and Navy nursing corps, the Women's Airforce Service Pilots (WASPs), and the Coast Guard's SPAR, a name taken from the service's motto "Semper Paratus—Always Ready."

The WAACs had a tough start. In the interwar years, several proponents of full military service and status for women advocated creation of an integrated women army corps. Top army brass and

1940-1945

many U.S. Congressmen hesitated though, fearing female intrusion into a formerly all-male world. As the United States approached war, however, in May 1941 Congress took up consideration of a bill creating the WAACs; it became law in May 1942, just as Japan was beating the United States out of its Philippine Island stronghold. But the WAAC was still an auxiliary force, and its members received no permanent rank or benefits. With the Navy, Marines and Coast Guard offering full military status, the WAAC was hard-pressed to attract volunteers, and as late 1942 brought key United States battles in both major theaters of the war, the army was feeling the manpower pinch. The War Department and Congress finally relented, the latter passing a bill in June 1943 converting the WAAC to the Women's Army Corps (WAC). Shed of its auxiliary status, the WAC became a strong force able to attract viable recruits.

Mobilizing the women forces was more difficult than it need have been. Arguments often erupted between male officers and women's corps directors; their disputes would have been comical were it not for the immediacy of the situation. When women made their obvious requests for bras and slips, requisition officers balked—after all, men didn't get them. In the army, early women recruits received uniforms obviously cut to fit men; it took some wrangling by women directors to acquire stylish uniforms with the proper cut and sizing. (The Navy sidestepped that issue by hiring fashion designers to design WAVE uniforms.) Should women be allowed to wear makeup? Can they serve if married? If so, can they serve if pregnant? The questions seemed unending.

Women served in a variety of jobs in all the services, in all theaters of the war. They were clerks and typists, decoders, intelligence officers, drivers, telephone operators and trainers. As always, nurses performed hazardous duty near the front lines in mobile and evacuation hospitals, and worked with thousands of wounded and dying men in the rear. In May 1942, Japanese troops conquering the Philippines captured sixty-six army nurses and eleven navy nurses. They held them in prison camps for the next three years.

Women in the WASP, too, had dangerous assignments. They test-piloted new aircraft, towed aerial gunnery targets, and flew military aircraft to delivery points inside the United States. At no time did United States women serve in combat roles, although more than thirty WASPs died in accidents.

While public hand-wringing over women in the armed forces would not end with World War II, women more than proved their mettle. At the end of the war in 1945, 100,000 volunteers were in the WACs; 86,000 in the WAVES; 18,000 in the Women Marines; 11,000 in SPAR; 57,000 in the Army Nurse Corps; and 11,000 in the Navy Nurse Corps. To their chagrin, many of the women veterans found upon their release from service that much of the American public discounted or denigrated their wartime efforts. Many people could not yet grasp that war now involved all elements of society; it was no longer a men-only game.

1940-1945 • THE AMERICAN RED CROSS IN WORLD WAR II

As it had responded in the First World War, the American Red Cross again responded in the Second. With the Battle of Britain raging in the skies over England in the summer of 1940, the American Red Cross began blood drives to collect blood and plasma for shipment to England. With the specter of war looming over the United States, it also began training volunteers at its many local chapters in the rudiments of first aid. As it happened, Red Cross first aid personnel were able to deliver treatment to victims of the attack on Pearl Harbor, December 7, 1941. As an integral part of the wider American home front mobilization, the Red Cross used volunteers to provide aid packages both for wounded American soldiers and for Europeans and Asians whom the war had injured, made homeless or orphaned.

1939-1945 • INDUSTRIAL MOBILIZATION ~ As in World War I, the United States had to adapt its peace-time industrial/economic base to support the war. But the first war had been a good training ground for the second, and mobilization, while not without glitches, went smoother this time. In truth, U.S. industry already had a leg up. During the Depression, Roosevelt's Public Works Administration had kept contracts working with naval shipbuilders. The outbreak of war in 1939, the country's halting efforts at early preparedness, and the Lend-Lease program to the Allied nations also helped. During the war, not only would American industry supply United States military services, but it sent equipment to the British, Soviets, and Free French as well.

Ultimately, the United States, a nation of 135 million people, wielded a work force of 73 million. That workforce, by 1945, had turned out an astonishing array of military equipment: 86,000 tanks; 120,000 artillery pieces; 14 million shoulder weapons; 2.4 million trucks and jeeps; 1,200 combat ships (including aircraft carriers); 82,000 landing craft and smaller ships; 96,000 bombers; 88,000 fighter aircraft; and 23,000 air transports. In 1944 alone American workers turned out a total of 96,000 aircraft. Perhaps most amazing is that, in 1945, while the economies of the other warring nations were strained to breaking, the United States was just hitting its stride.

Such production erased the Great Depression. Unemployment, as high in some places as fifty percent in 1933, fell to nothing. Anyone who wanted a job could have one. The few polls that recorded unemployment factored in people who simply did not want to work, or who were traveling from one war-job to another. War industry created another "Great Migration," as rural Americans, many for the first time, left their farms and sought work in industrial plants near cities. During the war years, farm populations fell by more than six million people even as agricultural production increased. Even more blacks left the South and headed, too, for war industry. While every state had some type of war industry, both coasts, the Detroit-Chicago region, and the Pacific Northwest attracted the most wartime migrants.

Harnessing this manpower became the government's job. Again, World War I had paved the way. At the start, the government preferred to let wage incentives freely attract labor to jobs, but quickly it learned that some jobs had too many applicants, while others, often critical, had too few. Wage wars between companies did not help. Quickly, in 1942, the government created the War Manpower Commission and the National War Labor Board. Both served to stabilize employment, train new employees for skilled jobs, and restrain wage fluctuations. The NWLB also worked with labor unions to avoid strikes that could cause critical work stoppages.

Seeing a need for an agency similar to the WIB in World War I, an agency that would coordinate military purchasing with industrial resource allocation and materiel output, Roosevelt's administration created the War Production Board (WPB) early in 1942. It had little success though, facing resistance from army and navy purchasers with their own long-standing purchasing relations, plus an array of other supply agencies. Finally, FDR scrapped the WPB in favor of the Office of War Mobilization (OWM). The president named James F. "Jimmy" Byrnes, a former senator and Supreme Court justice, as its head and gave him broad authority to centralize, once and for all, military purchasing and outputs.

(1942) A poster supporting American industry during World War II proclaims 'We Can Do It.' Women were becoming welders, electricians, tool and dye makers, crane operators and riveters, hence this famous poster of American women in war industries.

1941-1946 • WOMEN IN THE WORKPLACE ~ American women faired best in the industrial mobilization. Industry owners previously believed women could not do heavy work, but war-time male manpower shortages changed their minds. Soon women were becoming welders, electricians, tool and dye makers, crane operators and riveters (hence the collective *nomme de guerre* of American women in war industries—Rosie the Riveter). Employment for women rose fifty-seven percent during the war. Women could work as much as they wanted, some taking double shifts, although they always received less pay than their male counterparts. Women over the age of forty-five joined the work force in larger proportions than those younger; married women were more likely to work than single women. Women married to servicemen got a double boon—their own paycheck plus their husband's. (The government, too, forced men to send home a portion of their check—allotments—to keep them from squandering it in foreign ports of call.) That meant that many families could now put aside a sizeable nest egg, something unheard of a few years before in the Depression. Women, too, took over the financial affairs of the home, paying mortgages, rent, and bills and affecting repairs about the house.

Women helped build everything: aircraft carriers, landing craft, Sherman tanks, M-1 rifles, P-51 Mustang fighter planes, B-17 and B-24 bombers. The Allies could not have won the war as efficiently and quickly without American women in the workplace.

They knew, of course, that the stakes of their work were high. Every rivet had to be tight, every bolt secure, every wire connected. In bomber plants, as planes neared completion, women frequently wrote notes of encouragement, perhaps included photographs of themselves, and tucked them away in the framework of the plane for aircrews to find. Even as they did the dirty, heavy, strenuous work, they were still mothers, sisters and sweethearts.

1942-1945 • WAR AFFECTS WOMEN'S PRIVATE LIVES ~ The war affected women in their private lives as well. Marriage rates climbed during the war, as couples wed before men went overseas. Divorce rates also climbed. Some women, known as "Allotment Annies," married two, perhaps three, men at the same time so they could draw their servicemen husband's allotment checks. The government quickly moved to stop this practice, and later in the war passed "Dear John" laws to halt hasty divorces during war-time. The laws took their name from battlefront vernacular: soldiers frequently received letters from their wives saying they had filed for divorce. The letters so often began "Dear John" that soldiers generically called them all "Dear John" letters.

Birth rates climbed also. A miniature baby boom occurred in 1942 and 1943. Known as "Goodbye Babies," these children were conceived before men left for the uncertainties of war; some never saw their fathers who died in service. The end of the war in 1945, of course, brought *the* Baby Boom as soldiers returned home. The Baby Boomer generation—officially anyone born between 1946 and 1960—has impacted the nation's history and culture perhaps more than any other generation.

1942-1945 • AFRICAN AMERICANS AND THE WAR ~ War-time opportunities existed for blacks as well as women, but often the benefits were harder to come by. In the second war-time migration of the century, 1.5 million blacks sought war industry jobs outside of the South. Many southern whites also migrated, so that blacks in northern cities faced both transplanted southern racism and latent northern prejudice. Whites, fearful since the end of slavery that blacks would take their jobs and infiltrate their neighborhoods, believed those fears were coming true, and racial combat broke out in more than forty cities in 1943. Still, urban blacks picked up more economic power as more than 500,000 of them joined labor unions.

Almost 900,000 black men and women entered American military service. Most of those were in the army, but the naval services attracted recruits as well. Even as the United States fought a war against racism in Europe, it remained racist itself. Clashes between whites and blacks in camp, and the memory of the race conflicts in World War I, reinforced segregation. The army still routinely kept blacks out of combat, relegating them to rear echelon duty.

1943 • TUSKEGEE AIRMEN ~ Black groups did grab some of the glory of war. At the Tuskegee Institute in Alabama, some blacks received fighter pilot training. The government brigaded them into the 99th fighter squadron and sent to them North Africa in 1943. There they escorted bombers flying north over Europe. Ultimately they moved to Sicily, then Italy as Allies invaded the continent. Flying P-51 Mustang fighters with distinctive red tails, the "Tuskegee Airmen" racked up one of the best records of any escort group in the war. One veteran bombardier from a bomb group that received Tuskegee escort recalled, "It was sure a comfort to look out and see the red tails of those planes flying by."

(circa 1943) Two African-American soldiers smile while posing with mortar shells scrawled with anti-Hitler chalk messages.

1941-1944

1944 • RED BALL EXPRESS ~ In the Army, most black troops were assigned to the Services of Supply (SOS). There they performed non-combatant roles, but they earned glory nonetheless. After Allies invaded France in June 1944, black troops formed a vital artery that kept American armies ripping through France, Belgium and into Germany. Stretched supply lines and delivery problems plagued the armies as they advanced, sometimes quicker than planners had expected. Black soldiers formed the "Red Ball Express," a delivery convoy line of trucks that picked up supplies in France and delivered them to the front. The Express ran night and day from August through November 1944 during which time it delivered more than 412,000 tons of supplies to the front. After that, other trucking routes— again largely black—took over the job of supplying the front. Without those troops the penetration of Germany would have come much later.

Military achievement, economic power and newly achieved urban political influence proved a watershed for American blacks. World War II gave blacks the necessary push to more boldly stand for their own civil rights. It provided the base for the Civil Rights era of the 1950s and early 1960s.

1941-1942 • INTERNMENT CAMPS ~ Perhaps the biggest blotch on the American wartime home front was the internment of 120,000 Japanese-Americans in internment camps. After the Japanese attack on Pearl Harbor, many Americans on the West Coast feared they were next. West Coast ports, they thought, were prime Japanese targets; they did not reason that in reality, such long-distance attacks were tactical impossibilities for Japan in 1941-1942. Nevertheless, Americans, especially Californians, where a significant Japanese-American population lived, believed that Japanese-Americans would prove loyal to their ancestral homeland and form a domestic group of conspirators, sympathizers and spies to aid in a Japanese invasion. With President Roosevelt's approval, the government gave military commanders with domestic commands the power to arrest suspicious citizens if a threat existed in their jurisdiction. The threat was real enough in the minds of West Coast Americans, and the army began rounding up Japanese-Americans. Some of them were *Issei*, people born in Japan but who immigrated to the United States and became naturalized citizens. Most, some 77,000, were *Nisei*, native-born Americans.

The internees often received short notice, perhaps no more than forty-eight hours, to dispose of their property and move to relocation centers in the interior of the country. Speculators hovered around the Japanese-Americans, offering ridiculously low prices for homes and land, which, with no other option, the internees accepted.

At the internment camps, Japanese-Americans lived in shacks with little sanitation. They survived through personal industry and by reestablishing local communities, even behind fences. By 1944, with the war scare on the coast gone, the government began releasing them to rebuild their lives in freedom. The Japanese-Americans could not forget, however, that their nation had, in fact, betrayed them. A later generation of Americans would agree. In 1988, along with an apology, Congress authorized $20,000 restitution for each of 60,000 surviving internees.

1942-1945 • WAR BONDS ~ Other aspects of the Home Front war effort looked remarkably similar to that of World War I. First, the government had to finance the war, and it made American citizens partners in the process. Current taxes covered less than half of war costs. War bonds were a way for the government to generate revenue and let the public have an investment in the war. As in World War I, the government would pay off the bond with interest after the

Allied POW Camp in Japan, World War II

Several studies have shown that the best way to survive a period of imprisonment is to resist. The resistance doesn't have to be large, just enough to keep the captive from bowing to those trying to break his will. It is known that slaves in the antebellum American South resisted by breaking hoes and shovels or hurting the master's livestock—anything to cost him time and money. Slaves got away with it by passing themselves off as ignorant and incompetent, a stereotype white slave owners readily accepted. Jews who survived the Nazi death camps had a measure of luck, certainly, in evading the gas chambers, but they also practiced simple resistance to keep their sanity. Whether it was stealing an extra crust of bread or potato for a fellow captive, or hiding a condemned inmate in a typhus ward—where German guards would not go—they were resisting the evil that surrounded them.

A young American Marine, Otis H. "Karl" King, did the same thing to survive a Japanese POW camp. As he relates in his book *Alamo of the Pacific*, Japanese troops captured him after the fall of the Phillipines in 1942, and he rode out the rest of the war in Japan. But Japanese soldiers had no respect for prisoners of war; to them the prisoners should have died rather than allow themselves to be captured. Thinking that such inferior beings could cause them no trouble, Japanese guards thus paid little attention to King and his compatriots.

The prisoners found themselves working at a Japanese ship factory. King frequently was dispatched to warehouses to bring back supplies. He routinely took extra spools of cable – and tossed them into Tokyo Bay. He once casually set fire to a warehouse and escaped unnoticed. While riveting parts of naval vessels together, King's buddies made sure the rivets were not tight. As a result, eighteen of twenty-three ships they worked on had to return for repair. Another sank before it ever sailed. Even in captivity, these resourceful Americans were helping win the war.

war. While private corporations bought most of the war-time bonds, individuals bought many million dollars worth. War bond rallies, often featuring Hollywood stars or war heroes (in 1945, surviving members of the group who raised the American flag on Iwo Jima were in such a rally), encouraged Americans to buy.

1941-1945 • RATIONING ~ Americans also rationed. Depending on household and work needs, the government allotted them quotas of sugar, flour, oil, gasoline—essentially all consumer goods—per week. The surplus, of course, went to the Allied armies. Americans turned in old tires in rubber drives—the army could recycle them into new tires. School children collected aluminum foil—the air corps had discovered that dropping strips of it from airplanes confused enemy radar.

1941-1945 • ENTERTAINMENT ~ World War II left an indelible mark on American entertainment. As in World War I, the government sought to influence public opinion and keep public support rallied throughout the war. This time it did it with the Office of War Information (OWI), which utilized Hollywood movie studios.

Hollywood churned out training films for the armed services, and director Frank Capra created the now classic series of shorts *Why We Fight*. The series, certainly American propaganda, was designed to keep Americans behind the war as it dragged into its third and fourth years. It recounted the territorial takeovers, political scheming, and military aggression of Germany, Italy, and Japan as reminders of how the United States got into war. The films championed the U.S. and Great Britain as the last line of defense against worldwide tyranny.

Hollywood also made many war-time movies with war themes. Often low budget, movies usually followed the government's wishes: they played up American might and played down battlefield deaths. After all, the OWI wanted movies to reinvigorate patriotism. Too many mothers watching too many boys die onscreen might have detrimental effects to the war effort.

Bataan (1943), starring Robert Taylor and depicting the horrible conditions of American soldiers defending the Philippine peninsula of Bataan against Japanese assaults in 1942, was perhaps one of the most realistic of Hollywood's war movies. Others, like the *Flying Tigers* (1942) and *The Fighting Seabees* (1944), both starring John Wayne, and Humphrey Bogart's *Sahara* and *Action in the North Atlantic* (both 1943), depicted the volunteer spirit and ingenuity of Americans in special service around the globe. Some ranged to patriotic escapism, like *Four Jills in a Jeep* (1944), the story of four women working for a USO (United Service Organization) show, and *Hollywood Canteen* (1944), a song-and-dance movie set in the real-life Hollywood Canteen, which offered relaxation for West Coast servicemen.

1941-1945 • CELEBRITIES AT WAR ~ Hollywood stars also joined the armed forces. Clark Gable enlisted with the Army Air Corps, serving on a bomber crew. (Gable was a war widower: his wife, Carole Lombard, had died when her plane crashed after a war bond rally.) Gable was so popular an American icon, famous as Rhett Butler in 1939's *Gone With the Wind*, that Hitler reportedly put a bounty on his head. Jimmy Stewart, affable star of *Mr. Smith Goes to Washington* (1939) and *Philadelphia Story* (1940), also joined the air corps, becoming pilot of a B-24 bomber. Stewart made a full quota of bomb runs, and after the war stayed in the air force reserve, ultimately becoming a brigadier general. Future U.S. president Ronald Reagan, star of several "B" movies, also enlisted, but the army kept him stateside to make training films.

1941-1945 • MUSIC ~ World War II had its own beat, too, with swing music playing in canteens across the United States, in Pacific bases and in England. Glenn Miller, wildly popular after he and his orchestra scored hits with "In the Mood" and "Chattanooga Choo-Choo," also enlisted in the army in 1942. As a major, he organized an army orchestra and entertained troops in all theaters. In December 1944, Miller was reported missing after taking off on a flight from England to Paris; later authorities determined he had died in an air accident.

1935-1945 • THE HOLOCAUST ~ Nazi leader Adolf Hitler never made it a secret that he despised European Jews, that he considered them as a race to blame for Germany's interwar financial troubles. He also made no secret that he wanted to dispose of them.

The German Reichstag passed the Nuremburg Laws in 1935, making Jews essentially "non-citizens" of Germany. As Germany grabbed European territory, Nazis persecuted Jews in occupied regions, taking their belongings, impounding their assets, relocating them. Many thousands became refugees, seeking to flee Nazi tyranny. Some, in fact, escaped; many others did not, the Nazis having taken their passports. In November 1938, Hitler signaled a higher level of violence against Jews throughout the Third Reich (which by then included Austria and the Sudetenland) when Nazi troops broke the windows out of Jewish homes, shops, and places of worship. Witnesses said the broken glass on sidewalks sparkled like crystal in the streetlights. That description lent a poetic name to a horrid night—*Krystallnacht*.

Of course, Hitler would not be satisfied with only the intimidation of Jews. As his "Final Solution" to dealing with European Jews, Hitler intended to kill them all. Evidence began to surface in late 1939 that Hitler was moving to such a plan when stories filtered out of occupied Poland that German troops were murdering Jews. But it was not until Germany invaded Russia in June 1941 that Hitler began his program of mass murder. With Europe occupied to the English Channel and with German troops pushing to the east, Hitler had a sort of "buffer zone" in Germany and Poland where he could do as he pleased with Jews without any real threat of interference.

At first, Hitler dispatched roving gangs of troops to round up and execute Jews. But the method, apparently, was too sloppy and inefficient. Soon Hitler's SS was building concentration and death camps inside the Reich. While the main inhabitants would be Jews, Hitler also rounded up gypsies, homosexuals and communists.

The death camps were compounds surrounded by electric fencing. Above the gateway entrance Germans had hung a sign—"Work Will Set You Free." While Germans did indeed force Jews to work for them in some areas, their ultimate fate at the camps was to be death. Crowded barracks housed the prisoners. They subsisted on little, often no more than a soup made of potato peelings and water and a crust of bread. Their daily caloric intake has been estimated at less than 200 calories. Jews were tattooed

War Movies

The birth of America is marked by a single, monumental event, the American Revolution, and four other terrible wars: The Civil War, World War I, World War II, and Vietnam have left indelible scars on the American conscience. The great wars, and some of the lesser wars have been portrayed in depth by filmmakers, so that much of what Americans know about history has been conveyed through movies. Here is a sampling of modern American war movies.

CIVIL WAR
The Birth of a Nation (1915)
Gone with the Wind (1939)
Red Badge of Courage (1951)
Little Big Man (1970)
The Blue and the Gray (1982)
Gore Vidal's Lincoln (1988)
The Day Lincoln Was Shot (1998)
Glory (1989)
Gettysburg (1993)
Tad (1995)
Ride with the Devil (1999)

AMERICAN EXPANSION
The Alamo (1960)
The Alamo: 13 Days to Glory (1987)
The Rough Riders (1997)

WORLD WAR I
Wings (1927)
All Quiet on the Western Front (1930)
The Fighting 69th (1940)
Sergeant York (1941)
The African Queen (1951)
A Farewell to Arms (1957)
Paths of Glory (1957)
Lawrence of Arabia (1962)
The Guns of August (1964)
Doctor Zhivago (1965)
The Blue Max (1966)
Johnny Got His Gun (1971)
Von Richtofen and Brown (1971)
The Land That Time Forgot (1975)
Aces High (1976)
Gallipoli (1981)
Return of the Soldier (1981)
The Lighthorsemen (1987)

WORLD WAR II
Action in the North Atlantic (1943)
Air Force (1943)
Destination Tokyo (1943)
Guadalcanal Diary (1943)
Bataan (1943)
Passage To Marseille (1944)
The Fighting Seabees (1944)
The Fighting Sullivans (1944)
Thirty Seconds Over Tokyo (1944)
A Bell for Adano (1945)
They Were Expendable (1945)
Arch of Triumph (1948)
Battleground (1949)
Sands of Iwo Jima (1949)
Twelve O'Clock High (1949)
Operation Pacific (1951)
Flying Leathernecks (1951)
The Cruel Sea (1953)
From Here to Eternity (1953)
The Cain Mutiny (1954)
To Hell and Back (1955)

Away All Boats (1956)
The Bridge on the River Kwai (1957)
The Naked and the Dead (1958)
The Guns of Navarone (1961)
The Four Horsemen of the Apocalypse (1962)
The Longest Day (1962)
Hell Is For Heroes (1962)
The Great Escape (1963)
The Thin Red Line (1964, 1999)
36 Hours (1964)
Battle of the Bulge (1965)
In Harm's Way (1965)
King Rat (1965)
Tobruk (1967)
The Devil's Brigade (1968)
Battle of Britain (1969)
Where Eagles Dare (1969)
Mosquito Squadron (1969)
The Bridge at Remagen (1969)
Catch-22 (1970)
Patton (1970)
Kelly's Heroes (1970)
Tora! Tora! Tora! (1970)
Slaughterhouse-Five (1972)
Execution of Private Slovic (1974)
Midway (1976)
A Bridge Too Far (1977)
Ike: The War Years (1978)
Das Boot (1981)
Eye of the Needle (1981)
Sophie's Choice (1982)
Empire of the Sun (1987)
Fat Man and Little Boy (1989)
Memphis Belle (1990)
A Midnight Clear (1991)
Schindler's List (1993)
Hiroshima (1995)

The Tuskegee Airmen (1995)
The English Patient (1997)
Saving Private Ryan (1998)
Enemy at the Gates (2001)
Pearl Harbor (2001)
Windtalkers (2001)

COLD WAR
From Russia with Love (1963)
The Spy Who Came In From the Cold (1965)
Missiles of October (1974)
White Nights (1985)
The Russia House (1990)
13 Days (2000)

KOREAN WAR
Bridges at Toko-Ri (1954)
Pork Chop Hill (1959)
M*A*S*H* (1970)

VIETNAM
The Green Berets (1968)
Rolling Thunder (1977)
Coming Home (1978)
The Deer Hunter (1978)
Go Tell the Spartans (1978)
Apocalypse Now (1979)
Platoon (1986)
Full Metal Jacket (1987)
Hamburger Hill (1987)
Born on the Fourth of July (1989)
Casualties of War (1989)
In Country (1989)

GULF WAR
Courage Under Fire (1996)

1936-1946

with identification numbers and forced to wear vertically striped uniforms.

Under such conditions, many prisoners simply died. Others faced orchestrated death as German soldiers forced them into gas chambers for execution. Then Germans had to dispose of the bodies. The dominating building of the camps was the crematorium, two-story buildings with huge furnaces where bodies were placed for incineration. Tall smokestacks spewed greasy black smoke over the countryside. Germans killed so many millions of Jews that they had to keep the crematoria burning night and day in an effort to dispose of them.

Today the names of those death camps have become chilling notations in the annals of evil—Buchenwald, Bergen-Belsen, Dachau, Ravensbruck among them. Total, Nazi Germany created more than twenty of the death camps.

Such mass murder was hard to keep secret. Although he tried, Hitler did not effectively veil the genocide. Reports of the Holocaust began filtering out of the Reich soon after it began in 1941. By late 1942, Allies fighting Germany confirmed that some type of mass extermination was occurring.

1936-1946 • AMERICAN RESPONSES TO THE HOLOCAUST ～ Americans, isolationist until Japan drove them to war, were slow to believe the stories of Jewish persecution and death at the hands of the Germans. Stories of the persecutions of 1936-38, stories of *Kristallnacht*, all received considerable play in the American press. However, Americans could quickly recall World War I, knew they didn't want involvement with anymore European business and tried to ignore the news—or at least

---

Air War, World War II

～

Warfare is often a matter of making decisions – some large, some small; some life threatening, others not. A B-24 bombardier with the 15th Air Force, stationed in Italy late in the war, once told of a decision he and his crew frequently had to make.

Flying at high altitudes, the unpressurized cabins of the bombers could become quite cold. Thus, crewmen wore bulky, insulated suits to keep warm. There was always the danger of an enemy fighter damaging the bomber to the extent that the crew had to bail out, and they had parachutes just in case.

But there was also the danger that flak – anti-aircraft fire – from the ground could hit the plane with the same result. But flak, like a giant shotgun shell in the sky, could and often did puncture a plane, leaving it intact, but wounding its crew. Fortunately, airmen had flak jackets, early day bullet-proof vests that they could wear as protection.

There was the dilemma. In the bulky suits and cramped quarters of a bomber, a crewman could not wear both flak jacket and parachute. He had to decide which he wanted. Air crews would study maps and intelligence of AA battery placements. If their bomb run looked relatively free of flak, they might opt for the parachute. If it didn't, then they would wear the flak jacket. It was definitely a gamble.

pass it off as something Europeans, not Americans, needed to deal with.

Thousands of Jewish refugees fleeing Europe applied for immigration to the United States. Congress and FDR announced that the United States would take its full quota of German immigrants—20,000 in 1939—but would not raise that quota. Americans had long been nativistic, xenophobic and anti-immigrant. Regardless of the trouble in Europe, they did not want any more European Jews than necessary entering the United States.

Contrary to popular belief today, the mass murder of Jews did not come as a surprise to Americans at the end of the war in 1945; they had ample opportunity to learn of it as the war progressed. Newspapers regularly reported stories of executions. As the war progressed, so did estimates of Jewish deaths. By 1944 those estimates reached into the millions.

In 1941 and 1942, many Americans found the stories hard to believe. Perhaps it was all propaganda, they reasoned. Less naïve than they had been in World War I, Americans knew the value of propaganda. Perhaps the British were planting the stories to drag the United States into the war. Maybe the Russians were planting them, and anything "Red" must be a lie.

By 1943, when the stories seemed completely valid, help for the Jews seemed somehow impossible. American and British emissaries met in Bermuda in 1943 to discuss a possible rescue of European Jews, but such might very well mean opening the United States to floods of refugees, and Americans did not want that.

The United States has also been criticized for not bombing the death camps; after all, both Americans and British bombers were flying bomb runs over Germany regularly in 1943, 1944 and 1945. Such a criticism might seem oversimplistic. World War II was not the era of so-called "smart bombs;" while bombardiers using sophisticated Norden bomb sights could easily target regions of cities, surgically taking out the gas chambers or crematoria of a death camp while not harming its inmates was impossible. Any rescue or liberation of Jews from the camps would come only when Allies conquered Germany and occupied the Reich. By then, more than six million Jews would be dead.

1945 • WORLD WAR II ENDS ∼ The United States Navy turned the tide of war in the Pacific in mid-1942, bludgeoning the Japanese in the southern Pacific at the Battle of the Coral Sea, then again northwest of Hawaii at the Battle of Midway. From that point on, Japan was on the defensive. In 1943, the United States began pushing the Japanese defensive perimeter back. In the south, General Douglas MacArthur led troops in retaking New Guinea, then the Philippines in 1944. In the central Pacific, Admiral Chester Nimitz spearheaded a naval island-hopping campaign that took Americans to Japan's front door. By summer 1945, Americans and their allies were preparing to invade Japan, but American atomic attacks on Hiroshima and Nagasaki in August ended the war.

Americans entered the European war in November 1942 by participating in an Allied invasion of Vichy-held North Africa. The invasion, though clumsy, enabled American and English troops to consolidate control of the region, then use it to launch an invasion of Sicily and ultimately Italy in 1943. Progress there was slow, and Allies took Rome only two days

1945-1947

(1944) American soldiers dashing through a smoke screen in the Normandy village of Saintenay.

before the massive Allied invasion of France at Normandy on June 6, 1944. That invasion enabled Allies to sweep through France, liberating Paris, and then into Germany in 1945. Soviet troops were also pushing from the east and took Berlin in April 1945. Caught in a pincers and defeated on every European battlefield, Germany surrendered on May 2, 1945.

American celebrated victory twice, first with Victory in Europe—VE—Day in May, then Victory over Japan—VJ—Day in August. Businesses closed, Americans flocked into the streets of cities and towns. Bands played, people danced. The United States had won, and it had taken every American, from school children collecting tin foil to soldiers dying on lonely islands, to do it.

1945-1947 • RETURN HOME ~ The military services began discharging men in late 1945 and continued through 1946. Returning soldiers and sailors found warm welcomes, parades, congratulations and well wishes. But life would not be all joy.

Men discovered that life in the States had gone on without them. Many wives resented giving up their status as heads of the house. Women also hated giving up the good-paying industrial jobs when men wanted them back, but they had no option. Blacks, too, felt resentment. But white males had no guarantee of a job either, and post-war demobilization forced layoffs in late 1945 and 1946 that led to a temporary recession.

The nation also faced something it had not seen in twenty years—soldiers returning maimed, who faced long periods of rehabilitation. Flushed with victory in 1945, Americans soon realized that the war had changed their world, and they now had to find some way to adapt to it.

Hollywood, free now of government censor restrictions, began showing life as it really was. One of the most popular movies of 1946, *The Best Years of Our Lives*, depicted the trauma that many returning soldiers faced. Later in the decade, Hollywood brought a new realism to war movies. Movies such as *Battleground* and *Twelve O'Clock High* (both 1949), stripped away the patriotism of war-era movies to reveal the taught emotions of men at war.

America's economy righted itself in 1947. Veterans settled into jobs or went to school. As part of their reward for service, the government paid college tuition for hundreds of thousands of men with the G.I. Bill. New families moved to the suburbs, putting up thousands of look-alike homes. For them, *these* were the best years of their lives. The economic boom that began in 1947 continued, virtually uninterrupted, until the early 1970s.

World War II had indeed changed American society. Its people responded to the international crisis with courage and optimism, grit and determination. The nation had lost more than 400,000 men in the war (relatively few compared to the Soviet Union's tens of millions), and now set its sights on better days ahead.

1946-1951 • WAR CRIMES TRIALS
The end of World War II saw the victorious Allies implement something new in war—war crimes trials against their defeated enemies. The idea of such trials occurred to the western Allies as early as 1942 as they received intelligence of Hitler's genocide of the Jews behind German lines. Although the Allies of World War I had attempted to try some 900 Germans on charges of war crimes, the Treaty of Versailles turned the duty over to Germany. The state convicted only thirteen of the 900, and they received light sentences.

Post-World War II trials were different. They would see Allies charge both Nazi

---

1945-1951

General Dwight D. Eisenhower, supreme commander of the Allied forces in Europe during World War II, was probably the loneliest man in the world that early morning of June 6, 1944. He had just ordered the greatest invasion force in history to attack German-occupied France.

At 1900 hours the evening before, Ike visited the men of the 101st Airborne Division who were about to drop behind the amphibious landing zones on the beaches of Normandy, France. Their job was to capture and hold critical road junctions to allow invading troops outlet from the beaches.

Ike engaged the men in small talk, asking where they were from, chatting about fishing back home. The men read his mood. Ike had planned it, seen to it that the men were trained, gotten equipment in place, plotted the order of battle. Now it was out of his hands. One of the men piped up and told Ike to stop worrying, they could handle it.

Indeed, Ike had to let them go. But he didn't stop worrying. Eisenhower penned a terse note, just in case tomorrow, if things went wrong, he had to break the news to an anxious public. The note, which still exists, said:

"Our landings in the Cherbourg – Havre area have failed to gain a satisfactory foothold and I have withdrawn the troops. My decision to attack at this time and place was based upon the best information available. The troops, the air, and the navy did all that bravery and devotion to duty could do. If any blame or fault attaches to the attempt it is mine alone." As evidence of Ike's preoccupation of thought, he dated the note "July 5" instead of "June 5."

Eisenhower never had to release that note to the public.

1946-1951

and Japanese leaders with waging "aggressive war" and "crimes against humanity," something philosophically new. The trials would culminate in many executions and set a precedent for years to come.

1946-1949 • NUREMBERG TRIALS ~ The trial of accused German war criminals occurred between November 1945 and October 1946 in Nuremberg, Germany, a city in the American occupation zone and the only city in Germany with a court building and contiguous jail that remained standing. The International Military Tribunal ran the trials, with prosecutors from the United States, Great Britain, France and the Soviet Union trying the accused. U.S. President Harry Truman picked Justice Robert H. Jackson, a member of the United States Supreme Court, to start organizing the tribunal as early as August 1945.

On trial were twenty-two Nazis, including Hermann Goering, second-in-command to Hitler for much of the war; Rudolf Hess, next in the line of Nazi succession behind Goering early in the war; and Joachim von Ribbentropp, German foreign minister. The tribunal charged the Nazis with conspiring to commit aggressive war, violating extant rules of war and committing crimes against humanity by operating death camps and exterminating Jews and other social classes throughout German-occupied Europe.

The trial attempted to draw obvious contrasts between the victors and the losers; to paint clearly the contrast between good and evil, and to show that the Allies were capable of complete justice, even though angry, whereas the Nazis had been capable only of unspeakable horror. Jackson put it into words at the opening of the trial when he said the fact that the victors could "stay the hand of vengeance and voluntarily submit their captive enemies to the judgment of the law is one of the most significant tributes that power has ever paid to reason." Many, of course, raised eyebrows at the involvement of the Soviet Union in the tribunal, a country known to have purged many of its own people in political genocide before the war, and suspected of its own war crimes during the struggle.

On October 1, the tribunal convicted nineteen of the defendants and acquitted the other three. Hess and six others received prison sentences. Goerring, von Ribbentrop and ten others were sentenced to death. Those hangings occurred on October 16. Goering, however, escaped the noose—he committed suicide the day before.

Between 1946 and 1949, the United States staged twelve other war crimes trials in its zone of occupation. Americans tried 177 military leaders, SS officers, German industrialists, diplomats and doctors who had conducted bizarre and cruel tests on concentration camp prisoners. The trials resulted in twenty-four convictions and executions and thirty-five acquittals. The remainder received prison sentences ranging from life to a few hours.

1946-1951 • TOKYO WAR CRIMES TRIALS ~ In May 1946, the International Military Tribunal for the Far East opened its session in Tokyo to begin hearing war crimes trials of Japanese officials. While Great Britain, France, Australia, the Netherlands, the Philippines and China all conducted trials, the United States was the leader in the prosecutions. (At Nuremberg, the United States had been an equal partner in the trials.) The United States tribunal convened in 1946 would try twenty-five defendants; other trials would run intermittently until 1951. By then the tribunal had heard the cases of 5,600 accused war criminals. It had convicted more than 4,000 of them; some 900 of those were executed.

Among the convicted were Japanese Prime Minister Hideki Tojo; he was hanged in 1948. Japanese Foreign Minister Koki Hirota and General Matsaharu Homma, who presided over the horrible Bataan Death March in 1942, were among others sentenced to death by hanging.

The Japanese trials, like the German ones, were an attempt by the Allies to rescue justice from the trauma of World War II. The carnage of the war, plus the unspeakable atrocities committed in both theaters made Americans believe that only democratic-style justice, fairly imparted, could help bind the wounds of war.

1947 • THE COLD WAR ~ After World War II, a new and different kind of war was about to leave its mark on American society. People called it the Cold War, because most of its battles were waged not in open combat, but in the secret circles of espionage, hard-line diplomacy and arms buildups. It's major belligerents were the United States and the Soviet Union, allies in World War II but only because they had a common enemy, not a common philosophy or national interests. The Cold War raged until the Soviet Union collapsed in 1991. It left its own mark on society, a mark of fear, self-doubt, and suspicion.

After World War II, it soon became apparent that American and Soviet interests were markedly different. The Soviet Union had taken eastern Europe in its push toward Germany, and Josef Stalin intended to keep it under his influence. Having just fought to end the tyranny of one dictatorial government, the United States wanted a free Europe with no extension of Communist territory.

The United States could do little about the Soviet stance. It certainly did not want war with the Soviets. It did not want them spreading into western Europe either. It took a middle stance, adopting a foreign policy called "containment"—essentially containing Communism within its current borders.

President Harry Truman proposed two types of containment—political/military and economic. Truman enunciated his political and military intentions when he forwarded the Truman Doctrine in 1947 in response to a Communist incursion in Greece. Asking Congress for $400 million in aid for Greece, Truman said, "it must be the policy of the United States to support free peoples who are resisting attempted subjugation . . . If we falter in our leadership, we may endanger the peace of the world—we shall surely endanger the welfare of our own nation." The Truman Doctrine designated money for military aid, and implied that troops were available to stop the spread of communism. It was the backbone of containment until 1991.

Containment also had an economic arm; it surfaced that same year, 1947, with the Marshall Plan. Truman believed it necessary to create situations where Communism was not likely to grow; war-torn Europe, with wrecked economies, limited industry, broken governments, was a ripe target for it. Named for its architect, George C. Marshall, former army commanding general and now Truman's secretary of state, the plan provided billions of dollars to war-torn Europe. Soviet-bloc eastern European nations did not accept it, but western Europe did.

1947-1950 • COMMUNIST THREATS

While containment appeared successful in 1947, other crises awaited before the decade ended. Collectively they shook American confidence.

The first crisis came in 1948. Realizing he could not prevent Western powers from reestablishing a free West Germany, Stalin tried to squeeze Western powers out of West Berlin. He did it by cutting off communication between the city, which was entirely within Communist East Germany, and the West in June 1948 with a blockade. Faced with a test, Truman ordered bombers with nuclear capability to England. But, wanting to avoid war, he hit on another idea. He ordered American aircraft to start flying supply missions over West Berlin, dropping provisions to the 2.5 million West Berliners. This "Berlin Airlift" was a huge success, flying multiple missions every day for 324 days. Realizing he had lost this fight and could not dislodge the westerners, Stalin finally lifted his blockade of West Berlin.

The year 1949 was a year of uncertainty. It began with the creation of the North Atlantic Treaty Organization (NATO), a military coalition to protect Western Europe. Its creation shocked many Americans who believed the Berlin Airlift signaled American victory in the Cold War; the existence of NATO suggested that the Cold War was in fact not something the United States could easily win. The Soviets responded to the creation of NATO with the Warsaw Pact, a similar Communist alliance.

Also, China became Communist in 1949. Before World War II had temporarily united them, Communist Chinese under Mao Tse Tung were fighting Nationalist Chinese under Chiang Kai-shek. With the Japanese gone, they resumed their war, and in 1949 the Communist forces won. That added about one billion new Communists to the world; suddenly the world's largest and second largest countries were Communist.

Also that year, the Soviet Union exploded its own atomic bomb. American experts did not know how close the Soviets were to exploding an A-bomb. As it turns out they were closer than many suspected, thanks largely to an effective spy network stealing American nuclear secrets. Three agents—Klaus Fuchs, and Julius and Ethel Rosenberg—were convicted of espionage in 1950; the Rosenbergs were ultimately executed.

1949-1950 • THE SECOND RED SCARE

The mood of the American public was grim in 1949 and it darkened further with the realization that more spies might be infiltrating the United States. Efforts to root them out marked the Second Red Scare.

Whittaker Chambers, a seedy former reporter and editor of *Time* magazine, admitted that he had once been a member of the American Communist Party and that one of his contacts had been Alger Hiss, a U.S. State Department official. Young California Congressman Richard Nixon latched onto the Hiss case, keeping the investigation alive and in the public eye, and earning a reputation as a "Red Hunter" as he did so. Nixon's efforts landed Hiss in court, although the best prosecutors could do was win a perjury conviction for Hiss on his false testimony that he had never been a member of the American Communist Party.

Still, public doubt was there. Most realized that American borders could not possibly be protected against the insidious, invasiveness of communism. As early as 1947, Truman had scared the public when he called for background checks on more than three million federal employees. Observers believed that alcoholics, gamblers, debtors, adulterers, and homosexuals were easy targets for Communist blackmail, and thus easily lured into helping with Soviet espionage. By 1950, the government was firing many of these people, often on flimsy circumstantial evidence. (During the Depression in the 1930s, some Americans, many of them writers and philosophers, saw in the tumult the chance for communism to oust capitalism. Some espoused joining the American Communist Party, although its numbers were never large. The Stalinist purges of the era in the Soviet Union made it even less of a draw. It was still of no political consequence in the United States in the 1950s.)

1947-1950 • HOUSE UN-AMERICAN ACTIVITIES COMMITTEE ~ The House of Representatives, too, was Red Hunting. The House Un-American Activities Committee (HUAC), born during the Stalinist purges of the late 1930s (which sparked its own mini Red Scare), began inspecting Hollywood for Communists in 1947. Two world wars had already proven the effectiveness of movies in national propaganda; some wondered what would prevent Soviets from infiltrating the nation's film factories and slipping Communist propaganda into film scripts and direction. They feared that the unknowing public could quickly become brainwashed and ripe for Communist takeover.

HUAC set up shop in Hollywood, taking testimony from top stars, directors and writers. This produced the "Hollywood 10," people who refused to cooperate and were sent to prison. They included screenwriter Ring Lardner, Jr.

Conservative Hollywood producers closed ranks, opting to work with HUAC, and began blacklisting, or excluding from work, those who did not cooperate with HUAC or showed evidence of following the Communist line. About 240 people were blacklisted. In HUAC investigations, witnesses could respond in several ways. First, they could "name names"—testify about whatever they knew. They could "take the fifth"—that is, refuse to testify on grounds it might incriminate them. Those who did were usually blacklisted; investigators believed they must have something to hide. Others chose to "take the first"—oppose the hearings on grounds they infringed on First Amendment rights of free speech. Those people were usually jailed for contempt. Regardless of the option, those asked to testify were in a no-win situation.

1950-1953 • KOREAN WAR ~ All the Communist paranoia seemed justified in mid-1950 when the Cold War suddenly turned hot. Since World War II, Korea had been divided at the 38th Parallel, with Communists controlling the northern half of the Korean peninsula, an appendix of land tucked behind the Japanese islands. That summer, Chinese-backed Communists in North Korea invaded South Korea in an attempt to unify the country.

The battle see-sawed across the peninsula, with Communists first driving U.S.-supported South Koreans to a thumbnail of land at the tip of the peninsula known as the Pusan Perimeter. Containment was in jeopardy. The United Nations, formed after World War II to stave off further wars, voted to support South Korean troops with a U.N. coalition force. While British, Australian and Turkish troops were in the

1950-1953

(circa 1953) American Intervention. American soldiers formed ninety percent of the forces in Korea, and World War II veteran General Douglas MacArthur was its commander. Seen here are U.S. troops emerging from tandem helicopters onto an open field during the Korean War.

force, American soldiers formed ninety percent of it and World War II veteran General Douglas MacArthur was its chief.

MacArthur saw that staging a landing on the Pusan Perimeter would entail costly fighting and time. Instead, he put together an invasion which landed on September 15 at Inchon Harbor behind the enemy lines. With a significant force coming ashore in their rear, the North Koreans had no choice. They had to pull back across the 38th Parallel or risk being trapped between the Americans and the sea. MacArthur gave chase into North Korea, but going too near the Yalu River—the border with China—he prompted China to intervene. Chinese troops stormed across the border, pushing the American and allied troops back below the 38th Parallel. The war ultimately stalemated along that dividing line, and did not end until an armistice was struck in July 1953. The armistice left the country divided. The United States had accomplished containment, but at quite a price: $20 billion and 33,000 Americans killed.

The Korean War was more a symptom of the larger Cold War than it was the direct driver of social change in the United States. In fact, some writers have called Korea the "Forgotten War." Still, it embittered many Americans of the World War II generation who knew what military victory looked like and who could not fathom the "limited" wars that containment bred. The Korean War foreshadowed events in the 1960s.

1952-1953 • WOMEN IN KOREA ~ The limited nature of Korea played havoc with women troops as well. In 1952, with the war stalemated, the Department of Defense launched a drive to recruit more than 100,000 women for all the women's services. The drive, a debacle, fell hopelessly short. At its peak, women forces counted less than 50,000 in all five branches (a Women Air Force corps had been created in 1948 after the Air Force had been broken away from the Army).

While women served with honor and skill in Korea, and while army nurses had been some of the first American troops to land near Pusan after the crisis began, their overall lack of volunteerism mirrored the country's ambivalence, or perhaps dismay, over Korea. In her extensive book *Women in the Military* (1992), retired Major General Jeanne Holm (USAF) deftly cites poor timing and a general misread of the public mood by the Department of Defense for the low women volunteerism. Trying to get recruits in 1952, the Department of Defense missed the highest level of American public interest in Korea, which came before Christmas 1950. It also assumed that the great patriotic swell of World War II would be present again and supply women volunteers. Of course, the swell was not there. Without an overriding patriotism, male attitudes against women in the service became an obstacle to female volunteerism. Also, a good postwar economy and poor military pay scales made private-sector jobs more alluring than military ones.

1950-1953 • THE RED CROSS IN KOREA ~ The American Red Cross continued its World War II practice of collecting blood for troops in Korea, and in so doing abandoned a long-held practice of marking blood donated by blacks. By doing so, the Red Cross was leading the way in one form of desegregation. The first aid organization set up recreational facilities for United Nations troops in Korea, and, after the armistice of 1953, it helped organize the orderly transfer of prisoners of war between the belligerents.

1950-1954 • MCCARTHYISM ~ The overall mood of the United States during Korea set the scene for one final player in the Second Red Scare—Senator Joseph McCarthy of Wisconsin. With a reputation for drinking, brawling and failing to answer roll-call votes, McCarthy needed something to help him win reelection in 1952. He took note of Nixon's success with Red-hunting, and decided he would try it, too. He began wildly charging members of the American government as being Communist, representing an infiltration danger. While he could never back up his claims, he continued leveling charges at people and organizations. He used the media expertly, feeding them stories just before a deadline, which they had little time to check out. McCarthy became a master of the Big Lie—essentially telling stories so outrageous that people believed they must be true.

From 1950-53, McCarthy was the center of national hysteria. Of all the people he charged, not one was convicted, however many were fired or resigned. He even accused Truman, two secretaries of state, clergymen and the Red Cross of having involvement in Communist activities. The press loved him and kept him in the news. Most Republicans supported him just out of party courtesy. The public apparently liked him as well; his constituents re-elected him in 1952.

McCarthy finally went too far. In 1953-54 he charged that the upper ranks of the U.S. Army were loaded with Communists.

1950s

The Senate convened hearings to check his accusations. Known as the Army-McCarthy Hearings, they were the first big televised media event in history.

Television was young and, broadcast live, few knew how to manipulate it. There was no coaching, no preparations. McCarthy's years of drinking had bested him and it showed up on TV. He would arrive late for the hearings; he was unkempt, unshaven; he apparently dozed off or daydreamed. Americans saw him as he was. Amid one of McCarthy's tirades, an army lawyer got up and asked "Have you no sense of decency?" McCarthy crumpled on live TV.

Congress finally censured McCarthy. The Senate went on record as opposing his actions. Shunned by his colleagues, his drinking got worse. He died in 1958 of cirrhosis of the liver. From 1950 to 1953, McCarthy had enjoyed a measure of success because of the spirit of public fear in which he operated.

1950s • SOCIAL RESPONSE TO THE RED SCARE ~ The 1950s and 1960s hardened relations between the United States and Soviet Union, and they deepened American public fears. When the Soviets launched their satellite Sputnik, proving they had the missile technology to deliver nuclear warheads to the U.S., Americans panicked. Civil Defense organizations built public "fallout" shelters where Americans could go in case of nuclear attack. These shelters had stockpiles of food to last, in theory, for years. Many of those stockpiles were still there at the end of the Cold War. Many homeowners opted to install their own bomb shelters in backyards. Now clichéd as "make-out spots" for a generation of 1950s teenagers, the shelters were Americans' attempts to defend themselves against a new kind of war. Television and films depicted the horrors of a nuclear attack and the wasteland that ensued in the aftermath, pitting

Cold War Presidents: Ike and JFK

~

Dwight D. Eisenhower, hero of World War II, was elected president in 1952 and took office in 1953. His Secretary of State, John Foster Dulles, advocated a policy of "brinkmanship," that is, going to the brink of nuclear war to affect policy. But Eisenhower remained more moderate, opting to let Dulles and his vice-president, Richard Nixon, handle the Red-baiting rhetoric while he steered a middle course. While remaining an ardent Cold Warrior, he was pragmatic as well, and handled crises involving Iran, Guatemala and the Suez Canal. Late in his administration Eisenhower suffered two perceived setbacks—Fidel Castro's Communist takeover of Cuba in 1959, and the downing of an American U-2 spy plane in the Soviet Union in 1960.

John F. Kennedy assumed the mantle of Cold Warrior from Ike when he won the presidency in 1960. He quickly stumbled by granting the go-ahead for a CIA-planned invasion of Communist Cuba (which the agency had actually planned under Eisenhower). The invasion collapsed when Castro's Communists stopped it at the Bay of Pigs in 1961. In October 1962, however, Kennedy displayed steely nerves when he forced, on threat of nuclear war, Soviet Premier Nikita Khrushchev to pull nuclear-tipped missiles out of Cuba.

neighbor against neighbor and family members against each other as they competed for bomb shelter space and provisions. Public schools, too, instituted "national emergency" drills alongside fire and tornado drills. In case of a nuclear blast, children were to get on the floor and cover their necks with their hands. These feeble drills served more to remind Americans of the Soviet threat than to provide safety measures against a nuclear attack. Some schools provided "dog tags," a remnant left over from World War II, which children wore around their necks so they could be identified after an attack. (Even today the familiar triangle signs designating fallout shelters remain on thousands of buildings across the United States.)

1954-1963 • VIETNAM ~ The real Cold War threat to the American public, the event that changed American society, came from a little known country in Southeast Asia. The conflict in Vietnam would question American military might that was once so strong after World War II. It would cause great public rifts, cast doubt on American public officials and throw a shadow over domestic and foreign policy for the rest of the century.

Before World War II, Vietnam had been French Indochina, part of France's colonial empire, but Japan had seized it from Vichy France in 1940. After the war, the United States supported France in its bid to retake Vietnam, much to the dismay of Vietnamese nationalists who wanted independence. Nationalist Vietnamese leader Ho Chi Minh, a Communist though not necessarily in league with the Soviet Union, and his general, Vo Nguyen Giap, fought French colonial soldiers in the early 1950s, finally trapping a large contingent of them at Dienbienphu in 1954. Failing to get military help from Eisenhower, France left Vietnam, but the United States stepped into the power vacuum. At treaty accords in Geneva, Switzerland, the country was divided at the 17th Parallel, with Ho's Democratic Republic of Vietnam occupying the north, and the government of Bao Dai, a former French puppet, occupying the south. The U.S. soon replaced Bao with Ngo Dinh Diem, and, fearing they would go Communist, canceled elections in 1956 that were to decide on a government for all of Vietnam.

Meanwhile Diem, a hated Catholic in a country of Buddhists, quickly drew opposition, some of it military. By 1960, anti-Diem South Vietnamese, calling themselves the Vietcong, were waging guerrilla actions against the government. Soon Ho Chi Minh was sending money and supplies, then North Vietnamese troops, into the South to topple Diem. Diem, dictatorial by nature, proved fractious to the U.S., and in November 1963 President Kennedy approved an internal coup to remove him. The coup went too far, however, and murdered Diem, ironically just a few weeks before Kennedy, too, was assassinated.

1964-1966 • U.S. "ADVISORS" IN VIETNAM ~ By then, however, American soldiers were assuming the fight against North Vietnamese communists and Vietcong. Kennedy had begun sending military "advisors" to the country, ostensibly to teach South Vietnamese troops how to use American military equipment and how to execute tactics and strategy. But more and more they were becoming front-line troops. By the time of Kennedy's death, the United States had more than 16,000 advisors in South Vietnam.

1966-1968

1966 • GULF OF TONKIN RESOLUTION ~ Kennedy's successor, Vice-President Lyndon Johnson, politically could not be seen as any less of a Cold Warrior than his predecessors, and he stepped up U.S. involvement in Vietnam. In August 1964, when two American destroyers in the Gulf of Tonkin off North Vietnam reported that Communists had fired on them (a second report of Communist attack two days later now appears spurious), Johnson took the matter to Congress, who in turn passed the Tonkin Gulf Resolution, giving Johnson full reign to prosecute a war in Vietnam as he saw fit.

(1973) Two amputees take part in a parade through Times Square in New York City to commemorate the end of the Vietnam War and honor those who took part in it.

The resolution was as close to a declaration of war in Vietnam as the United States ever got. It was also a key turning point in the war. Retired United States Army Colonel Harry Summers, in his book *On Strategy* (1984), comments that the government failed to rally the United States at this point to support a conventional war in South Vietnam. The House vote on the resolution was 466 to 0; in the Senate it was 88 to 2. Summers concludes the government should have taken that vote as a public vote of confidence and proceeded to define its war objectives and muster public support as it had in two world wars.

But the government did none of that. At no time during the Vietnam War did the government attempt to gain public support. The draft had continued from World War II, so there was no need to promote its reintroduction; the Cold War had already propagated an industrial arms race, so there was no need to mobilize industry. The country just slipped from cold war to hot war with barely the blink of an eye.

1965-1969 • AMERICAN COUNTERINSURGENCY ~ Throughout 1965, 1966 and 1967, American commanders pursued counterinsurgency rather than conventional tactics. American troop strength escalated to 540,000 by early 1969, and American troops always had the advantage of firepower and technology. While they "won" nearly every engagement they fought, American G.I.s still had the nagging feeling they were losing the war. NVA and Vietcong troops were elusive, and the Communist manpower supply seemed unending. American soldiers also had trouble differentiating enemies from friends. NVA troops tended to be uniformed, but Vietcong were not, dressing instead in the style of millions of

South Vietnamese friendly to the United States. Such identification trouble caused confusion and demoralization among American G.I.s.

1965-1967 • DOMESTIC WAR PROTESTS ~ American soldiers were not the only ones demoralized. College campuses in 1965 became the scene of anti-war protests. Professors first questioned the validity of the Vietnam War, and their skepticism soon spread to students, many of whom were in college on draft deferments. Students staged sit-ins, demonstrations and protests. In 1967, 100,000 anti-war protesters marched on Washington. Young men began refusing to register for the draft; others, already registered, fled to Canada or Mexico to avoid the draft. Still others stood around bonfires and symbolically burned their draft cards.

1964-1968 • BLACKS PROTEST THE WAR ~ The anti-war protests melded with other social movements. The Civil Rights movement had begun in the late 1950s and continued into the early 1960s. Largely peaceful under the leadership of Martin Luther King, Jr., it became radicalized after 1964 and the growing influence of the more aggressive Malcolm X. Blacks began to sense that the Vietnam War was another violation of their Civil Rights. Sensing that, because they were unable to get draft deferments in the same proportion as whites, blacks began to see Vietnam as a white man's war/black man's fight. They were incorrect; blacks served in the army in a proportion that reflected the black/white population of the United States. Nevertheless, they joined the war protests.

1967-1969 • "PEACE AND LOVE" ~ Protesters offered peace and love as an alternative to war. Spurred on by the sexual liberation that the birth control pill had brought women in 1960, many young Americans opted to live in free-love communes where they listened to rock music, experimented with drugs and denounced the war. Music of the Grateful Dead and Jefferson Airplane became the anthems of the "Summer of Love"—1967—that emanated from the Haight-Ashbury district of San Francisco. The Woodstock music festival in New York in August 1969 became the ultimate expression of the youth culture. Psychedelic paintings, posters and T-shirts—the artistic manifestations of drug-induced trips—became the norm of the late 1960s, even filtering to the youth of conservative families.

Appalled by their behavior and appearance (long hair, faded and ripped blue jeans), American conservatives called the young Americans "hippies," and denounced anything associated with them. When hippies introduced the Peace sign, a stylized, upside-down and broken cross within a circle, Midwestern conservatives denounced it as the "footprint of the American chicken."

American society soon became torn, not just between pro-war and anti-war factions, but between young and middle-aged Americans. A "generation gap" had been born. The older group, raised in the Depression and veterans of World War II, could not understand the Baby Boomers' seeming lack of patriotism. The Boomers could not see the benefit of a war every decade, especially one where the enemy was not clearly delineated or vilified.

1970-1972 • AMERICAN CULTURE AND VIETNAM ~ Mainstream culture also began reflecting the war's tensions. On television, evening sitcoms began poking

1968-1972

fun at things military. Shows like *Hogan's Heroes* and *F-Troop*, neither set in Vietnam, denigrated military leadership. At the theater, 1970's *Kelly's Heroes* and *M*A*S*H* did the same. The television version of *M*A*S*H*, which debuted in 1972, followed its theatrical namesake in using Korea as a euphemism for Vietnam. Only one pro-Vietnam movie appeared in the Vietnam era, John Wayne's *The Green Berets* (1968). Out of touch with the public mood, Wayne cast his film in the traditional bounds of duty and honor. The most popular movie of 1970, *Patton* (1970), set in World War II, did not glorify war but instead harkened back to a time when heroes were easily recognizable and the United States knew how to win a war.

While there was no real evidence of it, the army maintained that the United States was winning the war in Vietnam. It offered as proof weekly "body counts" on the evening newscasts of the three main news networks, NBC, ABC, and CBS. American deaths were always underestimated; enemy deaths overestimated.

News agencies had reporters in Vietnam, and the war became the first one covered virtually live on television. Americans watching the evening news and talking about Vietnam over dinner began to notice something was wrong. Veterans of World War II, now in their forties, noticed it. Progress in World War II could be measured in ground gained and enemy positions taken. That wasn't happening in Vietnam. Yet General William Westmoreland maintained that victory was at hand.

1968 • TET OFFENSIVE ~ The North Vietnamese shattered the illusion of U.S. superiority in 1968 with the Tet Offensive. In January 1968, NVA and Vietcong troops struck all along the Ho Chi Minh trail, besieging the American base of Khe Sanh in northern South Vietnam as a diversion, then striking hard at the heart of American operations in the capital city of Saigon. Fighting there raged in the streets and in the courtyard of the American embassy. Television cameramen captured most of it.

Many Americans wondered how Tet could have happened if the United States was winning the war, as they were being told. Television journalists sought the answer. While many top TV reporters probed in South Vietnam, one in particular was in position to sway broad American public opinion. Walter Cronkite, anchor of the CBS Evening News, went on his own fact-finding mission to Vietnam. He returned disillusioned with the American war effort. In the spring of 1968, at the end of one of his newscasts, Cronkite offered a rare editorial opinion. He announced that he was convinced that the only way the United States could win in Vietnam was to withdraw from the conflict. In the White House, Lyndon Johnson habitually watched all three evening news programs. When he heard Cronkite's announcement he slumped. "If I've lost Cronkite," he reportedly said, "I've lost middle America."

The war, in fact, had eaten up Johnson. The year 1968 was an election year, but loss of public approval for the war and a poor showing in early primaries forced Johnson to reconsider his options. In March 1968, Johnson surprised millions of television viewers when he announced that he would neither seek nor accept the Democratic nomination for the presidency. Vietnam had claimed another casualty.

1968 • PRESIDENTIAL ELECTION PROTEST ~ Rioting spread throughout the election year. Racial and anti-war riots tore apart the Democratic National Convention in Chicago that year. Chicago police, under the order of Mayor Richard Daley, roughed up protesters. Meanwhile, Democrats nominated Vice-President Hubert Humphrey for president rather than the anti-war candidate, Eugene McCarthy.

Richard Nixon, defeated for the presidency in 1960, won the Republican nomination in 1968. Running on a platform of "law-and-order," aimed at anti-war protesters, and promises of reducing American involvement in Vietnam, Nixon won in November.

1969-1973 • VIETNAMIZATION

Taking office in January 1969, Nixon soon revealed his plan for Vietnam. He wanted to "Vietnamize" the war, hand over the fighting responsibility to South Vietnamese troops while U.S. forces withdrew "with honor." Nixon made good on his promise, quickly beginning to bring troops home. But, with peace talks ongoing and fearing the North would perceive the United States as dealing from a position of weakness, Nixon escalated the war in other areas.

In 1970 he ordered troops to invade Cambodia and get astride the Ho Chi Minh trail in an attempt to choke off supplies from Communists in the South. The invasion prompted a new wave of anti-war protests at home. At Kent State University in Ohio, National Guardsmen attempting to restore order to a protest demonstration fired on a crowd of students, killing four of them. The nation mourned, Nixon took a hard-line defensive stance and protests began anew.

1972-1973 • THE END IN VIETNAM; PUBLIC DISAFFECTION

Running for re-election in 1972, Nixon again promised Americans that the United States would soon be out of Vietnam. The evening before the election, Secretary of State Henry Kissinger announced a major breakthrough at the Paris peace accords, and Nixon won in a landslide the next day.

U.S. involvement in Vietnam was indeed to end in January 1973. But in December 1972 Nixon again escalated the war to keep North Vietnam bound to its obligations. This time he authorized carpet bombing—bombing that seemed to saturate or "carpet" large

(1969) Protest Flame. Protesters burn a U.S. flag during an anti-Vietnam war demonstration in Washington, D.C., showing their distrust of the Federal Government through the symbolism of the American Flag.

1971-1974

regions of the North (also known as the Christmas bombings for the season in which they occurred.)

For the United States, the Vietnam War did end in 1973. Troops withdrew; bomb runs ended, and American prisoners-of-war returned home. The American draft ended, and Congress passed the War Powers Act, which curtailed the war-time executive powers of a president so that nothing like Vietnam could ever occur again. The Vietnam War left in its wake a shaken society. Youth distrusted older Americans; citizens distrusted police; almost everyone distrusted the army; and, thanks to Nixon's handling of two episodes—the Pentagon Papers and Watergate—arguably extensions of Vietnam, most Americans distrusted government in general.

1971 • THE PENTAGON PAPERS ~ The Pentagon Papers case erupted in 1971 when a former Pentagon employee, Daniel Ellsberg, threatened to leak to the press copies of an internal report the Pentagon had commissioned examining its handling of the Vietnam War. The report was highly critical, and highly secret. Ironically, Nixon feared exposure of the report would undermine public trust in the federal government, and he moved to have them blocked. Nixon authorized a covert White House group, known as the "Plumbers" because their chief assignment was to plug "leaks," to discredit Ellsberg and, in turn, the Pentagon Papers themselves. The Plumbers broke into Ellsberg's psychiatrist's office and stole files on Ellsberg. The break-in obviously looked like just what it was, although the perpetrators remained unknown until Watergate hearings two years later exposed them.

1972-1974 • WATERGATE ~ During the 1972 election, Nixon authorized the Plumbers to wiretap the Democratic National Headquarters in the Watergate office complex in Washington D.C. Uncertain of his abilities to win reelection, Nixon wanted intelligence from the Democratic camp. On June 17, 1972, the Plumbers were caught breaking into the Watergate. Nixon won reelection by a landslide, but the ensuing scandal and investigation implicated Nixon in authorizing the break-in, then covering it up. Nixon resigned the presidency in August 1974; Vice-President Gerald Ford assumed the office. Some historians suggest that Nixon thought he was the only American politician capable of dealing with the Soviets, and thus he had to take drastic measures to ensure his reelection.

The Vietnam War and Watergate cast a shadow of doubt and distrust over the United States that American presidents and officials have never been able to fully dispel.

1991 • GULF WAR ~ After the end of the U. S. presence in Vietnam (1973) Americans lived in times of relative peace. American troops conducted invasions of Grenada in 1983, and Panama in 1989. But only one conflict, the limited Persian Gulf War 1991, gave younger Americans a true taste of American military might.

On August 1, 1990, Iraq invaded Kuwait, annexing the oil-rich country to its own borders. American President George Bush quickly mobilized American troops and built an international coalition to force Iraq out of Kuwait. The ensuing war accomplished the goal, and it reinvigorated the United States Army and American patriotism. As *Time* magazine quickly pointed out, the war also demonstrated the inadequacy of Soviet-made military hardware, which the Iraqis used to fight the war. Exposing the true nature of the Soviet equipment may have hastened the end of the Cold War with the USSR.

The government quickly and effectively mobilized public support for the short Persian Gulf War. Lack of support had killed the Vietnam war effort. But in 1990, patriotism was again in vogue. Americans flew flags from their homes and car antennas, and they wore patriotic slogans on their T-shirts. The public differentiated between anti-war protests (and there were some in 1991) and anti-soldier protests. While protesters may not have liked America's war aims, they made it clear they fully supported the men in battle. For a few weeks in 1991, a new American generation tasted the heady atmosphere of a victorious United States.

In one of television's most dramatic moments, CNN broadcast live from Baghdad the first American attack on the city; but the Army gave television news services only limited access to war information. Officers had long believed that television journalists had submarined their efforts in Vietnam. News teams in the Persian Gulf had to get their information through "pools" of selected reporters. Those who chose to go it alone did so at their own risk. One CBS news crew with reporter Bob Simon found themselves prisoners of Iraqis for much of the war. Such constrained coverage gave Americans less sophisticated understanding of any war since the birth of electronic and film media.

1991 • WOMEN IN THE GULF WAR

In what was perhaps a true measure of changing society and norms, women served in the Persian Gulf War in a greater percentage than in any other. They had served in Vietnam, although accurate numbers—oddly—are unavailable. But in

(1991) Two U.S. soldiers pose with the remains of an Iraqi SCUD missile, shot down by an army Patriot missile near Riyadh, Saudi Arabia during the Persian Gulf War. Despite initial claims of the Patriot's effectiveness, a 1992 U.S. General Accounting Office investigation showed that a Patriot actually hit a Scud in only nine percent of their encounters.

1991

the Persian Gulf they accounted for more than seven percent of the total deployed force. That compares with only about one percent in World War II.

In the Gulf, women were not specifically assigned combat roles, but many operated so close to the front that they were virtually in combat. Women helped identify targets, supply advancing columns and, serving as nurses, care for the wounded. Women were captured in the war, and women were killed.

Americans were stunned when one of those women, Major Marie Rossi, a Chinook helicopter pilot running supplies to the battlefront, died after her chopper hit a tower. The day before the ground attack began, Rossi, in a CNN interview, impressed millions with her courage and confidence, stating like the trained soldier she was, "I feel ready to meet the challenge." She died the day after the war ended.

1991 • TAILHOOK SCANDAL ~ The Persian Gulf War should have elevated women to an equal stature in the minds of male military personnel. But it did not, as the Tailhook Scandal of 1991 proved.

The Tailhook Association, a professional organization for Navy and Marine aviators, held its annual meeting at the Las Vegas Hilton, September 5-7. Before it was over, eighty-three women and seven men reported being assaulted, some sexually.

While most of the conference attendees were quite civil—indeed most never knew the assaults were occurring—other men, many of them drunk, forced women to run a "gauntlet" in a hotel hallway. In that ordeal, the women faced sexual groping and indecent exposure by the men. A Navy helicopter pilot, Lieutenant Paula Coughlin, disclosed the Tailhook molestations after she encountered the gauntlet.

In her disclosure, Coughlin charged that a Marine captain had molested her. Other female officers charged they had faced similar indignities.

In subsequent investigations, Pentagon investigators referred 119 Navy and twenty-one Marine Corps officers back to their respective branches for discipline. None of them ever went to trial. Charges against half of them were completely dropped for lack of evidence. The remaining defendants suffered internal disciplinary action that included fines and career penalties. While some top Navy brass saw their careers tarnished or abbreviated by Tailhook, the investigation into the scandal proved unsatisfactory to many observers. It simply underscored that, despite meritorious military service by women for decades, they were still little more than objects of sex and innuendo to many military men.

Undeterred, women still seek military jobs. In 1999 women made up more than fourteen percent of the U.S. Army's total force. They also accounted for about fifteen percent of candidates to United States service academies.

1991-PRESENT • LEGACY OF THE GULF WAR ~ The Persian Gulf War was indeed a spectacular victory to a generation of Americans who had never before witnessed their country victorious in a major war. But did the war foster a delusion on that generation? Unused to privation, as the World War II generation had been after surviving the Depression, Americans in 1991 saw little discomfort from the Persian Gulf War. It was quick; comparatively it lasted about as long as a video game. It was clean; gee-whiz, laser-guided smart bombs took out targets with surgical precision. Gone, seemingly, were the days when bomb raids took out whole city sections to destroy one installation. American deaths in the war were less than 300, severe enough for 300 families, to be sure, but of little notice to most Americans.

1991-Present • Gulf War Syndrome ~ A decade after the Gulf War, one aspect of the conflict still lingers—suspicion that thousands of American and Allied troops may have received exposure to chemical weapons that later affected their health.

Some months after the war, returning veterans began reporting instances of nausea, joint pain, chronic fatigue and memory loss. Soon, too, Gulf War veterans began producing children with birth defects. Veterans and Veterans' groups early began charging that some type of exposure, perhaps to chemical weapons, in the desert was causing the trouble. That chemical weapons should become suspect was natural, as it was widely known that Iraq had used them in its recent ten-year war against Iran.

The United States Department of Defense, however, denied that American troops ever received exposure to chemical weapons. In 1996 and 1997, evidence surfaced that such may not be the case. On March 10, 1991, after the end of the war, American combat engineers blew up an Iraqi weapons bunker at Kamisiyah. Not until 1996, however, was it learned that weapons containing deadly sarin gas were in the bunker. After consulting meteorological charts for the regions on that date, then running a computer analysis, the Department of Defense admitted that as many as 98,900 American troops could have been exposed to particles of the gas. However, the department steadfastly maintained that any exposure would have been so minimal as to cause no effects.

Veterans groups doubt that, and charge that such exposure coupled with fallout from the destruction of other weapons bunkers during the air-war phase of the Gulf War, are the culprits behind Gulf War Syndrome. Even others suggest that a combination of exposure to chemical weapons, smoke from rampant post-war oil fires and depleted uranium used in armor-piercing projectiles have caused GWS. The true cause remains a mystery, but recent years have seen the Department of Defense back away from its earlier denial of a problem and set up an office to investigate GWS and to help veterans afflicted with it.

The debate over Gulf War Syndrome is reminiscent to that over Agent Orange in the late 1970s and early 1980s. In the Vietnam War, the army used Agent Orange, a defoliant, to destroy millions of acres of jungle and crops in an effort to deny Communists their refuge and sustenance. Thousands of U.S. forces came in contact with the toxic material.

Late in the 1970s, Vietnam vets were becoming ill, many with cancer. Scientists linked their diseases to the contact with Agent Orange, which they said could also cause birth defects in the children of veterans. By the early 1980s, a veterans' group had brought a class-action suit against the makers of Agent Orange. In 1984, the suit was settled out of court, with veterans to receive a total of $180 million. Broken down, however, that amounted to only a few thousand dollars per individual veteran.

Conclusion

In the end, the Persian Gulf War seemed to gloss over the fact that the century it capped had been the bloodiest on record. That century had seen rapid and rampant military progress, and it had seen the United States rise to world power status from the smoke of wars that, at their outset, had been anything but certain.

The "Violent Century" saw changes in the attitudes of Americans toward war. Always reluctant to wage war, Americans after World War I and the rise of totalitarianism before World War II realized sometimes it was impossible to escape. Once committed to war, however, Americans wanted total victory. The Treaty of Versailles after World War I, they believed, had left a job undone and paved the way for World War II. During that conflict, Americans understood that all citizens, either on the battlefront or the home front, had become combatants. They thought nothing of working long hours in the factories to turn out bombers and landing craft; they willingly did without, rationing common goods so the boys at war would have plenty of supplies. They also didn't blink when the United States began bomb runs over Germany and Japan that killed upwards of 80,000 people in one strike; the Axis powers would do the same to them if they could, Americans reasoned. Thus, when they learned of the atomic devastation of Hiroshima and Nagasaki, they saw it as a practical way to end what had been a horrible war.

That notion of total victory, however, plagued Americans during the Cold War when "limited wars" made complete victory unattainable. Growing restlessness with the nation's inability to contain communism and win regional wars in Korea and Vietnam caused distrust between Americans and the government. The gray area of the Cold War did not sit well with Americans who liked to see things in black and white.

From the Civil War to the present, Americans have fared best in wars where they have crusaded against tyranny. In the Civil War the crusade was against slavery; in World War II it was against fascism, totalitarianism and genocide. The United States returned to such rhetoric in the 1990s. In 1990 and 1991, government and the press made many comparisons between Adolf Hitler and Saddam Hussein; in 1999, with American jets bombing Kosovo, they were making comparisons between Adolf Hitler and Slobodan Milesovich. As a society, Americans are not opposed to war, total and complete. The twentieth century proved, however, that Americans fight best when the cause is just and in line with the spirit of American democracy.

BIBLIOGRAPHY

Adkin, Mark. *Urgent Fury: The Battle for Grenada.* Lexington, MA: Lexington Books, 1989.

Blair, Clay. *The Forgotten War: America in Korea 1950-1953.* New York: Doubleday, 1987.

Bradley, James. Flags of Our Fathers. New York: Bantam, Doubleday, 2000.

Bullock, Alan. *Hitler and Stalin: Parallel Lives.* New York: Alfred A. Knopf, 1992.

Calvocoressi, Peter, and Guy Wint. *Total War: Causes and Courses of the Second World War.* New York: Penguin Books, 1979.

Colley, David P. *On the Road to Victory: The Red Ball Express.* www.thehistorynet.com/worldwarii/articles

Cronkite, Walter. *A Reporter's Life.* New York: Alfred A. Knopf, 1996.

DesPres, Terrence. *The Survivor: An Anatomy of Life in the Death Camps.* New York: Oxford University Press, 1980.

Feifer, George. *Tenozan: The Battle of Okinawa and the Atomic Bomb*. New York: Ticknor and Fields, 1992.

Freidel, Frank. *The Splendid Little War*. New York: Bramhall House, 1958.

Heller, Charles E., and William A. Stofft, eds. *America's First Battles, 1776-1965*. Lawrence: University Press of Kansas, 1986.

Herring, George C. *America's Longest War: The United States and Vietnam, 1950-1975*. New York: Alfred A. Knopf, 1986.

Holm, Maj. Gen. Jeanne. *Women in the Military: An Unfinished Revolution*. Rev. ed. Novato, CA: Presidio, 1992.

Jeffers, H. Paul. *Colonel Roosevelt: Theodore Roosevelt Goes to War, 1897-1898*. New York: John Wiley and Sons, 1996.

King, Otis H. "Karl." *The Alamo of the Pacific: The Story of the Famed "China Marines on Bataan and Corregidor" and What They Did to the Enemy as POWs*. Fort Worth, TX: n.p.,1999.

Lewy, Guenter. *America in Vietnam*. New York: Oxford University Press, 1978.

Lipstadt, Deborah E. *Beyond Belief: The American Press and the Coming of the Holocaust, 1933-1945*. New York: The Free Press, 1986.

Lord, Walter. *Midway: Incredible Victory*. New York: Harper and Row, 1967.

Manchester, William. *American Caesar: Douglas MacArthur, 1880-1964*. New York: Dell Publishing, 1978.

McCullough, David. *Truman*. New York: Touchstone Books, 1992.

Millett, Allan R., and Peter Maslowski. *For the Common Defense: A Military History of the United States of America*. New York: The Free Press, 1984.

Morgan, H. Wayne. *America's Road to Empire: The War with Spain and Overseas Expansion*. New York: John Wiley and Sons, 1966.

Norton, Mary Beth, et al. *A People and a Nation: A History of the United States*. 5th ed. Boston: Houghton Mifflin, 1999.

Patterson, James T. *Grand Expectations: The United States, 1945-1974*. New York: Oxford University Press, 1996.

Perret, Geoffrey. *A Country Made by War: From the Revolution to Vietnam – the Story of America's Rise to Power*. New York: Random House, 1989. Reprint. Vintage Books, 1990.

Prange, Gordon W. *At Dawn We Slept: The Untold Story of Pearl Harbor*. New York: Penguin Books, 1982.

Ryan, Cornelius. *A Bridge Too Far*. New York: Popular Library, 1974.

———. *The Longest Day*. New York: Popular Library, 1959. Reprint. 1974.

Schirmer, Daniel B. *Republic or Empire: American Resistance to the Philippine War*. Cambridge, MA: Schenkman Publishing, 1972.

Schwarzkopf, H. Norman. *It Doesn't Take A Hero*. New York: Bantam Books, 1992.

Shirer, William L. *The Rise and Fall of the Third Reich: A History of Nazi Germany*. New York: Simon and Schuster, 1960.

Smith, Robert Barr. "Justice Under the Sun: Japanese War Crime Trials." www.thehistorynet.com/world war II/

Stokesbury, James L. *A Short History of World War II*. New York: William Morrow and Co., 1980.

———. *A Short History of the Korean War*. New York: William Morrow and Co., 1988.

Summers, Harry G. *On Strategy: A Critical Analysis of the Vietnam War*. New York: Dell Books, 1984.

Van Doren, Charles, ed. *Webster's American Biographies*. Springfield, MA: Merriam-Webster, Inc., 1984.

Weigley, Russell F. *History of the United States Army*. Bloomington: Indiana University Press, 1967.

———. *The American Way of War: A History of United States Military Strategy and Policy*. New York: Macmillan Publishing, 1973.

Wheal, Elizabeth-Anne, Stephen Pope, and James Taylor. *A Dictionary of the Second World War*. Peter Bedrick Books for Military Book Club, 1990.

*Wilcox, Fred A. "Toxic Agents." In *The Oxford Companion to American Military History*. Edited by John Whiteclay Chambers, II. New York: Oxford University Press, 1999.

World Almanac and Book of Facts, 2000. New York: Primedia, 1999.

Young, Warren L. *Minorities and the Military: A Cross-National Study in World Perspective*. Westport, CT: Greenwood Press, 1982.

INTERNET RESOURCES

MILITARY HISTORY SITE

Curious about Rommel's desert strategy, or the role of women in combat? Guide Stephen C. Ural takes you on a historical tour of duty.
http://militaryhistory.about.com/index.htm (About Military History Site)

MILITARY HISTORY

Our nation in battle, from the start to now.
http://americanhistory.about.com/cs/militaryhistory/index_2.htm

http://americanhistory.about.com/cs/militaryhistory/index_3.htm

http://americanhistory.about.com/cs-new/cs/militaryhistory/index.htm

http://americanhistory.about.com/cs-new/cs/militaryhistory/index_2.htm

http://americanhistory.about.com/cs-new/cs/militaryhistory/index_3.htm

MILITARY HISTORY

A look at a wide variety of issues concerning the discipline of military history. Links to the major areas such as technological developments, tactics, strategy, theory, logistics, battles, wars, and all branches of military service.
http://militaryhistory.about.com/mbody.htm

HISTORY NET

Wide-ranging collection of resources covers world and American history, profiles of famous people, battle stories, and interviews.
http://www.thehistorynet.com/

GRUNTS.NET - HOME OF U.S. MILITARY HISTORY

Histories of the combat arms units of the US Armed Forces and the Veterans who served in the Army, Marines, Air Force and Navy
http://www.grunts.net/

CIVIL WAR CENTER

Louisiana State Univ. maintains this resource for Civil War research. Find histories, scholarly articles, upcoming events, statistics, and links.
http://www.cwc.lsu.edu/

NAVAL HISTORICAL EVENTS - SPANISH-AMERICAN WAR

Learn about the battles that took place on the sea during the conflict, including the sinking of the Maine and the Battle of Manilla Bay.
http://www.history.navy.mil/photos/events/spanam/eve-pge.htm

REMEMBERING THE KOREAN WAR
U.S. Center of Military History provides extensive material. Study maps, official histories, campaign summaries, and operation reports.
http://www.army.mil/cmh-pg/online/kw-remem.htm

WASHINGTONPOST.COM: IRAQ SPECIAL REPORT—IRAQ IN-DEPTH
Iraq Time Line Since the Iraqi invasion of Kuwait in August of 1990, Iraq's relations with the United States have been marked by confrontation. The time line reviews significant events in U.S.-Iraq relations since the Gulf War. 1990, 1991, 1992.
http://www.washingtonpost.com/wp-srv/inatl/longterm/iraq/timeline1990.htm

WORLD WAR II: THE HOMEFRONT
Timeline, Museum, Simulation, Resources.
http://library.advanced.org/15511

AMERICAN ACES OF WORLD WAR TWO
World War Two, U.S. fighter pilots.
http://www.acepilots.com/

WAR DOGS - U.S ARMY'S USE OF DOGS 1942-PRESENT
http://www.qmfound.com/War_Dogs.htm

The American Red Cross
www.Redcross.org

Information on Nazi death camps
www.Remember.org

United States Holocaust Memorial Museum's *The Holocaust: A Learning Site for Students*. Organized by theme, this site uses text, historical photographs, maps, images of artifacts, and audio clips to provide an overview of the Holocaust.
www.Ushmm.org/outreach

R. Steven Jones
Southwestern Adventist University
Keene, Texas

WORK AND THE WORKPLACE

~

(1965) An office girl travels from desk to desk via a scooter in the vast office area of a Honeywell plant in Fort Washington, Pennsylvania. The scooter is three wheeled and battery powered.

TIMELINE

1870-1913 ～ Rise of Mass Production

Widespread use of child labor (1870) / Railroads first to accomplish managerial revolution with professional managers (1880s) / Eight-hour work day inaugurated in Chicago (1886) / Henry Ford opens the Highland Park plant to begin mass-production (1913) / President Wilson establishes the United States Commission on Industrial Relations (1913)

MILESTONES: Indian Appropriation Act permits railroads to lay tracks across Indian lands (1871) • Yellowstone, the first national park, is established (1872) • First experiments with gasoline-powered engine (1876) • Invention of internal combustion engine (1876) • Sioux kill Custer's men at Little Bighorn (1876) • Louis Pasteur first demonstrates use of antibiotics in France (1887) • Modern electric motor opens way for consumer appliances (1888) • Henry Ford begins production of the gas-powered automobile (1896) • Alaskan gold rush begins after the discovery of gold in the Klondike (1897) • Jack Johnson becomes first African American heavyweight boxing champion (1910) • Ford Motor Company initiates mass production of the automobile (1913)

1914-1919 ～ Age of Industrial Violence

Mass migration of workers across the nation (1915-1919) / African Americans comprise more than 20 percent of the workers in the Chicago stockyards (1917) / President Wilson institutes the Federal Mediation Commission to resolve labor disputes (1917) / National War Labor Board functions to settle all industrial disputes (1918) / Workers demand an eight-hour day and equal pay for women (1918)

MILESTONES: Chemical warfare and airplanes introduced as new weapons of war (1914-1918) • Child labor abuse made a federal crime (1916) • Great flu epidemic begins in United States (1918)

1920-1929 ～ Welfare Capitalism

Over 800,000 workers invest more than a billion dollars in 315 companies (1927) / Over 350 companies give pensions; improve plant safety and working conditions, and provide medical care; sports and education for workers are subsidized by companies (1929) / Workers laid off and production is cut back due to over-production and large stocks of unsold inventory (1929) / Stock market crash propels economy into the worst economic depression in American history (October 1929)

MILESTONES: First commercial radio broadcast (1920) • First transcontinental airmail route established between New York City and San Francisco (1920) • Human growth hormone discovered (1922) • *The Jazz Singer*, first talking picture, is released (1927) • Amelia Earhart becomes the first woman to fly across the Atlantic, as a passenger (1928) • Discovery of vitamin C (1928)

1930-1939 ~ Depression

One-third of college professors are women (1930) / Unmarried women workers in the labor force are one-quarter of the female population (1930) / Construction falls by 78 percent, private investment drops by 88 percent; farm income, already low, falls another 50 percent (1932-1933) / Unemployment is 24.9 percent; 9,000 banks fail; 100,000 businesses fail (1932-1933) / Frances Perkins becomes the first woman cabinet member as President Roosevelt's Secretary of Labor (1933) / Child labor is banned (1933) / Passage of Social Security and the National Industrial Relations Act (1935) / American corporations spend $80 million dollars a year spying on their employees (1935) / Rise in formation of labor unions (1937)

MILESTONES: First jet aircraft put into service (1939) • 50,000 coal miners strike in Birmingham, Alabama against exploitation (1934) • Nazis banish Jews to ghettos (1936) • Sulfa drugs introduced to United States (1936) • Fair Labor Standards Act establishes minimum wages, maximum hours, and the abolition of child labor (1938) • Germany invades Poland, starting WWII (1939)

1940-1949 ~ Age of Industrial Democracy

30 percent of the workforce is white-collar (1940) / Five million women enter the labor force (1940-1944) / Fair Employment Practices Commission established (1941) / 35.5 percent of America's non-agricultural workers are in unions (1945) / 8 percent of all defense workers are African American (1945) / 86 percent of Americans believe married women should not work (1946) / Jackie Robinson integrates professional baseball — it takes another 12 years before every major baseball team has at least one black player (1947)

MILESTONES: Penicillin and blood plasma become available for battlefield use (1941) • *Enola Gay* drops an atomic bomb on Hiroshima (August 6, 1945) • *Mendez v. Westminister* desegregates Mexican American education rights (1946) • United States recognizes sovereignty of Israel (1948) • National Institute of Mental Health is established (1949)

1950-1979 ~ Age of Affluence

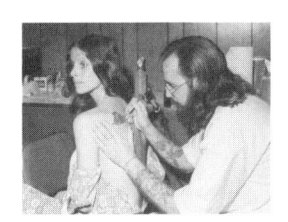

37 percent of the workforce is white-collar (1950) / Weekly earnings for production workers increase by 70 percent (1950-1970) / *Brown vs. Board of Education* rules that school segregation is unconstitutional (1954) / Contracts include paid vacations of up to four weeks for long-term workers (1960) / Opposition to union leadership becomes commonplace (1960s) / Bra burning protests have tremendous impact on the wardrobe of working women (1963) / Civil Rights Act prohibits discrimination in employment (1964) / 48 percent of the workforce is white-collar (1970) / Women make up 40 percent of the overall labor force reflecting a substantial increase in married women who work (1970) / *Dress for Success* becomes a bible for corporate America (1975)

MILESTONES: 33,600 American combat deaths and 20,600 non-combat deaths in Korean War (1950-1953) • Rosa Parks arrested, starting the Bus Boycott in Montgomery, Alabama (1955) • Soviet cosmonaut Yuri Gagarin is the first man in space (1961) • Surgeon general declares cigarette smoking a health hazard (1964) • *Woman's Day* adds articles on health and money management to help working women (1966) • Consumer Product Safety Commission provide a continuous review of consumer goods for risks (1972) • Soviet Union purchases $1 billion of U.S. wheat (1972) • President Nixon resigns over the Watergate scandal (1974) • Hostages taken from the U.S. embassy in Teheran (1979)

1980-1989 ~ Downsizing and the Contingent Workforce

Northeast and Midwest lose 1.5 million manufacturing jobs while the South and West gain 450,000 jobs (1980-1990) / Recession forces companies to "downsize," laying off many workers (1980s) / Rise in "contingent workforce" of temporary, leased, independently contracted, seasonal, and non-permanent part-time workers (1980s-1990s) / President Reagan disbands the Air Traffic Controllers union (1981) / Number of temporary workers more than doubles and the number of part-time workers increases by 40 percent (1980-1989) / Immigration Reform Act makes it illegal for employers to hire undocumented workers (1987)

MILESTONES: Attempted assassination of President Reagan (1981) • United States restores sovereignty to Native American nations (1982) • Sally Ride is the first American woman in space (1983) • Exxon *Valdez* oil spill in Alaska wreaks havoc on the environment (1986) • Fall of the Berlin Wall marks the beginning the of breakup of the Soviet Union (1989)

1990-1999 ~ Revolutions in Work Environment

The restaurant chain Denny's pays $50 million to settle discrimination suits (1991-1997) / Value of all corporate mergers increase nearly ten-fold (1992-1998) / Family and Medical Leave Act provides worker security during family emergencies (1993) / Number of farm workers declines from 13.6 million in 1915 to 2.85 million (1995) / Albertson's supermarkets pays over $29.4 million in a discrimination case involving women and Hispanics (1996) / Publix supermarkets pays $81.5 million to settle accusations that it had systematically denied promotions, raises, and preferred assignments to women (1997) / Many companies permit employees to work from their homes (1995-1999) / Computer and Internet revolution create many high-tech jobs (1997-1999) / Unionized workers earn nearly one-third more than nonunion workers and are more likely to receive health and pension benefits (1998)

MILESTONES: World Wide Web is created (1990) • United States increases efforts to stop illegal Mexican immigration (1990s) • Dissolution of the Soviet Union ends the Cold War (1991) • Clean Air Act requires automobile manufacturers to begin developing alternative fuel vehicles (1991) • Congress authorizes U.S. troops in Kuwait; Gulf War begins (1991) • U.S. scientists clone a male calf (1997)

INTRODUCTION

The United States is the Land of Freedom, the Land of Opportunity. In no other country is there such a concept as The American Dream. For millions of Americans that dream can be summed up by the words "security" and "prosperity." The heart of achieving such a dream for the vast bulk of Americans in the twentieth century lay in being rewarded for hard work. For the most part, it was work for wages or salary. Americans worked harder and longer than any other industrialized nation. The experience of work and the workplace is thus of crucial concern in understanding the social history of Americans in the twentieth century. And for many, the American Dream was elusive.

To a great degree, what kind of work one did determined the work experience. In the late nineteenth and early twentieth centuries, a large majority of working Americans were involved in some kind of physical, unskilled labor. By the 1920s and 1930s, huge numbers of Americans worked in factories. By the close of the twentieth century, the shovel or the drill press had been replaced for most American workers by the automated cash register or the computer.

America's working people were not always able to choose the work they did. Work type and availability were determined by objective factors such as education, skill-level, and the state of the economy but also by subjective social and cultural factors like dominant attitudes to ethnicity, race, and gender. Relationships to whiteness and masculinity have historically affected job prospects and opportunity for progression. One of the profound changes initiated in the twentieth century world of work was to introduce the potential for people of southern or eastern European heritage and of African or Hispanic or Asian descent to compete for skilled, professional, supervisory, or managerial jobs. Equally profound was the steady march of women into the paid workforce. While equality of opportunity for all Americans was not achieved, a start was made.

> "The 'working stiffs,' totally unorganized into labor unions, had to accept pretty much whatever wages, hours and working conditions the bosses decided upon. How little a worker's life was valued was illustrated one day when two rockmen, caught by a premature blast, were blown to bits. All we found of them was a shoe with a torn-off foot inside. The hard-boiled boss hefted this in hand a moment, and remarking, 'Well, I guess we can't have a funeral over that,' threw the grisly object into the swirling Columbia River."
>
> William Z. Foster, *Pages From a Worker's Life* (1939)
>
> "It doesn't matter how loyal you are to the company. If someone decides that you did something wrong or they don't like you or you didn't smile at them in the right way or their cousin's brother's uncle needs a job, then you don't have a job."
>
> Rebecca Amoto, waitress, quoted in the *New Yorker* (1996)

THE RISE OF INDUSTRIAL WORK AND INSTABILITY OF THE INDUSTRIAL SYSTEM 1870s-1933

From the 1870s the United States can be accurately described as a country in which industrial work characterized a major portion of the workforce. By the 1890s the vast bulk of goods for sale were mass-produced in identical fashion and an age of mass consumption dawned. So productive did the United States become that it moved from the world's sixth largest economy in 1890 to the world's largest shortly after 1900. By 1937, the United States produced 35.1 percent of the world's manufactured goods. Its Gross National Product (GNP), a measure of the size of the American economy, rose from $19 billion in 1900 to $97 billion in 1928. In order to achieve this transformation America's workers had to work harder and faster than their international competitors. Consequently, they suffered the highest accident rate in the industrial world. From small shops at the beginning of the period, America's workers labored in ever-larger factories and workplaces. As plants and companies increased in size, administering corporations became ever more complex, requiring a vast new army of administrative and supervisory workers. Conversely, during this time period the place of agriculture in American society was vastly reduced. The absolute numbers in farming became stagnant or were slightly reduced as urban America boomed. Trends in employment that became noticeable in the 1870s grew through the first part of the twentieth century and the work experience of Americans was profoundly changed.

1900-1930 • THE FACE OF THE WORKFORCE

By 1900, the composition of America's workforce was calculated as follows: 38 percent were farmers, tenants or sharecroppers, 25 percent were factory operatives or laborers, 11 percent were craftsmen or foremen, and 18 percent were deemed white-collar. By then, in addition to a vast expansion of work and the size of the workplace, workers experienced intense and repeated periods of profound economic downturns. Even during times of prosperity, employment was influenced by seasonal factors that affected product demand, by a mismatch between demand and production that led to times of massive stockpiling and consequent unemployment, and by rapid technological change that made some occupations obsolete and created others. Periodic unemployment was a fact of life for most workers during the rise of the industrial system. In the last decades of the nineteenth century, America's businesses engaged in fierce battles for increased market share that resulted in price and cost cutting and a mania to maximize production.

The tables below show different ways of tabulating the composition and distribution of America's workforce. In Table 1 the spectacular leap in the size of the total labor force between 1900 and 1933 is clearly displayed. It is noteworthy that, except in wartime, the size of the armed forces was very low especially when compared to other great powers. Similarly, except in periods of exceptional economic well being, the unemployed were usually far greater in number than we have come to expect today. Finally, the great increase in the total labor force can be pinpointed as occurring mainly among the non-farm employed.

Table 1: The Labor Force and Its Composition, 1900-1933

Year	Total Labor Force	Armed Forces	Civilian Labor Force	Total Employed	Farm Employed	Nonfarm Employed	Total Unemployed	Percent of Nonfarm Unemployed
1900	28.5m	124,000	28.38m	26.96m	11.05m	15.91m	1.42m	12.6
1905	32.41m	109,000	32.30m	30.92m	11.19m	19.73m	1.38m	9.5
1910	36.85m	141,000	36.71m	34.56m	11.26m	23.30m	2.15m	11.6
1915	39.77m	174,000	39.60m	36.22m	10.95m	25.27m	3.38m	15.6
1918	41.98m	2.90m	39.10m	38.54m	10.67m	27.87m	536,000	2.4
1920	41.72m	380,000	41.34m	39.21m	10.44m	28.79m	2.13m	8.6
1921	42.34m	362,000	41.98m	37.06m	10.44m	26.61m	4.92m	19.5
1925	45.43m	262,000	45.17m	43.72m	10.66m	33.10m	1.45m	5.4
1930	48.78m	260,000	48.52m	44.18m	10.34m	33.84m	4.34m	14.2
1933	51.13m	250,000	50.88m	38.05m	10.09m	27.96m	12.83m	37.6

SOURCE: Ben J. Wattenberg ed., *The Statistical History of the United States*. (New York: Basic Books, 1976)

Table 2 gives a clearer idea of what types of employment increased and by how much between 1870 and 1930. While agriculture showed considerable increase after 1870 until 1910, thereafter it decreased. It was the only type of employment to register an actual decline in numbers. While the census categories displayed here do not break down skill levels, they do give a good indication of the huge increases in categories associated with work necessary for production (Mining, Manufacturing, Construction, & Transportation) and the rise of white-

(circa 1913) Women's Trade Union. The vast increase in America's workforce between 1870 and 1933, from under 13 million to over 50 million, was made possible in part by a transformation in the organization of work. Seen here are suffragettes carrying the banner of the Women's Trade Union League of New York in a Labor Day Parade through the city.

Table 2: Industrial Distribution of Employed Workers, 1870-1930

Year	Total	Agriculture	Forestry & Fisheries	Mining	Manufacturing and hand trades	Construction	Transportation & Other Public Utilities
1870	12.9m	6.4m	60,000	200,000	2.25m	750,000	640,000
1880	17.4m	8.6m	95,000	310,000	3.2m	830,000	860,000
1890	23.7m	10.0m	180,000	480,000	4.8m	1.4m	1.5m
1900	29.1m	10.7m	210,000	760,000	6.3m	1.7m	2.1m
1910	36.7m	11.3m	250,000	1.1m	8.2m	2.3m	3.2m
1920	41.6m	11.1m	280,000	1.2m	10.9m	2.2m	4.2m
1930	48.8m	10.5m	270,000	1.2m	11.0m	3.0m	4.9m

Year	Finance & Real Estate	Trade	Educational Service	Other Professional Service	Domestic Service	Personal Service	Government Not Elsewhere Classified
1870	n/a	n/a	190,000	140,000	940,000	250,000	100,000
1880	n/a	n/a	330,000	190,000	1.1m	360,000	140,000
1890	n/a	n/a	510,000	350,000	1.5m	640,000	190,000
1900	n/a	n/a	650,000	500,000	1.7m	970,000	300,000
1910	520,000	3.4m	900,000	770,000	2.2m	1.5m	540,000
1920	800,000	4.1m	1.2m	1.1m	1.7m	1.6m	920,000
1930	1.4m	6.0m	1.7m	1.8m	2.3m	2.5m	1.1m

SOURCE: Ben J. Wattenberg, ed., *The Statistical History of the United States.* (New York: Basic Books, 1976)

1870-1933

collar work. Two other types of work are worthy of note in the second table. The importance and growth of domestic service and other personal service work is striking, as is the steady growth in government work from a very small base.

If we distinguish between manual, white collar, and service work we see that whereas in 1900 white-collar workers made up 17.6 percent of the workforce; by 1930 they had increased their share to 29.3 percent. Dominating the increase was the explosion of clerical workers whose share of white collar working overall jumped from 17.1 percent to 30.3 percent. The other major categories showed little change. Among manual workers the greatest increases were posted in the categories of "craftsmen & foremen" and "operatives" (factory machine tenders). Straight manual laborers posted a decline in share as a result of greater mechanization of tasks formerly requiring brute strength.

1870-1933 • TRANSFORMATION OF WORK ~ The vast increase in America's workforce between 1870 and 1933, from under 13 million to over 50 million, was made possible in part by a transformation in the organization of work. During this period, technological changes came thick and fast. Management was invented. The size of workplaces increased dramatically as did the firms that owned them. Handcrafts were replaced by machine manufacture that could turn out greater quantity, more uniformity, increased variety, and better average quality. A tendency toward what economists David Gordon, Richard Edwards, and Michael Reich have labeled the "homogenization of work" characterized employment. Between 1900 and 1930 a decline in the numbers of both skilled and unskilled workers and a rise in the number of semi-skilled machine operators became evident. The Ford Motor Company provides a clear example, as Table 3 indicates.

1870-1933 • Technological Change and the Nature of Work

Andrew Carnegie was a successful businessman by the 1870s. But after a trip to Britain, where he saw a fabulous new invention that allowed steel to be mass-produced for the first time, he became the second richest man in the United States. Carnegie used his wealth and access to credit to build the largest Bessemer converters ever built. To house them, he built the world's largest steel plant to that time. The scale of Carnegie's plans was awesome. By 1904 when he sold his company to the world's largest corporation, US Steel, it produced more steel annually than all of Great Britain, the nation that had led the world in steel production until just a few years earlier.

Before the 1870s, butchering cows and hogs had been a skilled affair undertaken by butchers who had passed apprenticeship training. Gustavus Swift started as a butcher in the apprentice system as well. By the time Swift reached the age of sixteen he decided to start his own business of butchery. With an initial investment of twenty dollars he invented the modern age of butchery. He changed the whole process by dividing down the process into the minutest tasks. Carcasses passed from one team of unskilled workers to another on overhead pulley systems. The famous historian of American business, Alfred Chandler Jr., described it as a "disassembly line." Swift and his major rivals established gigantic killing sheds in major railroad hubs like Omaha, Kansas City, and especially Chicago. The perfection of the refrigerated railroad car

Table 3: Homogenization of Work as Shown at Ford Motor Company:
Production Worker Employment Proportions, 1891-1917

Type of Production Worker	Detroit Metal Industries, 1891	Ford Motor Company, 1910	Ford Motor Company, 1913	Ford Motor Company, 1917
Skilled Workers	39.8%	31.8%	28.0%	21.6%
Semi-skilled Operatives	30.6%	29.5%	51.0%	62.0%
Unskilled Laborers	29.6%	38.6%	21.0%	16.4%

SOURCE: David M. Gordon, Richard Edwards, & Michael Reich, *Segmented Work, Divided Workers: The Historical Transformation of Labor in the United States* (Cambridge: Cambridge University Press, 1982)

made it all worthwhile as the meat and meat products emerging from his packing houses could now be kept reasonably fresh for the vast markets of the East Coast and even Europe. Instead of dozens of butchers, he employed thousands of packinghouse workers.

In the twentieth century, technological changes made the mass production of the automobile possible as parts could be made interchangeable through the development of precision engineering. Electricity could be applied to the powering of machines. Henry Ford revolutionized the new age of industry. In 1913, he opened the Highland Park plant and transformed both the automobile industry and the organization of mass-production generally. High volume resulting from the same kind of minute division of labor pioneered by Swift led to the ready availability of cars to many more Americans at prices they could afford. It was a social revolution.

1890s • THE INVENTION OF MANAGEMENT ~ Changing technology that allowed for a vast increase in production demanded large investment. Building bigger and larger factories required the development of larger companies. The capital required to invest in such enterprises led to a trend away from family-owned businesses and toward corporations owned by investors. As size became the goal, how to organize and control the work became a pressing concern. The first large companies to reorganize were the railroads. They not only had to solve problems that arose from hiring thousands of workers but also geographic problems due to the far-flung nature of their businesses. A layer of professional managers developed to plan, oversee, regulate, and coordinate. By the 1880s, the railroads had accomplished the managerial revolution. It was from the experience of the railroads that later large corporations drew.

What this meant for workers was closer supervision as managers delegated some of their power to supervisors and foremen. By the 1890s, the mania to maximize production and for control over the production process settled upon a concerted effort to shape workers to the demands of their machines. After years of experiments, Frederick Winslow Taylor found what he believed to be a scientific form of management. Taylor reasoned that workers were inefficient. He measured every movement taken to accomplish a particular task and the amount of time taken. Photography and the stopwatch became his preferred investigation tools. Famously, he hired a German immigrant to transfer coal from a railroad car to where it was needed at the Midvale Steel Company and paid him generously if he agreed to follow exactly the movements that Taylor dictated. The result was the removal of the coal pile in record time. For workers, Taylor's efforts meant the removal of individuality and their reduction to the level of automatons. While Taylor's recommendations were never universally applied, the individual autonomy of workers and control over their work did steadily diminish. Henry Ford's moving assembly line around World War I dictated the speed of work as workers sweated to keep up with the pace the machinery ran at and which was increased when they did. Control over the workforce, however, was both imperfect and incomplete before 1933. As America's workplaces became more authoritarian, worker resistance increased. Industrial relations were strained. By the 1890s, strikes were frequent. The period between 1910 and 1914 was described by

Graham Adams Jr. as "the Age of Industrial Violence."

1870-1933 • CHILD LABOR ~
Demand for labor was intense in American industry from 1870 to 1929 when the Great Depression struck. Child labor was common in many industries. While the employment of children increased after 1870, between 1880 and 1890 estimates suggest it declined by as much as 34 percent. Nevertheless, after decades of campaigning against child labor, according to the U.S. census of 1920, more than a million children between the ages of 10 and 15 were employed. Lewis Hine, the great American documentary photographer recorded the female child laborers of the Piedmont textile mills in North and South Carolina before 1910. His pictures showed filthy, dangerous, and unhealthy working conditions of these children textile workers.

In 1906, John Spargo wrote a book *The Bitter Cry of the Children*. In it he described what it was like for young boys to work in the coal mines. He wrote:

Think of what it means to be a trap boy at ten years of age. It means to sit alone in a dark mine passage hour after hour, with no human soul near; to see no living creature except mules as they pass with their loads or a rat or two seeking to share one's meal; to stand in water or mud that covers the ankles, chilled to the marrow by the cold drafts that rush in when you open the traps for the mules to pass through; to work for fourteen hours—waiting—opening and shutting a door—then waiting again.

Child labor was used all across American industry and was only finally banned in 1933 fifteen years after the U.S. Supreme Court had upheld the practice. By that time, the effects of campaigning against child labor, the abundance of adults needing work, the replacement in many industries of children by women earning little more, the changing demands of industry, and a new emphasis on the necessity of education meant that child labor decreased. Between 1900 and 1930, child labor decreased from 18 percent to 4.7 percent of the nation's workforce while attendance at high schools increased eight-fold.

1890-1970 • WOMEN AT WORK ~
One of the most notable employment trends of the twentieth century was the steady increase in the number of women into the paid labor force. There had, of course, always been women who worked for wages, but in the nineteenth century with the ideals of "true womanhood," it was thought that the proper place for women was at home. Much of the agitation made by labor unions in the late nineteenth and early twentieth centuries centered on the notion of the "family wage." According to this, men should be paid enough to support their family, including their wife and children.

Reality usually dictated otherwise to those at the bottom of society, to most non-whites, and to widows and single women of working families. Even so, there was tremendous pressure on women, especially married women, to stay out of the paid labor force. Many managed to supplement family income by working at home. As Eileen Boris has shown, there was an immense hidden economy of women home workers, from the immigrant Jewish women who supplied parts for clothing to small manufacturers to women of all ethnic backgrounds who made money by taking in boarders.

Table 4: Women in the Paid Labor Force, 1890-1970

Year	% Total Labor Force	% Female Population	Employed Married Women as % of Female Labor Force
1890	16	18	14
1910	21	24	15
1930	22	24	29
1950	29	31	52
1970	38	43	63

Tables 4 and 5 show the influence of women in the nation's economy. In the first table, it can be noted that up to 1930 women formed a small but substantial part of the overall labor force, that women workers were not quite one-quarter of the female population in America, and that of those women who did work for wages, few were married. After 1930, the trend shows a sharp upward turn. Far more women were in employment and they formed a much greater share of the overall labor force, approaching 40 percent by 1970. Most spectacularly, the proportion of married women in the female labor force showed a dramatic increase.

In Table 5 we can see the evolution of occupations that attracted the greatest number of women. The segregated nature of these occupations becomes apparent when the small variety of most common occupations over the decades is considered. The census data sometimes reflects a shift in categories but the various branches of domestic service dominated female employment until 1930, followed by farm work. The rise of segregated white-collar work is also clearly visible. In 1890 and 1910, only teachers made it into the top five occupations of waged women. Even so, almost everywhere they were forced to resign if they got married. By 1930 four of the top five women's occupations were white-collar.

1870-1933 • JOBS FOR WOMEN

One of the reasons more women entered the paid labor force between 1870 and 1933, was that child labor declined and women workers filled the empty spots, especially in industries like textiles, tobacco, and agriculture. Many employers were happy to hire women for their reliability and low wage expectations, which were barely above those paid to children. Department stores, mail-order companies, telephone exchanges, and administrative offices of all kinds were filled with women by 1930. Participation rates of women in paid labor varied considerably according to ethnicity and race. While the participation of black women was traditionally high, not least because the wages and employment opportunities of black men were so much less than for whites, most immigrants from conservative rural cultures kept women at home as much as possible. Among Italians in Buffalo in 1905, for example, less than 2 percent of wives held regular jobs. Jewish, German, and Irish immigrant women however, worked outside the home at consistently far higher rates than most immigrant women.

Table 5: The Leading Ten Occupations For Women, 1890-1970

1890
1) Domestic Servants
2) Agricultural Laborers
3) Dressmakers
4) Teachers
5) Farmers, Planters, Overseers
6) Laundresses
7) Seamstresses
8) Cotton Mill Operatives
9) Housekeepers & Stewards
10) Clerks & Copyists

1910
1) Servants
2) Farm Laborers
3) Laundresses
4) Teachers
5) Dressmakers & Seamstresses
6) Farm Laborers
7) Cooks
8) Stenographers & Typewriters
9) Farmers
10) Saleswomen

1930
1) Servants
2) Teachers
3) Stenographers & Typists
4) Other Clerks
5) Saleswomen
6) Farm Laborers
7) Bookkeepers & Cashiers
8) Laundresses
9) Trained Nurses
10) Other Cooks

1950
1) Stenographers, Typists, Secretaries
2) Other Clerical Workers
3) Saleswomen
4) Private Household workers
5) Teachers (Elementary)
6) Waitresses
7) Bookkeepers
8) Sewers & Stitchers
9) Registered Nurses
10) Telephone Operators

1970
1) Secretaries
2) Sales Clerks
3) Bookkeepers
4) Teachers (Elementary)
5) Typists
6) Waitresses
7) Sewers & Stitchers
8) Registered Nurses
9) Cashiers
10) Private Household Cleaners & Servants

Few industries hired women to work alongside men. For the most part, women were segregated into positions that seemed to require the extension of skills women had traditionally displayed in the home. They were hired for manual dexterity and in all sorts of nurturing and support positions like nursing or waiting on customers in a variety of capacities. Even among the best-educated women, job segregation continued to be the norm. Among college-educated women, social work was a new field they came to dominate. While a few women triumphed over the odds to become doctors and lawyers, the professions and managerial positions were still very much dominated by men.

Three broad categories of work drew most women who worked for wages in the non-agricultural sector—domestic service, factory work, and sales clerking. Each was accompanied by distinctive social attitudes. Sales clerking was open only to white women, mostly to the native-born but also to those who looked the part and spoke without a foreign accent. While the pay was low, hours were long, and expenses for good clothes required to wait upon customers were high, to be a sales clerk was to be considered the most respectable among all working women without higher education. Factory work contained the possibility of respectability for women. At the bottom of the job hierarchy, domestic servants, usually foreign-born or black, worked twelve hours a day, seven days a week.

Rose Schneidermann, later a leader of the Women's Trade Union League, recalled the disappointment of her mother when she left a job as a sales clerk for a better paying factory job. Adele Lindner related her thoughts when she changed jobs: "Very slowly, I buttoned my apron, the badge of the servant. I knew Minnie and Sadie and all the other girls who worked in shops and offices would stop associating with me. I had dropped out of their class." Even *within* jobs, hierarchies reflected a sense of status. Agnes Nestor remembered her years in a glove factory, "like the gloves they made, the kid glove makers felt that they were superior to the rest of us and used to refer to us as the 'horsehide girls.'"

1870-1921 • IMMIGRATION, ETHNICITY AND WORK

Work patterns and work experiences were very much influenced by the waves of immigration experienced by the United States between 1870 and 1921. Indeed, the Carnegie Steel Company among others sent recruiters to Europe to encourage immigration to the United States in order to staff their factories and mines. The bulk of immigrants, especially after 1880, came from rural cultures and in wage-work terms were unskilled. They became laborers and machine tenders, miners and construction workers.

As Melvyn Dubofsky, John Bodnar and others have pointed out, individual ethnic groups in certain cities or regions often gravitated toward work in a particular industry. In New York City and elsewhere, Italians tended toward construction; in Pittsburgh and elsewhere, Slovaks and Hungarians sought employment in the steel mills; Mexican workers in the Southwest and California became miners and agricultural workers; and the Irish whose English-language skills were a tremendous advantage stereotypically sought employment in government work at the city or state level. According to David Brody, in the years before World War I, close to 60 percent of all workers in America's basic industries were foreign-born. In the Carnegie steel mills in Pittsburgh in 1907, of the company's 14,359 common laborers, 11,694 were Eastern Europeans.

In the basic industries that typically produced goods through factory production and in America's mines, the workforce at the turn of the twentieth century was often quite mixed with unskilled workers from a variety of immigrant groups. Foremen and supervisors tended to be Irish or German immigrants of long standing or

Anglo-Americans born in rural areas. Managers and supervisors tended to be overwhelmingly Anglo-Americans, especially in the large industries. In the West, as the frontier receded and big business moved in to exploit mineral wealth, immigrants became a major source of labor.

In 1911, the United States Immigration Commission reported on the copper mines of Butte, Montana. It noted that the camp had been established for about 40 years:

"The labor supply at first was almost equally composed of Irish and English, with a scattering of Swedes, Norwegians, Germans, and native-born. These races were employed in varying proportions with the Irish and English always most numerous, as they are today, until, late in the nineties, members of the Finnish, North Italian, and various Austrian races began to assume importance as elements in the labor supply. About the same time a small number of Greeks and Russians were also given employment. The Montenegrins had been added within the two years previous to the time of the investigation. Most of them come from construction work on the railroads."

In many industries, employers consciously set out to hire workers from multiple ethnic and racial groups. Summarizing their investigation, the U.S. Immigration Commission reported in 1911, "in many cases the conscious policy of the employers [is] mixing the races in certain departments and divisions... preventing concert of action on the part of the employees." They thought that they could divide-and-rule the workers and thus defeat efforts at self-activity on the part of workers to resist greater employer control and to organize themselves into labor unions to improve their situation.

1870-1933 • RACE AND WORK

America's workforce between 1870 and 1933 was characterized by a galaxy of different ethnic groups. It was made even more diverse by different racial groups. Table 6 displays the racial composition of railroad workers in the Pacific Northwest in the spring and summer of 1909.

Table 6: Racial Composition of Common Laborers on Pacific Northwest Railroads, Spring & Summer 1909

	Oregon Railroad & Navigation Co.	Oregon Short Line	Northern Pacific	Great Northern
Chinese	N/A	68	132	N/A
Japanese & Korean	397	779	444	215
East Indian	14	30	5	N/A
Greek*	N/A	794	45	743
Italian* (includes Greek)	930	357	894	851
Mexican	N/A	3	N/A	N/A
Miscellaneous White	587	310	1656	1070

SOURCE: Carlos A. Schwantes, *Hard Traveling: A Portrait of Work Life in the New Northwest* (Lincoln & London: University of Nebraska Press, 1994)

1870-1933

In many areas of the United States, non-white labor was even more significant. On the West Coast, Chinese labor was important in the salmon canning industry and found a niche in commercial laundry work by 1900. Japanese labor—so obviously influential in the table above—had diversified into small-scale agriculture by 1920. Indeed, in 1902 in a famous strike, Japanese and Mexican farm laborers combined to demand better wages and working conditions from the farm owners of Oxnard, California. In the South, while kept out of the Piedmont textile factories, black workers found jobs in the new coal and steel industries of Birmingham, Alabama. From the 1890s onward black workers found work in some tobacco factories. They also found work on the docks of Southern ports. Probably the most well known profession for black workers was found in growing cotton.

After 1915, as the Great Migration got under way, increasing numbers of black Americans moved north and found positions in the great industries. By 1917, more than 20 percent of the workers in the Chicago stockyards were African American. In 1919, at the time of the Great Steel Strike, 14 percent of Pittsburgh steel workers were black. Henry Ford made it a policy to hire 10 percent of his Detroit workforce from the black community. Assigned the dirtiest, most dangerous or lowest ranking jobs, these workers often felt grateful not to be chopping cotton for starvation payment.

1880s-1890s • GROWTH OF WHITE SUPREMACY ~ Non-white workers usually did not find it easy to co-operate

(1902) Old scenarios like the one seen here still continue to dominate the black worker's life after World War I. Here, black women are educated for segregated work as seamstresses.

with white workers. In many occupations, white workers refused to work alongside non-whites. Southern white women refused to work in laundries or in textile, glass, or tobacco factories if blacks were employed alongside them. Quite often, different sections of a factory were racially segregated. In San Francisco, when immigration restrictions limited the number of Chinese servants previously available, white women refused to enter a "degraded" occupation.

One feature of the growth of white supremacy in the 1880s and 1890s was the gradual exclusion of African Americans from skilled occupations throughout the United States. Reflecting this, many labor unions representing craftsmen wrote racial exclusion clauses into their union constitutions. One effect of white exclusion of African Americans was their frequent use by employers during strikes, leading to a popular misconception that all African Americans were strikebreakers. Everywhere, if a white worker was available and willing to work for the wages offered, he would be hired in preference to a non-white. Non-white Americans were usually last in and first fired.

In some cases, racial stereotyping by employers led to the clustering of working people of color. In the beet fields of California where non-white labor was the norm, growers in 1911 compared the different racial groups. According to a report made to the U.S. Government by employers of beet field labor on the attitudes of laborers, Mexicans were preferred to Japanese because of their tractability even though they worked more slowly; the Chinese, a declining force in the California fields by this time were preferred above all; and a new group, the East Indians, were acceptable as slow, honest, steady and exceedingly tractable.

1870-1930 • WHITE-COLLAR WORK

~ The extraordinary growth of white-collar work after 1870 transformed the experience of work for millions of Americans. To take one example, in 1880 there were estimated to be fewer than 32,000 sales workers in America, about one-quarter of whom were women. By 1940, the number had jumped to around 2 million. A little over 40 percent were women. It was not just in the rise of retailing that white-collar work showed a dramatic increase. The table below indicates both the absolute rise in the number of white-collar workers in America between 1900 and 1930 and the rise of white-collar work as a proportion of the total labor force.

In manufacturing, the vast increase in size of firms had consequences also. One large consequence was the development of bureaucracies to run corporations requiring more white-collar workers. Large amounts of white-collar workers were needed for the separation of functions of

Table 7: Proportion of White-Collar Workers in the Economically Active Population, 1900-1930

	In 10,000s	As a % of the Economically Active Population
1900	336	12
1910	556	15
1920	793	19
1930	1,092	22

SOURCE: Adapted from Jurgen Kocka, *White Collar Workers in America*, 1890-1940 (London & Beverly Hills: Sage, 1980)

1870-1930

(circa 1935) A man sits at a machine, packaging change into rolls for a bank. There are cloth bags full of bank notes on a cart beside him.

Table 8: Blue-Collar Workers & White-Collar Workers in Manufacturing, 1919-1933

Year	Blue Collar Workers Employed (000s)	White Collar Workers Employed (000s)
1919	8,482	1,384
1920	8,413	1,343
1921	6,487	1,087
1922	7,198	1,152
1923	8,206	1,286
1924	7,618	1,272
1925	7,873	1,270
1926	8,048	1,316
1927	7,866	1,362
1928	7,863	1,381
1929	8,386	1,503
1930	7,330	1,468
1931	6,179	1,273
1932	5,246	1,085
1933	5,787	1,003

SOURCE: Jurgen Kocka, *White Collar Workers in America, 1890-1940* (London & Beverly Hills, Sage, 1980)

planning, preparation, and administration from the larger production requirements of the company. This new "bureaucracy" also increased division of labor within the managerial functions. The increase in administration and supervisory functions in large businesses required much more paperwork, again more white-collar workers were needed. Some of this paperwork also was required by the government to keep contact between business and government strong after the mistakes of the Progressive Era.

Table 8 shows the numbers of white-collar workers as compared with blue-collar workers in American manufacturing. The fall in overall numbers in certain years can be explained by the intrusion of severe economic downturns between 1919 and 1921 and again after 1929. Note, however, that the decline in manufacturing employment was steeper for blue-collar workers after 1929 than for white-collar workers.

As demand for a more educated workforce for the industrial economy increased, education expanded. So too did the employment of teachers. A parallel development toward the end of the nineteenth century was the systematic training of those entering the professions and the professionalization of previously low-status occupations like school teaching. Doctors and lawyers received specific training and qualifications, as did teachers, engineers, and many managers. Universities established schools of engineering, medicine, education, and law. Recognizably modern curricula demonstrated the emergence of new academic disciplines and the professionalization of others, such as history. Between 1870 and 1930, members of the professions increased their share of the labor force from 2.6 percent to 6.7

percent. They formed an elite whose social status other white-collar workers might attempt to mimic.

1890-1920 • FOREMEN AND SUPERVISORS ~ The role of foremen and supervisors underwent a dramatic transformation, especially after World War I. Factories in the nineteenth century and until about 1920, as historian and author Daniel Nelson observed, were the "foremen's empire." Foremen had immense power. They could hire and fire workers, assign tasks, determine the pay rate (by the piece or the day), decide who would be laid off and who would get overtime, and resolve all disputes. Thus foremen could favor relatives and friends. They could punish pieceworkers not only with fines or dismissal but also by delaying the delivery of parts to those who had run out of work or by failing to insure the dispatch of repairmen if the machine had broken down. The power of the foreman actually increased as factories and companies grew ever larger.

Operators in factories were far more under the control of foremen than craftsmen. Foremen tended to be drawn from the ranks of the skilled and the skilled also were far more vital in the production process as they were not easily replaced. Some foremen were absolute tyrants and complaints against foremen were among the most frequent causes of unrest. It was not uncommon for foremen to use brute force to coerce workers to accept their orders. When the Pullman Company, for example, decided to transfer workers from day work to piecework and to slash the rates for such work in 1894, it was the foremen who carried out the orders, punching, cursing and waving clubs in the faces of angry workers. Complaints of violence against foremen were common even under more settled circumstances. Resentment by women workers against sexual harassment, including sexual favors and rape in return for keeping their jobs or preferment in task assignments, was strong and common as it was usual for all supervisory positions to be filled by men.

As giant corporations consolidated themselves, the rule of foremen generated considerable hostility on the part of workers and consequently increased problems for higher management in the smooth operation of the corporation. To compensate, the development and refinement of modern management severely compromised the traditional autonomy of the foreman. Similarly, the mechanization of production imposed control over workers by technology rather than directly between worker and supervisor or boss.

Despite the advice of scientific management guru Frederick Winslow Taylor to increase the number of foremen eightfold, firms began to limit foremen to the task of transmitting the orders of others. Simply put, they were often more trouble than they were worth. To take one example, at the Ford assembly plant in Detroit in 1914, so many workers were fired or quit as a result of oppressive working conditions that five hundred new workers had to be hired each day to keep the work force at 15,000.

The foreman's previous task of setting the speed of production and routing work and production supplies was removed and vested in specialists who would advise him. Skilled workers designated as his assistants now achieved work inspection, troubleshooting, and setting up tasks. Discipline was taken out of his hands altogether with the development through the 1920s of personnel management. The mechanization of production at Ford and elsewhere created a situation where control was achieved over workers without the need for the traditional foreman. By the end of 1914 at Ford, only 255 men supervised the 15,000 laborers. There was, therefore, one supervisor for every 58 men, an impossible ratio before foremen were no longer needed to direct the sequencing or pace of work. In other corporations, the same process was achieved only after 1920.

1886-1920 • CONDITIONS OF WORK
~ American workers worked hard and dangerously. In mining, construction, and manufacturing, hours were long and conditions were often brutal. Social reform movements achieved success in several states before World War I in reducing levels of child labor and in restricting the hours required of women workers.

The drive for the eight-hour day, which had begun in Chicago in 1886, gradually bore fruit for workers. The Edison works in Schenectady, New York, were quite typical. In 1892, production workers worked a ten-hour day, office personnel nine hours, while both worked an hour less on Saturdays. A 1913 survey at a Boston evening school for women found that 33.5 percent of the office employees, 4.8 percent of the factory workers, and 5.8 percent of the saleswomen worked less than eight hours per day. However, 89.4 percent of the office workers, 94.1 percent of the saleswomen but only 59.6 percent of factory workers worked less than nine hours per day. World War I accelerated a trend toward the reduction of hours overall and differentials existed between the average work week of blue-collar workers and white-collar workers. In the steel industry however, as late as 1920, it was still common for most laborers to work a seven-day work week of twelve hour shifts. In 1919 in the Pittsburgh district, laborers in blast furnaces averaged 82 hours a week, open hearth workers 78.5, and plate mill workers 70.3 hours.

The drive to create large corporations, the enlargements in the size of workplaces, the desire for control, the power of foremen, periodic unemployment, and the mechanization of production processes all made conditions of work after 1900 the subject of great worker resentment. Workers were confronted on all sides by the power of the corporation and their consequent lack of influence over their own lives. Universally, employers militantly resisted efforts by workers to organize themselves collectively in unions to negotiate for better conditions and pay. As a labor investigator in Pittsburgh in 1911 remarked, "The man working for the United States Steel Corporation sees on every side evidence of an irresistible power, baffling and intangible. It fixes the conditions of his employment; it tells him what wages he may expect to receive and where and when he must work." To speak out would bring rebuke, dismissal or indifference. The result was discontent that boiled over often into spontaneous action.

So many strikes costing so many lost working days accompanied with so much violence led in 1913 to the establishment by President Wilson of the U.S. Commission on Industrial Relations. The Commission held hearings nationwide and reported its findings in 1915. It found an attitude of class-consciousness on both sides of industry. As the historian of the Commission, Graham Adams Jr. noted, "In conflict after conflict, either one or both sides struck a posture of unyielding obduracy which produced open violence. Regardless of cause, geographic location, type of industry, or ethnic grouping, turbulence in industrial relations flared all over the United States. It rocked large cities and small towns, manufacturing areas and agrarian communities. On labor's side, native Americans as well as immigrants plunged into battle. Many management leaders of old American stock willingly employed the tactics of war. Industrialization had outdistanced American social attitudes and institutions. In many cases this led to a collapse of civil authority, to near-anarchy, and to military rule. The Commission warned that American industrial relations were so poor that they constituted a threat to American democracy itself. Matters had barely improved by the time of the great steel strike of 1919, just the largest in a year that saw the greatest number of American workers on strike in the nation's history.

1917-1918 • THE EFFECT OF WORLD WAR I ON WORK IN AMERICA ~

The Progressive movement that had dominated American politics in the first two decades of the twentieth century had effected some changes in work relations by passing piecemeal legislation at state and federal levels aimed at protecting workers from some of the worst abuses of employers. The U.S. Commission on Industrial Relations had heightened public awareness of the brutal state of America's workplaces, but nothing produced such change as America's entry into World War I.

The demands of total war concentrated government attention on the efficient production of war matériel. Labor's cooperation was critical. In 1917, few concrete steps were taken to secure it and, as prices rose, strikes broke out on a scale even larger than before the war. President Wilson instituted three important mechanisms that impacted work in America. First, special wage adjustment boards were established. Second, a federal Mediation Commission was set up to resolve labor disputes. Finally, in April 1918, the National War Labor Board (NWLB) functioned as the final court of appeal to settle all industrial disputes that could not be resolved through other means. Even more than this, for the first time, government recognized the importance of workers in the war effort by including representatives of labor in the critical work-related bodies concerned with planning and managing production.

The role of the federal government was thus transformed during World War I from one in which its sole concern was to keep order in industry, usually through the dispatch of troops when necessary to support the rights of property and thus employers, to one in which order was to be secured through winning the support of labor. The NWLB recognized labor's right to organize into unions and to bargain collectively with employers, rights that had previously been denied or ignored. It recognized that employers should not in any way deny or abridge those rights.

The eight-hour day was to be applied as far as possible, women entering industry were to be given equal pay for equal work, and there was complete acceptance of the right of all workers to a "living wage." Membership in labor unions soared. By 1919, union membership stood at 4.125 million, more than twice the figure for 1910 and well over four times the number in unions in 1900. Even so, most unions were exclusive rather than inclusive. Most unions only organized skilled workers, excluding the bulk of production workers, immigrant workers, African Americans, and women.

For production workers in particular, the war also brought higher wages and more overtime. Demand for service in the military drew primarily on male workers. Immigrant workers were subject to intense Americanization campaigns and during the war many became citizens. With many skilled and semi-skilled workers in the military, these new American citizens were able for the first time to acquire better skills and jobs. To replace them, groups of people previously at the margins of American society were called upon. The migration of southern blacks became a torrent as between 200,000 and 300,000 were drawn to regions associated with heavy industries and primary metal products. Similarly, Mexican Americans and Mexican citizens were recruited to Northern centers of war production. A third group in the new wartime workforce was women where they found work for the first time in foundries, steel mills, public transportation, and anywhere else labor was needed.

Gains made by workers from World War I did not last far beyond the end of hostilities. The war was followed by perhaps the greatest labor upheaval ever in American history. Employers aggressively sought to reassert their control over workers and the workplace. Government abruptly cancelled its interest in labor-management harmony. Prices outstripped wages. America fell into depression. Finally, the country was struck by the fear of Communism, or the Red Scare.

1920s • Welfare Capitalism
The economy was restored by 1922 and went on to enjoy unprecedented prosperity. As corporations became even larger and fewer, the cut-throat business competition of the pre-war years faded. Good management now required both efficiency and stability. Tyrannical foremen were replaced by ordered mechanisms to regulate production and minimize resentment. Large corporations became sensitive to public opinion upon which they depended for market share. Many large corporations took a new interest in their workers as they tried to prevent high turnover. They discovered a community of interest between managers and workers. Steel magnate Charles Schwab, speaking in 1927, discussed workers' rights. Among other things he listed steady employment, a voice in the regulation of their working conditions, the opportunity to save and to own stock, and some guarantee of security in old age. Successful management, according to Schwab in 1928 while addressing an audience of engineers, depended upon good industrial relations: "Industry's most important task in this day of large-scale production is management of men on a human basis."

Still committed to dealing directly with workers and to keeping out labor unions where possible, managers developed a number of mechanisms that altered the experience of work for millions of Americans. Companies developed programs to help employees save money, acquire property, and purchase company stock. By 1927, over 800,000 workers had invested more than a billion dollars in 315 companies. Other programs protected workmen and their families from the monetary disasters that might accompany accident, illness, old age, and death. By 1929, over 350 companies offered pensions. In addition, companies improved plant safety and working conditions, provided medical care for workers and their families, subsidized sports and education for workers, provided land for gardening, and assisted workers with personal problems.

Perhaps the most celebrated experiment of the 1920s was the employee representation plan. ERPs allowed workers to discuss matters of concern and incidentally to improve efficiency. However, as David Brody observed, "In practice, welfare capitalism fell far short of the boasts of the speechmakers. For all the fine talk, companies failed to act on the most challenging problems." He noted that even the most advanced companies under welfare capitalism did virtually nothing to protect against joblessness. ERPs also failed to retain the enthusiasm of workers for long. They were too transparently the creatures of management. Even more important, welfare capitalism in the 1920s was a minority phenomenon limited to large prosperous corporations. By the end of the 1920s, even the enthusiasm of many corporations for welfare capitalism waned and was replaced by more directly job-related incentives for workers.

1930s • WORK AND THE GREAT DEPRESSION

The prosperity of the 1920s had been general but not universal. Workers in mining, textiles and agriculture had experienced a prolonged depression while production workers experienced more job consistency, improved safety and overall work conditions, and better pay. By the end of the decade though, the broader economy showed signs of a slowdown. 1928 witnessed a decline in consumer spending and a slowdown in housing construction, an early indicator of changing economic conditions. The following year, workers were laid off and production cut back due to over-production and large stocks of unsold

(circa 1935) Ahoy There Maties. In order to find new ways to bring in more revenue, business owners tried all kinds of gimmicks. This is a seafood bar in a grocery store with a counterperson in mock-Navy uniform standing behind a counter made to look like a ship.

inventory. The stock market also showed signs of increasing volatility. When the stock market crashed at the end of October 1929, the economy began a deep descent into what became the worst economic depression in American history. Between 1929 and the winter of 1932-33, the gross national product fell by one half. In certain sectors, the decline was even more pronounced. Construction fell by 78 percent, and private investment dropped by 88 percent. Farm income, already low throughout the 1920s, fell another 50 percent. Unemployment, which had stood at 3.2 percent in 1928 leapt to 24.9 percent—even higher among industrial workers. Finally, 9,000 banks went bust and 100,000 businesses failed.

At first, businesses attempted to rally together to stop the decline. Promises were made to workers that they would be protected. Wages would be guaranteed. Work would be shared to avoid unemployment. Assurances of this kind did not last long. Welfare capitalism was abandoned as too expensive, though dividends continued to be paid in many instances to shareholders. Businesses scurried to protect themselves and did so with a frenzy of price and cost cutting. Workers were stunned. The rising numbers of unemployed, as Melvyn Dubofsky pointed out, were generally passive, discouraged, demoralized.

The Great Depression was the culminating evidence that America's industrial system was unstable and unpredictable. The shock of the Depression posed a challenge that all members of society were forced to confront. How could the depression be overcome? How could the industrial system be stabilized?

THE ERA OF STABLE WORK AND INDUSTRIAL STABILITY 1933-1970

In the early 1930s critics offered a myriad of plans to fix the industrial system. The election in 1932 of Franklin D. Roosevelt

Table 9: Employees on Nonagricultural Payrolls, 1933-1970: (1) Production

Year	Total	Mining	Construction	Manufacturing
1933	23.7m	744,000	809,000	7.4m
1935	27.1m	897,000	912,000	9.1m
1937	31.0m	1,015,000	1,112,000	10.8m
1940	32.4m	925,000	1,294,000	11.0m
1942	40.1m	992,000	2,170,000	15.3m
1945	40.4m	836,000	1,132,000	15.5m
1947	43.9m	955,000	1,982,000	15.5m
1950	45.2m	901,000	2,333,000	15.2m
1955	50.7m	792,000	2,802,000	16.9m
1960	54.2m	712,000	2,885,000	16.8m
1965	60.8m	632,000	3,186,000	18.1m
1970	70.6m	622,000	3,345,000	9.4m

SOURCE: Ben J. Wattenberg, *The Statistical History of the United States* (New York: Basic Books, 1976)

as president marked a real sea-change in the way America's industrial system operated though the efforts at reform he spearheaded took fifteen years to reach fruition. For workers, Roosevelt's New Deal and the subsequent reforms instituted during World War II marked a decisive shift in the quality of their working life. Roosevelt instituted what Steve Fraser and Gary Gerstle termed "The New Deal Order." Remarkably effective, it lasted until around 1970. It produced the most profound extended period of economic expansion in American history. It closed the divide between the richest and poorest members of society and created the most stable working environment up to that time in the most stable industrial system.

Tables 9 and 10 give indicators of the changing balance between the major sectors of employment between 1933 and 1970. Striking patterns in Table 9 are: (1) the decline in mining—even more marked after 1970—due to the mechanization of mining and the rise of alternative energy sources; (2) the steady rise of the construction industry from the depths of depression in 1933 to the long steady increase following World War II, with the sole exception of 1945 when war orders ceased and the housing boom had yet to begin; and (3) the spectacular increase in the number of manufacturing employees under both political parties and at all levels, especially after World War II. In 1945, the United States produced 50 percent of world manufacturing output.

Table 10 shows the major categories of service producing employment in the same years. Most spectacular is the fourfold increase in the number of government employees at all levels from 1933 to 1970, with more than half the increase occurring from 1950 to 1970, when the severe challenges of the Depression and World War were over. A shifting emphasis in employment patterns in the econo-

Table 10: Employees on Nonagricultural Payrolls, 1933-1970: (2) Service Producing

Year	Transportation & Public Utilities	Wholesale & Retail Trades	Finance, Insurance & Real Estate	Services	Government, Federal, State & Local
1933	2.7m	4.8m	1.3m	2.9m	3.2m
1935	2.8m	5.4m	1.3m	3.1m	3.5m
1937	3.1m	6.3m	1.4m	3.5m	3.8m
1940	3.0m	6.8m	1.5m	3.7m	4.2m
1942	3.5m	7.1m	1.5m	4.1m	5.5m
1945	3.9m	7.3m	1.5m	4.2m	5.9m
1947	4.2m	9.0m	1.8m	5.1m	5.5m
1950	4.0m	9.4m	1.9m	5.4m	6.0m
1955	4.1m	10.5m	2.3m	6.3m	6.9m
1960	4.0m	11.4m	2.7m	7.4m	8.4m
1965	4.0m	12.7m	3.0m	9.1m	10.1m
1970	4.5m	14.9m	3.7m	11.6m	12.5m

SOURCE: Ben J. Wattenberg, *The Statistical History of the United States* (New York: Basic Books, 1976)

my is also noteworthy. While transportation and public utility employment remained almost static after 1945, the other major categories—mainly composed of white-collar workers—rose significantly.

The composition of America's workforce thus changed dramatically between 1933 and 1970. For example, between 1900 and 1950, the proportion of women in the workforce had risen 10 percent. Between 1950 and 1970, the increase was another 12 percent for a total of 40 percent of women in the workforce. In that period, the numbers of married women doubled as a proportion of all women working. Agriculture and mining, "the traditional work of a traditional society," in Robert Zieger's memorable phrase, declined from 25 percent of the work force in 1940 to 5 percent in 1970. White-collar work, meanwhile, continued its steady rise. In 1940 it was estimated that 30 percent of the workforce was white-collar. By 1950, the figure had climbed to 37 percent and by 1970 to 48 percent. By 1960 it had outdistanced blue-collar work for the first time as the largest occupational category.

1933-1935 • A NEW DEAL FOR WORKERS ~ When Franklin Roosevelt entered office in March 1933, the country was at the absolute depths of Depression and on the verge of complete economic freefall. While he had no blueprint to tackle the unprecedented economic problems, he did have expert advice and his own personal experience to draw upon. As Assistant Secretary to the Navy under President Woodrow Wilson, Roosevelt was in government during World War I. He was convinced that America's problems in the 1930s required a mobilization as broad as during the war effort if they were to have any chance. He knew that government would have a key role to play in solving America's economic and industrial problems and that it alone could bring together both sides of industry to work together on the issues. This was in sharp contrast to the ideas of his predecessor, Herbert Hoover, who shared the notion that economic questions were private matters best left to business owners.

In his first one hundred days in office, Roosevelt sent a blizzard of legislation to the Congress to enact measures to provide relief, recovery, and reform. The cutthroat competition that had returned during the early days of the depression was suspended as government brought together firms in each industry to cooperate on an industrial code of conduct that would stabilize the industry and prevent further decline. The National Industrial Recovery Act (NIRA) that set up the machinery to accomplish this also contained a clause—Section 7(a)—that acknowledged the rights of workers to bargain collectively with their employers through representatives of their own choosing. For the first time, it seemed to workers in America's mass production industries, most of whom had not previously been members of labor unions, that the federal government was on their side.

Frances Perkins, the first woman cabinet member and Roosevelt's Secretary of Labor, expressed the government's interest in labor questions: "As a Nation, we are recognizing that programs long thought of as merely labor welfare, such as shorter hours, higher wages, and a voice in the terms and conditions of work, are really essential economic factors for recovery, and for the technique of industrial management in a mass production age."

Workers flooded into unions and major strikes broke out. Unions in textiles and coal mining, industries that had been devastated during the 1920s, aggressively sought to sign up workers, sometimes erroneously allowing workers to think that the country's president wished every worker to join. In the midterm elections of 1934, the most radical Congress in history was returned, a reflection of rising hope and indignation in the country at large. The outcome for workers was the passage in 1935 of Social Security and the National Labor Relations or Wagner Act. The former gave a measure of financial support in old age to the vast bulk of workers across the country for the first time.

The Wagner Act revolutionized America's industrial relations system. Government was required to perform the role of impartial referee between workers and bosses. It stated as a right that workers could choose representatives to bargain for them with management. Elections should be held to see if and who workers wanted to perform that task. The legislation provided machinery to enforce its wishes and outlined what was and was not fair for employers to do to persuade workers that labor unions were not needed. It was no coincidence that Roosevelt was re-elected by a landslide in 1936 or that industrial workers were among his most solid supporters.

Simultaneously with New Deal legislation, unions dissatisfied with the defensive stance of the American Federation of Labor formed a committee to organize mass production workers enthused as never before with the ideal of "industrial democracy." Between 1937 and 1941 millions of mass production workers poured into newly formed unions and new relationships were forged between America's workers and the giant corporations that employed them. Threatening both the New Deal itself and the new dawn for America's labor unions was the U.S. Supreme Court. In a series of decisions in 1935, the Supreme Court struck down as unconstitutional the major legislation underpinning the New Deal, including the NIRA. A constitutional crisis was provoked. Only when this was successfully navigated by Roosevelt was the Wagner Act safe and "industrial democracy" given a chance to grow and prosper.

1930S-1960S • INDUSTRIAL DEMOCRACY ~ At the beginning of the 1930s, the term "industrial democracy" was already of some vintage. It first enjoyed currency during 1917 as the United States came together to fight in World War I. It was a convenient phrase for employers who allowed shop committees of workers to advise on means to increase productivity and just enough say in the workplace to forestall the introduction of unions. For the government, similarly, it was a useful phrase to aid in the harmony it wanted to maximize production in factories producing for the war effort.

For industrial workers, however, it meant a great deal more. It meant securing the right of workers to influence or control working conditions, to bring into the workplace the ideals of political democracy. Through the 1920s, the American Federation of Labor and the Taylor Society developed the concept. So by the 1930s the term industrial democracy had a widely understood meaning. Franklin Roosevelt and the New Deal agencies saw in it a mechanism for putting American industry back on its feet. In its most well developed form the concept was explained by Clinton Golden and Harold Ruttenberg in their 1942 book, *The Dynamics of Industrial Democracy*. Industrial democracy, they maintained, would ensure industrial peace as labor unions brokered relations between workers and employers to maximize production. This concept of industrial relations came to dominate the mass-production industries from the 1940s through the 1960s. To a remarkable degree, industrial peace was attained.

1870s-1930s • INDUSTRIAL SPIES ~ Industrial harmony was hard won. From the 1870s through the 1930s, corporations, in addition to tolerating harsh conditions of work, labored mightily to keep out unions. Many firms demanded employees sign "yellow dog" contracts promising never to join a union. Breaking the contract was grounds for immediate dismissal. Private security forces were established in factories to police the workforce and intimidate workers. Stockpiles of arms and tear gas were kept in case of strikes. Large and small firms retained detective agencies to spy on their employees.

In 1936, the LaFollette Civil Liberties Committee investigated the abuses. Their findings were popularized in two books. One, by Edward Levinson was called *I Break Strikes*. The other by Leo Huberman was titled *The Labor Spy Racket*. The committee estimated that in 1935, American corporations spent $80 million dollars a year spying on their employees. Though operating secretly, it was estimated that the 230 agencies providing such services to corporations employed between 40,000 and 135,000 agents. One labor leader called before the committee stated that he never "knew of a gathering large enough to be called a meeting but small enough to exclude the spy."

Of all the corporations obsessed with keeping control over their workers by keeping out unions the Ford Motor Company was perhaps the worst. From the late 1920s until 1941, Henry Ford delegated labor policy to Harry Bennett, who built a paramilitary force of over 3,000 men. To keep order in the gigantic River Rouge plant outside Detroit, Bennett's Service Department regularly roughed up workers on the assembly lines, beat and even flogged them. In 1932 and again in 1937 as workers attempted to organize into unions, Bennett's men opened up with clubs, blackjacks, pistols and rifles.

1920s-1930s • UNIONS AND THE WORKPLACE ~ While such tactics as those used at Ford were not the norm, industrial discipline in factories was often grim. In retreat throughout the 1920s, labor unions aggressively organized throughout the nation, encouraged by the role of the government after 1933 and by a spontaneous upsurge in strike activity by unorganized workers.

Table 11: Membership in Labor Unions, 1897-2000

Year	Number	Year	Number
1897	350,000	1929	3,440,000
1900	868,000	1933	2,900,000
1904	2,000,000	1940	8,900,000
1910	1,560,000	1945	14,800,000
1917	3,000,000	1954	18,000,000
1919	4,125,000	1962	16,800,000
1923	3,500,000		

SOURCES: Melvyn Dubofsky & Foster Rhea Dulles, *Labor in America: A History*. Sixth Edition. (Wheeling, IL: Harlan Davidson, 1999); Robert H. Zieger, *American Workers, American Unions, 1920-1985*. (Baltimore: The Johns Hopkins University Press, 1986)

An idea of the achievement of organized labor may be gained from a look at the percentages in Table 12. In 1917, 18 percent of non-farm workers were organized into labor unions. In 1935, before the great upsurge, 13.2 percent were in unions. By 1940 the figure was 26.9 percent. At the end of World War II it stood at 35.5 percent and thereafter declined. In 1954 it was at 35 percent. In 1962 it had slid to 30 percent and by 1965 to 25 percent of all workers. Between 1980 and 1995, the fall in union membership had become dramatic, from 20 percent to 15 percent. At the beginning of the twenty-first century, it was at 11 percent. By 1945, it was widely recognized that America's unionized workers were now not only a power in the land but they were the richest labor movement in the world, its members paid relatively more dues than workers in any other country. In comparative terms, however, America's workers had not achieved the kind of solidarity and broad-based industrial democracy achieved elsewhere.

When the Steel Workers Organizing Committee opened its doors in Pittsburgh in 1937, it was overwhelmed with workers wanting to sign up and quickly ran out of membership cards. Similarly, the rubber workers and packinghouse workers flooded into unions. Hard battles were fought against reluctant auto manufacturers and the corporations collectively known as Little Steel. Throughout the nation during 1936 and 1937 workers sat down on the job refusing to move until their grievances and desires to be represented by unions were met. By the end of 1937, major contracts were signed between unions and General Motors, U.S. Steel, the big meatpacking corporations and Akron's tire manufacturers. A new era of industrial relations was ushered in. During World War II, the remaining giants of manufacturing signed contracts with labor unions to form an industrial partnership and practice a form of industrial democracy.

The labor upsurge of the 1930s led to a change in work relations and the expe-

Table 12: Union Membership as a Percentage of the Non-Agricultural Employed Labor Force in Selected Industrial Countries, 1965

Country	Union Membership (000s)	Total Number Employed (000s)	Percentage of Organization
Austria	1,540	2,247	68.5%
Sweden	2,165	3,302	65.6%
Belgium	1,700	3,407	49.9%
Italy	6,320	14,242	44.4%
Australia	1,475	3,448	42.8%
England	8,757	22,621	38.7%
Netherlands	1,430	3,978	35.9%
Germany	7,996	23,733	33.7%
France	3,071	10,243	29.0%
United States	17,299	60,770	28.5%

SOURCE: Derek C. Bok & John T. Dunlop, *Labor and the American Community*. (New York: Simon & Schuster, 1970.)

rience of work in manufacturing. Its success can be accounted for through two main factors. First was the Depression itself. Profitability for companies plummeted. To restore profits, managers needed to make the labor process more stable and predictable. The search for profits throughout the 1920s which had seen the drive system and continual speed-up of work had led to much disruption through rapid turnover of workers, resistance and consequent firings, and an uneven level of production throughout the year as production and demand fell out of step.

In the 1930s as recovery from the worst of the Depression occurred, companies attempted to solve labor problems through a variety of means. Sanford Jacoby noted that between 1929 and 1935 the number of corporations employing 250 or more workers with personnel departments nearly doubled. The number of large firms with centralized hiring and selection increased by half. The percentage of large companies applying formal rating systems for internal promotions increased by 75 percent.

Second, through their own actions, workers aided in this transformation of work from arbitrary management to stable, fair policies. The level of strikes after 1932 increased almost five-fold and their effectiveness climbed. After union recognition and restoration of wage cuts, the most common demands expressed by strikers were for greater fairness and some measure of control over their work. They resisted technological change that altered the social relations of work and disrupted their work routines. They demanded a say in determining the pace and quality of work to be done. Concerns over lack of individual or collective influence over work and the workplace were reflected in demands for grievance procedures. And they wanted an end to arbitrary and divisive management practices with regard to promotions and supervi-

(circa 1973) Labor rights leader Cesar Chavez (third from right) and Coretta Scott King (fourth from right), widow of Dr. Martin Luther King, Jr., lead a demonstration in New York City supporting a consumer boycott of lettuce.

sion. Such anxiety crystallized into spreading demands for seniority systems to root out discrimination and favoritism. Whether or not they were affected by strikes, worker activity spurred large companies in many industries to make the changes noted above.

1940-1945 • WAR AND WORK ～ The change in workplace relations and policies was far from complete by 1940. The necessity of production for the war effort brought government, corporations, and labor unions into much closer contact. For unions, this meant a greater commitment to accommodation with government and business and a sharp rise in union membership. For the duration of the war, both major labor union federations volunteered to keep a No-Strike Pledge. For business, whose profits were guaranteed by war contracts, labor and production stability became even more pressing. Many more businesses signed contracts with labor unions that agreed to police the contract for its duration. Grievances were quickly taken off the shop floor and placed before arbitration bodies. The numbers of supervisory personnel were dramatically increased to counter union influence in matters of grievance and seniority and many firms used the war to increase the speed of production. By war's end, accommodation between unions representing workers and employers in the large, mass-production industries had set the broad outlines of industrial relations in American manufacturing that lasted at least until the 1970s.

1940-1944 • WOMEN DURING THE WAR ～ While the numbers of women in the paid labor force had steadily grown in the twentieth century, World War II represented a great step forward, at least temporarily. Job segregation had characterized the experience of work for women up to 1933. Barriers had broken down somewhat in the Depression years as men were thrown out of work and in some cases replaced by women who could be paid less. Yet during the Depression, unemployment was historically high and social attitudes tended to be hostile to women working outside the home. War, on the other hand, witnessed a frenzied rush to expand the economy and an insatiable need for workers. Even more than during the brief period of World War I, industry ran short of male white workers. Five million women entered the labor force between 1940 and 1944. The government issued a non-discrimination directive early in 1942 and followed it with aggressive campaigns to recruit women workers for traditionally male jobs. "Rosie the Riveter" became a representative of America's patriotic working women. She appeared in magazines, a movie was made, and a song of the same name trumpeted how she was "making history working for victory."

For black women the change effected by war was dramatic. A far greater percentage of black women had worked before 1940 than was the case among white women so the proportion of black women entering the paid workforce for the first time was consequently smaller. Discrimination and prejudice still affected their potential choices. As white women moved from laundries into factories, black women gladly left domestic service and filled their jobs. Only after 1941 with the threat of an embarrassing public demonstration by African Americans did the president establish the Fair Employment Practices Commission. Even then, progress was often slow. In Detroit, large factories imported hundreds of rural whites. It took nearly two years of demonstrations, the storming of a Ford plant by busloads of black women, the active support of government agencies, and threats of citywide strikes by unions for black women to gain employment in the city's factories.

However, for women, World War II brought little of lasting benefit. As Alice Kessler-Harris remarked, "what happened in the war and immediate postwar years represented a response to emergency rather than a shift in attitude." The general pattern of women's employment after 1945 remained much the same as before 1940. The shift to clerical and office jobs continued, but only a slightly greater share of manufacturing jobs were retained by women.

1950-1970 • INDUSTRIAL RELATIONS ~ The enormous rise in union membership as a result of events during the Great Depression and World War II meant that by 1945, 35.5 percent of America's nonagricultural workers were in unions, an historic high. Broken down, the figures are even more startling. In manufacturing, over two-thirds of production workers were covered by collective bargaining agreements. In transportation, coal and metal mining, steel, automobiles, meatpacking, rubber and other basic industries, union coverage ran between 80 percent and 100 percent.

Workers were no longer on their own in confronting the dictates of employers. During World War II, the power of foremen and supervisors was further undermined by the rise of shop stewards, elected by workers in a section to represent them. As they became co-equal with foremen in practice, the caliber of foremen dropped sharply. The increasingly difficult position of foreman was reflected in their own embrace of unionization after 1941. Labor had become a power in the land. Workers commanded respect as never before. The strike wave of 1946 told the story. Gone were the days of employer private paramilitary forces in league with local law enforcement and even state or federal legal and military power. While management was keen to reassert its "right to manage" after what it regarded as the erosion of that power in wartime conditions, in manufacturing it did so in the context of bargaining with the representatives of the workers to produce binding contracts.

Unions were able to use their power through the principle of seniority to assert influence in personnel actions like promotion, layoff, transfer and rehire. Further, they pushed beyond seniority to make issues of job content, operation rates, and other production issues matters for discussion. Even more alarming for managers, unions sought to discuss financial policies as they related to wage determination. In negotiations with General Motors in 1946, United Automobile Workers (UAW) president Walter Reuther challenged them to open their books and prove they could not afford to offer workers a better wage. GM obstinately declined, preferring to wait out a 113 day strike, despite government encouragement to settle on a "fair" raise.

To keep their managerial prerogatives, GM fiercely continued to police its right to manage but in return opened up a new day for production workers in America. In 1948, GM proposed to peg wage rises to the cost-of-living index and to increases in productivity. This was a tremendous break-through for workers. The company also recognized the union as a permanent presence by accepting that new employees should join the union. In a 1953 study of eighteen companies, the National Planning Association concluded that company executives "appeared to look upon the union as a means of implementing a large range of managerial functions. For this reason they were not apprehensive of union interference with the exercise of managerial functions. At the same time the union was actually extending its control of the jobs of its members by assuming some responsibility along with management for exercising these functions. The result was a remarkable degree of compatibility of interests."

1950-1970 • GAINS FOR WORKERS
∼ What emerged by 1950 was a system of industrial relations bounded by contracts in which managers struggled with unions over the retention of managerial prerogatives in return for higher wages, incentive pay, and fringe benefits. The results for production workers were remarkable. Between 1950 and 1970, real weekly earnings increased by 70 percent. Contracts included paid vacations of up to four weeks for long-term workers by 1960, up from one week before World War II. By 1967, three-quarters of all workers under forty were able to move to the suburbs. Rising rates of home ownership, cars and other consumer durables attested to rising expectations among workers, as did the high incidence of installment buying and the doubling in the number of working wives between 1945 and 1960. As David Brody noted, "For the industrial worker of this era, the union contract was becoming the passport to a better life."

Throughout the industrial world, the early part of the twentieth century saw the development of what was called the "welfare state." This was the obligation of the government to make sure that its citizens had access to quality health care, pensions for disability and old age, unemployment relief, and equal access to education. In other words, the right of each citizen to minimum standards of life without the worry they would starve or be abandoned was to be guaranteed. In the United States, the concept of the welfare state had not been accepted in the same way. At best, by 1946, it was incomplete; at worst, it was completely inadequate.

As the dream of the welfare state in America faded, it came to labor unions to try to establish it for their members. During World War II health and insurance benefits were negotiated by some unions. Beginning with the United Mineworkers in their 1946 contract, welfare and retirement benefits funded from a royalty on coal tonnage set the standard for other union contract negotiators. By 1949-50, pensions were generally established in the basic industries. In 1955, the UAW and Ford agreed to set up a Supplementary Unemployment Benefit (SUB) to provide up to 26 weeks of unemployment payments for laid-off employees.

In return, managers in the 1950s and 1960s expected unions to control shop-floor militancy and to put a hold on disruptions of production by workers. Indeed, government legislation held unions legally responsible for actions by workers that violated signed contracts. To be effective in bargaining with employers, unions had to be able to keep workers united and in line with the contract. Just like managers, unions were committed to what was called the "workplace rule of law."

By the late 1960s, the incidence of workers voting down union-negotiated contracts began to rise. Opposition to union leadership hardly known in the

1933-1970

1950s became commonplace in the 1960s. In part it was due to the distance that had evolved between well-paid union leaders used more to dealing with employer counterparts and the minutiae of highly complex contract negotiation and enforcement than with their own members. It was also due, however, to a complex set of circumstances connected to generational change, the anxieties of the Vietnam War era, social and racial pressures, and the oppressive nature of work. The incidence of strikes rose. Absenteeism grew. Rank and file militancy re-emerged.

1940-1970 • RACE AND WORK ~ As in World War I, the quest to maximize production for World War II drew on workers previously marginalized. Almost one million black workers entered the labor force during World War II. By 1945, they constituted 8 percent of all defense workers. In all of manufacturing, black workers increased their presence by 150 percent from 1940 to 1945. The influx of blacks into northern cities and new destinations like Los Angeles, led to violent white backlashes that worked themselves out not only in acts of petty discrimination but in race riots across the nation.

Labor unions, especially those in industrial plants affiliated with the Congress of Industrial Organizations (CIO) recognized that their success depended on organizing black workers just as it did every other worker. The UAW became a powerful force in the quest for black civil rights. In Detroit it prevented racial tensions becoming even more serious and even took over its local at the Packard aircraft engine facility when its white members struck against the presence of African Americans. Other unions were not always so enlightened. Important unions in the defense industries like the

(1947) Body Shop. By 1947, African Americans had successfully broken through a "color ceiling" into many more types of work. Even so, most black workers were in low-wage jobs outside the core of large industrial corporations. Seen here, an African-American man in coveralls smokes a cigarette next to rows of tires outside an auto body shop in Pittsburgh.

1890 ~ WORK AND THE WORKPLACE

International Association of Machinists (IAM) and the Boilermakers respectively banned black members entirely and imposed discriminatory practices on its black membership.

As a result of war, black workers found greater possibilities, and some of their gains lasted. Between 1939 and the mid-1950s the median annual income of black workers rose from 45 percent of that of white workers to 57 percent. The possibilities of industrial work and the rapid expansion of government work, especially after President Harry Truman's Executive Order of 1948 banning discrimination in federal employment both increased job security and increased earning potential. Advances on the legal front also aided black workers from the 1940s through 1970. Nevertheless, patterns of discrimination and deeply entrenched attitudes, fears, and resentments against people of color continued to inform white attitudes.

As black migration from the rural South continued after 1945, the number of blacks exceeded the jobs available to them. They concentrated in the deteriorating ghettos of inner cities. In these circumstances, black employment came to consist mainly of low-wage jobs outside the core of large industrial corporations, some jobs in the core industrial sector in industries to which blacks had already gained some access before World War II, and in the rapidly expanding service sector. In almost all situations, blacks were more likely to be placed in low-wage positions with little or no potential for promotion or specialized training opportunities.

During the 1960s, patterns of black occupation did change, largely as a result of actions by black people themselves and by government reforms including affirmative action programs. Black male employment in core goods industries increased from 502,000 in 1960 to 682,000 in 1970. The proportion of black males employed as managers rose from 2.1 percent to 3.5 percent. The rapid expansion of federal welfare programs provided an alternative to low-paying employment, forcing employers to look to Puerto Ricans, Chicanos, Mexican immigrants, and other people of color. Title VII of the 1964 Civil Rights Act prohibited discrimination in employment. Yet progress remained stubbornly

Table 13: Unemployment Rates, 1949-1979

Year	All Workers	White Males	Nonwhite Males	White Females	Nonwhite Females
1949	5.9	5.6	9.6	5.7	7.9
1954	5.5	4.8	10.3	5.6	9.3
1959	5.5	4.6	11.5	5.3	9.4
1964	5.2	4.1	8.9	5.5	10.6
1971	5.9	4.9	9.1	6.3	10.8
1974	5.6	4.3	9.1	6.1	10.7
1979	5.8	4.4	10.3	5.9	12.3

SOURCE: David M. Gordon, Richard Edwards & Michael Reich, *Segmented Work, Divided Workers: The Historical Transformation of Labor in the United States* (Cambridge & London: Cambridge University Press, 1982)

slow and uneven. Even if employers tried to make changes, all-white work forces resisted change. A number of unions continued to insist on segregated locals. Throughout the nation, unions often served as gatekeepers controlling or even excluding black applicants for apprenticeships and skilled jobs, thwarting the law's intent through antiquated application and seniority procedures.

In the South and many Northern cities, previously all-white industries like textiles saw the integration of black workers or even the creation of all-black work forces as a result of employer desire for cheaper labor and the exit of white workers for less strenuous office and clerical work. By the second half of the 1960s, work rights and civil rights had forged a powerful partnership. Civil rights leader Martin Luther King Jr., was assassinated in Memphis in 1968 as he worked to end discrimination among the city's garbage workers demanding dignity, decent wages, benefits, and job security.

(1963) Switchboard. In the thirty years after 1970, the American economy was transformed yet again. Seen here is the old way of telephone operation. Two women sit at a reception desk, wearing headsets and connecting customer calls at the Western Electric Company offices.

THE POST-INDUSTRIAL SYSTEM, THE RISE OF THE SERVICE SECTOR & THE DIGITAL REVOLUTION, 1970-2000

In the thirty years after 1970, the American economy was transformed yet again. Manufacturing industry, which had been concentrated in the Northeast and Midwest, moved much of its capacity to the South and West or overseas as employers looked for cheaper labor and to escape labor unions. Between 1980 and 1990 for example, the Northeast and Midwest lost 1.5 million manufacturing jobs while the South and West gained 450,000 such jobs. Manufacturing workers showed a dramatic decline as a proportion of the workforce, even while their overall numbers held steady. Table 14 shows the stagnation of Agriculture, Mining, and Manufacture, and the spectacular increase in the service, or post-industrial economy.

1970s • A Decade of Challenge ~ By the end of the 1960s, the American economy faced some severe problems. Finally restored from the devastating effects of World War II, Japan and western European countries were able to challenge U.S. domination of world and domestic markets. One effect of the Vietnam War was to stimulate inflation and to adversely affect America's ability to compete in foreign markets. The dollar was in trouble. In steel, automobiles, and electronics during the 1970s, foreign-made goods were cheaper, better made, and claimed an ever-greater share of the American market. Prices on basic goods were driven up as a result of unforeseen or natural disasters like the 1974 oil embargo. Unem-

Table 14: The Labor Force, 1960-1998

Year	Agriculture	Mining	Manufacture	Construction	Trade	Other	Total
1960	5.97m	0.71m	17.15m	3.64m	14.05m	32.55m	74.06m
1970	3.46m	0.52m	20.75m	4.82m	15.01m	34.13m	78.68m
1980	3.36m	0.98m	21.94m	6.22m	20.19m	46.61m	99.30m
1990	3.22m	0.72m	21.35m	7.76m	24.62m	60.85m	117.91m
1997	3.40m	0.63m	20.84m	8.30m	26.77m	69.61m	129.56m
1998	3.38m	0.62m	20.73m	8.52m	27.20m	71.01m	131.46m

SOURCES: *Historical Statistics of the United States, Colonial Times to 1970* (Government Printing Office: Washington D.C., 1975); *Statistical Abstract of the United States, 1998* (Government Printing Office: Washington D.C., 1998)

---

ployment rose. Between 1965 and 1979, corporate profits were cut in half.

1980s • RE-STRUCTURING AND SPECULATION ~ By the late 1970s, businessmen shifted resources and priorities in their companies. Barry Bluestone among others referred to the "de-industrialization" of America. Plants were shut down or had their capacities reduced. Production was moved to low-wage regions or outside the United States altogether. Resources were shifted from low-profit manufacturing to less capital-intensive services. Investments were refocused from production to speculation. The case of General Electric shows the change. In the course of the 1980s, GE sold off its consumer electronics division, its small appliance division, and its semiconductor division, the heart of the industrial giant's traditional business. At the same time it acquired the entertainment corporation RCA, including television network NBC, investment firm Kidder Peabody, credit card company Montgomery Ward, the Burton Group Financial Services and Travel Mortgage companies, and the Employers Reinsurance Corporation. In a decade, one of America's great manufacturing companies transformed itself into a conglomerate of service corporations.

REBOUND: THE GREAT BOOM OF THE 1990S

The malaise and feelings of decline that had characterized much of American economic life after 1970 were startlingly reversed in the 1990s, at least as far as American productivity and competitiveness were concerned. By the late 1990s, unemployment, inflation, mortgage rates, and oil prices had fallen to levels not seen in 30 years. The stock market saw its index rise four-fold between 1991 and 1999. Key industries like steel, automobiles, telecommunications, microchip manufacturing, computer software, entertainment, aircraft, and finance were once again creative, innovative, and profitable. As around the turn of the twentieth century, again in the 1920s, the 1950s, and the 1980s, a wave of corporate mergers produced a new set of powerfully competitive companies. Between 1992 and 1998, the

1970-2000

value of all corporate mergers advanced nearly ten-fold.

American success was based partly upon the misfortunes of its competitors—the incredible costs of German reunification and the collapse of the Japanese economy brought on by crisis in its banking and real estate sectors—and partly by changes in the United States. During the 1990s American companies adopted the best of their competitors' organizational and technological techniques. A revolution in telecommunications that made fax machines, E-mail, cell phones, and overnight package delivery universal led to tremendous gains in productivity in America's factories, offices, and hospitals.

Fortune Magazine's Best Companies to Work For in 1999

1. Container Store (Dallas, TX)
2. Southwest Airlines (Dallas, TX)
3. CISCO Systems (San Jose, CA)
4. TD Industries (Dallas, TX)
5. Synovus Financial (Columbus, GA)
6. SAS Institute (Cary, NC)
7. Edward Jones (St. Louis, MO)
8. Charles Schwab (San Francisco, CA)
9. Goldman Sachs (New York, NY)
10. MBNA (Wilmington, DE)
11. CDW Computer Centers (Vernon Hills, IL)
12. Scitor (Sunnyvale, CA)
13. Frank Russell (Tacoma, WA)
14. Qualcomm (San Diego, CA)
15. Great Plains (Fargo, ND)
16. Finova Group (Phoenix, AZ)
17. Plante & Moran (Southfield, MI)
18. AFLAC (Columbus, GA)
19. Graniterock (Watsonville, CA)
20. Pfizer (New York, NY)

Even more important, advances in computers finally made their mark throughout American industry and business. Software programs developed to the point where complex operations previously only possible for highly skilled technicians could be carried out, as one Princeton economist memorably put it, by "numbskulls." The Internet and World Wide Web were equally important. Comparing the computer revolution of the 1990s to earlier revolutionary developments like steam power, the railroad, electricity, and the internal combustion engine, the authors of the text *Who Built America?* noted, "Like these technologies, computerization promised a revolutionary transformation in the structure of production, the organization of society, and the meaning of work." Like all revolutionary changes before it, computerization did not benefit all of America's workers evenly or even positively.

1980s • THE CONTINGENT WORK FORCE ~ One of the startling effects of the revolutionary shift from a manufacturing-based economy to a service-based economy was on job security. One of the great goals of labor unions from the turn of the twentieth century until World War II was to regularize employment. Great victories were achieved when, for example, the practice of casual hiring of longshoremen on a day-to-day basis was ended on the West Coast in the 1930s and the principle of seniority was established in manufacturing during the decade. Companies themselves strove to put an end to high turnover of production workers in the automobile industry during the 1920s. From 1945 until the 1980s, most workers in America could expect to join a company and if they chose, stay with it for their entire working life. One of the

Table 15: The Contingent Work Force, 1995

	Independent Contractors	On-Call & Day Laborers	Temporary Help Agency Workers	Workers Provided by Contract Firms	Total Contingent Workers
Manufacturing	2%	1%	2%	1%	6%
All Services	6%	2%	1%	1%	10%
Transportation & Public Utilities	5%	2%	1%	1%	9%
Wholesale & Retail Trade	4%	1%	0.4%	0.2%	5.6%
Finance, Insurance & Real Estate	10%	0.4%	1%	1%	12.4%
Other Services*	8%	2%	1%	0.4%	11.4%
Public Administration	0.4%	1%	0.2%	1%	2.6%

* Includes business & repair services, personal services, entertainment & recreation services, and professional services.

SOURCE: Stephen A. Herzenberg, John A. Alic & Howard Wial, *New Rules For A New Economy: Employment and Opportunity in Postindustrial America* (Ithaca: ILR Press, 1998)

---

most profound changes beginning in the 1980s was the decline of a long-term commitment between employer and employee. Instead, there was a growing part of the workforce described as contingent. The contingent workforce consisted of temporary, leased, independently contracted, seasonal, and non-permanent part-time workers.

Spurred on by the problems of the 1970s in addition to downsizing workforces to cut costs, employers strove to avoid costs related to benefits such as employer-funded health care programs. Between 1980 and 1989 the number of temporary workers more than doubled and the number of part-time workers increased by 40 percent. Half of all new jobs in the period were part-time jobs. Women, who made up 47 percent of the workforce nevertheless filled more than two-thirds of the temporary and part-time jobs. Some sought more flexibility in their employment but contingent workers overall received lower hourly pay and fewer employer-paid benefits. In a 1989 study, John Sweeney and Karen Nussbaum noted that less than 25 percent of all part-time workers received health coverage on the job while 75 percent of all full-time workers did; less than 25 percent of part-time workers were members of a pension plan while over half of all full-time workers were.

Simple arithmetic yields the information that 11 percent of manufacturing workers were non-permanent while 33 percent of all service workers were non-permanent in 1995-96. The numbers become even more significant if we track changes in the numbers of workers employed in these sectors. Table 17

Table 16: Part-Time Workers* in Manufacturing and Major Service Industries, 1979-1996

	1979	1989	1996
Manufacturing	4%	4%	5%
All Services	23%	23%	23%
Transportation, Communications & Utilities	9%	9%	10%
Wholesale Trade	7%	8%	8%
Retail Trade	38%	38%	37%
Finance, Insurance & Real Estate	13%	12%	12%
Business & Repair Services	20%	19%	16%
Personal Services	46%	38%	34%
Entertainment & Recreation Services	40%	36%	37%
Professional Services	23%	25%	24%
Public Administration	7%	7%	6%

* Part-time work is defined as less than 35 hours per week

SOURCE: Stephen A. Herzenberg, John A. Alic & Howard Wial, *New Rules For A New Economy: Employment and Opportunity in Postindustrial America* (Ithaca: ILR Press, 1998)

shows clearly that as employment in the service industries rose dramatically, median hourly wages in most sectors fell, a reflection of the increase in contingent and part-time workers. Wage losses fell most heavily on women, blacks and Hispanics, and those with the least education.

1980S-1990S • EARNINGS, EDUCATION, AND THE WORKING POOR

The poor were "rediscovered" with the 1962 publication of Michael Harrington's *The Other America*. This book revealed that around 20 percent of all Americans lived in poverty during America's age of affluence. Similarly, in the 1980s, the term "working poor" entered the national public vocabulary. These were not the traditional poor—the unemployed or long-term sick or disabled. They were able-bodied, doing their best to work to keep themselves and their families above crippling debt. In 1997, there were 9 million people identified by the Department of Labor as living in poverty of whom one-quarter worked full-time, year round. It found that nearly 60 percent of the working poor were women and that minority women were twice as likely to be poor as white women. Almost 3 million poor workers were in families with children under six.

The new economy of the 1980s and 1990s continued a growing gap between the best-paid workers and the worst. By the late 1990s the top 10 percent of full-time workers averaged $1,200 per week in earnings while the bottom 10 percent averaged $275. The key to better earnings lay in more education. In 1979 the average college graduate earned 38 percent more than the average high school graduate. By 1999, the gap had widened

Table 17: Employment & Wages in Manufacturing & Major Service Industries, 1979-1996

	1979	1989	1996	Employment Change, 1979-1996	Wages Change, 1979-1996*
Manufacturing	22.0m	20.8m	19.7m	-10%	-10%
All Services	58.3m	74.6m	83.8m	44%	-4%
Transportation, Communications & Utilities	6.2m	6.8m	7.3m	18%	-17%
Wholesale Trade	3.3m	3.9m	4.4m	33%	-10%
Retail Trade	13.9m	17.3m	19.3m	39%	-12%
Finance, Insurance & Real Estate	5.3m	7.0m	7.0m	32%	10%
Business & Repair Services	2.8m	5.6m	6.2m	121%	-7%
Personal Services	2.9m	3.6m	3.5m	21%	2%
Entertainment & Recreation	0.9m	1.1m	2.0m	122%	-6%
Professional Services	17.9m	22.7m	27.4m	53%	9%
Public Administration	5.2m	6.5m	6.6m	27%	-3%

* Wages change reflects median hourly wages in 1996 dollars.

SOURCE: Stephen A. Herzenberg, John A. Alic & Howard Wial, *New Rules For A New Economy: Employment and Opportunity in Postindustrial America* (Ithaca: ILR Press, 1998)

Table 18: Changes in the Wage Gap Between White Males and Everyone Else, 1970-1998

Year	White Men	Black Men	Hispanic Men	White Women	Black Women	Hispanic Women
1970	100%	69.0%	N/A	58.7%	48.2%	N/A
1975	100%	74.3%	72.1%	57.5%	55.4%	49.4%
1980	100%	70.7%	70.8%	58.9%	55.7%	50.5%
1985	100%	69.7%	68.0%	63.0%	57.1%	52.1%
1990	100%	73.1%	66.3%	69.4%	62.5%	54.3%
1995	100%	75.9%	63.3%	71.2%	64.2%	53.4%
1998	100%	74.9%	61.6%	72.6%	62.6%	53.1%

SOURCE: National Committee on Pay Equity, "The Wage Gap: Myths and Facts" in Paula S. Rothenberg ed., *Race, Class, and Gender in the United States*. Fifth Edition (New York: Worth, 2001)

to 71 percent. Real wages for male high school graduates fell in those 20 years by 20 percent while those without a high school diploma fell by one-third.

Wages have also been affected by union membership. In 1998, unionized workers earned overall nearly one third more than nonunion workers and were more likely to earn health and pension benefits. African-American union workers earned 45 percent more than non-unionized African-American workers.

1970-2000

Unionized Hispanics earned 54 percent more than their non-unionized counterparts. Race and gender still mattered and made a difference in earnings potential even when education and skills levels were equal.

1965-1999 • THE CHANGING COMPOSITION OF THE WORK FORCE ~ Since 1965, massive immigration has changed the face of America and its workplaces. One result is that the racial composition of the work force has altered dramatically. The educational level of the workforce has also changed, a factor with an important impact on career opportunity. In 1970, fewer than 54 percent of all adults over 25 had completed high school and only 10 percent had completed college. By 1997, 83 percent of all adults over 25 had completed high school and 24 percent had completed college. Within these figures, the racial balance of educational attainment also shifted. For the first time in 1997, the high-school graduation rate of young blacks and whites was on a par at 86 percent and 88 percent respectively.

Hispanics, however, were stuck at 62 percent, a level that had not changed from the previous decade. It could partially be explained by the continued immigration of people of Hispanic origin and the generally lower high school completion rates of all immigrants.

At the college level more women than men enrolled, a factor that tended toward the narrowing of levels of women's and men's wages. Disparities of race also persisted. Despite the narrowing of high school graduation rates, only six out of ten young blacks enrolled in college compared to nearly seven out of ten whites and five out of ten Hispanics. Furthermore, while 25 percent of all whites over 25 graduated college, only 13 percent of all blacks and 11 percent of all Hispanics graduated. Asians and Pacific Islanders outpaced all groups at 42 percent, though.

Finally, the gender balance of the workforce continued its historic shift. In 1940, 28 percent of American women were employed. In 1967, 41 percent of women worked for wages. By 1999 it had risen to 60 percent. Within those figures the proportion of employed women working year-round rose from 52 percent to 70 percent. During the same period the labor force participation rate of men actually declined from 80 percent to 75 percent while the proportion of employed men working year-round rose only slightly from 74 percent to 77 percent. By 1999 almost one in four wives earned more than their husbands, an increase of 7 percent over 1981. Increasingly, women worked before childbirth and returned to work while their children were still of a pre-school age, a phenomenon particularly prevalent among women who maintained families on their own. Single-parent families rose in the United States from 16 percent in 1975 to 26 percent in 1998. By 1999, 66 percent of single mothers with children under the age of 18 worked, as did 60 percent of single mothers with children under the age of 6.

1990s • WORKING CONDITIONS ~ In a Department of Labor report, *Futurework*, published in 1999, workplace conditions were examined as a prelude to making predictions concerning the first fifty years of the 21st century. The report stated: "Today, American workers are healthier and more productive than ever. Young workers are better protected against workplace injuries. Families suffer fewer workplace-related tragedies. Employers can focus resources on increasing their competitive positions, rather than paying workers' compensation for preventable injuries and illnesses."

In 1913, the Bureau of Labor Statistics reported 23,000 industrial deaths among the U.S. work force of 38 million, or 61 deaths per 100,000 workers. In 1998, there were 6,026 workplace deaths, or less than 5 per 100,000 workers. According to the Centers for Disease Control, if the 1999 labor force of 130 million were subject to the same risk of dying from occupational injury as those in 1933, an additional 40,000 workers would have died from preventable occupational hazards. Blowing its own trumpet, the Department of Labor report made the case for government regulation. It reported that work death rates dropped by 38 percent between 1948 and 1970, when the Occupational Safety and Health Administration (OSHA) was created. In the 22 years following its establishment, however, work death rates dropped 61 percent.

Government regulations have also revealed the extent of occupational diseases in America. Such deaths and disabilities often have a long latency period. Prolonged exposure to hazardous chemicals or physical agents resulted in cancers, silicosis and other lung diseases, and hepatitis. In 1999 occupational injury resulted in 600,000 needle-stick injuries in the health care professions with potentially lethal consequences while 38 percent of nurses endured back injuries during their career. Among coal miners, benefits paid to miners with black lung disease topped more than $1 billion per year in the 1990s, a sum attributable to mechanization in the industry that raised more dust than previously. One consequence of the digital revolution that included the universal use of computers was the rise in musculoskeletal disorders, such as carpal tunnel syndrome and other repetitive motion disorders. By 1998, 34 percent of all lost-workday injuries and illnesses and one out of every three dollars spent on workers' compensation was attributed to such ailments.

1990s • Race, Gender, and Discrimination ~ Despite changes mandated since 1948 when President Truman ordered the integration of the armed forces and the federal government, and laws passed by Congress since the landmark Civil Rights Act of 1964, discrimination on the basis of race and gender continued in the workplace. Women were able to make far more of a contribution to family incomes and became a major force in business and political life. The black middle class grew. Hispanics and newer immigrants emerged as strong contributors to the U.S. economy. Even so, in 1998 alone more than 12,500 claims of discrimination filed with the U.S. Equal Employment Opportunity Commission based on race or color, national origin, gender, religion, age, or disability, were upheld or resolved in favor of the complainant. Discrimination in hiring persisted at the end of the 1990s. In one study, Hispanic testers received 25 percent fewer job interviews and 34 percent fewer job offers than other testers. Another study revealed that when researchers sent comparably matched resumés of men and women to restaurants, in high-priced establishments men were more than twice as likely to receive an interview and five times as likely to receive a job offer than a woman.

As minorities and women moved in larger numbers through higher education and sought positions in management, a new concept became current: "the glass ceiling." This was the notion that an invisible barrier existed through which women and minorities could not pass in their quest for promotion and equality of opportunity. According the report of the Glass Ceiling Commission in 1995 only 0.6 percent of senior management positions in the nation's largest companies were held by blacks, 0.4 percent by Hispanics, and 0.3 percent by Asian Americans. Women held between 3 percent and 5 percent of these positions. On the other hand although men made up only 43 percent of the work force they held 95 percent of the senior management jobs.

Fortune Magazine's Top 20 Companies For Minorities, 1999

1. Union Bank of California (San Francisco, CA)
2. Fannie Mae (Washington D.C.)
3. Public Service Company of New Mexico (Albuquerque, NM)
4. Sempra Energy (San Diego, CA)
5. Toyota Motor Sales (Torrance, CA)
6. Advantica (Spartanburg, SC)
7. SBC Communications (San Antonio, TX)
8. Lucent Technologies (Murray Hill, NJ)
9. Darden Restaurants (Orlando, FL)
10. Wal-Mart Stores (Bentonville, AR)
11. Allstate (Northbrook, IL)
12. Chase Manhattan (New York, NY)
13. Marriott International (Bethesda, MD)
14. US West (Denver, CO)
15. Federal Express (Memphis, TN)
16. Southern California Edison (Rosemead, CA)
17. Bank of America (Charlotte, NC)
18. Hyatt (Chicago)
19. TIAA-CREF (New York, NY)
20. Xerox (Stamford, CT)

The reasons become obvious when legal cases are examined. Headlines were made, for example, when excerpts from an audiotape made at a meeting of Texaco executives, was reported in the *New York Times* in 1996. On it three senior executives were discussing a class-action lawsuit brought by black employees who charged that the oil company had discriminated against them and created a racially hostile atmosphere. Racial epithets, the belittling of black cultural observance in the form of Kwanzaa, and discussion of destroying records to protect themselves provided ample independent support for the EEOC ruling, which stated there was reason to believe Texaco guilty of company-wide racial bias.

Between 1991 and 1997, the restaurant chain Denny's paid $50 million to settle discrimination claims in their franchises across the nation. Perhaps the worst of these cases against the company involved the refusal of service to six African-American secret service agents in Maryland in 1993. Supermarkets seemed particularly prone to discriminate against their workers. In 1997, Publix supermarkets, one of the largest chains in the nation, paid $81.5 million to settle accusations that it had systematically denied promotions, raises, and preferred assignments to women. The suit covered more than 100,000 women who had worked for the company since 1991. In 1994, Lucky Stores paid out $107 million covering 14,000 women, and in the same year Safeway settled for $7.5 million. In 1996, Albertson's was judged to pay $29.4 million in a discrimination case involving women and Hispanics. Promotion discrimination against women also cost home improvement giant Home Depot $87.5 million in 1997.

Continued discrimination on the basis of gender and race did not always come from managers or a corporate ethos. Reporting on a case brought against the airline American Eagle, the *Wall Street Journal* noted in April 1999, "In interviews, company documents and court depositions, current and former employees said that racial slurs were as common as tire changes." Despite elaborate company policies on racial discrimination, black mechanics were harassed by co-workers and supervisors. Complaints to management were ignored. Similar claims made by a New York City police officer were reported in a *New York Times* article in September 1998. Double standards at the police academy, sexual harassment by squad commanders, retaliation and cover-ups in response to complaints were all reported. The paper had disclosed systematic racism in the Manhattan office of the U.S. Marshal's service the previous year including discrimination against black employees, the use of racial slurs and threats against a black Deputy Marshal, and using a picture of Martin Luther King Jr. for target practice. They were not isolated incidents.

1980s • FAMILY FRIENDLY EMPLOYEE BENEFITS ~ Employee benefits grew over the course of the twentieth century. Initially introduced by companies such as Ford before World War I as mechanisms to keep down labor turnover among the skilled and semi-skilled, with the New Deal of the 1930s government became convinced that employee benefits were a public responsibility. By 1975, about 95 percent of all full-time office and plant workers had some type of employer-sponsored medical coverage and life insurance. By the end of the 1980s when both spouses worked in more than half of all married-couple families, it became less and less common for women to leave the workforce for any significant period following childbirth. Working wives contribution to family income exceeded 30 percent. In the 1980s, new kinds of employee benefits that reflected the changing rate of women's labor force participation were introduced. Such new kinds of benefits were dubbed "family-friendly" in recognition of women's double burdens for work responsibilities and those associated with the family, from childcare to elder care.

In any given year after 1978 and before 1995, between 9 percent and 11 percent of all women in full-time employment had no benefits at all. It found that, even for a benefit so universally accepted as health insurance, for all women, average income, level of education, duration of marriage, and length of full-time employment were positively related to the number of years of coverage. Even government-mandated benefits were not available to all. The Family and Medical Leave Act of 1993, for example, was found three years later to provide coverage to only 66 percent of the nation's full-time workforce.

Perhaps more disturbing given the obvious improvements in the lives of working women brought about by the creation of family-friendly benefits, the study found that those women who took advantage of them often found themselves, as with similarly situated men, with career-related disadvantages compared to colleagues who spent greater "face-time" with each other. The dismissive notion of the "Mommy track" identified with family-friendly benefit usage together with employer non-compliance with the acts establishing such benefits helps explain the small utilization rates found in family leave studies during the mid-1990s.

1970-2000

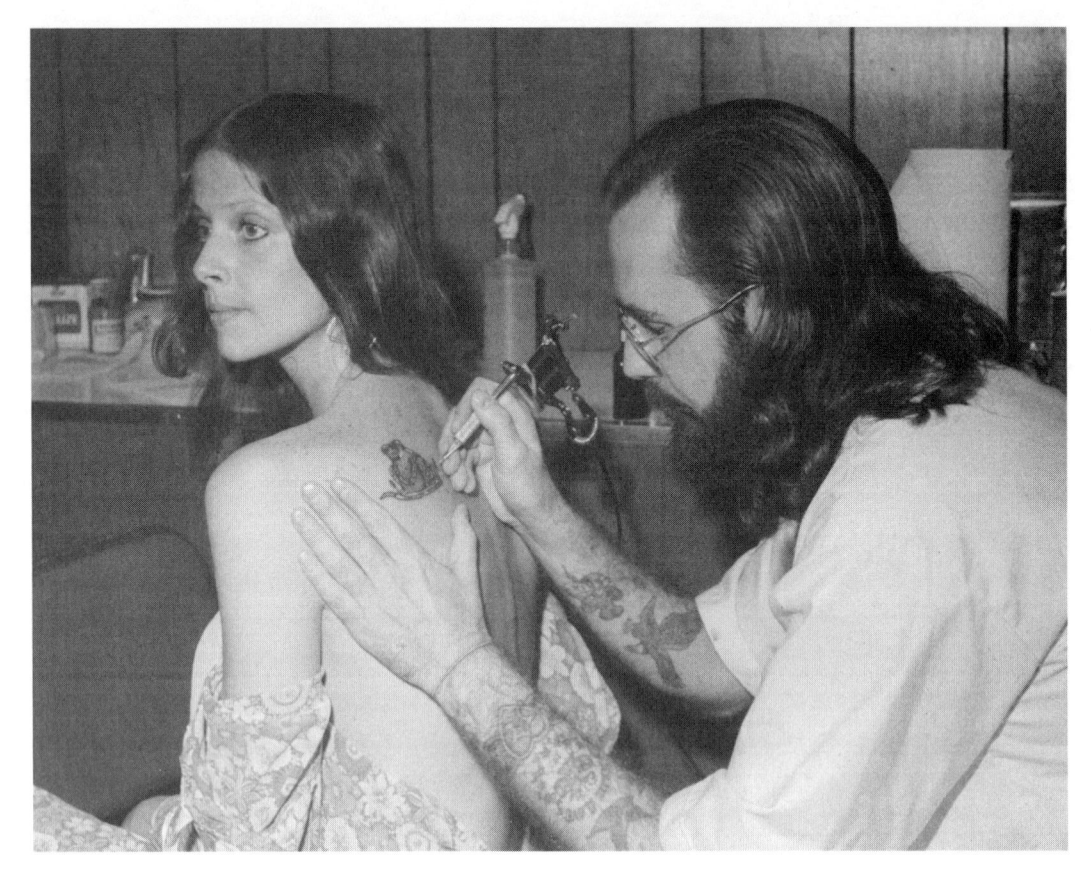

(1973) Women went outside the stereotypes of traditional work wardrobe, helping transform the tattoo industry into mainstream fashion.

Table 19: Percentage of Working Women Enjoying Traditional Benefits, 1978-1995

Benefits	1978	1985	1988	1991	1995
Medical	77	78	73	82	95
Life Insurance	55	67	61	68	82
Retirement	56	63	59	70	85
Training	43	61	59	58	66
Profit sharing	18	24	20	23	28
Stock Options	15	20	16	18	N/A
Free Meals	15	18	16	16	N/A
Free Merchandise	20	28	20	20	N/A
Paid Sick Leave	69	76	68	76	N/A
Paid Vacation	75	80	73	82	N/A

The above table shows the extent of employee benefits as traditionally defined among women. It is based on a long-term survey of women between 1978 and 1995.

SOURCE: Richard K. Caputo, "The Availability of Traditional and Family-Friendly Employee Benefits among a Cohort of Young Women, 1968-1995," in *Families in Society: The Journal of Contemporary Human Services*, 81 (July 2000).

Finally, women of color were far less likely to enjoy employee benefits than white women. Much of the reason for this had to do with problems of initial access to benefit-related jobs and to the number of years they were likely to hold such jobs.

CONCLUSION

The nature and experience of work and the workplace underwent enormous change in the course of the twentieth century. At the beginning of the twentieth century, a majority of young people entering the workforce could expect to spend a lifetime in back breaking manual labor punctuated by periods of seasonal, short-term, and long-term unemployment. By the end of World War II, a majority of people entering the workforce could expect to spend a working lifetime in some branch of manufacturing supported by union benefits won through a negotiated contract with a large employer.

At the end of the century, a majority of people entering the workforce could expect to spend a working life in an office but also to change careers at least three times. By the end of the century, work experience was less affected by the exclusion of categories of people from particular occupations and career possibilities than in 1900. Education became a better determinant of income expectation and job advancement. Industrial relations had become less violent and confrontational. For those with limited educational achievements, a series of contingent or part-time work could well mean that two or three jobs held at the same time were needed to stay above poverty levels.

Lest too rosy a picture emerge, it should be remembered that relations between employers and employees did not essentially change. The drive for profit and

Table 20: Percentage of Working Women Enjoying Family-Friendly Employee Benefits, 1978-1995

Benefits	1978	1985	1988	1991	1995
Paid Maternity	24	47	35	40	N/A
Unpaid Maternity	29	49	25	26	N/A
Flexible Work Hours	N/A	45	39	41	45
Child Day Care	N/A	05	04	06	N/A
Paid Personal Time	N/A	N/A	37	46	N/A
Time Off for Child Care	N/A	N/A	13	10	N/A
Time Off for Elder Care	N/A	N/A	N/A	16	N/A
Flexible Menu of Benefits	N/A	N/A	N/A	23	N/A
Subsidized Child Care	N/A	N/A	N/A	N/A	10
Leave	N/A	N/A	N/A	N/A	84
Other	N/A	17	16	10	N/A

SOURCE: Richard K. Caputo, "The Availability of Traditional and Family-Friendly Employee Benefits among a Cohort of young Women, 1968-1995," in *Families in Society: The Journal of Contemporary Human Services*, 81 (July 2000).

efficiency was always in tension with the expression of individual identity so necessary to humankind. Supervisors, managers, and workers remained in conflict. The so-called "New Economy" continued to co-exist with the so-called "Old Economy." In their highly optimistic introduction to "The New Economy Index: Understanding America's Economic Transformation" (1998), Robert D. Atkinson and Randolph H. Court noted that the New Economy was still maturing. They produced a table that showed the ideal differences in the two types of economy. Bill Gates, Microsoft, and the high-tech industries were clearly in the New Economy. Rebecca Amoto—quoted at the beginning of this chapter—and millions of others remained in the Old Economy: service workers from fast-food restaurants like McDonald's and Denny's and a majority of the newer immigrants, some of whom had made possible a resurgence of the old "sweatshops" in the textile industry. It is still too soon to learn if their typology is an accurate or universal reality for workers and companies in the New Economy.

Table 21: Keys to the Old and New Economies

Issue	Old Economy	New Economy
Economy-wide Characteristics		
Markets	Stable	Dynamic
Scope of Competition	National	Global
Organizational Form	Hierarchical, Bureaucratic	Networked
Industry		
Organization of Production	Mass Production	Flexible Production
Key Drivers of Growth	Capital/Labor	Innovation/Knowledge
Key Technology Driver	Mechanization	Digitization
Source of Competitive Advantage of Scale	Lowering Cost Through Economies	Innovation, Quality, Time-to-Market, and Cost
Importance of Research/Innovation	Low-Moderate	High
Relations With Other Firms	Go It Alone	Alliances & Collaboration
Workforce		
Policy Goal Incomes	Full Employment	Higher Real Wages &
Skills Training	Job-Specific Skills	Broad Skills & Cross-
Requisite Education	A Skill or Degree	Lifelong Learning
Labor-Management Relations	Adversarial	Collaborative
Nature of Employment Opportunity	Stable	Marked by Risk &
Government		
Business-Government Relations Opportunities	Impose Requirements	Encourage Growth
Regulation	Command & Control	Market Tools, Flexibility

SOURCE: Robert D. Atkinson & Randolph H. Court, *The New Economy Index: Understanding America's Economic Transformation* (Washington D.C.: Progressive Policy Institute, 1998)

BIBLIOGRAPHY

Baron, Ava, ed. *Work Engendered: Toward a New History of American Labor.* Ithaca: Cornell University Press, 1991.

Brody, David. *Workers in Industrial America: Essays on the 20th Century Struggle.* Second Edition. New York: Oxford University Press, 1993.

Cobble, Dorothy Sue, ed. *Women and Unions: Forging a Partnership.* Ithaca: ILR Press, 1993.

Department of Labor. "Futurework: Trends and Challenges for Work in the 21st Century." (1999) http://www.dol.gov/dol/asp/public/futurework/report/letter.htm

Dubofsky, Melvyn and Foster Rhea Dulles. *Labor in America: A History.* 6th ed. Wheeling, IL: Harlan Davidson, 1999.

Edwards, Richard. *Contested Terrain: The Transformation of the Workplace in the Twentieth Century.* New York: Basic Books, 1979.

Herzenberg, Stephen A., John A. Alic and Howard Wial. *New Rules For A New Economy: Employment and Opportunity in Postindustrial America.* Ithaca: ILR Press, 1998.

Jones, Jacqueline. *A Social History of the Laboring Classes: From Colonial Times to the Present.* Malden, MA & Oxford, UK: Blackwell, 1999.

Katzman, David M. *Seven Days A Week: Women and Domestic Service in Industrializing America.* Urbana: University of Illinois Press, 1978.

Kessler-Harris, Alice. *Out To Work: A History of Wage-Earning Women in the United States.* New York: Oxford University Press, 1982.

Kocka, Jurgen. *White Collar Workers in America, 1890-1940: A Social-Political History in International Perspective.* London & Beverly Hills: Sage, 1980.

Menzies, Heather. *Whose Brave New World? The Information Highway and the New Economy.* Toronto: Between the Lines, 1996.

Piore, Michael J. and Charles F. Sabel. *The Second Industrial Divide: Possibilities For Prosperity.* New York: Basic Books, 1984.

Romero, Mary. *Maid in the U.S.A.* New York & London: Routledge, 1992.

Theriault, Reg. *How To Tell When You're Tired: A Brief Examination of Work.* New York: W.W. Norton, 1995.

Schwantes, Carlos Arnaldo. *Hard Traveling: A Portrait of Work Life in the New Northwest.* Lincoln & London: University of Nebraska Press, 1994.

Zieger, Robert H. *American Workers, American Unions, 1920-1985.* Baltimore: The Johns Hopkins University Press, 1986.

INTERNET RESOURCES

AFL-CIO
This comprehensive site is that of the largest federation of labor unions in the United States. It includes information on affiliates, campaigns, how and why people join unions.
http://www.aflcio.org/front/unionand.htm

BUREAU OF LABOR STATISTICS
Any kind of statistics on industry, companies, and their workers is likely to be found here, as well as how the economy is doing. Sections on the site provide links to the Economy at a Glance, Career Guides, Inflation & Spending, Working and Looking for Work, How Much People Earn, Worker Safety & Health, Productivity, International Statistics, Online

Magazines, Economic Analysis, and more.
http://www.bls.gov

EQUAL OPPORTUNITIES PUBLICATIONS INC.
The site contains a series of career magazines directed to forwarding the cause of equal opportunities. They include: Equal Opportunity, Woman Engineer, Minority Engineer, Careers & the Disabled, and Workforce Diversity for Engineers and IT Professionals.
http://www.eop.com

FAMILIES AND WORK INSTITUTE
A non-profit organization committed to finding research-based strategies to foster mutually supportive connections among workplace, families, and communities. A gem of a site it contains sections on Policy Worksite research, including its important National Study of the Changing Workforce, and Evaluation and Technical Assistance for business, government, community organizations on design, implementation, and evaluation of work life solutions. They publish around twelve new research reports each year.
http://www.familiesandwork.org

GEORGE MEANY CENTER FOR LABOR STUDIES
The closest there is to a national repository of labor's history in America. It is sponsored and funded by the AFL-CIO. Most fascinating for the purposes of this chapter is the Archives Section.
http://www.georgemeany.org

NATIONAL LABOR RELATIONS BOARD
This site reflects the work of the organization set up in 1935 under the Wagner Act or National Labor Relations Act. Its purpose is to organize secret ballots to see if, and by who, workers in a particular plant wish to be represented in their negotiations with management and to investigate charges of "unfair" labor practices against their workers by managers. The site contains facts, a weekly summary, press releases, public notices, decisions, and rules and regulations. It is a good place to check out how labor relations are going in America.
http://www.nlrb.gov

Stephen Burwood
SUNY, Geneseo

Timeline

1500

1492 ~ Christopher Columbus lands in the New World

c. 1500 ~ Nicolaus Copernicus, a Polish mathematician, develops new theories of a sun-centered universe

1565 ~ Spanish settle the first American city, St. Augustine, Florida

1600 ~ Isaac Newton makes significant contributions to mathematics, physics, astronomy, and optics

1600s ~ Francis Bacon envisions the power of science as the savior of the human race

1600s ~ Johannes Kepler and Galileo Galilei develop theories about the existence of other planets and their motion

1607 ~ Establishment of Jamestown

1610 ~ Establishment of Santa Fe

1619-1808 ~ American colonies import slaves

1619 ~ First African slaves arrive in America at Jamestown, Virginia

1622 ~ First Indian attack on Jamestown

1628 ~ William Harvey describes the circulation of blood, in England

1630 ~ Establishment of Boston

1630 ~ John Winthrop lectures Puritans on board ship about model behavior before arriving in America

1678 ~ Model steam carriage made in China

1688 ~ Organized horse racing begins at Malvern Hill, near Richmond, Virginia

1698 ~ The Royal Theater in London holds regular boxing matches

1700s ~ Richard Arkwright invents the spinning jenny and the power-driven spinner

1775 ~ Boston Tea Party protests taxation without representation

1776-1779 ~ American Revolution

1786 ~ Three-wheel, steam-powered carriage developed in Britain

1787 ~ Constitutional Convention ratifies the Constitution for the new republic

1789 ~ Congress authorizes recruitment of marshals to serve warrants and subpoenas

1790-1820 ~ State legislatures introduce policies of mandatory retirement for some public officials

1790 ~ Naturalization Law excludes non-whites from citizenship

1796 ~ Edward Jenner develops smallpox vaccination in England

1800

early 1800s ~ Thomas Jefferson designs his house Monticello, the Rotunda at the University of Virginia, and the Virginia state capitol in Richmond, setting the style for Neoclassical architecture for monumental buildings

early 1800s ~ Eli Whitney invents interchangeable parts, making mass production possible

early 1800s ~ New Orleans forms police force to control slavery

1800 ~ Congress occupies the first section of the Capitol, the north wing

1800 ~ Philadelphia becomes the largest city

1800 ~ President John Adams moves into the newly constructed White House

1800s ~ Society regards wealth as a sign of virtue

1803 ~ Louisiana Purchase doubles the size of the U.S.

1805 ~ Oliver Evans builds the first steam-powered motor vehicle in the U.S.

1806 ~ Congress authorizes construction of the first federally financed road, Cumberland Road

1810 ~ Federal census surveys occupations for the first time

1814 ~ British troops set fire to the White House

1820-1860 ~ Decline of the apprenticeship system

1820s-1830s ~ Factories employ entire families of immigrants

1827 ~ *The Freedom Journal* is the first African American newspaper

1829 ~ Introduction of railroad sleeping cars

1830

1830-1870 ~ Old Immigration from England, Ireland, Scandinavia, and Germany

1830-1930s ~ Steamboat era causes towns to flourish along major rivers

1830 ~ First public railroad, the Baltimore and Ohio, begins operation

1830 ~ Joseph Smith Jr. publishes the *Book of Mormon* – the holy book for The Church of Latter-day Saints

1830 ~ Indian Removal Act forces southern Indian tribes to relocate west of the Mississippi

1830s-1840s ~ Emerson and Thoreau popularize Hinduism in America

1830s-1900 ~ "Cult of Domesticity" advocates women as the protectors of morality

1831-1838 ~ Thousands of Indians die during forced relocation on the "trail of tears"

1831-1840 ~ Alexis de Tocqueville publishes his classic book *Democracy in America*

1832 ~ Steam-powered buses in use in London

1835 ~ Texas Revolution against Mexico cedes the Texas territory to the U.S.

1837 ~ Economic crisis brings high unemployment, bread riots, and rent strikes

1838 ~ Americans adopt the London Prize Ring Rules for Boxing

1838 ~ Boston forms police department

1840

1840-1950s ~ Steam-powered railroad opens the American West to settlement

1840 ~ 70% of American males over the age of 65 still work

1840s ~ George Goodyear invents rubber tires

1842 ~ First use of anesthetic [ether] on humans in the U.S.

1844 ~ New York forms police department

1844 ~ Provisional Government of Oregon bans slavery and orders all free blacks age 18 or older to leave the territory

1845 ~ Beginning of Manifest Destiny doctrine that justifies taking western territory

1846 ~ Texas joins the union

1847 ~ Michigan abolishes capital punishment

1848 ~ First skyscraper, a five-story, iron factory building is completed in New York
1848 ~ Gold rush begins in California
1848 ~ Mexico cedes California to the U.S.
1848 ~ Women hold first Women's Right Convention in Seneca Falls, New York
1849 ~ Mechanization of tin can production inaugurates factory canning

1850

1850 ~ Census shows a great increase in the types of occupations
1850 ~ Congress makes the first federal land grants for developing U.S. railroads
1850 ~ Debates rage over restricting slavery in the western territories
1850 ~ Feminist Theology emerges – the argument that the biblical story of creation is proof of man and woman's equality
1850 ~ Fugitive Slave Law requires whites to return runaway slaves
1850s ~ Female moral reformers attack prostitution as the product of male lust
1850s ~ Invention of the elevator by Elisha Otis paves the way for skyscrapers
1850s ~ Invention of the Bessemer steel process
1850s ~ Machines make possible the mass production of boots and shoes
1851 ~ Land Act gives whites in California control over Mexican territory
1853-1929 ~ Orphan trains transport homeless or impoverished children from urban to rural areas
1853 ~ Gadsden Purchase adds southern Arizona and southern New Mexico to U.S. territory
1853 ~ Japan opens doors to the U.S. for trade
1857-1866 ~ Americans lay first transatlantic telegraph cable to Europe
1857 ~ *Dred Scott* case establishes slaves as legal personal property
1858 ~ Colorado gold rush begins
1859 ~ Darwin's *Origins of the Species* theorizes that man is descended from apes
1859 ~ Edward Drake discovers in Pennsylvania the first oil well
1859 ~ Great American Tea Company pioneers supermarkets
1859 ~ Oregon "Bill of Rights" contains a Negro Exclusion Law that remains on the state's law books until 1926

1860

1860-1880 ~ Silver rush populates Nevada and the Dakotas
1860-1900 ~ Children under the age of 15 produce 20% of the family income
1860 ~ Three million slaves live in southern states
1860s ~ Improved meat packing plants and railroads make transporting meat more accessible
1860s ~ Proliferation of sewing machines
1860s ~ Some states begin to require judges to retire due to advancing age
1861-1865 ~ One-fifth of the American population die in the Civil War
1862-1867 ~ Widespread Indian uprisings
1862-1869 ~ Irish and Chinese laborers build transcontinental railroad across the U.S. connecting it at Promontory Point, Utah

TIMELINE ~ 1909

1862 ~ Congress establishes a system to provide pensions for disabled soldiers

1862 ~ Homestead Act provides free land to pioneer settlers

1864 ~ Chinese workers comprise one-fourth the population of Hawaii

1865-1870 ~ Great cattle drives roll from Texas northward

1865 ~ Congress authorizes the Secret Service

1865 ~ Ice making machines produced

1866 ~ First labor union formed in the U.S.

1866 ~ Fourteenth Amendment declares that all persons born or naturalized in America are citizens

1867-1868 ~ Freed slaves elect sharecropper farming over paid wages

1867 ~ Joseph Lister creates antiseptics for use in surgery in England

1867 ~ U.S. purchases Midway Islands

1868 ~ Florida passes state law banning convicted felons from voting

1868 ~ U.S. purchases Alaska

1869 ~ First full service advertising agency inaugurated

1869 ~ Panama Canal construction begins; completed 1914

1869 ~ Wyoming is the first state to grant women the vote

~

1870

early 1870s ~ The Stein Manufacturing Company of Rochester, New York mass produces caskets in many styles, colors, and grades

1870s ~ Introduction of electricity for streetlights and factories

1870 ~ Fifteenth Amendment declares all men eligible to vote without regard to race

1870 ~ John D. Rockefeller forms Standard Oil of Ohio

1870 ~ Seven out of ten working women hold jobs as domestic servants

1870 ~ Widespread use of child labor

1870 ~ Women in Montana gain the right to sue, enter into contracts, and serve on juries

1870s-1880s ~ "Passionless marriages" control birth rate

1870s-1880s ~ Germans Carl Benz and Gottlieb Daimler create the essential elements of the gasoline automobile, including the spark plug

1870s ~ Henry Heinz invents new methods of packing under steam to make the large-scale production of pickling possible

1870s ~ Police exchange photos of criminals

1870s ~ Refrigerated railcars permit long-range shipment of meats, fruits and vegetables

1871 ~ During the Great Fire of Chicago, many of the iron buildings melt, causing designers to turn to steel supports

1871 ~ Formation of the National Association of Professional Baseball Players

1871 ~ Indian Appropriation Act permits railroads to lay tracks across Indian lands

1872 ~ Establishment of Yellowstone — the first national park

1873 ~ Comstock Law prohibits possessing any book, pamphlet, paper, writing, advertisement, circular, print, picture or drawing of an immoral nature, including educational materials

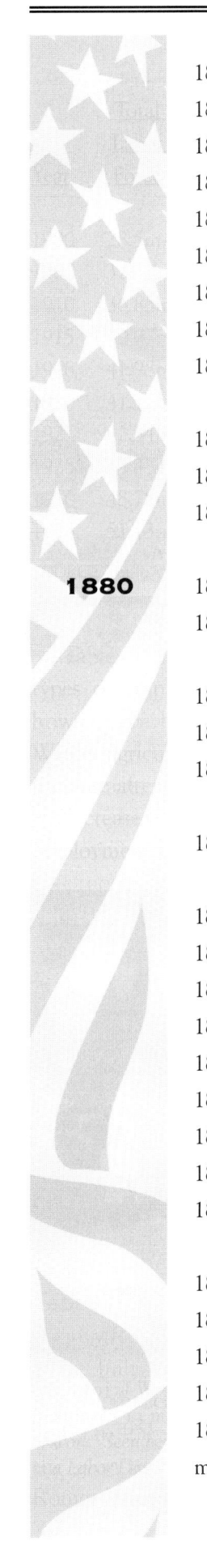

1875 ~ American Express establishes the first railroad pension plan

1875 ~ Kentucky Derby is founded by Colonel M. Lewis Clark

1876 ~ Alexander Graham Bell assisted by George Watson invents the telephone

1876 ~ First experiments with gasoline powered engines in the U.S.

1876 ~ First national restaurant chain, Harvey House, is founded

1876 ~ Sioux Indians slaughter Custer's men at Little Bighorn

1876 ~ Thomas Edison invents the phonograph

1877-1907 ~ Widespread labor violence

1877 ~ President Hayes removes all federal troops from southern states, ending Reconstruction

1878 ~ Massachusetts is the first state to collect unemployment statistics

1879 ~ Thomas Edison invents the light bulb

1879 ~ Wanamaker places first full page advertisement, in Philadelphia

1880

1880-1900 ~ Proliferation of birth control devices

1880-1900 ~ Russell Conwell becomes famous for his sermons on the virtues of wealth, which he preaches 6,000 times

1880-1930 ~ New Wave immigration, mainly from Southern and Eastern Europe

1880 ~ Coffee roasting technique is developed

1880 ~ The weekly *Independent* is the most influential religious paper in the country, with over 6,000 clergymen on its mailing list

1880s-1890s ~ Interracial alliances of workers and farmers forge the first national union, the Knights of Labor

1880s-1920s ~ Mexican Americans throughout the Southwest began printing more newspapers

1880s ~ Cafeterias become popular in large cities

1880s ~ Construction of sod houses

1880s ~ Increase in tenement housing in cities

1880s ~ Increase of poor immigrants and migrant farmers into cities

1880s ~ Introduction of electric rail transport and gasoline powered automobiles

1880s ~ Railroad companies create the first professional managers

1880s ~ Using alternating current, Nikola Tesla develops dynamos, motors, and transformers

1881-1900 ~ State courts rule that labor reform laws violate the rights of employers to enjoy the freedom to operate their businesses

1881 ~ Creation of the American Red Cross

1881 ~ Thomas Edison invents the one horsepower generator

1882 and 1884 ~ Chinese Exclusion Act restricts Chinese immigration

1882 ~ German physician Robert Koch discovers the tuberculosis bacterium

1883 ~ Completion of the Brooklyn Bridge in New York City

mid 1880s ~ Business begins to regard unemployment as a distinctly different problem from poverty

1885 ~ Children's Aid Society of New York City offers a summer home for children at Bath, Long Island

1885 ~ First professional football game takes place in Latrobe, Pennsylvania

1885 ~ First funeral chapel built in the U.S.

1885 ~ Invention of the safety bicycle

1886 ~ Capture of Geronimo ends formal warfare between whites and Native Americans

1886 ~ Chicago establishes eight-hour work day

1886 ~ Coca Cola is developed

1886 ~ Henry Grady delivers his New South speech in New York

1886 ~ Knights of Labor call a strike against the railroads

1887 ~ Congress passes the Interstate Commerce Act to control certain economic practices of railroads

1887 ~ Dawes Act calls for a redistribution of Indian reservation land

1887 ~ General Allotment Act wipes out the communal lands of Native American nations

1887 ~ Louis Pasteur first demonstrates use of antibiotics, in France

1887 ~ U.S. College of Embalming opens

1888 ~ George Eastman invents celluloid rolls of film for use in Kodak cameras

1888 ~ Modern electric motor opens the way for consumer appliances

1888 ~ Thomas Edison invents the motion picture camera

1889-1932 ~ Two African Americans are lynched every week

1889 ~ Pan American Union established to deal with matters of common concern in Western Hemisphere nations

~

1890

1890 ~ Embalming replaces ice as the main method of preserving the appearance of dead bodies

1890 ~ Development of diptheria antitoxin in Germany

1890 ~ Indians are massacred at Wounded Knee

1890 ~ First forest set aside for conservation, the Sierra redwood groves

1890-1910 ~ Emergence of the New Woman and the ideal of companionate marriage

1890 ~ Introduction of subway systems

1890s ~ Construction of high-rise residential buildings

1890s ~ Proliferation of two- and three-story American Queen Anne frame houses

1890s ~ Fusion alliance threatens the white supremacy wing of the Democratic Party

1890s ~ States enact statutory rape laws

1890s ~ Electric trolleys replace walking as the main form of transportation in cities

1890s ~ Development of modern submarines

1890s ~ Indoor bathrooms prevalent in urban homes of the wealthy

1890s ~ Women begin to express favorable opinions about enjoying sex

1890s-1910s ~ Illuminated and talking advertisements introduced

1890s-1920 ~ Consumer activists help improve working conditions in factories

1891 ~ First American electric car produced

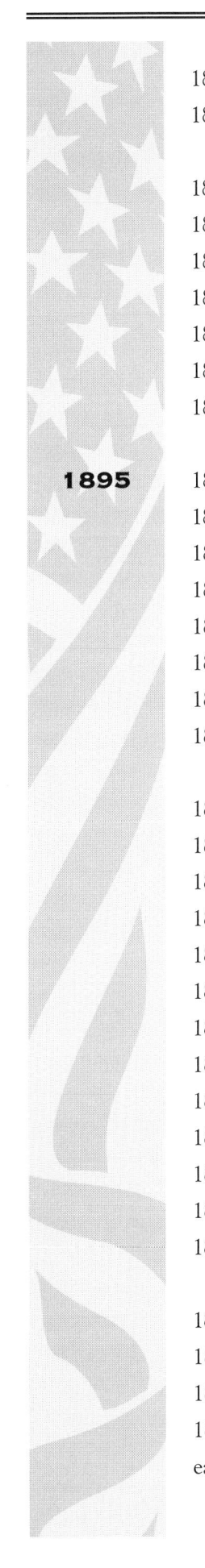

1891 ~ Federal meat inspection laws enacted

1891 ~ Dr. James Naismith invents basketball at the YMCA Training School in Springfield, Massachusetts

1891 ~ Forest Reserve Act gives presidents the authority to proclaim permanent forest reserves

1891 ~ First federal prison opens

1892 ~ Foundation of the National Consumer League

1893 ~ World Columbian Exposition held in Chicago presents new technology and products

1893 ~ First American gas-powered automobile produced

1894 ~ New York City conducts investigations into police corruption

1894 ~ Origination of Hockey in the United States

1895

1895 ~ Completion of America's largest residence, the Biltmore House near Ashville, NC

1895 ~ Congressional legislation prohibits the transport of any lottery material across state lines

1895 ~ Marconi invents ship-to-ship communications

1895 ~ Wilhelm K. Roentgen discovers X-rays, in Germany

1896-1915 ~ U.S. manufacturers produce 35,000 electric cars

1896 ~ Free rural postal delivery proliferates mail order catalogs

1896 ~ Henry Ford experiments with the production of gas-powered automobiles

1896 ~ *Plessy v. Ferguson* declares it illegal for blacks to ride in the same railroad car as whites and that a person with mixed blood is black

1897 ~ Alaskan gold rush begins after the discovery of gold in the Klondike

1897 ~ Construction of Steeplechase Park at Coney Island

1897 ~ Development of the Stanley Steamer auto

1897 ~ Establishment of the first police training school, in New York

1897 ~ First Zionist World Congress

1897 ~ John Torrance invents condensed soup

1898-1899 ~ Spoiled food and yellow fever kill U.S. troops in Cuba

1898-1925 ~ Proliferation of installment credit plans

1898 ~ 200,000 men volunteer for the Spanish American War

1898 ~ Annexation of Hawaiian Islands

1898 ~ C.W. Post invents Grapenuts cereal

1898 ~ Establishment of the first Buddhist temple in the U.S.

1898 ~ Only 17,000 U.S. troops of the 200,000 men who volunteered make it to Cuba in time to fight in the Spanish American War

1898 ~ U.S. fleet conquers the Spanish navy in a one-day fight at Manila Bay in the Philippines

1899 ~ Annexation of the Samoan Islands

1899 ~ Open door trade policy with China initiated

1899 ~ The term "home economics" is first used and leads to academic study

early 1900s ~ Publication of social protest novels and essays that deal with relationships of racial and class oppression

1900

early 1900s ~ Women become involved in the conservation movement

1900-1910 ~ Frank Lloyd Wright designs 'Prairie' houses

1900-1910 ~ Poor city services, crowded unsanitary conditions, and undernourished people in tenements cause squalor and proliferate diseases

1900-1910 ~ Proliferation of 'bungalow' houses in California

1900-1915 ~ Mail order houses, complete in every detail, replace some custom construction

1900-1915 ~ Reform movement replaces elaborate Victorian houses with the rustic bungalow or the modest colonial home

1900-1915 ~ Robber barons of industry rule

1900-1919 ~ Andrew Carnegie gives $350 million for social causes

1900-1919 ~ Rapid expansion of the railroads across the country

1900-1920 ~ "Social gospel" expects churches, not government, to deal with social injustice

1900 ~ Size of middle class families falls by half, from an average of seven or eight children per couple in 1800 to about four children per couple in 1900

1900 ~ About 20% of Americans die before reaching age 5; less than half survive to age 60

1900 ~ Color photo reproduction provides cheap, eye-catching images for ads

1900 ~ Formation of United States Civil Service Retirement Association

1900 ~ German physicist Max Planck publishes his quantum theory of energy stating that heated objects emit units in quanta instead of being discharged continuously

1900 ~ Marriage rates steadily decline beginning in 1850; by 1900, 10% of marriageable women choose to remain single

1900 ~ Non-whites are excluded from most union membership

1900 ~ Only effective drugs available for treating disease are digitalis, quinine, and opium

1900 ~ Pension plan for soldiers and federal employees consumes 30% of the federal budget

1900 ~ Significant segment of the American population consider gambling a sin

1900 ~ U.S. Army Yellow Fever Commission confirms mosquitoes as the disease carrier of malaria

1900 ~ U.S. bans all Chinese immigration except for diplomats, students, and merchants

1901 ~ Electrolux and Hoover introduce the first vacuum cleaners

1901 ~ New York City introduces the first law governing speed

1901 ~ NYC Tenement House Act requires that no new tenement could occupy more than 70% of its lot, thereby making tenements more livable

1901 ~ Queen Victoria dies, ending the repressive Victorian era; Edwardian era begins

1901 ~ Spindletop oil plume gushes and the Texas black gold rush begins

1902-1906 ~ Ten major magazines, exploiting the trend toward exposés, have a combined circulation of three million copies

1902 ~ President Theodore Roosevelt inaugurates his Square Deal program

1902 ~ U.S. Public Health Service identifies the hookworm parasite devastating the South

1903; 1907 ~ Supreme Court rules against unions, giving business full reign over labor

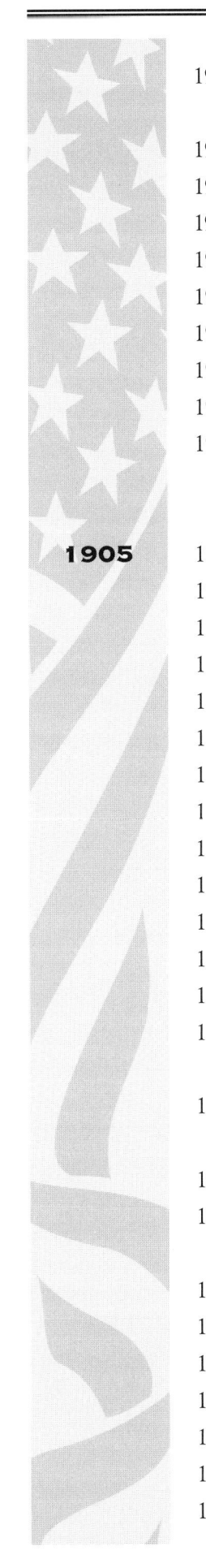

1903 ~ Director D.W. Griffith produces the first feature-length film, *The Great Train Robbery*, which lasts eleven minutes

1903 ~ Formation of the American Power Boat Association

1903 ~ Formation of the Ford Motor Company

1903 ~ Mexicans strike against the Pacific Electric Railway Company for equal wages and parity

1903 ~ W.E.B. Du Bois opposes racial discrimination in *The Souls of Color Folk*

1903 ~ Wright brothers' gasoline-engine aircraft successfully flies at Kitty Hawk

1904 ~ Formation of International Professional Hockey League

1904 ~ Olympic games held in St. Louis at the Louisiana Purchase Exhibition

1904 ~ Scotland Yard demonstrates fingerprinting at the St. Louis World's Fair

1904 ~ Union Station in Washington, D.C. is the only complete example inspired by the City Beautiful movement

1905

1905 ~ Andrew Carnegie endows a foundation for the retirement of college teachers

1905 ~ Einstein theorizes that light is composed of particles that he calls photons

1905 ~ Last yellow fever epidemic in the U.S. strikes New Orleans

1905 ~ Oregon hires the first policewoman in America

1905 ~ Pennsylvania establishes the first highway patrol

1905 ~ Physician William Osler argues that men should retire from work at the age of 60

1905 ~ President Theodore Roosevelt is the first president to be submerged in a submarine

1906 ~ Construction of the Bronx River Parkway begins

1906 ~ Creation of the FBI

1906 ~ Lee De Forest invents the vacuum tube, essential to the development of electronics

1906 ~ Pure Food and Drug Act sets standards for food and drug control

1906 ~ U.S. Census Bureau reports the divorce rate at one in fifteen marriages

1907-1917 ~ Nine states abolish or sharply limit the death penalty

1907 ~ Albert A. Michelson becomes the first American scientist to win a Nobel Prize for his invention of the interferometer to measure stellar spaces

1907 ~ Indiana is the first state to pass a sterilization law; twenty-nine additional states pass sterilization legislation by 1935

1907 ~ Leo Hendrik Baekeland patents the first completely synthetic plastic, Bakelite

1908 ~ First mental health organization established, the Connecticut Society for Mental Hygiene

1908 ~ First compulsory pasteurization law enacted, in Chicago

1908 ~ Ford introduces the first inexpensive car, the Model T

1908 ~ Formation of the General Motors Corporation

1908 ~ Foundation of Federal Council of Churches by 33 denominations

1908 ~ Hybrid corn is the United States' most valuable crop, adding $1.6 billion to the economy

1908 ~ Supreme Court rules in favor of restricting working hours for women

1909 ~ First use of photography to catch speeders

TIMELINE ~ 1915

1909 ~ Foundation of National Association for the Advancement of Colored People

1909 ~ Gibson Girl anticipates modern woman's wardrobe

1909 ~ Karl Landsteiner classifies blood groups, in Austria

1909 ~ Paul Poiret discards the corset as a fashion necessity

1909 ~ Seven thousand Japanese plantation workers in Hawaii stage a four month long strike

1909 ~ The Indianapolis 500, a 2.5 mile automobile race, begins

1909 ~ Alice Ramsey becomes the first woman to drive a car across the U.S., capturing Americans' imagination and interest in automobiles

1909 ~ Commission on Economy and Efficiency calls for compulsory retirement at age 70 and supports the creation of a pension fund financed at employee expense

~

1910

1910-1919 ~ Development of large apartment buildings and cooperative apartments in New York City

1910 ~ Boy Scouts of America founded

1910 ~ Einstein develops his theory of relativity

1910 ~ Enrollment of women in college rises from 20% in 1870 to 40% in 1910

1910 ~ Epidemics of yellow fever, malaria, cholera, and smallpox decline

1910 ~ Flexner Report is the first study to question the inadequacy of American medical schools and poor training of physicians

1910 ~ Inauguration of airmail service

1910 ~ Jack Johnson becomes first African American heavyweight boxing champion

1910 ~ Public health programs begin to be effective

1910 ~ Salvarsan first used to combat syphilis

1910 ~ Theodore Roosevelt is the first president to ride in an airplane

1910 ~ Vaudeville is at the peak of popularity

1910s ~ Development of standardized tests to determine racial intelligence

1910s ~ Eugenics movement declares that one's destiny is determined by one's genes, and supports sterilization of genetically inferior people

1910s ~ Mass production of blouses in sweatshops

1911 ~ Discovery of measles as a viral infection

1911 ~ First publicly advertised maternity wear

1911 ~ First American transcontinental flight

1911 ~ Harriet Quimby becomes the first American woman to earn a pilot's license

1911 ~ Mann Act prohibits transporting women across state lines for immoral purposes

1911 ~ Polish chemist Casimir Funk creates vitamins

1912 ~ African American Garrett Morgan invents the gas mask to keep firefighters from being overcome by smoke

1912 ~ British luxury liner, the *Titanic*, sinks, killing 1,500 passengers

1912 ~ Congress creates United States Public Health Service

1910

1912 ~ Discovery of Vitamin A

1912 ~ F.W. Woolworth has 600 stores

1912 ~ Formation of the Chamber of Commerce

1912 ~ Native American Jim Thorpe relinquishes his gold medals in the pentathlon and decathlon in the Stockholm Games when officials learn he had played professional baseball and football

1913-1917 ~ President Wilson enacts laws to support unions and workers

1913 ~ Approval of Hetch Hetchy dam amid protests of destroying National Park lands

1913 ~ Development of mammography to detect breast cancer

1913 ~ Ford begins the mass production of automobiles and perfects assembly line production

1913 ~ Foundation of the Cremation Society of America

1913 ~ Foundation of the American Cancer Society

1913 ~ Initiation of water chlorination for water purification

1913 ~ Introduction of the first mass-produced candy, Life Savers

1913 ~ Kenyon Law prohibits the sale of alcohol in states that want to ban it

1913 ~ Personal income taxes levied (Sixteenth amendment)

1913 ~ President Wilson establishes the U.S. Commission on Industrial Relations

1913 ~ The only foreign born residents in the U.S. ineligible for citizenship are Asians

1914-1918 ~ Introduction of chemical warfare and airplanes as new weapons of war

1914-1918 ~ World War I

1914-1920 ~ In the U.S., German-language press has a circulation of one million, the Polish and Yiddish press each have one million subscribers, the Italian American press has 700,000, and the Swedish American press has 500,000

1914 ~ Christian Scientists, whose religion objects to military service, support the war effort by sending supplies to Europe

1914 ~ Clayton Anti-Trust Act is designed to strengthen the Sherman Anti-Trust Act by prohibiting corporate practices such as price fixing

1914 ~ Completion of the Panama Canal

1914 ~ Federal Trade Commission Act is designed to prevent unfair methods of competition in interstate commerce such as trade boycotts, mislabeling and adulteration of commodities, and false claims to patents

1914 ~ First voice communication by radio

1914 ~ Henry Ford institutes the five-dollar day for his factory workers, greatly improving their wages and quality of life

1914 ~ Margaret Sanger risks arrest by opening up birth control clinics and importing and distributing contraceptives illegally

1914 ~ Mayo Clinic opens in Minnesota

1914 ~ Theodore W. Richards becomes the first American to win a Nobel Prize for chemistry for his work with atomic weights

1915

1915-1919 ~ Mass migration of workers across the nation

1915-1925 ~ Ku Klux Klan revives

1915 ~ 17,000 weeklies, semi-weeklies, and tri-weeklies are published

1915 ~ Age discrimination worsens as companies require older employees to take physical exams

1915 ~ Establishment of the first transcontinental phone line between New York City and San Francisco

1915 ~ Ford Model T costs $290, down from $950 in 1908

1915 ~ Landmark film, *The Birth of a Nation*, about the Civil War, portrays the Ku Klux Klan in a heroic role

1915 ~ Release of first pornographic film, *A Free Ride*

1916 ~ U.S. government makes child labor a federal crime

1916 ~ Creation of the National Park Service

1916 ~ Discovery of Heparin, an anticoagulant

1916 ~ Election of the first woman to Congress, Jeanette Rankin from Montana

1916 ~ Federal Aid Road Act begins government assistance to construct roads

1916 ~ White Castle food chain invents the hamburger steak

1917 and 1918 ~ Revenue Acts raise money for World War I

1917-1918 ~ 53,000 American soldiers die in battle in WWI; many more soldiers die of influenza

1917-1918 ~ AFL demands and receives better wages for workers

1917-1918 ~ Churches rally to mobilize support of troops in World War I

1917-1918 ~ Diseases and unsanitary conditions in the WWI trenches claim many lives

1917-1918 ~ Fashion industry creates comfortable clothes for wartime working women

1917-1918 ~ War economy problems include transportation, production, and finance

1917-1919 ~ World War I provides new roles and opportunities for women

1917-1921 ~ Race riots erupt in St. Louis, Chicago, Washington, DC, and Tulsa, Oklahoma

1917 ~ Secretary of War Newton D. Baker orders the prohibition of alcohol from military camps and removal of "bawdy houses" from surrounding neighborhoods

1917 ~ 200,000 U.S. troops arrive in France under the command of General John J. Pershing

1917 ~ 26 states prohibit alcohol

1917 ~ A million acres of vacant city lots are turned into gardens to support the war effort

1917 ~ African-Americans comprise more than 20% of the workers in the Chicago stockyards

1917 ~ Creation of the War Labor Board and federal Mediation Commission to protect labor during World War I

1917 ~ Discovery of Vitamin D

1917 ~ Espionage Act prohibits open criticism of the U.S. government

1917 ~ First mass advertising campaign to win support for war

1917 ~ Formation of the War Industries Board to coordinate pending war efforts

1917 ~ George Hale constructs a 254 centimeter telescope and learns that galaxies other than the Earth's Milky Way exist

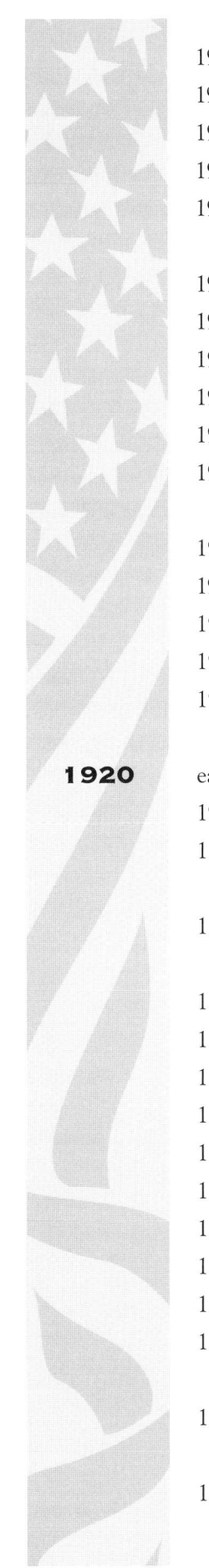

1917 ~ Puerto Rico becomes a U.S. territory

1918 ~ 675,000 Americans die during the influenza epidemic, far more deadly than World War I

1918 ~ Cincinnati police strike for better wages

1918 ~ General John J. Pershing breaks the German front in France and ends WWI

1918 ~ More than 12,000 Native Americans join the U.S. Army and Navy during World War I and serve with distinction

1918 ~ Sabotage Act and the Sedition Act are designed to control anti-government activities

1918 ~ United States Army pilots begin first air mail service

1918 ~ Workers demand and receive an eight-hour day and equal pay for women

1918 ~ World War I halts Housing Construction

1919-1920 ~ Unions fall into government and public disfavor

1919 ~ Anti-black race riots break out in Elaine, Arkansas as African Americans attempt to push for higher wages

1919 ~ Discovery of curative effect of sunlight on rickets

1919 ~ Eighteenth Amendment prohibiting the sale of alcoholic beverages begins prohibition era

1919 ~ Formation of the Chicago Crime Commission to oversee police corruption

1919 ~ Grand Canyon becomes a national park

1919 ~ Taking a stolen car across state lines is made a federal crime

1920

early 1920s ~ Helena Rubenstein and Elizabeth Arden start their cosmetic businesses

1920 and 1924 ~ Japanese and Filipino farm workers strike against Hawaiian plantation owners

1920 ~ Congress passes a law that allows civil service officials to receive retirement benefits at the age of 70; mechanics, letter carriers and clerks at 65; and railway clerks at 62

1920 ~ Establishment of the first transcontinental airmail route between New York City and San Francisco

1920 ~ First commercial aircraft flights for passengers and cargo begin

1920 ~ First diesel railroad engine put into service

1920 ~ For the first time more Americans live in urban than in rural areas

1920 ~ Formation of RCA

1920 ~ Formation of the Negro National League in baseball

1920 ~ Forty-six percent of Americans own their own homes

1920 ~ Half of American homes have electricity

1920 ~ Infant death rates fall by 20 percent

1920s-1930s ~ Emergence of brand name products

1920s-1930s ~ Foundation of the Consumer Research and Consumer Cooperative to educate consumers about products

1920s ~ "Flappers" frequent speakeasies, smoke cigarettes and engage in promiscuous sexual activity

1920s ~ Ninety-two percent of college coeds engage in petting, and one third in sexual intercourse, laying Victorian morality to rest

1920

1920s ~ Art Deco becomes the most popular style for buildings in America's cities

1920s ~ Automobile deaths dramatically increase

1920s ~ Chrysler Building in New York City symbolizes the dominance of corporate America

1920s ~ Cleveland establishes the first police radio band

1920s ~ Commercial sponsors advertise on radio programs

1920s ~ Construction of the first New York skyscrapers

1920s ~ Development of traffic signal technology by Garrett Morgan, an African American

1920s ~ Elite society prefers Georgian, Tudor or French Classical architecture for homes

1920s ~ Harlem Renaissance produces renowned African American writers, artists, and musicians

1920s ~ Hays Code restricts film makers from ridiculing the law

1920s ~ Invention of Freon makes widespread home refrigeration feasible

1920s ~ One out of every eight Americans work in an automobile-related industry, including rubber, steel, and petroleum

1920s ~ Presbyterians and Baptists split into smaller denominations

1920s ~ Proliferation of indoor bathrooms

1920s ~ Proliferation of organized crime

1920s ~ Restricted Filipino immigration; unlimited Western Hemisphere immigration

1920s ~ Standardization of building and housing codes

1920s ~ Welfare capitalism by businesses reduce the power of unions over workers

1920s ~ Widespread real estate speculation, especially in Florida

1921, 1924, 1927 ~ U.S. imposes permanent immigration quotas

1921 ~ Bessie Coleman becomes first African American female pilot, earning her license in France because of segregation in the U.S.

1921 ~ Discovery of Vitamin E

1921 ~ Hermann Rorschach introduces the inkblot psychological test

1921 ~ Invention of first modern lie detector

1921 ~ KDKA in Pittsburgh, the first public radio station in the U.S., begins broadcasting on November 2, 1921

1921 ~ Pig Stand in Dallas is the first drive-in restaurant

1921 ~ Tariffs close foreign markets to farmers

1922 ~ Cable Act declares that an American woman married to an alien loses her citizenship

1922 ~ Discovery of the human growth hormone

1922 ~ Founding of *Reader's Digest* for the "lowbrow" reader

1922 ~ RCA introduces the console radio

1922 ~ Use of insulin to treat diabetes

1923 ~ Development of whooping cough (pertussis) vaccine

1923 ~ Development of antitoxin for streptococcus

1923 ~ Henry R. Luce and Briton Hadden found *Time* magazine

1923 ~ Invention of the electrocardiograph

1923 ~ *Moore v. Dempsey* establishes federal due process protections for defendants on trial in state courts

1923 ~ Robert A. Millikan wins a Nobel Prize for his work with electrons

1924 ~ Charles Birdseye develops a quick-freeze technique, making frozen foods possible

1924 ~ First shopping mall opens, in Kansas City

1924 ~ J. Edgar Hoover becomes director of the FBI

1924 ~ Publishing of the first national road atlas by Rand McNally

1925

1925 ~ John T. Scopes, a schoolteacher in Tennessee, is arrested for teaching evolution to his students

1925 ~ Formation of Chrysler Corporation

1925 ~ *Harper's* emphasizes up-to-date articles on current questions

1925 ~ First motel is built, in San Luis Obispo, California

1925 ~ Discovery of iron as a major factor in the formation of red blood cells

1925 ~ Production of first miniature camera, the Leica, in Germany

1925 ~ Federal Trade Commission officially recognizes manmade textile filaments

1925-1929 ~ Mail order catalogues and magazines bring fashion awareness to every household

1926 ~ Introduction of the pop-up toaster

1926 ~ Diets rich in liver control pernicious anemia, usually a fatal disease

1926 ~ Construction begins on Route 66, originating in Chicago and ending in Santa Monica (Los Angeles); it will be fully paved by 1937, crossing 8 states and 3 time zones creating America's first major highway system

1926 ~ Congress expands benefits to people already retired

1927 ~ Supreme Court decides in *Buck v. Bell* that involuntary sterilization for eugenic purposes is constitutional

1927 ~ Sixty-three percent of Americans live in homes with electric lights

1927 ~ Over 800,000 workers invest more than a billion dollars in 315 companies

1927 ~ Development of iron lung for patients who cannot breathe on their own

1927 ~ Philip Farnsworth invents the television picture tube

1927 ~ *The Jazz Singer*, first talking picture, is released

1927 ~ Babe Ruth hits sixty home runs

1927 ~ Production of the last Model T Ford

1927 ~ 55 chains control 230 major newspapers

1927 ~ First national radio networks begin, NBC (1926), CBS

1927 ~ Charles Lindbergh completes nonstop transatlantic flight on "The Spirit of St. Louis"

1927-1933 ~ Committee for the Suppression of Irresponsible Censorship, comprised of 40 authors, denounces all forms of censorship

1928 ~ Amelia Earhart becomes the first woman to fly across the Atlantic, as a passenger

1928 ~ George Eastman invents the Kodak color film process

1928 ~ George Papanicolaou develops the Pap test for diagnosing cervical cancer

1928 ~ Discovery of Vitamin C

1928 ~ Alexander Fleming discovers penicillin in molds

1928 and 1932 ~ Collective bargaining laws strengthened, giving unions more power

1929 ~ Total advertising budget for the major newspapers rises to $860 million

1929 ~ Building of first public parking garage, in Detroit

1929 ~ Walt Disney creates the first animated motion picture, *Steamboat Willie*

1929 ~ 23,000 registered movie houses estimate 100 million admissions each week

1929 ~ First national radio comedy show, *Amos 'n' Andy*, airs

1929 ~ Issuing of uniform classification of crimes by Chiefs of Police

1929 ~ Workers laid off and production cut back due to over-production and large stocks of unsold inventory

1929 ~ Union strike in Elizabethtown, Tennessee turns violent

1929 ~ Vladimir Zworykin, a Russian, demonstrates the first practical, completely electronic television system

1929 ~ A&P supermarket has 4,621 stores nationwide

1929 ~ Use of insulin shock to treat schizophrenia

1929 ~ Over 350 companies give pensions; plant safety and working conditions improve, medical care is provided; and sports and education are subsidized

1929 ~ Wickersham Commission investigates police work and crime

1929 ~ Coca Cola is sold in 66 countries

October 1929 ~ Stock market crash propels economy into the worst economic depression in American history

1929-1935 ~ Experimental broadcasting of television

1929 ~ German Hans Berger invents the electroencephalograph (EEG) to measure electrical activity in the brain

~

1930

1930-1932 ~ Roman Catholics call for government sponsored social programs

1930-1938 ~ Property values plummet due to oversupply and foreclosures

1930-1939 ~ Infant mortality rates decline by 25%

1930-1980 ~ Industrial occupations and farming greatly decrease

1930 ~ 30,000 Americans die in car accidents

1930 ~ Common cold virus is discovered

1930 ~ Ernest O. Lawrence's cyclotron accelerates nuclear particles to smash atoms and release their energy

1930 ~ Establishment of the National Institutes of Health

1930 ~ First jet aircraft put into service

1930 ~ First psychoanalytic institute for training analysts opens in Boston

1930 ~ One-third of college professors are women

1930 ~ Percentage of women in clerical positions rises from 34% in 1910 to 49%

1930

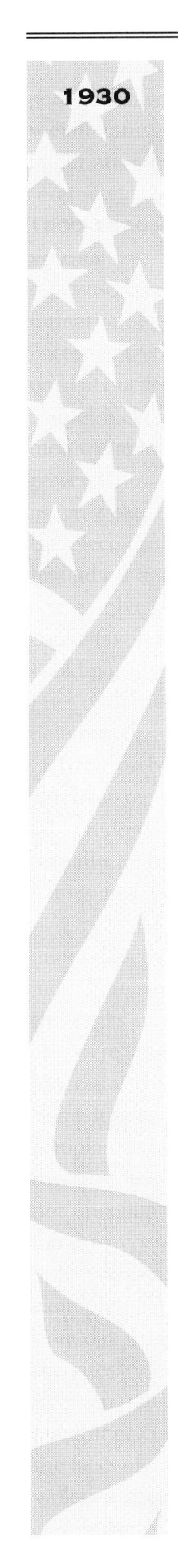

1930 ~ Under pressure, the movie industry enacts the Production Code, regulating crime, sex, vulgarity, obscenity, profanity, costumes, dancing, and religion in films

1930 ~ Victor Houtoff creates the Branch Davidians, a sect of the Seventh Day Adventists

1930 ~ Women dominate the professions of teaching, nursing, and social work

1930 ~ Working wives publicly criticized as selfish and "a menace to society"

1930s-1940s ~ Hybridization yields significantly better seeds

1930s ~ Chicago establishes a police complaint bureau

1930s ~ Conservatives lash out against non-Protestants

1930s ~ FBI arrests famous gangsters and solidifies its public image

1930s ~ Foundation of The Nation of Islam

1930s ~ Guglielmo Marconi develops radar and microwave ovens

1930s ~ Labor unions gain foothold among semi-skilled workers

1930s ~ Nobel Prize winning geneticist, Hermann J. Muller, attacks the eugenics movement for "lending a false appearance of scientific basis to advocates of race and class prejudice"

1930s ~ Police establish fingerprint data banks

1930s ~ Proliferation of radio soap operas, detective shows, and daytime programming

1930s ~ Proliferation of African American newspapers

1930s ~ Sports, religious, and public affairs programming on the radio increase

1930s ~ Streamliners popularize railroad travel

1931 ~ Alka-Seltzer becomes widely used

1931 ~ First culture of poliomyelitis virus is produced

1931 ~ Nevada legalizes gambling, founding the economic basis for Las Vegas

1931 ~ Satirical magazine *Ballyhoo*, aimed at advertisers, is launched with enormous success

1931 ~ Supreme Court rules that "malicious, scandalous, and defamatory" journalism can be suppressed

1931 ~ Wiley Post and Harold Gatty are the first people to circle the globe in an airplane

1932-1933 ~ Construction falls by 78%, private investment drops by 88%; farm income, already low, falls another 50%

1932-1933 ~ Unemployment is 24.9%; 9,000 banks fail; 100,000 businesses fail

1932 ~ Amelia Earhart is the first woman to complete a solo transatlantic flight

1932 ~ Discovery of Vitamin C and Riboflavin

1932 ~ Economy Act stipulates that married women be discharged from their jobs

1932 ~ Federal Home Loan Bank provides a reserve system for lending institutions

1932 ~ Franklin D. Roosevelt appoints women to prominent posts within his administration

1932 ~ Listerine advertising creates fear (don't lose your job) of bad breath and begins fear tactic advertising

1932 ~ President Hoover's programs fail and the American banking system is on the verge of total collapse

1932 ~ Supreme Court rules for due process in the Scottsboro Boys case

1933 ~ Adolf Hitler rises to power in Germany

1933 ~ Civilian Conservation Corps provides jobs to millions of Americans

1933 ~ Creation of the Blue Cross hospital insurance program

1933 ~ Emergency Banking Act closes, then reopens failing banks

1933 ~ Federal Deposit Insurance Corporation is established to guarantee the safety of deposits

1933 ~ First usage of sodium pentothol as an anesthesia

1933 ~ First successful lung surgery removes cancerous lung

1933 ~ First use of electric shock to reverse potentially fatal ventricular fibrillation

1933 ~ Frances Perkins becomes the first woman cabinet member

1933 ~ Government develops hog and corn subsidy programs

1933 ~ President Roosevelt inaugurates his New Deal programs and his radio fireside chats

1933 ~ Richard M. Hollingshead, Jr. of New Jersey patents the first drive-in movie theater

1933 ~ Studies show that fluoride helps reduce tooth decay

1933 ~ Thomas Hunt Morgan becomes the first American to win a Nobel Prize in medicine and physiology

1933 ~ Twin engine Boeing 247, the first modern commercial aircraft, is put into service

1933 ~ U.S. introduced to the modern architecture of the German Bauhaus group

1934-1990s ~ Neo-Paganism, a movement to re-harmonize humans with the natural and sacred worlds, is associated with the practice of witchcraft

1934 ~ 50,000 coal miners strike in Birmingham, Alabama against exploitation

1934 ~ Federal Housing Administration federally insures long-term mortgages to encourage lending institutions to make loans in a difficult market

1934 ~ Passage of the Social Security and the National Industrial Relations Acts

1934 ~ Restriction of Filipino immigration to 50 people a year

1935

1935 ~ *Reader's Digest* has a circulation of over 1,000,000 readers

1935-1939 ~ United Mine Workers (UMW), one of the nation's few interracial organizations, provides the organizational foundation for the emergence of industrial unionism

1935 ~ American corporations spend $80 million a year spying on their employees

1935 ~ Completion of Hoover dam

1935 ~ Farm Security Administration helps protect farmers from bankruptcy

1935 ~ First FM radio stations are licensed

1935 ~ Founding of Alcoholics Anonymous in New York City

1935 ~ Production of the first wearable hearing aid

1935 ~ Production of 1.5 million latex condoms in the U.S. each day

1935 ~ Rate of unemployment increases for workers over 65 to more than 50 per cent

1935 ~ Resettlement Administration relocates Dust Bowl farmers

1935 ~ Rural Electrification Act brings electricity to rural areas

1935 ~ Social Security Act shifts pension responsibilities from local to federal government

1935 ~ Works Progress Administration launches the Federal Theater

1936-1974 ~ Indian nations continue to lose around 13,000 acres of land per year

1935

1936 ~ African American Jesse Owens wins three gold medals at the Olympic Games in Berlin, dispelling Hitler's theory of Aryan superiority

1936 ~ Creation of Vitamin B

1936 ~ Frank Lloyd Wright designs his most famous residence, Fallingwater

1936 ~ Henry R. Luce begins *Fortune* for businessmen and *Life* for family readers

1936 ~ Introduction of sulfa drugs to U.S.

1936 ~ Nazis banish Jews to ghettos

1936 ~ Soil and Water Conservation Act provides government assistance for soil-saving efforts

1937 ~ Angiocardiography introduced to open clogged arteries in heart attack victims

1937 ~ Charities and churches are permitted to hold bingo games legally in Rhode Island

1937 ~ First antihistamine treatment for allergy

1937 ~ First successful treatment of bacterial infection with sulfanilamide

1937 ~ Miller-Tydings, known as the Fair Trade Act, compels local retail merchants to sell nationally advertised products at the manufacturers' suggested retail price

1937 ~ Rise in the number of labor unions

1937 ~ Theologians Reinhold and Helmut Richard Niebuhr reevaluate the Christian heritage

1937 ~ Vitamin B12 isolated

1938 ~ Earl Tupper begins producing plastic gas masks and signal lamps for the military and later develops Tupperware storage products

1938 ~ Al Gross develops the two-way radio, or walkie-talkie, widely used during WWII

1938 ~ Electroconvulsive therapy, ECT or "shock" therapy is used to treat mental illness

1938 ~ Euthanasia Society of America is established

1938 ~ Fair Labor Standards Act establishes minimum wages, maximum hours, and the abolition of child labor

1938 ~ Pellagra successfully treated with niacin

1938 ~ Wallace H. Carothers at the E.I. Dupont chemical company develops the synthetic fiber nylon

1939-1940 ~ U.S. provides war materials to the Allies

1939-1945 ~ Holocaust results in the massacre of millions of Jews and disenfranchised people in Germany and Eastern Europe

1939 ~ African American opera diva Marian Anderson sings before 75,000 at the Lincoln Memorial

1939 ~ Discovery of Vitamin K

1939 ~ Discovery of the Rh factor in human blood

1939 ~ First commercial televisions displayed at New York World's Fair

1939 ~ First experimental food stamp program initiated, in Rochester, New York

1939 ~ Germany invades Poland, starting WWII

1939 ~ Heart disease, cancer, and stroke replace contagious diseases as the leading causes of death

1939 ~ Immigrant Igr Sikorsky builds the first successful helicopter

1939 ~ *Queen Mary* is commissioned for use as a troop carrier to and from Australia during World War II

1939 ~ Synthetic hormone diethylstilbestrol treats menopause symptoms

1940

early 1940s ~ Claire McCardell designs clothes for the American career woman

1940 ~ 30% of the workforce is white-collar

1940 ~ 54% of American adults gamble in one form or another

1940 ~ Congress approves a rearmament budget; peacetime conscription of soldiers begins

1940 ~ Discovery of plasma as a substitute for whole blood in transfusions

1940 ~ First Freeway, Pennsylvania Turnpike, opens

1940 ~ Lanham Act authorizes housing construction at defense plants and military bases

1940 ~ Percentage of teenagers finishing high school increases from 50% in 1930 to 75% in 1940

1940 ~ Selective Service Act permits conscientious objectors to serve in non-combat positions

1940 ~ Two Oceans Navy Bill appropriates funds to build 1.3 million tons of new warships

1940 ~ U.S. freezes Japanese assets

1940 ~ Women outlive men by four years

1940s ~ Development of new vaccines against typhus and tetanus

1940s ~ Development of chemical sprays to control diseases spread by insects

1940s ~ Development of penicillin, erythromycin, tetracycline, and other antibiotics

1940s ~ Over fifty tabloids are in circulation

1940s ~ Television enhances the popularity of professional boxing

1940s ~ *Women's Day, Family Circle,* and *Better Living* become actively engaged in social issues

1941-1942 ~ Shipbuilding booms

1941-1945 ~ 25,000 Native Americans join the Army, Navy, or Marine Corps; another 40,000 support the war industries at home

1941-1945 ~ World War II restricts production of consumer goods and controls agricultural production

1941 ~ Atlantic Charter proclaims the U.S. and Britain will respect the sovereign rights of other nations

1941 ~ Clinical trials of penicillin begin

1941 ~ First treatment of pneumonia with sulfanilamide

1941 ~ First performance of cardiac catheterization

1941 ~ Japanese bomb Pearl Harbor, forcing the U.S. into WWII

1941 ~ National Housing Act authorizes FHA mortgages in defense areas

1941 ~ Penicillin and blood plasma become available for battlefield use

1941 ~ Westinghouse Science Talent Search is organized to identify high school students who have extraordinary scientific potential

1942-1944 ~ Expansion of coal, petroleum, steel, aluminum and rubber production

1942-1944 ~ First use of radio to sell war bonds

1940

- 1942-1944 ~ Wartime restrictions on goods cause fashion to become more austere
- 1942-1945 ~ 300,000 Americans die in battle in World War II, and another 115,000 die of non-combat accidents and diseases
- 1942-1945 ~ Brewery workers are granted draft deferments and 15% of the beer produced is reserved for the military
- 1942-1945 ~ Farmers dramatically increase crop production for the war effort
- 1942-1945 ~ Military leaders regard venereal disease prevention as a major priority
- 1942-1945 ~ Once considered inappropriate, swing dancing becomes an acceptable method of releasing wartime tension
- 1942-1945 ~ Recruitment of 3,600 Navajos in the 382nd Platoon serve as "code talkers," using phrases from the Navajo language to transmit intelligence data over the airwaves
- 1942 ~ Allies secure the Suez Canal, restricting German ships into North Africa
- 1942 ~ Establishment of national policy of rent control
- 1942 ~ Executive Order 9066 requires internment of Japanese Americans living on the West Coast
- 1942 ~ General Eisenhower invades North Africa
- 1942 ~ Japan conquers the Philippines
- 1942 ~ Luxury liner, *Normandie* burns in New York City harbor as it is being turned into a U.S. troop carrier
- 1942 ~ Radioactive iodine therapy replaces surgery for overactive thyroid
- 1942 ~ U.S. troops defeat the Japanese at Guadalcanal
- 1942 ~ U.S. ships defeat the Japanese navy at Midway Island, marking a turn in the war with Japan
- 1942 ~ War Production Board coordinates production of war materiel with industry and labor
- 1942 ~ Women, blacks and immigrants increase the work force from 46 million in 1940 to 60 million in 1945
- 1943-1946 ~ "War brides" immigration permitted
- 1943 ~ Aircraft industry expansion
- 1943 ~ Availability of the new drug penicillin to treat venereal disease changes attitudes and caution about intercourse
- 1943 ~ Discovery of streptomycin, an antibiotic
- 1943 ~ Edward R. Murrow pioneers live war reportage
- 1943 ~ Efforts to enforce occupational and residential segregation causes race riot in Detroit
- 1943 ~ Establishment of the All-American Girls Professional Baseball League
- 1943 ~ Russians hold Stalingrad against the German on-slaught and turn the war on the Eastern front
- 1943 ~ Frank Sinatra draws thousands of "bobby-soxers" to concerts
- 1943 ~ Madame Chiang Kai-Shek of China visits the United States, leading to the repeal of the Chinese exclusion law that prohibited Chinese immigration
- 1943 ~ First atomic explosion occurs in Los Alamos, New Mexico

1945

1943 ~ Roosevelt demands unconditional surrender of the Germans

1944 ~ G.I. Bill of Rights guarantees loans to veterans for home purchases and education

1944 ~ Isolation of DNA

1944 ~ Allied invasion at Normandy begins the end of WWII

1944 ~ Founding of *Seventeen Magazine*

1944 ~ Rome liberated from the Nazis

1944 ~ Introduction of aureomycin as the first broad-spectrum antibiotic

1944 ~ Allied tank divisions race across France and into Germany

1944 ~ Massey-Ferguson introduces the first combine farm machine

~

1940-1944 ~ Five million women enter the labor force

1944 ~ Allied troops invade Normandy on D-Day on June 6

1945-1970 ~ "Ghetto," once referred to as a broad range of ethnic residential enclaves, is now almost exclusively applied to African American and Latino neighborhoods. "Urban renewal" is openly referred to as "Negro removal"

1945 ~ 35.5% of America's non-agricultural workers are in unions

1945 ~ 8% of all defense workers are black

1945 ~ American Cancer Society is founded

1945 ~ Atomic bombs dropped on Hiroshima and Nagasaki, Japan, leading to the end of WWII

1945 ~ Capture of Iwo Jima and Okinawa put Japan within range of heavy American B-29 bombers

1945 ~ Introduction of oral penicillin

1945 ~ Significant immigration of Muslims, who found The Federation of Islamic Associations of the U.S. and Canada

1945 ~ Unconditional Surrender of German forces on May 7, 1945

1945 ~ Veterans Emergency Housing Program provides subsidies to create housing

1946-1949 ~ Increase in non-farm employment

1946-1949 ~ Prefabricated housing helps fulfill housing shortage

1946-1949 ~ War crime trials held for German and Japanese atrocities

1946-1952 ~ Young brides and women in their 30s begin having post-war babies

1946-1960 ~ Union influence declines

1946 ~ 86% of Americans believe married women should not work

1946 ~ Development of the first electronic computer, ENIAC

1946 ~ Farmers Home Administration makes loans available for farmers to buy or modernize their houses

1946 ~ First television sets go on sale

1946 ~ Full Employment Act is passed to promote increased employment but does not specify how the government will accomplish this

1946 ~ Hill-Burton Act restricts certain medical practices to hospitals

1946 ~ Marshall Plan to restore Europe is implemented

1945

1946 ~ *Mendez v. Westminister* desegregates Mexican American education rights

1946 ~ National School Lunch Act provides food for needy children

1946 ~ President Truman ends workers' strikes

1946 ~ Production of synthetic penicillin

1947-1948 ~ General Agreement on Tariffs and Trade expands trade opportunities

1947 ~ Carbon 14 dating methods accurately date objects thousands of years old

1947 ~ Christian Dior introduces his "New Look" for American women

1947 ~ First units of the Levittown suburban development constructed

1947 ~ First self-service gas station

1947 ~ House Committee on Un-American Activities begins communist "witch hunt"

1947 ~ Housing and Rent Act controls rents and provides subsidies for garden apartments

1947 ~ Jackie Robinson becomes first black to join major league baseball

1947 ~ Prefrontal lobotomy brain surgery used to treat schizophrenia

1947 ~ Taft-Hartley Act limits unions' political activities, and prohibits a long list of labor practices, as well as empowers the president to postpone major strikes for an 80-day "cooling off" period

1947 ~ Test pilot Chuck Yeager breaks the sound barrier in an experimental aircraft, the Bell X-1

1947 ~ Transistors invented, which will revolutionize electronics

1947 ~ Truman Doctrine aligns U.S. with Western Hemisphere nations

1948-1952 ~ The Keynesian Revolution proposes lowering interest rates, sponsoring public works projects, and undertaking massive government spending in order to increase employment

1948 ~ Citation wins the Triple Crown; no other horse duplicates his achievement during the next twenty-five years

1948 ~ Comedian Milton Berle becomes television's first superstar

1948 ~ Dior becomes the first designer to license his name for ready-to-wear clothing

1948 ~ Emigrés George Gamow and Hans Bethe, with American physicist Ralph Alpher, propose the big bang theory to explain the origins of the universe

1948 ~ Introduction of 45 RPM records

1948 ~ Kinsey report on sexual behavior of the human male is published

1948 ~ *Lamp Unto My Feet*, a Sunday morning religious show originally aimed at children, begins and will continue for more than thirty years, making it one of TV's longest-running shows

1948 ~ Truman's Fair Deal extends Social Security and the minimum wage to more workers

1948 ~ U.S. recognizes Israel as a sovereign state

1949 ~ Establishment of the National Institute of Mental Health

1949 ~ Establishment of NATO

1949 ~ Housing Act provides for slum clearance and community redevelopment

1949 ~ Lithium used to treat psychiatric disease

1949 ~ Mao Zedong's Communist party seizes power in China

1949 ~ Sickle-cell anemia, prevalent among African Americans, is described as a molecular disease

~

1950

early 1950s ~ Mainstream radio stations begin to broadcast hillbilly, country, and rhythm and blues music

1950-1953 ~ 33,600 American combat deaths and 20,600 non-combat deaths in the Korean War

1950-1959 ~ Baby boomer children inspire diversity in clothing

1950-1970 ~ Weekly earnings for production workers increase by 70%

1950-1980 ~ Asian intellectuals are permitted to immigrate

1950 ~ United Auto Workers (UAW) signs a national union contract with General Motors that includes seniority provisions, a pension plan, cost-of-living allowances, and wage increases

1950 ~ 10 billion cans of foods are produced each year in the U.S.

1950 ~ Baby Boom, low unemployment, and increase in life expectancy create more housing demand; housing starts reach 1.7 million

1950 ~ Diner's Club introduces the first general-purpose credit card

1950 ~ Dinosaur Monument controversy suspends plans to build a dam and starts the modern preservation movement

1950 ~ First nuclear submarine, the *Nautilus*, is put into service

1950 ~ Gerard Blitz creates the first Club Med with 23,000 members

1950 ~ Introduction of blood tests for tuberculosis

1950 ~ North Korean troops invade South Korea, starting the Korean War

1951 ~ President Truman dismisses General MacArthur for expanding the Korean War

1950 ~ Patient whose heart stopped in surgery is revived through heart massage

1950s-1960s ~ Federal home loan programs discriminate against minorities

1950s-1980s ~ U.S. Buddhists westernize their rituals

1950s ~ 70,000 civilian American males aged 15-34 die from accidents and homicide

1950s ~ Baby boomers create enormous demand for products, fueling the economy

1950s ~ Beat generation considers itself pilgrims on a spiritual quest

1950s ~ Decade of 'correct' fashions and complicated rules of behavior

1950s ~ Establishment of nationwide motel chains

1950s ~ Heyday of television dramas

1950s ~ Military spending grows exponentially, creating many defense industry jobs

1950s ~ Proliferation of regional shopping centers in suburbia

1950s ~ Proliferation of television and air conditioning in homes

1950s ~ Proliferation of ranch-style houses

1950s ~ Red scare causes black unions to be disenfranchised

1950s ~ Senator Kefauver investigation of organized crime

1950

1950s ~ Special police squads saturate high-crime neighborhoods

1951 ~ Development of the first full body X-ray machine

1951 ~ First coast-to-coast television broadcast

1951 ~ *I Love Lucy* premieres

1951 ~ U. S. luxury liner *United States*, the fastest ocean liner ever built, is commissioned

1952 ~ Airlines offer first transatlantic tourist fares

1952 ~ Artificial pacemaker regulates heart rhythm

1952 ~ Bishop Sheen's "Life Is Worth Living" premieres on NBC television

1952 ~ First heart attack patient to be revived by electric shock

1952 ~ First McDonald's opens

1952 ~ Heart-lung machine developed

1952 ~ Launching of National Educational Television

1952 ~ McCarran-Walter Act permits Japanese to apply for citizenship

1952 ~ Polio rate at an all-time high

1952 ~ President Truman refuses to use atomic weapons against China

1953 ~ Creation of Department of Health, Education and Welfare

1953 ~ Establishment of the Church of Scientology by L. Ron Hubbard

1953 ~ First color television broadcast

1954 ~ Swanson introduces the TV dinner

1953 ~ Julius and Ethel Rosenberg, avowed Communists, are executed for transmitting atomic secrets to the Soviets

1953 ~ Kinsey reports that more than half of the nation's women are not virgins when they married

1953 ~ President Truman ends racial discrimination in government

1953 ~ With no victory, the U.S. and U.N. negotiate an armistice with North Korea

1954 ~ *Brown vs. Board of Education* rules that school segregation is unconstitutional

1954 ~ Congress inserts "under God" into the Pledge of Allegiance and adds "In God We Trust" to the currency

1954 ~ Edward R. Murrow's exposé of Joseph McCarthy begins investigative reporting

1954 ~ Founding of The Unification Church by the Reverend Sun Myung Moon – dedicated to the coming of the "Lord of the Second Advent" who will finish the work Christ

1954 ~ *Hernandez v. Texas* rules that Mexican Americans are white

1954 ~ Introduction of open-heart surgery

1954 ~ Marlboro Man advertisement introduced, to enormous success

1954 ~ Mass trials of Salk polio vaccine begin

late 1950s ~ Federal urban renewal program attempts to revive inner cities

1955 ~ Church membership rises from 50% in 1940 to 75% in 1955

1955 ~ Two thirds of college women drop out to marry or to make themselves more eligible for marriage

1955

1955 ~ Arrest of Rosa Parks starts the Bus Boycott in Montgomery, Alabama

1955 ~ Disneyland opens

1955 ~ First successful kidney transplant

1955 ~ Louise Arner Boyd is the first woman to fly over the North Pole

1955 ~ Montgomery Bus Boycott propels Martin Luther King, Jr. into national prominence

1955 ~ Pruitt-Igoe public housing project builds 2,800 apartments in St. Louis, which the tenants hate

1955 ~ Sabin live polio vaccine introduced

1956 ~ American Cancer Society announces relationship between smoking and lung cancer

1956 ~ Elvis Presley releases his first single

1956 ~ Federal troops intervene to enforce Little Rock integration orders

1956 ~ First television remote control

1956 ~ First fully enclosed shopping center opens in Minnesota

1956 ~ Interstate Highway Act funds a vast network of high-speed roads

1956 ~ Invention of kidney dialysis machines

1956 ~ Social Security provision permits women to retire at age 62

1957 ~ Civil Rights Act protects voters against violence

1957 ~ Martin Luther King, Jr. founds the Southern Christian Leadership Council

1957 ~ Poultry Inspection Act regulates poultry commerce

1957 ~ President Dwight D. Eisenhower is the first president to dive in an atomic submarine

1957 ~ Sputnik satellite launched by the Soviet Union, causing pandemonium in the U.S. and escalating the Cold War

1957 ~ Supreme Court rules that a literary work containing explicit materials must be judged as a whole and not by its parts

1957 ~ Supreme Court rules that obscenity be judged on "community standards," allowing for more daring films

1958 ~ American Association of Retired Persons (AARP) founded

1958 ~ Federal Food, Drug and Cosmetic Act prohibits using cancer causing additives to foods, drugs, and cosmetics

1958 ~ First coronary artery cauterization

1958 ~ First nuclear submarine, the *Nautilus*, passes underneath the North Pole

1958 ~ First use of ultrasound to examine fetuses in the womb

1958 ~ First National Conference on air pollution

1958 ~ Invention of the microchip launches the technological revolution

1958 ~ Italian influence in design comes to America

1959 ~ U.S. Postal Service uses the first fax machines1958

1959 ~ Alaska and Hawaii become states

1959 ~ Bank of America introduces credit cards to compete with Diner's Club cards

1959 ~ Barbie doll creates public debate about her unattainable body standard

1959 ~ Combined vaccine for whooping cough, diphtheria, and polio released

1959 ~ Development of pressure test for the eye disease, glaucoma

1959 ~ Formation of the American Football League to rival the NFL

1959 ~ Housing Act authorizes loans to private nonprofit corporations to build elderly housing projects

1959 ~ Housing Act authorizes loans to private nonprofit corporations to build elderly housing projects

1960

early 1960s ~ Mary Quant creates the miniskirt

1960-1964 ~ Attorney General Robert Kennedy leads the war against organized crime

1960 ~ Beginning of the retirement industry

1960 ~ Civil Rights Act makes it a federal crime to transport explosives across state lines

1960 ~ FDA approval of the oral contraceptive pills

1960 ~ First Lady Jackie Kennedy sets standards for elegance

1960 ~ Hazardous Substances Labeling Act requires warnings on dangerous household products

1960 ~ Invention of laser technology

1960 ~ The U.S. Olympic hockey club wins the gold medal

1960 ~ Union contracts include paid vacations of up to four weeks for long-term workers

1960s ~ Annual number of deaths due to homicide double over the decade

1960s ~ Civil Rights atrocities published in the press aid the movement

1960s ~ Development of Boeing's jumbo 747 jet

1960s ~ Expansion of mobile home and condominium apartments market

1960s ~ FBI's authority dramatically expanded

1960s ~ Gross National Product, driven by increased military expenditures to fund American involvement in Vietnam, nearly doubles

1960s ~ Importance of television news programming emerges

1960s ~ Liberation Theology movement, largely Roman Catholic, is concerned about the political, economic, and social oppression of Latin America

1960s ~ Ms. magazine reflects a revolution in women's thinking

1960s ~ Number of deaths due to automobile accidents increases 46%

1960s ~ Opposition to union leadership becomes commonplace

1960s ~ Supreme Court applies the Bill of Rights to state court proceedings

1960s ~ U.S. adopts a policy to "contain" the Soviet Union to its current borders

1960s ~ Women's liberation movement encourages smaller families and free access to the birth control pill

1961 ~ AFL-CIO founds the National Council of Senior Citizens to lobby for Medicare

1961 ~ Congress authorizes grants to states and cities to finance mass transportation

1961 ~ Cuban Americans, with the aid of the CIA, attempt to invade Cuba at the Bay of Pigs

1961 ~ Housing Act includes mortgage interest subsidies for low- and moderate-income rental housing and condominiums, and a subsidy for apartments for the elderly in public housing projects

1960

1961 ~ Housing Act extends mortgage insurance to condominiums

1961 ~ Intrauterine contraceptive devices developed

1961 ~ President Kennedy commits to landing Americans on the moon by 1969

1961 ~ President Kennedy signs bills designed to provide investment tax credits, greater depreciation allowances, and increased government spending to expand the number of jobs

1961 ~ Soviet cosmonaut Yuri Gagarin is the first man in space

1961 ~ Supreme Court rules that evidence seized in illegal searches cannot be used in state court trials

1961 ~ Vaccination for Rh-negative mothers prevents their antibodies from affecting future pregnancies

1962 ~ Alan B. Shepherd, Jr. becomes the first American in space

1962-1964 ~ Boston Strangler murders thirteen women

1962 ~ Cuban Missile crisis finalizes split between Cuba and the U.S.

1962 ~ First successful reattachment of a severed arm

1962 ~ First kidney transplant

1962 ~ John H. Glenn, Jr., becomes the first American to orbit the Earth

1962 ~ Kennedy administration introduces Civil Rights legislation, which will not pass until 1964

1962 ~ Model criminal code standardizes sentencing

1962 ~ President Kennedy initiates the first deliberate use of fiscal policy to ignite and sustain economic expansion

1962 ~ President Kennedy vows support to West Germany

1962 ~ Rachel Carson's *Silent Spring* calls national attention to pollution

1962 ~ Rubella (measles) virus isolated

1962 ~ Sam Walton establishes the first Wal-Mart

1962 ~ Telstar satellite makes worldwide communication possible

1963 ~ 200,000 Civil Rights supporters march on Washington with Dr. Martin Luther King, Jr.

1963 ~ Betty Friedan's *The Feminine Mystique* attributes women's problems to a sex-based society and not the personal failure of women, starting the women's liberation movement

1963 ~ Boeing 707 explodes over Elkton, MD, becoming the first lightning caused American air disaster

1963 ~ Bra burning protests symbolize women's liberation and have tremendous impact on the fit of clothing and the undergarment industry

1963 ~ First human liver and lung transplants

1963 ~ Assassination of President John F. Kennedy

1963 ~ Introduction of Valium to treat nervousness and hyperactivity

1963 ~ Supreme Court expands the availability of habeas corpus to state prisoners

1964-1975 ~ Consumer activism influences Civil Rights success

1964 ~ Civil Rights Act declares that American citizens cannot be segregated in public accommodations or discriminated against in employment

1964 ~ Executive order bars discrimination in the sale, lease, or occupancy of residential property owned or operated by the federal government

1964 ~ Federal Trade Commission requires cancer-warning labels on cigarette packages

1964 ~ Gulf of Tonkin Resolution begins official U.S. involvement in Vietnam

1964 ~ Introduction of a new fertility drug, Pergonal, resulting in multiple births

1964 ~ Marine theme park, Sea World, opens

1964 ~ Multi-billion dollar tax cut prompts greater consumer spending and capital investment

1964 ~ NBC TV introduces color programming

1964 ~ Neshoba County, Mississippi sheriff's department aids and abets the murder of three young Civil Rights workers by Ku Klux Klansmen

1964 ~ New Hampshire is the first state to reinstate lotteries

1964 ~ Surgeon general declares cigarette smoking a health hazard

1964 ~ The Beatles appear on *The Ed Sullivan Show*

1964 ~ Wilderness Act sets aside huge tracts of land for wilderness preservation

1965

1965 ~ Alabama Attorney General investigates the Ku Klux Klan

1965 ~ Assassination of Malcolm X

1965 ~ Department of Housing and Urban Development (HUD) established to oversee federal projects in cities

1965 ~ Discovery of the female hormone estrogen to prevent osteoporosis

1965 ~ Early Bird, first commercial communications satellite, relays television programs between U.S. and Europe

1965 ~ Enactment of Medicare and Medicaid

1965 ~ Fierce race riots occur in Los Angeles, Cleveland and New York

1965 ~ Freedom Riders firebombed on buses

1965 ~ Housing Act authorizes rent supplement subsidy to low-income families

1965 ~ Immigration and Nationality Act removes Japanese quota restriction

1965 ~ Older Americans Act specifies a series of goals to improve the lives of the elderly

1965 ~ Voting Rights Act

1966-1973 ~ 131,000 Americans die of homicide; 50,000 die in the Vietnam war

1966 ~ Child Protection Act bans toys containing hazardous substances

1966 ~ First national women's basketball championship tournament

1966 ~ Introduction of MasterCard

1966 ~ Medicare provides health care coverage for people over 65

1966 ~ Militant Black Power movement begins

1966 ~ Miranda decision forces police to read a suspect his rights

1966 ~ Model Cities Act authorizes construction of turnkey projects for low-rent housing

1966 ~ National Historic Preservation Act makes the protection of historic buildings a national policy

1965

1966 ~ Truth in Packaging Act responds to growing public dissatisfaction with deceptive advertising

1966 ~ Usage of staples in surgery instead of sutures

1966 ~ *Woman's Day* adds articles on health and money management to help working women

1967 ~ *Apollo 1* launch pad fire kills 3 astronauts

1967 ~ Clean Air Act sets pollution guidelines

1967 ~ Ford Foundation provides seed money to establish the Public Broadcasting network

1967 ~ Government indicts Muhammad Ali for evading the draft; the New York State Athletic Commission suspends his boxing license; and the World Boxing Association, noting that he could not defend the title, voids Ali's heavyweight championship

1968-1975 ~ Political rebellion causes anti-establishment dress codes

1968 ~ Assassinations of Martin Luther King, Jr. and Robert Kennedy

1968 ~ Bombing of the Army Math Research Center at the University of Wisconsin by student protesters

1968 ~ Concerned parents form Action for Children's Television to force networks to provide more programming than advertising

1968 ~ Film industry drops the Hays Code, lifting its ban on political and moral content in movies

1968 ~ First production of meningitis vaccine

1968 ~ Housing Act includes provisions designed to assist low-income families in becoming homeowners

1968 ~ My Lai massacre of women and children horrifies the American public

1968 ~ Newly elected President Nixon implements his "Southern Strategy" of stalling on court-ordered desegregation, cutting welfare assistance programs, and cracking down on anti-war protesters in an attempt to enlist white southerners into the GOP

1968 ~ President Nixon promises to end the Vietnam involvement

1968 ~ Race riots across America, destroying many inner-city areas, start after Martin Luther King's assassination

1968 ~ Supreme Court rules that police can stop and frisk suspects

1968 ~ Tet Offensive turns the Vietnam war in favor of the Viet Cong

1969 ~ A riot ensues after New York City police raid a gay bar giving rise to groups who will work for the repeal of laws that prohibit homosexual conduct

1969 ~ American astronauts Neil Armstrong and Buzz Aldrin become the first people to walk on the moon

1969 ~ California is the first state to permit "irreconcilable differences" divorce, leading the way to no-fault divorce

1969 ~ Creation of Environmental Protection Agency to control pollution

1969 ~ First artificial heart transplant is performed, but patient dies 30 hours after surgery

1969 ~ Housing Act authorizes FHA insurance for mobile home loans up to $10,000

1969 ~ Invention of videocassettes

1969 ~ Louis Ketner proposes the living will

1969 ~ Poverty rate declines from 20% in 1960 to 12% in 1969 because of government assistance program

1969 ~ *Sesame Street* premieres

1969 ~ The Gap clothing store opens, catering to "generation gap" buyers

1969 ~ Woodstock Music Festival attracts 400,000 young people to a 3-day outdoor "happening"

1970

1950-1970 ~ Family income triples

1970 and 1973 ~ Endangered Species Act protects species from extinction

1970-1975 ~ Vietnam refugees are permitted to immigrate into the U.S.

1970 ~ 48% of the workforce is white-collar

1970 ~ Clean Air Act attempts to minimize vehicle produced pollution

1970 ~ Comprehensive Drug Abuse Prevention and Control Act attempts to control illegal drugs and trafficking

1970 ~ Electrically powered light rail systems put into service

1970 ~ First nerve transplant

1970 ~ First Earth Day calls attention to environmental problems

1970 ~ Four students are killed by the Ohio National Guard at Kent State University

1970 ~ Norman E. Borlaug, a plant pathologist, receives the Nobel Prize for genetically creating a strain of high yield dwarf spring wheat and is credited with saving millions from dying of starvation

1970 ~ Occupational Safety and Health Act sets safety standards in the workplace

1970 ~ Rail Passenger Service Act establishes Amtrak to transport passengers on intercity routes

1970 ~ Supreme Court vindicates Muhammad Ali, ruling that the government had violated his constitutional rights, clearing the way for his return to the ring

1970 ~ U.S. escalates Vietnam war into Cambodia

1970 ~ United Farm Workers' five-year grape boycott succeeds

1970 ~ Women make up 40% of the overall labor force and represent a substantial increase in married women who work

1970s-1980s ~ Womanist theology begins in an effort to expose Christian sexism as oppressive to both men and women

1970s ~ Creation of pre-fabricated and modular housing

1970s ~ Creation of housing clusters: duplexes, triplexes, and fourplexes

1970s ~ Dramatic rise in median prices of new conventional single-family homes

1970s ~ Emergence of "relevance" television

1970s ~ Ethnic studies curriculum inaugurated in colleges

1970s ~ First utilization of alternative energy sources

1970s ~ Houses are viewed as a hedge against inflation

1970s ~ Magazine advertisers begin profiling and segmenting readers

1970

1970s ~ NASA engineers build Skylabs, orbiting scientific laboratories, predecessors of the International Space Station

1970s ~ Preservation Movement provides tax incentives to save historic buildings

1970s ~ Public opposition to atomic reactors increases

1970s ~ Renewed support for the death penalty

1970s ~ Rise of environmental terrorism

1970s ~ Use of single, double-wide, and triple-wide mobile units as permanent homes

1970s ~ Use of wood-burning stoves, fireplaces, and solar energy to conserve oil

1970s ~ Realization of the dangers of lead paint, radon gases, asbestos, and fiberglass

1970s ~ White flight to the suburbs increases urban deterioration

1971 ~ Federal laws require use of safety belts

1971 ~ First broadcast of *All Things Considered* on National Public Radio

1971 ~ First dual heart and lung transplants

1971 ~ President Nixon adopts "détente" policy (easing of tensions) toward China and the USSR

1972 ~ Congress eases trade restrictions on China

1972 ~ Consumer Product Safety Commission provides a continuous review of consumer goods for risks

1972 ~ Demolition of Pruitt-Igoe public housing project in St. Louis, built in 1955

1972 ~ Development of Computerized Axial Tomography (CAT) in England to provide cross sectional X-rays

1972 ~ Dr. Robert C. Atkins publishes a block-buster diet book

1972 ~ First authorization of oil exploration in Alaska

1972 ~ Pornographic film, *Deep Throat*, produced in six days at a cost of $24,000, grosses an estimated $5,000,000 in its first year

1972 ~ President Nixon approves Strategic Arms Limitation Talks with the USSR

1972 ~ President Nixon is the first American president to visit China

1972 ~ President Nixon agrees to cooperate with Soviets in space exploration

1972 ~ Social Security benefits are indexed to the Consumer Price Index

1972 ~ Soviet Union purchases $1 billion of U.S. wheat

1972 ~ Supersonic *Concorde* put into service for passenger flight

1972 ~ Title IX requires schools to provide for girls' sports

1972 ~ United Nations sponsors first global environmental conference

1973 ~ American Indian Movement occupies Wounded Knee for two months

1973 ~ Arab Oil Embargo creates gas crisis in U.S.

1973 ~ Cable use of satellites begins

1973 ~ Courts upholds a woman's right to privacy (making abortion legal) in *Roe v. Wade*

1973 ~ Deep Ecology movement espouses appreciating the natural world for its inherent value apart from any benefits it provides humanity

1973 ~ OPEC embargo of oil and gas from the Middle East raises energy awareness in construction design

1973 ~ President Nixon imposes soybean embargo

1973 ~ Tennis superstar Billie Jean King defeats Bobby Riggs, and women symbolically assert their strength, in the so-called Battle of the Sexes in straight sets before a record crowd at the Houston Astrodome and a television audience of 50 million

1973 ~ U.S. signs cease fire in Vietnam

1973 ~ U.S. sponsors Mideast mediation between Egypt and Israel after the Yom Kipper war

1973 ~ Watergate scandal breaks, alleging that President Nixon spied on his political opponents

1973 ~ Watergate hearings became the top rated program on television

1974 ~ Introduction of the Heimlich maneuver as first aid for choking

1974 ~ KPFK radio in Los Angeles refuses to turn over to the FBI Symbionese Liberation Army kidnapping tapes, continuing a series of battles between the press and law enforcement officials about sources of information

1974 ~ President Nixon resigns over the Watergate scandal

1974 ~ Ultrasound diagnostic techniques invented

1975

1975 ~ U.S. troops pull out of Saigon, which falls into Viet Cong control, ending the U.S. presence in Vietnam

1975 ~ Fair Packaging and Labeling Act sets standards for labeling additives to food

1975 ~ District court rules that deadly force can be used by police only when life itself is endangered or great bodily harm is threatened

1975 ~ Home Box Office (HBO) becomes the first national cable network

1975 ~ Introduction of VCRs: Betamax (1975), VHS (1976)

1975 ~ Lyme disease is identified

1975 ~ Social Security benefit levels increase five times since 1965

1975 ~ *Dress for Success* becomes a bible for corporate America

1975 ~ Viet Cong change the name of Saigon to Ho Chi Minh City

1975-1990 ~ Cuban refugees are permitted to immigrate into the U.S.

1975 ~ Fair Packaging Labeling Act forces disclosure of a product's nutritional value

1975 ~ Tennis champion Martina Navratilova defects to the United States from Czechoslovakia and becomes a U.S. citizen

1976 ~ Deregulation of airlines and railroads from government control, making these industries more competitive

1976 ~ Supreme Court ruling protects advertising as free speech

1976 ~ Mysterious disease kills dozens of Legionnaires during a convention

1976 ~ Vegetarian movement advocates eliminating meat products for the diet

1977 ~ Construction of the Alaskan pipeline begins

1977 ~ Apple II computer first appears on the market

1977 ~ Disco music has a profound impact on fashion

1977 ~ Invention of magnetic resonance imaging (MRI) scanners

1977 ~ Balloon angioplasty procedure reopens diseased arteries

1977 ~ Congress approves tax cut totaling $34 billion, raises the minimum wage by 50%, increases farm price supports, and eases environmental restrictions on industries

1978 ~ Age Discrimination and Employment Act raises the age for mandatory retirement from 65 to 70

1978 ~ Arno Penzias and Robert W. Wilson win the Nobel Prize for developing the "Big Bang" theory of the beginning of the universe

1978 ~ First "test-tube baby" is born in England

1978 ~ U.S. Presbyterian Church officially welcomes homosexuals to worship

1979 ~ Supreme Court limits strip searches

1979 ~ Panama Canal control scheduled for return to Panama in 1999

1979 ~ President Carter protects some Alaskan land from oil drilling

1979 ~ Three Mile Island meltdown causes backlash to nuclear reactors

1979 ~ American Byron Allen crosses the English Channel in a mylar and polystyrene aircraft

1979 ~ Deposed Shah of Iran comes to the U.S. for medical treatment

1979 ~ American embassy personnel are taken hostage by the Iranian government and held for over a year

1979 ~ Jerry Falwell founds Moral Majority, Inc. and pledges to use its political influence to return America to traditional values

late 1970s ~ Development of the "green culture" which advocates environmental responsibility

late 1970s ~ Residents along the Love Canal are re-located because of pollution

1980

1980-1989 ~ Cardio-vascular disease falls 30%

1980-1989 ~ Number of temporary workers more than doubles and the number of part-time workers increases by 40%

1980-1990 ~ Northeast and Midwest lose 1.5 million manufacturing jobs, mostly in cities, while the South and West gain 450,000 jobs

1980-1995 ~ U.S. permits Soviet refugees to immigrate

1980-1997 ~ Passage of hate crime legislation in every state

1980 ~ President Carter imposes a grain embargo and a U.S. boycott of the Moscow Summer Olympics in response to the Soviet Union's invasion of Afghanistan

1980 ~ World Health Organization announces the worldwide eradication of smallpox

1980s-1990s ~ Public's insatiability for intimate details about celebrities gives rise to paparazzi journalists

1980s-1990s ~ Rise in 'contingent workforce' of temporary, leased, independently contracted, seasonal, and non-permanent part-time workers

1980s ~ Adoption and use of racial profiling by police forces

1980s ~ Commercial advertising appears on religious networks

1980s ~ Corruption is discovered in the Department of Housing and Urban Development

1980s ~ Establishment of state lotteries in Arizona, California, Colorado, Florida, Idaho,

1980

Indiana, Iowa, Kansas, Kentucky, Missouri, Montana, Oregon, South Dakota, Virginia, West Virginia and Wisconsin

1980s ~ Failure or merger of 900 federally-insured thrift institutions

1980s ~ High inflation, high interest rates, high unemployment reduce housing starts

1980s ~ Increase in single person households creates demand for condominiums

1980s ~ Microwave ovens become popular despite fears of causing radiation poisoning

1980s ~ Movement begins to restore old houses in urban neighborhoods

1980s ~ Proliferation of attached two-story single-family housing in suburbia

1980s ~ Proliferation of black music, musicians, and athletes into mainstream America

1980s ~ Reagan revolution against environmental regulation

1980s ~ Recession forces companies to "downsize," laying off many workers

1980s ~ Rise of talk radio

1980s ~ U.S. attempts to stabilize Central American countries

1980s ~ War on drugs targets minorities

1980s ~ Warehouses turned into fashionable apartments in old industrial cities

1981 ~ Attempted assassination of President Reagan

1981 ~ Congress passes the Economic Recovery Tax Act, decreasing personal income taxes by 25% and lowering the maximum tax rate from 70% to 50%

1981 ~ Congress cuts federal spending on domestic social programs by $41 billion, severely curtailing or abolishing welfare payments, food stamps, Medicaid, medical care for the indigent, and public housing programs

1981 ~ Congress approves $1.6 trillion expansion of the military budget designed to enhance national security and stimulate the domestic economy

1981 ~ First successful surgery performed on a fetus

1981 ~ Music television (MTV) begins

1981 ~ President Reagan disbands the Air Traffic Controllers union

1981 ~ Recognition of AIDS as responsible for a worldwide death toll and the first diagnosis of the disease in the U.S.

1981 ~ The first space shuttle, *Columbia,* is launched

1982-1988 ~ President Reagan promotes supply side economics designed to increase consumption

1982-2000 ~ Some Native American economies prosper from casino gambling

1982 ~ Depository Institutions Act allows thrifts to offer federally-insured money market accounts to invest in residential and commercial real estate loans

1982 ~ First permanent artificial heart is implanted in a human

1982 ~ National Cancer Institute publishes dietary guidelines for reducing cancer risks

1982 ~ U.S. restores sovereignty to Native American nations

1983 ~ Acceptance of the first women into the rabbinate – the study to become a rabbi

1983 ~ Barbara McClintock becomes the first woman to win a Nobel Prize, not shared by other scientists, for her work in gene behavior

1983 ~ Housing and Urban-Rural Recovery Act provides funds for housing for the elderly, handicapped, and homeless

1983 ~ Performance of the first liposuction surgery

1983 ~ Premiere of *Larry King Live*

1983 ~ Russell Higuchi becomes the first scientist to clone an extinct animal's DNA segment

1983 ~ Sally Ride is the first woman in space

1984 ~ First baby born from a donated embryo to an infertile mother

1984 ~ Performance of first dual heart and liver transplant

1984 ~ U.S. Supreme Court upholds the right of colleges and universities to sign independent contracts with television networks

1985

1985-1987 ~ Fashion industry creates Supermodels to conceal the fact that fashion is in a slump

1985-2000 ~ Congress considers but rejects most gun control legislation

1985 ~ Country singer Willie Nelson hosts the first Farm Aid benefit

1986-1989 ~ Proliferation of VCRs

1986 ~ Amendment to the Olympic Charter calls for the Winter and Summer Games to be held alternately every two years

1986 ~ *Challenger* space shuttle explodes killing six astronauts and the first private citizen, teacher Christa McAuliffe

1986 ~ Exxon *Valdez* oil spill in Alaska wreaks havoc on the environment

1986 ~ U.S. grants amnesty to illegal immigrants in the U.S.

1986 ~ *Voyager* airplane flies nonstop around the world in nine days without refueling

1987-1999 ~ 400,000 Americans die of AIDS

1987 ~ Housing and Community Act establishes a housing voucher program

1987 ~ Immigration Reform Act makes it illegal for employers to hire undocumented workers

1987 ~ Stock market loses more than 500 points and nearly 20% of its value in a single day

1987 ~ U.S. and the U.S.S.R agree to destroy some nuclear and conventional weapons

1988 ~ Founding of the Human Genome Organization

1988 ~ Indian Housing Act assists Native Americans and Alaska Natives in securing housing loans

1988 ~ Savings-and-loan institutions begin collapsing, causing the worst banking crisis since the Depression

1989 ~ AZT approved for treating AIDS in 1987 is shown to delay the onset of AIDS

1989 ~ Department of Housing and Urban Development Reform Act reorganizes HUD after criminal allegations

1989 ~ Fall of the Berlin Wall begins the breakup of the Soviet Union

1989 ~ AIDS becomes the second leading cause of death (following accidents) among American men aged 25-34

1989 ~ Financial Institutions Reform, Recovery, and Enforcement Act reorganizes the many insolvent thrift institutions

1989 ~ First U.S. liver transplant using a living donor

1989 ~ Inauguration of Channel One, targeted at children

1990

early 1990s ~ 26 states repeal their anti-sodomy laws, and at the local level, many laws are enacted to protect homosexuals from discrimination

1990 ~ *Oregon v. Smith* defends the rights of Native Americans to use peyote, a hallucinogenic drug, during religious ceremonies

1990 ~ A four-year-old American girl is the first person to undergo gene therapy

1990 ~ Creation of the World Wide Web

1990 ~ Development of Intelligent Transportation Systems

1990 ~ First major housing act since 1974 provides matching funds for new construction and rehabilitation of renter-occupied and owner-occupied housing

1990 ~ Globalization of environmental concerns, especially global warming

1990 ~ GM introduces the first mass-marketed electric car, the Saturn EV1

1990 ~ Iraqi troops invade Kuwait, starting the Gulf War

1990 ~ National Opinion Research Report finds that a majority of whites believe that African Americans are "innately lazy and less intelligent and patriotic than whites," and prefer welfare to work

1990 ~ Norplant implantable contraceptive is approved for women

1990 ~ Number of working mothers increases from 12% in 1950 to 60% in 1990

1990 ~ Nutritional Labeling and Education Act enables consumers to know about the fat, fiber, and caloric content of foods

1990 ~ Performance of the first gene therapy on a human to treat an immune deficiency

1990 ~ Smoking banned on all U.S. domestic flights of less than six hours

1990 ~ START Treaty between the U.S. and Russia reduces nuclear weapons

1990s ~ 25% of teens do not graduate from high school

1990s ~ Cable forces network television to air "alternative" programs

1990s ~ Female Spirituality movement begins as lesbian theologians attempt to reinterpret religious traditions for women

1990s ~ Home shopping network and ATM machines encourage spontaneous buying

1990s ~ HUD authorizes demolition of some of its worst public housing projects

1990s ~ Primetime television broadcasts sexually explicit programming

1990s ~ Research shows how stem cells can be used to alleviate the symptoms of Parkinson's disease and other nervous disorders, raising ethical questions since the stem cells were taken from human embryos

1990s ~ Scientists develop irradiation as a safety measure to kill bacteria and toxins such as *E. coli* in meat, vegetables, and fruits

1990s ~ Some people spend as much as a third of their lives in retirement

1990

1990s ~ Surge in construction of luxury apartment buildings

1990s ~ Thrift institutions are no longer a force in home mortgage lending

1990s ~ Two-car garages are replaced in many wealthy neighborhoods with three- and four-bay garages

1990s ~ U.S. increases efforts to stop illegal Mexican immigration

1990s ~ U.S. commits troops for peacekeeping missions to Africa and the Balkans

1990s ~ Women's magazines reshape their focus from home and fashion to questions of dating, sex, gays/lesbians, mental health, and health problems

1991-1997 ~ Restaurant chain Denny's pays $50 million to settle discrimination charges

1991 ~ Basketball superstar "Magic" Johnson announces he has AIDS and retires from professional basketball

1991 ~ Clean Air Act requires automobile manufacturers to begin developing alternative fuel vehicles

1991 ~ Congress authorizes U.S. troops in Kuwait; Gulf War begins

1991 ~ Dissolution of the Soviet Union ends the Cold War

1991 ~ Dr. Jack Kevorkian assists patients who want to commit suicide

1991 ~ Establishment of The Promise Keepers, an organization to help men assert themselves and become better fathers and husbands

1991 ~ Gulf War ends in decisive defeat for Iraq

1991 ~ U.S. Presbyterian Church forbids same sex marriages

1991 ~ Performance of the first successful heart surgery on a fetus in the womb

1991 ~ Rodney King is videotaped being clubbed and kicked by Los Angeles police, an incident that forces police department reviews nationwide

1991 ~ U.S. National Women's Soccer Team wins the first Women's World Cup

1991 ~ Use of economic sanctions on Iraq after the Gulf War halts the exportation of oil

1992-1998 ~ Value of corporate mergers increase nearly ten-fold

1992 ~ Announcement that placing sleeping babies on their backs leads to a decrease in Sudden Infant Death Syndrome

1992 ~ April Larson becomes the first female bishop in The Evangelical Lutheran Church

1992 ~ Implementation of free agency in the National Football League as part of the settlement in a 1987 lawsuit with the Players Association

1992 ~ Travel and tourism is the second largest industry in the U.S. after health

1993 ~ ATF assaults the Branch Davidian Compound in Waco, Texas, leading to a 51 day stand off and the deaths of all the inhabitants, many women and children

1993 ~ EPA labels second hand smoke a carcinogen

1993 ~ Family and Medical Leave Act provides for workers' job security during family emergencies

1993 ~ North American Free Trade Agreement opens trade borders to Mexico and Canada

1993 ~ Production of the first Internet browser, Mosaic

1993 ~ Religious zealot Michael Griffin shoots and kills Dr. David Gunn at his clinic where he performs abortions

1993 ~ Terrorist bombing of the World Trade Center

1993 ~ The federal government withdraws funding for the Superconducting Super Collider, which scientists had used for high energy physics research

1994 ~ Episcopal Diocese of Newark, NJ declares there is nothing in the scriptures to preclude a homosexual relationship to become a holy union

1994 ~ Former President Ronald Reagan reveals he has Alzheimer's disease

1994 ~ Passage of Brady Bill for control of handguns

~

1995

mid-1990s ~ U.S. troops committed to the Balkans

mid-1990s ~ U.S. sends troops for peacekeeping missions in Africa

mid-1990s ~ Attacks on affirmative action

1995 ~ Number of farm workers declines from 13.6 million in 1915 to 2.85 million in 1995

1995 ~ African American football superstar O.J. Simpson is acquitted of charges of murdering his Caucasian wife

1995 ~ Louis Farrakhan, the spiritual leader of The Nation of Islam, organizes the Million Man March – the call for black men to take more of a role with their families

1995 ~ FDA approval of a chicken pox vaccine

1995 ~ Bombing of the Murrah Federal Office Building in Oklahoma City kills 168 people and is the worst act of terrorism in the U.S. until 2001

1995-1999 ~ Many companies permit employees to work from their homes

1995-2000 ~ Trendy teen glossies, *Teen Vogue*, *Cosmogirl*, *Teen People*, *Teen*, and *Elle Girl*, publish frank articles about self-empowerment, racism, eating disorders, rape, sexual diseases, pregnancy, and depression

1996 ~ United Methodist Church declares that homosexual marriages are not to be preformed by Methodist ministers

1996 ~ Albertson's supermarket pays over $29.4 million in a discrimination case involving women and Hispanics

1996 ~ Scottish doctors clone a sheep, Dolly

1996 ~ A pipe bomb explodes in Centennial Olympic Park, Atlanta, during the summer Olympic games, killing two persons

1997 ~ First significant decline in AIDS deaths is attributed to new protease inhibitors

1997 ~ U.S. Supreme Court uphold states' rights to outlaw physician-assisted suicide

1997 ~ The First Methodist Church in Omaha, Nebraska challenges the prohibition from the United Methodist Church and marries a lesbian couple

1997 ~ U.S. scientists clone a male calf

1997 ~ Huntington F. Wilard makes the first artificial human chromosome

1997 ~ Introduction of Viagra, a drug to treat sexual dysfunction in men

1997 ~ Publix supermarkets pays $81.5 million to settle accusations that it had systematically denied promotions, raises, and preferred assignments to women

1997-1999 ~ Computer and Internet revolution create many high-tech jobs

1998 ~ Southern Baptist Convention amends its Articles of Faith to read that a woman ought "to submit graciously to the servant leadership" of her husband

1998 ~ Unionized workers earn nearly one-third more than nonunion workers and receive health and pension benefits

1998 ~ A million households apply for personal bankruptcy

1998 ~ e. Coli bacteria in contaminated hamburgers in Jack-in-the-Box restaurants kills several people

1998 ~ Westboro Baptist Church of Topeka, Kansas declares that the killing of Mathew Shepard because he is gay is justified

1998-2000 ~ E-commerce companies vie for Internet consumers

1999 ~ Fewer men and more women smoke cigarettes

1999 ~ With the retirement of Wayne Gretzky, the NHL loses the most popular player in its history

1999 ~ Heart disease, cancer, and strokes account for 60% of all deaths

1999 ~ Death by cancer decreases 8% between 1990 and 1999

1999 ~ Homicide rate decreases by 33% between 1990 and 1999

late 1990s ~ High definition televisions become available

late 1990s ~ Rampage killing by students in their own schools

2000

2000 ~ Congress approves Everglades National Park restoration

2000 ~ For the first time, the Hispanic population equals the African American population

2000 ~ Inauguration of high speed passenger trains between Washington, Boston, and New York City

2000-2001 ~ Twenty-five-year old Tiger Woods wins four consecutive major championships and increases his career earnings to $28 million

2000 ~ Mapping of the first complete plant genome sequence, the mustard weed

2000 ~ Mapping of the human genome, one of the twentieth century's most outstanding scientific accomplishments

2000 ~ One of every four Americans is obese and 60% are overweight

2000 ~ Organic food industry grows to $6 billion annually

2000 ~ U.N. inspection teams are forced to withdraw from Iraq

2001 ~ Supreme Court rules that a child of an American mother, regardless of where it is born, automatically becomes a U.S. citizen while the child of a foreign mother by an American father must apply for citizenship

2001 ~ Formation of the Alliance for Retired Americans to lobby for retired trade unionists

2001 ~ Number of eligible Social Security recipients is expected to double while the number paying taxes into the system will increase by less than 20% between 2001 and 2030

2001 ~ Terrorists hijack four U.S. commercial aircraft, crashing two of them into the twin towers of the World Trade Center, New York City, one into the Pentagon, Washington, D.C., and the 4th crashed in the countryside near Pittsburgh, Pennsylvania

INDEX

A
A&P supermarket, 678
Aaron, Hank (baseball star), 1252
AARP, 1529
Abilene, KS, 1681, 1757
Abortion, 212, 1077, 1340, 1605, 1467, 1489
Abrams v. U.S. (1918), 967
Abrams tank, 1663
Acid rock, 1075, 1121
Acuff, Roy (musician), 1116
Acupuncture, 725
Addictive substances, 713
Adkins v. Children's Hospital (1923), 969
Adventures of Huckleberry Finn, 1045

Advertising and Consumerism, 1
Advertising
  Beginnings, 14
  Billboards, 120
  Children, 41
  Cigarettes, 35
  Consumer education, 25
  Depression (effects of), 24
  Electrical ads, 15
  Fear tactics, 17, 25
  Government regulation, 37
  Nutrition, 676
  Promoting war, 19, 320
  Purpose of, 16
  Race, 18
  Radio, 21
  Religion, 1391
  Sex, 1609
  Targeting audiences, 41
  Televangelists, 40
  Television, 36, 40, 1344
  War propaganda, 27, 1802
Consumerism
  Automobiles, 13
  Beginnings, 5
  Boycotts, 34
  Civil Rights (influence on), 33
  Credit card debt, 39
  Critics of, 32
  Food, 688
  Growth of, 22, 29
  Immigrants, 11
  Impact on emotions, 460
  Installment buying, 908
  Middle class, 9
  Political power, 30
  Post-WWII, 363

Race, 12
Revolt against, 637
Self indulgence, 31
Shopping centers, 635, 1015, 1027
Social conscience/progress, 8, 33
Teenage, 31
World War I, 312; (1920s), 326

Affirmative action, 1250, 1305
AFL-CIO, 155, 342
African cuisine, influence of, 657

African Americans
  Brown vs. the Board of Education, 427, 525, 880, 1232
  Citizenship for former slaves, 522
  Classes of, 526
  Cold War, 1232
  Cultural influence, 639, 645
  Definitions of "slave," 520
  Effects of factory closings, 1235
  End of Reconstruction, 523
  Excluding blacks from skilled labor, 1204
  Families, 567
  Farmers, 1222
  Hate groups, 527
  Housing, 787, 1223
  Influence on fashion, 639, 645
  Lynching, 199, 1205, 1274
  March on Washington (1941), 1288; (1963), 1293
  Migration/riding the rails, 1722
  Music, 1094, 1102, 1112, 1118, 1215
  Nation of Islam, 1429
  Negro (baseball) League, 1283
  Newspapers, 1181
  Progress, 526
  Putting blacks in their place, 1213
  Quality of life (1950s-60s), 880; (1970s), 1024
  Race riots, 186, 204, 213, 795, 947, 1203, 1224, 1236, 1279, 1298, 1304
  Race and work, 1890
  Racial and ethnic prejudice in cities, 756
  Radio programming, 1337
  Religion (during slavery), 1424
  Restricting freedom for slaves, 520
  Right to vote, 522
  Role of black soldiers (Civil War 1861-1865), 521
  Segregation, 524 (also see separate section "Segregation")
  on trains, 1723
  Service in the Spanish-American War, 1619
  Strikes
    Labor, 1218

Roanoke Rapids textile, 1238
  Sanitation workers, 1242
  Sit-down, 1220
 Television programming, 1333
 Universal Negro Improvement Association, 1216
 Vietnam war protest, 1845
 War on drugs, 1246
 World War I, 1805, 1808
 World War II servicemen, 1825
 World War II labor, 1223, 1288

Age discrimination, 1517
Agriculture (see **Farming**)
Agricultural Adjustment Act (1933), 149, 334, 588, 972
Agricultural science, 1546

AIDS
  Causes of, 729
  Insurance policies, 257
  Recognition of, 241

Air Commerce Act (1926), 1733
Air Traffic Controllers strike, 157, 1244, 1736

Air transportation
  Air Traffic Controllers strike, 157, 1244, 1736
  Airmail service, 1732
  Barnstorming, 1730
  Breaking the sound barrier, 1734
  Civil pilot training, 1735
  Disasters, 1737
  Early test flights, 1729
  First parachute jump, 1730
  First passenger service, 1732
  First seaplane, 1730
  First transatlantic flight, 1730
  Government regulation of, 1734
  Improvements in aircraft, 1733
  Presidential aircraft, 1735
  Space flight, 1737
  Special duty aircraft, 1735
  Women pilots, 1731, 1735

Aircraft industry (WWII), 347
Aircraft technology, 1554
Airmail service, 1732

Airplanes (see also "Air Transportation")
  Barnstorming, 1730
  Early test flights, 1929
  First person to die in, 1730
  First seaplane, 1730
  Invention of the airplane, 1728
  World War I, 1634, 1644
  Wright Brothers, 1728

Alaska
  Exxon *Valdez* oil spill, 492
  Gold rush, 882
  Oil discovered, 884
  Purchase of, 75

Alcohol (see also "Prohibition")
  Alcoholics Anonymous, 1059
  Alcoholism (troops in Vietnam), 1658
  And morality, 1051
  Consumption and temperance, 674

Alger, Horatio and the American dream, 872
Ali, Muhammad (prize fighter), 1236
All in the Family, 1338
Allen, Byron (pilot), 1735
Alternating current, 907
Alternative medicine, 735
Amalgamated Union of Iron, Steel and Tin, 139
Amendments to the Constitution, 963
American Federation of Labor, 138
American Dream (see **Individual Prosperity and the American Dream**)

American Expansion, 47
  Asia, 74
  California, 68
  Canada, 76
  Caribbean, 74
  Confiscation of Indian territory, 1216
  Culture, 101
  Dollar Diplomacy, 93
  Entertainment, 102
  Great Plains, 80
  Hawaii and the Philippines, 88, 1270
  Manifest Destiny, 66
  Military expansion, 96
  Northwest, 55
  Oregon, 67, 1198
  Panama Canal, 92
  Products, 102
  Puerto and Cuba, 89, 1619, 1793
  Roosevelt Corollary, 93, 1797
  Slavery, 72
  Southwest, 51
  Space, 98, 1737
  Sports, 101

Texas, 59
Westward migration, 57, 881

American Cookery (cookbook), 696
Americans with Disabilities Act (1991), 816
Amos 'n' Andy, 1319
Amtrak, 1718
Anderson, Marian (singer), 1287
Anesthesia, 713
Anger, 456
Annapolis, MD, 1675
Anti-imperialism, 89
Anti-Saloon League, 1384
Anti-semitism, 846
Antibiotics, 729
Antitrust, 309, 311, 323, 340
Apartments (also see **Housing and Architecture**)
  Boom in the 1920s, 761, 763
  Apartments and rental houses, 780, 796
Apollo spacecraft tragedies, 1739
Appliances, 9
Arab oil embargo, 492
Arabs (Oklahoma City Bombing), 1249
Architecture (see **Housing and Architecture**)
Aries, Philippe, 249
Arkwright, Richard (inventor), 902
Armstrong, Louis (musician), 1103
Armstrong, Neil (astronaut), 1739
Army pension program, 1514
Artificial hearts, 738
Artificial insemination, 610
Artillery (WWII), 1642
Asbestos poisoning, 806

Asian Americans
  Chinese Americans
    Chinese in Hawaii, 530, 1270
    Chinese Exclusion Act (1882), 531, 1268, 1271
    Equal protection, 1268
    Immigrants 1820-1860, 528
    Laborers, 529
    Migration to cities, 531
    Opportunities for work, 530
    Repealing Chinese exclusion, 532, 1288
    Transcontinental railroad, 529
  Japanese Americans
    Economic success, 534
    Hostilities toward, 533, 1272
    Immigrants 1868-1924, 532
    Internment during WWII, 533, 852, 972, 1289, 1826
    Laborers, 532

  Filipino Americans
    Discrimination against, 1285, 1301
    Hawaiian workers, 535, 1271
    Increased immigration to the U.S., 535
    Strikes and unions, 535, 1286

Asparagus, 678
Assassinations, 210, 936
Assemblies of God, 1392
Assembly line automobile production, 907
Assembly line clothing production, 628
Assimilation of immigrants, 845, 851
Atkins diet, 694
Atlantic Monthly, 1167

Atomic bomb
  Dropped on Japan, 1639
  Fear of, 250
  Invention of, 915
  Religion and, 1410

Atomic Energy Commission (AEC), 1553
Atoms for Peace, 481
Atwater, Wilbur O. (nutritionist), 670
Aunt Jemima and Uncle Ben, 657
Automats, 666

Automobiles
  Accidents, 1713
  Assembly line production, 280, 907
  Automotive culture, 1714
  Autos and policing, 942
  Billboards, 120
  Cost of, 114, 875
  Early history, 114, 1704
  Early models, 1704
  Early roads, 1708
  Fashion, 624
  Federal Aid Highway Act (1938, 1944, 1952, 1954), 1710
  First national highway system, 1710
  First automobiles, 1706
  Freight transportation, 1712
  Impact on society, 279
  Impact of interstate highways, 1711
  Improvements in, 1715
  Influence on small towns, 1687
  Law and order, 1707
  Model T, 114, 875, 907, 1706
  Motels, 119
  National Highway System, 1713
  Road expansion, 1710, 1766

Safety, 123, 1714
Suburbs, 117, 764, 1711
Use for leisure, 995, 998, 1028

Automobiles and Highways, 107 (see also **Transportation**)
Automobiles
Assembly line production, 907
Autos and policing, 942
Billboards, 120
Cost of, 114, 875
Fashion, 624
First patent, 114
Growth of suburbs, 764, 1711
History, 110, 1705
Influence on small towns, 1687
Model T, 114, 875, 907, 1706
Motels, 119
Safety, 123, 1714
Suburbs, 117, 1711
Use for leisure, 995, 998, 1028
Highways
Billboards, 120
Early roads, 115, 1708
Fast food, 121
First national highway system, 1710
Interstate highways, 785, 1711
Modern roads, 116, 1710

Axis Sally (WWII radio propagandist), 1650

B
Baby boom
  Housing, 182
  Start of, 1825
Bad Axe, Battle of, 509
Baekeland, Leo Hendrik (inventor), 1540
Baez, Joan (musician), 1121
Baha'i Faith, 1455
Bailey bridge, 916
Bakersfield, California, 884
Bakker, Jim and Tammy Faye (TV evangelists), 1343
Baldwin, Lola (policewoman), 939
Bankhead-Jones Farm Tenancy Act (1937), 341
Banking Act (1935), 338

Banks (also see **Economy**)
  Bankruptcy of rural banks, 599
  Failure (1933), 334; savings and loan, 376
  Mergers and consolidation, 385
  Regulation, 334, 387

Baptism, 1362
Baptists, 1361, 1390
Barbecues, 689
Barber, Samuel (composer), 1115
Barbie (doll)
  Measurements, 1013
  Wardrobe, 637
Barnett, Ida Wells (activist), 1723
Barth, Karl (theologian), 1404
Barton, Bruce (writer), 1391
Baruch, Bernard (economist), 345

Baseball
  Discrimination, 1252, 1274
  Immigrant stars, 1282
  Integration, 1297
  Negro League, 1283

Bataan, Battle of, 1647
Bauhaus Group (architects), 773
Beach Boys (musicians), 1118
Beard, James (chef), 689, 696
Beat writers, 1416
Beatles, 1119
Beaumont, Texas, 884
Bebop, 1110
Bell, Alexander Graham (inventor), 906
Bell Curve, The: Intelligence and Class Structure in American Life, 1246
Bell bottom pants, 641
Bell, Susan (scientist), 1560
Bennett, Henry (industrial guard), 1884
Benz, Carl (inventor), 1705
Berle, Milton (TV star), 1326
Berlin, Irving (composer), 1101
Berry, Chuck (musician), 1118
Best companies to work for, 1894
Betty Crocker Picture Cookbook, 669
Big band/swing, 1007, 1063, 1104, 1108
Big Bang theory, 1554, 1560
Bikini swimwear, 634, 1068
Bilingual Education Act (1968), 429
Biltmore Estate, 753
Bingo, 1061
Birdseye, Clarence (frozen foods), 678

Birmingham, Alabama
  Civil Rights march of 1957, 186
  KKK burns a church, 213
  Miners strike, 1218

Birth control, 1076, 1604, 1048, 1064, 1467, 1585, 1594

Birth control pill, 1076, 1604
Birth of a Nation, 910, 1274
Bismarck, Otto von (German Chancellor), 1798
Black Panthers, 1299
Black (African American) press, 1181
Black power, 187, 1299
Blitzkrieg, 1817
Blonde bombshell, 1069
Blood plasma, 1643
Blue Grass Boys (band), 1113
Blue Cross insurance plan, 720
Bluegrass music, 1113

Blues music
  Country, 1095, 1102
  Electric, 1111
  Rhythm and Blues, 1116, 1119
  Urban, 1104

Bobbitt, John Wayne (victim), 1608
Boeing aircraft, 1733, 1768
Bohr, Niels (physicist), 1542
Bolshevik Revolution, 1809 (see also "Red Scare")
Book of Mormon, The, 1451
Borlaug, Norman E. (geneticist), 1562
Borrenson, Kari (feminist writer), 1445
Bossa nova, 1123
Boston Cooking School Cook Book, 669
Boulder Dam, 479

Boxing
  Benny Leonard, 1283
  Jack Johnson, 1274
  Muhammad Ali, 1236

Boy Scouts of America, 478
Boycotts, 34
Boyd, Louise Arner (pilot), 1735
Bradford, William (minister), 1355
Bradley, Tom (politician), 1301
Bradley Fighting Vehicle, 1663
Branch Dividians, 1491
Brand names, 7
British rock bands, 1119, 1124
Broken windows policing, 951
Brotherhood of Sleeping Car Porters, 1223, 1286
Brown vs. the Board of Education, 427, 525, 880, 975, 1232
Brownmiller, Susan (writer), 216
Brubeck, Dave (musician), 1122

Bryan, William Jennings (politician/lawyer)

Cross of Gold, 293
  Position on evolution, 1386
  Scopes monkey trial, 422, 1387

Buchman, Frank (minister), 1395
Buck v. Bell (1927), 969
Buckminster, Joseph Stevens (minister), 1369
Bucks Stove decision, 140

Buddhism, 1417
  Assimilation of, 1418
  Jodo Sinshu, 1417
  Nichiren, 1417
  Tibetan, 1417
  Zen (Beat writers), 1416

Buffalo soldiers (Indians), 1619
Bungalow houses, 757
Bureau of Customs, 938
Bureau of Indian Affairs, 510
Bureau of Land Commissioners, 517
Bureau of Narcotics, 938
Bureaucratizing death, 250
Burger King, 690
Burke Act (1906 Indians), 511
Bush administration policy (environment), 495
Bush, Vannevar (engineer), 1550, 1552
Bushido Code (Japanese), 1647

Business and Labor, 127 (see also **Work and the Workplace** and **Occupations**)
Business
  Businessmen (respect for), 137, 143
  Civil War, 134
  Colonial America, 131
  Corporate spiritualism, 1484
  Great Depression, 146, 1217, 1879
  Hoover's policy toward, 322
  Industrialization, 136
  Lowell labor system, 132, 1145, 1678
  Opposition to immigration restrictions, 842
  Opposition to unions, 1208
  Rhode Island labor system, 132
  Southern plantations, 133
  Trade associations, 144
  Welfare capitalism, 144, 1878
Labor
  Apprenticeship system, 1142
  Blue collar opportunities (1990s), 393
  Breaking strikes, 1221, 1242, 1244 (see also "Strikes")
  Brotherhood of Sleeping Car Porters, 1223
  Catholic Worker Movement, 1398

Child labor, 415, 550, 969, 1142, 1867
CIO (Congress of Industrial Organization), 151, 1219, 1286, 1890
  Decline of (1990s), 380
  Depression era labor, 1218
  Depression era strikes, 1218
  Discrimination against Mexican labor, 1206
  Excluding blacks from skilled labor, 1204
  Factory closings, 1235
  Flint Michigan strike, 1244
  Foremen and supervisors, 1875
  Gains for workers, 1889
  Hostility towards (1920s), 325
  Immigrant, 137, 1199, 1870
  Industrial democracy, 1883
  Industrial relations 1950-1970, 1888
  Interracial cooperation, 1202
  Jewish garment workers strike, 1275
  Knights of Labor, 138, 1199, 1202
  Labor and class, 1208, 1871
  Labor and white supremacy, 1872
  Lowell labor system, 132, 1145, 1678
  Mexican labor 1880-1900, 517
  National Labor Relations Board, 150, 342, 1805, 1823
  Opposition to unions, 1208
  Police unions, 941
  Rhode Island labor system, 132
  Sharecropping, 135
  Southern plantation labor system, 133
  Support from religious groups, 1393
  Support of immigration restrictions, 843
  Supreme Court decision, 140, 1209
  Sweatshop garment production, 626, 1275
  Taft-Hartley Act (1947), 346
  Unions (beginning of), 138
  Unions, history of, 1884
  Universal Negro Improvement Association, 1216
  Violence, 139, 145
  War Labor Board (WWII), 153
  Worker benefit victory at GM, 1230
  Worker solidarity, 1210, 1276
  Working conditions, 132, 137
  World War I, 320
  World War II, 151, 349, 1887

Byrnes, James F., 346

C
Cable Act, 1281
Cafeterias, 666
Cage, John (composer), 1123
California
  Discrimination against Asians, 1273
  Farming, 604
  Los Angeles (see Los Angeles)
  Manifest Destiny, 68

Calley, William (Lieutenant), 1659
Camping, 1765
Canadian immigration, 850
Canals
  Importance to the development of towns, 1673
Cancer, 240, 724
Candy, 661, 692
Canned
  Milk, 659
  Soup, 660
Canning, 659
Cannon, James (minister), 1384
Car theft, 942
Caribbean immigration, 858
Carjacking, 942
Carnegie, Andrew (industrialist/philanthropist), 1371
Carothers, Wallace H. (synthetic fibers), 631, 914
Carson, Rachael, 486
Carter family (musicians), 1106
Carter, Jimmy (president)
  Economy and labor policy, 157
Cash, Johnny (musician), 1116
Casinos
  Native American, 513
  Gambling, 1080
Caskets, 253
Castro, Fidel, 859
Casual business dress, 647
CAT scans, 737

Catholics
  and communism, 1465
  Early settlers, 1362
  Influence of Bishop Sheen, 1411
  Liberation theology, 1447
  Orthodox Catholic Church, 1456
  and patriotism, 1464
  Positions on sex and abortion, 1467
  Prejudice against, 1383
  Priesthood, 1468
  Support for social reform, 1395
  Vatican Council II, 1466
  Women in the priesthood, 1473
Catholic Hour, 1411
Catholic Worker Movement, 1398
Cattle drives, 284

Cattle towns, 1681
Catwalk, The (fashion), 645
Celebrities at war (WWII), 1828
Cemeteries, 260
Censorship, 1045, 1057
Central Park, 993
Challenger space craft, 1739
Chambers, Whittaker (communist), 1838
Chanel, Coco (clothes designer), 625
Chanute, Octave (inventor), 1728
Charity (gambling), 1061
Charleston, the (dance music), 1104
Charleston, South Carolina, 1677
Chemical weapons (WWI), 1627
Chesapeake Bay towns, 1675
Chiang Kai-Shek, Madame, 532
Chicago Defender, 1183
Chicago stockyards, 658, 668
Child, Julia (chef), 696

Children (also see **Family Life**)
  Advertising, 41
  Child labor, 415, 550, 969, 1142, 1867
  Child-rearing, 547, 563
  Children in same-sex marriages, 1607
  Children's Aid Societies, 670, 674
  Clothes, 636
  Death rate in childbearing, 236
  Disabled, 424, 430
  Discrimination against Mexican foster parents, 1206
  Diseases, 713
  Entertainment, 991, 1012
  Handicapped, 430
  Labor, 415, 550, 969, 1142, 1867
  Lowell labor system, 132, 1145, 1678
  Malnutrition, 673, 693
  Mortality rate, 712
  Prenatal care, 721
  Psychology, 556
  Reformers, 994
  Rhode Island labor system, 132
  Role in family, 546
  School lunch boxes, 689
  School lunch programs, 684
  Sexual activity, 1609

Children's Television Workshop, 1341
Children's Aid Society, 670, 674
Chin, Vincent (victim), 1301
China
  Open Door policy, 92
Chinese Americans (see "Asian Americans")

Chinese Exclusion Act (1882), 531, 1271, 1288
Chisholm Trail, 1681
Chittenden, Russell Henry (nutritionist), 671
Chocolate candy, 661
Chopra, Deepak (spiritual leader), 1485
Christ as businessman, 1391, 1487
Christian Broadcasting Network, 1343
Christian capitalists, 1487
Christian Scientists, 1381
Christianity and the Social Crisis, 1375
Chrysler Building, 766
Church of Jesus Christ of Latter-day Saints, 1450
Church of the Nazarene, 1392
CIO (Congress of Industrial Organization), 151, 155, 342, 1219, 1286, 1890

Cities, 163
  Bankruptcy, 188
  Civil rights, 186
  Demographics, 184
  Entertainment, 177
  Ethnicity, 170, 993
  First American cities, 167
  Growth of, 168, 190, 754
  Housing, 171 (see also **Housing and Architecture**)
  Immigrant settlements, 836, 839
  Immigrants, 170
  Importance of, 168
  Interstate highways, 785, 1711
  Largest, 837
  Migration to, 171, 872
  Minorities, 184
  Model cities programs, 794
  New urbanism, 188
  Police, 198
  Political machines, 174, 1270
  Poverty, 178
  Race riots, 186, 204, 213, 795, 947, 1203, 1224, 1236, 1279, 1298
  Racial and ethnic prejudice, 756
  Renewal, 185
  Services, 173
  Slums, 181
  Smart growth, 189
  Traffic, 190
  Trolleys, 172
  Urban renewal, 788, 790, 813, 814, 1234, 1241
  White flight to the suburbs, 1300
  Zoning, 173

Civil Aeronautics Board (1938), 339, 1734
Civil disobedience (non-violent), 1426

Civil rights (see also **Race and Minorities** and "African Americans")
  (Act of 1957), 212
  (Act of 1960), 213
  (Act of 1964), 213, 428, 880
  (Act of 1965), 213
  (Act of 1968), 795
  Birmingham march, 186
  Brown vs. the Board of Education, 427, 525, 880, 975, 1232
  Cities, 186
  Court decisions, 975
  Demonstrations, 525
  Movement in the South, 1292
  Race riots, 187, 795, 1298
  Religion, 1425
  and sexuality, 1078

Civil Service Act (1883), 1518
Civilian Conservation Corps, 337, 422
Civilian involvement in WWII, 1648
Clambakes, 657
Clear and present danger (Supreme Court ruling), 967
Clinton, Bill, 1085 (president)
Clinton administration policy (environment), 494
Cloning farm animals, 610
"Clothing" vs. "Fashion", 622
Club Med, 1769
CNN, 1345
Co-ops (apartments), 797
Coal and petroleum (WWII), 347
Cobb, Jerrie (space pilot), 1739
Coca-Cola, 661
Code talkers (Navajo soldiers), 512
Coffee, 662
Cohan, George (composer), 1099
Coin's Financial School, 292

Cold War (1946-1991)
  Atomic bomb, 1410
  Communist China, 1838
  Communist threats
    Communist China, 1838
    NATO, 1838
    West Berlin, 1838
  Demand for interstate highways, 1711
  Effect on class struggle, 1231
  Effects on minorities, 1231
  Fear of atomic bombs, 250
  Military spending, 154
  NATO, 1838
  Opportunities for science, 1556
  Origins, 1408
  Policy of containing the Soviet Union, 1837
  Red scare, 142, 155, 202, 967, 1231, 1279, 1290, 1811
  Second Red scare, 1838, 1842
  Space race, 1558
  Sputnik (impact of), 153
  Truman Doctrine, 1837
  U.S. money to fight communism, 96
  West Berlin, 1838

Coleman, Bessie (pilot), 1731
Collective bargaining, 145
Collectors, 1018, 1031
College entrance board exams, 418
Colonial America
  Business, 131
  Cities, 167
Colonial Williamsburg, 774
Colored American (newspaper), 1181
Colt .45 pistol, 1631
Coltrane, John (musician), 1122
Combine (farm machine), 602
Commentary, 1163
Commercial farms, 287, 596
Committee of 100 (WWI), 1378
Communalism, 1421
Communism (also see "Cold War")
  Crusade against, 1409
  Catholics, 1466
Community (concept of), 1673
Community policing, 951
Companionate family ideal, 554
Complexity and Contradiction in Architecture, 1692
Compromise of 1850 (slavery), 73
Compromise of 1877 (Reconstruction), 523
Compulsory education beginnings, 414
Computers
  Invention of, 921
  Use in leisure, 1029
Comstock, Anthony (reformer), 1044
Condominiums, 796
Coney Island, 993
Conglomerate farming, 601
Congregationalist, 1361, 1672
Construction methods, 777, 786
Consumers and social reform, 8, 10
Contingent work force, 1894
Contraception, 1076, 1604, 1048, 1064, 1467, 1585, 1594

Conwell, Russell H. (minister), 1372
Cookbooks, 663, 669
Cooke, Sam (songwriter), 1215
Copland, Aaron (composer), 1114
Copland (movie), 1249
Corn and soybean production, 614
Corn loan program, 589
Cornflakes, 664
Corporal punishment in schools, 437
Corporate spiritualism, 1484
Cosby, Bill (comedian), 1333
Cosmetics, 627
Cosmopolitan, 1177
Cotton, John (religious leader), 1359
Coughlin, Fr. Charles E. (radio priest), 1396
Council of National Defense (1940), 345
Council of Senior Citizens, 1529
Count Basie (musician), 1104, 1110

Counter-culture
  Beliefs, 1017
  Clothing, 638
  Environmentalists, 482
  Music, 1121, 1123

Country blues, 1095, 1102
Country music, 1113
Cowboy singers, 1114
Cowboys, 85
Cowell, Henry (composer), 1099
Crackers (food), 661
Creationism, 1479
Credit cards, 39, 876
Creech, The Reverend Jimmy (minister), 1475
Creel, George (journalist), 1173, 1803
Cremation, 258
Creole music, 1096, 1114

Crime and Justice, 195
  Assassination, 210
  Civil Rights era, 212
  Crime prevention techniques, 198
  Death penalty, 206
  Drugs, 215
  Federal police power, 200
  Hate crimes, 217
  Ku Klux Klan, 202
  Labor violence, 200
  Last meals (execution), 210
  Lynchings, 199, 1205
  Murders, 203
  Prohibition, 200, 1052

  Race riots, 186, 204, 213, 795, 947, 1203, 1224, 1236, 1279, 1298, 1304
  Rampage killers, 221
  Serial killers, 214
  Women, 216

Cronkite, Walter, 1846
Cruelty to farm animals issues, 612

Cuisine (influences on)
  African, 657
  Farm and frontier, 658
  Immigrants, 662
  Italian, 663, 673
  Reformers, 663, 669, 695
  Southern plantation, 657

Cryonics, 259
Cuban refugees, 859
Cugar, Xavier (band leader), 1112
Curley, James (Irish leader), 1276
Curriculum advances, 417
Curtiss, Glenn (inventor), 1730
Cyclotron, 1548

D
Daimler, Gottlieb (inventor), 1705
Dali Lama, 1417
Daly, Mary (feminist writer), 1445
Dancing (WWII), 1007
Dapper Dan (men's clothing style), 627
Darrow, Clarence (lawyer), 1387
Darwinism, 1161
  Social Darwinism, 1268, 1203, 1370, 1789, 1791
Davenport, Charles B. (Eugenics leader), 1548
Davies, Joseph (plantation owner), 523
Davis, Miles (musician), 1122
Dawes Plan (German reparations), 331, 968, 1267
Day, Dorothy (religious leader), 1398
DDT pesticide, 486
Dearborn Independent, 846

Death, 227
  (1900), 712
  (1950), 722
  (1999), 727
  Bureaucratizing death, 250
  Caskets, 253
  Cemeteries, 260
  Changing perceptions of, 245
  Cremation, 258
  Cryonics, 259

De-emphasizing death, 454
De-sensitizing death, 462
Death rates, 232, 235, 711
Dignity, 266
Embalming, 257
Flu epidemic of 1918, 234
Fraud, 256
Funeral homes, 257
Funeral industry, 252, 254
Grandparents, 243
Grief, 454, 455
Home burial, 252
Hospice, 269, 465
Hospitals, 250
Leading causes of
  (1900), 712; (1950), 722; (1999), 727
Life expectancy, 231, 238, 711, 723, 727
Miracle drugs, 236
Mourning customs, 246
Obituaries, 248
Old parents, 243
Physician-assisted suicide, 268
Privatizing death, 249
Prolonging, 265
Public health, 233, 235
Religions role, 262
Right to die movement, 267
Science and death, 263, 264
Siblings, 245
Undertakers, 254
Work related, 1899

Death penalty, 206
Debs, Eugene (labor leader), 139, 1173
Deep Ecology, 1442
Defenders, The, 1332
Deficit spending (1970s), 368
DeForest, Lee (inventor), 910
Delayed families, 569
Delmonico's restaurant, 666
Denny's discrimination law suit, 1900
Department stores, 6, 990, 1015
Department of Transportation, 1740
Depression (see Great Depression)
Deregulation of industry, 371
Designer jeans, 642
Development of commercial agriculture, 287
Dewey, John (educator), 419, 1269
Dianetics, 1438
Dick Van Dyke Show, 1332
Diem, Ngo Dinh (Vietnamese president), 1843

Diets/dieting
  Clothes for overweight Americans, 647
  Diet programs, 694
  Early 1900s, 664
  Fat free/healthy foods, 697, 699
  Food reformers, 664, 670
  Influence on fashion, 641

Diet for a Small Planet (cookbook), 696
Digital imaging, 1564
Dignity in dying, 266
Dilbert (cartoon), 1247
Dillingham Commission, 838, 840
Dinosaur National Monument controversy, 484
Dior, Christian (clothes designer), 633
Disabled people
  Children's education, 424, 430
  Handicapped access, 815
Disco, 1023, 1126
Discount stores, 635

Discrimination
  Age, 1517
  Asians, 1271, 1273, 1301
  Beginning of the 20th century, 1267
  Blacks, 1890
  Chinese, 1199, 1271
  Filipino, 1285, 1301
  Job, 1899
  Loans, 1233
  Mexican foster parents, 1206
  Mexican labor, 1206
  Movies, 1274
  Post-WWII discrimination against blacks, 1890
  Publix, Albertson's and Safeway law suits, 1900
  Race and gender, 1899
  Reverse discrimination, 1250
  Sports, 1252, 1273
  Supermarket jobs, 1900
  Wage, 1610, 1896
  Women, 1901
  WWII discrimination, 1289

Diseases (see **Health and Medicine**)
  Decline in infectious diseases, 236
Disneyland, 1014
Dissenters, 1357
Divine Principle, The, 1453
Divorce, 571, 800, 1049, 1066, 1598
Dixieland jazz, 1097
DNA, 1557, 1568
Doctors (see "Physicians")

Dodge City, Kansas, 1683
Dogfighting (aircraft), 1628
Dollar-a-Year men, 315
Dollar Diplomacy, 93
Domestic science, 669
Doppler, Christian (inventor), 906
Doughboys, 1630
Douglass, Frederick (abolitionist), 1767
Dr. Spock (child psychologist), 562
Draft (WWII), 1820
Dred Scott decision, 521
Dried foods, 688
Dress for Success, 641, 1610
Drew, Timothy (religious leader), 1431
Drover's Cottage, 1682
Drugs (illegal), 215
Drugs, war on, 1246
Du Bois, W.E.B., 1182, 1200, 1214, 1252, 1269, 1277
Dudley, William (conservative critic), 1394
Dudley, Paul (biologist), 1543
Due process in criminal law, 204, 975
Duryea, Charles and Frank (inventors), 1706
Dust bowl (causes of), 479
Dylan, Bob (musician), 1121

E

e. Coli outbreak, 610
E-commerce, 389
Earhart, Amelia (pilot), 1731
Earth First movement, 1443
Earth Day, 474
Eastman, George (inventor), 912
Eating disorders, 730
Echo Park Dam, 484
Economic Recovery Tax Act (1981), 821
Economic downturn (1937), 343

Economy, Part I: 1865-1900, 273 (see also
  Business and Labor)
  Assembly line production, 280
  Automobile (impact of), 279
  Cattle drives, 284
  Cattle industry, 284
  Decline of western farming, 286
  Development of commercial agriculture, 287
  Foundation 1860-1910, 276
  Gold rush, 283, 882, 1680
  Grievances 1880s-1890s, 288
  Inventions, 276
  Mass production, 280
  Mining, 283
  Oil, 277, 279

Railroad time, 282
Railroads, 281
Silver rush, 283
Tariffs 1870s-1890s, 289
Taylorism, 279, 1210, 1866
Water and irrigation, 285

Economy, Part II: 1900-1945, 303
  Agricultural Adjustment Act (1933), 334
  Civilian Conservation Corps, 337
  Clayton Antitrust Act, 311, 965
  Consumerism (1920s), 326
  Corporate capitalism, 297
  Corporate revolution of the 1890s, 299, 301
  Corporations (rise of), 294
  Depression, causes for
    Credit structure, 330
    Debt structure, 331
    Disposable income, 330
    Early signs of trouble, 328
    Economic diversification, 329
    Hoover's inaction, 332
    Overseas commerce, 330
  Dollar-a-Year men (WWI), 315
  Economic crisis of the 1890s, 299
  Economic downturn (1937), 343
  Economy Act (1932), 1598
  Emergency Banking Act (1933), 334
  Federal Trade Commission, 310, 965
  Financing WWI, 317, 319
  Financing WWII, 1827
  Food Administration (WWI), 316, 1806
  Fuel Administration (WWI), 316
  German reparations, 331
  Gold vs. silver standard, 291
  Industrial psychology, 325
  Inflation (WWI), 318
  Labor (1920s), 325
  Management (1920s), 326
  Mergers and consolidations (1920s), 327
  National Industrial Recovery Act (1933), 334, 336, 971
  New Deal 334, 344, 1882
  Panic of 1893, 300
  Preparation for WWII, 345
  Prosperity (post-WWI), 321, 324
  Reconstruction Finance Corp, 333
  Rockefeller, John D., 296
  Standard Oil of Ohio, 296
  Stock market crash (1929), 328; (1987), 377
  T. Roosevelt's economic and business policy, 307
  Taft's economic and business policy, 308
  Trusts/antitrusts, 290, 309, 311, 323, 340

War Industries Board (WWI), 314, 1805
Wilson's economic and business policy, 310
World War I economy, 312
World War II economy, 345

Economy, Part III: 1945-Present, 353
Banks, 385
Deficit spending (1970s), 368
Deregulation, 371
E-commerce, 389
Eisenhower's economic policy, 360
Energy crisis (1970s), 370
Federal Reserve, 381
Internet revolution, 388, 396
Kennedy's economic policy, 366
Keynesian economics, 359, 369
National debt, 376
New economy (1990s), 380
Post-WWII economy, 358
Reagan's economic policy, 372
Savings and loan crisis, 376
Stock market (1990s), 382, 887
Stock market crash (1987), 377
Supply-side economics, 372
War on poverty (Lyndon Johnson), 367

Edison, Thomas (inventor), 906, 909

Education and Literacy, 411
Bilingual education, 429
Brown vs. the Board of Education, 427, 525, 880, 975, 1232
Child labor and education, 415
Civil Rights changes, 427
College entrance board exams, 418
Compulsory education beginnings, 414
Concern for quality, 430
Corporal punishment, 437
Curriculum, 417
Depression, 422
Disabled children, 424
Education for handicapped children, 430
Education for illegal immigrants, 430
Education and work, 1145, 1898
G.I. Bill, 423
Girls sports, 430
Home schooling, 431
Illiteracy, 438
Immigrants, 416
Magnet schools, 433
Multiple-choice testing, 420, 1270
Prayer in schools, 424
Professional schools, 1150

Progressive ideas, 419, 1270
Public, 416
Rampage killers in schools, 221
Religion and education, 1478
School buses, 423
School violence, 436, 1251
Science emphasis, 425
Separate but equal schools, 418
Setting standards, 433
Sex education, 1609
Teaching the theory of evolution, 421
Vocational, 419, 420, 1146
Women's education in the 19th C., 1589

Education for All Handicapped Children Act (1975), 430
Education of Mentally Retarded Children Act (1958), 424
Educational Orders Act (1939), 345
Edwards, Jonathan (minister), 1366
Eight-hour work day, 1876
Einstein, Albert (phyiscist)
   Theories of relativity and light, 1542
Eisenhower, Dwight D. (general and president)
   Economic policy, 360
   World War II, 1835
El Spectator, 1179
El Heraldo de Mexico, 1179
Elderly (see **Retirement** and **Travel**)
   Medicine, 728
Electing minorities to government, 1301
Electric blues music, 1111
Electric automobile starters, 1706
Electricity, 906
Elementary and Secondary Education Act (1965), 428
Elitist press, 1166
Ellington, Duke (musician), 1104, 1110
Ellsberg, Daniel (Pentagon Papers), 1848
Elroy, James (novelist), 1248
Ely, Richard T. (social scientist), 1374
Embalming, 257
Emergency Banking Act (1933), 334

Emotional Change, 443
Anger, 456
Child psychology, 556
De-emphasizing death, 454
De-sensitizing death, 462
Gender and emotions, 451, 453
Grief, 454, 455
Guilt, 456

History of emotions, 450
Hospice, 465
Informalization of emotions, 459
Jealousy, 448
Jealousy, 457
Love and sex, 457
Motherly love, 456
Political behavior, 463
Psychoanalysis, 461
Public display of emotions, 446
Restraining emotions, 466
Road rage, 465
Sibling rivalry, 448
Social expectations, 452
World War II, 1008

Empire State Building, 766
Employment opportunities for immigrants, 838
Endangered species, 489

Energy (see also **Environment**)
  Crisis (1970s), 370
  Conservation, 805
  From farm crops, 613

Enfield rifle, 1630
Eno, William (traffic rules), 1707

Entertainment (see **Leisure**)
  In towns, 1688
  Urban, 177
  World War II, 1644, 1828

Environment, 471
  Bush administration policy, 495
  Clinton administration policy, 494
  Counter-culture environmentalists, 482
  Dinosaur National Monument controversy, 484
  Dust bowl (causes of), 479
  Earth Day, 474
  Endangered species, 489
  Environmental protection, 487
  Everglades National Park cleanup, 494
  Farming, 608
  Forest Reserve Act (1891), 476
  Grassroots environmental movement, 488
  Legislation and agreements, 493
  Los Angeles, 176
  National Park Service Act (1916), 483
  Nuclear technology, 480, 1551
  Oil embargo, 492
  Pollution, 486

Popularizing nature, 490
Preservation vs. conservation, 477
Recycling, 488
T. Roosevelt's environmental policy, 476
Tennessee Valley Authority, 480
Transportation, 1741
Water reclamation, 478
Wilderness Act (1964), 485

Environmental protection, 487
Epidemic diseases, 728
Episcopal
  system of church government, 1357
  view on homosexuality, 1478
Equal Opportunity Employment Commission, 1250
Equal Pay Act (1963), 1605
Equal Rights Amendment, 1605
Erotic literature, 1070
Eskimo Pie, 678
Espionage Act (1917), 967, 1173, 1803
Espionage (WWII), 1649
Ethanol production, 612

Ethnic Minority Groups, 499
  African Americans
    Citizenship for former slaves, 522
    Classes of, 526
    Cultural influence, 639, 645
    Definitions of "slave," 520
    End of Reconstruction, 523
    Hate groups, 527
    Migration/riding the rails, 1722
    Progress, 526
    Restricting freedom for slaves, 520
    Right to vote, 522
    Role of black soldiers in the Civil War, 521
    Segregation, 524
    Service in the Spanish-American War, 1619
    World War I, 1805, 1808
    World War I veterans, 1214
    World War II labor, 1223
    World War II servicemen, 1825
  Asian Americans
    Chinese
      Chinese Exclusion Act (1882), 531, 1271
      Chinese in Hawaii, 530
      Immigrants 1820-1860, 528
      Laborers, 529
      Migration to cities, 531
      Opportunities for work, 530
      Repealing Chinese exclusion, 532, 1288
      Transcontinental railroad, 529

Filipinos
  Hawaiian workers, 535, 1271, 1282
  Increased immigration to the U.S., 535, 849
  Laborers, 1281
  Strikes and unions, 535, 1286
Hispanic Americans
  Ancestry, 518
  Assimilation, 519
  Chicanos, 514
  Coalition groups, 1247
  Education, 519
  Greaser Act, 516
  Immigration, 1228
  Labor, 517, 1206, 1224, 1281
  Land Act, 517
  Restrictions against Mexicans, 1870s, 516
  U.S. relations with Mexico 1840s, 514
  War with Mexico, 515
Japanese Americans
  Economic success, 534
  Hostilities toward, 533, 1272
  Immigrants 1868-1924, 532
  Internment during WWII, 533, 852, 972, 1289, 1826
  Laborers, 532
  Discrimination against, 1271, 1285, 1301
  Success of Asian Americans, 536, 1240

Ethnic Press, The, 1163

Ethnicity
  Cities, 170
  Entertainment, 993
  Foods, 699
  Press, 1162
  Television, 1010

Eugenics movement, 1269, 1547
  Sterilization, 969
European brain drain, 848
Evans, Hiram Wesley (Imperial Wizard KKK), 1383, 1391
Everglades National Park cleanup, 494
Evolution (see also "Darwin")
  And religion, 1386
  Theory of, 421
Exxon *Valdez* oil spill, 492
Expansion (see **American Expansion**)
Explorer spacecraft, 1559

F
Fair Deal, 358

Fair Employment Practices Commission (1941), 358, 1887
Fair Labor Standards Act (1938), 342
Fair Packaging and Labeling Act (1975), 695
Fair Trade Act (1937), 339
Fairs (tourism), 1761
Falling Water (house), 775
Falwell, Jerry (TV evangelist), 1470

Family Life, 541
  Abortion, 212, 1077, 1605
  Contemporary family concerns, 570
  Delayed families, 569
  Divorce, 571, 800, 1066, 1079, 1598
  Family demographics, 570
  Leisure activities, 1030
  1950s
    Child-rearing practices, 563
    Dr. Spock, 562
    Entertainment for children, 1012
    Gender roles, 1014, 1600
    Housewives, 563, 1009, 1014, 1603
    Housing, 563
    Post-war birthrates, 561
    Post-war marriages, 561, 1068, 1600
    Religion, 563, 1584
    Role dissatisfaction, 564
  1960s
    Families in turmoil, 565
    Generational conflict, 566
    Working women, 566, 880
    African-American families, 567
    Government assistance to families, 569
    Sexual behavior and pregnancy, 1076
  Nineteenth Century
    Birth control, 1048, 1467, 1585, 1594
    Child labor, 550, 1142
    Child-rearing practices, 547
    Divorce, 1049, 1066, 1598
    Education, 547
    Frontier families, 552
    Impact of industrialization, 544
    Income for working class families, 551
    Living conditions, 548, 551, 553, 1211
    Marriage, 548, 552, 888, 1049
    Role of children, 546
    Role of women, 545, 553, 1584
    Sexual practices, 546, 1585, 1590
    Women's rights movement, 1586
    Working class families, 549
    Working women, 1588
  Reunification of immigrant families, 857

Sex education, 1609
Twentieth Century
    Companionate family, 554
    Courtship, 1594
    Depression assistance to families, 559
    Depression finances, 558
    Effect of the Depression, 557
    Effect of WWII, 559
    Family related legislation, 556
    Flapper society, 555, 1055, 1592
    Role of women, 554
    Single women, 1589, 1593
    Youth culture, 555
Typical family, 544
Working women
    1920s, 1592
    Family friendly benefits, 1901
    History of, 1867
    WWII, 560, 1793

Faraday, Michael (inventor), 906
Fard, W.D. (religious leader), 1429
Farm Security Administration (1935), 341

Farming, 577
Agricultural Adjustment Act, 149, 334, 972
Agricultural science, 1546, 1561
Alternative jobs for farmers, 597
Artificial insemination, 610
Bankhead-Jones Farm Tenancy Act (1937), 341
Bankruptcy of rural banks, 599
Bioengineered crops and livestock, 1568
Black farmers, 1222
California farming, 604
Cloning farm animals, 610
Commercial farms, 596
Controlling food surpluses, 586
Converting farming to war, 593
Corn and soybean production, 614
Corn loan program, 589
Cruelty to animals issues, 612
Decline of farms, 597
Decline of western farming, 286
Declining farm population, 592
Development of commercial agriculture, 287
Environmental issues with farming, 608
Ethanol production, 612
Farm Aid concerts, 600
Farm machines, 660
Farm Security Administration (1935), 341
Food safety, 606, 610, 694
Foreign markets, 614
Genetic corn controversy, 609, 611
Genetic engineering of seed, 591
Government assistance to farmers, 586
Grain embargoes, 598
Great Depression, 587
Grievances 1880s-1890s, 288
Hog farming, 605
Hog subsidies, 588
Homestead farm project, 583
Immigrant, 837
Increase in production (1950s), 362
Infectious farm animal diseases, 609
Jerusalem artichoke, 613
Living History Farms, 580
Machines, 660
Modern farms and conglomerates, 601
Murray, William G., 580
Number of farms 1915-1995, 581
Old-fashion farm, 582
Organic farming, 607, 698, 1562
Pioneers in agriculture, 615
Politicians and farming, 584
Railroads, 285
Relocating Dust Bowl farmers, 770
Rural electrification, 589
Rural Electrification Administration (1935), 341
Seed hybridization, 590
Sick chicken case, 150
Soil and water conservation, 590
U.S. grain surpluses, 584
U.S./Soviet agricultural relations, 597
Water and irrigation, 285
World War II, 349
    food production, 593

Farmer, Fanny (chef), 669
Farnsworth, Philip (inventor), 905, 1324
Farrakhan, Louis (religious leader), 1435, 1474

Fashion, 619
Assembly line clothing production, 628
Barbie's wardrobe, 637, 1013
Bell bottoms, 641
Bikini swimwear, 634, 1068
Casual business dress, 647
Children's clothes, 636
Clothes and ideology, 640
Clothes for overweight Americans, 647
"Clothing" vs. "Fashion", 622
Correct fashion and proper behavior (1950s), 635
Cosmetics, 627
Counter-culture clothing, 638

Dapper Dan, 627
Depression years fashion, 629
Designer jeans, 642
Designs for the wealthy, 623
Diets and panty hose, 641
Dior's revolution, 633
Effect of World War I on clothing, 627
Effect of World War II on clothing, 632
Fashion shows and profession models, 646
Flapper attire, 627, 1592
French couture in America, 630, 638
Generation gap (The Gap) clothing, 639
Gibson Girl look, 624
Granny look, 640
Hair coloring, 640
Home decoration fashion, 647
Influence of
  Disco and punk, 642
  Italian designers, 636
  Jackie Kennedy, 638
  Madonna, 645
  Musicians, 640
  Ronald Reagan and Princess Diana, 643
  Vietnam, 640
  Women's liberation, 639
Little black dress, 625
Maternity wear, 626
Military clothing, 633
Mini dress, 638, 1610
Movie star fashion and influence, 629, 641, 644, 996
Oriental influence, 644
Plastic surgery and cosmetics, 645
Poiret's vampish designs, 624
Protest and fashion, 639
Sexual dress, 1610
Shopping centers and discount stores, 635, 1014, 1027
Supermodels, 645
Sweatshop garment production, 626
Synthetic fibers, 631, 914
Unisex styles, 639
Women in pants, 627, 641
Yuppi styles, 644
Zoot suit, 632

Fast food
  Beginning, 667
  Drive-through windows, 691
  Fast food industry, 690
  McDonalds and Howard Johnson's, 681

Father Divine (religious leader), 1430

FBI, 936, 938, 944
Federal Aid Highway Act (1938, 1944, 1952, 1954), 1710
Federal Art Project (1935), 342, 1004
Federal Dance Project (1935), 342
Federal Housing Administration, 770
Federal Housing Authority, 180, 1233
Federal National Mortgage Association (1938), 771
Federal Power Commission (1935), 338
Federal Reserve, 318, 381
Federal Road Act (1916), 1710
Federal Savings and Loan Insurance Corp, 770
Federal Surplus Commodities Corp, 684
Federal Theater Program (1935), 342
Federal Writers Program (1935), 342
Federalist Papers #10, 1159
Federation of American Zionists, 1401
Female teen readers, 1176
Feminism (see "Women")
Feminism (Catholic position), 1468
Feminist theology, 1444
Femme fatale, 1069
Ferdinand, Franz (Archduke), 1799
Ferguson, Miriam (governor), 1387
Fermi, Enrico (atomic physicist), 915, 1551
Fertility treatment, 739
Fiber optics, 924
Field's Code, 205
Fifth Amendment (self-incrimination), 949
Filipino Americans (see "Asian Americans")
Film noir, 1067
Film industry, 1067
Finger printing, 945
First modern war, 1787
Fitzgerald, John (Irish leader), 1276
Flapper attire, 627, 1592
Flapper society, 555, 1055, 1592
Fleming, Alexander (medical research), 1065
Fletcher, Horace (food reformer), 664
Flint Michigan strike, 1244
Florida real estate speculation, 884
Flour, 658
Flu epidemic of 1918, 234, 714

Food, 651
  Additives, 694
  Advertising nutrition, 676
  Alcohol consumption and temperance, 674
  Beginning of fast food, 667, 681
  Cafeterias and automats, 666
  Canning, 660
  Chicago stockyards, 658, 668

Coffee, 662
Cookbooks, 663, 669
Crackers, Coca-Cola, margarine, gelatin, candy, 661
Diet of Colonial Americans, 656
Dieting, 694
Diversity and abundance, 698
Domestic science/home economics, 669
Eating during the Depression, 683
Farm and frontier cuisine, 658
Farm machines, 660
Feeding the soldiers, 686
Food and status, 696
Food Nutrition Board, 685
Food on the home front, 687
Food packaging and storage, 688, 691
Food safety, 606, 610, 668, 694
Food stamps, 684
Food standards, 674
Food surpluses, 586
Genetic engineering, 697
Government assistance food programs, 684
Heat and eat food, 700
Impact of the Industrial Revolution, 658
Influence of African cuisine, 657
Influence of immigrants, 662
Malnutrition, 673, 693
New Nutrition, 669
Newer nutrition, 676
Nutrition reform for the poor, 669
Organic, 698
Outdoor cooking, 689, 784
Preservation, 659, 678, 914
Preventive nutrition, 693
Processed food, 660
Radio shows, 681
Reformers, 663, 669, 695
Refrigeration, 660, 685, 910
School lunch boxes, 689
School lunch programs, 693
Scientific research on food, 670
Southern plantation cuisine, 657
Standardizing the American diet, 682
Supermarkets, 678
TV dinners and dried foods, 688
Vitamins, 676, 678, 721
War on poverty, 693
World War I, 672, 1806
World War II poor nutrition, 685

Food safety
  Farming, 606, 610, 668, 694
  Standards, 694

Food Administration, 316, 1806
Food Nutrition Board, 685
Ford, Henry (inventor/industrialist), 846, 907
Ford Motor Company, 1706
Ford-Ferguson (contribution to WWII), 593
Fordney-McCumber Tariff (1922), 968
Foreign agricultural markets, 614
Foremen and supervisors, 1875
Forest Reserve Act (1891), 476
Formaldehyde toxic gas in homes, 806
Fortune, T. Thomas (black labor leader), 1202
Four-minute men, 1803
Fourteenth Amendment (1866), 522
France (invasion of WWII), 1637, 1649
Frank, Leo trial (for rape), 204
Frank, Robert (lynch victim), 1274
Franklin, Benjamin, 902, 1158, 1365
Fraud, 256
Free enterprise
  Court decision about, 965
Freed, Alan (musician), 1116
French couture in America, 630, 638
French resistance (WWII), 1649

Frontier
  Cow towns, 85
  Cowboys, 85
  Families, 552
  Homestead Act, 81, 881
  Mexico, 59
  Population growth, 62
  Railroads, 80
  Slavery, 72
  Society, 57
  Women, 57

Frozen foods, 678
Fuel Administration, 316
Fugitive Slave Laws (1795, 1850), 521
Fundamentalists, 1390
Funeral homes, 257
Funeral industry, 252, 254
Funk music, 1024, 1125
Fusion alliance, 1203
Fusion music, 1125

G
G.I. Bill
  Loans to veterans, 779
  Veterans go to school, 423, 878
G.I.s (WWII)
  Entertainment, 1644

Holocaust, 1651, 1829
Medicine, 1643
Outfitting, 1640
Rations, 1643
Weapons, 1641

Gadsden Purchase, 74
Gambling, 892, 1053, 1060, 1066
  for charity, 1061
Game shows, 890
Games
  Board, 991
  Video, 1029
Gangsters, 938
Garvey, Marcus (black leader), 1182, 1214, 1282
Gated communities, 820
Gates, Bill, 888
GATT, 95
Gays (see "Homosexuals")
Gelatin, 661
Gender (see "Women," **Sex and Gender,** and **Family Life**)
Gender and emotions, 451, 453
General Allotment Act (1887), 1216
General Motors (Flint Michigan strike), 1244

Generation gap
  Clothing, 639
  Conflict, 566
  Families in turmoil, 565
  Music 1121, 1128, 1248

Generation X, 1128

Genetic engineering, 697, 1563
  Corn controversy, 609, 611
  Food, 697
  Seed production, 591

Genome and DNA research, 1567
Gentrification, 804
Georgia Tom (composer), 1112
German reparations, 331
Germany (invasion of WWII), 1638
Gershwin, George (composer), 1106
Getz, Stan (musician), 1122
Ghandi (spiritual leader), 1426
Gibson Girl look, 624
Gideon v. Wainwright, 976
Gillespie, Dizzy (musician), 1111
Ginsberg, Allen (poet), 1416
Girls sports in schools, 430

Glenn, John H. (astronaut), 1560, 1739
Global economy, 394
God Is Dead controversy, 1493
Gold rush, 283, 882, 1680
Gompers, Samuel (labor leader), 138
Good Humor Bar, 678
Goodman, Benny (musician), 1110, 1287
Gordy, Berry (songwriter), 1117
Gorsuch, Anne (Dept of the Interior), 493
Gospel music, 1112
Gospel of wealth, 1370
Gourmet Magazine, 691
Grace, Sweet Daddy (religious leader), 1429
Grady, Henry (newspaper editor), 136
Graham, The Reverend Billy (minister), 1412
Graham, William Sylvester (food reformer), 664
Graham cracker, 664
Grain embargoes, 598
Grain surpluses, 584
Grand Ole Opry, 1106, 1112
Grand Teton National Park, 1765
Grandparents, 243
Granny look, 640
Grant, Madison (author), 846
Grapes of Wrath, 1223, 1768
Grassroots environmental movement, 488
Greaser Act, 516
Great Awakening, 1364, 1366

Great Depression
  Black farmers, 1222
  Causes for, 328
  Credit structure, 330
  Death rates decline, 236
  Debt structure, 331
  Disposable income, 330
  Early signs of trouble, 146, 328
  Economic diversification, 329
  Education during, 422
  Effect on families, 557
  Entertainment, 1004
  Farming, 587
  Fashion, 629
  Federal assistance to families, 559
  Food, 683
  Hoover's inaction, 332
  Housing, 767
  Impact on farming, 587
  Overseas commerce, 330
  Redistribution of wealth, 1217
  Religion, 1392
  Relocating Dust Bowl farmers, 770

Travel during, 1767
Work, 1879

Great Migration (music), 1102
Great Plains housing, 751
Great Plains towns, 1683
Great Society (Lyndon Johnson), 367
Great White Hope, the (boxer), 1274
Greek Orthodox Church, 1457
Green tourism, 1773
Greenspan, Alan (economist), 381, 800, 1244
Grief, 454, 455
Griffith, D.W. (director), 910, 1274
Griggs, Sutton E. (writer), 1212
Gross, Al (walkie-talkie inventor), 916
Grumann fighter planes, 1635
Grunge and rap music, 1128
Guadalcanal (WWII battle), 1633
Guardian, The, 1183
Guilt, 456
Gulf of Tonkin Resolution, 1655, 1844
Gulf War syndrome, 1851
Gurus (Hindu), 1419
Gutter journalism, 1168

H
Hair coloring, 640
Hale, George (astronomer), 1545
Haley, Bill (musician), 1117
Halfway Covenant, 1368
Hamburger (invention of), 667
Hammer v. Dagenhart (1918), 969
Handicapped (see Disabled)
Handicapped access, 815
Handicapped children's education, 430
Handy, W.C. (Composer), 1095
Harassment
  Religious, 1487
  Sexual, 217, 1901
Harding, Warren G. (president), 322
Harlem Renaissance, 1103
Harrington, Michael (author), 365, 692, 1297, 1896
Harrison, William Henry (president)
  Indian policy, 509
Harvey House, 666
Hate crime, 217
Hate groups, 527
Hauptmann, Bruno (kidnapper), 937

Hawaii
  Annexation, 88
  Chinese workers, 530
  Filipino workers, 535

Hawley-Smoot Tariff (1930), 968
Hawthorne Experiment, 1210
Hays Code (Hollywood), 941, 1061

Health and Medicine, 705
  Addictive substances, 713
  Advances during WWI and the Depression years, 720
  Advances in the 1960s, 726
  AIDS, 241
  Alternative medicine, 735
  Anesthesia, 713
  Cancer, 240
  Decline in death rates, 711
  Discovery of micro-organisms, 710
  Doctors and death, 252
  Eating disorders, 730
  Elderly, 728
  Epidemic diseases, 728
  Flu epidemic 1918, 714
  Health awareness, 721
  Health Bureaucracy, 730
  Health care cost, 730, 739
  Health Maintenance Organizations, 732
  Heart disease and cancer, 239, 724
  Hospitals, 718, 737
  Life expectancy, 711, 723, 727, 231, 238,
  Medicaid and Medicare, 726
  Medical research, 725
  Medical technology, 737
  Nurses, 718, 725, 736, 1796, 1807
  Physicians
    American Medical Association, 717
    Dot.com doctors, 735
    Medical training, 716, 718, 733
    Practice, 715, 718
    Salaries and fees, 724, 732
    Victims of anti-abortionists, 1489
  Public health, 233, 235
  Vaccinations, 713

Hearst, Patty (revolutionary), 1336
Hearst newspapers, 1165
Heart disease, 239, 724
Heatter, Gabriel (reporter), 1321
Heavy metal music, 1124
Heinz, Henry J. (food processor), 660
Helicopters (WWII), 1646
Helmets (WWII), 1640
Henderson, Fletcher (musician), 1109
Hendrix, Jimi (muscian), 1121, 1125, 1302

Herbs (medical), 736
Hernandez v. Texas (1954), 1232
Hershey, Milton S. (candy maker), 661
Herzl, Theodore (journalist), 1399
Hetch Hetchy Valley/Dam, 477
Hickok, Wild Bill (lawman), 1682
High rise buildings, 753
Highland Beach, Maryland, 1767
Highway patrols, 934
Highways (see **Automobiles and Highways** and **Transportation**)
Hill-Burton Act, 251
Hillbilly music, 1106
Hindenberg explosion, 1737

Hinduism, 1419
  Influence on the Civil Rights movement, 1426
  Origins in America, 1419
  Transcendental meditation, 1420

Hippies
  Clothing, 639
  Lifestyle, 1845
  Religion, 1421

Hirabayashi v. U.S., 972

Hispanic Americans
  Ancestry, 518
  Assimilation, 519
  Chicanos, 514
  Education, 519
  Greaser Act, 516
  Labor, 517, 1224
  Land Act, 517
  Restrictions against Mexicans, 1870s, 516
  U.S. relations with Mexico 1840s, 514
  War with Mexico, 515

Historic preservation, 821
Hitler, Adolf, 1816
Ho Chi Minh trail, 1656
Hog farming, 605
Hog subsidies, 588
Holding Company Act (1935), 338
Holiday, Billie (singer), 1287
Holocaust, 1651, 1829, 1832
Holy Koran, The, 1431
Home Box Office, 1342
Home burial, 252
Home decoration fashion, 647
Home economics, 669

Home entertainment, 1026
Home health hazards, 806
Home Owners Loan Corp, 179
Home ownership, 758, 877
Home schooling, 431
Homelessness, 768
Homestead farm project, 583
Homestead strike, 139, 200

Homosexuals
  Changing attitudes, 1606
  Culture, 1024
  Gay Rights movement, 1078
  Religion, 1475
  Same sex marriages, 1475, 1607
  Violence against, 1489

Hooker, Thomas (dissident minister), 1358
Hoover Dam, 479
Hoover, J. Edgar (FBI director), 936, 938

Hoover, Herbert (president)
  Economic crisis, 147
  Food Administration head, 672
  Policy toward business, 322
  Reconstruction Finance Corp, 333, 968
  Response to economic crisis (1931), 332
  Tariffs, 968

Hooverized diets, 673
Hopalong Cassidy (cowboy), 689
Horse Bend, Battle of, 507
Hospice movement, 269, 465
Hospitals, 250, 718, 737
Hostile takeover, 377
House Un-American Activities Committee, 1067, 1327, 1331, 1839
Housewives, 563, 1009, 1014, 1603

Housing and Architecture, 745
  Apartments, 761
  Apartments and rental houses, 780, 796
  Baby boomers, 182
  Bungalow houses, 757
  Cities, 172
  Colonial Williamsburg, 774
  Construction methods, 777, 786
  Depression era, 179
  Depression woes, 767
  Discrimination for loans, 1233
  Energy conservation, 805
  Excluding African Americans, 787, 1233

Expanding suburbs, 783, 875, 1711
Failed government housing programs, 789, 801
Federal backing of mortgage banks, 769
Federal Housing Administration
  Creation of, 770
    Discrimination for loans, 1233
    Housing programs in the 1960s, 793
Gated communities, 820
Gentrification, 804, 1242
Government housing loans, 789, 1233
Government loans, 180
Great Plains housing, 751
Growth of Cities, 754
Handicapped access, 815
High rise buildings, 753
Historic preservation, 821
Home health hazards, 806
Home ownership, 758, 877
Homelessness, 768
House of Tomorrow, 774
Household demographics, 760
Housing and apartment boom 1920s, 763
Housing conditions, 751, 760, 781
Housing starts, 776, 778, 782, 791, 797, 799, 807, 817
Housing Styles
  1920s, 765
  Bungalow, 757
  Colonial, 805
  International, 773
  Neo-French, 805
  Neo-Tudor, 805
  Postmodernism, 805
  Prairie, 756
  Queen Anne, 752
  Ranch, 785
  Regional, 813
  Usonian, 774
  Wealthy, 753
  Working class, 772
HUD, 795, 803, 812
Immigration and migration late 1800s, 750
Inflation and housing prices, 799
International style, 773
Loans to veterans, 779
Mail order houses, 757
Mobile homes, 772, 792, 798
Model cities programs, 794
Mortgages, 758
Orthodox Church architecture, 1458
Post-war boom in housing, 778, 781
Prairie style houses and Progressive reform, 756

Pre-fab housing, 807
Progressive movement concerns, 756
Prosperity and housing, 819
Public housing, 780, 797
Racial and ethnic prejudice in cities, 756, 1223
Ranch houses, 785
Rejection of Victorian style, 757
Relocating Dust Bowl farmers, 770
Savings and Loan crisis, 809
Single family houses, 752
Skyscrappers, 766
Subsidized housing, 803, 816, 877
Suburban development, 764
Tax breaks, 182
Townhouses, 814
Urban renewal, 788, 790, 813, 814, 1234, 1241
Vanderbilt estate, 753
World War I, 761
World War II, 776
Wright, Frank Lloyd, 756, 774
Zoning laws, 765

Housing Act (1959), 790
Housing Act (1961), 793
Housing Act (1965), 793
Housing Act (1968), 794
Housing and Community Act (1987), 811
Housing conditions, 751, 760, 781
Housing loans (government), 789, 793
Housing programs (government), failed, 789, 801
Housing starts, 776, 778, 782, 791, 797, 799, 807, 817
Housing styles (see **Housing and Architecture**)
Howard Johnson's restaurants, 681
Howdy Doody (TV star), 1329
Howl, 1416
Hubbard, L. Ron (Scientology), 1438
Hubble, Edwin (astronomer), 1545
HUD, 795, 803, 812
Hughes, Langston (writer), 1215
Human Sexual Response, 1604
HUMVEES, 1663
Hutchinson, Anne (religious leader), 1358
Hyde, Ida (scientist), 1549

I

I Spy, 1333
I Love Lucy, 1113, 1328
Ice makers, 659

Illegal aliens
  1990s, 861, 1305
  Arguments supporting restrictions, 862

Education of, 430
Illiteracy, 438

Illustrated magazines, 1169
Immigrant Press and Its Control, 1162

Immigration, 831
  Assimilation, 845, 851, 1268
  Canadian, 850
  Caribbean, 858
  Chinese discrimination, 1199, 1271
  Christian attitudes after WWI, 1383
  Dillingham Commission, 838, 840
  Employment opportunities, 838
  European brain drain, 848
  Family reunification, 857
  Farmers, 837
  Filipino, 849
  First settlers, 834
  Illegal aliens
    (1990s), 861, 1305
    Arguments supporting restrictions, 862
  Immigrant enclaves in cities, 838
  Immigrants with special skills, 853, 857
  Internment of Japanese Americans, 533, 851, 972, 1289, 1826
  Jewish immigration, 846, 847
  Literacy tests, 843
  Main waves of immigration, 835, 1759
  Mexican, 850, 857, 1228
  Music, 1099, 1111
  Pan American, 849
  Population centers, 836, 839, 856
  Profile of immigrant workers, 1870
  Racism
    Immigrants, 846, 1194
    Police brutality, 949
    Sports, 1274
  Refugees, 858
    Jewish, 847
    Cuban, 859
    Vietnamese, 860
    Russian, 861
  Restrictions
    (1882-1924), 840
    (1990s), 862
    Act of 1965, 855
    Asian, 841, 1271
    Consequences of, 847
    Opposition by business, 842
    Support by intellectuals, 843
    Support by labor, 843
    World War I, 1279
    World War II, 1833
  Terrorists, 866
  Travels of immigrants, 1754

Immigration and Nationality Act (1965), 535
Immigration and Naturalization Service, 938
Immigration Reform Act, 1294

Imperialism, 87
  Anti-imperialism, 89
  Imperialism and race, 1207, 1270
  Vietnam, 1297

In God We Trust, 973, 1413
Income for working class families in the 19th C., 551
Income tax (personal), 966
Indian Affairs, Bureau of, 510
Indian Appropriation Act (1871), 511
Indians (see "Native Americans")

Individual Prosperity and the American Dream, 869
  Credit cards, 876
  Florida real estate speculation, 884
  G.I. college education, 878
  Gambling, 892, 1053
  Game shows, 891
  Home ownership, 758, 877
  Horatio Alger and the American dream, 872
  Klondike gold rush, 882
  Levittown, 877
  Lotteries, 893, 1061, 1080
  Marriage and money, 888
  Migration of Americans, 872, 881
  Quality of life
    (1890-1925), 874
    (1945-1970), 874, 877
  Stock market boom (1920s), 885, (1990s), 887
  Subsidized housing, 877
  Sweepstakes, 895
  Texas oil boom, 884
  Walmart and Microsoft, 888
  Westward migration, 881

Industrial democracy, 1883
Industrial spies, 1884
Industrial Workers of the World, 141

Industrialization
  Effect on cities, 169
  Impact on families, 544
  Influence on food, 658

Infectious farm animal diseases, 609
Inflation (WWI), 318
Inflation and housing prices, 799, 817
Influence of Sea Power upon History, 1791
Inside North Vietnam, 1334
Installment buying, 908
Intellectuals
  Jewish, 1295
  Minority, 1302
Intelligence and ethnicity, 1246
Intelligent design, 1483
International law, 965, 979
International style (architecture), 773
Internet (morality), 1084
Internet, 1563
Internet revolution, 388, 396
Internment camps for Japanese, 533, 852, 972, 1289, 1826
Interstate Commerce Commission (1935), 339
Interstate highways, 785, 1711

Inventions, 897 (see also **Science** and **Technology**)
  Airplane, 1728
  Atomic bomb, 915
  Automobile, 907, 911
  Computers, 921
  Early American inventors, 902
  Economic importance, 276
  Electricity, 906
    Inventing uses of, 908
  Fiber optics, 924
  Industrial Revolution, 902
  Installment buying, 908
  Labor saving devices, 913
  Microchips, 920
  Milestones, 903
  Motion picture, 909
  Nylon, 914
  Phonograph, 909
  Photography, 912
  Plastics, 918
  Radar, 906
  Radio, 905
  Refrigeration, 910, 913
  Scientific revolution (1600-1700s), 901
  Space technology, 918, 920, 1737
  Synthetics, 911
  Telephone, 906
  Television, 918
  Transistors, 919
  Two way radio, 916
  Vacuum tube, 910

X-ray, 905

Iowa Jima and Okinawa (invasion, atomic bomb), 1639
Irish
  Irish Americans and northern blacks, 1201
  Irish power, leaders and entertainers, 1276
Iron Curtain, 1409
Irradiation, 1569
Islam in America, 1454, 1490
Italian influence on
  American cuisine, 663, 673
  American fashion, 636
Itinerant preachers, 1365
Ives, Charles (composer), 1098

J

Jackson, Andrew (president)
  Battle of Horse Bend, 507
  Indian policy, 507, 1197
Jackson Hole, Wyoming, 1765
Jackson Index (newspaper), 1181
Japan trade, 74
Japanese Americans (see "Asian Americans")
Japanese Americans, internment of, 533, 851, 972, 1289, 1826
Japanese Bushido Code, 1647
Jazz, 1062, 1096, 1105, 1110, 1122
Jealousy, 448, 457
Jeans (designer), 642
Jefferson, Thomas (president)
  Indian policy, 507
  Inventor, 902
Jeffries, James (boxer), 1274
Jello, 683
Jerusalem artichoke, 613

Jews
  Activists, 1276
  Actors and musicians, 1287
  Conservative Judaism, 1461
  Cuisine, 663
  Differences among Jews, 1462
  Early settlers, 1362
  Entertainers, 1276
  Garment workers, 1275
  Holocaust, 1651, 1829, 1832
  Immigration, 846, 847
  Intellectuals, 1295
  Judaism in the 1930s, 1399
  Orthodox, 1459
  Reform Judaism, 1460
  Sports stars, 1283

Zionism, 1399, 1461

Jim Crow, 1095, 1201
John Deere (contribution to WWII), 593
Johnson, Jack (boxer), 1274
Johnson, James (composer), 1104
Johnson, Lady Bird (highway beautification), 1712
Johnson, Lyndon (role in Vietnam), 1657
Jolson, Al (entertainer), 1282
Jones, George (musician), 1116
Joplin, Scott (musician), 1094
Joy of Cooking, The 669
Judiciary Act (1789), 935
Jungle, The (novel 1906), 668, 1213

K

Kahanamoku, Duke (athlete), 1277
Kaltenborn, H.V. (reporter), 1321
Kansas (school board decision on evolution), 1479
Kellogg, John Harvey (food reformer), 664
Kellogg-Briand Pact (1928), 968, 1401
Kelly, Grace (princess), 889
Kennedy, Jackie's influence on fashion, 638
Kennedy, John F. (service in WWII), 1636
Kennedy's economic policy, 366
Kent State massacre by National Guard, 1847
Kenton, Stan (musician), 1122
Kentucky Fried Chicken, 690
Kerner Commission, 947
Kerouac, Jack (writer), 1416
Keynesian economics, 359, 369
Kilgore, Texas, 884
King, B.B. (musician), 1111
King, Bille Jean (tennis star), 1021
King James I, 1356

King, Martin Luther, Jr.
  Birmingham jail, 186
  Montgomery, 526
  Nonviolent civil disobedience, 1427
  Religious ideas, 1427
  Vietnam war views, 1236

King, Rodney (victim), 949, 1304
Kinsey, Alfred (sexologist), 1069, 1603
Kinsey Report, 1070, 1078
Kipling, Rudyard (poet), 1271
Klein, Calvin (clothes designer), 642
Klondike gold rush, 882
Knights of Labor, 138, 1199, 1202
Kodak film, 913

Korean War
  Battlefield conditions, 1654
  Beginning of, 1652
  Military campaign, 1839
  Red Cross, 1841
  Women in the war, 1841

Koresh, David (spiritual leader), 1491
Krag-Jorgensen rifle, 1621
Ku Klux Klan, 202, 212, 846, 946, 1274, 1280, 1383
Kwaskwami (Indian chief), 509
Kyoto Protocol, 493

L

L.A. Confidential, 1248
Labeling (food), 695, 697
Labor (see **Business and Labor**)
Labor and white supremacy, 1872
Labor saving devices, 913
Ladies Home Journal, 1174
Lagasse, Emeril (chef), 700
Lambert, John William (inventor), 1706
Lamp unto My Feet, 1330
Land Act, 517
Land Ordinance of 1785, 50
Langmuir, Irving (physicist), 1543
Las Vegas, 893, 1066, 1966

Latin America
  Music, 1112
  Roosevelt Corollary, 93, 1797
  Trade with the U.S., 95

Laurel's Kitchen (cookbook), 695
Laurent, Yves St. (clothes designer), 641
Law, Ruth (pilot), 1731

Law Enforcement, 929
  Apprehending gangsters, 938
  Civil Rights, 946
  FBI, 936, 938, 944
  Highway patrols, 934
  Lie detectors, 949
  Lindbergh baby kidnappng, 937
  Miranda warning, 950
  Murder rate decline, 951
  Policing
    Automobiles 942, 1707
    Black officers, 947
    Brutality, 948
    High-speed chases, 943
    Origins, 932

Policewomen, 939
Policing and movies, 940
Scandal and reform, 945
Speeding, 942
Unions, 941
Race riots, 947, 1224, 1236, 1279, 1298, 1304
Reforming police functions, 933
Religion, 1489
Secret Service, 935
Strip searches, 950
Wickersham Commission, 933

Laws and the U.S. Legal System, 955 (see also separate section "Supreme Court Rulings")
Administrative law and the New Deal, 969
Amendments to the Constitution, 963
Conservative Court, 978
Domestic law 1980s-1990s, 980
Due process in criminal law, 975
Espionage Act (1917), 967, 1803
Free enterprise
  Legal decision, 965
International law, 965, 979
Methods of changing the law
  Administrative action, 962
  Court decision, 961
  Direct action of the people, 963
  Legislation, 962
Personal income tax, 966
Reforming the legal system, 981
Religion, 1489
Sedition law upheld, 967, 1173, 1803
Sherman Anti-Trust decision, 966
Supreme Court rulings
  Civil Rights era, 974
  New Deal programs, 971
  WWII, 972
Technology and the law, 978
Treaties and pacts, 968
Types of federal cases, 960
Warren court, 976

Le Corbusier (architect), 773
Leadbelly (musician), 1097, 1215
League of Nations, 1382, 1811
Lear, Norman (TV writer), 1338
Leary, Timothy (LSD proponent), 1121, 1421
Legionnaire's disease, 728

Leisure, 985
Cars, 1028
Children, 991, 1012
Children and reformers, 994
Children in the 1950s, 1012
Collectors, 1018, 1031
Computers, 1029
Conspicuous consumption, 989
Consumerism, 10
Counterculture, 1017, 1021, 1120, 1416, 1421, 1845
During WWII, 1005
Gender roles in the 1950s, 1014
Home entertainment, 1026
Malls, 1027
Middle-class leisure
  (1890s), 990
  (1920s), 995
  (1960s), 1019
  (1970s), 1019, 1023, 1025
  Influence of the telephone, 991
  Touring, 991, 998
Movies and restaurants, 1003
Nineteenth century, 988
Paint-by-the-numbers, 1010
Physical fitness, 1020, 1026
Political influences on, 1004
Radio, 1001
Reading, 1004, 1025
Seniors, 1031
Single life, 1015
Small town, 995, 1688
Structuring leisure time, 1030
Subcultures, 1023
Technology and leisure, 999, 1016
Teenagers
  1950s, 1011
  During WWII, 1007
  Female teen readers, 1176
  Sexual behavior, 1066, 1070
  Shopping malls, 1028
Television, 1008, 1020, 1032
Travel, 1031
Vaudeville and movies, 997
Video games, 1029
Working-class leisure, 992
Yuppies, 1026

Lend-Lease Act (1941), 1820
Leopold and Loeb trial (traitors), 203
Let Us Now Praise Famous Men, 1222
Levittown sub-development, 784, 877
Lewinsky, Monica (Congressional intern), 1084
Lewis, Gilbert N. (physicist), 1542
Lewis, John L. (labor leader), 151, 342
Lewis, Sinclair (writer), 1687

Libel, protection against, 1169
Liberty loans (WWI), 319
Lie detectors, 949
Life expectancy, 231, 238, 711, 723, 727
Life Is Worth Living, 1330, 1412
Ligutti, Luigi (social reformer), 583
Limbaugh, Rush (radio host), 1348
Lindbergh, Charles A. (aviator)
  First transatlantic flight, 1730
  Lindbergh baby kidnapping, 203, 937
Lister, Joseph (physician), 713
Listerine, 17
Literacy requirements to vote, 843, 1204
Literature and morality, 1056
Little black dress, 625
Little magazines, 1166, 1171
Little Rock school integration orders, 428
Living conditions in the 19th C., 548, 551, 553
Living History Farms (living museum), 580
Living Newspapers, 1004
Lo Opinion, 1179
Lochner v. New York (1905), 965
Lollipops, 661
London, Jack (novelist), 1213
Long Boom, The (1990s economy), 383

Los Angeles
  Creation of, 175
  Elections, 1301
  Environmental problems, 176
  L.A. Confidential, 1248
  Police brutality, 949, 1225
  Public housing failures, 186
  Rodney King incident, 1304
  Watts riot, 187

Lotteries, 893, 1080
Louisiana Purchase, 51
Love and sex, 457
Love Canal, 487
Lowell labor system, 132, 1145, 1678
Lowell, Massachusetts, 1678
Lunch boxes, 689
Lusitania, 1378, 1800
Lutherans, 1472, 1477
Lyme disease, 728
Lynching, 199, 1205, 1274

M

M & M's, 686
*M*A*S*H*, 1338
MacArthur, General Douglas, 1638, 1653, 1840
Machen, J. Gresham (theologian), 1389
MacKenzie, Douglas (seminarian), 1380
Mad cow disease, 609
Madonna's influence on fashion, 645
Magnet schools, 433
Mahan, Alfred Thayer (military strategist), 87, 1791
Mail order houses, 757
Main Street, 1687
Maine (battleship), 1794
Malcolm X, 1433
Mambo, 1112
Man Nobody Knows, The, 1391
Managed Care health plans, 730
Management
  1920s, 326
  Scientific, 279

Manifest Destiny, 64
  California, 68
  Caribbean, 75
  Mexico, 74
  Native Americans, 509
  Oregon, 67
  Texas, 66

Manila Bay, battle of, 1795
Mann Act, 200, 211, 1047, 1588
Mapp v. Ohio, 976
March on Washington
  (1941), 1288
  (1963), 1293
Marconi, Guglielmo (inventor), 905
Margarine, 661
Marlboro cigarette ads, 36
Marley, Bob (musician), 1126
Marriage (also see **Family Life**)
  (1950s), 561
  Marrying for money, 888
  in the 19th C., 548, 552, 1049

Marshall Plan, 95, 1837
Mary Tyler Moore Show, 1338
Mason and Bell jars, 659
Mason, Captain John (religious leader), 1359
Mass consumption (see **Advertising and Consumerism**)
Massachusetts Bay Company, 1356
Massey-Ferguson, 594
Mastering the Art of French Cooking, 696
Masters and Johnson (sexologists), 1603
Maternity wear, 626
Maude, 1340

Mauldin, Bill (cartoonist), 1647
Maxwell House coffee, 662
Mayflower, 1355
Mayflower Compact, 1355
Mayo, Elton (industrial psychologist), 325
McAuliffe, Christa (teacher), 1739
McCarthy, Joseph (senator), 155, 1067, 1841
McCarthyism, 155, 1067, 1841
McCartney, Bill (spiritual leader), 1474
McClintock, Barbara (scientist), 1549
McCoy, Joseph G. (cattleman), 1681
McDonalds restaurants, 681, 698
McFadden, Bernard (publisher), 1168
McFarland, James, 200
McLaurin v. Oklahoma State Regents, 975
McVeigh, Timothy (terrorist), 1492
Meade, Margaret (sociologist), 685
Measles, 713
Meat Inspection Act (1906), 668
Medicaid and Medicare, 726
Medical research, 725
Medical technology, 737
Medicine (see **Health and Medicine**)
Medicine (WWII), 1643
Meir, Golda (prime minister), 1400
Melting Pot, The (play), 1268
Mendes, Sergio (musician), 1122
Merchant Marine Act (1935), 339
Methodist view on homosexuality, 1475

Mexico (also see "Hispanic Americans")
  (1900-1920s), 850
  (1950s), 1229
  (1960s-1990s), 857
  Immigration, 1228
  Labor, 517, 1206, 1224, 1285
  Land grants to Americans, 59
  Mexican American press, 1164, 1179
  NAFTA, 395
  Race, 1232
  School desegregation, 1291
  War with U.S., 61, 515

Michelson, Albert A. (physicist), 1543
Mickey Mouse Club, 1329
Micro-organisms, discovery of, 710
Microchips, 920, 1561
Microsoft, 888
Microsurgery, 738
Microwave ovens, 700
Midway Island (WWII battle), 1633, 1833
Migration of Americans, 872, 881

Militancy and rebellion, 1299
Militant black newspapers, 1182
Military clothing, 633
Military Policy of the United States, 1791
Military-Industrial Complex, 154, 364
Miller-Tydings Act (1937), 339
Millikan, Robert A. (physicist), 1543
Mills, Eno (environmentalist), 483

Milk
  Advertising, 677
  Canned, 659
  Powdered, 688
  Purity of, 668

Minersville School District v. Goitis (1940), 973
Mingus, Charles (musician), 1122
Mini dress, 638, 1610

Mining, 283
  California gold rush, 81, 1680
  Klondike gold rush, 882
  Mining towns, 1680

Minnow, Newton (critic of TV), 1331
Minority intellectuals, 1302
Minstrel shows and stereotyping, 1201
Miracle drugs, 236
Miranda, Carmen (musician), 1112
Miranda warning, 206, 950, 976
Missouri Compromise (slavery), 73
Missouri Crisis (slavery), 72
Mitchell, Billy (aviator), 1814
Mobile homes, 772, 792, 798
Moby Dick, 1223
Model cities programs, 794
Model minority (Asian Americans), 1240
Models (fashion), 646
Modern Woman, The: The Lost Sex, 1602
Modernist architecture, 1692
Monk, Thelonious (musician), 1111
Montgomery, Benjamin (black plantation owner), 522
Montgomery bus boycott, 1723
Moon landing, 1560
Moon, The Reverend Sun Myung (spiritual leader), 1452
Moonies, 1452
Moore, John W. (printer), 1160
Moorish Science Temple, 1431
Moral majority, 1083

Morality, 1037

Abortion, 212, 1077, 1605
Alcohol, 1051
Anthony Comstock, 1044
Attacks on schools and libraries, 1082
Attitudes toward sexuality, 1048
Birth control, 1048, 1467, 1585, 1594
Blonde bombshell, 1069
Casinos, 1080
Censorship, 1045, 1057
Civil rights and sexuality, 1078
Clinton sex scandal, 1084
Contraceptives, 1064
Crime, 211
Erotic literature, 1070
Film industry, 1067
Flappers, 1920s, 1054, 1592, 1594
Gambling, 1053, 1060, 1066
Gambling for charity, 1061
House Un-American Activities Committee, 1067
Internet, 1084
Las Vegas, 1066
Literature, 1056
Lotteries, 1080
Mann Act, 1047, 1588
Margaret Sanger, 1049, 1594
Marriage and divorce, 1049, 1068, 1598
Moral majority, 1083, 1343, 1469
Movies, 1057
No-fault divorce, 1079
Obscenity in literature, 1057
Obscenity standards, 1071
Pornography, 1072, 1609
Production code for movies, 1061, 1067
Prostitution, 211, 1046, 1586, 1587
Rating system, 1073
Religion and morality, 1042
Repeal of prohibition, 1058
Right to Life movement, 1078
Rock music, 1075
Secular humanism, 1081
Sexual behavior and pregnancy 1960s, 1076
Sexual behavior of soldiers during World War II, 1063
Sexual revolution, 1069
Sodomy, 212
Temperance and prohibition, 1050
Vice societies, 1044
Victorian, 1043
Women in sex-related occupations, 1078
Women's responsibility for sexual behavior, 1065, 1585, 1601
World War I morality, 1056, 1813

Morgan, Garrett (inventor), 903, 1707
Morgan, Thomas Hunt, (biologist), 1543
Mortgages, 758
Morton, Jelly Roll (musician), 1096
Mosley, Walter (novelist), 1249
Motherly love, 456
Motion picture, 909
Motor Carrier Act (1935), 339
Motown, 1118
Mourning customs, 246

Movies/theaters/stars
  (1920s), 996, 998
  (1930s), 1003, 1057
  (1950s), 1011
  (1970s), 1022
  About Military life, 1657
  Appeal to the working class, 993
  Discrimination, 1274
  Early movies, 910
  Production code, 1061
  Protest, 1248
  Rating system, 1073
  Small town, 1688
  Vaudeville, 997
  War, 1830
  World War II, 1828

Movie star influence on fashion, 629, 641, 644
MRI, 737
Ms. Magazine, 1174
MTV, 1345
Muckraking journalism, 1165, 1802
Muhammad Ali (boxer), 1236
Muhammad, Elijah (religious leader), 1432
Muir, John (environmentalist), 477
Muller, Herman J. (scientist), 1548
Multinational corporations, 364
Multiple-choice testing, 420
Munroe, Bill (musician), 1113
Munsey, Frank A. (publisher), 1167
Murder, 203
Murder rate decline, 951
Murray, Charles (writer), 1246
Murray, Margaret (writer), 1441
Murray, William G. (professor of agriculture), 580
Murrow, Edward R. (reporter), 1321, 1331

Music, 1089
  Acid rock, 1075, 1121
  African American, 1215
  Beatles, 1119

Bebop, 1110, 1227
Big band/swing, 1007, 1063, 1104, 1108, 1287
Bossa nova, 1123
Counterculture/protest, 1121, 1123, 1248, 1845
Country/Bluegrass, 1113
Country blues, 1095, 1102
Disco, 1023, 1126
Electric blues, 1111
Funk, 1024, 1125
Fushion, 1125
Gospel, 1112
Grunge and rap, 1128
Harlem Renaissance, 1103, 1214, 1281
Heavy metal, 1124
Hillbilly, 1106
Immigrant, 1099, 1111
Jazz, 1062, 1096, 1105, 1110, 1122, 1227
Latin, 1112
MTV, 1345
Music from the Great Migration, 1102
Musical theatre, 1099
Orchestral, 1098
Progressive jazz, 1122
Punk and New Wave, 1127
Radio, 1317, 1323, 1335
Ragtime, 1094
Recorded, 1107
Reggae, 1126
Rhythm and Blues, 1116, 1119
Rock 'n' Roll, 1011, 1117
Rockabilly, 1116
Soft rock/Motown, 1118
Soul, 1119
Stride piano, 1104
Sweet jazz, 1105
Tin Pan Alley, 1100
Turn of the century, 1093
Urban blues, 1104
World War I, 1631
World War II, 1829

Musicians (also see **Music**)
  Influence on fashion, 640
  Disco and punk, 642
Musical theatre, 1099
Muslims, 1454
Mustard and chlorine gas (WWI), 1627

N
NAACP, 423, 427
Nader, Ralph (activist), 804, 1740
NAFTA, 380, 395

Naked and the Dead, 1223
Nashville sound, 1116
National Consumer League, 8
National debt, 376
National Defense Act (1916), 1807
National Defense Research Council, 1550
National Guard
  Enforcing integration in Arkansas, 428
  Kent State massacre, 1847
National Historic Preservation Act, 791
National Housing Act (1934), 770, 776
National Industrial Recovery Act (1933), 334, 336, 971
National Institutes of Health (NIH), 1553
National Labor Relations Act (1935), 150, 342, 971, 1883
National Labor Relations Board, 150, 342, 1805
National Labor Union, 138
National Organization of Women, 1604
National Origins Act (1924, 1927), 1281, 1294, 1383
National Park Service Act (1916), 483
National Recovery Administration, 149
National Restaurant Association (founding), 667
National Science Foundation, 1552
National Textile Workers Union, 145
National War Labor Board, 1823, 1877
National Youth Administration, 423

Native Americans
  Assimilation, 54
  Bureau of Indian Affairs, 510
  Burke Act (1906), 511
  Casinos, 513
  Christianity, 507
  Citizenship, 1267
  Confiscation of territory, 510, 1216, 1267
  Defeat, 79
  Eastern tribes, 55
  European relationship, 504
  French and Indian wars, 506
  Indian Appropriation Act (1871), 511
  Indian removal policy, 507
  Land settlement by whites, 53
  Mass migration, 509
  Plains Indians, 77
  Poverty, 365
  Religion, 1362
  Relocation after WWII, 512
  Removal from territories, 507, 1196
  Resistance to Europeans, 505
  Restoration of sovereignty, 512
  Role in WWI and WWII, 511

Sand Creek massacre, 77
Scientific observations, 1537
Service in the Spanish-American War, 1619
Sioux, 77
Trail of Tears, 508, 1198
Treaties, 506, 508
Tribes, 504
Wars in the Northwest, 55
Wars of the 1860s, 76

NATO, 97
Nature Conservancy, The, 490
Nautilus (submarine), 1728
Nazis, fleeing from, 847, 1833
Negro (baseball) League, 1283
Neo-Paganism, 1441
New Age spiritualism, 1440
New Communities Program, 802

New Deal, 334ff, 344, 1882
  Administrative law, 969
  Agricultural Adjustment Act, 149, 972
  Color barriers, 1286
  National Recovery Administration, 149
  Programs, 149, 1882

New economy (1990s), 380
New England food in the 1700s, 657
New England towns, 1674, 1678
New Orleans jazz, 1096
New Republic (magazine), 1167
New urbanism, 188, 1693
Nichols, Mark L. (inventor), 1545
Niebuhr, Reinhold and Helmut (theologians), 1404
Nimitz, Admiral, 1638
Nine Power Treaty (1928), 968
Nirvana (musical group), 1128

Nixon, Richard (president)
  Communist hunter, 1838
  Southern strategy, 1237
  Vietnam policies, 1847

No-fault divorce, 1079
No-man's land (WWI), 1627
Nobel Prize winners in science, 1543
Noble savages, 1197
Norma Rae, 1238
Norris, Frank (novelist), 1213
Norris-LaGuardia Act, 146
Norteño (Mexican) music, 1093
North Africa (invasion of WWII), 1636

Northwest Ordinance of 1787, 51
Northwest Territory, 51
Not in my back yard, 1692
Nuclear reactors, 1551
Nuclear technology (environment), 480
Nuremberg trial (WWII), 1836
Nurses, 718, 725, 736, 1796, 1807

Nutrition
  Better eating habits, 682
  Fat free/healthy foods, 697
  Government relief during the Depression, 684
  New ideas about, 669, 676
  Preventive nutrition, 693
  Prior to World War II, 685
  Reformers, 663, 669

Nutrition Labeling and Education Act (1990), 697
Nutrition reform for the poor, 669
Nylon, 914, 1548

O
Obesity, 730
Obituaries, 248
Obscenity in literature, 1057
Obscenity standards, 1071
Ocean liners, 1763

Occupations, 1135
  (1850s), 1139
  Apprenticeship system, 1142
  Child labor, 1142
  Early 1900s, 1139
  Education and occupations, 1145
  Eliot, Charles (educator), 1150
  Emerging occupations, 1150
  Expanding occupations, 1142
  Land Grant Act, 1146
  Morrill, Justin Smith (congressman), 1146
  Morrill Act, 1146, 1538
  Professional schools, 1150
  Settlers' occupations, 1138
  Smith-Hughes Act (1917), 420, 1146
  Snedden, David (educator), 1147
  Textile industry, 1144
  Transferring job skills, 1148, 1151
  Vocational training, 1146
  Women, 1140, 1144

Office of Economic Stabilization (1942), 346
Office of Price Administration (1942), 346
Office of Production Management (1940), 346, 593

Oil, 277, 279
Oklahoma City Bombing, 1249, 1492
Old parents, 243
Oldsmobile, 1706
Olmstead, Frederick Law (landscape designer), 754
Olmstead v. U.S. (1925), 969
On the Road, 1416
OPEC, 370
Open Marriage: A New Lifestyle for Couples, 1604
Operation Breakthrough, 802
Orchestral music, 1098
Oregon
  Banning blacks, 1198
  Dispute with Britain, 67
Oregon Trail, 71
Organic farming, 607, 698, 1562
Organic food, 695, 698
Organized Social Justice, 1396
Oriental influence on fashion, 644
Orthodox Catholic Church, 1456
OSHA, 1899
Osler, William (physician), 1516
Other America, The, 365, 692, 1297, 1896
Our Country: Its Possible Future and Its Present Crisis, 1374
Outdoor cooking, 689
Owens, Jesse (athlete), 1287

P
Pacific islands campaign (WWII), 1638
Paint-by-the-numbers, 1010
Palestine, 1400
Palmer raids, 142
Pan American immigration, 849
Panty hose, 641
Paparazzi, 1168
Parachutes, 1730
Parker, Charlie (musician), 1111
Parks, Rosa (activist), 1723
Passing of the Great Race, 846
Patou, Jean (clothes designer), 646
Peace Mission Movement, 1430
Pearl Harbor, 1818
Pearl Jam (musical group), 1128
Penn, William (founder of Pennsylvania), 1360
Penicillin
  Discovery, 1065
  Importance in WWII, 1643
Penny lunches, 670
Pentagon Papers, 1848
Perkey, Henry (food reformer), 664
Perkins, Frances (cabinet member), 1882

Pershing, General John J. (Blackjack), 1619, 1623

Persian Gulf War (1991)
  Background, 1848
  Causes for, 1662
  Desert equipment, 1662
  Gulf War syndrome, 1851
  Legacy of the war, 1850
  Tailhook scandal, 1850
  Women soldiers, 1849

Petroleum
  Alaskan oil, 492, 884
  Arab oil embargo, 492
  Dependence on, 124
  Exxon *Valdez* oil spill, 492
  History, 112
  Pipelines, 1717
  Texas oil boom, 884
  World War II

Philippine Islands annexation, 88
Phonograph, 909
Photography, 912
Physical fitness, 1020, 1026

Physicians
  American Medical Association, 717
  Dot.com doctors, 735
  Medical training, 716, 718, 733
  Physician assistants, 725
  Physician-assisted suicide, 268
  Practice, 715, 718
  Salaries and fees, 724, 732

Pickles, 660
Piggly Wiggly, 678
Piggy sow subsidy, 589
Pilgrims, 1355
Pill, the (birth control), 1076, 1604
Pilots, women, 1731, 1735
Pin-up girls, 1063, 1069
Pinchot, Gifford (environmentalist), 476
Pink Floyd (musician), 1124
Pipelines, 1717
Pizza, 691
Planck, Max (physicist), 1542
Plastic, 1540
Plastic surgery and cosmetics, 645
Plastic wrap, 688
Plastics, 918
Playboy magazine, 1071, 1177, 1604

Plessy, Homer (civil rights), 1202
Plessy v. Ferguson (separate but equal), 525, 1202
Plow, sow, cow experiment, 583
Plunger (submarine), 1727
Plymouth Plantation, 1356
Poiret, Paul (clothes designer), 624
Poland (start of WWII), 1817

Policing
   Automobiless, 942, 1707
   Black officers, 947
   Brutality, 948
   Corruption, 218
   Discrimination, 1901
   High-speed chases, 943
   Origins of, 932
   Policewomen, 939
   Policing and the movies, 940
   Reforming police functions, 933
   Scandal and reform, 945
   Speeding, 942
   Unions, 941

Polio, 713, 720, 723

Political influence
   Behavior of politicians, 463
   Consumerism, 30
   Leisure, 1004
   Political machines, 174
   Power, 30

Politicians and farming, 584
Pollution, 486
Polk, James K. (president)
   Oregon territory, 67
   Policy toward Mexico, 515
Polygamy, 1451
Polygraph testing, 949
Poor People's Campaign, 1237
Pope John Paul II, 1468
Popeye, 678
Population centers of immigrants, 836, 839, 856
Pornography, 1072, 1609
Port Tobacco, Maryland, 1676
Porter, Cole (composer), 1101
Portland, Oregon, 189
Post, C.W. (food reformer), 664
Post, Wily (pilot), 1731
Post-WWII boom in housing, 778, 781
Postal Service, contribution to transportation, 1741
Postum (coffee substitute), 664

Pot pies, 688
Poultry Inspection Act (1957), 694
Poverty, 365, 379
Powderly, Terence V. (labor leader), 138
Prairie style houses and Progressive reform, 756
Prayer in schools, 424
Pre-fab housing, 807
Preparation for WWII, 345
Preppy Handbook, The, 643
Presbyterians, 1361, 1389, 1476
Preservation (food), 659, 678, 914
Preservation vs. conservation (environment), 477
Presidential aircraft, 1735
Presley, Elvis (musician), 1117

Press and Democracy, The, 1155
   African American press, 1181
   Consolidation of newspapers, 1167
   Darwinism, 1161
     Social Darwinism, 1268, 1203, 1370, 1789, 1791
     Teaching evolution, 422, 1387, 1479, 1547
   Elitist press, 1166
   Ethnic and immigrant press, 1162
   Female teen readers, 1176
   Freedom and the press, 1159, 1184
   Illustrated magazines, 1169
   Immigrant, 1162
   Intellectual discourse and political dissent, 1161, 1171
   Little magazines, 1171
   Mexican American press, 1164, 1179
   Nineteenth century newspapers, 1161
   Political abuse, 1173
   Power of the press, 1162
   Profiling readers, 1177
   Protection against libel, 1169
   Reader surveys, 1174
   Reader's Digest, 1170
   Subliminal persuasion, 1177
   Syndicated news, 1172
   Tabloids and paparazzi, 1168
   Time, *Fortune*, and *Life*, 1170
   Women's magazines, 1173
   Women's magazines and social concerns, 1175
   Yellow journalism, 1165, 1793

Preventive nutrition, 693
Priesthood (Catholic), 1468
Primary care health treatment, 732
Printer's Ink magazine, 14
Princess Diana's influence on fashion, 643
Privatizing death, 249
Processed food, 660

Production code for movies, 1061, 1067
Profiling, racial, 949
Profiling readers, 1177
Progressive education, 419

Progressive Era
　Attitudes about race, 1212, 1268, 1269
　Attitudes about class, 1212
　Consumerism, 8
　Crusade against prostitution, 1046, 1587
　Environment, 476
　Food activists, 667
　Housing, 756
　Law, 965, 966
　Newspapers and the press, 1165
　Science, 1541
　Social Darwinism, 1268, 1203, 1370, 1789, 1791

Progressive jazz, 1122

Prohibition era
　Backlash, 1385
　Organized crime, 201
　Religions and alcohol, 1384
　Repeal of, 1058
　Temperance movement, 675, 1050
　Unpopularity of, 201

Promise Keepers, 1474
Propaganda (war), 27, 1322, 1650, 1802
Prosperity and housing, 819
Prosperity after WWI, 321, 324
Prostitution, 211, 1046, 1586, 1587

Protest
　Clothes and ideology, 640
　Influence on fashion, 639
　Literature, 1212
　Movement, 1787, 1845
　Music, 1121, 1123, 1248

Pruitt-Igoe housing complex, 789, 797
Psychoanalysis, 461
PT squadrons (WWII), 1636
Public education beginnings, 416
Public health, 233, 235
Public housing, 780, 789, 797, 801
Puente, Tito (band leader), 1112
Pullman, George (inventor), 139
Pulp magazines, 1170
Pulsars, 1560
Punk and New Wave music, 1127

Pure Food and Drug Act (1906), 713
Puritans, 1356ff, 1674
Pynchon family, 1678

Q
Quonset huts, 916
Quakers, 1360, 1381
Quant, Mary (clothes designer), 638
Queen Anne houses, 752
Quimby, Harriet (pilot), 1731

R
Race (also see "African Americans" and **Ethnic Minority Groups**)
　Affirmative action, 1250, 1305
　Asian Americans: The Model Minority, 1240
　Asian immigration restrictions, 1271
　Assimilation of immigrants, 1268
　Chinese immigrants, 1199
　Class warfare in the 1950s, 1229
　Class and taxes, 1242
　Class relations and the workplace, 1196
　Class and the new economy, 1247
　Cold War (effects of), 1231
　Definitions of race, 1194, 1201, 1265
　Depression era labor and protests, 1217
　Depression jobs, 1284
　Desegregating Mexican American education, 1291
　Discrimination (also see "Discrimination")
　　Beginning of the 20th century, 1267
　　Filipino, 1285
　　Mexican, 1206, 1285
　　Movies, 1274
　　Post-war discrimination against blacks, 1890
　　Sports, 1273
　　World War II, 1289
　Elections, 1193, 1202, 1204
　Ethnic community organizations, 1274
　Eugenics movement, 1269, 1547
　Filipino and Mexican laborers, 1281
　Immigration Reform Act, 1294
　Imperialism and race, 1207, 1270
　Indian abuses, 1216
　Indian removal from territories, 1196
　Intelligence and ethnicity, 1199, 1246
　Interracial cooperation on labor issues, 1202
　Irish Americans and northern blacks, 1201
　Irish power and Jewish activists, 1276
　Jack Johnson and the Great White Hope, 1274
　Jewish garment workers, 1275
　Ku Klux Klan, 1280
　Labor (excluding blacks), 1204

Labor and class, 1208, 1871
Labor and white supremacy, 1872
Latino coalition groups, 1247
Law, 1267
Literacy requirements to vote, 1204
Living conditions for the working class, 1211
Los Angeles police, 1225
Lynching, 1205, 1274
Mexican immigrants (stratification of), 1228
Minorities and electoral politics, 1294
Minstrel shows, 1201
Music (black), 1215, 1227
Music, movies, and television, 1283, 1303
Non-Asian immigration restrictions, 1273
Oklahoma City Bombing and Arabs, 1249
Opposition to unions, 1208
Oregon (banning blacks from), 1198
Popular Front culture, 1286
Post-war opportunities, 1290
Progressivism and Social Darwinism, 1268
Protest literature, 1212, 1222
Protest music, film and literature, 1248
Putting blacks in their place, 1213
Racial exclusion for citizenship, 1195
Racism against immigrants, 1194
Racism and the communist scare, 1290
Reconstruction (attitudes toward blacks during), 1200
Reformers, 1212
Restrictions on immigration, 1279
Return to mainstream racism, 1246
Richard Nixon's Southern strategy, 1237
Ruling that Mexicans are white, 1232
Separate but equal, 1232
Show business and sports, 1276, 1282, 1286
Sit-down strikes, 1220
Southern Civil Rights movement, 1292
Strikes, 1221, 1242, 1244
Trail of tears, 1198
Union victory for worker benefits, 1230
Union sunset, 1243
Urban renewal and black neighborhoods, 1234, 1241
Urban rebellion, 1235
Vietnam war, 1237
Violence and blacks, 1279
War on drugs, 1246
Welfare Queen, 1244
Worker solidarity, 1210, 1230
WWI jobs for minorities, 1278
World War II, 1223, 1227
Opportunities for minorities and blacks, 1288, 1887

Zoot-suit riots, 1224

Race and Class, 1189
Affirmative action, 1250, 1305
Asian Americans: The Model Minority, 1240
Attitudes of Progressive reformers, 1212
Attitudes toward blacks during Reconstruction, 1200
Banning blacks from Oregon, 1198
Black music, 1215, 1227
Breaking strikes, 1221, 1242, 1244
Chinese immigrants, 1199
Class and the new economy, 1247
Class and taxes, 1242
Class relations and the workplace, 1196
Class warfare in the 1950s, 1229
Definitions of race, 1194, 1265
Definitions of racial purity, 1201
Depression era labor and protests, 1217
Discrimination against Mexicans, 1206
Effects of the Cold War, 1231
Erasing Indian heritage, 1216
Excluding blacks from skilled labor, 1204
Imperialism and race, 1207, 1270
Indian removal from territories, 1196
Intelligence and ethnicity, 1246
Intelligence and the size of skulls, 1199
Interracial cooperation on labor issues, 1202
Irish Americans and northern blacks, 1201
Labor and class, 1208, 1871
Labor and white supremacy, 1872
Latino coalition groups, 1247
Literacy requirements to vote, 1204
Living conditions for the working class, 1211
Los Angeles police, 1225
Lynching, 1205, 1274
Minstrel shows, 1201
Oklahoma City Bombing and Arabs, 1249
Opposition to unions, 1208
Protest music, film and literature, 1212, 1222, 1248
Putting blacks in their place, 1213
Race and elections, 1193, 1202, 1204
Racial exclusion for citizenship, 1195
Racism against immigrants, 1194
Return to mainstream racism, 1246
Richard Nixon's Southern strategy, 1237
Ruling that Mexicans are white, 1232
Sit-down strikes, 1220
Stratification of Mexican immigrants, 1228
Striking down "separate but equal", 1232
Trail of tears, 1198
Union sunset, 1243

Union victory for worker benefits, 1230
Urban rebellion, 1235
Urban renewal and black neighborhoods, 1234, 1241
Vietnam war, 1237
War on drugs, 1246
Welfare Queen, The, 1244
Worker solidarity, 1210, 1230
World War II, 1223, 1227
Zoot-suit riots, 1224

Race and Minorities, 1261
  Allying with Japan to resist Chinese communism, 1291
  Asian immigration restrictions, 1271
  Assimilation of immigrants, 1268
  Definitions of race, 1194, 1265
  Depression jobs go to white men, 1284
  Desegregating Mexican American education, 1291
  Discrimination
    Beginning of the 20th century, 1267
    Filipino, 1285
    Movies, 1274
    Post-war against blacks, 1890
    Sports, 1273
  Ethnic community organizations, 1274
  Eugenics movement, 1269, 1547
  Filipino and Mexican laborers, 1281
  Immigration Reform Act, 1294
  Imperialism, 1270
  Irish power and Jewish activists, 1276
  Jack Johnson and the Great White Hope, 1274
  Jewish garment workers, 1275
  Ku Klux Klan, 1280
  Law, 1267
  Mexican discrimination, 1285
  Minorities and electoral politics, 1294
  Music, movies, and television, 1283, 1303
  Non-Asian immigration restrictions, 1273
  Popular Front culture, 1286
  Post-war opportunities, 1290
  Progressivism and Social Darwinism, 1268
  Racism and the communist scare, 1290
  Restrictions on immigration, 1279
  Show business and sports, 1276, 1282, 1286
  Southern Civil Rights movement, 1292
  Violence and blacks, 1279
  WWI jobs for minorities, 1278
  WWII discrimination, 1289
  WWII jobs for blacks and minorities, 1288, 1887

Race riots, 186, 204, 213, 795, 947, 1203, 1224, 1236, 1279, 1298

Racial polarization, 1297
Racial profiling, 949
Radar, 906
Radburn, New York (model town), 765

Radio and Television, 1312
Radio
  Advertising, 21, 681
  African American and Latino programming, 1337
  Beginning of radio, 905, 1315
  Car radios, 1331
  Censorship of war material, 1322
  Civic programming, 1322
  Commercial radio, 912, 1315
  Commercial sponsors, 21, 681, 1316
  Constituency programming, 1348
  Detective programs, 1319
  FM radio, 1337
  First stations, 912
  Homogenization of American culture, 1314
  Leisure, 1001, 1314
  Live news reportage, 1321, 1322
  Modern news broadcasting, 1336
  Music, 1002, 1107, 1317, 1323
  National Public Radio, 1336
  Programming, 1317
  Protecting news sources, 1336
  Radio propaganda (WWII), 1650
  Radio sets, 1316
  Revival of radio, 1335
  Serving the civic cause, 1322
  Shows, 681
  Soap operas, 1319
  Sound effects, 1318
  Sports, religious, and public affairs programming, 1320
  Talk radio, 1348
  World War II broadcasting, 1321, 1650
Television
  (1970s), 1020, 1022
  (1990s), 1032
  Advertising, 36, 40
  Animals on TV, 1341
  Beginning of, 918, 1324
  Cable TV, 1342, 1344
  Children's shows, 1329, 1341
  CNN, 1345
  Competing for ratings, 1346
  Cooking shows, 700
  Courting younger viewers and women, 1346
  Criticizing programming, 1331
  Eclipsing radio, 1326

Emmy Awards, 1343
Ethnicity, 1010
Evangelism programs and networks, 1343
Game shows, 891
High Definition TV, 1347
House Un-American Activities Committee broadcast, 1327, 1331
I Love Lucy, 1113, 1328
Invention of, 918
Mini-series, 1341
Minorities, 1010, 1333
MTV, 1345
Network competition, 1347
News programming, 1333
Programming, 1325
Programming for teens and the elderly, 1332
Programming for the youth culture, 1334
Public affairs programming, 1330
Rating system, 1073
Ratings, 1346
Relevancy programming, 1337, 1339
Religious and quiz shows, 1330, 1331
Sex, 1347
Sit-coms, 1327
Soap operas, 1340
Sports and variety shows, 1328
Teens and elderly programming, 1332
Televangelists and advertising, 40
TV dinners, 688
Unleashing the networks, 1342
VCR, 1345
Vietnam war reportage, 1333, 1846
Watergate, 1338
Younger viewers and women, 1346
Youth culture programming, 1334

Ragtime, 1094
Rail Passenger Service Act (1970), 1718

Railroads
Accidents, 1718
Building the transcontinental railroad, 529
Illegal passengers (hoboes), 1720
Impact on western development, 1757
Importance to the economy, 281
Importance to the development of towns, 1673
Orphan trains, 1719
Pension plans, 1512
Refrigerated cars, 660
Rise and decline, 1718
Segregation on, 1723
Transcontinental, 1717
Use for leisure travel, 1756

Railroad time, 282
Railway Labor Act, 146
Rainey, Grandma "Ma" (musician), 1104
Rampage killers, 221
Ramsey, Alice (adventurer), 1709
Ranch houses, 785
Randolph, Philip A. (black leader), 1223, 1235, 1286, 1288
Rape (cause for lynching), 1205
Rape, 216, 1604
Rappelyea, George (evolution proponent), 1387
Rappers (musicians), 1129
Rating system, 1073
Rationing (civilian WWII), 1828
Rations (soldiers WWII), 1643
Rauschenbusch, Walter (social theorist/minister), 1373, 1375
Reader surveys, 1174
Reader's Digest, 1170

Reagan, Ronald (president)
Air Traffic Controllers strike, 157, 1244, 1736
Critics of, 373
Decline and recovery, 374
Economic policy, 38, 372
Economy and labor, 157
Influence on fashion, 643
Social consequences, 375, 378
Supply-side economics, 372
Reclamation Act (1902), 478
Reconstruction, end of (Civil War), 136, 523
Reconstruction Finance Corporation, 148, 333, 345, 684, 968
Recorded music, 1107
Recycling, 488
Red Ball Express, 1826
Red Barron, the (pilot), 1628

Red Cross
Korean War, 1841
Malnutrition services, 674
World War I, 1809
World War II, 1822

Red Pipestone Quarry controversy, 510
Red scare, 142, 155, 202, 967, 1231, 1279, 1290, 1811, 1838, 1842
Reed, Ralph (Christian leader), 1470
Reformers, 663, 669, 695
Reforming the legal system, 981

Refrigeration, 660, 685, 910, 913

Refugees, 858
  Cuban, 859
  Jewish, 847
  Russian, 861
  Vietnamese, 860

Refugee Escape Act (1957, 1965), 859
Reggae music, 1126

Religion and American Life, 1351
  American response to Jewish persecution, 1407
  Andrew Carnegie's philanthropy, 1371
  Anne Hutchinson and the New Hampshire colonies, 1358
  Atomic bomb, 1410
  Attitudes toward prohibition, 1384
  Baha'i Faith, 1455
  Baptists and Fundamentalists, 1390
  Battle over evolution, 1386, 1478
  Bishop Sheen: Life Is Worth Living, 1412
  Branch Dividians, 1491
  Buddhism in America, 1417
  Catholic positions on sex and abortion, 1467
  Catholic Worker Movement, 1398
  Catholicism and patriotism, 1464
  Catholics and communism, 1465
  Catholics and Jews, 1362
  Christian pacifism, 1401
  Christian response to war, 1404
  Christian Right and the Moral Majority, 1469
  Coming to America, 1356
  Connecticut colonies, 1358
  Conscientious objections to the war, 1380
  Conservative backlash, 1394
  Conservative Judaism, 1461
  Contemporary religion summary, 1493
  Contemporary religious issues
    Ecumenism, 1471
    Education, 1478
    Homosexuality, 1475
    Men's issues, 1473
    Women's issues, 1472
  Corporate spiritualism, 1484
  Counterculture, 1416, 1437
    Deep Ecology, 1442
    Feminist theology, 1444
    Neo-Paganism, 1441
    New Age spiritualism, 1440
    Scientology, 1438
    Vietnam era, 1845
  Womanist theology, 1445
  Crusade against communism, 1410, 1465
  Decline of religious zeal, 1368
  Differences among Jews, 1462
  Disharmony after the war, 1382
  Division among believers, 1366
  Edwards, Jonathan, 1366
  Escaping persecution, 1355
  Evolution v. creationism, 1478
  Fr. Charles E. Coughlin and the Union for Social Justice, 1396
  Gospel of wealth, 1370
  Great Awakening, 1364, 1366
  Great Depression, 1392
  Hinduism in America, 1419
  Immigrant and nativism, 1383
  Institutionalizing Social Gospel, 1377
  Intelligent design, 1483
  Islam in America, 1454
  Islamic terrorists, 1490
  Itinerant preachers, 1365
  Jews (see separate entry "Jews")
  John Winthrop, 1367
  Josiah Strong and Social Gospel, 1374
  Judaism in the 1930s
  Law and religion, 1489
  Liberation theology, 1447
  Martin Luther King, Jr., 1426
  Mormons, 1450
  Nation of Islam, 1429
  Native Americans, 1362
  Oklahoma City terrorist attack, 1492
  Origins of the Cold War, 1408
  Origins of religious democracy, 1357
  Orthodox Catholic Church, 1456
  Orthodox Judaism in America, 1459
  Piety, 1364
  Presbyterians, 1389
  Priesthood, 1468
  Prohibition backlash, 1385
  Prosperity and religion, 1369
  Protestant response to WWII, 1402
  Puritan Legacy, 1367, 1370
  Quakers in Pennsylvania, 1360
  Reading the Bible literally: division within the church, 1388
  Reform Judaism, 1460
  Religions' role in society, 262
  Religious diversity, 1361
  Religious protests of war practices, 1407
  Resurgence of religious activity, 1414
  Reverend Billy Graham, 1412

Revival of the Social Gospel, 1393
  Roger Williams and the Rhode Island colonies, 1358
  Russell Conwell and the acres of diamonds, 1372
  Scientology, 1438
  Self-expression and self-realization as religion, 1420
  Slave religion, 1424
  Social Gospel, 1373
  Social justice and Roman Catholicism, 1395
  Unification Church, 1452
  Vatican Council II, 1466
  Vietnam War, 1422
  Violence and religion, 1489
  Walter Rauschenbusch and Social Gospel, 1375, 1381
  World War I, 1377
  Zionism, 1400, 1461

Resettlement Administration (1935), 341
Resolution Trust Corporation, 811
Resorts, 1756
Reuther, Rosemary (womanist theologian), 1445
Reversing affirmative action, 1305
Resettlement Administration (1935), 341
Resolution Trust Corporation, 811
Resorts, 1756

Restaurants
  (1800s), 666
  (1930s), 1003
  Chinese, 663
  Effect of Prohibition, 675, 679
  First chain, 666
  New types of, 680
  Take out, 700
Restrictions on immigration
  (1882-1924), 840
  (1990s), 862
  Act of 1965, 855
  Asian, 841
  Consequences of, 847
  Opposition by business, 842
  Support by intellectuals, 843
  Support by labor, 843
  World War I, 1279
  World War II, 1833

Reuther, Rosemary (womanist theologian), 1445
Reversing affirmative action, 1305

Retirement, 1507
  Age discrimination, 1517
  Army pension program, 1514
  Debate over retirement age, 1516
  Economics of retirement, 1512
  Elderly and politics, 1529
  Federal government, 1518
  Mandatory retirement, 1511
  Pension system, 1520
  Poor houses, 1515
  Private pensions, 1512
  Prosperity for retirees, 1527
  Retirees as the leisured class, 1526
  Retirees at work, 1530
  Retirement benefits, 1525
  Social Security, 1521ff
  Women in retirement, 1528
  Worker productivity and social progress, 1517
  Working all your life, 1510

Rhapsody in Blue, 1106
Rhode Island labor system, 132
Rhythm and Blues music, 1116, 1119
Rickenbacker, Eddie (pilot), 1628
Ridgway, General Matthew, 1653
Right to die movement, 267
Right to Life movement, 1078
Riis, Joseph (reformer), 1212
Rio environmental conference, 493
River towns, 1678
Rivers, The Reverend Eugene (minister), 1436
Road rage, 465
Roanoke Rapids textile strike, 1238
Roberts, Kenneth (author), 846
Robertson, Pat (TV evangelist), 1343, 1470
Robeson, Paul (athlete, entertainer), 1287
Rock 'n' Roll, 1011, 1117
Rock music, 1075
Rockabilly, 1116
Rockefeller Center, 766
Rodgers, Calbraith (pilot), 1730
Rodgers, Jimmie (musician), 1106
Rodney King incident, 1304
Roe v. Wade (1973), 1077
Roentgren, W.K. (inventor), 905
Roger and Me, 1244
Role dissatisfaction, 564
Role of women in the 20th C., 554, 1014
Rolling Stones, 1124
Roman Catholics (see Catholics)
Roosevelt Corollary, 93, 1797

Roosevelt, Franklin D.
  Color barriers, 1286
  Early administration, 334
  New Deal, 148, 1882

Support from unions, 151

Roosevelt, Theodore
　Airplane ride, 1730
　Economic policies, 306
　Environmental policy, 476
　Panama Canal, 92
　Philippines, 1795
　Roosevelt Corollary, 93, 1797
　Rough Riders, 91, 1619, 1622, 1792
　Submarine ride, 1727

Rosenberg, Julius and Ethel (spies), 1557
Ross, Diana (musician), 1119
ROTC, 1660
Route 66, 1710, 1766
Rubber (WWII), 349
Rural Electrification Act (1935), 589
Rural Electrification Administration/Commission (1935), 341, 685
Russia (Alaska sale), 75
Russian Orthodox Church, 1457
Russian refugees, 861
Rutherford, Ernest (physicist), 1542

S
Sacco and Vanzetti trial (treason), 203, 968
Safety in transportation, 1740
Salk, Jonas (polio), 723
Sanger, Margaret (feminist), 1049, 1064, 1594
Santa Fe Trail, 71
Saturday Night Live, 1339
Savannah, Georgia, 1677
Savings and loan crisis, 376, 809
Schechter Poulty Company, 338
Schenck v. U.S. (1917), 967
Schlafly, Phyllis (activist), 1605
Schlieffen Plan, 1798
School buses, 423
School lunch programs, 693
School violence, 436, 1251
Schools and libraries (attacks on), 1082

Science, 1533
　Agricultural, 1546
　Atomic Age, 1551
　Atomic physics, 1542, 1545
　Atomic research, 1557
　Backlash to science, 1547
　"Big Science", 1561
　Bioengineering, 1568
　Cold War opportunities for science, 1556
　Consumer products, 1566
　Death, 263, 264
　Deductive v. inductive logic, 1536
　Deep space exploration, 1570
　Depression-era science, 1548
　Digital imaging, 1564
　Education, 425
　Eugenics, 1547
　Food, 670
　Foreign scientists in the U.S., 1555
　Genetic research, 1543
　Genome and DNA research, 1567
　Going to the Moon, 1559
　Health, 1544
　Information Age, 1563
　Medicine, 1569
　Moon, 1559
　National Science Foundation, 1552
　Organic farming, 1562
　Periods of modern science, 1537
　Popularizing science, 1566
　Post-WWII science, 1554
　Practical applications for research, 1560
　Public perception, 1539
　Renaissance of American science, 1550
　Scientific freedom, 1539
　Scientific Research, 1564
　Space race, 1558
　Space shuttle, 1565, 1739
　Support and dissent,
　Transition of American science, 1538
　Women and immigrant scientists, 1549
　World's Fair (1904), 1540

Scientology, 1438
Scopes, John T. (teacher), 421, 1387, 1547
Scott, Winfield (military leader), 515
Scottsboro Boys decision, 205
Seaplanes, 1730
Seaside, Florida, 1694
Seattle Sound (music), 1128
Seawolf (submarine), 1728
Secret Service, 935
Secular humanism, 1081
Sedition Act (1917), 967, 1173, 1803
Sedition law upheld, 967, 1803
Seed hybridization, 590

Segregation (see also "Race")
　Brown vs. the Board of Education, 427, 525, 880, 975, 1232
　Discrimination for loans, 1233

Housing, 180, 183, 788
Little Rock school integration orders, 428
Plessy v. Ferguson (separate but equal), 525, 1202
School, 188, 212, 428, 1232
Transportation, 1723

Selden, George B. (inventor), 1706
Selective Service Act (1917, 1941), 1807, 1820
Senior citizens (see Retirement)
Seniors travel, 1031
Separate but equal, 418, 525
   Brown vs. the Board of Education, 427, 525, 880, 975, 1232
Separatists (religious sect), 1355, 1358
Serial killers, 214
Sesame Street, 1341
Seton, Ernest Thompson (environmentalist), 478
700 Club, 1343
Seventh Day Adventists Sanatorium at Battle Creek, Michigan, 664
Sex (Catholic position on), 1467

Sex and Gender, 1579
   Activism among women, 1590
   Backlash to feminism, 1605
   Birth control, 1048, 1467, 1585, 1594ff
   Challenging traditional roles, 1603
   Courtship, 1594
   Equality and the women's liberation movement, 1604
   Femininity and domesticity, 1600
   Gender roles, 1608
   Homosexuality, 1606
   Legalizing abortion, 1606
   Morality in the 1920s, 1593
   Return to traditional values, 1597
   Sexual attitudes, 1590
   Sexual double standard, 1600
   Sexual revolution, 1603
   Single women, 1589
   Wage discrimination, 1610, 1896
   Wartime (WWII) jobs for women, 1599
   Wartime sex, 1599
   Women after the war, 1599
   Women and slaves, 1587
   Women as the weaker sex, 1583
   Women in government, 1598
   Women in the workplace, 1588
   Women providing moral guidance, 1583
   Women reformers, 1586
   Women's education, 1589
   Women's rights movement, 1586

   Working women in the 1920s, 1591

Sex and the City, 1347
Sex Pistols (musical group), 1127

Sexual behavior
   (1960s-1970s), 1076, 1603, 1604
   (1980s-1990s), 1608
   Abortion, 212, 1077, 1605
   Advertising, 1069
   Birth control, 1048, 1467, 1585, 1594
   Catholics, 1467
   Children's sexuality, 1609
   Civil Rights, 1069, 1978, 1604
   Clothes, 1610
   Double standard, 1600
   Education, 1609
   Flappers, 1054, 1592
   Harassment, 217
   Kinsey report, 1070, 1078
   Love and sex, 457
   Masters and Johnson, 1603
   Morality, 1048, 1590
   Nineteenth century, 546, 1584, 1590
   Pornography, 1072, 1609
   Practices in the 19th C., 546
   Sex-related occupations, 1078
   Sexual Revolution, 1069, 1603
   Soldiers during WW II, 1063
   Teens, 1066, 1070
   Television, 1347
   Women during WWII, 1599
   Women in sex-related occupations, 1078
   Women's responsibility for, 1065, 1585, 1601, 1609
   World War II

Sexual Behavior in the Human Male, 1069
Sexual harassment, 217, 1901
Sexual revolution, 1069
Sexuality, attitudes toward, 1048
Sharecropping, 135
Sheen, Bishop Fulton (TV minister), 1330, 1411
Shepherd, Alan B. (astronaut), 1739
Sheppard-Towner Act (1921), 721
Sherman Antitrust Act, 140, 290, 966
Shipbuilding (WWII), 347
Shipping disasters, 1727, 1763
Shopping, 1014
Shopping centers, 635, 1015, 1027
Short wave radio, 905
Show boats, 1679
Shredded wheat, 664

Siblings, 245, 448
Sicily (invasion of WWII), 1637
Sick chicken case, 150
Sierra Club, 484
Silent majority, 1238
Silent Spring, 486
Silver Pallette Cookbook, 696
Silver rush, 283
Simmons, Charles A. (journalist), 1181
Simms, Naomi (model), 639
Sin (gambling), 1053
Sinclair, Upton (novelist), 1213
Single family houses, 752
Single life, 1015, 1021
Skyscrapers, 766

Slavery (see also "African Americans")
  Compromise of 1850, 73
  Economy, 131
  Northern opposition, 72
  Religion, 1424
  Southern plantation labor system, 133
  Western territory, 72
  Women reformers, 1586

Small, Albion W. (social scientist), 1374
Smart growth (cities), 189
Smith, Alfred E. (governor), 1386
Smith, Bessie (musician), 1104
Smith, Jr., Joseph (Mormon leader), 1451
Smith v. Allwright, 972
Smothers Brothers (comedians), 1334
SNCC, 1428
Snyder, Gary (poet), 1443
Social gospel, 1373, 1393
Social Security Act (1935), 343, 1521
Socialist press, 1166
Society for the American Indians, 1275
Society of American Indians, 511
Sod houses, 751
Sodomy, 212
Soft rock, 1118
Soil and water conservation, 590
Solidarity (labor), 1210, 1230

Soldiering: Life in Combat, 1615
  Korean War (1950-1953)
    Battlefield conditions, 1654
    Beginning of, 1652
  Persian Gulf War (1990-1991)
    Causes for, 1662
    Desert equipment, 1662

  Spanish-American War (1898-1902)
    Disease and medical care, 1622
    Equipment problems, 1620
    Rough Riders and Buffalo soldiers, 1619, 1622, 1792
    Transportation and food problems, 1621
  Vietnam (1964-1975)
    Airpower, 1656
    American escalation, 1655
    Combat conditions, 1656
    Fragging, 1659
    Stress on troops, 1660
    Tet offensive, 1657
    Troop morale, 1658
    Vietnamese women in combat, 1659
  World War I (1917-1918)
    Airplanes, 1628
    Americans arrive in Europe, 1624
    Breaking the German lines, 1624
    Chemical weapons (WWI), 1627
    Conditions on the battlefield, 1625
    Crossing "No-man's land", 1627
    Dogfighting and Eddie Rickenbacker, 1628
    Doughboys, 1630
    Music, 1631
    Trench warfare, 1625
    Uniforms and weapons, 1630
  World War II (1941-1945)
    Agriculture, 349
    Aircraft industry, 347
    Airplanes, 1644
    Airpower, 1634, 1644
    Allied invasion of France, 1649
    America enters the war, 1632
    Artillery, 1642
    Battle of Bataan, 1647
    Civilian involvement in the war, 1648
    Coal and petroleum, 347
    Dropping the atomic bombs, 1639
    Educational Orders Act (1939), 345
    Entertainment, 1644
    Espionage, 1649
    G.I.s and the Holocaust, 1651, 1829
    Invading Germany, 1638
    Invading Sicily and France, 1637
    Invasion of North Africa, 1636
    Iowa Jima and Okinawa, 1639
    Island hopping in the Pacific, 1638
    Japanese Bushido Code, 1647
    Labor, 349, 1223
    Medicine, 1643
    Midway and Guadalcanal, 1633

Outfitting the G.I.s, 1640
　　Radio propaganda, 1650
　　Rations, 1643
　　Rubber, 349
　　Service aborad ship, 1634
　　Shipbuilding, 347
　　Steel and aluminum, 348
　　Submarines and PT squadrons, 1636
　　Tanks, 1642
　　War economy, 345ff
　　War Resources Board (1939), 345
　　Weapons, 1641
　U.S. Military after Vietnam, 1661

Sosa, Sammy (baseball star), 1252
Soul music, 1119
Souls of Colored Folk, 1269
Sound barrier, breaking, 1734
Soup (canned), 660
South, The
　New South, The, 136
　Unions, 145
South Dakota (gold rush), 1680
Southern plantation cuisine, 657
Southern plantation labor system, 133
Southern strategy (Nixon's), 1237

Space
　American space program, 1737
　Moon mission, 99
　Space race, 98
　Technology, 918, 920, 1737

Spanish-American War (1898-1902)
　Alfred Thayer Mahan's professional navy, 1791
　American imperialism, 88
　Background, 1797
　Battle of Manila Bay, 1795
　Battles of Kettle and San Juan hills, 1796
　"Butcher" Weyler's tactics in Cuba, 1793
　Causes for, 1792
　Cuban campaign, 1619, 1793
　Disease and medical care, 1622
　Emory Upton's professional army, 1791
　Equipment problems, 1620
　Firearms, 1620
　Food problems, 667, 1621
　Imperialism, 1783, 1789
　Military and Social Darwinism, 1791
　Sinking of the battleship *Maine,* 1794
　Teddy Roosevelt and the Rough Riders, 81, 1619, 1622, 1792
　U.S. troop strength, 1790, 1795
　Women (role of), 1796
　Yellow journalism, 1793

Spanish press, 1178
　Mexican American, 1164, 1179
Speed limits, 943
Spencer, Herbert (social theorist), 1371
Spies (industrial), 1884
Spies, 1557
Spinach, 678
Spindletop oil well, 884
Spiritual Motivation movement, 1394
Spock, Dr. Benjamin (child psychologist), 562

Sports
　Boxing 1236, 1274
　Discrimination/racism, 1273
　Fashion, 630
　Immigrant and minority participation
　　(1920s), 1282
　　(1930s), 1287
　　(1940s-1950s), 1296
　　(1960s-1980s), 1303
　Integration, 1297
　Kahanamoku, Duke (athlete), 1277
　Leisure, 1000, 1008, 1029
　Sports programs in schools, 430, 1021
　Surfing, 1277
　Tiger Woods, 1306

Springfield, Massachusetts, 1678
Sputnik satellite, 153, 917, 1558
Stalin, Josef, 1408
Standardized testing, 420, 1270
Standardizing the American diet, 682
Standards for schools, 433
Star Trek, 1332
StarLink (genetic corn), 609, 611
Steel and aluminum (WWII), 348
Steinbeck, John (novelist), 1223, 1768
Stem cell research, 1569
Stephens, Uriah (labor leader), 138
Stephenson, David C. (Ku Klux Klan), 202
Sterilization, 969, 1548
Stern, Howard (radio/TV host), 1348
Stewart, Martha (chef, entrepreneur), 700
Still, William Grant (composer), 1104
Stock market boom (1920s), 885, (1990s), 382, 887
Stock market crash (1929), 328; (1987), 377
Stresemann, Gustav (German chancellor), 331

Strikes
  Air Traffic Controllers, 157, 1244, 1736
  Breaking, 1221
  Depression Era, 1218
  Filipino, 535, 1286
  Flint Michigan, 1244, 1890
  Japanese plantation workers in Hawaii, 1276, 1282
  Jewish garment workers, 1275
  Miner's, 1218
  Roanoke Rapids textile, 1238
  Sit-down, 1220

Stride piano, 1104
Strip searches, 950
Strong, Josiah (minister), 1375
Student protests, 429
Subliminal persuasion in advertising, 1177
Submarine warfare (WWI), 1636, 1800

Suburbs
  Consumerism, 30
  Discrimination for loans, 1233
  Growth of, 117, 172, 764, 875, 1711
  Post World War II, 181, 783

Subsidized housing, 803, 816, 877
Subways, 1716
Suffragette movement, 1591
Sunday, Billy (preacher), 1383, 1385
Supermarket job discrimination, 1900
Supermarkets, 678
Supermodels, 645
Supply-side economics, 372

Supreme Court Decisions
  Abortion, 977, 1605
  Affirmative action, 1251, 1305
  Antitrust, 966
  Asian Indian eligibility for citizenship, 1280
  Capital punishment, 977
  Child labor, 969
  Chinese rights to public education, 1268
  Divestiture of theater chains, 1326
  Due process, 205
  Education for illegal immigrants, 430
  Environment, 496
  Espionage, 967
  Executive privilege, 977
  Fair competition, 149
  Free speech, 429
  Gun-Free School Zones, 222
  Habeas corpus, 206
  Internment of Japanese Americans, 533, 851, 972, 1289, 1826
  Japanese eligibility for citizenship, 1280
  Labor, 140, 1209
  Lie detectors, 950
  Miranda warning, 206, 950, 976
  National Industrial Recovery Act (1933), 337
  Overthrow of government, 969, 974
  Pledge of Allegiance, 973, 1413
  Police power, 948
  Polygamy, 1451
  Primary voting restrictions, 972
  Public housing, 804
  Race defined (Mexicans), 1232
  Religion, 977
  Religion in public schools, 424
  Religious behavior, 1488
  Restrictions on New Deal programs, 972, 1883
  Reverse discrimination, 1250
  Right to legal counsel, 976
  School prayer, 977
  Segregation, 525
  Separate but equal, 975, 1202
  Slavery, 521
  Special education, 430
  Sterilization, 969, 1548
  Strip searches, 950
  Suppression of malicious journalism, 1169
  Unreasonable search, 969, 976
  Violence against Women, 222
  Working hours, 965

Surfing (sport), 1277
Surveillance activities (FBI), 936
Swanson, C.A. (TV dinners), 688
Sweatshop garment production, 626
Sweatt v. Painter (1950), 975
Sweepstakes, 895
Sweet jazz, 1105
Swift, Gustav (meat packer), 660
Swing music, 1007, 1063, 1104, 1108
Symbionese Liberation Army, 1336
Syndicated news, 1172
Synthetic fibers, 631, 911, 914
Synthetics, 911

T
T-shirts, 640
Tabloids, 1168
Taco Bell, 690
Taft, William Howard (president)
  Latin America, 93

Philippines, 1271
Taft-Hartley Act (1947), 357
Tailhook scandal, 1850
Tammany Hall, 1201
Tanks (WWII), 1642
Tape v. Hurley, 1268
Tariffs (1870s-1890s), 289
Tatum, Art (musician), 1104

Taxes
  Breaks for housing, 182
  Breaks for upper income brackets, 1242
  Personal Income tax, 966

Taylorism, 279, 1210, 1866
Tea rooms, 680
Technology and leisure, 999, 1016

Teenagers (also see **Family Life**)
  1950s, 1011
  During WWII, 1007
  Female teen readers, 1176
  Sexual behavior, 1066, 1070
  Shopping malls, 1028

Telephone companies, 388

Television
  (1970s), 1020, 1022
  (1990s), 1032
  Advertising, 36, 40
  Animals on TV, 1341
  Beginning of, 918, 1324
  Cable TV, 1342, 1344
  Children's shows, 1329, 1341
  CNN, 1345
  Cooking shows, 700
  Criticizing programming, 1331
  Eclipsing radio, 1326
  Emmy Awards, 1343
  Ethnicity, 1010
  Evangelism programs and networks, 1343
  Game shows, 891
  High Definition TV, 1347
  House Un-American Activities Committee, 1327, 1331
  I Love Lucy, 1113, 1328
  Invention of, 918
  Leisure, 1009
  Mini-series, 1341
  Minorities, 1010, 1333
  MTV, 1345
  Network competition, 1347
  News programming, 1333
  Programming, 1325
  Public affairs programming, 1330
  Rating system, 1073
  Ratings, 1346
  Relevancy programming, 1337, 1339
  Religious and quiz shows, 1330, 1331
  Sex, 1347
  Sit-coms, 1327
  Soap operas, 1340
  Sports and variety shows, 1328
  Teens and elderly programming, 1332
  Televangelists and advertising, 40
  TV dinners, 688
  VCR, 1345
  Vietnam war reportage, 1333, 1846
  Watergate, 1338
  Younger viewers and women, 1346
  Youth culture programming, 1334

Telemarketing, 41
Tellico Dam controversy, 489
Temperance and prohibition, 1050
Tennessee Valley Authority, 480
Terrell, Mary Church (activist), 1767
Terrorism (religious), 1490
Terrorist immigrants, 866

Texas
  Annexation, 64
  Cattle, 84
  Land grant from Mexico, 59
  Oil boom, 884
  Revolution with Mexico, 61
  Status of Americans with Mexico, 60

Theory of evolution, 421
Theory of the Leisure Class, 1754
Thomas, Clarence (Supreme Court justice), 217
Thomas Cook travel company, 1757
Thorndike, Edward L. (educator), 419
Three Mile Island reactor, 481
Time, Fortune, and *Life*, 1170
Tin cans, 659
Tin Pan Alley, 1100
Titanic, 1763
Tobacco crops, 1676
Today Show, The, 1331
Tokyo Rose (WWII radio propagandist), 1651
Tokyo war trial (WWII), 1836
Tonight Show, The, 1331

Tootsie Rolls, 662
Toqueville, Alexis de (social historian), 1159
Toquevillian paradox, 1159, 1169, 1172

Tourism
  Destinations/theme parks, 1772
  Environmental concerns, 1773
  Leisure activities, 995
  Impact on countries' economies, 1769
  Importance of, 1774
  Tourist boom in the 1920s, 1765

Townhouses, 814

Towns, 1667
  Automobiles (influence of), 1687
  Canals and railroads (importance of), 1672
  Changes in towns (1900-1920), 1685
  Changing function of towns, 1689
  Community (concept of), 1673
  Definition of, 1670
  Depression (effect of the), 1689
  Downtown (compounding the problems), 1691
  Entertainment, 1688
  Founding of towns, 1670
  Not in my back yard movement, 1692
  Pre-Revolutionary towns (1650-1775)
    Cattle towns, 1681
    Chesapeake Bay, 1675
    Great Plains, 1683
    Mining towns, 1680
    New England industrial, 1678
    New York to Florida, 1677
    New England, 1674
    River towns, 1678
  Returning to traditional town life, 1693
  Seaside, Florida, 1694
  Small town society, 1686
  Structure and pattern of towns, 1671
  New Urbanism, 1693
  Urban sprawl, 1692

Townsend Plan, 1521
Toys and games, 1012
Trade associations, 144
Trade with Latin America, 94
Traffic, 190
Traffic rules, 1707
Trail of Tears, 508, 1198
Transcendental meditation, 1420
Transcontinental flight, 1730
Transistors, 919

Transpersonal psychology, 1440

Transportation, 1699
  Air transportation
    Air Traffic Controllers strike, 157, 1244, 1736
    Airmail service, 1732
    Barnstorming, 1730
    Breaking the sound barrier, 1734
    Civil pilot training, 1735
    Disasters, 1737
    Early test flights, 1729
    First
      Parachute jump, 1730
      Passenger service, 1732
      Seaplane, 1730
      Transatlantic flight, 1730
    Government regulation of, 1734
    Improvements in aircraft, 1733
    Invention of the airplane, 1728
    Presidential aircraft, 1735
    Space flight, 1737
    Special duty aircraft, 1735
    Women pilots, 1731, 1735
  Automobiles
    Accidents, 1713
    Automotive culture, The, 1714
    Early models, 1704
    Early roads, 1708
    Federal Aid Highway Act (1938, 1944, 1952, 1954), 1710
    First automobiles, 1706
    First national highway system, 1710
    Freight transportation, 1712
    Improvements in, 1715
    Interstate highways (impact of), 1711
    Law and order, 1707
    National Highway System, 1713
    Road expansion, 1710, 1766
    Safety, 1714
  Government's role in
    Environmental issues, 1741
    New technologies, 1740
    Postal Service contribution, 1741
    Safety, 1740
    World War II, 317
  Pipelines, 1717
  Railroads
    Accidents, 1718
    Illegal passengers (hoboes), 1720
    Orphan trains, 1719
    Rise and decline, 1718
    Segregation on, 1723

Transcontinental, 1717
Subways, 1716
  Water transportation
    Natural waterways, 1723
    Ports, 1724
    Presidents at sea, 1727
    Racing boats, 1726
    Recreational boats, 1725
    Shipping disasters, 1727, 1763
    Ships, 1725

Travel, 1749 (see also **Transportation**)
  Airplane travel, 1768, 1770
  Automotive leisure travel, 1764
  Fairs, 1761
  Ocean liners, 1763
  Post World War II, 1768
  Railroad travel, 1756
    Decline of, 1771
  Shipping disasters, 1727, 1763
  Tourism
    Destinations/theme parks, 1772
    Environmental concerns, 1773
    Impact on countries' economies, 1769
    Importance of tourism
    Facilitates immigration, 1775
    Major contributor to world trade, 1775
    Promotes world culture, 1774
    Tourist boom in the 1920s, 1765
  Travels/migration of immigrants, 1754
  Travels of the wealthy, 1755
  Vacations
    (1870-1900), 1760
    Depression Era, 1767
    Middle class, 1760
    Minorities, 1766
    Working class, 1761
  Work v. play, 1753

Treaties and pacts, 968
Treaty of Versailles (WWI), 1382, 1810
Trench warfare (WWI), 1625
Triple Alliance, 1798
Triple Ententre, 1798
Trolleys, 172, 993
True Story Magazine, 1168
Truman Doctrine, 1837
Truman, Harry (president), 358, 1837

Trusts/antitrusts, 290, 309, 311, 323, 340
  Clayton Antitrust Act, 311, 965
  Consumerism (1920s), 326
  Corporate capitalism, 297
  Corporate revolution of the 1890s, 299, 301
  Corporations (rise of), 294
  Dollar-a-Year men (WWI), 315
  Economic crisis of the 1890s, 299
  Federal Trade Commission, 310, 965
  Financing WWI, 317, 319
  Food Administration (WWI), 316, 1806
  Fuel Administration (WWI), 316
  Gold vs. silver standard, 291
  Industrial psychology, 325
  Inflation (WWI), 318
  Labor (1920s), 325
  Management (1920s), 326
  Mergers and consolidations (1920s), 327
  Panic of 1893, 300
  Prosperity (post-WWI), 321, 324
  Rockefeller, John D., 296
  Roosevelt's (Theodore) economic and business policy, 307
  Standard Oil of Ohio, 296
  Stock market crash (1929), 328; (1987), 377
  Taft's economic and business policy, 308
  War Industries Board (WWI), 314, 1805
  Wilson's economic and business policy, 310
  World War I economy, 312

Tuberculosis, 234, 720
Tupperware, 688
Turner, Frederick Jackson (historian), 1673
Tuskegee Airmen, 1825
TV dinners, 688, 918
Twenty-One, 1330
Twiggy (model), 638
Two way radio, 916
Tyler, John (president), 66

U
U.S./Soviet agricultural relations, 597
U.S. v. Butler, 972
U-boats, 1800
Uncle Sam (creation of), 1803
Undertakers, 254
Uniform Crime Reports (FBI), 936

Unions (labor)
  Beginning of, 138
  Collective bargaining, 145
  Decline of (1970s), 1244
  History of, 1884
  Homestead strike, 139, 200, 881

Industrial Workers of the World, 141
National Labor Relations Board, 150, 342, 1805, 1823
Operation Dixie, 155
Opposition to, 1208
Opposition to free trade, 158
Race, 1890
Red scare and the decline of unions, 142, 155, 1231
Support from Wilson, 141
Worker benefit victory at GM, 1230

Unisex clothing styles, 639
United Mine Workers, 1202, 1218
United States Housing Authority (1938), 771
Universal Negro Improvement Association, 1216
Unsafe at Any Speed, 1740
Upton, Emory (military strategist), 1791
Urban blues music, 1104
Urban renewal, 788, 790, 813, 814, 1234, 1241
Urban sprawl, 1692

V
Vaccinations, 713
Vacuum tube, 910
Valentine Massacre (gangsters), 939
Valery, Paul (French poet), 1403
Van Allen Radiation Belts, 1559
Vanderbilt estate (Biltmore House), 753
Vanguard spacecraft, 1559
Vatican Council II, 1466
Vaudeville, 997
Veblen, Thorsten (social scientist), 1754
Venturi, Robert (architect), 805, 1692
Versailles, Treaty of, 1382, 1810
Veterans
  Loans to, 779
  Pension program, 1514
Viagra, 739
Vice societies, 1044
Victorian morality, 1043
Victorian style, rejection of, 757
Victory gardens, 595
Victory girls, 1599
Video games, 1029

Vietnam War (1964-1975)
  Abrams tank, 1663
  Airpower, 1656
  Alcoholism, 1658
  American escalation, 1655
  Background, 1843
  Bradley Fighting Vehicle, 1663
  Calley, William (Lieutenant), 1659
  Class differences, 1237
  Combat conditions, 1656
  Counter-insurgency, 1844
  Culture, 1845
  End of the war, 1847
  Fragging, 1659
  Gulf of Tonkin resolution, 1655, 1844
  Ho Chi Minh trail, 1656
  HUMVEES, 1663
  Johnson, Lyndon (role in Vietnam), 1657
  Pentagon Papers, 1848
  Protest movement, 1787, 1845
  Refugees, 860
  Religion, 1422
  ROTC, 1660
  Stress on troops, 1660
  Troop morale, 1658, 1660
  TV reportage of the war, 1333, 1846
  U.S. advisors, 1843
  Vietnamese women in combat, 1659
  Views of minorities, 1298

Virginia City, Nevada, 1680
Vitamins, 676, 678, 721
Vocalists, 1110
Vocational education, 419, 420, 1146
Vogue magazine, 1177
Volcker, Paul (economist), 1244
Volstead Act, 1384
Von Braun, Werner (rocket scientist), 1555
Voting, 1193, 1202, 1204

W
Wagner Act (1935), 150, 342, 971, 1883
Walkie-talkie, 916
Waller, Fats (musician), 1104
Walmart, 888
Walton, Sam (businessman), 888

War and the U.S. Military, 1779
 American Civil War (1860-1865)
    Economic cost, 134
    First modern war, 1787
  Between the Spanish-American War and WWI, 1797
  Between WWI and WWII, 1812
    Armed forces, 1813
    Germany and Hitler, 1816
    Hedonism, 1813
    Italy, 1815
    Japan, 1815, 1818
    Rise of air power, 1814

Cold War (1946-1991)
  Atomic bombs (fear of), 250
  Class struggle (effect on), 1231
  Communist threats
    Communist China, 1838
    NATO, 1838
    West Berlin, 1838
  Military spending, 154
  Opportunities for science, 1556
  Policy of containing the Soviet Union, 1837
  Red scare, 142, 155, 202, 967, 1231, 1279, 1290, 1811
  Second Red scare, 1838, 1842
  Space race, 1558
  Sputnik (impact of), 153
  Truman Doctrine, 1837
  U.S. money to fight communism, 96
Gulf War (1991)
  Background, 1848
  Gulf War syndrome, 1851
  Legacy of the war, 1850
  Tailhook scandal, 1850
  Women soldiers, 1849
Korean War (1950-1953)
  Military campaign, 1839
  Red Cross, 1841
  Women in the war, 1841
  McCarthyism, 155, 1067, 1841
Post-war challenges (1947-1947)
  Returning soldiers, 1834
  War crimes trials, 1835
Spanish-American War (1898-1902)
  Alfred Thayer Mahan's professional navy, 1791
  Battle of Manila Bay, 1795
  Battles of Kettle and San Juan hills, 1796
  Butcher Weyler's tactics in Cuba, 1793
  Causes for, 1792
  Emory Upton's professional army, 1791
  Imperialism, 1783, 1789
  Military and Social Darwinism, 1791
  Role of American women, 1796
  Sinking of the battleship *Maine*, 1794
  Teddy Roosevelt and the Rough Riders, 81, 1619, 1622, 1792
  U.S. troop strength, 1790, 1795
  Yellow journalism, 1793
Vietnam (1964-1975)
  Background, 1843
  Counter-insurgency, 1844
  Culture, 1845
  End of the war, 1847
  Gulf of Tonkin resolution, 1655, 1844

  Pentagon Papers, 1848
  Protest movement, 1787, 1845
  Tet offensive, 1846
  TV reportage of the war, 1333, 1846
  U.S. advisors, 1843
World War I (1917-1918)
  African Americans at war, 1808
  American military mobilization, 1801, 1806
  Bolshevik Revolution, 1809
  Creation of Uncle Sam, 1803
  Espionage and Sedition Acts, 1803
  European causes of, 1798
  European mobilization, 1799
  Four-minute men, 1803
  Industrial and financial mobilization, 1804
  Isolationism, 1783
  Labor (effect on), 1877
  National Defense Act (1916), 1807
  Propaganda and civilian support, 1802
  Red Cross, 1809
  Red scare, 1811
  Schlieffen Plan, 1798
  Selective Service Act (1917), 1807
  Sinking of the *Lusitania*, 1378, 1800
  Submarine warfare, 1800
  U.S. neutrality, 1799
  Versailles peace treaty, 1382, 1810
  War turns in U.S. favor, 1810
  Women and African Americans at home, 1805
  Women at war, 1807
  Zimmerman telegram, 1800
World War II (1941-1945)
  African Americans at home and abroad, 1825
  Celebrities at war, 1828
  Civilian contribution, 1784
  Draft, 1820
  End of WWII, 1833
  Entertainment, 1828
  Fighting the enemy while captured, 1827
  German invasion of Poland, 1817
  Holocaust, 1651, 1829, 1832
  Industrial mobilization, 1823
  Japan bombs Pearl Harbor, 1818
  Japanese internment camps, 533, 851, 972, 1289, 1826
  Labor, 1823
  Mobilization, 1819
  Newsreels, 1785
  Rationing, 1828
  Red Ball Express, 1826
  Red Cross, 1822
  Supplying U.S. allies, 1820

Tuskegee Airmen, 1825
War bonds, 1827
War movies, 1830
Women at war, 1821
Women in the workplace, 1785, 1824

U.S. Peacekeeping role worldwide, 1786

War bonds (WWII), 1827
War crimes trials, 1835
War economy (WWII), 345
War Industries Board, 314, 1805
War Labor Board, 153
War of the Worlds, 1320
War on drugs, 1246
War on poverty (Lyndon Johnson), 367, 693, 1297
War Production Board (1942), 346
War Resources Board (1939), 345
Warren and Keeney (developers), 1684

Warren Court
  Due process decisions, 205
  Liberal decisions, 976
  Miranda warning, 206, 976

Washington, Booker T. (scientist), 1183, 1216, 1277
Water and irrigation, 285
Water reclamation environmental issue, 478

Water transportation
  Natural waterways, 1723
  Ports, 1724
  Presidents at sea, 1727
  Racing boats, 1726
  Recreational boats, 1725
  Ships, 1725

Watergate
  Background, 1848
  Television coverage, 1338
Waters, Muddy (musician), 1111
Watt, James (inventor), 902
Watt, James (Secretary of the Interior), 493
Weapons (see **Soldiering, War and the U.S. Military,** and each of the individual wars by name)
Webb-Kenyon Law, 1384
Welfare capitalism, 144, 1878
Welfare Queen, the, 1244
Wells, Alice (policewoman), 939
Wells, Ida B. (activist), 1278
Wesley, John and Charles (ministers), 1365
West Virginia Board of Education v. Barnett (1944), 973

Westward migration, 881
Weyler, "Butcher," (military captain), 1793
Wheelwright, John (religious leader), 1359
White Castle (hamburger) chain, 667, 681
White flight to the suburbs, 1300
Whitefield, George (minister), 1365
Whiteman, Paul (music arranger), 1105
Whitney, Eli (inventor), 907
Whitney v. California (1927), 969
Who Wants to Marry a Millionaire?, 890
Whole Earth Catalog, 486
Wichita Falls, KS, 884
Wickersham Commission, 933
Wigglesworth, Michael (religious poet), 1368
Wilderness Act (1964), 485
Williams, Roger (dissident minister), 1358
Williams Sonoma, 691
Wilmington massacre, 1203
Winrod, Gerald B. (conservative critic), 1394

Wilson, Woodrow (president)
  Latin America, 94
  Support of unions, 141
  World War I, 1378

Winthrop, John (minister), 1356, 1367
Wobblies, 141, 200
Womanist theology, 1445

Women (see also **Emotional Change, "Children," Family Life, Sex and Gender,** and **Morality**)
Abortion, 1077, 1605
Activism, 1590
Birth control, 1048, 1467, 1585, 1594
Blonde bombshell, 1069
Careers, 880, 1611
Courtship, 1594
Crime, 216
Death rate in childbearing, 236, 711
Domestic science/home economics, 669
Eating disorders, 730
Education, 880, 1611
Entertainment, 998
Fashion (see entire chapter), 619
Female teen readers, 1176
Feminism, 1300, 1600
Fertility treatment, 739
Flappers, 1054, 1592
Food, 695, 699
Friendship between women, 1584
Frontier, 58
Gender roles, 1014, 1600, 1608

Harassment, 217, 1487, 1901
Housewives, 183
Issues in religion, 1472
Ku Klux Klan (support of), 203, 212
Leisure-time wives, 1001
Lesbian parents, 1607
Magazines, 1173
Mann Act, 200, 1047, 1588
Marriage and money, 888
Men's spiritual movement, 1474
Military service and sex, 1064
Morality, 1920s, 1593
New Woman, The, 1048, 1054, 1590
1950s
   Birthrates, 561
   Child-rearing practices, 563
   Housewives, 563, 1009, 1014, 1603
   Marriage, 561, 1068
   Role dissatisfaction, 564, 1603
Nineteenth Century
   Child-rearing practices, 547
   Divorce, 1049
   Education, 1589
   Marriage, 548, 552, 1049
   Reformers, 1586
   Role in the family, 545, 553, 1584
   Sexual practices, 546, 1584, 1590
   Spanish-American War, 1796
No-fault divorce, 1079
Nurses, 718, 725, 736, 1796, 1807
Pants fashion, 627, 641
Physical fitness, 1020, 1026
Physicians, 727
Pornography, 1072, 1609
Prenatal care, 721
Prostitution, 1046, 1586, 1587
Rape
   Cause of lynching, 1205
   Feminist scholarship on, 216
   Increase, 1604
Reading preferences, 1025
Religious leadership, 1359, 1584
Retirement, 1528
Role in the family, 554, 1597
Scientists, 1549
Sexual behavior
   (1960s-1970s), 1076, 1603, 1604
   (1980s-1990s), 1608
   Civil Rights, 1978, 1604
   Soldiers during WW II, 1063
   Teens, 1066, 1070
   Women during WWII, 1599, 1825

Women in sex-related occupations, 1078
   Women's responsibility for, 1065, 1585, 1601, 1609
Sexual revolution, 1603
Single women, 1589
Slavery, attitudes toward, 1587
Sports programs in schools, 430, 1021
Suffragette movement, 1591
Television programs, 1338, 1346
Temperance and prohibition, 1050
Women's Liberation movement, 1586, 1604, 1608
   Influence on fashion, 639
Working women
   (1850-1900), 1588
   (1910-1930), 1140, 1592
   (1930s), 1587
   (1950s), 1600, 1602
   (1960s), 566
   Careers, types of, 880
   Education, 1898
   Family friendly benefits, 1901
   Government jobs, 1598
   Gulf war, 1849
   History, 1867ff
   Job discrimination, 1899
   Korean War, 1841
   Professional, 1141
   Textile, 1144
   Wage discrimination, 1610, 1896
   Wages in the 19th C., 1588
   WWI, 1805
   WWII war front, 1821
   WWII home front, 151, 1598, 1599, 1785, 1824, 1887

Women pilots, 1731, 1735
Women's Christian Temperance Union, 1590
Women's liberation movement, 1604
Women's magazines, 1173
Wonderful World of Disney, 1329
Wood, Sylvia (union leader), 1216
Woods, Tiger (golfer), 1306
Woodstock festival, 1121

Work and the Workplace, 1857
   Benefits for working wives, 1901
   Best companies to work for, 1894
   Business boom of the 1990s, 1893
   Changing composition of the workforce, 1898
   Child labor, 1867
   Contingent work force, 1894
   Demographics of the workforce, 1862
   Discrimination against blacks, 1890

Effect of World War I, 1877
Foremen and supervisors, 1875
Great Depression work, 1879
History of unions, 1884
Industrial democracy, 1883
Industrial growth, 1862
Industrial relations and gains 1950-1970, 1888
Industrial spies, 1884
Invention of management, 1866
New Deal work programs, 1882
Profile of immigrant workers, 1870
Profile of the workforce 1933-1970, 1880
Race and class, 1871
Race, gender and discrimination, 1899
Restructuring business in the 1980s, 1893
Technology and work, 1865
Transformation of skilled jobs, 1864
Wage discrimination 1980s-1990s, 1896
Welfare capitalism, 144, 1878
White supremacy, 1872
White-collar work, 1873
Women, 1867ff
Working conditions 1886-1920, 1876
Working conditions in the 1990s, 1899
World War II, 1887

Working class families in the 19th C., 549
Works Progress Administration (1935), 341, 422
World Trade Center bombing, 1490
World War II economy, 345ff
Wounded Knee, 1299
Wright Brothers (inventors), 1728
Wright, Frank Lloyd (architect), 756, 774
Wrigley, William (chewing gum magnate), 662

World War I (1917-1918)
    African Americans, 1214, 1808
    Airplanes, 1628
    American military mobilization, 1801, 1806
    Bias against immigrants, 844
    Bolshevik Revolution, 1809
    Buffalo soldiers (Indians), 1619
    Chemical weapons, 1627
    Colt .45 pistol, 1631
    Dogfighting (aircraft), 1628
    Dollar-a-Year men, 315
    Doughboys, 1630
    Economy, 312, 314
    Enfield rifle, 1630
    Espionage and Sedition Acts, 1803
    European mobilization, 1799
    European causes of the war, 1798

Financing the war, 317, 319
Food Administration, 316
Four-minute men, 1803
Fuel Administration, 316
Housing, 761
Industrial and financial mobilization, 1804
Inflation, 318
Influence on clothes, 627
Influence on foods, 672
Isolationism, 1783
Job opportunities, 1278
Krag-Jorgensen rifle, 1621
Labor, 320, 1877
Liberty loans, 319
Morality, 1056
Multiple-choice testing of soldiers, 420
Music, 1631
Mustard and chlorine gas (WWI), 1627
National Defense Act (1916), 1807
No-man's land (WWI), 1627
Nurses, 718, 1807
Pershing, General John J. (Blackjack), 1619, 1623
Post-war prosperity, 321, 324
Propaganda and civilian support, 1802
Red Barron, the (pilot), 1628
Red Cross, 1809
Red scare, 1811
Religion, 1377
Rickenbacker, Eddie (pilot), 1628
Schlieffen Plan, 1798
Selective Service Act (1917), 1807
Sinking of the *Lusitania*, 1378, 1800
Spiritual crisis, 1403
Submarine warfare, 1800
Transportation, 317
Trench warfare, 1625
U.S. neutrality, 1799
Uncle Sam (creation of), 1803
Uniforms and weapons, 1630
Versailles peace treaty, 1382, 1810
War Industries Board, 314, 1805
War turns in U.S. favor, 1810
Women at war, 1807
Women and African Americans at home, 1805
Yellow fever, 1623
Zimmerman telegram, 1800

World War I to World War II (1919-1941)
    Armed forces, 1813
    Germany and Hitler, 1816
    Hedonism, 1813
    Italy, 1815

Japan, 1815, 1818
Rise of air power, 1814

World War II (1941-1945)
  African Americans at home and abroad, 1825
  Agriculture, 349
  Aircraft industry, 347
  Airpower, 1634, 1644
  Alcohol consumption, 1059
  Allied invasion of France, 1649
  America enters the war, 1632
  Artillery, 1642
  Atomic bomb, 1639
  Axis Sally (radio broadcaster), 1650
  Bataan, Battle of, 1647
  Bushido Code (Japanese), 1647
  Celebrities at war, 1828
  Civil pilot training, 1735
  Civilian involvement in the war, 1648, 1784
  Coal and petroleum, 347
  Draft, 1820
  Educational Orders Act (1939), 345
  Effect on clothing, 632
  Effect on families, 559
  End of the war, 1833
  Entertainment, 1644, 1828
  Espionage, 1649
  Fighting the enemy while captured, 1827
  Food production, 593
  Food for soldiers, 686
  France (invasion of), 1637, 1649
  French resistance movement, 1649
  German invasion of Poland, 1817
  Germany (invasion of), 1638
  G.I.s
    Entertainment, 1644
    Holocaust, 1651, 1829, 1832
    Medicine, 1643
    Outfitting, 1640
    Rations, 1643
    Weapons, 1641
  Grumann fighter planes, 1635
  Guadalcanal, Battle of, 1633
  Helicopters, 1646
  Helmets, 1640
  Holocaust, 1651, 1829, 1832
  Housing, 775
  Industrial mobilization, 1823
  Internment of Japanese Americans, 533, 852, 972, 1289, 1826
  Iowa Jima and Okinawa (invasion, atomic bomb), 1639
  Island hopping in the Pacific, 1638
  Japan bombs Pearl Harbor, 1818
  Japanese Bushido Code, 1647
  Japanese internment camps, 533, 851, 972, 1289, 1826
  Jobs for blacks, 1288
  Kennedy, John F. (service in WWII), 1636
  Labor, 349, 1223, 1823, 1887
  Leisure, 1005
  MacArthur, General Douglas, 1638, 1653, 1840
  Mauldin, Bill (cartoonist), 1647
  Medical advances during, 724
  Medicine, 1643
  Midway Island, Battle of, 1633, 1833
  Minority veterans, 1227
  Miracle drugs, 237
  Mobilization, 1819
  Newsreels, 1785
  Nimitz, Admiral, 1638
  North Africa (invasion of), 1636
  Nutrition, 685
  Pacific islands campaign, 1638
  Post-war challenges
    Returning soldiers, 1834
    War crimes trials, 1835
  Protestant response, 1402
  PT boats, 1636
  Radio propaganda, 1650
  Rationing (civilians), 1828
  Rations (troops), 1643
  Red Ball Express, 1826
  Red Cross, 1822
  Ridgway, General Matthew, 1653
  Rubber, 349
  Scientific research, 1550
  Service aboard ship, 1634
  Sexual behavior of soldiers, 1063
  Shipbuilding, 347
  Sicily (invasion of), 1637
  Steel and aluminum, 348
  Submarines, 1636, 1800
  Supplying U.S. allies, 1820
  Tanks, 1642
  Tokyo Rose (radio propagandist), 1651
  Tuskegee Airmen, 1825
  Unions, 152
  War Resources Board (1939), 345
  War movies, 1830
  War bonds, 1827
  War economy, 345
  Weapons, 1641
  Women in the workplace, 151, 560, 1785, 1824
  Women at war, 1821

X
X-ray, 905

Y
Yeager, Chuck (test pilot), 1554, 1734
Yeager, Jeana (pilot), 1735
Yellow fever, 1623
Yellow journalism, 1165, 1793
Yellow Peril (Chinese immigrants), 1199
You Are There, 1331
Youth culture, 555
Yuppi styles, 644
Yuppies, 1026, 1030

Z
Zahniser, Howard (environmentalist), 484
Zangwill, Israel (playwright), 1268
Zen
  Beat poets, 1416
Zeppelin, Led (musician), 1125
Zimmerman telegram, 1800
Zionism, 1399, 1461
Zoning laws, 173, 765
Zoot suit, 632, 1007
Zoot-suit riots, 1224
Zworykin, Vladimir (inventor), 905

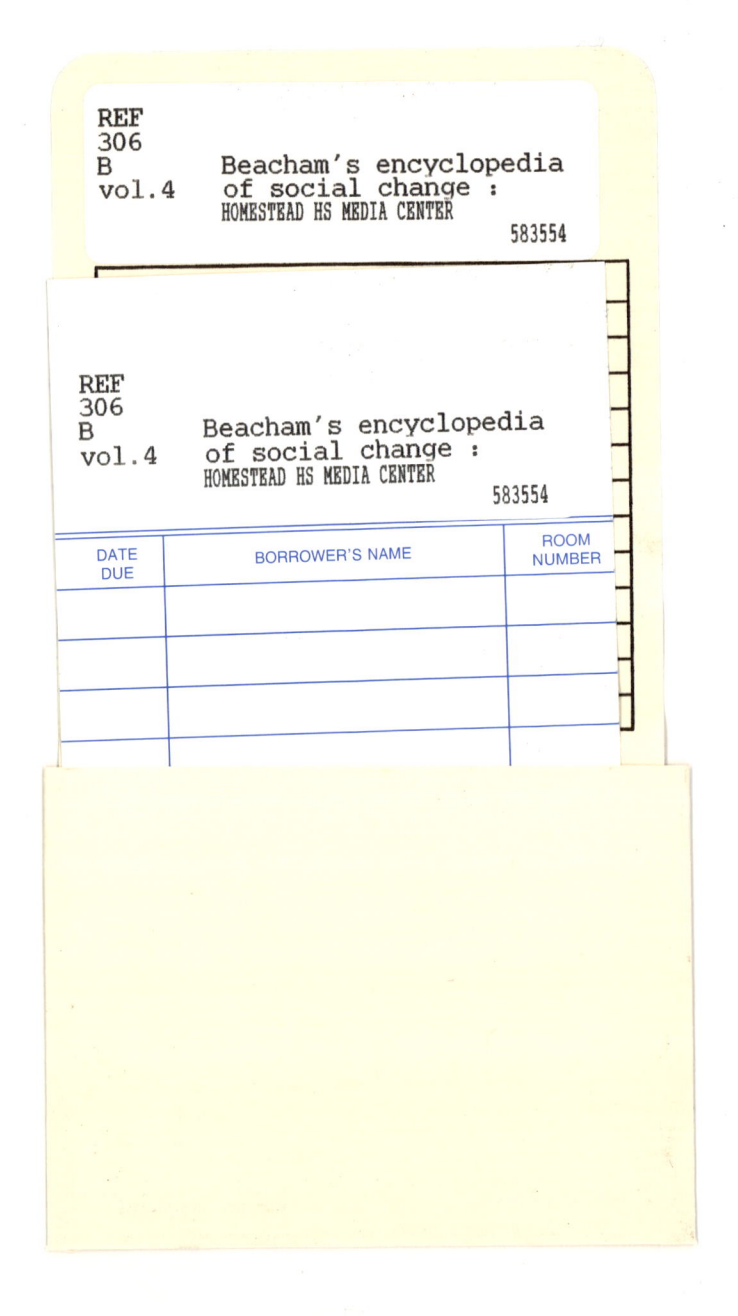

```
REF
306
B           Beacham's encyclopedia
vol.4       of social change :
         HOMESTEAD HS MEDIA CENTER
                              583554
```

```
REF
306
B           Beacham's encyclopedia
vol.4       of social change :
         HOMESTEAD HS MEDIA CENTER
                              583554
```

DATE DUE	BORROWER'S NAME	ROOM NUMBER